◼ A Century of Stories

A Century of Stories

The History of the Iowa City Public Library,
1897–1997

by Lolly Parker Eggers

Bitsy –
more than you want
to know, I'm sure
Lolly
5-3-04

Building on a Century of Service

The Iowa City Public Library Friends Foundation

In memory of Suzanne Richerson (1934-1996)

■ Contents

■ Preface

At midlife, after nearly forty years as a regular and enthusiastic library user, I became a public librarian and spent all my professional career at the Iowa City Public Library.

During that time, I was consistently surprised at how little the general public and even the library's most regular and frequent users knew about the public library—its history, basic values, operational methods, and even its financing.

Books on American political and social history and studies of U.S. cultural life and institutions provide little information about public libraries. In the acknowledgments section of many books, writers dutifully thank libraries and librarians for their research help, but no general historian has evaluated the role that libraries—especially public libraries—have played in our history, or acknowledged the existence of 8,000 public libraries in this country as a hallmark of our democratic society, as one of our nation's most notable accomplishments.

We have no record of what the public library has meant to those who have been its greatest supporters and heaviest users—the child, the curious, the political activist, the volunteer, the teacher, the editor, the creative doer, the voracious reader—or how society in general has benefited from the ideas and work of those who were enriched by what they learned at the library.

My history of the Iowa City Public Library will not fill this educational hole but I hope it offers a start. I hope that by telling some of the interesting Iowa City library stories I will leave the reader wiser about ICPL and its place in the history of Iowa City and of the American public library. Also, I hope it will better inform the general reader about the accomplishments and failures of public libraries in our history and culture and about the philosophy, ethics, goals, techniques, and conventions that create quality library service.

It is impossible to separate the history of a single institution from its sister institutions, from the environment in which it exists, or from the larger social movements from whence it came. In telling the Iowa City Public Library story, I have tried to make some of these connections.

I had four goals: Document the library's history and celebrate its centennial; relate the library's history to the history of Iowa and especially Iowa City; link ICPL to the development and history of public libraries in general; and increase the general reader's awareness about public library philosophy, operations, and traditions.

The library is now one hundred years old. For nearly one-half of that time I have observed the community and used the library as an Iowa City resident; between 1969 and 1994 I served as cataloger, reference librarian, and director. This is Iowa City Public Library history from my perspective. Starting with chapter 7, it is frequently told in my voice.

■ Acknowledgments

Writing this history has been a journey I never expected to take, and without the help, guidance, and encouragement of many people I would never have found my way nor reached my destination. First, Suzanne Richerson convinced me I should try and then guided and corrected my first efforts. Charlie Drum generously stepped in when Suzanne left us so suddenly. He spent hours and hours unsnarling my convoluted sentences and sometimes garbled ideas. Both were tough yet supportive editors and friends.

I am indebted to Irving Weber who offered a flood of stories, useful historical tidbits, and ideas on where to find more information. He critiqued the early chapters, but sadly, did not live to see the completed book. Thanks also to all the folks with library connections that gave me hours of their time and provided information about former library directors and past library events and to the many friends and colleagues who encouraged me by suggesting they were looking forward to reading the book!

I am grateful to everyone at ICPL who helped and supported me. I found out firsthand why, as director, I always received so much praise for the library's information service. Especially I thank Sara Brown, Maeve Clark, Linda Dyer, Larry Eckholt, Debb Green, Carol Spaziani, and, of course, Susan Craig who always saw that I had the resources I needed. Thanks, too, to the Iowa City Public Library Friends Foundation for its financial support and to Denice Connell who corrected my spelling and punctuation and found many misused words and awkward phrases.

Finally, thank you, Del, for postponing and rescheduling our retirement adventures for a couple of years. Your support was essential.

—March 28, 1997

◼ Introduction   Setting the Scene: Iowa City in 1897

In 1897, the year the public library opened, Iowa City was two years away from its sixtieth birthday. The Old Settlers' Association was already planning its 1899 Semicentennial Reunion. William McKinley had been elected U.S. president in the fall of 1896 after a long campaign against William Jennings Bryan. During the last four months of that year only the presidential campaign and the subsequent plans of the new federal administration received more news coverage in the local newspapers than the civic drive to found a public library in Iowa City.

After rapid expansion during its first thirty years, Iowa City had grown very little since 1870 when the population reached almost 6,000. In 1895 the official census takers tallied 7,526 people living in 1,700 households. In the fall of 1897 this included 1,325 University of Iowa[1] students, nearly 60 percent of them enrolled in the professional schools of medicine, law, dentistry, and pharmacy. During the same time period the state's population increased 130 percent, to just over 2 million. Cedar Rapids exploded with a sevenfold increase from 2,900 to 21,500. Eleven Iowa cities that are now considerably smaller than Iowa City— Boone, Burlington, Clinton, Council Bluffs, Fort Dodge, Fort Madison, Keokuk, Marshalltown, Muscatine, Oskaloosa, and Ottumwa—all recorded more residents than Iowa City in the 1895 tally.

The incorporated town was only eighteen blocks long from Brown Street on the north to Kirkwood on the south and fifteen blocks wide, bounded by the Iowa River on the west and by a few named additions and subdivisions about two blocks east of Summit Street. It was at most a fifteen-block walk to the center of town from either the northeast or southeast corner of the city, but only a few streets—much of the business district and the residential areas of Clinton, College, and Summit streets—provided an all-weather surface.

On the west side of the Iowa River a few homes on the bluffs overlooked the river; farther west lay some small acreages and estates. The 1876 Centennial Bridge on Iowa Avenue led to the Hutchinson rock quarry—part of the western bluffs, which were not part of Iowa City proper but known locally as the "West Side." Beyond the bluffs, farmlands stretched westward.

In Johnson County—like most of Iowa in the 1890s—most families lived on farms. The 1895 county census listed 3,100 farmers and with their families they accounted for 12,000 to 15,000 of the total population, twice the number living in Iowa City. In fact, there were more *retired* farmers living in Iowa City—and in the whole state of Iowa—in 1895 than workers in any but the major occupations like day laborers, clerks, teachers, domestics, and merchants.

As Gerald Mansheim said in his 1989 Iowa City history, "Iowa City had *been* the West in the 1840s and 1850s,"[2] not to mention the westernmost point on the railroad until 1860. Not until 1869 did zeal for a railroad to the Pacific push construction of tracks west of Council Bluffs. Because of the disruption of the Civil War, Mansheim noted, "Iowa City had the look—and perhaps the spirit—of the West throughout the 1870s."[3] In the late 1870s and during the next decade Iowa City businessmen and investors tried to establish an industrial base to balance the growing university. Throughout the 1880s they tried breweries, distilleries, packing plants, and factories, producing fence and wire, glass, cutlery, gloves, linseed oil, paper, perfume, and jewelry. "Some prospered for awhile, others failed; many burned."[4]

The 1895 Iowa census dramatically illustrated Iowa City's failure to build an industrial-based economy. In that year, with a total value of $170,000 in manufactured goods, Johnson County ranked in the bottom third of the state while twelve Iowa counties each produced goods worth $2 million dollars or more. Only 220 people worked in manufacturing jobs in Johnson County compared to nearly 700 just ten years earlier.

The merchandising sector, however, did prosper. "The retail trade of the city is in splendid shape," wrote the anonymous author of an article on Iowa City in the *Atlas of Johnson County, Iowa, 1900,*[5] citing a reason familiar in Iowa City to this day—the presence of university students throughout most of the year. There were more merchants, teachers, students, and hotel and restaurant keepers in Iowa City than in several cities twice its size. The presence of the university accounted for proportionately more single residents, fewer persons per household, fewer births per capita, and a larger share of population over eighteen years of age—68 percent in Iowa City versus an average of 58 percent statewide.

While the presence of the university dominated Iowa City's social, political, and economic life, it was not the only educational institution. A prominent local educator, W.A. Willis, owned and directed Iowa City Commercial College and the Iowa City Academy, a private high school popular with rural residents whose children were not eligible to attend Iowa City schools. In 1897 the commercial college was featuring a course in typewriting.

The Iowa City Conservatory of Music, with a faculty of twelve—all identified as pupils of important teachers from New York City, Chicago, and Boston—provided music instruction to both townspeople and university students; the university had not yet established any fine arts departments.

In addition to the public schools—a high school, grammar or middle school, and six elementary schools—the community offered St. Agatha's Seminary for "young ladies," St. Patrick's School run by the Sisters of Charity, and St. Mary's Parochial School under the direction of the Sisters of St. Francis.

Iowa City had a higher percentage of females—54 percent—than any other city in Iowa. In all of Iowa, women accounted for 48 percent of the total residents. The larger number of females in Iowa City was most likely due to the presence of the university, the commercial college, the conservatory, and St. Agatha's Seminary. Women were rapidly replacing men in clerical jobs in the 1890s. Nationwide, female office workers increased their share of such employment from less than 6 percent to over 38 percent between 1880 and 1910.[6]

Fewer native-born residents (80 percentof the total population) resided in Iowa City than in the state in general (84 percent) and in 1895 Iowa City led the state, including Cedar Rapids, in the number of residents who were first- or second-generation Bohemians. Germans, Irish, and Welsh followed Bohemians as the largest Iowa City ethnic groups. For the 2,500 Iowa City residents born in the United States outside Johnson County, most came from four states: Illinois, New York, Ohio, and Pennsylvania.

The 1895 census contained considerable information about religious preferences in Iowa City. In response to the question, "What is your religious belief irrespective of church affiliation?" 141 Johnson County residents listed a diverse array of religious and political beliefs: Deist, Liberal, Friend, Spiritualist, Jewish, Dunkard, Agnostic, Adventist, Christian Scientist, Communist, Latter-Day Saint, and Moravian. Most of the respondents, however, identified themselves as either Catholic (27 percent), Methodist, Lutheran, Presbyterian, Christian, Congregationalist, Episcopalian, Baptist, Evangelical, or United Brethren, in that order. Thirty-four percent gave no religious preference or said "none."

Four newspapers were published regularly in Iowa City in the fall of 1896 in addition to two produced by university students. Two papers, the *Iowa City Republican* and the *Iowa City Citizen*, identified themselves as Republican and issued both daily and weekly editions. The Democratic *Iowa State Press* and the

A Century of Stories

Independent-Herald came out weekly, although the *Press* absorbed the *Herald* early in 1897. The combined circulation of the town newspapers was over 4,000—heavy newspaper reading in a town of 1,700 households.

The newspapers carried little local news without inserting editorial comments: A major story, for example, would typically be sprinkled with judgmental comments—"the miserable cur," "the scoundrel"—and the accused was often presumed guilty long before the trial began. In addition, long columns of editorials provided lively reading. Often unsigned, the editorials lashed out at local government and controversial community issues, but most frequently at positions taken on these topics by editors of the competing papers and leaders of the opposition political party. With annual—and highly partisan—city council elections that included party caucuses to choose candidates from the city's five wards, city politics was seldom absent from editorial columns. The editors aggressively defended their own party actions and officeholders, often quoting a rival paper's comments extensively and then dissecting the arguments at length.

In his 1976 history of Iowa, Joseph Wall noted, "Iowa was fortunate from its earliest territorial days in having a lively press whose impact upon the cultural and political education of its readers cannot be overestimated."[7]

[1] In this book we use the terms University of Iowa, university, or UI, although its official name is still the State University of Iowa (SUI). Since 1964 the university has used the shorter version, partially to avoid confusion with Iowa State University (ISU).

[2] Gerald Mansheim, *Iowa City: An Illustrated History* (Norfolk, VA: Donning Co., 1989), 78.

[3] Ibid., 78.

[4] Ibid., 81.

[5] As cited by Mansheim, 81.

[6] Klaus Musmann, *Technological Innovations in Libraries, 1860-1960* (Westport CT: Greenwood Press, 1993), 11.

[7] Joseph Frazier Wall, *Iowa, A Centennial History* (New York: Norton, 1976), 193-94.

■ 1.   Getting Started: Crime Helps Open Library Doors

Initially spurred into action in August of 1896 by news of a violent assault committed by six local young men, a citizens group formed almost immediately "to consider the advisability of establishing a reading room and games room for the young people of Iowa City." This initial group was part of the organization that opened a library in January 1897. By March 1897, just six months after the crime report appeared in the newspapers, the library proponents won voter approval for ongoing tax support for a municipal public library. The events of this six-month period form the first story in the history of the Iowa City Public Library.

The Crime

The newspaper accounts[1] described the "debauchery" of August 24, 1896, in flamboyant prose. Six young men, well known in the area for their previous "drunken revels," lawlessness, and convictions for various misdemeanors, were joined by an "unknown tramp" for an all-night drinking bout "near the quarries on the West Side" of the Iowa River.

Supplied with at least two kegs of beer, they spent the entire night "making the welkin ring with their ribald songs and coarse obscene language." One of them lured a "simple-minded" sixteen-year-old Bohemian girl from a dance at the National Hall,[2] held her against her will, and, according to eyewitnesses, repeatedly assaulted her.

The "heinous crime" did not go unnoticed. Early Tuesday morning as District Judge Martin J. Wade was driving to town, he met University of Iowa professor Frank Nipher near the latter's west side residence. Nipher reported that he had heard the disturbance, "just rods from his home," all night long. The *Iowa State*

Press quoted a nearby camper who said the men were holding the girl against her will and "were treating her in a most brutal manner."

Judge Wade, a popular local official and an 1886 graduate of the University of Iowa Law School, hurried into town. According to the *Iowa City Citizen* report, he found no policeman on duty, so he collected a posse of seven men.

This bluff on the west side of the Iowa River was the scene of the crime that sparked public outrage. Today it is primarily occupied by Burlington Ave. and Hillcrest dormitory.

Irving B. Weber

Some of them drove back to the ongoing crime scene in the police wagon. Wade and two others followed in Wade's buggy.

On being confronted, the drunken gang, described as "wise in the ways of the local police," refused to be arrested by the ad hoc posse, and by the time Wade arrived, several blows had been exchanged. The toughs "greeted him [Wade] with epithets" and a demand that he show a warrant if they were to be arrested. Wade drew his revolver and told the men his gun "was his warrant and that he was ready, even anxious to show them its force."

Two of the group turned and ran away. The posse herded the other five, including the stranger, into the police wagon, but before it reached the Burlington Street bridge the "toughs" tried to push their captors from the wagon. Deputy sheriff Zeke Clark, who had joined the posse at the crime scene, "took several blows" before he pulled his gun and shot the "tramp."

After the shot, the other four rioters "were cringing in their servility . . . stretching themselves out in the bottom of the wagon." The wagon delivered the men to the jail, then headed to the hospital with the wounded man, but he died before it arrived. In the *Iowa City Republican* version, "He gave a few gasps as the wagon stopped . . . in front of the old hospital, and with a final gurgling groan, passed away."

Police officers then returned to the west side to round up the two who had run away. One, according to the *Iowa State Press*, was a friend of the arresting officer and did not want to be seen riding through town in the police wagon, so the officer walked back with him.

The next day the young girl, taken into protective care by several women of the community, filed charges. All six men were arraigned, and in October, at separate trials reported to have cost the county over $5,000, five of the six were convicted of assault. County Attorney George Ball served as prosecutor for the trials. Judge Wolfe, from the Clinton district, presided at the trials since Judge Wade had been involved in the arrest of the defendants. A group of twenty women took turns attending the trials to give support to the young girl and to make it easier for her to give testimony.

Large crowds attended the trials and especially the sentencing of the criminals, frequently overflowing the courtroom. Jacob Reizenstein, city editor for the *Republican*, noted that "there seemed but one terminus to the thoroughfares in Iowa City . . . the court house . . . . Every seat, as well as every nook and cranny in the courtroom was filled."[3]

When he sentenced the men, Judge Wolfe said that while their past records were not in their favor, he "did not feel like inflicting the extreme penalty." He gave them each from seven to ten years. The *Press* described the sentences as "merciful."

In addition to the news coverage of the trials by all the local papers, W.H. Conant, editor of the *Citizen*, wrote at least eight long editorials between August 28 and November 20 about the problems that this incident represented to the community.[4] Again and again, he railed against the "loud, surly, rude young men" that were making conditions unpleasant on the streets and in other public places. He denounced the Democratic city administration for allowing saloons and billiard and gambling rooms to operate in opposition to the law and for generally lax law enforcement.[5] He frequently demanded the resignation of Police Marshall James Mara who he said was sometimes drunk on duty. He further charged that Mara and his law officers were "too friendly" with those causing the problems. He wrote that a careless government and an indifferent community had not heeded his warnings of nearly a year on the consequences of unchecked rowdyism and illegal taverns and gambling halls.

The events of August 24 had shocked the community, and if local newspapers are an accurate indication, the "heinous crime" was widely discussed. According to the *Republican*, the incident "caused the indignation of the citizens to raise to almost a fever heat." The *Press* used similar language and added that "dire results will follow if these beastly practices are continued."

The Campaign for a Public Library Begins

The collective hand-wringing that follows a shocking and upsetting community event and the desire of the general citizenry to take immediate action probably motivated representatives of the local churches to meet in the First Christian Church just four days after the crime to consider the idea of establishing a reading and game room for the young people of Iowa City.

Samuel Kirkwood (S.K.) Stevenson, representing the Presbyterian Church, called the meeting to order and was elected chairman. The group set a "popular meeting" in ten days and appointed Stevenson, Alice Luscombe, and a "Mr. Huggins" (possibly George Hummer) to canvass for money and report at the next meeting. From its first meeting the group recognized the necessity of finding funds to operate the proposed reading and game room.

F.V. Brock, a twenty-five-year-old shorthand instructor at Iowa City Commercial College, served as secretary for most of the early meetings. Despite his training in recording speech quickly, he kept his minutes brief, in the style of the period. As the only existing official record, the minutes fail to fully explain the evolution from the idea of a reading and game room to that of a fully equipped public library.

The citizens group moved ahead rapidly. On Thursday, September 6, they held their popular meeting at City Hall. According to Brock's minutes this meeting was held "for the purpose of organizing a public library society." The chairmanship was turned over to Judge Wade so Stevenson could give his reports. In just six days Stevenson and his committee had drafted a proposed constitution and bylaws for the library. They also identified at least three possible sites for the library and reading room in existing downtown buildings: second-floor rooms over the new C.O.D. Steam Laundry at 211-213 Iowa Avenue; over Startsman Jewelry Store, 109 East Washington; and over Greer's former jewelry store at 106 South Clinton. Committee members estimated the cost of running a library would be least $1,200 for one year.

S.K. Stevenson had represented more than the Presbyterian Church at the August 28 meeting of religious leaders. As the current superintendent of schools for Johnson County he had established libraries in many of the ninety-five county schools. Joining him at the September 6 meeting was Professor W.F. Cramer, who was both superintendent of the Iowa City schools and high school principal in 1896. Stevenson would succeed Cramer as Iowa City superintendent in 1897. Together, Cramer and Stevenson introduced the motion that a reading room and library be established, "which motion, after an extended discussion, was adopted." Five people—Cramer, Stevenson, Brock, Wade, and Luscombe—were asked to plan a "mass meeting of the people of Iowa City" for Monday evening, September 21.

During the next two weeks the group worked to help assure a large audience for the meeting. They asked ministers of all Iowa City churches to make announcements from their pulpits. They sent invitations to four hundred local businesses and asked Luscombe, a teacher at the grammar school, to send notices "to a number of Iowa City ladies inviting them [to the meeting] and asking [for] an expression of their views."[6] Both the *Citizen* and the *Press* carried notices.

The Community Gathers

The mass meeting of September 21 was held at Smith's Armory, a triple-front, three-story building located on the southwest corner of College and Linn streets.

Getting Started

Many civic and social groups used this building for lectures, business expositions, political meetings, university dances, fire company balls, and roller-skating. State and national election returns were telegraphed there and announced to the waiting crowds.[7]

Neither the newspapers nor the minutes reported the exact number of people who attended the meeting. The *Republican*[8] called it a "large and enthusiastic audience . . . representative . . . of Iowa City's best business and professional men and women." The gathering featured more than a simple discussion of the merits of the library proposal. It combined elements of a concert in the park, town meeting, camp meeting, and fund-raiser. The newspaper report noted that in addition to the "stirring words of noble, enterprising men and women," those present heard the "well-drilled Semi-Centennial Chorus of forty voices," conducted by Joseph Ruggles, director of the Iowa City Conservatory of Music.

S.K. Stevenson was active in public library affairs from the first organizational meeting in August 1896 until he left the library board in 1929.

The number of speakers confirms the staying power of the crowd attending the meeting. Stevenson set the stage for speechmaking by giving the audience some facts about the status of libraries in Iowa. He pointed out that twenty-six Iowa communities had public libraries, each offering from 5,000 to 16,000 volumes. The roster of twelve speakers that Stevenson introduced included Judge Wade, Professor Bohumil Shimek, University of Iowa President Charles Schaeffer, University Law Chancellor Emlin McClain, County Treasurer Dennis Maher, Rev. Dr. E.N. Barrett, Rev. Dr. M.A. Bullock, businessmen W.S. Thomas and W.P. Hohenshuh, and three women—Mrs. Alexander Sortor, a widow; Mrs. J.W. Sterling, whose husband owned the Marble Works; and Mrs. Isaac Loos, spouse of a university political science professor. All attested to the city's need for a public library.

Each speaker linked the need for a library to the need to help the boys and girls of the community. The public library will be a "destroyer of street loafing," said Mrs. Sortor. It would "keep our youth off the street corners," where, she warned, "boys are learning obscene and vile language under the street lamps." Mrs. Sterling echoed the sentiments of several speakers, arguing that the library's purpose was more than "keeping boys and girls off the streets." A library, she said, could provide "elevating, cultivating entertainment. The mental, physical, and moral nature of man should be developed and only the right kind of physical, intellectual, and spiritual food will accomplish that end."

Several speakers said the library would complement the public school system while others described their experiences with public libraries in other communities and wondered why Iowa City had waited so long. Schaeffer observed that although the existence of the university library might be partially blamed for the failure of Iowa City to have a public library, the university library "is scarcely adequate to meet the demands of the great and growing body of [its own] students."

Both Wade and Shimek stressed the practical need to provide resources and opportunities for young people forced to leave school and go to work, or those who lived with only "the bare necessities." Shimek painted a particularly compassionate scene. "Year after year," he said, "young people of Iowa City, though hungry for knowledge, have been compelled to quit school to begin the real battles of life." Warming to his subject, he testified that "over and over many have begged me to give them at night the instruction they could not afford to go to school to secure." Wade, in less emotional terms, noted that "many young people, many wage-earners in Iowa City . . . are without the facilities for reading and studying," and told the audience that the best way to help them is to found a public library.[9]

Many of the speakers took the opportunity to urge Iowa Citians to contribute generously to a fund to start the library. Members of the committee passed out subscription blanks to audience members as they left the meeting.

If there were any in attendance who expressed doubts or disagreement, *Republican* reporter Reizenstein failed to record them. His paper's headlines summed up the general tenor of the meeting: "ALL FOR A PUBLIC LIBRARY. A Grand Mass Meeting Held at Smith's Armory. Leading Citizens Make Speeches. Prominent Men and Women Grow Eloquent in a Good Cause—Pledge their Voices and Purses for the Uplifting of Youth—Success Sure."

After the choral concert and at least twelve speeches on the "noble," "elevating," "wholesome," "spiritual," and "worthy" benefits of a public library, the organizers appointed a large committee, dubbed the "Council of Thirty," to adopt the drafted constitution for the proposed library association. This group of six women and twenty-eight men—from the university, the public schools, and county government as well as professionals and local businessmen—was typical of the mix of groups throughout the nation that have started public libraries and served as trustees. Lawyers, bankers, teachers, newspaper editors, doctors, college professors, small business owners, and their wives established, built, and still govern this country's public libraries.

As noted in the *Republican*'s headlines, members of the council represented the power structure of the community. They included university officials and distinguished faculty members Amos Currier, Bohumil Shimek, Thomas H. Macbride, Emlin McClain, and George Patrick; newspaper editors W.H. Conant, Jacob Reizenstein, and S.W. Mercer; lawyers George Ball, A.E. Swisher, Paul Korab, and Martin J. Wade; influential businessmen Moses Bloom, Max Mayer, D.F. Sawyer, Peter Dey, W.P. Hohenshuh, W.F. Main, Patrick J. Regan, W.S. Thomas, George Hummer, and W.P. Coast, plus county treasurer Dennis Maher, superintendent W.F. Cramer, teacher Alice Luscombe, and assistant university librarian Bertha Ridgway.

The make-up of this group sent a signal that community leaders fully supported the project. Over one hundred other people followed their lead and pledged over $2,500 to the fund to finance the library's first year of operation. The list of contributors included twenty-five schoolteachers and principals, ten doctors and dentists, several attorneys, university faculty members, and businessmen, many of them familiar names in Iowa City history to this day.[10]

Of those publicly involved in the library campaign to this point, 75 percent belonged to mainstream Protestant churches and lived in all parts of the city except the Third Ward. Professor Shimek was the lone representative from that Bohemian and Catholic stronghold of northeast Iowa City, known locally as Goosetown.

Can a Public Library Diminish Youthful Lawlessness?

In the *Citizen,* Conant voiced reservations about the public library as a front-line defense against youthful lawlessness and apparent aimlessness. Like many of the middle class at the end of the nineteenth century, he was wrestling with some of the consequences of an increasingly industrialized society. In the midst of oratory expressing democratic ideals and the redeeming value of universal education lay the often unspoken fear of egalitarianism and the consequences of losing control to others with different moral and cultural values.

Conant, a young father of two who had come to Iowa City in 1894 following several reporting and editorial jobs between Iowa and his native Maine, offered a simple solution: Laws should be enforced and parents, rich and poor alike, should take responsibility for their children.

After the meeting at Smith's Armory, Conant published one of his long editorials acknowledging the incalculable benefits a library would bring to the community.[11] He quoted the words of University Law Chancellor Emlin McClain, who told the armory audience that "the city needs to supplement its splendid public school system with a library . . . just as much and as forcibly as the university needs to be provided with a library to assist its students." And Conant added his own conviction that it would benefit "those who can't afford the books they would like to read."

Conant issued a note of caution, however, suggesting that the church-related efforts to start a public library may be a wise step but not the best solution to the difficulties brought to the public's attention by the events of August 24. He worried in print that the library might be an example of "Christian complacency"—one of his favorite demons—and a rush to an easy and respectable solution to complex community problems. Earlier he had described two types of children and young people who alarmed Iowa City and needed the community's help. He used the terms of turn-of-the-century social reformers fighting the consequences of industrial development, the division of labor, and technological change. In his opinion, the "powers of darkness"—a phrase he frequently applied to the lure of liquor, drugs, and gambling—brought together two groups: the children of "discouraged or vicious poverty" and "the offspring of pampered comfort turned out by parental impatience or indifference." The same powers of darkness, he wrote, "keep one from rising to respectability and drag the other down to shame and disgrace."

Offsetting these "black influences," Conant wrote, "has been the aim of philanthropists and humanitarians for years." He thought some of their schemes would "work good results" but others he called "chimerical, serving to make more complacent [the already] complacent Christianity." He lumped Iowa City with other communities harboring complacency, saying that it was "in this respect . . . no exception to the rule." He then attributed the drive for a public library to efforts to offset those powers of darkness, asserting that "to help this condition is largely the cause of the movement to establish a public library in this community."

Although a strong supporter of a public library, Conant made his priorities very clear. He ended with two points he had made in his earlier editorials in response to the August 24 assault. A public library, he assured his readers, "would not take the place of parental supervision on the one hand and energetic legal repression on the other. If we can't have but one we would rather see a general awakening of parental responsibility . . . and a general awakening of public sentiment demanding energetic enforcement of law and order."

Making the Library a Reality

Members of the Council of Thirty met at City Hall on September 28, a week after their appointment. According to Brock's minutes, a majority of the members attended to review the constitution drafted by Stevenson for the September 6 meeting. It was read and approved article by article, "carefully discussed, slightly amended . . . and then adopted unanimously." Article I documented the intent of the organizers to focus on young people. It cited the fostering of a "love for good reading on the part of our young men and women" as one of the proposed association's four objectives and added the option, if it appeared useful, to "establish an amusement room and gymnasium" in connection with the reading room.[12]

The constitution gave the new organization an official name, the Iowa City Public Library Association, and provided for a temporary board of nine directors to be selected to serve until the first annual meeting of the association scheduled for the third Wednesday of December. Members of the selection committee included Stevenson, Cramer, Shimek, Ball, and W.S. Thomas, co-owner of Thomas & Lichty Hardware. The committee was also charged with appointing subcommittees to help with the community-wide campaign to raise funds for the association library.

By October 12 the committee had selected nine persons to serve on the temporary board of directors. In addition to Stevenson, Wade, Ball, Shimek, Luscombe, and Ridgway, who had all participated in the organizational activities, the committee chose three businessmen to balance the lawyers and educators: George Hummer, the owner and manager of a large wholesale food business; W.P. Coast and Max Mayer, who owned clothing stores at 10 South and 28 South Clinton Street. (Iowa Citians have been buying clothes at these locations for over 125 years. Today they are the sites of Land's End Outlet Store and Ewers Men's Store.)

The temporary board met on October 21, 1896, just seven weeks after the exploratory meeting at First Christian Church on August 28. All but Coast were present. As its first order of business the board elected officers: Judge Wade, president; Bertha Ridgway, vice president; S.K. Stevenson, secretary; and George Hummer, treasurer.

After each new board member signed the Articles of Incorporation for the association, President Wade appointed Stevenson, Ball, and Hummer to continue the search for suitable rooms to house the proposed library, a search that Stevenson and Luscombe had started in early September.

On October 28 the board empowered the rooms committee to begin negotiations for a lease with the owners of the Kenyon and Ham Building, which housed the C.O.D. Steam Laundry. The board members agreed to a figure "not to exceed $270 a year including heat." They were unable to get an agreement at this price and a week later, on November 7, they met again to increase the "not to exceed" limitation to $350 per year, adding the stipulation that "privileges continue for up to five years."

On November 18 the association board of directors held a meeting in the rooms above the C.O.D. Steam Laundry so board members could look over the recommended facilities. They formally approved a one-year lease for the two second-floor rooms at $375 including heat, $105 over their initial offer.

In a recently constructed brick building next door to First Christian Church, the two rooms over the C.O.D. Steam Laundry at 211-213 Iowa Avenue mea-

sured about thirty feet wide by one hundred feet deep, with windows on both the east and west sides and across the front on the north, plus an outside stairway. A wheelwright and a blacksmith worked out of a separate building on the back of the site.[13]

At this same meeting the board reviewed five applications for the position of librarian. No record exists of what the directors wanted from their librarian or of how the job was advertised. Public meetings, newspaper reports, and fund-raising activities had publicized plans for the library, so job applicants may have offered their services unsolicited. Two applicants were teach-

The first Iowa City Public Library was located at 211 Iowa Avenue on the second floor over the C.O.D. Steam Laundry. The building remains to this day.

ers, two were unemployed, and one, A.C. Howell, was a bookkeeper and a member of the Council of Thirty. Howell was unanimously "elected" for one year, with a salary of six hundred dollars.

With facilities and a librarian chosen, board members turned their attention to two other important items: a collection of books and policies and procedures for operating. Following the detailed language of the association constitution Article VII, Wade set up five committees and made appointments: an executive committee, an administrative committee, and three book committees. The executive committee handled staffing and financial issues and the administrative group planned and monitored library facilities and operations.

Wade appointed the three book committees responsible for selecting books and periodicals. He outlined the subject groupings as found in Stevenson's constitutional language and assigned the members: history, travel, philosophy, sociology, and religion to Stevenson, Ball, and Hummer; literature, including fiction and juvenile, language, arts, and reference to Ridgway, Coast, and Wade; science, magazines, and newspapers to Shimek, Luscombe, and Mayer.

The board scheduled a meeting for the following Tuesday to select books for the new library. There are no minutes from this selection meeting, but if the constitution was followed, the chairmen of the book committees plus the president were empowered to make the final decision on all book orders. It would be interesting to know what books were discussed and how this committee system worked, but at least the record of what was ordered has been preserved. Beginning with the initial purchase and for sixty years after, the library maintained a volume-by-volume listing of all books and bound volumes of magazines added to the collection by purchase or gift.

At its first annual meeting in December, the new Iowa City Public Library Association elected the temporary directors to the first permanent association board. The board met frequently in December and January to make decisions about the books, magazines, equipment, and furniture needed to turn the rented space into a library.

The directors purchased bookcases, newspaper racks, tables, chairs, a desk for the librarian, five hundred sheets of letterhead, blank library cards, "thirteen 16-candle power lamps with porcelain shades," board games—crokinale, archrena, checkers, chess, and Parcheesi—and some basics like a wastebasket, inkstand, stamp pad, broom, and dustpan. They ordered a sign and an electric globe to hang outside the suite of second-floor rooms.

Two newspapers announced in early December that the library would open on January 1, but as the date neared, the book committees still had not decided which bookseller would receive the new library's first order. After several meetings to consider proposals from a local bookstore, Lees and Ries, and from the New York-based Scribner's, they accepted the bid from Scribner's for 1,300 volumes—1,000 general and 300 juvenile.[14] The committee approved the book order on January 2; the board postponed the opening date to January 21.

The *Republican* reported that the books began arriving on January 13. "Five cases arrived yesterday containing about 1,200 of the 1,300 volumes .... Librarian and Mrs. Howell are busily engaged today, putting the books in order, classifying, recording, etc. The collection is a fine one—the books being representative of the best in fiction, history, travel, and various ologies. Mrs. Bertha Ridgway, assistant librarian at the university, is contributing much time and labor to the work that must necessarily antedate the opening of a new library."

Librarian Howell had started work on December 15. The first month's rent was paid on January 2 following some modest reworking of the shafting to reduce noise and vibration from the laundry below. Bookshelves had been constructed and basic equipment and supplies were in place. Newspapers published the rules for the new library on January 15: It would be open to anyone age ten or older, ten hours a day, six days a week, plus four hours on Sunday; one book per person for up to two weeks; five cents a day fine on books past due.

Current issues of about twenty magazines and newspapers began to arrive.

S.K. Stevenson contributed seventy-five back copies of several of the magazines ordered: *Century, Scribner's, Harper's, Review of Reviews,* and *McClure's.*

Most of the books ordered from Scribner's had been accessioned (listed and numbered as part of the library's official inventory) labeled, and prepared for use by January 16. With a good share of the new books as well as many gift volumes from local residents processed for check-out, the library was ready. After the opening ceremonies on the evening of January 20, the library would officially open for business at 9:00 a.m., Thursday, January 21, 1897.

The Dedication Ceremonies

The community turned out en masse for the dedication ceremonies. As Reizenstein described the evening, the "audience . . . packed the rooms to the very doors, while a throng, unable to gain admittance, assembled on the stairs and stretched in a long dense line, a half-block to the Dubuque St. corner."

The *Press* described the event as a "love feast," reporting that the great interest already shown by Iowa City residents "culminated in one grand burst of feeling . . . The rooms . . . were totally inadequate to contain the people who wished to hear and see last night . . . . The hallways were [also] jammed and many were on the sidewalk seeking admittance."

A mandolin quartet provided musical entertainment and at least eight dignitaries offered speeches of tribute to the "noble men and women who had worked so hard" to establish the public library and congratulated the community on its good fortune.

Historians give several reasons why communities establish public libraries: civic pride, preserving their local history, humanitarian and democratic ideals, even economic development. But on this occasion these community leaders, the economic and social elite of Iowa City, were expressing concern for the young people of the community. They wrapped these concerns in egalitarian concepts plus an almost quasireligious belief in the power of books and libraries to transform and redeem.

The most famous speech on this occasion was written but not delivered by Judge Wade, president of the Iowa City Public Library Association. In Wade's absence, Ball presided at the ceremonies and read the speech, which may have disappointed the audience, for Wade was a well-known and popular orator. The speech became a legacy to the Iowa City Public Library; it is the only one for which the text has been fully preserved and has given the library quotable material throughout its history.

As read by Ball, Wade first apologized for his absence and then congratulated the library organizers on progress up to that point. He promised that it was only a start, a foundation on which to build "a thoroughly equipped library, ample in its proportions and in the diversity of its literature . . . to meet the desires and supply the tastes of everyone." He then took several paragraphs to define "everyone," affirming the democratic principles on which the public library movement was officially based, telling the assembled crowd:

One fact should be clearly appreciated at the start: . . . this library is and will be public in the fullest sense of the word. It belongs to no person nor class of persons. It is to be under the control of no particular race nor creed. Its doors are to be ever open to the workman in overalls with the dinner bucket upon his arm, as well as to the rich or well-to-do.

The boy or girl who earns a weekly stipend by manual labor can feel that here at least they have the same rights as those upon whom fortune has smiled more kindly. Parents may feel that their children in coming here for books, whether they be rich or poor, are placing themselves under obligation to no one. They are simply exercising a right.

. . . Every person in the city shall feel perfectly free to seek the advantages of this library. It was to promote this spirit—to broaden the influence of the library—that it was made absolutely free to everyone.

Acknowledging that in most matters Iowa City had been progressive, Wade closed his prepared speech with words of regret, "but in the matter of a public library [Iowa City] has been many years behind most of the progressive cities of the state," and a plea echoed in other speeches of the evening: The citizens of Iowa City would need to approve a tax levy for the library if they wanted to see the library continue and improve.

In his story for the *Republican*, Reizenstein printed quotations from the speakers who followed—Mayor Charles Reno, Judge John Joseph Ney, A.E. Swisher, Professor Bohumil Shimek, Dennis Maher, and S.K. Stevenson.

Martin J. Wade, lawyer, judge, congressman, and first president of the Iowa City Public Library Board of Trustees

Photo courtesy State Historical Society of Iowa-Iowa City

Wade had really said it all and with style, but those who followed gave their own sermons.

Mayor Reno used a common platitude: "If one boy or one girl is saved from ruin and led into the path of right living, the efforts of these workers will not have been in vain."

Attorney Swisher pointed out that the advantages of a public library were as obvious as the benefits of schools or education: "Let children come in contact with great thinkers and great thoughts, to learn faith without fear, reverence without superstition."

Judge Ney also promised great results for the children of the community. He said they would find ideas that would be an "incentive to noble living . . . . Books like *John Halifax* or *Vicar of Wakefield* will leave an everlasting impression upon the mind of the young [and] tend to make good men and women of all young people who read them." All the speakers, using a variety of rhetorical flourishes, made two main points: The library would save the children, and citizens must be willing to pay taxes to support it.

Professor Shimek claimed that "the presence of long rows of [books] containing the best thought of human minds was more eloquent than any speech," but nevertheless continued his remarks. He insisted on the absolute necessity of a public library in any respectable community, "a place where poor boys and girls and rich boys and girls can meet on an equal footing, and the poor can find relief from the daily drudgery of life, with healthful, helpful amusement and instruction."

Speakers throughout the evening gave Stevenson credit for being the driving force behind the library campaign. In the last, and in Reizenstein's opinion the "most eloquent and elaborate speech of the evening," Stevenson got down to practicalities, explaining in some detail the potential costs to taxpayers through the proposed one-mill levy. He challenged the audience by asking, "Are you willing to vote for this to destroy the habit of reading vicious, yellow backed literature that is ruining so many young lives, and to inculcate in its stead the habit of frequenting a library where may be found good literature, the works of the world's greatest men?"

The speeches over, hundreds attended the reception, "examined the beautiful books and expressed their joy over the fact the great work had been so successfully inaugurated," reported the *Republican*. "The crowd was loath to leave and lingered late inspecting the rooms and books," wrote the *Press* reporter.

Reizenstein finished his editorial with a verbal salute: "Praise and honor be to the parents of the movement! May the people of Iowa City do their duty as nobly!" Records show he was at the library early the next morning, the fifth person to get a library card from the new Iowa City Public Library.

Tax Support for the New Library

At this juncture, as the library became increasingly popular and the campaign for tax support gained momentum, the strategy of the library's key founders became clear: Establish the library association as the governing organization, raise enough funds for the first few months, and open a library to give members of the public a demonstration of library service before they are asked to vote on tax support. The private money would not only fund the opening expenses, but would provide library service for the fifteen months between the vote and the time the tax funds would first be available.

The strategy's vital last step, the campaign to convince voters to accept the idea of a tax-supported municipal library, really started in the fall of 1896 during discussions about the need for a public library. Tax support had been mentioned obliquely as early as the September 21 meeting at Smith's Armory. Newspaper editorials took up the banner, upholding a drive for tax support in their editorial campaign for the library. Through the fall and winter as the campaign developed, references to the need for permanent tax support, in both newspapers and speeches, got more detailed and precise.

Stevenson, the most purposeful and the best-informed library advocate, had made the first reference to long-term funding at the September 21 meeting. At that time, Stevenson told the audience gathered to consider the possibility of a public library. "It will require $1,800 . . . to keep the library in force for one and a half years," he said. "[During this time] it will be securing a firm and permanent footing."

The *Republican* had reported on Stevenson's plan to raise $1,800 by subscription for the first year and a half, "after which time it is hoped that other and permanent means of support will be secured." Both Stevenson and the newspaper were vague about the definition of "permanent." At that point the emphasis had to be on raising the funds or "the plan" would not work.

In the September 25 *Citizen* Conant wrote, "The agitation for a public library should be kept up until such an institution is secured for Iowa City, but this agitation should at once assume the form of working up public sentiment in favor of a small tax for that purpose." He went on to argue what librarians and library boards would be arguing for the next hundred years. "Public libraries are not an experiment . . . . They should be a branch of the public work of every municipality as much as sanitation, street improvements, or the system of public schools."

While Conant was the first to use the word "tax" in print, he indicated that the total tax level should not be raised and used the library campaign to criticize the local Democratic administration: "We do not advocate an increase of taxes for the purpose of establishing a public library, but that our municipal business be conducted in such a manner that sufficient money . . . may be saved from what is now frittered away and actually wasted."

Unlike the *Republican* writers, whose editorials and reporting of meetings rarely mentioned taxes, Conant boldly wrote of the need for tax support of the library. In his October 2 report on the follow-up meeting of the Council of Thirty and later, on November 13, he argued for a tax. Pointing to the success of the

15

fund drive, which had yielded almost twice the goal of $1,800, he expressed assurance that the community would "instruct the municipality to use some of the public revenues for support [of the library] . . . as is done in many other places."

At a special meeting on January 5, 1897, to meet the requirements of the Iowa Code, the library board hurriedly passed a resolution asking the city council to put the question of tax support for the library on the March 1 ballot and instructed Ball and Stevenson to present it to the city council. If approved, the library would receive tax funds starting April 1, 1898. The gift funds had to cover library start-up costs and operating expenses through 1897. Start-up costs included purchase of the initial book collection, bookshelves, furniture, the installation of electric lights, painting, and the carpentry work to reduce noise from the laundry below.

Because the board took action on getting tax revenues before the January 20 dedication ceremonies, both library operations and the *official* campaign for the library's tax support were launched that evening. At the end of his January 20 dedication speech Wade had expressed confidence that the community would do the right thing: "It is only necessary to submit the question [to the voters] in order that the same may be favorably voted on." In addition, Swisher had appealed to their pride in doing at least as well as other communities. "The slight tax required to keep a good library in the city where [I] formerly resided was never complained of by a single citizen."

Stevenson laid out the facts: "Johnson County's taxable property is $2,266,888. A tax of one mill on this would magnificently support the institution and yet not make itself oppressive or even felt by any one citizen. If you possess a piece of property valued at $1,000 and assessed—as is the custom—at $300, your tax will be 30¢." After that he switched into high gear with his emotional appeal, telling his captive audience of citizens waiting to view the new library, "Do this [vote yes] and you will make good citizens of your boys and girls. Save your boys and girls and you save the city. Save your city and save the state and nation."

After the dedication ceremonies, the board focused on convincing the townspeople to vote "yes" for a levy to support a municipal library. The only existing evidence that the board made a concerted effort to educate and inform the voters outside the pages of the local newspapers is a brochure found in a scrapbook of early library documents. It states the need for the library and its cost. It could not have been printed much before February 20, ten days before the election, for it says the library has been open one month.

The immediate popularity of the library and the reports in local newspapers made the board's task easier. The *Republican* and the *Citizen* gave the campaign effort their strong and frequent editorial support. The *Republican* carried three lengthy editorials in January and February full of the sentiments expressed at the January 20 dedication. On February 24, a news article reported on the heavy traffic at the library since it had opened. "The person who has entertained for a minute the false idea that the institution is not a success, should drop into the rooms almost any afternoon and view the throng of book-readers and borrowers." "In juvenile [books]," Reizenstein in the *Republican* reported, "*Little Lord Fauntleroy* like Abou Ben[15] 'leads all the rest.'" The story publicized the success of the institution by noting that in its first three weeks the library had issued 836 cards, loaned 2,226 books, and received 4,407 visitors. Despite his general support for the library, Conant continued his am-

A FREE PUBLIC LIBRARY

IS NEEDED In Iowa City to furnish suitable reading matter for our citizens, both young and old; to supplement and continue the work begun in our schools; and provide an attractive place where our youth can spend their leisure hours and be surrounded by good influences.

ITS VALUE The good a Free Public Library will do can not be computed in dollars and cents. The establishment of this Library will increase the value of all property in Iowa City because it will make it a more desirable place in which to live.

ITS COST The citizens of Iowa City have subscribed $3,000 to establish a Free Public Library. It is proposed to donate the books and other property which has been purchased with this sum to the city of Iowa City on condition that the citizens vote to accept the benefits of Sec. 461 of the Code of Iowa. To do this and maintain the Library a one mill tax will be necessary. **If a person owns a House and Lot Valued at $1,000, his share of this Tax would only be 40 Cents. Furthermore the aggregate Taxes of Citizens will not be Increased** because the City Council propose to reduce the bridge Tax from 2½ mills to about one-half mill. Thus one mill of the bridge tax can be used for library purposes and the aggregate tax still be reduced one-half mill.

WILL IT BE USED? The Iowa City Library has been open to the public one month during that time 2,782 Books have been loaned and 5,730 persons have visited the Library and Reading Room. Facts are more convincing than words. These facts prove that there is a need for a Public Library in Iowa City and that it will be widely used.

VOTE FOR IT! It will benefit your children, your home, your city. Its privileges will be free to all.

Campaign poster promoting a "yes" vote for a tax-supported free public library. Voters gave the measure 81 percent approval on March 1, 1897.

bivalent, independent crusade in the *Citizen*. He called the public library a great resource for the "many in Iowa City outside the charmed university community who would like some of the advantages enjoyed by those who swing in the [university] circle," but said it was not the solution to Iowa City's street and youth violence. Throughout January and February he printed news about the library and added editorial support. Near the end of February, his editorials focused on the defeat of Mayor Reno and the Democrats as the only way to save Iowa City from complete control by the "powers of darkness." From this point on until the election, he ignored the library issue.

Both the *Republican* and the *Citizen*, in campaigning for "yes" votes on the referendum, told their readers that the library association had "shown a remarkable amount of determination" in getting the library opened and operating. Now the association was offering the community an opportunity to preserve that beginning by providing tax support. The *Republican* wrote on February 10: "The board of the library association proposes to donate the books and other property which has been secured to Iowa City on condition that the city takes charge of the library and makes it a permanent institution."

The only publicly recorded controversy about the appropriateness of voting for the library tax took place in mid-February, three weeks before the election. From the beginning, the Democratic *Press* gave less space and attention to the library campaign than either of the two Republican papers. It took either a neutral or supportive stance until February 10 when one of the paper's weekly editorials—signed by "Veritas" whom the community assumed to be editor C.S. Mercer—put a Faustian twist on the idea that the association was giving the city a great gift. After admitting that the association had started a very creditable public library and had given the public "a monument that speaks highly of its energy and taste for the more beautiful things of life," the writer went on to question the repercussions of the gift: "But what to do with it, now that their work is done." The editorial noted that the board had raised $3,000 and invested it all in the library; it deemed the directors "morally responsible to render a lasting account of their stewardship." Suggesting that private donations would not be sufficient to maintain what had been started, the library was "something like a worthy [white] elephant." The library board members had been taking the glory, ready to receive all the honors, but now were trying to find a way out of maintaining financial support. They would "unload the burden on the city," the editorial warned, and went on to equate the tax levy with cruel and repressive measures. "To accept their gift is to agree to maintain the library . . . and therefore, one more mill of taxes will be permanently added to the city's tax burden."

Veritas and the *Press* questioned the sincerity of the Republican papers and the association. It accused them of using egalitarian arguments simply to get the vote of the washerwoman and the laborer, and questioned whether the library could remain free to all. "Books will fall into irresponsible hands and it will be impossible to get the book wanted, unless a cash deposit is required. When you do this, the washerwoman is no longer on equal terms with the banker." He raised these issues, he wrote, so people would not "allow fine theories to hurry them beyond the facts."

The public responded with indignation. The February 17 *Republican* reported that the editor of the *Press* did not "realize the unpopularity of his move until he found himself confronted by a number of the most prominent citizens, who proceeded to call him down for his utterances." The story went on to say that when he realized there were men in his own political party who did not think this was a matter where political preference was relevant, he "stammered out something of a mingled apology and excuse."

The following week, Veritas backed down in print but denied that anyone had spoken to him personally on the topic. He came out in favor of tax support, writing, "I would advise thoughtful people to vote the tax," but repeated his accusation that the association and the other papers were using false arguments to get the vote. "My sympathy is with the success of the library, but I do not allow fanciful theories to lead me into stirring the souls of poor washerwomen and poor laborers, by raising them to the level of bankers and bankers' wives, to induce them to vote the tax." He protested against statements that were both "a delusion and a snare."

Getting Started

In the *Citizen* Conant crowed, "Veritas . . . thought it would be a popular thing to oppose the library tax that will be voted on at the coming . . . election. On Wednesday evening he backed down from his position and advocated passage of the tax."

By the end of February both Republican papers had turned away from the library issue and were carrying columns and columns of invective about the current Democratic mayor and the alleged unprofessional and unethical activities of his appointee, James Mara, as police chief. In the annual orgy of debating city politics before the city election, the *Republican* attacked the incumbent Democrats and the *Press* attempted to defend them. The skirmish created by Veritas in the *Press* over the viability of a library levy referendum soon died and all papers returned to their respective battlefields, aiming charges at or defending city officials and employees and their ability to budget and spend tax funds wisely.

Ironically, the showdown over the administration that was seen by some as allowing crime and lawlessness to flourish in Iowa City and the solution that some hoped would help diminish that crime, a permanent public library, came together on the March 1 ballot. The library tax won handily, receiving 81 percent approval from 1,582 voters. Reizenstein wrote, "Only a few mistaken voters opposed it." Democratic Mayor Charles Reno, son of one of Iowa City's pioneer mayors, was defeated 910 to 1,005 as were most of the Democratic aldermen up for reelection. Only the Democratic, Bohemian, and Catholic Third Ward held its Democratic representatives.

In his last day in office, as one of his final official acts, Mayor Reno appointed all members of the Iowa City Public Library Association Board of Directors to the first board of trustees of the newly approved municipal library. On March 15, 1897, it officially became the Iowa City Public Library.

1. Descriptions of the crime taken from three newspaper accounts: *Iowa City Republican,* Aug. 26, 1896; *Iowa State Press,* Aug. 26, 1896; *Iowa City Citizen,* Aug. 28, 1896.

2 "National Hall" is the English translation of the Bohemian phrase "Narodni Sin." It was a popular place for dances and other social events in the Bohemian community. Built by Joe Slezak in 1875, it was on the second floor over Slezak's hotel, dining room, grocery store, and stable. On the northeast corner of Linn and Bloomington, the building has been in the Slezak family since it was constructed and today is the site of Pagliai's Pizza and the Holub Apartments. Irving Weber, "Narodni Sin Remembered," *Iowa City Press-Citizen,* April 18, 1981.

3 *Republican,* Oct. 14, 1896.

4 Both the *Republican* and the *Citizen* published daily and weekly editions. Since only the weekly versions for this period are extant, there is no way to determine the news or editorial content on this crime in the daily editions. Many articles in the weekly are labeled "From Tuesday's Daily," etc.

5 The 1899 City Directory lists six billiard halls and twenty six saloons, up from three billiard halls and eighteen saloons in the 1897 edition.

6 Minutes of the library committee, Sept. 15, 1896.

[7] Irving Weber, *Irving Weber's Iowa City,* vol. 3. (Iowa City Lions Club, 1985), 61.

[8] The *Republican* of Sept. 30, 1896, gave the fullest report and along with the minutes provided the details for this description of the Sept. 21, 1896 meeting.

[9] As quoted by Reizenstein in the *Republican,* Sept. 30, 1896.

[10] Contributors included Emil Boerner, O.A. Byington, Samuel Calvin, W.D. Cannon Jr., Mrs. Helen Close, Solomon and Stevens Coldren, Elizabeth Felkner, John Hands, Gertrude Howell, W. Musser, Lee and Reis Bookstore, Charles Reno, J.W. Rich, John P. Sanaxy, Frank Stebbins, Byron Stillwell, Pratt and Strub General Store, and H.J. Wieneke—153 pledges in all. All but six were paid in full.

[11] *Citizen,* Sept. 25, 1896.

[12] Article I, Sections 1 and 2, Constitution of the Iowa City Public Library Association. Minutes book for the pre-election period.

[13] The building is relatively unchanged from when it was built in 1895. The name C.O.D. Laundry was resurrected in 1970 and attached to a bar. Today the sports bar Que is on the first floor and the second floor, with a bandstand, tables, and chairs, is rented out for private parties or when Que sponsors a band.

[14] The Scribner family was one of the first families of American publishing and bookselling. Scribner's operated a large bookstore on Fifth Avenue near the other well-known New York bookstores—Dutton's, Putnam's, Bretano's—as well as a publishing house for books and the popular *Scribner's Magazine.*

[15] Reference to a poem by Leigh Hunt, Abou Ben Adhem. Written about 1835, it still appears in many anthologies of favorite poems.

■ 2.   Looking Back: Libraries Before 1897

It was nearly fifty years after the start of the American public library movement that the doors of the Iowa City Public Library opened for the first time. After leading Iowa into territorial recognition and statehood, Iowa Citians established a university and built public schools; opened private academies, meeting halls, bookstores, and opera houses; founded historical and literary societies, social and study clubs; published books and newspapers; and even helped pass state legislation for the founding of municipal libraries many years before the campaign to start a local public library began in the fall of 1896.

If a brutal crime and concern over the resources available to the young people of the community were the short-term causes driving community leaders to quickly convince both financial contributors and voters to support the new institution, it is also interesting to speculate on the reasons why Iowa Citians waited significantly longer than many other Iowa and university communities to provide the general public free access to a collection of reading materials.

Public Library Development before 1897

If a public library is defined as a collection of reading materials that is publicly supported, publicly controlled, and available free to the general public, the modern American public library movement began around 1850. Before 1850 the term "public library" often referred to various kinds of shared book collections, but the public library as recognized today evolved over a much longer period. Libraries began with the preservation of written records, but before the eighteenth century they were primarily storehouses, not institutions for the distribution of knowledge, a key purpose of the modern public library.

A Century of Stories

The early colonists brought the first libraries to America—their private collections. These early settlers had a relatively high rate of literacy and a strong and early interest in books. Philadelphia is said to have had as many libraries and bookstores in 1760 as any European city of comparable size. Leaders of the colonial era not only owned books, they read and used them effectively in formulating the ideas instrumental to the founding of the United States. Numerous journals, diaries, and books reveal the effect of private libraries on the world of colonial ideas. Early colleges had also established libraries for students and scholars. But neither private nor college libraries could meet general community needs.

Thomas Bray (1656-1730), a colonist and clergyman of the Church of England, took an early step toward establishing the public library concept. Deeply concerned over the inability of colonial ministers to obtain books, he founded the Society for Promoting Christian Knowledge. The society collected money and purchased over 35,000 volumes. Bray organized libraries all along the eastern seaboard aimed at serving ministers and laymen, and while they fell far short of his expectations, they were undoubtedly the first free lending libraries in the New World.

In the fourth decade of the eighteenth century, people of similar background, income, and social level began to organize voluntary associations—termed "social libraries" by one authority—to provide themselves access to a shared collection of books and periodicals. One type, called "proprietary libraries," was based on a joint stock principle. Members purchased shares in the property of the group. Men of some wealth and social standing frequented the reading rooms of the library and owned and used the collections, which usually consisted of serious books intended more for education than entertainment.

In 1731 Benjamin Franklin started the first and perhaps most famous of the other type of social library, the "subscription library." His Philadelphia Library Company supplied books and information to colonists during the Revolution and to delegates to the Constitutional Convention in 1787. By 1800 his subscription form of library had become very popular. It required only an annual membership fee and marked a further step toward popularizing knowledge, for unlike proprietary associations, subscription libraries admitted people who could not afford to invest in collections of books. Annual fees bought services only, not title to the property. Subscription libraries often catered to particular kinds of users or to special reading interests. There were lyceum libraries, mercantile libraries, libraries for mechanics, for apprentices, for factory workers. Some women's clubs also operated libraries. Members of these associations enjoyed companionship, recreation, and entertainment while pursuing their common goal of education and self-improvement.

After 1851 social libraries organized by members of the Young Men's Christian Association (YMCA) gained wide popularity throughout the country, including Iowa City. By 1875 over 180 local YMCA chapters or associations had been established in the U.S. Although initially these library collections aimed at the moral improvement of young men with the study of the Bible as a central theme, the libraries gradually expanded to include more general reading matter. YMCA reading rooms, sometimes open to the public, offered newspapers, periodicals, and general reading and reference works. In addition, their popular custom of remaining open evenings and Sunday afternoons influenced the practice of extended hours for public libraries. Money for books came from membership fees and from sponsored lecture courses for the general public. In many places sponsorship of an annual lecture series was the original reason for organizing.

Labeled "social" because of their general public purpose, both proprietary and subscription libraries were corporations, first chartered by each state and later granted their powers through state legislation. The act of incorporation allowed the members of association libraries and the shareholders of proprietary libraries to work together without surrendering their personal rights or threatening their personal property if the corporation should acquire debts or fail—which happened frequently. The act of incorporation gave the library the right to own property and receive gifts and allowed it to elect officers and a board of control that could formulate rules and regulations binding on its members in a basic governance structure found in most public libraries to this day.

During the colonial period and the first half of the nineteenth century, corporate structure provided many of the municipal functions that later became the province of government agencies. Corporate associations under special charter supplied water, built bridges, provided fire protection, maintained roads, and operated educational and charitable efforts for the poor. The thousands of social libraries—public library historian Jesse Shera[1] records over 1,000 in the six New England states by 1850—were corporations "not because of an inherent virtue in the corporation as an instrument of book distribution but because other social agencies coexistent with the social libraries were organized in a similar manner."[2] It was easy and natural for citizens to turn to forms used in their communities.

Both types of social libraries were important forerunners of the public library. Their inherent weakness, however—reliance on voluntary support—drove communities to look for more permanent sources of funds. These association libraries continually faced the problem of maintaining memberships or shareholders in numbers large enough to finance adequate collections. In addition, many of them relied on a few individuals to keep the library going. When these individuals died, moved away, or simply "burned out," support for the library rapidly evaporated. Thus, while subscription and proprietary libraries provided a public library system based on the ability to pay for the service desired, the "shifting sands of voluntary support [were] not a sufficiently solid foundation upon which to build a universal library service."[3]

During this same period, circulating or rental libraries were making their own contribution to evolving ideas about public libraries. The term "circulating library" dates back to an earlier time when most libraries did not allow their books to leave the library. Circulating or "rental" libraries permitted people to take books home for a small rental fee. While men with enthusiasm for good literature usually selected the book collections of the social libraries, the circulating libraries reflected more popular tastes. Because they were commercial enterprises, the business owners chose popular and ephemeral titles over more substantive works, with fiction the most popular category. The circulating library catered to the current demands of borrowers, who paid quarterly or annual membership dues for a predetermined number of books or paid for each volume borrowed, with the fee usually based on the size of the book. Sometimes they operated independently, but many of the most successful circulating libraries were based in bookstores and other businesses. Though most rental libraries had short lives, a few retained their vitality well into the twentieth century by supplying in the later period what many public libraries avoided—popular collections of Westerns, mysteries, and detective stories. Circulating libraries remained sensitive barometers of popular reading tastes, reflecting the culture if not the form of the institutions from which the public library emerged.

The popularity of both social and circulating libraries reflected the interest in and concern for providing educational and cultural opportunities for citizens of the new republic. Reading was not only a popular pastime, it could be the passport to a professional career in this period when colleges provided classical studies, not practical or professional training. During the nineteenth century support for the common (free) school was widespread, but the preparation of teachers, mechanics, lawyers, and many others for the tasks society required was still relatively unstructured; books and reading were the prime resource. In addition, as the number of immigrants arriving increased, the need to educate and to acclimate them to society's mores and values loomed large in the minds of many political and community leaders.

The first formal affirmation of the principle that it was the duty of the state to help provide libraries as well as schools for the general public came in 1835. In that year New York enacted a state law permitting tax-supported, free library service in each school district through school district libraries open to the general public. About twenty other states followed the New York example. But school district libraries proved ineffective as public libraries. The units were too small, the amount of tax money raised annually too limited, and the number of volumes too meager to attract the general public. However, the libraries did establish certain principles which form the basis of our present public library system: Libraries are educational agencies and logically extend the idea of universal free public education, taxes should support free library service, and state aid to local libraries can encourage local efforts. The acknowledgment of the importance of free library service meant that social and circulating libraries, with their limited constituencies, could no longer be expected to serve the broad range of citizens seeking access to good literature and reference books or wanting to read new fiction, newspapers, and magazines.

Using the definition of a public library as a book collection publicly supported, publicly controlled, and free to the public, only a few public libraries existed before 1850. Though several New England communities claim earlier free tax-supported collections, Petersborough, New Hampshire, is usually credited with establishing the first municipally supported free public library in 1833. By 1896 the number of municipal libraries with at least 1,000 volumes had grown to 971—plus hundreds of others with smaller collections—assuring the public library a permanent place in the life of the nation.[4]

The passage of state laws enabling local governmental units to levy taxes for the support of public libraries—New Hampshire in 1849 and Massachusetts in 1851—and the establishment of the first great public library in Boston in 1854 marked the beginning of the modern public library movement. The Boston form of library governance by a lay board followed the pattern of the many social libraries of the period. It protected the library from the often unscrupulous conflicts of city politics.

The Ticknor Report,[5] submitted by the Boston Public Library board to the Boston City Council in 1852, set forth what is generally considered the first credo of the public library. It still stands as one of the best single statements of the relation of the library to the social order.[6] If there is an argument for free public schools, Ticknor said, then it follows that free public libraries are also required. Schools awaken a taste for reading and train men and women to acquire knowledge from books, but furnish nothing to read. Books are the basic instrument of education and both the graduates themselves and public and social institutions benefit from the general diffusion of knowledge. Ticknor ended the report with some details of proposed library operations: All residents of Boston—men and women, employed and unemployed—should be allowed to use the library without charge, with books supplied in enough variety and quantity to allow access to popular materials within a reasonable period of time.

Especially during its early years, the Boston Public Library influenced every aspect of the American library movement. By 1875 the Boston Public Library, with a collection of nearly 300,000 volumes, circulated over 1 million volumes per year from its main building and several branches. The library board stressed the educational, social, and political advantages of a public library that served every class in the community, and after considerable controversy, it had begun supplying books for entertainment as well as enrichment and instruction. Its egalitarian policies set the standard for American public library service.

Library Development in Iowa before 1897

H.H. Hoeltje in his 1927 *Iowa Journal of History* article on the history of lecturers and lecturing in Iowa, notes that contrary to its "isolated pioneer" stereotype, Iowa was not a cultural wasteland during the first fifty to sixty years of its settlement. The existence of association libraries, touring lecturers and drama groups, hundreds of churches, opera houses, and newspapers, and by 1872, over 12,000 school districts, all suggest a literate if not wealthy population who desire and need access to a variety of reading materials.

From the day it became a territory in 1838, Iowa began planning for a state-supported library. The U.S. Congress allotted $5,000 for the purchase of a library under the supervision of the Iowa governor. In that same year Governor Robert Lucas, in his first message to the first territorial legislative assembly, reported he had assembled a list and ordered standard works appropriate for a "public library." This was the seed from which the Iowa State Library grew. The State Law Library in Des Moines still houses many of these volumes; others were returned to the library in Iowa City's Old Capitol when it was restored in 1976.

In 1839 the legislative assembly of the Iowa Territory passed an act "for the incorporation of public libraries." Like legislation passed earlier in many eastern states and discussed above, the act allowed for the establishment of subscription or proprietary libraries with the powers and protection of a corporate structure. These social libraries, frequently called public or association libraries by their operators, predominated in Iowa until the 1870s, issuing stock, owning property, assessing dues, and setting rules of operation for their members. In 1853 Jefferson County first used the 1839 law to start a subscription library. Under continuous operation since it began more than 140 years ago, it later became the municipal library of Fairfield, Iowa's oldest public library. While no other library can match Fairfield's record, in the late 1850s and 1860s several other communities started association libraries that eventually evolved into municipal libraries: Maquoketa (1857), Cedar Falls (1859), Keokuk (1863), and Dubuque (1865), as well as Council Bluffs, Des Moines, Davenport, Burlington, and Manchester before 1870.

The Thirteenth General Assembly adopted legislation in 1870 to allow cities and towns to levy a tax in support of a municipal library. In 1872 the Fourteenth General Assembly amended the law to require a vote of the people to create a free tax-supported library. Modeled after the Illinois Public Library Act, the legislation tied funding to assessed property valuation, allowing automatic increases as the value of property increased. Cities with populations of less than 25,000 could levy one mill per $1,000 assessed value. The law enumerated the powers and responsibilities of the board of directors and directed appointment of trustees by the mayor with approval by the city council. This governance pattern, influenced by the corporate structure of association libraries and refined by the Boston Public Library board to protect the library from the whims of city politics, characterized libraries throughout the country.

By the end of 1873 the citizens of Independence had voted to approve tax support for a library, and it became Iowa's first municipal free public library. Ten more communities followed in the next ten years: Osage, Sioux City, Nevada, Cedar Falls, Council Bluffs, Des Moines, Washington, Fort Dodge, Indianola, and Manchester. By 1897, the year of the vote in Iowa City, thirty-one cities had approved a local levy for a municipal library. This number included half the cities with populations over 5,000. Another fourteen cities had viable association libraries that had been providing access to book collections to some persons in their communities for as long as forty-five years. Though not publicly supported or controlled, and generally not free or available to all citizens, these long-term association libraries built a strong foundation for library service in their communities and many became so widely used that the step to municipal support was almost pro forma.

In 1890 Iowa libraries and librarians, growing in number, joined forces to form the Iowa Library Association. Only New York had formed such a professional organization before Iowa. University librarian Ada North, the moving force behind the first Iowa gathering, spent three years at the Des Moines Association Library in the 1860s, was state librarian from 1871 to 1878, and then came to Iowa City as administrator of the University of Iowa Library from 1879 to 1892.

Early Iowa City Libraries

Iowa City went through the same phases of library development the country had experienced since colonial days. Between 1857 and 1873 townspeople organized two association libraries, one proprietary library, and a circulating library. Unlike the long-term success of association libraries in places like Fairfield and Cedar Falls, these libraries suffered the same fate as many libraries before them, failing for lack of patronage, continuing sources of financial support, or profitability.

In 1857 Iowa City lost the seat of state government, but gained other important state institutions: the State Historical Society and the first state university.

The third and final Iowa Constitution, written and approved in Iowa City, contained a compromise that said while the capital would move to Des Moines the university would be permanently sited in Iowa City with no branches in other communities, thus dropping earlier efforts to place university outposts in Dubuque, Mount Pleasant, and Fairfield.

Since its establishment in 1846, the university had struggled to get financed and organized. In 1857 university officials appointed mathematics professor Frederick Humphrey to organize a collection of five hundred books built from an initial gift of fifty volumes two years earlier. In his first year Humphrey opened the doors of the new university library in the old Mechanics Academy on Iowa Avenue; with books divided into five classes—theology, jurisprudence and politics, science and art, belles lettres, and history—he prepared a book catalog and urged the legislature to give the growing university an annual book budget.

The State Historical Society was established in Iowa City in the same year. Members of the Sixth General Assembly and representatives to the Iowa Constitutional Convention of 1857 agreed that an organization to collect and preserve Iowa history should be located in Iowa City "in connection with, and under the auspices of, the State University." Benjamin Shambaugh, in his 1939 Iowa City history, *Old Stone Capitol Remembers*, eloquently described the convictions of the time, writing that the pioneers of the 1830s and 1840s "were part of a great movement that some day would be recorded in the pages of history." The state legislators approved a permanent annual appropriation for the historical society, and when the state officers moved to Des Moines they gave the society quarters in the abandoned capitol building.

Citizens' Library Association, 1857. In the shadow of these historic events, the establishment of the Citizens' Library Association in November 1856 received little attention. In Iowa library history, nevertheless, it has generally been recorded as the first attempt in Iowa City and the fourth in Iowa—following Fairfield, Davenport, and Dubuque—to provide a community with a general purpose library, although the preamble to its constitution says little to imply a public purpose [emphasis added]:

> *We,* the subscribers . . . being desirous of extending the means by which *we* may promote the best interests of *our* social, intellectual and moral intercourse and to extend *our* information upon subjects of general utility; do associate *ourselves* together for the purpose of collecting a Library, establishing a Reading Room, and organizing a course of instruction by Lectures; . . . and other means of *mutual* improvement as may contribute to *our* well being.

While the constitution proposed a library, a reading room, and a course of instruction via lectures, the board of trustees evidently gave higher priority to the public lecture course and the reading rooms for members than to building a book collection. At the end of the year their financial report recorded no money spent on the purchase of books.

According to its published rules, the association assessed an initiation fee of one dollar and charged dues of two dollars per year. Visiting friends of members could use the rooms free for two weeks; other nonmembers paid ten cents per week in advance for up to four weeks.

The reading room, located "four doors north of the post office" on the west side of the 100 block of north Clinton Street, was open twelve hours every day except Sunday. While the room contained no books, the 142 members of the association could choose from twenty-two daily newspapers, nine weeklies, and twelve periodicals. Rules prohibited talking and smoking and urged the use of spittoons. The atmosphere resembled that of a private club, with the silence broken only by the rustle of papers and the zing of tobacco juice hitting the spittoons.

Twelve members served on the board of trustees during 1857.[7] They included editors, legislators, bankers, county and state officials, lawyers, and merchants. Many played important roles in the history of Iowa and Iowa City. Charles Hobart—later a lawyer, an editor of the *Republican,* and a land agent—served as president and librarian of the association at a salary of twenty-five dollars for the year. He resigned after six months "because business of a more profitable character demands my . . . attention. . . . The association would [be better served by someone] better qualified with influence and means than myself." When Hobart resigned, John Pattee, brother-in-law of soon-to-be-governor Samuel Kirkwood and the first librarian for the State Historical Society, took over as president. Trustee George McCleary, a county judge in 1857, was one of the founders of Iowa City's Old Settlers' Association and would serve three terms as Iowa City mayor in the 1860s. R.H. Sylvester started several newspapers in Iowa City; John Teesdale, editor of the *Republican,* left Iowa City the next year to buy a newspaper in Des Moines and to become Iowa State Printer.[8] Hugh Downey is generally described as Iowa City's first banker. Franklin D. Wells, superintendent of public Instruction in 1857, later took the post of university librarian. All were men interested in books and ideas who evidently could afford the membership fees.

According to a lengthy report written by lecture course chairman Frank Ballard, the association expended its biggest effort on the lecture course of 1856-57, a "Course of Literary and Miscellaneous Lecturers" sold via season tickets. Before the railroad arrived in 1856, lectures generally featured local talent because of the uncertainties of touring by stagecoach. Aurner, in his 1912 history of

Johnson County, makes the point that lawyers, judges, and others interested in ideas and public affairs had much lighter workloads in the 1840s and 1850s. With time on their hands, they hungered for intellectual entertainment.[9] Two meeting halls, Market Hall and Athenaeum Hall, had been constructed in 1856 to accommodate public gatherings. An advertisement by the owners of Market Hall in the 1857 City Directory described it as "Iowa City's largest and finest public hall." Athenaeum Hall, "built with taste and beauty," seated seven hundred people. Market Hall was at the corner of Iowa and Dubuque streets and the Athenaeum was on Clinton Street north of Jefferson.

While ten lectures were ultimately given, the Citizens' Library Association lecture committee faced several problems. First of all, members did not start planning the series until after November 12, the date of their incorporation, taking over a series under preparation by others. Lecture chairman Ballard described the lectures as "an unusual array of talent and promising a most attractive feast of reason,"[10] but members grumbled that the speakers did not reflect the association's interests and expectations. Ballard's report also claimed that some of the general public expressed fear that the originally published list of lecturers was merely an enticement to induce ticket sales and that there would be substitutions or eliminations from the announced schedule. While the lecture committee vigorously denied the allegations, a string of unlucky events made the denials subsequently appear false. Six of the original speakers dropped out, three from illness and death. Another three, including Horace Mann, failed to appear despite signed contracts.

Wendell Phillips and Horace Greeley, the best-known names in this first Iowa City lecture series, did speak to audiences as promised that winter of 1856-57. Phillips, a lawyer and abolitionist, delivered his most famous lecture, "The Lost Arts," in Iowa City in the winter of 1857. He reportedly gave this speech over 2,000 times before he died in 1884. Greeley, the often controversial but very popular editor, reformer, and abolitionist, had left the Whig Party to join the new Republican Party just before his Iowa City appearance. Mrs. Eliza Woodson Farnham, philanthropist, novelist, and feminist, lectured on women's rights. At one time she directed the female wing of Sing Sing prison and over a period of years started several establishments for destitute women. Henry Giles, long-time popular orator and another abolitionist, had left the Catholic priesthood to become a Unitarian minister. Except for Wendell Phillips's lecture on "The Lost Arts," Ballard's report on the lecture series does not link lecturer and topic, but the titles he cited included "Yankee Land," "The West," "Mary, Queen of Scots," "Civilization," and "Temperance."

In addition to the late start and the several deletions and substitutions to the program, a long and hard winter that year caused fewer people to attend. Expenditures for the series exceeded receipts by $69.67, "which amount has been generously made up by individuals interested in the welfare of the association," according to the president's year-end report. He was optimistic about the impact of the series, however. The "public lectures produced not only a vast amount of positive good, but they suppressed a vast amount of evil." He claimed that they had supplied the community with a "healthy, wholesome system of amusements, which otherwise would seek gratification in demoralizing and pernicious shows and exhibitions."

A receipt dated March 4, 1857, issued by the Citizens' Library Association for library privileges. The association apparently lasted only one year.

I.C. Public Library Archives

With a balance in the treasury of $2.04 and thirty-three new members lined up to join the original 142, President Pattee was downright bullish about the coming year. "I congratulate you . . . upon the success of this . . . enterprise and . . . recommend that we do not halt in the work. Let the best of lecturers be secured early for the coming winter and lecture season; let the best of papers and magazines be taken; let the reading room be suitable and convenient, and kept in good order; let the proper officers solicit a large membership, and the permanent existence and future success of the Citizens' Library Association will be secured." The existence of the Citizens' Library Association seems to end with this report; the association never owned any books and died with $2.04 in the treasury after the 1856-57 season.

Wieneke Circulating Library, 1859. In the spring of 1859 Henry J. Wieneke briefly opened a circulating library in his grocery store on Jefferson Street between Dubuque and Clinton streets, the second recorded attempt to provide some kind of library service to residents of Iowa City. Public response to this service, at five cents per day per book, quickly built the collection to 1,000 volumes, but Wieneke did not find it profitable enough to continue and closed the library after a few months.[11] Shera's exhaustive look at circulating libraries in New England in a slightly earlier period suggests that five cents was on the high end of fees charged.[12]

Wieneke had come to Iowa City in 1845 at the age of eight and was involved with books and bookselling for much of his life. In 1861 he enlisted for service in the Civil War; in 1904 he told J.W. Rich that, when ordered to Fort Randall on the northwest frontier, he took 150 volumes with him to share with his infantry company. Many of the remaining volumes were still in his private collection in

1904, according to Rich.[13] Following the Civil War, he managed and later owned a bookstore on Clinton Street. His daughter, Carrie, ran the Wieneke/Arcade Bookstore at 114 East Washington until 1938. For many of those years the younger Wieneke offered a rental library in the bookstore like her father had done eighty years earlier.

YMCA Social Hall and Reading Rooms, 1863–70. Iowa City's YMCA officially started on June 24, 1864, with a social hall and reading room on north Clinton Street, probably near the rooms that housed the 1857 Citizens' Library Association. The area was sometimes referred to as the Post Office Block.[14] Membership was limited to men and cost three dollars a year. J.W. Rich, an officer of the organization in its early years, wrote in 1904 that he was uncertain if a library was an avowed objective of the YMCA when organized, but its reading room soon began to fill up with books. He wrote, from personal memory and from an 1867 report, that reading room bookshelves contained several hundred volumes. The 1868-69 City Directory reports, "The YMCA occupies a commodious public library and reading room in their hall in the post office block. Reading rooms are open 2 to 5 and 6:30 to 9:30 daily." The reading rooms were open to the general public; there is no record of rules for borrowing books.

The YMCA appears to have been successful during the first few years despite a fire in the fall of 1867. The October 2, 1867 *Republican* reported that the damage done by the fire had been repaired and the rooms were open to the public each weekday evening from seven to nine-thirty.

A very successful lecture series during the winter of 1867-68 brought in a profit of over two hundred dollars. After the Civil War, lectures remained a major source of education and entertainment for cities and towns of the Midwest. With the expansion of railroad travel they became an even more viable and reliable attraction. The YMCAs in Iowa and neighboring states had even organized a speaker's bureau in Chicago, booking lecturers for all its forty members.

The lecture circuit of 1867-68 included two of the most popular speakers of the post-war years. John Gough, a reformed alcoholic and very effective temperance speaker, claimed to have made 9,600 lectures and received 140,000 written pledges from individuals promising never to drink alcohol. Only Gough, who has been described as perhaps the greatest speaker on the lecture circuit in the post-Civil War years, could compete in popularity with Anna Dickinson, a Quaker from Philadelphia who had been lecturing since she was seventeen, primarily on Negro and women's rights. This was the second consecutive year that Gough and Dickinson had appeared in Iowa City, and each of them drew twice the audience of any of the other six lecturers.

In addition to Gough and Dickinson, Iowa Citians heard lectures by B.F. Taylor, popular poet of everyday life; William Milburn, a blind Methodist circuit

rider; John H. Vincent, called the father of the American Sunday School movement and one of the founders of the Chautauqua Institution in New York; E.P.
Whipple, literary critic and essayist; J.G. Holland, medically trained but better at
discussing everyday problems with everyday people in a way that built a large
following; and Petroleum Nasby, a popular and famous political satirist from the
Toledo *Blade*.

In May 1869 the YMCA moved to new quarters over G.W. Marquardt's Jewelry Store, on the east side of Clinton Street between Washington and College,
possibly for economic reasons. By the next spring the YMCA made a public appeal for funds and raised $230, according to the *Republican*. The paper also reported that the library had five hundred volumes and was receiving eight daily,
forty weekly, and sixteen monthly publications. Financial problems continued,
however, and a few months later, in October 1870, the YMCA offered the library to any association that would carry on "the work begun."

Iowa City Library Association, 1870–73. The response to this plea created the
fourth attempt at a "public library" for Iowa City. Between October 6 and December 10, 1870, a group of nineteen "incorporators" organized the Iowa City
Library Association, sold shares at five dollars each, negotiated an agreement
with the YMCA for the transfer of its books and other property, assumed its
lease, and issued rules and regulations for use of the reading rooms and collection
through detailed bylaws. The articles of incorporation described the
association's purpose as "the formation and maintenance of a public library." By
January 1, 1871, the group had completed all the legal and practical steps and
claimed to have over $1,000 in subscribed stock.

The fee schedule made the Iowa City Library Association the kind of proprietary library that sold both shares and memberships. A five dollar share guaranteed all the privileges of the library as well as a vote at the annual stockholders
meeting for the first year. After that a shareholder paid two dollars per year dues
or forfeited his stock. In addition, the association offered memberships for two
dollars or three dollars a year (both figures are given), which carried the right to
use the reading room and borrow books but no voting rights.

The bylaws called for a seven-member board of directors, with four officers
and three committees—executive, library, and lecture. The previously accessible
collections of books and periodicals of the YMCA were now available only to
those who paid a minimum fee of two dollars per year. The reading rooms were
open each week day from 3 to 5 p.m. and 7 to 9 p.m. with slightly longer hours
from April 1 to October 1. The bylaws also stated that the librarian "shall keep
the . . . rooms in perfect order and shall not be absent . . . during the time . . . open
to visitors without consent of a member of the library committee," and continued with details on required records and reports. Members and stockholders

could borrow one volume at a time for up to two weeks. The overdue fee was ten cents per week "or fraction thereof" and damages would be assessed for ink spots, torn pages, and so on. One sentence summarized the rules for behavior: "All loud talking, laughing, spitting on floor or carpet, and all boisterous and improper conduct in the rooms of the association is strictly prohibited."

An 1871-72 shareholders list carried the names of 156 men and ten "stock subscribers but not paid." Of the 120 identified, half were business owners, investors, and bankers, and about a third were professionals—lawyers, doctors, editors, professors, and ministers. The remaining shareholders worked in skilled trades, as employees of local businesses, or as farmers. Many held offices in the community or in churches and lodges. Fifteen had held elected city offices— mayor or city council member. Fourteen had served as county officials—treasurer, supervisor, or school superintendent. Several had been state legislators and six had served on the Iowa City school board. Many had also held appointed offices from time to time: postmaster, police chief, city assessor, state librarian, board of regents. They belonged to lodges, boat clubs, agricultural societies, temperance groups, the State Historical Society, YMCA, and the Old Settlers' Association. All whose religion could be identified from directories and histories of the period were Protestants. No obviously Bohemian names appeared on the list.

By the end of 1871, financial troubles loomed despite the comfortable start. The association had taken over all the assets of the YMCA library for only the $145 YMCA debt. In 1871 the association board spent all but $70 of the $860 capital raised from the sale of stock: $400 for books and retirement of the YMCA debt and $360 for rent, salaries, fuel, and light bills. The latter, along with new books and periodical subscriptions, would be annual expenses. Only ten men purchased memberships at two dollars each in 1871 and members and shareholders paid only ten dollars in fines. Even if each of the 172 shareholders would pay his two-dollar dues in the coming year, and the number of members would double, 1872 income would be less than four hundred dollars. Without additional income from new members, stock sales, or a lecture course, the association faced ongoing financial difficulties.

Problems continued to multiply. The board of directors never met regularly as the bylaws required. Crises generated most meetings. Plans to recruit new members and to sponsor fund-raising events were discussed but seldom carried out. When the directors met in October of 1871 they passed a motion asking the lecture committee to make arrangements for a series of six lectures by "the best lecturers whose services can be procured." The minutes did not say "at this late date," but like the Citizens' Library Association before them, the committee had probably waited too long to book outstanding speakers for the 1871-72 season.

After a grim financial picture presented at the November 6 stockholders meeting, stockholders John P. Irish and M.T. Close suggested for the first time, but certainly not the last, that the association solicit donations. Again, fund-producing activities were discussed but nothing was decided.

Despite the dire need for funds and fund-raising activities, the group did not sponsor a lecture series—potentially the major source of income besides shares and memberships—in the winter of 1872. President W.C. Hammond, a law professor, told the board in January he would be gone most of the year and urged them to replace him, but the board declined. At a May 1872 meeting they decided to raise $150 "at once" to purchase books. By August the lecture committee had lined up three speakers for the 1872-73 season, including John Gough, one of the big draws of the YMCA lecture series of 1867-68, and the Mendelssohn Quintette Club, a local musical group.

At the second annual stockholders meeting in November 1872, the stockholders were so upset by the financial report that they elected seven new directors. No financial details appear in the minutes, but Professor S.N. Fellows immediately moved that the directors be instructed to submit the question of a tax for the support of the library to the citizens of Iowa City at the next municipal election. The motion, while not seconded, proposed an alternative solution to the library's financial problems using new legislation passed earlier that year.

The new board members tackled association problems in a series of three meetings between November 1872 and January 1873. They asked that arrears of stockholders be collected "in order to replenish our treasury, sufficient for current expenses." They instructed their president and former mayor Moses J. Morsman to "visit our citizens in person and solicit memberships, collect dues, or accept donations of money for the library association." And they asked the new lecture committee "to canvass the field and if thought expedient, to secure a few additional lectures" to those already approved by the retired board. They subsequently added three names and dropped one from the original lecture schedule. To cut expenses they decided to open the library only two days a week: afternoons and evenings on Wednesdays and Saturdays.

The board did not meet again until the following May. The nation experienced a severe financial depression in 1873 and it was probably a poor year to expect shareholders to bail out the library. After hearing a verbal financial report that board members said must be written up and "spread upon the record," they appointed a committee to meet with the Amateur Drama Club to explore the idea of a benefit performance. Professor Fellows of the library committee reported that the reading rooms no longer had a librarian.

On September 19, 1873, the board met for a "general discussion on the propriety of closing and winding up the affairs of the association caused through the general indisposition on the part of the stockholders to pay dues or contribute funds to the association." By the next meeting the treasurer reported debts of $112 and cash of $75. L.B. Patterson, one of the former board members, suggested they auction off the books and other property of the association and divide the net proceeds among current stockholders. He and two others were appointed to carry out the resolution, which included scheduling a general meeting of the stockholders for their approval of the plan. Nine months later, in June 1874, Patterson reported the results of the auction and announced that stockholders holding the forty-one shares of association stock would receive eight dollars per share. Thus he distributed the proceeds of two library associations among thirty-five of Iowa City's business, professional, and academic citizens.

From the beginning, the Iowa City Library Association suffered all the classic problems of association libraries. Only a few members actively participated, and even their interest waned between emergencies. The group was unable to attract new members or to organize fund-raising events, and income from dues and the sale of stock was inadequate to support operations. While one member had suggested the possibility of establishing a tax-supported municipal library, there did not seem to be any understanding among the other members about this option.

Library Activity between 1873 and 1896

Between the failure of the Iowa City Library Association in 1873 and the sudden activity of 1896 no other groups or individuals attempted to provide a collection of books and periodicals to the general public nor establish a bona fide public library. We can only speculate as to reasons for this apparent lack of interest in a tax-supported library during these twenty-three years, but comments made during the 1896-97 campaign provide evidence that there had been no sustained efforts. Several participants and commentators referred to the libraries of "twenty years ago" and expressed dismay at the failure of Iowa City to act sooner on this matter.

W.H. Conant, editor of the *Citizen,* noted in the fall of 1896 that "the conditions are just about the same in this city as they were when the Young Men's Christian Association organized and maintained a library . . . twenty years ago." At the September 1896 public meeting to enlist community-wide support and contributions for the proposed library, Superintendent Stevenson attempted to spur or shame citizens into action. "If a map of the larger towns of Iowa were hung up before you, you would see that twenty-six of them already had public libraries and reading rooms," he said. Wade continued this theme in his letter read at the formal opening of the new library on January 20, 1897, when he said that Iowa City was many years behind other progressive cities of Iowa in establishing a public library.

In the years since 1873, despite a cooling down from the heady days of its first two decades—settlement, territory legislatures, statehood, and constitution writing—Iowa City continued to play an important role in the political and cultural life of the state. The university produced many college graduates (including women after 1860),[15] most of the state's medical practitioners, and a long list of lawyers, judges, and elected officials. Newspaper editors and legislators from other communities, envious of Iowa City as the home of the university and the State Historical Society, seldom missed an opportunity to criticize Iowa City. According to *Citizen* editor Conant, local residents were very sensitive to these comments and frequently voiced fear of losing these prestigious institutions. In 1890 the Iowa City City Council gave its one-block city park (bounded by Iowa, Dubuque, Jefferson, and Linn streets) to the university, supposedly to head off attempts by the legislature to move the university to Des Moines. In 1896 Conant accused Iowa City officials of trying to cover up the West Side assault because statewide knowledge of it could harm the university, and both Davenport and Muscatine papers editorialized about sending the state's young people to Iowa City in light of the "horrible act."[16]

In a city where newspapers, public and private schools, bookstores, lodges, literary societies, women's study clubs, lecture courses, theaters, an opera house, and a major university all flourished, by the late 1880s at least, a public library appears to be one of the most conspicuous exceptions to Iowa City's list of cultural institutions.

Historians have cited a natural rivalry among communities to become cultural centers as a strong reason for establishing a public library. A public library on Main Street was becoming the symbol of a modern and progressive community, replacing the church on the square of European towns and villages. Iowa City could point to the university and a rich history as the first capital of the state. By 1885 Reizenstein in the *Republican* had already nicknamed Iowa City the "Athens of Iowa," but a list of things "needed to make Iowa City a better place," published in the fifty-year (1890) anniversary edition of the paper, did not mention a public library. The wish list included streetcars, residences for workingmen, a canning factory, and a "first class glass house."

Photo courtesy State Historical Society of Iowa-Iowa City

Jacob Reizenstein, Iowa City journalist from 1885 to 1961, wrote colorful prose about the library for over fifty years. Known to many as "Jake" or "Jakey", he always signed his newspaper columns "J.E.R."

Sometimes a desire to preserve the history of a town and conserve its historical records has impelled citizens to organize a library as a storehouse for their past, but early Iowa City history was the history of

Iowa and, by the 1890s, the State Historical Society and the Old Settlers' Association had been recording Iowa and Iowa City history for over twenty-five years.

In many communities philanthropy was an important impetus to organizing a library. Families with large fortunes endowed libraries and built buildings. In Iowa local families funded Dubuque, Muscatine, Burlington, Boone, Centerville, Grinnell, and Fort Madison library buildings. The post-Civil War dream of Iowa City's businessmen to build a strong industrial base in their community had faded by 1896, and the community had not produced successful industrialists with tax-free fortunes and the desire to attach their family name to a local institution. By 1896 Iowa City was primarily a college town, and while a crime committed by a few rowdy young laborers could arouse citizens to action, most boys came to town to get an education, not a job. There was not much danger in Iowa City of the long-term labor conflicts or large-scale poverty and crowding produced by "this new industrial age," but neither was there much hope that a local industry would produce a fortune and endow a library.

On the other hand, since the period of school district libraries in the 1840s and the Ticknor Report of the Boston Public Library in 1852, the idea of public libraries as potential partners with the public schools and as instruments of universal public education had grown increasingly popular. Education-based arguments for a public library dominated the 1896 Iowa City campaign, with school officials and teachers active, visible, and vocal. In addition to the contention that the library supports children in and out of school, the campaigners expounded heavily on the redeeming value of reading. Reading leads to desirable ends, they said, and books have the power to alter people for the better. This educational and civilizing aim of a public library had not been expressed in Iowa City before. No one had advocated library services to young people below the university level in any of the 1857-73 activity; rather, the specific needs and interests of the association libraries' members and shareholders shaped their small collections.

Library historians today debate the motives of the nineteenth century founders of public libraries.[17] Did they wish to empower individuals and prepare them to function in a democratic society or were they hoping to perpetuate the established social order by maintaining control over the growing number of relatively uneducated laboring classes and immigrants? Fourth of July oratory often included public libraries as one of the ways to make democracy work. Public library advocates agreed with Jefferson who said informed and intelligent citizens would never consent to the destruction of their liberties. By educating citizens to vote intelligently and participate in local community affairs, a public library provided the means to develop responsible townspeople. Iowa City, surrounded by and partially supported by educational institutions, with a history of high participation in both state and local politics and with a highly literate citizenry, evidently felt little need for further educational opportunities for its citizens. Opening its high school in 1872, Iowa City was relatively early in Iowa in offering local children a free post-grammar school education. Only when faced with undisciplined young men threatening the community's peace and safety did they begin to understand the possibility of the library as an instrument of social control.

The University and the Public Library. The presence of the University of Iowa Library was one of the basic reasons for the lack of efforts to start a public library after the demise of the Iowa City Library Association in 1873, but the relationship between the university library and the lack of a public library is more complex than it might appear.

After starting with a mere five hundred books in 1857, the year of the Citizens' Library Association, by 1873 the university library owned 5,600 volumes, and between 1873 and 1896 the collection grew to over 32,000. For twelve years starting in the late 1860s, Amos Currier, a shareholder of the 1870 Iowa City Library Association, served as university librarian in addition to his faculty position. He "put the library in shape," according to Mildred Throne in her 1943 history of the library.[18] He created catalogs, increased hours to six a day, six days a week, started reserve and accession systems, and raised the amount spent annually on books to over $750 a year. When he left in 1879 the library owned 12,000 books and university officials had accepted his recommendation of a full-time librarian.

Ada North, with experience at two major libraries in Des Moines, was probably at the time the best-known librarian in the state. She took charge of the university library and made more improvements, including a card catalog and books classified in the Dewey Decimal System. North responded to requests from students for more hours and more newspapers, and she extended library privileges to undergraduates. By the 1890s the library offered over one hundred periodicals and more than forty newspapers. Bertha Ridgway and Joseph Rich, both future Iowa City Public Library trustees, joined the staff as librarians in 1892 when North left.

Who would benefit from an improved university library besides college students? Faculty members, whose work depended on a well-stocked library, were the chief advocates of improving that library. They, along with the business and professional leaders of Iowa City, had made several unsuccessful attempts in the third quarter of the nineteenth century to create for themselves and their peers a place where some books, but especially newspapers and periodicals, were available at a cost they could afford. There is no record of what the business and professional group did after 1873 or if they ever used the university library as it grew and improved. Discouraged by their attempts to keep an association library going, they faced limited choices to satisfy their reading needs: bookstores and newsstands, books shared informally among themselves, or, possibly, loans from the university library. While a reading room richly furnished with newspapers and periodicals appeared to be attractive to educated men of the nineteenth century and probably essential if they wished to follow technological, business, financial, and political trends in Iowa and nationwide, it is doubtful they would share space comfortably with university students or if there was even room for them to do so.

In 1882 the university library moved from Old Capitol to a forty-by-one-hundred-foot second-story room next door in North Hall. It shared some of the space with the chapel until 1892 when the chapel was moved to the new YMCA building (Close Hall). This small area housed 9,000 books when the library opened in North Hall, but the collection had grown to 25,000 by 1897. Open only six to nine hours a day during the school year, with no evening hours until 1898, there was an average of 290 visitors a day in 1891. Space was severely limited. Often seats were full and many were forced to stand to use library materials. For many of these years access to the book stacks for anyone but faculty, graduate students, and seniors was limited to Friday afternoons. In the summer the library closed except for one half-day per week. There was no assistant to the librarian until 1887 and it was 1896 before a third person was added. Student complaints about the facilities appeared frequently in the campus newspaper.

Librarian Rich reported in 1894, however, that nonstudents accounted for 13 percent of the library's two-week loans. (Overnight and faculty loans were counted separately.) Some individuals besides students and faculty were evidently borrowing books from the university library, but the desire for a comfortable reading space manifested in the facilities of all three earlier association libraries was probably not being satisfied.

If the presence of the university library reduced the actual or assumed need for a public library in Iowa City, it was not the practice followed by nineteen other communities with major state universities in ten Midwestern states. All but two established public libraries before or a few years after the founding of the university. Only East Lansing and Iowa City waited fifty years or more to start their municipal libraries.[19]

Women's Clubs and Public Libraries. In many cities and towns throughout the state and nation, women labored for libraries, but in Iowa City no women joined any of the 1857, 1863, or 1870 association libraries, and several women's clubs organized in the 1880s (some extant to this day) failed to advocate for a public library or even to join the successful campaign for a library initiated in late 1896. The university library hired Ada North in 1879 and other women followed in

1887 and 1892, but the appointment of Alice Luscombe to a committee at the public library's first organizational meeting in August 1896 is the earliest record of an Iowa City woman volunteering for any kind of public library support activity. By contrast, groups of women and formal women's clubs were the organizing agents in over twenty Iowa communities between 1865 and 1900, helping to build strong association libraries and later municipal libraries. Algona, Boone, Carroll, Cedar Rapids, Des Moines, Dubuque, Mount Pleasant, Newton, Oskaloosa, Tipton, and West Liberty were some of the communities to benefit from these pioneer library advocates.[20] Records of the efforts of Iowa women and women throughout the country appear in archives of community libraries, in histories of women's clubs, and in fiction about women of the nineteenth century.

In Cedar Rapids Ada Van Vecten organized the City Federation of Ladies Literary Clubs in 1895, combining eight literary clubs into one. These women subsequently led the fight for a community library using the power of an 1894 law giving Iowa women the right to vote on certain local tax issues. They fought off heavy opposition both to the idea of a tax-supported library and to women voting, and carried the election by a margin of fifty-nine votes in March 1896, just one year before the easily approved all-male referendum in Iowa City.[21]

In the final thirty years of the 1800s women organized themselves into secular clubs for the first time and began the women's club movement. Equal education for women was still a recent addition to the premises of a democratic society and equal rights for women, especially the right to vote, was a developing and controversial issue. The women's club movement was much less radical or political than the burgeoning feminist and suffrage groups of the period and thus was immensely popular to a wide spectrum of women—rural and urban, middle and upper class, professional and homemaker, but generally well-educated. As in Cedar Rapids, these clubs became the nuclei of organized women in this period who worked to form public libraries, both for their self-improvement and to improve their communities.

Women journalists, barred from a New York Press Club meeting with Charles Dickens, are generally credited with starting the first U.S. women's club, Sorosis, in 1868. But the concept developed spontaneously across the country—women joining together to pursue educational goals and seeking intellectual fulfillment with other women not of the same "class, clique, or caste" but with similar personal objectives. The Conversational Club started in Dubuque, Iowa, in the same year as Sorosis, and members of that group claimed there had been reading circles in Dubuque since at least 1857. A Maquoketa ladies literary club started the same year, followed by the first Cedar Rapids Ladies Literary Club organized in 1879. By the 1880s women in many communities in the state, including Iowa

City, had established small groups of like-minded women and set up formidable courses of study with frequent meetings and serious rules for preparation and presentation.[22]

In preparing for topics such as "The Athenian Commonwealth," "The German Reformation: Its Cause, Leaders, and Results," "The Origins of Language," "The Spirit and Progress of Italian Arts," and "History of Financial Systems in Europe," women discovered the need for resource materials. The idea of starting a club or community library surfaced about the same time in many areas. Some clubs limited membership to between fifteen and twenty-five; others grew larger and broke into "departments" organized by topics. Several clubs nurtured the formation of other clubs in their communities with the plan to join ranks, Cedar Rapids-style, when they wished to undertake a broader project such as establishing a library.

To celebrate its twentieth anniversary, Sorosis issued a call in 1889 for representatives of women's clubs from all over the nation to assemble in New York and form a national federation of clubs. Five Iowa clubs, including Iowa City's Nineteenth Century Club (est. 1883), were among the sixty-nine organizations that sent delegates. Many others sent letters of support. By 1890 the General Federation of Women's Clubs had been organized, and at its first biennial meeting in 1892 the federation cited Iowa as a "pioneer in club work" and as the fourth state to begin a statewide federated organization.

But neither a national federation of clubs nor civic activities to improve the local community seemed to interest the women's clubs of Iowa City. Nineteenth Century Club instructed its representative, Ellen G. McClain, to vote against federation at the 1889 national meeting. The club also declined an invitation to join the Iowa State Federation in 1892 and an invitation to join other Iowa City clubs in hiring a joint hall for club meetings. The club did sponsor two lectures on women's legal rights in Iowa and an appearance by reformer and suffragist Julia Ward Howe in the 1880s, but the only other attempt to address a local issue before 1900 was a suggestion by Mrs. Amos Currier in 1899 that members join others in petitioning the city council to prevent spitting on the public sidewalks. "The club formed its own ivory tower of concentrated self-education," reported one history of the organization.[23]

Iowa City's N.N. Club (est. 1886) attended the first state meeting of Iowa federated clubs in 1892, and while it kept its membership in the state federation until 1942, club minutes show little active participation. Except for two projects in the late 1890s—helping to organize the Women's Improvement League (a Project Green precursor) and a short-lived committee "to assist schools"—the club has remained a study group, not an action group, for over 110 years.

Raphael Club (est. 1884) was the third women's study club to organize in Iowa

City before 1900. The club's records have not been preserved to the extent of the other two, but profiles of the organization from its fiftieth and one hundredth anniversaries make it clear that this organization was devoted from its first day to the study of art and art history and undertook no community-wide projects.

The study topics undertaken by these Iowa City women's study clubs were as challenging as those recorded in Croly's 1898 history of the General Federation of Women's Clubs. The members of these clubs displayed a serious interest in a wide range of topics, yet there was no University of Iowa College of Liberal Arts until 1900, and thus little post-high school, general education for them to pursue. Raphael concentrated on art history while Nineteenth Century Club and N.N. Club sampled history, literature, and the social sciences. Their ambitious agendas in the last two decades of the nineteenth century included thirteen to twenty meetings a year, sometimes with as many as four reports per meeting. For many years sessions would last several hours before and after a shared lunch or dinner. A four-year study of English history (N.N. Club, 1890-94) or two-year studies of Elizabethan literature (Nineteenth Century Club, 1889-91) and early German history (Nineteenth Century Club, 1893-95) required resource materials. Sometimes the groups included bibliographies in their annual printed programs, but where did these lists or the books they represented come from? Did they rely on their personal libraries? Did their own academic members or their university faculty spouses give guidance and loan them materials? Or did they, as seems likely with the business and professional men stranded after the end of the earlier library association efforts, turn to the university library and in doing so remove themselves from the roster of Iowa Citians most likely to demand a public library in Iowa City?

Another type of organization, the local book club, may have inadvertently helped delay the opening of an Iowa City public library. While many other communities, recognizing the need for a communal collection of books and periodicals, were working to establish public libraries, at least one Iowa City book club bought and shared books among its own members. They were people with the means, respect, and leadership skills to organize and advocate the need for giving everyone access to books, but in what may have been a typical college community "town and gown" division, they chose another route. The Iowa City Book Club, started in the fall of 1888, organized to select, jointly purchase, and circulate two books a month to each member household. Members paid dues of up to five dollars a year, hired a messenger to deliver the books on a carefully planned schedule, and, at the end of the year, held an auction among themselves so members could purchase titles from the past year's selection for their private libraries. The club limited membership to twenty households, primarily university and professional families including many names familiar in the public life of Iowa

City during the last quarter of the nineteenth century: McClain, Currier, Calvin, Macbride, Shambaugh, Schaeffer, Dey, Bloom, and Carson. The club continued to operate well into the twentieth century, probably until the beginning of World War II.[24]

Civic Leaders and the Public Library. Public librarians understand that their institutions serve several constituencies: those seeking knowledge and wisdom and the "civilizing" effects of reading good books and great literature; those seeking to become better informed citizens of a democratic society; and those seeking to fulfill basic utilitarian needs for job improvement, vocational training, school assignments, personal hobbies and interests, or leisure and recreational reading. But despite the library community's claim that the public library is the "people's university," it is the educated classes that have always exercised the dominant force in its governance and have been its heaviest users. Without their support a public library does not begin nor does it survive.

There is some evidence that of the Iowa Citians who belonged to the several library associations and book and study clubs started in the latter half of the nineteenth century, few were active in the 1896-97 movement to establish a public library. While both groups—the club/association members and the public library activists (Council of Thirty and contributors to the library's first-year fund)—were dominated by professionals, faculty, business owners, and their families, there was little overlap in membership of the two groups. Few members of the club/association group registered for library cards in the library's first six months, and even five years later in 1901 the card holder list carried few club/association family names.[25]

When a community provides many of its civic leaders alternative paths to library resources, these leaders—the very people who know how to articulate the need and to organize for action—fail to exert pressure on the community for public library service. Consequently, many who might have benefited from the treasures of a public library once opened are denied the opportunity. In the 1890s many clerks and laborers worked twelve-hour days, sometimes six days a week, and had little enough time to seek education or entertainment through reading, let alone advocate for a public library. Joseph Wall, in his 1970 biography of Andrew Carnegie, quotes a steelworker, ". . . but after my day's work, I haven't been able to do much studying. . . . After working twelve hours, how can a man go to a library?"[26]

It appears that in Iowa City, until public school officials and other concerned citizens in 1896 used an upsetting and cruel crime to open an avenue of attention to the library and reading needs of schoolchildren, especially those less well-served by current community conditions, no strong voice proclaimed the value of public library service. Many of the academic, economic, and social leaders of the community had found other means for satisfying their reading and information requirements and felt no urgency to establish a public library.

A final irony: Six months after the opening of the Iowa City Public Library, on June 16, 1897, the University of Iowa Library—the institution that may have unwittingly slowed the public library's founding—suffered a serious fire and lost two-thirds of its collection. By October of the same year North Hall was repaired and rebuilt and the university library moved back after a temporary stay in the old Unitarian Church on the northeast corner of Clinton and Iowa streets. The 4,000-square- foot room in North Hall was about the same size as the first site of the public library on Iowa Avenue.

---

[1] Jesse Shera, *Foundations of the Public Library* (University of Chicago, 1949), 69.

[2] Ibid., 66.

[3] Ibid., 78.

[4] George S. Bobinski, *Carnegie Libraries: their history and impact on American Public Library Development* (American Library Association, 1969), 5-7.

[5] Written by George Ticknor and Edward Everett. Ticknor was a Harvard faculty member, known especially for his *History of Spanish Literature*. After 1854, he traveled in Europe for fifteen months to buy books for the Boston Public Library and left his valuable personal collection to the library. Everett was the "other" speaker at Gettysburg. Both were members of the first Boston Public Library Board of Trustees.

[6] Shera, 181.

[7] *Constitution, By-laws, and List of Officers of the Citizens' Library Association.* J. Teesdale, printer, 1857.

[8] Teesdale bought the *Iowa Citizen,* changed the name to the *Iowa State Register,* and declared it "the official paper of the state of Iowa." Both its statewide scope and the word "Register" remained and it eventually evolved into the *Des Moines Register.* "The Newspaper that captured a state: The Des Moines Register, 1849-1985," The *Annals of Iowa,* vol. 54, no. 4, fall 1995.

[9] Charles Ray Aurner, *Leading Events in Johnson County, Iowa, History* (Cedar Rapids: Western Press, 1912), vol. 1, 570.

[10] *Reports of the President and other Officers of the Citizens' Library Association for the Year 1857.* Iowa City, Crum and Boye, printers, 1857, 9.

[11] J.W. Rich, *Memo of the History of Library Movement in Iowa City, Iowa.* Typescript of remarks given at the dedication of the Carnegie building, 1904, 2.

[12] Shera, 128.

[13] Rich, 3

[14] This block, bounded by Clinton, Capitol, Jefferson, and Market streets, was called the Post Office Block in pre-Civil War days. It was filled with businesses of all kinds including the Post Office from 1839 to 1868. This block is now the location of the Pappajohn Business Administration Building, opened in 1993.

[15] The University of Iowa was the first state institution of higher learning to admit women on the same basis as men.

[16] *Republican*, September 9, 1896. The paper quotes the critical comments of both the Davenport and Muscatine papers and replies. After 1860 Iowa newspapers continually criticized all aspects of Iowa City life, so much so that the ability to serve and preserve the university was the prime consid-

eration when Johnson County residents chose their legislators. See also "A Fact a Day about Iowa City," *Press-Citizen*, Aug. 27, 1934, for more examples.

[17] See Dee Garrison, *Apostles of Culture; the Public Librarian and American Society, 1876-1920* (Free Press, 1979), xi-xv, and Michael H. Harris, "The Purpose of the American Public Library; a Revisionist's Interpretation of History," *Library Journal,* 98 (Sept. 15, 1973), 2509-14.

[18] Mildred Throne, *History of the State University of Iowa Libraries.* Unpublished master's thesis, University of Iowa, 1943.

[19] Founding dates of public libraries in Midwestern university communities: Champaign/Urbana, 1876/1874; Bloomington, 1821; Lafayette, 1882; Cedar Falls, 1865; Manhattan, 1857; Minneapolis, 1885; Ann Arbor, 1856; Lincoln, 1877; Madison, 1875. The Ames public library was started in 1903, thirty-three years after Iowa State University in 1869. East Lansing was established in 1923, nearly sixty-five years after Michigan State University.

[20] Iowa Library Commission. *First Biennial Report,* 1903.

[21] *The Cedar Rapids Public Library; the First 100 Years.* Cedar Rapids Public Library. n.d., 1-4. Richard Lord Acton and Patricia Narsif Acton. *To Go Free; a Treasury of Iowa's Legal Heritage* (Iowa State University Press, 1995) Page 174 gives text of the 1895 law.

[22] If there were women's clubs in Iowa City earlier than 1883 no historical records have been found.

[23] Kate Rousmaniere, *The Nineteenth Century Club,* typescript, 1980, 7. Nineteenth Century Club papers, State Historical Society, Iowa City.

[24] Records for the years 1888-98 are at the State Historical Society, Iowa City. Local resident Betty Keyser Means remembers her family's participation at least as late as 1939.

[25] The early rosters of the Iowa Library Association, Iowa City Book Club, Nineteen Century Club, N.N. Club, and Raphael Club were compared to the Council of Thirty, the list of contributors to the 1896-97 library fund, and the library's list of card holders, 1897-1901. Many names could not be identified so conclusions may be open to debate.

[26] Joseph Wall, *Andrew Carnegie* (New York: Oxford Press, 1970), 580.

■ 3.   Keeping It Going: The First Five Years, 1897—1901

Iowa Citians lined up to get borrower's cards on January 21, 1897. A.K. Corbett, a harness maker, received the first Iowa City Public Library card. Next was the manager of the local Western Union office, J.A. Chapman, followed by one of the Close brothers who owned the Close Linseed Oil Works, near the Close Mansion at Gilbert and Bowery streets. Newspaper editors William Conant and Jacob Reizenstein, two people who strongly supported the establishment of a public library, received cards four and five. Next were a printer from the *Republican*, local lawyer S.A. Swisher, and two employees of the Chicago, Rock Island and Pacific Railroad. Nora Donohoe, wife of a local plumber, was the first woman to get a card. A group of teachers from the Iowa City schools took the next ten, and later came the children of a furniture dealer and a saloon keeper, a druggist and a carpenter. Stenographers and bookkeepers seemed to come in pairs: two from the Citizens Savings Bank, two from Athens Press, and two more who worked for W.F. Main, jewelry manufacturer. By the end of the day a banker and an insurance agent, a mason and a painter, a blacksmith who was also a city councilman, a grocer, and the secretary of the Iowa Commerce Commission had requested their cards. None of the visitors that day were listed in the 1897-98 City Directory as the "washerwoman" whom Veritas had worried about during the library campaign, but there were several widows who may have filled that category. And we will never know if the carpenter or the house painter wore "his overalls and carried his dinner bucket under his arm" like Judge Wade predicted in his dedication remarks, but from the first day, residents of all ages and all parts of the community began to use their new library.

In the first ten days librarian Howell issued 577 cards, nearly 60 a day and more than 10 percent of all the cards issued in the first five years. By the end of 1901, five year later, area residents had made nearly 300,000 visits to the library, and 5,292 card holders had checked out the library's 6,000 books 135,000 times.

The First Trustees

In the story of these first five years, however, the enthusiasm for the library was shown not only in the numbers of people who checked out books, but also by the volunteers who chose to serve. During the last one hundred years 115 men and women[1] have served on the Iowa City Public Library Board of Trustees, but it was the first nine persons appointed by outgoing Mayor Reno in March 1897, plus one 1898 replacement, who took on the difficult task of beginning and nurturing the new institution.

In the fall and winter of 1896-97, before their official appointment, the founding nine trustees made all the initial decisions of place, equipment, collection content, rules, hours, and library staff. They orchestrated the opening ceremonies to the obvious delight of the overflow crowds who attended. Starting Thursday, January 21, 1897, they had the responsibility to see that the public library they had promised to the electorate was open and operating every day. After the resounding vote of approval on March 1, they knew they had created an institution destined to serve Iowa City for a long time.

At a meeting in early March the board members reelected the officers they had selected the previous year: Judge Martin Wade, president; Bertha Ridgway, vice president; S.K. Stevenson, secretary; and George Hummer, treasurer. This election established a pattern that continued for many years. A male president held the position for as long as he was willing or until he left the board. A female vice-president presided when the president was absent but displayed little leadership on policy issues. Sometimes she helped with day-to-day operations of the library, especially in these first years. The secretary and treasurer were both very important jobs in the early years but their duties gradually decreased as the library staff increased, the librarian took on more responsibilities, and the city staff began to assist with budget and finances.

Despite the absence of women in the library campaign, there have never been fewer than two women serving on the board in its history. Since 1897 40 percent of all local library trustees have been female, with three to five women the pattern after the late 1930s. In contrast, the Madison (Wisconsin) Public Library had no female board members for its first thirty-three years. It took Minneapolis sixteen years to appoint a woman to its library board, and then only five in the first fifty years. Detroit, a pioneer library established in 1865, had just three women trustees in its first one hundred years. Five women served as trustees for the San Diego

Public Library in its first fifty years, with no woman until thirteen years after it was founded.

There was a vigorous mix of gender, religion, political party, ethnic background, and middle class occupations among the first ten Iowa City library trustees: Democrat and Republican; Catholic, Unitarian, Presbyterian, Methodist, and Jew; business owner, teacher, professor, librarian, lawyer, judge, and school superintendent; immigrants from England, Ireland, Bohemia, and Germany; ages ranging from twenty-six to fifty-five. If not representative of the broadest range of Iowa City residents, the membership was probably more varied than library boards in many communities.[2]

Few trustees in ICPL history can match the time and years of service contributed by this original group and few boards can match these individuals in accomplishment, talent, and community service. These remarkable men and women served a total of 129 years and directed the library in its crucial early years.

Martin J. Wade, 1896–1902. Judge Wade served as president of the board from the early pre-opening meetings through 1903 when his election to the U.S. House of Representatives forced him to resign from the board. This young and popular Democratic judge was born in Vermont in 1861 but spent most of his youth on a farm north of Independence, Iowa. He completed a classical course at St. Joseph's College in Dubuque before he went on to receive a law degree from the University of Iowa in 1886. His parents emigrated from Ireland and Wade was an active Catholic layman and lifelong Democrat. He was appointed (1893) and later elected judge of the Eighth Judicial District Court. After one term in Congress (1903-05) he practiced law until President Wilson named him to the United States District Court in 1915. From 1891 to 1905 he also served on the university faculty as a professor of medical jurisprudence. Always a popular orator in Iowa City and across the country, he spent several seasons on the lecture circuit in the Midwest. In his later years he wrote and spoke frequently about the Constitution and the importance of education for citizenship, devoting much effort and his own funds to publishing and distributing his ideas. Today, however, his speech read at the opening of the public library is probably the best known of his many books, pamphlets, and speeches. He had a national reputation and his death in 1931 brought officials and friends from all over the United States to Iowa City to say goodbye to a much-beloved "Judge Wade."

Bertha Ridgway, 1896–1904. Bertha Gilchrist Ridgway was the original vice-president of the Iowa City Library Board. Born in Pennsylvania in 1865, she came to Iowa City in 1891 by way of Detroit, Michigan, where her daughter, Jessie, was born in 1888 and where her husband evidently died. Little is known about her life before or after her years in Iowa City. She became assistant librarian at the university library in 1891 and was promoted to librarian in 1898 after

J.W. Rich (ICPL trustee 1903-17) left the position. Whether she had formal library training before Iowa City is unknown, but her responsibilities at the university library suggest she had a certain amount of experience. Ada North had started the card catalog at the university library, but Ridgway and Rich found many "non-accessioned" documents and periodicals after taking a detailed inventory and Ridgway began to add these records to the catalog. When Rich left the university library in 1898, Ridgway began rebuilding and revitalizing the library after the disastrous fire of 1897. The public library relied heavily on Ridgway's expertise during these first five years, but she left the ICPL board and the university in 1903 for a position at the Purdue University Library. She died, however, at University of Iowa Hospitals in 1910 "after a long illness."[3]

Bertha Ridgway, library trustee, 1896-1904

S.K. Stevenson, 1896–1929. Samuel Kirkwood Stevenson could be tagged the father and grandfather of the Iowa City Public Library. Only twenty-nine years old in 1896, Stevenson had left law school four years earlier when he was elected superintendent of schools for Johnson County. He organized and chaired the first meeting to consider establishing a public library in August of 1896, and participated in every aspect of the library's organizational activities from that first meeting until he left the board thirty-three years later at the age of sixty-two. Stevenson, a Republican repeatedly elected to the county schools office in a heavily Democratic county, was recruited by the Iowa City Board of Education to become superintendent of schools for Iowa City just four months after the public library opened. He was the chief spokesman for the public library as a support system for the public schools, and demonstrated his belief in the importance of schoolchildren's access to books and reading by establishing small lending libraries in most of the ninety-five school districts of Johnson County while he held the office of superintendent and by giving papers at meetings of the Iowa State Teachers Association on how to start school libraries.

Born and raised on a farm in Scott Township and the youngest of eight children, Stevenson attended Johnson County schools. He graduated with honors from the Iowa City Academy and from the university in 1893 with a bachelor of philosophy degree. Stevenson first revealed his talents for organization and leadership during his college days. An active debater who made the commencement address for his class, he also led the Zethagathian Literary Society, organized the University Lecture Bureau, and served as business manager for the *Vidette-Reporter*, a student newspaper.

On graduation Stevenson was elected a ruling elder of the Presbyterian Church in Iowa City and served as Sunday school superintendent for over twenty-five years. During his public school superintendency he formed the Johnson County Teacher's Association and edited the monthly paper, *Johnson County Teacher*. He also started an organization of Johnson County school officials to bring together the school boards in each of the county's twenty-two townships. He was known throughout the area for his Johnson County School of Methods, "largely attended by progressive teachers of eastern Iowa because of the high quality of instruction given."[4]

The chief mover behind the organizational efforts of 1896, chairing public meetings, writing bylaws, serving on all committees, and campaigning for votes for the March 1, 1897 election, Stevenson took a more low-profile role for the next thirty-three years. Never president, he served continuously as secretary for sixteen years and for several other terms in the 1920s. He was always willing to take on special assignments and there were many such opportunities in the early years when the board managed every detail of library business. He attended nearly 90 percent of all the board meetings—more than 350—during his years of service. Stevenson left the Iowa City superintendent's job in 1906, finished law school, and practiced law in Iowa City until 1931.

In that year Stevenson was disbarred for mismanaging client funds, just five days after his chief partner in founding the library thirty-five years earlier, Judge Wade, was buried with highest honors. In the midst of accolades for Wade and public speculation about the career of Stevenson, neither man was remembered for his contribution to the public library. Stevenson moved to California in 1937 and died in San Francisco in 1938.

George W. Ball, 1896–1905. George Ball was one of most active of the original board members during the library's organizational period. He was county attorney at the time and in addition to prosecuting the young men found guilty of the August 1896 assault, he hosted many of the first meetings of the Iowa City Public Library Association board in the Baker and Ball law offices. Ball was an active and experienced Democrat and a member of the city council in the early 1880s, serving in the Iowa General Assembly 1886-87. After his term as county attorney he was elected a state senator, 1901-04, while still serving as a library trustee. He left the board in 1905 when he was elected mayor of Iowa City, the first Democrat to fill that position since Reno lost to Stebbins in the March 1897 city election that established the public library. In the library's early years Ball often served as a go-between with the mayor and the city council. Despite his active political life, Ball attended 83 of 116 scheduled meetings during his eight years on the board.

Ball was born in 1847 in Jefferson County and attended rural schools near

Fairfield. He attended Fairfield and Iowa Wesleyan colleges before graduating from the University of Iowa Law School in 1870. After a short time in Des Moines, he established the Baker and Ball law firm in 1874. His wife, Estella Walker, attended Simpson College and was a charter member of Nineteenth Century Club in 1883. His son, George Ball Jr., worked at the library while a student during this period and his granddaughter, Virginia Ball Hendershot, spent her entire life in the Iowa City area. The Iowa City law firm of Hayek, Hayek, Brown, and Engh is a direct descendant of Baker and Ball.[5] Active in the Masonic Lodge, Ball served as Grand Prelate, Grand Master, and Grand High Priest for the state of Iowa before he died in 1915.

MAYOR GEO. W. BALL

From "Our Live Ones," circa 1907

George Ball, library trustee, 1896-1902

Bohumil Shimek, 1896–1907. Shimek is probably the best known today of this original group. Iowa City has named two elementary schools and state officials have named a state forest in southern Iowa in honor of this distinguished university botanist and lifelong community leader. He never held an office during his fourteen years on the library board but seemed always willing to take on special assignments. For the first six years he personally selected and ordered the magazines and newspapers for the library including German and Bohemian-language papers and journals. It wasn't official, by any means, but there seems to have been a "Bohemian seat" on the board during the first twenty years. Shimek was succeeded by Frank Horak in 1911, and Paul A. Korab replaced Horak in 1917. All three were very active in the Bohemian community of Iowa City.

Photo courtesy State Historical Society of Iowa-Iowa City

Bohumil Shimek, library trustee, 1896-1910

Shimek's parents emigrated from Bohemia in 1856, bringing two children with them. Shimek was born in 1861 in a rural area near Shueyville and was the youngest of five children. His mother died in 1866 and his father in 1880. Biographers like to relate that Shimek earned his own way from the age of eleven, although the pinch didn't really come until he was sixteen when his father became seriously ill. These same biographers describe Shimek's parents as poor, struggling farmers. This was fairly accurate for their years in the United States, but Shimek's father, Francis Joseph, was politically active in Bohemia, known as an orator and "man of persuasion." He had little formal education, but was widely read in philosophy, religion, and topics related to politics and history prohibited by the Austrian government. A horticulturist and later a shoemaker, Francis Shimek suffered persecution for his activities during the revolutionary period of 1848-49 and he sought asylum from the government when he came to the U.S. in 1856. Raised as Catholics, Shimek's parents disavowed all connection with the church and became "free thinkers." Shimek worked with others to establish the first Bohemian newspaper in the U.S. and continued his political activities as long as his health permitted.[6]

Based on this background, young Shimek's early interest in education, his long interest in perpetuating Bohemian culture and language, and his lifelong career in botany is not so surprising even for an eleven-year-old orphan from a poor farming family. Like his father and contrary to most Iowa Citians of Bohemian heritage, Shimek was a Unitarian.

Shimek earned a degree in civil engineering from the university in 1883 and worked as the Johnson County surveyor before becoming a science teacher at the Iowa City Academy and later, Iowa City High School. After two years of teaching zoology at the University of Nebraska, he joined the University of Iowa faculty in 1890, becoming a full professor of botany in 1902. By the time he retired in 1932 he was considered the foremost plant ecologist in the United States, and was part of the university's powerhouse team in the natural sciences during this period—Macbride, Calvin, and Shimek.

In addition to his professional and library activities, Shimek served on the city council from 1883 to 1887, was elected to six terms on the school board between 1891 and 1917, joined the Iowa City Park Board after leaving the library board, and was president of the board of the Unitarian Church and various state and national Bohemian, science, and engineering societies. He died in 1937.

George Hummer, 1896–1912. Born in 1842, George Hummer joined Ball and Coast as the oldest members of the original board. Hummer served as treasurer until 1907 when he became president for the four years preceding his death in 1912. Along with Stevenson, Hummer was the driving force behind the fund drive that the library association started in 1896 to pay for the first year's operation before the tax levy became available in March of 1898. He helped collect pledges and continued to raise new money throughout 1897 until the total reached $3,500. Hummer was the chief financial officer of the library in the early years. At that time city officers were not yet involved in holding and disbursing library funds, and the librarian had no authority to commit or expend these monies.

Hummer's father came to Johnson County in 1839, according to the records of the Old Settlers' Association. Young Hummer started a grocery store in the 1870s. By 1890 the business grew into the George Hummer Mercantile Co., wholesale grocers. He had other business interests and became relatively wealthy. Hummer Mercantile, at 229-231 Washington Street, was still in business in 1926. An active Catholic layman, Hummer volunteered in many Iowa City organizations.

W.P. Coast, 1896–1907. William Phillip Coast, an Iowa City businessman, served the library from its founding until 1907, including two years as president. Born in 1841, he came to Iowa City from Ohio in 1854. He attended Oberlin College and later the University of Iowa. He took over his father's real estate business and in 1890 he opened a clothing store at 10 South Clinton Street. In business until 1933, the Coast shop headed a long list of clothing stores at that site: Bagwell's, Towner's, Seiferts, and Land's End. (The word "Coast" can still be seen on the sidewalk outside the building.) According to Irving Weber, Coast made a fortune from his store and his vast real estate holdings, but his sons, Will and Preston, were less successful. Mrs. Coast was an avid reader and joined both the Nineteenth Century and Raphael clubs in the late 1890s. Son Will was a charter member of the Iowa City Rotary Club in 1915, the year the elder Coast died.

Max Mayer, 1896–1914. Max Mayer was the second clothing retailer on the original library board. His business, started by his father-in-law Moses Bloom, is one of two long-term clothing stores on Clinton street, continued by Ewers Men's Store to this day. Mayer was one of the less active trustees on the first library board. He was never an officer and his attendance record was spotty. He accepted special assignments, however, and showed up for crucial decisions like hiring a new librarian, financial crises, or issues related to library facilities.

Mayer was born in 1858 in Washington, Iowa. He attended schools there and took a "classics course" in New York. He father, an immigrant from Germany, ran a clothing store in Washington. Mayer came to Iowa City in 1885 when he married Laura Bloom and joined his father-in-law in the clothing business. After the death of Laura three years later, he married her sister, Julia, and spent the rest of his life in the Bloom and Mayer and later Max Mayer Clothing Store at 28-30 South

From "Our Live Ones," circa 1907

MAX MAYER

Max Mayer, library trustee, 1896-1914.

Clinton Street. In the late nineteenth century Bloom and Mayer had one of the largest stocks in the state, and owned stores in Peoria, Hastings, and other cities.

Father-in-law Bloom, a former state senator and Iowa City mayor, was one of the most successful businessmen in the late 1800s.

Mayer was always active in the cultural and social life of the city and became known for his strong support of university football players. He has been described as the "father of Iowa football" and the "grandfather of Iowa athletics" for his intense interest and financial support.[7] He served on the board of directors for the Iowa City Chautauqua for many years and died in 1939 at the age of 81.

Alice Luscombe, 1896–1898. Luscombe served the shortest time of the original nine but she participated more fully than any other woman in the library campaign. She attended the first meeting and was appointed to the original fund-raising and bylaws committee along with Stevenson and Hummer. She was given the task of recruiting various "Iowa City ladies" to the mass meeting. A teacher at the grammar school, Luscombe served with two other teachers on one of the fund-raising subcommittees. They evidently worked vigorously, for over 20 percent of those pledging to the campaign were public school teachers and principals. Except for fellow trustee Bertha Ridgway, these educators were the only women who contributed.

Luscombe was born in England in 1870 and in 1896 was living with her widowed mother, older brother James and his wife, and her younger sister. She arrived in the U.S. and Iowa City sometime between 1870 and her sister's 1874 birth in Iowa City. She started teaching at the Second Ward School in 1891, moving to the grammar school in 1893, but left her job, the library board, and Iowa City when she married in 1898. Brother James had a photography shop on Dubuque Street next to Smith's Restaurant for many years.

Elizabeth Felkner, 1898–1898. The first replacement trustee to join the original board, Elizabeth Felkner was appointed to replace Alice Luscombe in May of 1898. She remained on the board for twenty-two years. Her name first appeared in relation to the library on the contributors list of the 1896-97 fund drive. Like Luscombe, she represented the public schools. In the 1890s she was principal of the Third Ward School but later city directories listed her as simply a teacher. Felkner was vice president from 1908 until 1916 and served as a member of the committee to recommend and plan a children's room in 1906.

Born in 1850, Felkner was one of about twelve children (sources vary on the number) of Henry Felkner, one of the Iowa City's best-known pioneers. The elder Felkner came to Johnson County in May of 1837, the seventh man to arrive, according to the 1883 *History of Johnson County, Iowa*. No one had more entries in the index of that 1883 history. He claimed 1,000 acres near Clear Creek, and has a stream of "firsts" to his credit: first flour mill, member of the first Johnson County Board of Supervisors, Johnson County representative to the first session of the Iowa legislature, first-year officer of the Old Settlers' Association, and elected to one of Iowa City's first city councils in 1856. His memoirs of the early years were published in the State Historical Society's *Annals of Iowa* in the 1880s. Mansheim called him "one of the most important gentlemen historians who wrote about Johnson County."[8] Elizabeth Felkner gave a talk at the 1912 Old Settlers' Reunion about what the Johnson County pioneers contributed to the development of this area, giving anecdotes about her father and her family. Weber remembers that she was considered something of a local historian in her later life.

From First Librarian to Pioneer Businessman

The delayed resignation of librarian A.C. Howell was the first problem the new board faced after celebrating its success at getting the library opened. On January 27, 1897, one week after the opening but four weeks before the election, President Wade appointed "Shimek and Stevenson to confer with Librarian and try and have . . . [the] resignation deferred until March 1st." It was not a good time politically to lose Howell. He had received considerable praise in the press for his skill and zeal in getting the collection organized and the library operating, and they were in the midst of convincing the public to make this a permanent tax-supported position. Howell evidently stayed through the election, but promptly after the successful vote the board reviewed applications, and on March 17, their

first official meeting as the Iowa City Public Library Board of Trustees, they agreed to meet "in special session . . . on March 24th . . . to consider the question of electing a librarian and assistant librarian." They also agreed to split the monthly fifty-dollar salary they were giving Howell into thirty-five dollars for a librarian and fifteen dollars for an assistant.

We can only speculate on why Howell decided to leave after just six weeks on the job. There may have been an agreement that Howell would stay only a few months, through a shake-down period perhaps, but undoubtedly longer than six weeks. That

Andrew C. Howell, first ICPL librarian (Dec. 1896-Mar. 1897), pictured with his wife, Bessie, and son, Lloyd, in 1897

Shimek and Stevenson had to try to convince him to stay at least six more weeks until after the election implies some kind of unhappiness or unexpected development. Howell, thirty-one years old in 1896, had worked first for the Chicago, Rock Island and Pacific railroad and since 1890 as a bookkeeper at the Close Linseed Oil Works, which had closed in 1896. Married and the father of a six-year-old son, Howell was, at best, between jobs. By at least 1898 (and probably 1897) he had taken a position as a bookkeeper for the Citizens Savings and Trust. There is some evidence that Howell's bookkeeping experience was what the board members felt they needed to get the new collection received and organized and they were evidently willing to pay for it. It would be 1903 before the trustees again paid their librarian fifty dollars a month. But after the pre-opening preparations did they expect him to operate the library—open daily for a total of sixty-four hours a week—without assistance? Does their rapid decision to split both the job and the salary into two positions indicate this may have been their plan all along? Perhaps Howell had recommended it or they had observed the necessity of the change themselves.

Whatever the exact circumstances and despite his short tenure, Andrew Craven Howell went into the record book as the first librarian for the Iowa City Public Library. Although he spent the rest of his life in Iowa City, Howell's distinction as Iowa City's first public librarian faded and was forgotten by the community. In 1899 he joined pioneer druggist W.E. Shrader in founding the Shrader Drug Company, manufacturers of livestock mineral feeds, and continued in the business until his death in 1949. For the last twenty-five years of his life he was the senior member of the firm, by then known as the Howell-Shrader Company and located for many years on the northwest corner of Gilbert and Prentiss streets. His son and daughter-in-law, Lloyd and Henrietta Rate Howell, continued the business until Lloyd's death in 1956. A.C. Howell's 1949 obituary, headlined "Pioneer business man dies," described sixty years of community service: church offices, school board, fraternal organizations, Chamber of Commerce, Chautauqua board, and public librarian. His job as librarian had become a volunteer community service. In 1995 it was news to his grandson Rate Howell, a retired lawyer in Worthington, Ohio, that his grandfather had this connection to the Iowa City Public Library. When asked if the elder Howell had a strong interest in books and libraries, he replied, "I'd like to say A.C. had a lifelong interest in books, but honestly, not that I know of. All the time I was growing up I had, of course, been in my grandparents' home on Summit Street [447 South Summit] many times, but they had [few books]."[9] Howell's apparent lack of interest in books is further evidence that he was hired in 1896 for his clerical and organizational skills, not his knowledge of books or libraries.

Three Years, Four Librarians

Library board members selected four men to serve as librarian between November 1896 when Howell was hired and February 1900 when they finally found someone who would stay longer than sixteen months.

The rapid turnover of librarians in the first three years causes one to wonder if the persons applying for the librarian's position in those early years understood the scope, or lack of scope, of the duties. The library board, like most library boards of the period, retained authority and responsibility for all aspects of the library. In all but the largest cities, boards were primarily looking for a clerk/janitor, not an administrator. Library historian Jesse Shera describes the early librarian as a "glorified janitor and a 'keeper' in the most elementary sense."[10] The hours were long, the pay low, the duties fairly simple, and with the board so thoroughly in control, the prestige of the position rather slim. Only as library operations became larger and more complex would the board relinquish authority to an increasingly professional librarian.

The Iowa City job, however, appeared to be popular and sought after. Twenty-two men and twenty women applied for the job openings from the fall of 1896 through February 1900. Several persons applied more than once. Of the applicants identified, the women seemed to be older and to have more experience—teachers, clerks, widows. The men were students, unemployed, or too new in town to appear in the city directory.

The repeated selection of men when older women with experience and community roots were applying and reapplying suggests that, at least for the first few rounds, men were preferred. Only the ongoing turnover and the continuing discontent over salaries and duties convinced the board that they needed, or at least could only afford, a woman.

There were few women working independently outside the schoolroom at this time, but they were beginning to take over the clerical positions they would fill almost exclusively for much of the twentieth century. In all but the largest public libraries, women were gradually taking most of the jobs. In 1876, male librarians accounted for 90 percent of the attendees at the first American Library Association national meeting. By 1902, 75 percent were women. Consistently low salaries had driven men out of public libraries.

Samuel H. Sperry, April 1897–August 1898. It took seven ballots on March 24, 1897, for the board to "elect" Sperry from a list of "ten applicants who had applied for the position." Gilbert A. McElroy, evidently a close runner-up, received the new assistant's job on the first ballot.

We know very little about Sperry and there is some confusion over his name. He was evidently called "Harry," yet some documents cite "Samuel H." and board secretary Stevenson listed him as "H.S. Sperry" when he was hired. Like Howell, it appears that Sperry was between jobs. The *Citizen* for February 19, just five weeks earlier, reported that "S.H. Sperry has disposed of his interest in the *West Liberty Review,* a paper he established something over a year ago. He has returned to Iowa City." The 1899 City Directory lists Harry Sperry as city editor of the *Press.*

In the interval he took on the job of librarian but not without some dissatisfaction. On April 21, just four weeks after he was hired, Sperry wrote to the "gentlemen" of the board: "I am very pleased with my position and am trying to serve the patrons of the library in the best possible manner. I desire to retain my place, and there is only one thing lacking to make me thoroughly contented in so pleasant a situation. I refer to the salary. In view of the responsibility, care and necessary experience, to say nothing of the long hours each day and Sunday afternoon, I feel justified in asking you to raise the librarian's salary to $50.00 per month."[11] He undoubtedly had discovered what Howell was paid when he took over the library's records.

Evidently not moved to act on his appeal, the board deferred the matter to a future meeting. The salary question was not addressed until a year later at a special meeting held in April of 1898 to elect a librarian and assistant librarian for the coming fiscal year. Nine applications were read, including Sperry's and McElroy's. It is not clear if accepting fresh applications indicated a dissatisfaction with Sperry or just the new board's method of dealing with a requirement that all staff must be reappointed annually. As the Iowa Code required, the board first set the salaries for "the term of employment." As soon as the motion was approved to set the salaries at forty dollars and twenty dollars a month for the year commencing April 1, 1898, the board suddenly deferred the election to a future meeting and adjourned. By the next regular meeting Sperry had submitted his resignation. There would be no fifty dollars a month, and based on the long balloting of the year before and the new applicants of 1898, maybe not even a job.

As Sperry had mentioned in his letter, hours were a legitimate concern. Sperry was scheduled to be on the job ten hours a day, six days a week, plus Sunday afternoons. During these first two years the library was also open on all holidays. His only free times were the noon and dinner hours when the library closed for ninety minutes. In January of 1898 he asked the board to close the library at 9:00 p.m. instead of 10:00 p.m., but the board agreed only to move closing to 9:30 p.m. For someone accustomed to the independence of running a newspaper, the library regime may have seemed quite rigid.

At the time of Sperry's resignation in May, assistant librarian McElroy was scheduled to leave for duty in the Spanish-American War. The board hired a woman, Adelaide Lloyd, to replace McElroy, and Sperry remained on the job through August. He received an extra five dollars a month during this period evidently to take over the janitorial duties performed by McElroy and not thought proper for the new female assistant. The board addressed its ongoing discontent with the physical condition of the library rooms and the issue of who performed janitorial duties head-on in the resolution officially hiring returning soldier McElroy to replace Sperry in September of 1898. "Moved and carried that the Sec'y [sic] be instructed to cast the ballot of the board for G.A. McElroy as Librarian at a salary of forty dollars per month, said salary to include sweeping the library but not dusting."

Discontent with Sperry and the board's eagerness to get McElroy back to stay were reflected in two documents written by Secretary Stevenson. One was a resolution to S.H. Sperry thanking him for his faithful services in the position of librarian, "which he filled in a satisfactory manner." He later wrote a letter to Colonel Lambert of the 50th Iowa Volunteers requesting that McElroy, home on leave from the Spanish-American war and in charge of the library, be excused from returning to Des Moines to be mustered out of the army, "as it is quite difficult to secure anyone to do his work as librarian."

Gilbert A. McElroy, September 1898–August 1899. We know even less about McElroy than about Sperry. We know of his brief volunteer service in the army and that he was a sophomore at the university in 1897-98.[12] His name does not appear in any records after his months as Iowa City Public Library librarian. A minority of the board had evidently backed him in those seven ballots before electing Sperry, and the trustees had been very generous in giving him leave for his army service and promising, by resolution, a position for him when he returned.

The few library records that exist today suggest that he was an organized, orderly fellow who kept careful records of library activities and frequently brought suggestions to board meetings about specific library needs and problems. In 1899 he began breaking down circulation records into subject and format categories, giving information for the first time about the amount of juvenile, fiction, and subject materials that were checked out each month, and he entered his monthly reports into the minutes. After a few months of this analysis, he took care to explain why such a large share of circulation came from juvenile titles and fiction: Many books classed as juvenile were on subjects; stories, for both children and adults, were read and returned quickly while books on history, religion, and philosophy took much longer; many came to the library to use reference books and newspapers and then took home a book of fiction. He pointed out that the number of visitors each month was generally about double that of items loaned, although it appears visitors were estimated in round numbers that could easily have been inflated. His penchant for explaining library traffic surfaced again a few months later. He counted forty-three visitors one evening in February 1899 when the temperature was twenty degrees below zero. Later that month he counted the Saturday traffic in terms of men and women and the number who entered who actually "used the reading room." Only 50 of the 455 visitors that day (265 men and 190 women) "did no reading in the library." He began to compare monthly circulation and the number of cards issued in the same month in the previous year, and he made other comparisons probably of interest then and now only to a fellow librarian.

Leslie Switzer, August 1899–February 1900. McElroy's enthusiasm seemed to wane, however. His reports became briefer and by June 1899 he submitted his resignation, effective August 1. In the minutes of June 21, 1899, immediately following the acceptance of McElroy's resignation is the following entry: "The subject of librarianship was then taken up and discussed." The board next accepted the motion of Max Mayer to "cast the ballot" for Leslie Switzer as librarian with the understanding that Switzer would work with McElroy during July, "familiarizing himself with details in [the] library and this month to be without salary." At the same time, Lloyd was confirmed to stay on as assistant at the same salary. Thus Switzer, twenty-one years old, another Spanish-American war veteran and currently a college freshman, was hired at forty dollars a month and would be assisted by a thirty-eight-year-old university graduate who already had fifteen months experience at the library.

Like Howell, Switzer's stay at the library was short, but his life in Iowa City continued for many years. Born in 1878, he was the eldest of seven children of Jacob Switzer and his second wife, Carolyn. The family lived at 819 Kirkwood Avenue for many years. The elder Switzer was assistant cashier at the Iowa City State Bank. Leslie was a bugler in the same volunteer National Guard unit as McElroy. According to Reizenstein in a 1931 *Press-Citizen* Fact-A-Day column,[13] the company never got farther than Florida. Following his job at the library, Switzer worked as a city editor for the *Republican* like Reizenstein before him, then served in the U.S. Navy and worked as a tire salesman. Back in Iowa City in 1940, he was appointed commander of the Iowa Soldiers' Home at Marshalltown. By then the *Press-Citizen* described him as a "Spanish-American war veteran who served throughout the war as a first lieutenant."[14] There are no library records reflecting Switzer's six months of work at the library.

Adelaide Lloyd: Stability and Skill

When Adelaide Lloyd joined the library staff as assistant librarian in 1898, she was thirty-eight years old and had taught in the Johnson County schools for about sixteen years. After serving under Sperry, McElroy, and Switzer, she undoubtedly knew more about the library than anyone in the community. She continued the extensive record keeping and analysis of library operations begun by McElroy and enlarged the reports. There was good statistical accounting and some narrative reports for her entire tenure, 1900 through 1905. She began to provide multiyear reports about library operations and in 1902 wrote a five-year history of the library that was published in the *Republican*.

Lloyd, who called herself Ada until the third month of her tenure as librarian when she began signing her name "Adelaide C. Lloyd," was born in Iowa City, one of three daughters of a pioneer Iowa City physician who came to the community from England in 1856. Frederick Lloyd was a founding member of the Johnson County Medical Association in 1857 and served in the Civil War as surgeon for the 16th Infantry. A member of the Iowa City Library Association in 1871, Dr. Lloyd was elected to several terms on the school board, was appointed to the curators board of the State Historical Society, and served as editor of the *Annals of Iowa* in 1866, writing articles about John Brown and his operations in Iowa. In 1890, as one of the guest editors of the Republican's semicentennial commemorative edition, he wrote a long critical essay about all the men who had been editors of both the *Iowa City Republican* and the *Iowa State Press* since 1856. He continued his medical practice at 112_ East Washington Street until he died in 1899.

It appears that none of the three daughters married and all were employees of the Johnson County and Iowa City school systems for many years. Louise and Adelaide, at least, were graduates of the University of Iowa, Louise in 1879 and Adelaide in 1882. Louise was principal of the Fourth Ward School for many years and contributed to the fund for the new public library in 1896. Youngest sister Edith worked as a stenographer and later as a nurse at the high school until her death in 1918.

Lloyd's impact on library operations was immediate. In February she prepared data on the number and use of cards issued to persons living outside the city limits. Lloyd's figures showed that while less than 2 percent of the cards issued since 1897 were to nonresidents, they constituted 22 percent of those issued in January of 1900. Nonresidents were obviously a growing component of the library's card holder list. The board adopted a resolution barring further issuance of such cards but did not recall those currently in effect. While Judge Wade's opening day speech celebrated the new library as an institution that would "meet the desires and supply the tastes of everyone within the limits of Johnson County," the taxpayers of Iowa City were contributing all of the library's annual budget and the question of fairness had been raised at an earlier meeting. This brief confrontation between service to county residents versus fairness in support of the library was the first in a century-long county-city dialogue on the issue that continues to this day.

Lloyd, whose father was the city's health officer for many years, brought another difficult issue to the board's attention during her first year. Since the 1870s, librarians had been discussing what to do with library books used by persons with contagious diseases. At the end of the nineteenth century it was still a matter of some controversy as to how various diseases were transmitted and the theory that germs were carriers of disease was not fully accepted. By 1900 germ theory was generally in command but officials disagreed about the danger of transmission via books. Epidemics of scarlet fever, smallpox, and diphtheria were very real, however, and library officials had to decide what to do. The often-ridiculed warnings of librarians about washing one's hands before handling library books and of not licking one's finger to turn a page originated not from a concern for preserving library books in pristine condition but from fear that these habits might spread disease. There were two generally recommended methods of dealing with books returned from a family quarantined with one of the feared diseases: disinfection or destruction through burning. Since 1898 the Iowa City library had operated under an informal policy of burning books that were identified as returned from someone with a contagious disease, but in late 1900 Lloyd reported that a list of "infected houses" was available from the mayor and that the city clerk could notify the library of all new cases. Of the twenty-six families infected at that time, twenty-three had library cards but only a few had borrowed items recently, Lloyd reported to the board. Since 1898 the library had burned fourteen books returned following epidemics of smallpox, diphtheria, and two of scarlet fever. At the same meeting the board adopted the following motion: "Resolved that all persons in whose families any contagious disease exists, or who have been exposed to any contagious disease are hereby prohibited from visiting the library during such time as quarantine is maintained . . . and . . . in case such persons have [library] books . . . they shall be forthwith delivered to the health officer of Iowa City to be destroyed."[15]

In November Lloyd convinced the board to close the library on four holidays—Thanksgiving, Christmas, Memorial Day, and Independence Day—by demonstrating through library records that the attendance on U.S. legal holidays for the previous four years had been one-fourth or less of the average daily attendance. "We, the servants of the people, solemnly declare that on four of these legal holidays . . . we desire not to serve . . . and we respectfully submit our petition to the library board, that upon the said legal holidays the Iowa City Public Library be closed." This policy change was the first retreat from opening the library 365 days a year. By this time the library was open eleven and one-half hours each day except Sunday, when it was open 2:30 to 5:00 p.m. The ninety-minute closings at noon and dinner had been reduced to one hour only at noon. The library opened at 8:30 a.m. and closed at 9:00 p.m. By eliminating most of the mealtime closings and opening at 8:30 a.m. instead of 9:00 a.m. Lloyd and the board were able to increase library hours from sixty-one to seventy-one hours a week.

Trustee Bertha Ridgway, who since 1898 had headed the university library, was undoubtedly a mentor and tutor for Lloyd, and was perhaps more influential with Lloyd than she could have been with the earlier male librarians. A former assistant of Ridgway's, Mary Heard, was hired to assist with cataloging the collection in November 1899. Ridgway apparently had done some cataloging earlier and the first card catalog case had been purchased in 1898. Ridgway would have understood the mechanics of publishing a book catalog of the library's holdings, a task which the board agreed to do in November 1900. Heard received $12.50 a week, a rate higher than any of the ICPL librarians had received, evidently for her library cataloging skills and experience.

The board granted Lloyd permission to attend the very first session of a six-week Summer Library School held at the University of Iowa each year into the 1930s. She returned armed with new ideas about the library and new acquaintances among library officials and other library workers. Alice Tyler, the executive secretary of the new Iowa State Library Commission (est. 1900), directed the summer session and evidently visited the Iowa City Public Library that summer. She advised Lloyd on getting spine labels with author letters and class numbers for the book collection. "While she [Tyler] was talking, I [realized] that a library was not a library unless thus equipped. The purpose of these labels is that the books may be placed and found readily upon the shelves. One librarian [at summer school?] said to me, 'I don't see how you find the books at all without an author letter.' If they are one of the library essentials, they should be placed on the books before the printed catalogue is made for they are the 'call number' in [this proposed] 'finding list.'"[16]

Lloyd described her first "experiment as to whether library books can be used by children in connection with their school work. Eleven children from Miss Cavanaugh's room in the Third Ward report . . . having read one book each . . . during the past term." This is the first record of direct cooperation between an Iowa City public school and the public library.[17]

At the end of her first year, Lloyd prepared a narrative and statistical report for the trustees including accomplishments of the year and outlined "the work for 1901." In her narrative report she included her definition of the ideal library book: "good print for the eyes; good language for the mind; good morals for the soul." She reminded the board that while the number of check-outs of fiction and juveniles was very large, they could not be compared with the time it took to read a serious title in one of the other classifications. (No generic term like "nonfiction" was used in this period.) Also, such books were consulted by the thousands in the reading room but not included in the circulation count. This argument was very similar to one McElroy gave in his 1898 annual report and is evidence that everyone, board and staff, was anxious to prove the seriousness of their institution's mission which, in the minds of many, did not include reading fiction.

The national debate over whether libraries should include fiction had been loud and widespread during the last two decades of the nineteenth century but was pretty well played out by 1900. The sheer popularity of fiction, accounting for nearly 75 percent of public library circulation to adults, helped shift the question from "fiction or no fiction" to "what quality of fiction should be acquired?" This latter controversy continues in some form to the present day.[18]

Lloyd also noted in her report that nearly 20 percent of the books added to the collection were gifts and gave name-by-name credit to all donors. She claimed that the addition of the card catalogue, book pockets, and spine labels had proved "not only a convenience to the public but also invaluable to the library force in promoting accuracy and rapidity of work." In her section labeled "Work for 1901" she outlined the need to continue her spine labeling project, to make preparations to publish a book catalog, and to acquire a bulletin board for posting reading lists for special subjects and special days, plus taking an inventory of the collection and purchasing more bookshelves and chairs before the move to the new quarters agreed to by the board late in 1900. By the end of her first year as librarian, Lloyd had enriched her knowledge of library work, improved library service, and demonstrated she was capable of helping to plan library improvements and of providing the board with a constant flow of suggestions.

Financing the Library: From Private Funds to Public Taxes

In addition to the problems of retaining a librarian and establishing a reasonable working relationship between the board and the librarian, the trustees also faced the major task of keeping the library operating on gift funds for fifteen months from January 1897 to April 1, 1898. While the referendum was held in March of 1897, the authorization for the levy did not become effective until fiscal year 1898 which started on April 1. The board used a major portion of the gift monies for the many up-front costs required in the early months: an opening day collection (about $1,000 for 1,300 volumes), magazine subscriptions, shelving, furniture, and supplies plus painting and carpentry work ($400). Salaries, rent, and utilities were costing about $90 a month that first year, so by July of 1897 the board had spent over $2,000 with another $850 or more in overhead expenses due before the city levy became available April 1, 1898. This sum did not include money for additional purchases of books.

Of the $2,500 pledged in the fall of 1896, only $1,300 had been paid by July 1. A small number of individuals paid their pledges in full early in 1897, but most had made a fifteen-month commitment, paying in six quarterly installments with the last payment not due until April 1, 1898. If Board Treasurer George Hummer had not continued to raise funds informally and apparently single-handedly, the board would have been short of funds from the first day. Building on the enthusiasm generated at the opening ceremonies and by the surge of citizens who immediately started using the reading room, getting cards, and borrowing materials, Hummer had collected $880 in additional gift funds by June, half of it in January during the library's first month of service.

Pledge payments and Hummer's $880 gave the board $2,100 to cover the first six months. With no more pledge payments due until October and ongoing salaries and rent to pay, the board obviously needed to find alternative sources of funds. Hummer continued his fund-raising and deposited $247 in the third quarter of the year, but at the June board meeting he also raised the issue of a bank loan. He received board authorization to borrow $400. At the July meeting he reported that he had not yet used the trustees' authorization to borrow, and asked that the amount be raised to $500 for a loan due April 1, 1898. There is no record of a second loan in the minutes, but in March 1898 the board approved payment of $750 plus interest on notes, and the expenditure report for all of 1898 lists $145 in interest paid.

The loans only increased the long-term financial commitments of the board, so at the same meeting in June when the idea of borrowing money was first raised, the trustees also discussed sponsoring a fund-raising event. The minutes of June 23, 1897, record a motion asking that "St. Mary's Dramatic Association be invited to give an entertainment early in the fall for the benefit of the library."

By September the board was deep into planning for this event. Hummer and Mayer worked on the plans originally but all trustees got involved—from booking Coldren Opera House to soliciting ads for the program to working competitively to sell tickets. Between November 3 and the performance on November 26, the board held five special meetings devoted to the project, including one which was called "to consider the advisability of giving the play" to benefit the library. This last meeting occurred after the opera house had been booked, and indicates there may have been some internal dissension or last-minute misgivings about going ahead with the project. Francis Sueppel attended as a representative of St. Mary's Lyceum Company and as the director of the proposed dramatic event. But just five days later at another special meeting, the board gave final approval to the play—*Honor Before Wealth*, the date—November 26, and the ticket price—fifty cents. Board members were all given assignments regarding ticket and ad sales, printing tickets, posters, and the programs. There were incentives for anyone selling tickets: one free gallery seat for every five sold, or one free main floor seat for every ten sold.

St. Mary's Lyceum Company, a troupe of fifteen young men and women, had performed in dramatic and musical fund-raising productions at St. Mary's Catholic School since they were ten to twelve years old. Most of this particular group graduated from St Mary's in 1895, few had married, and the group stayed together to stage many theatrical productions over the next ten years, continuing to give the proceeds from their very popular events to St. Mary's School. The season of 1897-98 was one of their most successful. They opened with *Honor Before Wealth*, and after restaging it for the library benefit in their first-ever appearance at the opera house, they went on to produce *My Friend from India* and *The Regiment*. Scheduled dates for *My Friend from India* sold out immediately and an extra performance was added.

This company of extraordinarily talented amateurs did not go unnoticed by the community or by one of its more prolific commentators, Jacob Reizenstein at the *Republican*. He reviewed all their productions and, often using superlatives, compared them to productions he saw in his annual theater-attending visits to New York City.

ST. MARY'S LYCEUM COMPANY

Photo courtesy State Historical Society of Iowa-Iowa City

1902 photograph of St. Mary's Lyceum Company. Pictured from left to right: (front row) Mary Bashnagel, Dr. John C. Mueller, Francis N. Sueppel, Will P. Mueller, Celia Bashnagel; (middle row) Louis F. Cerny, John A. Eppel, Louis J. Bashnagel, Henry S. Corso; (back row) Mary C. Stach, Joseph E. Stach, Agnes E. Sueppel.

One critic from an unnamed Chicago paper wrote: "St. Mary's Lyceum Co. of Iowa City, Iowa is an example of what may be done for the advancement of drama in a small community by properly directed amateurs. It is a stock company maintained under the auspices of St. Mary's Catholic Church and plays in its own theater [Columbus Hall], which is properly equipped. The Company opened its third season with *Honor Before Wealth* as adapted from the French by Octane Feuillot. The performances usually run for several nights and they are much better than those professional companies that tour small towns. At the Lyceum, the 'standing room only' sign is always out."[19]

The opera house where St. Mary's troupe would perform for the first time was on the southwest corner of Clinton and College streets. It was purchased by J.N. Coldren in 1897 and thereafter called Coldren Opera House. Built by bankers Clark and Hill in 1877, the building housed the Iowa City State Bank on the first floor and the opera house on floors two and three. For thirty-five years, traveling theater and musical troupes played there. Like opera houses in nearly every town in Iowa in the latter half of the nineteenth century, few operas were performed. The name "opera house" was simply a more respectable term than "theater."[20] For a similar reason, undoubtedly, the word "theater" or "drama" did not appear in the name or programs of St. Mary's Lyceum Company. Coldren's elaborate thirty-foot frescoed ceiling with portraits and inscriptions on the walls celebrating the "dramatic and lyric muses," sixty-four gas jets, some "double-armed globes" under the balcony, and gas footlights capable of simulating "morning, noon, or night," were described by the *Press* when the house opened in 1877. "McVicar's in Chicago is the only theater finer," the paper said, referring to regions west of Chicago. In 1897 after some remodeling, it seated 314 on the main floor plus 531 in the two balconies. The stage was sixty by thirty feet with a proscenium twenty-two feet wide and eighteen feet high. There were eleven dressing rooms and three stage traps. In 1897, still lighted by gas, it was the site of many community events, especially those that required a stage, including high school graduations and productions by local theater groups like St. Mary's Lyceum Company.[21]

On November 24, two days before the performance, the *Republican* published both a news story and an editorial promoting the library's event and explaining the financial needs of the library. Noting that the library had been supported by voluntary subscriptions ever since it opened, the articles explained that they must continue on gift funds "until the first of next April" and added that there was a constant demand for more books, especially in the children's department. "From the very hour of its organization . . . the public library has been used to a remarkable extent. . . . No class has employed [it] so constantly as . . . the boys and girls of this city. [They] have found it a constant source of pleasure and profit. But they have read through most of the books suitable for their use and now, like Oliver Twist, they ask for `more.'" After describing the play scheduled for November 26, the editorial instructs its readers that "it is the duty of every citizen to support this effort. The boys and girls of Iowa City ask it of you. . . . [T]he scholars in our schools are so much interested in this enterprise that they are [helping with] the sale of tickets. . . . Don't turn them away with a refusal." The poster promoting the production said the proceeds would be used to buy "additional books for the public library."

And the schoolchildren did their part, selling 123 of the total 460 tickets sold. Treasurer Hummer, continuing his fund-raising efforts for the library, sold about 160 tickets, more than anyone, even the children. In addition to the $230 from tickets, board members, especially Max Mayer, sold advertisements in the program that brought in $80—nearly enough to pay the $90 in expenses—so the library cleared $217.80. The complete financial record was published in the December 7 issue of the *Republican*.

Reizenstein had already reviewed the lyceum company's first production of the play earlier in the fall.[22] "Once more has an audience sat for three hours, entranced with the pleasures of the play, charmed with the talent and art of the players," he wrote in just one sentence from his fifteen-paragraph review. He goes on to evaluate the performances of Francis and Agnes Sueppel, Louis Cerny, John Eppel, Celia Bashnagel, and especially Mary E. Stach. "Her acting was exquisitely skillful and again marked her as one of the conspicuously brilliant members of the Lyceum." After the special performance on November 26, Reizenstein continued his praise. "The able young actors of St. Mary's Lyceum have duplicated the success scored a few weeks ago. Upon a professional stage, with a large audience, and a wider scope for their talents, they have presented the play to the entire satisfaction of one and all. . . . The play was staged exquisitely . . . the scenic effects were frequently applauded."[23]

The trustees, evidently pleased with the financial success of *Honor Before Wealth,* appointed a committee at the very next meeting in December 1897 "to devise further means of raising money and report at the next meeting." Just two weeks later the Committee on Entertainments for the Benefit of the Library (Shimek, Stevenson, and Mayer) reported in favor of having a course of five or six lectures. The board accepted the recommendation and in late January the committee announced that Judge Wade and professors Macbride, Shimek, Gilchrist, and Wilcox had each consented to give one lecture. The board set a price of one dollar for the course or twenty-five cents per lecture. There are surviving copies of the posters printed to advertise the lecture course, and the *Republican* published a short article promoting the series two days before the first scheduled lecture, "Life and Death of a Tree" by Professor T.H. Macbride, on February 17, 1898. The final four were planned for March: "Law of the Land" by Judge Wade, "English Cathedrals" by Dr. J.G. Gilchrist, "Calamity Howler" by Professor W.C. Wilcox, and "Glimpses of Man in the Tropics" by Professor B. Shimek. "Illustrated by a Stereoptican and Illuminated with Wit, Wisdom and Eloquence," the poster promised. The turnout for the series is not recorded in the existing papers for the period and the minutes of the board never reported on the financial outcome. Whatever the success of the lecture series, this would be the last fund-raising event for over seventy-five years, until the library began holding annual book sales in 1974.

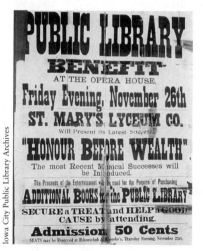

Poster for the benefit performance of Honor Before Wealth by St. Mary's Lyceum Company held at Coldren's Opera House, November 26, 1897

With or without income from the lecture course, the board stretched its funds to April 1. In addition to the successful theater performance, $900 in final pledge payments and $570 from further efforts by Hummer brought the fifteen-month total library income to $3,700. The board ordered $100 worth of children's books (about 120 volumes) in December, but money for books would be very short throughout 1898 as the loan and interest had to be repaid and the first year's one-mill tax levy brought only $2,315. In all, the board received about 89 percent of the $2,500 in pledges; thirty people failed to pay or to complete their pledges. Hummer's work, the loan, and the play with the somewhat ironic title, *Honor Before Wealth,* had made the difference. The cash flow problem of mid-summer was behind them and they ended the fiscal year with sufficient funds to pay off the debt.

April 1, 1898, had arrived and for the first time tax revenues were available. While some of the details of the transactions and year-end reports are missing, it is very clear from the 1898 minutes that tax revenues required a new relationship between city staff and council and the library board.[24] Until this time, George Hummer, as treasurer, had handled both the revenues and the expenditures. He was receiving the income, paying the bills, and giving a treasurer's report—rarely detailed—at each board of trustees meeting. As soon as tax funds were available the question arose about who would handle the funds. Trustee Ball was assigned to talk to the city solicitor, an elected official in those days, who ruled that the library would have to set up a warrant system authorizing the city treasurer to pay library bills upon the signature of the president and secretary of the library board. This system was established early in fiscal year 1898 and has continued with increasing complexity to this day.

The board did enjoy some other forms of financial independence from the city in these years. First, trustees had complete control of gift funds, kept in a separate bank account. Secondly, the board simply requested its millage allotment from the council. The amount available to public libraries varied from time to time according to changes in the Iowa Code, but the council felt compelled to give the library the codified amount and exercised no oversight on how the funds were spent. For many years the annual resolution sent to the council, with the full text included in the board minutes through 1912, read:

Resolved by the Board of Trustees of the Iowa City Public Library the amount of money necessary for the maintenance of the Iowa City Public Library, aforesaid, for the period of one year is the sum of [amount], and we do hereby fix the amount to be appropriated for the maintenance of said library for the ensuing year at the said sum of [amount], and the President and Secretary are hereby instructed to certify this resolution to the City Council of Iowa City, Iowa in order that said Council may fix the levy for said fund as by law provided.

Finally, any funds not expended in one fiscal year were carried over in the library's account by the city. After the relationship with the city was worked out and a quarterly report from the city treasurer to the board was established, there is little record of financial concerns in the minutes of 1898-1901.

Tracing the trustees' annual resolutions through library board minutes reveals a discrepancy between what the law allowed, what the citizens voted to approve, and what was actually levied in these first years. Since 1894 the Iowa Code had allowed cities of 25,000 population or less to levy up to two mills for the support of a municipal library, yet the Iowa City Public Library Association Board of Directors campaigned on the need for only one mill to support the library. The 1897 ballot asked the electorate for permission to establish the library under the Iowa Code of 1873 which limited the maximum levy to one mill. This limitation was cited on the ballot. Evidently the library board and city council did not realize the code had been revised until after the election and it is unclear when the Iowa City taxpayers learned they were paying nearly twice the levy they had voted for. It is very obvious, however, that without the two-mill upper limit, the library would have been in financial trouble after 1898, apparently the only year the library received just one mill of income. After the first year's request to the council for $2,300, the library board told the council to levy $3,500 for 1899, 1900, and 1901. In July 1901 the board's annual resolution rose to $3,750 for the 1902 budget. The city was growing, total assessed valuation had increased slightly since 1897, and the one-mill levy had suddenly become two. The amount available for the library increased accordingly.

Expenses for the library were also increasing. With Lloyd at forty dollars a month, two assistants at fifteen each, some janitorial help at five dollars a month, and a temporary librarian getting $12.50 a week for forty-two hours of cataloging, the monthly payroll was now more than twice the fifty dollars of the first year. The next major increase to expenditures would follow an unexpected offer to relocate the library.

New Quarters: From Iowa Avenue to College Street

There were only a few hints in the board minutes of the first three years that the Iowa Avenue quarters were not entirely satisfactory. Several motions in 1897 and 1898 spoke to the need to improve the lighting in the long narrow room with windows on two sides only. Additional lights, however, increased the electric bill to the point where the board asked the staff to turn lights off whenever possible. The "problem of heating the library" was referred to the executive committee in the spring of 1897 and by January the board had an agreement with the owners to heat the rooms for seventy-five dollars a year if the board paid ten dollars for additional pipes. Fans, screens, and awnings were discussed with the landlord in the heat of the Iowa summers. Other repair and maintenance problems—faulty railing, defective toilet, floors needing oiling, and walls painting—appeared from time to time. The Iowa Avenue lease was renewed a second time with Kenyon and Ham for 1900, but when W.D. Cannon Jr. came to the board with an offer of new quarters in a building to be constructed at 212 College Street, the board members immediately expressed interest. They held a special meeting on October 8, 1900, to discuss Cannon's proposition for new space for $540 per year. They agreed to offer him $500, to include rent and heat and a three-year lease with privileges to continue for up to ten years. Their offer was $125 more per year than they were paying Kenyon and Ham for the second-floor rooms over C.O.D. Steam Laundry just two blocks north at 213 Iowa Avenue. Eight days later, on October 16, both parties signed the lease.

The three-year agreement between the library board and W.D. Cannon Jr. and his partner, W.I. Pratt, promised occupancy by January 1, 1901, "if possible to do so," built according to "the plan agreed on between them . . . with at least two rooms in addition to the public library room, two toilet rooms and a stairway six feet wide." Granting the $500 per year and the ten-year option the board had requested, the lease further promised veto power over the kind of businesses that could rent the first floor, ample light and blinds on at least three sides, and comfortable heat with rooms wired for electric lights and "properly piped for gas light."

Additional space, better light, and quarters built to its specifications appear to be the advantages the board was purchasing for the additional $125 per year. The College Street site, at fifty-five by eighty feet, would contain nearly 1,000 square feet more space than the long and narrow thirty-by-one-hundred-foot quarters on Iowa Avenue. The wide and open staircase in the center of the building would help overcome the relative invisibility of a second-floor location.[25] It is not clear if any partitioned spaces existed in the first location, but the minutes of 1897 described a small dispute over the location of the librarian's desk. It needed to be in a public area at least until there was a second person to prepare orders and receive and catalog new books in some kind of nonpublic area. McElroy had asked for a partition when he was assistant librarian. Today, while the newer Cannon & Pratt building is gone, the Iowa Avenue building remains. Windows have been added to the west side and part of the west side stairway has been enclosed; otherwise the room remains essentially as it was in 1897-1900 but with no evidence of any kind of partitions or interior walls.[26]

After the lease was signed in October there is little mention of the new quarters in the minutes so it must be assumed that the main responsibility for planning and executing the move fell to Lloyd. She had already asked for additional bookcases and furniture in her 1900 annual report and reported that she planned to inventory the collection. She had more time than expected to prepare for the move; promised for January or soon after, the new rooms were not ready until June. A note in Lloyd's 1901 annual report says the library "moved to the Cannon & Pratt building on College Street, June 17 [1901]." There were few additional details about the move or the new building. The missing daily circulation records for June 5 through June 23 confirm the terse line in the board meeting of June 22: "Library ordered open on Monday, June 24." The only evidence of additional costs generated by the move is a nineteen-dollar bill for six and a half days of labor and an authorization to order three more tables plus a dozen chairs and to construct shelves in the "workroom." In June of

In 1900 the library moved to the Cannon & Pratt building at 212 East College Street. Today most of this site is occupied by the present public library building.

Photo courtesy State Historical Society of Iowa-Iowa City

1901 the Iowa City Public Library settled into the first of three locations on College Street it would occupy during the next ninety-six years.

Building the Library's Collections

The first board of trustees approached no task with more enthusiasm and attention to detail than building the library's book and periodical collections. Throughout the five-year period, despite the problems of keeping a librarian, a shortage of funds, attention required by fund-raising events, and other details of operations, the majority of decisions made by the board had to do with the collection. And until late 1901, when the board gave librarian Lloyd authorization to "secure a dozen copies of current books," including duplicate copies "if best in her judgment," to beef up the selection of current popular titles, there were no exceptions to the unwritten but solid policy that the trustees made every decision about what books were purchased for the collection. On motions regarding matters of operations which were frequently initiated by the librarian, especially Lloyd, the librarian was "authorized" to carry out the task, but on motions about the collection the librarian was generally "instructed."

From the first day, the demand for library materials outstripped the board's ability to provide them. When the doors opened on Thursday, January 21, 1897, those first eager readers found about 1,050 books on the shelves. By the end of January, 992 had been checked out. In month two the collection grew to 1,200 volumes but with 2,606 loans, each book had already been used an average of three times in the first six weeks. Roughly arranged by subject or category—there was no catalog or list of holdings—this small collection was read and reread in 1897 at a rate that would wear out any collection. On average that year the library owned 1,625 books, reaching 1,825 books by December, and they were checked out just under 25,000 times, a "turnover rate" of fifteen. Turnover rate is a library term for measuring the average number of times each book in a collection is used in a particular period, usually one year. Today a public library would be pleased with a turnover rate of four to seven. A lower rate indicates an excess of rarely used volumes; higher than seven or eight means that frequently there will be few titles on the shelf to choose from. With a rate of fifteen during the library's first months, there must have been days when the shelves were nearly empty.

What did Iowa Citians have to choose from during those first months? The book collection consisted of the same three major components that make up public library collections to this day: fiction, nonfiction, and children's books—generally referred to as "juveniles" in those days and thus the traditional small "j" before library call numbers to indicate a book belonging to the collections designed for children. "Nonfiction" has always been an awkward term in library terminology, but if fiction is defined as imaginative works of prose, especially novels and short stories, then nonfiction, conveniently, is everything else.

Works for children can also be divided between stories and all other forms and topics. In 1897 juvenile books were primarily stories for children aged ten and above plus a smattering of nonfiction titles, especially in science and history. There were very few picture books appropriate for reading to the young child. A contemporary children's librarian would probably not recognize about 70 percent of the titles purchased in this first batch. The rest were classic titles or less well-known titles by classic authors. Louisa May Alcott, Mark Twain, Hans Christian Andersen, Lewis Carroll, Joel Chandler Harris, Rudyard Kipling, Andrew Lang, Howard Pyle, Anna Sewell, Jules Verne, and Daniel Defoe formed a small but solid core of standard authors, and books like *The Arabian Nights, Little Lord Fauntleroy, The Little Lame Prince, Grimm's Fairy Tales, The Peterkin Papers, The Wonder Book, Tales from Shakespeare, Robin Hood, Gulliver's Travels,* and *Hans Brinker* beckoned to children from the first day.

Of the 1,300 volumes ordered from Scribner's for the library's "opening day" collection, 32 percent were fiction, 40 percent nonfiction, and 28 percent juvenile, based on entries in the library's first accession book. History and biography comprised well over 50 percent of the nonfiction, with another quarter devoted to literature—poetry, drama, essays, and criticism. Board members had also chosen from one to twenty-five titles in each of the other major categories of the Dewey classification system and most of those were in religion, philosophy, government, and science.

Although there was a lot of oratory in the library campaign and opening ceremonies about meeting the needs of working men and women, little in this opening day collection had practical application. The Dewey 600s—applied technology—contained four titles on first aid, glassmaking, and ocean steamships. A practical science series called *The Wonders of . . .* addressed optics, heat, water, heavens, meteors, the moon, the sun, acoustics, and electricity. A handbook on wild flowers, *Electricity in Daily Life,* and *Ants, Bees, and Wasps* also promised useful information. There were some helpful reference volumes: *Webster's International Dictionary,* a concordance to the Old and New Testaments, a gazetteer and an atlas, *Bartlett's Quotations,* a *Cyclopedia of Painting,* and a dictionary of mythology. Trustees Hummer and Shimek agreed to loan their "Britannica and American cyclopedias" to the library early in the year until the board could afford to buy a set or two for the library's collection. It should be noted that these popular reference volumes added to the count of volumes owned but were not eligible for loans, thus making the actual turnover rate even higher.

Classic titles and authors in many fields were represented: Shakespeare and Spenser; Milton and Pope; Plato and Aurelius; Keats and Browning; Burns and Wordsworth; Bunyan and Bellamy; Agassiz and Darwin; Ruskin and Mill; Longfellow, Emerson, Lowell, Whittier, Bryant, Thoreau, Holmes; Thomas Carlyle and Thomas Huxley; and most of the works of the American historians Francis Parkman and William Prescott. Prescott's three-volume *The History of the Conquest of Mexico* remained in the collection until 1955, the last of the original 1,300 titles to be withdrawn. There were two books by a man soon to have a great impact on Iowa City: *Triumphant Democracy* and *American Four-in-Hand in Britain* by Andrew Carnegie.

The first book added to the Iowa City Public Library collection was *Waverly* by Sir Walter Scott. Twenty-four other Scott novels were followed by the works of Thackeray, Dickens, Stevenson, Hawthorne, Dumas, Cooper, Eliot, and Howells and at least one or two titles by Jane Austen, the Brontës, Henry James, Kipling, Trollope, Hugo, Cervantes, and Clemens. Cooper led with thirty-two titles, but only a few would be familiar to today's reader. Examples of novelists apparently popular with Iowa City readers in 1897 that have disappeared from all but academic collections today include Edward Bulwer-Lytton, George Cable, Edward Eggleston, Frank Stockton, Henry Kingsley, Charles Reade, and F. Marion Crawford. The opening day collection contained from three to eight titles by each of these now-forgotten fiction writers.

Library trustees selected minor American writers—Octave Thanet, Sarah Orne Jewett, Mary Wilkins Freeman, Bret Harte, Edward Everett Hale, Wilkie Collins, Harriet Beecher Stowe—and chose some of the big names in translation—Maupassant, Turgenev, Tolstoy, and Balzac in addition to Hugo and Cervantes. A translation of Feuillet's *Romance of a Poor Young Man,* the basis for the play *Honor Before Wealth,* appeared on this early list. Other now-classic English novelists included Oliver Goldsmith, George Meredith, and Thomas Hardy.

Novels with more than one copy in the opening day collection provide another peek at what was popular with Iowa City readers at the end of the nineteenth century. There were six copies of Alexander Dumas's latest, *The Vicomte de Braggelone,* and four copies of his *Count of Monte Cristo.* The board ordered three copies of Anthony Trollope's *Last Chronicle of Barset,* and two of *Vanity Fair* (Thackeray), *Hazards of New Fortunes* (Howells), *Three Musketeers* (Dumas), and *Middlemarch* and *Daniel Deronda* (Eliot). Some of the less familiar writers today who earned double shelf space on opening day in 1897 included Henry Kingsley, George Ebers, Berthold Auerbach, Helen Hunt Jackson, and the controversial Mary Augusta Arnold Ward, always known as Mrs. Humphrey Ward.

At the turn of the century authorities on English and American fiction thought there were about one hundred writers worthy of serious consideration, although established public libraries fequently had from 1,200 to 2,500 fiction authors in their collections. Of the twenty most popular novelists in 1903, John Cotton Dana, one of the best-known librarians of the period, thought only one of major importance.[27] Iowa City's opening day collection of fiction, with only about 110 authors represented, had titles by about half of this top twenty, but the board's proportion of classic writers to popular novelists was much higher than the one to 120 or 250 suggested by Dana. Subsequent demand for popular fiction reduced the share of quality titles markedly and by the end of 1901 all but one of Dana's top twenty authors and 75 percent of the top ten bestsellers for 1895-1900 were in the collection. But even then at least a fifth of the 380 authors represented would qualify as writers of "serious consideration" by Dana and other turn-of-the-century critics.

Not only did board members seem very interested in selecting books appropriate to their idea of a quality public library collection, it is evident that they were under pressure to increase the quantity of materials available for check-out. Motions to "get prices as soon as possible and call a special meeting," "buy some more books immediately," and "spend $500 at once!" are sprinkled throughout the minutes of this five-year period. In January 1899, in the board's last major purchase made through local bookstores—last because of the bookstores' inability to provide a wide range of titles without months of delay—a resolution urging Lee and Ries to fill the library's order as soon as possible began, "In view of the urgent demand for books in the library. . . ."

One method of making more books available was to juggle the rules for loans. By March of 1897 the board had already established a seven-day loan period for "popular titles." This was expanded in 1900 to all new books. Board rules declared a reserved book would not be held for longer than twenty-four hours and borrowers would have to pay one cent for a postcard notification.

The heavy use of the collection produced another problem. The books were wearing out and needed rebinding. Both the expense and the time required to get popular books through this process seemed to surprise the trustees. They tried several companies in Iowa City and Cedar Rapids and frequently complained to the librarian about the delay. "Get books bound at once. If it can't be done promptly, go elsewhere," one resolution in the summer of 1899 read. By this time the library was sending from sixty to one hundred books a month to be rebound at an unplanned cost of about fifty-eight cents per volume.

The board continued to use its committee system to prepare lists of books to be purchased but was always looking for a wider net of ideas. When members felt rushed they frequently turned the decisions over to Bertha Ridgway, but they also tried several methods to get input from the community. In 1898 they asked community literary and study clubs as well as "reading circles" to submit lists of books for general reading or for "a special study project of their organization." They explained they could not promise to buy every title suggested but said they would procure as many as possible. The board promised the organizations some circulation priority for the books they suggested. The board evidently received at least some responses, for trustees referred to an order with a list A and list B from the "reading circles."

In 1899 the board extended a general invitation to anyone who wished to submit a list of titles. The following year, still feeling they were not systematically identifying titles essential to satisfying the interests and demands of the public, the board appointed a five-member "consulting committee" to prepare a list of at least two hundred titles "suitable for use in the library." The five included a university professor, a minister, a teacher at the Iowa City Academy, and the wife of trustee W.P. Coast who was very active in several literary clubs. The committee worked rapidly and by January 1901 trustees were demanding a quick turn-around on prices for their list. "Call a special meeting" when it is ready, they told librarian Lloyd.

The sisters of St. Agatha's Seminary provided the final list received in these five years from groups or individuals not on the board. Their request was combined with lists prepared by trustees S.K. Stevenson and George Ball to form the last major book order in 1901.

While the board responded with serious intent and creative methods to the interests and demands of the general library user, the building of the reference and periodical collection seemed to be more of a labor of love. Some library historians have said that an intense interest in having access to newspapers and magazines on the part of those involved in establishing public libraries was one of the driving forces behind the library movement.[28] The concept of a reading room as distinct from a library proper was evident in the history of social or association libraries including those in Iowa City. A reading room furnished with a rich array of newspapers and magazines was one of the primary goals of many library pioneers. Descriptions of the proposed Iowa City Public Library in 1896 often read "public library and reading room."[29]

Mass circulation magazines were a rather recent phenomena. In 1885 there were no modern mass circulation periodicals but by 1900, with the help of favorable postal rates, there were about twenty. The circulation of monthly magazines soared from 18 million in 1890 to 64 million in 1905, exceeding daily papers and weeklies and becoming, according to one expert, "the major form of repeated cultural experience for people in the United States."[30]

Both the *Iowa City Daily Press* and the *Iowa City Daily Republican* helped build local demand for periodicals by regularly printing contents and article summaries from the latest issues of these popular magazines. These features would sometimes fill two to three newspaper columns.

Trustee Shimek selected the titles of almost all the current newspapers and periodicals that the library subscribed to from 1897 through the proposed list for 1902. He placed personal orders for the newspapers and was reimbursed from library funds. The periodicals were ordered through a local bookstore and cost about $125 a year by the end of the period. The board approved twenty magazines and ten newspapers for the first year of the library. By 1902 the magazine list had grown to sixty titles and the newspapers to about fifteen, not including Iowa City papers and other local and Iowa papers that were usually contributed. In addition to buying Iowa papers from Dubuque, Keokuk, Des Moines, and Council Bluffs, Shimek chose two Omaha papers, a German-language paper from Illinois, plus the *Chicago Chronicle,* the *Louisville Courier-Journal,* the *New York World,* and the *St. Paul Pioneer-Press.* Each newspaper cost less than one dollar a year except the Chicago and St. Paul titles.

Of the original twenty magazines, nine—*Atlantic Monthly, Harper's Bazaar, Harper's Magazine, Ladies Home Journal, Library Journal, National Geographic, Popular Science Monthly,* and *Publishers' Weekly*—have been received at the library continuously for the last one hundred years; another two, *North*

American Review and *Saturday Evening Post,* ceased publishing for some years in the middle of this century but are now back and appear regularly on the shelves of ICPL and many other libraries. By 1902 the list of sixty included an interesting variety of popular and scholarly titles covering special interests such as art, gardening, music, homemaking, teaching, and a broad range of subjects: psychology, history, forestry, world affairs, religion, literature and criticism, science, industry, and economics. The library always subscribed to four or five titles for or about children during this period including *St. Nicholas, Youth Companion,* and *Little Folks.* Magazines for children seem to go out of style faster than mainstream titles and none from this period lingered much after 1925.

While Shimek took the leadership for selecting specific periodicals, all seemed very interested in two other aspects of an attractive and useful periodical collection—buying back files and getting current issues bound. At many meetings trustees reviewed the holdings of dealers and discussed the availability and cost of back runs of major periodicals. The library purchased forty-three years of *Harper's,* 1850-93, for sixty dollars in 1898. The next year the trustees picked up back issues of *Forum, Century, Scribner's, Review of Reviews,* and *Atlantic Monthly.* In 1900 they added several years of *St. Nicholas* and *Popular Science Monthly* to the collection. Sometimes these back issues were already bound, sometimes that was an additional cost. All through 1899 they worked out policy statements on what titles to bind automatically. This included most magazines but only a few newspapers: the Iowa City dailies, the *Iowa City Republican* and the *Iowa State Press,* plus the *Des Moines Register* and the *Des Moines Leader.* (The Des Moines papers merged about 1902.) In 1900 the trustees added the *Chicago Tribune.* As the library entered its sixth year, the periodical collection certainly qualified as one of the early strengths of the new institution.

By 1900 the trustees were also able to spend money on some important series and titles to enhance the reference collection. Many trustees came to meetings with specific titles to propose and to seek approval for their purchases. Some major titles acquired included *Larned's History of Ready Reference* (two vols.), *Appleton's Cyclopedia of American Biography* (six vols.), *American Statesman Series, World's Best Orations, Abbott's Biographical Histories* (thirty-two vols.), *Appleton's Scientific Library, Personal Recollections from Washington to Lincoln* (two vols.), and *Ellis' Illustrated History of the United States* (eight vols.). These sets could cost anywhere from five to sixty-five dollars. Sometimes the resolution would say "offer $8" or "try for no more than $35."

Gifts were another source for library materials during this period. Like those that still arrive at libraries every day, the selection ranged from extraordinary to forgettable—or regrettable, if the library makes the mistake of adding materials not suitable for its constituency. The librarians and the board seemed to make a strong effort to recognize and thank those who contributed to the collection. They were always listed in the minutes, often in the annual report, and frequently the newspaper included donor names and book and magazine titles in the long columns of local news. Many people contributed magazines, both single issues and long runs. These were useful to fill in worn or missing issues or to exchange with other libraries. The Iowa State Library ran a magazine exchange during this period and the board authorized its use two or three times. In 1897 the library received a major gift of seventeen years of *Scientific American, 1849-66.* These volumes were held by the library until 1930 but the board entered no current subscription to this well-known journal during this five-year period.

Gift books were more of a mixed blessing. Small gifts of two or three titles often consisted of good editions of standard titles and would be welcomed. Large gifts sometimes appeared to be the result of attic cleaning: old, often on religious topics, or by unknown authors. During the nineteen months from May 1897 until January 1899, only one major shipment of new books arrived at the library. The balance was made up of gifts, sometimes of doubtful value, but they did help fill up the shelves during this very busy but impoverished period. One category of "gift" books—government documents—was solicited and welcomed. The library received the tenth U.S. Census, Iowa Geological Survey reports, *Iowa Official Registers,* railroad commissioners' annual reports, and a wide variety of other state and federal documents.

At the board's first official meeting in March of 1897, the trustees were given the opportunity to serve one of the community's ethnic minorities. Two representatives of the P.J. Safarik Lodge, #75, C.S.P.S., Paul Korab and J.W. Dvorsky, offered to loan the library 150 volumes of books in Bohemian "to be loaned out to the public under the same rules as other books of the library . . . [and] . . . to revert to said Lodge should the Iowa City Public Library cease to exist." The board accepted the offer and adopted a resolution of thanks, but, according to circulation records for 1897-1900, the books received limited use. In November 1900 the lodge requested that the board return the books so the group could form a library in its recently constructed hall on North Johnson Street (now the Preucil School of Music). At the same meeting the board appointed three members—Stevenson, Shimek, and Mayer—to a committee to "prepare a plan for starting a branch library in the new C.S.P.S. Hall." The committee was directed to report at a special meeting of the board. No further reference to this idea or the committee was ever recorded in the minutes.

Who Used the Library and What Did They Read?

The wide variety of first-day visitors described earlier continued at least through the first six months. An analysis of the occupations of the 1,600 individuals who received library cards from January 21 through June 30, 1897, gives a profile of the library's earliest card holders. The gender breakdown of 53 percent female and 47 percent male misses the 1895 census figures (54 to 46 percent) by less than 1 percent. Minor children can be identified by matching home addresses to surnames of adults appearing in the directories, although distinguishing between children and unemployed wives is difficult. Based on the use of diminutive names like Willie, Robbie, Eddie, and Lizzie, and other clues, it appears that about 30 to 35 percent of the registrants were minor children.

Using a sample of one-fourth of the 1,600 card holders, 55 percent of the names could be linked with an occupation either for the working parent or for any adult children living with parents. A minor child was tallied under the occupation of the adults in the household. Under this method, which, of course, has a wide margin for error and misinterpretation, the occupations represented included all the socio-economic classes the library was intended to serve. Twenty percent could be classed as professional: teachers, professors, lawyers, doctors, ministers; 28 percent were related to managing or owning large and small businesses: manufacturing, printing, contractors, insurance agents, retail merchants, undertakers; 45 percent used clerical, craft, and technical skills in their jobs: business and retail clerks, shoemakers, painters, dressmakers, tinners, railroad engineers, barbers, plumbers, lathers, masons, telegraph operators, postal clerks; 5 percent were listed as laborers; and 3 percent as students. The most underrepresented categories were day laborers and domestics, who comprised about 26 percent of the labor force in 1895. The sample from just the first 577 cards issued in January of 1897 had proportionally more men and children, more professionals, laborers, and students, and fewer business, clerical, and skilled workers. Of the entire 1,600 card holders only forty-four—less than 3 percent—gave addresses from other Johnson County communities or from the "West Side."

Did the rush for cards and the heavy use of the library's small opening day collection represent a pent-up demand for access to free reading materials? There had been bookstores in Iowa City from about 1857, at least two from about the mid-1870s and three from 1887 forward. Books were cheap by today's standards and relatively cheaper than they had been before many of the technological improvements to printing and publishing in the latter part of the nineteenth century. The average cost of a book to the library in the first years was about eighty-five cents but this was a discounted price. With a salary of forty dollars a month, librarians after Howell and others with similar income found one dollar a major expense. One of the cheapest sources of books in 1897 was the Sears, Roebuck catalog. The 782-page catalog listed many paperbound editions for as little as five cents a volume. While some of the books were in the "dime novel" category that libraries hoped to compete with successfully, the catalog also offered, like today's remainder houses, sales on reference books, classic titles, and respected authors. The number of titles published in the United States tripled between 1881 and 1900, from 2,100 to 6,536.[31] The actual number of volumes printed is unknown, but the large Sears assortment indicated there were many more than could be sold at their original prices.

Reading had little competition for leisure time in these years. The library was founded to challenge saloons, gambling, and pool halls, not the automobiles, movies, radio, television, home videos, and computers that have appeared since. Musmann in his history of library technology believes the height of the book's popularity was between the years 1890 and the beginning of World War I. For centuries since the invention of moveable type, the book was the first and only carrier of information besides memory and art, and recorded knowledge was described and honored in terms of the physical carrier of that information. The book represented "the embodiment of knowledge and thought" and was considered as fundamental an invention as the wheel.[32] Books and reading were not only an important passport to education, income, security, power, and prestige, they satisfied curiosity and supplied vicarious adventure and relief from anxiety in an increasing complex society in a way that no other pastime of the day could match.

Iowa Citians, eager to drink from this new cup of knowledge and entertainment, borrowed and borrowed and borrowed, and we must assume that the favorite titles and authors of the day nationally were in high demand. When borrowed from the library, the books of Mrs. Humphrey Ward, J.M. Barrie, and "other merchants of glucose"[33] as well as semireligious writers like Hall Caine and Harold Fredric were respectable when pastimes like pool or poker were not. *Quo Vadis* by Henryk Sienkewicz was the top seller in 1897 along with one classic, Stephen Crane's *The Red Badge of Courage*. H.G. Wells published *War of the Worlds, The Invisible Man,* and *The Time Machine* during the library's first five years. *David Harum* and *When Knighthood was in Flower* claimed the top slots in 1899 along with Finley Peter Dunne's first Mr. Dooley title and *Richard Carvel,* the second big seller by the American Winston Churchill. Two well-known authors, one from each end of the quality spectrum, were missing from the library's 1901 collection: Joseph Conrad and Burt Standish. Standish was the author of over 750 Frank Merriwell stories and was probably too close to the dime novel category to merit consideration. Conrad was possibly too avant garde for the general reader of 1897.

In 1949 Shera claimed that "the members of social libraries had much the same reading habits as those who frequent the public library of the present." Fiction, literature, history, travel, and biography were the popular topics. He noted that many libraries appeared to have large religion and theology collections, but this was because people too often judge a library collection "by its remnants. . . . The more popular are used and worn out"—or at least checked out.[34] During this period sociology was replacing theology for insights into humans and their world. As noted earlier, religious titles dominated many of the gifts received by the library.

The circulation records for 1899, 1900, and 1901, the only years before 1902 which are broken down by category and class number, confirm Shera's comments about the most popular topics and categories with library readers. Over 90 percent of the adult books checked out during these three years consisted of fiction, literature, history, and biography. One percent of titles chosen were from the religion section and the balance came from all the other general Dewey categories: philosophy, social studies, languages, science, applied technology, and the arts. And like the pattern in almost every public library then and today, fiction was the largest single category. In those years before the nonfiction collection was as varied and rich as in a contemporary library, over 50 percent of the check-outs came from the fiction shelves. Children's titles—juveniles—accounted for about one-third of all books checked out, and less than 20 percent of the public's choices were from the various Dewey classified categories.

With the inventory that Lloyd took early in 1901 before the move to College Street, we can see that the library's collection over a four-and-a-half-year period grew from 1,300 to 5,600 volumes but the shape of the collection changed from about one-quarter nonfiction to nearly 60 percent nonfiction. The 517 nonfiction volumes had expanded to 2,500 while juvenile and fiction collections were only two and half times larger, 359 to 862 volumes and 417 to 967 volumes respectively. There was significant growth in philosophy, religion, social sciences, science, and the arts, while the more popular topics of history, literature, and biography merely doubled, indicating the board's determination to provide a balanced and varied collection of nonfiction. Use of some of these categories lagged behind, but the library was beginning to build strength in all areas of the collection. Continued high turnover rates of fiction and juvenile titles (twelve to thirteen uses per year) kept the staff busy repairing, rebinding, and replacing, but the low to moderate use of nonfiction (one and one-half to three check-outs per year) helped keep those collections in good physical shape while they grew in scope and depth. Even practical subjects changed much more slowly at the turn of the century so few if any would be removed because they were outdated. In 1901 the religion collection—at a turnover rate of one-half per volume—was the least-used collection in the library.

A monthly pattern of use established itself in the first year and continued throughout the period except for 1898 when the heavy circulation of the new collection and the inability to buy many new books caused loans to dip nearly 14 percent below the library's opening year. Check-outs peaked each March, leveled off in the summer, and climbed back again in the fall after the lowest traffic in September. Saturday was always the busiest day, averaging nearly three hundred check-outs in March and November. Loans on other days varied from week to week and season to season, but Sundays were always busy for the two and one-half hours the library was open.

Both staff and trustees expended a great deal of time and energy improving the methods available for readers to find specific books in the collection, especially after Lloyd joined the staff. As the nonfiction collection expanded, these methods and procedures became increasingly important. From Lloyd's realization about the usefulness of spine labels to the production of a book catalog of all library holdings (it would become available early in 1902), the library made great progress toward an organized and usable collection. The card catalog expanded to two units and Mary Heard was hired to see that every title was properly cataloged. In late 1900 the board voted to pattern a book catalog after those of the Cleveland and Des Moines public libraries. In 1901 the board took bids from several printers and hired a part-time clerk to help proofread the galleys before the final printing.

Why the board and staff gave this $250-300 project such a high priority is unclear. In her introduction to the book catalog Adelaide Lloyd wrote, "The purpose of the catalogue is to render the resources of the library available to the public." Unlike the card catalog, the book was out of date the day it appeared. In addition to being considered a prestigious thing for a library to do, it may also have been intended as an aid to those selecting books for the library. Did the board and staff expect to sell copies to local residents for use at home or work? They ordered 2,000 copies and the financial report for 1902 lists income from sale of catalogs as a type of receipt, but the report shows no income. The article in the *Republican* announcing the publication of the catalog suggests copies were given away. The newspaper reported that card holders could receive one copy per family on request.[35] Two copies are in the library's current collection and summarize nicely the collection work of those first five years.

Visitors to the library had two choices. They could browse the collection to see if they could find a book they wanted to take home for up to two weeks, or they could stay a while to read newspapers and magazines or to consult reference books. There are no clues as to how visitors to the library were counted, and in some years many of the daily counts end in zero or five, indicating they were estimated, but for the entire five years the number of visitors was always about twice the number of check-outs, and in 1898, when circulation dropped, the number of visitors was nearly triple the circulation. The number of visitors topped 60,000 in four of the five years, equal to eight annual visits per capita.

Subtract the one visit per book required to check it out and there were nearly 30,000 visits each year just to use reading room materials. If this logic holds, then the careful work of the board in building a quality collection of current and back files of newspapers and magazines was paying off. Twice in this period the librarian reminded the board when looking at circulation totals not to forget the many uses that materials received in-house. Libraries have always measured themselves in terms of books owned, acquired, and loaned, and have wrestled with how to measure use of materials not checked out.

The pattern of visitors by month during these five years parallels that of circulation, with peaks in the spring and the fall. The exception is 1898 when circulation dropped but in-library use rose, further evidence of the attraction of the more stable and accessible periodical collection at a time when circulating books were scarce, picked over, and wearing out.

Keeping the reading room quiet and comfortable for library users challenged the board in the first few weeks of operations. The young people that the library founders had been anxious to attract to the library were coming in. On April 21, 1897, at their third meeting, the trustees adopted the following carefully worded resolution: "Resolved that the grown people—the fathers and mothers—be requested to visit the library especially upon Saturdays and Sunday afternoons, when the attendance of young people is large, their presence acting as a stimulus to the young to greater effort in the broad field of education and investigation which the library affords." How this resolution was transmitted to the "fathers and mothers" is unknown. A report in the newspapers was not found. In December the problem evidently continued for it was "moved and carried that M.J. Wade and Geo. Ball be a committee to ask the city council to pass an ordinance governing the conduct of persons using the library." On May 18, 1898, the city council adopted ordinance number 44, providing punishment for any person who disturbs the "order and quiet of the public library by making noise, loud talking or whispering or by using obscene, profane, or vulgar language . . . or violate the rules . . . adopted by the library board." The penalty of twenty-five dollars also applied to persons guilty of keeping or defacing any books, papers, or magazines belonging to the library. The mayor was empowered to appoint the librarian and assistant librarian special police officers without compensation authorized to arrest any person violating the provisions of the ordinance. A form of this ordinance remains in the city code to this day.

Looking at the First Five Years

If the trustees had wished to hold an evaluation session for their first five years, they could have used as a guide the goals they had written in 1896 for the Iowa

City Public Library Association constitution. Article II entitled *Object* listed four goals:

1. To provide good and elevating literature for the citizens of Johnson County,
2. To maintain comfortable reading rooms open to the public,
3. To seek to inculcate a love for good reading on the part of our young men and women, and
4. To promote intelligent and patriotic citizenship.

Although there is no record of the trustees specifically referring to these goals again, their work may be judged by these self-imposed standards.

Board members could give themselves high marks for the first two goals. By the end of 1901 they had built a quality collection of books and periodicals and had started a substantial reference collection. The statistics on the number of people visiting the building suggest that the reading room was heavily used and the board had moved quickly to prevent young people from disrupting the decorum of the small area. The continuity of the board and, after several attempts, the continuity of the librarian had allowed the library to build collections and services gradually.

To actively promote a love of reading and intelligent citizenship as listed in goals three and four was clearly beyond the power and resources of this group during its first five years. The members spent their years learning the basics about selecting staff and books, about providing reasonable hours in clean and adequate quarters, and about organizing their resources for the convenience of their public.

The trustees had met their major financial crisis with calm, creativity, and determination. They had moved the library into larger, better-equipped quarters, and by the end of 1901 they had already taken preliminary steps to secure a permanent home for the library. And, as we shall see, the original nine trustees plus one would see this dream come to fruition in just a few years.

---

[1] See appendix A for a chronological list of all trustees.

[2] There is overwhelming evidence that public library trustees have been almost entirely male, white, well-educated, and usually professional or businessmen. Studies by Joeckel [1939], Garceau [1949], and Prentice [1973] have confirmed this. Shera noted the same regarding early association libraries. Also see Garrison, 50.

[3] *Iowa Library Quarterly*, vol. 16, 1911, 88.

[4] Aurner, vol. 2, 343.

⁵ Ray Yenter replaced Ball in 1915 and Will Hayek replaced Yenter in 1926. John Hayek reports that the safe in his firm's office has "Baker and Ball" painted on it. Telephone call of January 8, 1995.

⁶ *History of Johnson County, Iowa,* Iowa City, 1883.

⁷ Dick Lamb, *75 Years with the Fighting Hawkeyes* (University of Iowa Athletic Department, 1964), 9-10. Weber, vol. 2, 259.

⁸ Mansheim, 19.

⁹ Letter to author from Rate Howell, August 11, 1995.

¹⁰ Shera, 107

¹¹ Comparative annual salaries of public employees in 1897: sheriff, $400; county school superinten-dent, $1,078; janitors, $225-$500; second highest salary at UI, Law Chancellor Emlin McClain, $3,200. From various issues of the *Republican,* fall of 1897 and early 1898.

¹² The 1897-98 City Directory contains a list of all university students by class.

¹³ *Press-Citizen,* April 25, 1931. Reizenstein joined the *Press-Citizen* when the papers merged in 1920 and wrote his daily column on Iowa City history from 1927 to 1960.

¹⁴ *Press-Citizen,* June 2, 1940.

¹⁵ Library board minutes for December 19, 1900. A fuller discussion of this issue in public libraries generally can be found in Musmann, 64-69.

¹⁶ Librarian's monthly report for November, 1900. Library archives.

¹⁷ Library board minutes for January, 1901, 118. Library archives.

¹⁸ See "Moral Passage: the Fiction Problem" in Garrison. Also Patrick Williams, "The Fiction Prob-lem, 1876-1896," in *American Public Library and the Problem of Purpose* (Greenwood Press, 1988), and Esther Jane Carrier, *Fiction in Public Libraries, 1876-1900* (Scarecrow Press, 1965).

¹⁹ From the scrapbook of Mae Strach, a member of the company, in the private collection of her nephew, Carl Strach Jr., Iowa City, IA.

²⁰ George D. Glenn, *Opera Houses of Iowa* (Ames: Iowa State University Press, 1933), 4.

²¹ Glenn, 128-129. Weber, vol. 1, 85.

²² *Republican,* October, 25, 1897.

²³ *Republican,* weekly edition, December 1, 1897.

²⁴ Budgets and year-end financial reports were not always included in the minutes. All minutes were handwritten into a journal book and it was not easy to include a report that was prepared on another sheet of paper. The librarians were typing their monthly and annual reports by 1898 and then copy-ing them into the minutes book. It was 1909 before a typed report was occasionally pasted into the book and at least 1928 before the journal book was abandoned for a punched notebook. (The min-utes book for 1928-1943 is missing.)

²⁵ The 1906 Sanford fire map (State Historical Society, Iowa City) shows the six-foot-wide staircase between the first floor businesses. Weber (*Press-Citizen,* September 27, 1978) quotes William Goodwin who used the library at this location. He described the wide stairway and remembered Merchants Cafe on the east and Emmons & Emmons Grocers on the west.

²⁶ The immediate successor to the library on Iowa was a bowling alley. The C.O.D. Steam Laundry remained until 1912 when it became New Process Laundry. The C.O.D. name was resurrected in 1974 and used for a vegetarian deli and bar at that location. Today the bar remains and is call QUE. The upstairs has a small bandstand at the south end and the room is sometimes booked for public performances or private parties.

²⁷ John Cotton Dana, "Fiction readers and the libraries," *Outlook,* 74 (June 27, 1903), as quoted in Carrier, vol. 2, 28. Dana didn't name the author of "major importance," but the best-known names on his list were Alexander Dumas, Conan Doyle, and Winston Churchill.

²⁸ For example, see Shera, 93-94.

²⁹ See minutes of the Iowa City Public Library Association, August 24, 1896 and many of the articles and editorials in the *Republican* and *State Press* in the fall of 1896.

[30] Richard Ohmann, *Selling Culture: Magazines, Markets and Class at the Turn of the Century* (London: Verson, 1996).

[31] U.S. Bureau of Census, *Historical Statistics of the United States; Two Centuries of the Census, 1790-1990* (Greenwood Press, 1993).

[32] Henry Bliss, *The Organization of Knowledge in Libraries and the Subject Approach to Knowledge* (New York: Wilson, 1934), 3, and Virginia H. Holtz, "Measures of Excellence:the Search for the Gold Standard," *MLA Bulletin* 74 (Oct. 1986), 307-308. Cited in Musmann, 16.

[33] Perelman, S.J., introduction to reprint of the *1987 Sears Roebuck Catalog* (Broomall, PA: Chelsea House, 1968).

[34] Shera, 114.

[35] *Republican*, March 26, 1902.

■ 4.   Building the "People's Palace," 1902–1904

On March 14, 1902, James Bertram, personal secretary to Andrew Carnegie, signed letters awarding grants for public library buildings to thirty-five communities in fifteen states. It was just another workday for Bertram, who sent these grant notifications at the rate of one every other day during the first three years of the new century, but it was a very important date for Iowa City. One letter confirmed that Carnegie would give Iowa City $25,000 "for the erection of a Free Public Library Building" if the city would provide a suitable site and a promise of no less than $2,500 a year in library support.[1]

Why Seek a Carnegie Building?

Was it a dire need for more space or a judicious response to Andrew Carnegie's standing offer to provide funds for library buildings that motivated the library board to quietly send off an inquiry to Carnegie in the summer of 1901 just after the move to College Street? Did the move to new quarters alert the trustees to the advantages of a permanent building?

There was a tremendous increase in library use after the move and all through 1902. Twenty-five percent more visitors checked out 21 percent more books from the Cannon & Pratt building on College Street in 1902 than during the previous year which was divided between two locations. Did this represent new demands for library services based on the growth of the community and the needs of its residents, or did the news about the Carnegie gift and the site dispute that followed stir interest in the library? The library's collection had grown more than 40 percent, to over 7,000 volumes, since the move to College Street in mid-1901. The combination of a larger collection and increased traffic plus five years of experience as a reliable and respected community library easily made a case for more space and a permanent building.

The library board and city council had more in mind than just following a popular national trend in seeking funds for a new library. The years 1901 and 1902 saw great growth for Iowa City. Business and community leaders were working "for the betterment of the Athens in all . . . phases of municipal life," as the *Press* wrote in its report of the Commercial Club's first annual banquet in February 1902. Besides talks about improving the riverfront, purchasing property for parks, and attracting new industry, members of the year-old organization heard a report on public buildings from Max Mayer, local retailer and library trustee.

"We need them and need them badly," Mayer declared. "No honorable method to attain [them] ought to be neglected." In addition to a library building he mentioned the new high school already planned, the post office building under consideration by Congress, and some new university medical buildings proposed for approval by the state legislature. By the end of 1902 all had been funded. The new courthouse and Schaeffer Hall had opened the year before.

Iowa City's promoters could point to other civic and business accomplishments in this period. During 1902 Mayer had become the first president of the new Retail Merchants Association and organized Iowa City's first country club;[2] a franchise for an electric street railway was approved; and a question about annexing land on the west side of the Iowa River was on the ballot. Two new hotels and one hundred new homes had been completed in the previous twelve months. As a speaker at that first Commercial Club banquet noted, Iowa City was looking for every possible way to grow and improve, "to become the hub of [Iowa's] educational world even more than it is now."

Library trustees were involved in most of these efforts to build a greater Iowa City and were among the most influential Iowa City citizens. Along with Mayer, trustees Wade and Coast spoke at the Commercial Club banquet. And all three, plus George Ball, served on the board of directors for the new organization. Ball, now a state senator, and Wade, who had just announced he would not run again for district judge, were both mentioned as possible Democratic candidates for Congress in the November election.

Getting a permanent library building for Iowa City would provide library users better service, of course, but a Carnegie award would also be another step in the community's growth "from a hamlet to a city through the energetic efforts of all its citizens," Judge Wade told the business community in his remarks to the Commercial Club that evening.[3]

After five years it was time for a permanent library building and such an effort fit nicely with the long-term plans of Iowa City's business community.

Building the "People's Palace," 1902–1904

Andrew Carnegie: Life and Legend

By 1902 Andrew Carnegie was easily one of the most famous men in America. Today his reputation is often that of a cold-blooded, insensitive industrialist who sought fame as well as redemption for his years of business sins by giving away some of his massive wealth to over 1,400 U.S. communities in the form of public library buildings. While this $40 million philanthropic project had a major impact on the development of public libraries in the United States, it was only a part of his contribution to libraries throughout the English-speaking world and was a very small portion of the $333 million he donated to an amazingly wide variety of causes before his death in 1919.

Carnegie is one of the best examples of a Horatio Alger rags-to-riches career. He was born in Dunfermline, Scotland, where his father was a master weaver. The elder Carnegie would soon be replaced as power looms changed the cottage industry of damask linen to a factory-based operation. Brought up among politically radical relatives fighting social inequality and the threat of approaching technology under the banner of the People's Charter or Chartism, young Carnegie was drilled from birth on the reform program of the working class: manhood suffrage, secret ballot, and the abolition of property qualifications for membership in Parliament. An early reader, Andrew used the Tradesman's Subscription Library which his uncle had helped found.

In 1848, "seeing his fellow weavers queuing daily in bread lines and at soup kitchens,"[4] Andrew's father took his small savings and brought his family to Allegheny, Pennsylvania, where relatives lived. William Carnegie never recovered economically or psychologically from the loss of his job and his independence as a handloom weaver. By 1850, at the age of fifteen, young Carnegie was the principal wage earner for his family—father, mother, and a younger brother. He first worked as a bobbin boy in a cotton factory, then as a messenger boy and operator at the Pittsburgh telegraph office. By 1853 he was the chief telegraph operator for the Pennsylvania Railroad and the protege of Superintendent Thomas A. Scott.

With no formal schooling after leaving Scotland, Carnegie remained a voracious reader and became a serious one. He had great difficulty finding books and so he greatly appreciated the opportunity to borrow from the four-hundred-volume private library of Colonel James Anderson. Carnegie remembered reading many classics of American literature and history for the first time from the Anderson collection, and once said Anderson's library "opened to me the intellectual wealth of the world." Anderson's offer was to any young working boy who wanted to borrow a book for a week's time. Just a year or two after Carnegie began borrowing from him, Anderson gave his library to form the Mechanics' and Apprentices' Library. Carnegie's first published writing—he wrote books and magazine articles throughout his lifetime—was an anonymous letter to the Allegheny newspaper in 1853 complaining that since he was not an apprentice he was being forced to pay for the use of a collection he formerly used for free. Signing his letter "Working Boy," he wrote again, provoking an editorial from the paper, and when the dispute came to Anderson's attention the rule was changed to let all working boys under a certain age, whether a bound apprentice or not, use the library free.[5] The Mechanics' and Apprentices' Library eventually became Allegheny's first public library and the first U.S. public library built from the Carnegie fortune. (Dunfermline, Carnegie's birthplace, received the very first library in 1881.)

In his amazingly successful career, first as an investor in railroad cars, then a builder of bridges, and finally as the world's largest producer of iron and steel, Carnegie made his first million by his early thirties and sold his holdings to the organizers of United States Steel in 1901 for $300 million. He then spent more than thirty years at the serious job of giving away his fortune.

He became the friend of presidents, statesmen, scholars, and other public figures participating in political and world affairs and corresponded regularly with many famous and influential individuals. From the late 1880s he was preoccupied with the abolition of war and the world peace movement. He provided the funds and some of the ideas for The Hague, his "Temple of Peace," and, according to Joseph Wall's definitive biography, he gave Wilson the term "League of Nations." He contributed $10 million to establish the Carnegie Endowment for International Peace in 1910. He was involved in negotiations for a potential arms-reducing treaty between the United States, Germany, France, and England just before the start of World War I.[6]

In what was probably his best-known work, *The Gospel of Wealth*,[7] Carnegie said a man may accumulate great wealth in a democracy, but he has a responsibility to return that wealth in a way that will not destroy society's own responsibility to preserve individual initiative. "Surplus wealth should be considered as a sacred trust to be administered by those into whose hands it falls, during their lives, for the good of the community," Carnegie wrote in one of the essays.[8] Under the rubric of "The Best Fields for Philanthropy," he listed what he considered the best uses to which a millionaire could devote his surplus funds: colleges and universities, libraries, art museums, concert and meeting halls, parks, gardens and swimming pools, hospitals and research labs. Antichurch and committed to democracy, he gave only limited approval to gifts to churches. He considered these to be not gifts to the community but rather to special classes.

An evolutionist—he read both Darwin and Herbert Spencer and became a close friend of Spencer—Carnegie believed in the possibility of a continually improving social organization. Prejudice, hatred, superstition, in short all the evils born of ignorance, constituted the greatest threat to progressive civilization. Like the advances he fostered in the processing of iron ore that succeeded in removing disruptive elements and allowed the production of steel, so, he thought, would the glories of advancing civilization be achieved by "dephosphorizing" man of his unruly characteristics.

Education was the formula for this transformation, and the public library was the place where practical general knowledge to enhance a man's ability to function effectively was dispensed. As a student of Spencer, as were many U.S. educational reformers at the end of the nineteenth century, Carnegie agreed that education should be practical and made interesting to the student. Also the ultimate goal of the library was to implant a taste for reading in the working classes in order to start them on the road to higher intellectual achievements. Carnegie supported the sometimes controversial policy of supplying large numbers of novels to public library readers, not only to sow the seeds for better literature but also to give emotional relief "to the tired and weary toiler [who] is subjected to monotonous labour day after day, week after week. . . ."[9] He also was uninterested in having libraries provide a narrow list of accepted "good books" as some of his critics suggested. "Every free library . . . should contain . . . all contributions bearing upon the relations of labor and capital from every point of view— socialistic, communistic, co-operative, and individualistic—and librarians should encourage visitors to read them all," Carnegie once wrote.[10]

His enthusiasm for funding public libraries was part of a strong interest in promoting educational opportunities for the workingman and for generally supporting educational institutions. Carnegie funds financed the Flexner report that helped revolutionize medical education. He used his fortune to endow several technical and vocational colleges in the U.S. as well as the major universities of Scotland and to establish the Foundation for the Advancement of Teaching. From his desire to provide pensions for college teachers he created the College Teachers' Pension Fund, the first retirement program for academicians and the beginning of today's massive TIAA/CREF fund found at most major colleges and universities.

Attacked then and now for the way he exploited his workers through low pay and long hours, Carnegie, always a man of ideas and intellectual pursuits, believed that the prevailing political and economic system produced the capital investment required to create jobs. He argued that it was not in the worker's interest to have higher wages. This "indiscriminate distribution of wealth stifled initiative, and the trifling sums handed out in the form of wage increases would result in funding earthly pleasures beneficial to neither rich or poor." The distribution of wealth through the establishment of cultural agencies created gains of a "higher spiritual type." The worker received his share of the profits in the form of a public library, for instance, which was, after all, built mostly for the benefit of the wage-earner, was supported by his taxes, and was subject to his control as a citizen of the community. Carnegie frequently celebrated "the precious heritage of poverty" because it gave a person born poor a chance to fight his own way upward, and "it is from the ranks of the poor [that] so many strong eminent, self-reliant men have always sprung and always must spring."[11] Carnegie thought that through public libraries he was giving the ambitious poor worker the tools to do just that.

The Carnegie Impact

No matter how you evaluate Carnegie the man—the powerful and wealthy industrialist, the lifelong writer and intellectual, the ambitious philanthropist—the impact of his contributions to public libraries cannot be denied. And despite major initiatives and huge sums of money spent in other areas, he is best remembered today for his library philanthropy.

Most historians agree that Carnegie's gifts were the most important turn-of-the-century stimulus to a public library movement well established by the last quarter of the nineteenth century. In many places, and especially in smaller communities, public libraries critically needed larger quarters and better yet, permanent buildings. In some communities the Carnegie offer generated interest in organizing a library for the first time, but about 65 percent of libraries getting a Carnegie grant for a building were already in operation. The timing was perfect; the country was growing and urban centers were accumulating growing numbers of workers, immigrants, and others with limited means and limited education. Not the creator but rather the patron saint of the American public library, Carnegie structured his awards in a way that made it clear that public libraries were the responsibility of local government and guaranteed that they were free and under local control. The sheer size and number of his gifts gave increased standing and importance to public libraries in general and gave clear evidence about the central role that books, reading, and education played in society in general and for individuals struggling to improve themselves.

Finally, the construction of more than 1,600 buildings with Carnegie dollars helped develop and define library architecture. The boom in the building of libraries benefited the growing profession of architecture and generated firms specializing in Carnegie libraries. Over time the awards carried more architectural requirements, and local officials received more advice and oversight from Carnegie staff and were more apt to turn to established library architects for their design.

After 1911, Bertram and the Carnegie Corporation sent each award winner a booklet called "Notes on the Erection of Library Buildings." This publication included several sample floor plans, and both the plans and the narrative strove to encourage libraries designed primarily for the efficient distribution of books. While these guidelines and Bertram's increased oversight helped produce buildings that were more functionally efficient than some earlier buildings where the architectural design was determined by each locality, what was gained in efficiency may have been lost in architectural variety. Wall described it this way: "In small towns all over America, there came to be an architectural style popularly known as Carnegie Classical, as easily recognizable as another small town standard, Wesley Romanesque. A stranger in the community had little difficulty in spotting the Carnegie Library and the Methodist Church, which in many towns confronted each other across the square."[12]

This impression is confirmed by Abigail Van Slyck in her 1995 architectural and social history of Carnegie libraries.[13] She found that despite pleas by the Carnegie staff to eliminate domes, columns, and other architectural flourishes, only 10 percent of Carnegie libraries varied from the classical styles she terms "Temple Front" or "Triumphal Arch." The interior floor plans, while equally uniform, conformed closer to Carnegie recommendations, and the open plan with a central charge desk, flanking reading rooms, and books shelved around the walls—known in some circles as the "Carnegie rectangle"—influenced library design until World War II.

The Carnegie Award-Making Process

There were several ways that Iowa City library officials would have known about the availability of Carnegie funds in addition to the nationwide publicity Carnegie regularly received for his library philanthropy. The newly formed State Library Commission, established in 1900, provided information and advice to Iowa communities seeking Carnegie money. Also, by 1902 thirteen Iowa communities had successfully qualified for Carnegie awards and were planning, constructing, or occupying Carnegie libraries. Fairfield received $30,000 in 1892—the fourth U.S. library that Carnegie funded—primarily at the request of Senator James F. Wilson, an old friend of Carnegie who had been helpful to him in building railroads in Iowa. Wilson was president of Fairfield's Jefferson County Library Association. Other Iowa beneficiaries were Carroll in 1898, Davenport in 1899, Ottumwa in 1900, and Cedar Rapids, Clinton, Dubuque, Eldora, Fort Dodge, Hawarden, and Marshalltown in 1901. Newton and Estherville received notification in early 1902 and six Iowa cities in addition to Iowa City were mailed Bertram letters on March 14, 1902.[14] Thus, while Iowa City was late in establishing its public library, it was relatively early among the the ninety-nine Iowa libraries to receive Carnegie building awards before the flow of money was turned off by the Carnegie Corporation in 1919. Carnegie gave nearly $1.5 million to build public libraries in Iowa.[15]

The requirements for receiving funds from Andrew Carnegie to construct a library building gradually became more restrictive and also more uniform as the number of awards increased. In what Carnegie himself called his "retail" period, 1890 to 1896, he funded fourteen buildings in six communities (including Fairfield). In the "wholesale" era, from 1898 to 1919, Carnegie, his staff and, after 1911, the Carnegie Corporation approved 1,665 buildings in 1,406 U.S. communities. In the peak year of 1903 he offered Philadelphia, for example, $1.5 million to build a main library and twenty-four branches. His largest gift went to New York City in 1899—$5.2 million for sixty-six buildings. After 1898 library giving became a business, "as efficient and standardized in procedure as the filling of orders for steel billets" from one of Carnegie's steel plants, according to Carnegie biographer Joseph Wall.[16] The thirty-five buildings approved on March 14, 1902, gave local color to this prodigious operation.

The initial inquiry about a Carnegie award could be submitted by anyone—librarian, trustee, teacher, women's club representative. Carnegie and Bertram both insisted that all business pertaining to a gift be carried on by mail, so on receipt of an inquiry, a standard letter of reply was sent stating the major requirements: an official letter from the mayor or city council saying that the community could provide a site and levy a tax equal to 10 percent of the Carnegie grant for the annual support of the library. Also, each community received a "Schedule of Questions" to complete, asking the town's population and information about current library facilities. Later versions of the questionnaire asked about the assessed valuation of the city. Some communities were turned down because Carnegie officials felt the community's current accommodations adequate or because the request was for a type of library not within Carnegie guidelines. Carnegie funded only communities in English-speaking countries. Any town of 1,000 or more with a locally controlled municipal library was eligible.

Carnegie's representative next sent out a tentative letter of approval, like the one received by Iowa City Mayor Frank Stebbins in March of 1902, promising funds of a certain amount if the site and annual support requirements were met. In fact, the Stebbins letter, carefully preserved by the library since its receipt in 1902, is almost word-for-word the letter received by the hundreds of U.S. Carnegie libraries found in the Carnegie archives and analyzed by George Bobinski for his 1969 study of U.S. Carnegie libraries.[17] Before any money was received, however, communities had to provide proof of their ability to provide annual support at the level requested (10 percent of the amount granted), describe the site, and show proof of community ownership.

Getting everyone to agree on a location was a big issue in many communities.

Towns bisected by a river were the most prone to controversy, according to Bobinski. Most such disputes were resolved by placing the building on one side of the river or the other. For Waterloo, Iowa, however, Carnegie finally raised his gift from $30,000 to $45,000 and "main" buildings were built on both sides, a rarity among communities of any size. Cedar Rapids initially planned to build its Carnegie library on the island in the Cedar River where other municipal buildings now stand until a flood in 1902 drowned public support for that location and it was constructed farther east on Third Avenue.[18]

The amount of the gift depended on the community's population according to the latest official United States census. The standard was about two dollars per capita usually rounded off to the nearest thousand. Communities used all kinds of appeals and statistics to argue that the latest census figures misrepresented their community. Bertram said in 1903 that "the local population statements, if believed, would give the United States a population of 150,000,000," nearly double the 1900 census total.[19]

The gift money was never sent in advance nor in one large sum. As proof of progress on the building was submitted, Bertram sent a letter to Carnegie's cashier, Robert F. Franks—later the treasurer of the Carnegie Corporation—authorizing payment of the approved share of the award. Carnegie's money continued to earn interest for Carnegie until the community had to pay its construction bills.

On completion of the building Carnegie staff asked the community to send a simple, unmounted photograph of the building plus a complete set of plans, "preferably on a sheet not more than twelve by sixteen inches." Despite hundreds of requests, Carnegie rarely attended dedication ceremonies and when asked to provide a bust or picture to display in a new building, Bertram would supply names and addresses of commercial outlets that could sell the library various forms of Carnegie's likeness.

The Library Site War

The library board began its formal pursuit of Carnegie dollars in mid-1901 and had hoped to get $35,000 or more from the first. Although seeking the Carnegie gift was never mentioned in board minutes until July of 1902, the newspaper report announcing the $25,000 gift which appeared in the *Press* on March 22, 1902, eight days after Bertram's letter, said the board had been endeavoring for more than a year "to secure a donation of $35,000."[20] To be exact, the board wrote Carnegie on July 16, 1901. It was signed by all members of the library board and the city council and stressed that Iowa City already levied two mills a year for the library and that two mills currently produced over $3,700. Also, the signers reported that they were expecting funds from "private endowment, so that the income may be safely placed at four thousand dollars a year." After describing the "phenomenal" growth, "exceeding by far the record of any other public library established in the state in cities of equal, or even one-third greater, population," they promised to furnish a site "suitable for a structure which will cost forty thousand dollars, or such other sum as you may in your kindness feel disposed to donate."[21]

As noted above, Carnegie looked at population, not current library income, when determining the size of an award. Based on the *Press* report, however, and from the emphasis in the board's letter on having $4,000 per year in income to match their plan for a $40,000 structure, it appears the board misinterpreted one of Carnegie's basic requirements. While Carnegie required that at least 10 percent of the value of his gift be pledged for annual support, the Iowa City library officials believed, as quoted in the newspaper, that it was "Mr. Carnegie's custom to make a gift of ten times the library's annual income." The same story said that the library board and library friends had "figured hitherto" on about a $40,000 building. The board indeed had expected more from Carnegie and the search for at least an additional $10,000 began the day Bertram's letter arrived.

With the final amount still undetermined but with at least $25,000 guaranteed, the library board immediately began searching for a site. At the April 14, 1902 meeting, trustees discussed the merits of several sites, and the *Press* report of the meeting speculated on various other locations including the southwest corner of Linn and College streets and the northeast corner of Washington and Linn. It appears that the trustees gave serious consideration only to the Koser-owned site on the southeast corner of Linn and College and to the Calkins Laundry site at the southwest corner of Iowa and Linn. (See table of proposed sites, page 99 and site map, page 101.)

At this same April 14 meeting the trustees empowered their committee to negotiate an option for the Iowa and Linn corner—the Calkins Laundry site—at a price not to exceed $6,500. Their resolution said "subject to city council approval," but the very next day the *Press* reported that the library board had bought the Calkins corner. The paper said the council would be asked to ratify the purchase, "but the deal is binding and will be cared for by private parties if necessary."[22] By this step, in the midst of its search for an additional $10,000, the board set off a "library site war"[23] that would not be resolved for several weeks. The agreement with owners W.E.C. Foster and F.D. Lindsey was a five-day option to buy at $6,500 but with a net cost of about $5,000 after the income from selling the buildings on the land. This corner site was 160 by 80 feet with the longer dimension on Linn Street.

Before board members had a chance to discuss their choice with the council, a group of fifty taxpayers led by lawyer Ira J. Alder appeared at the next council

Building the "People's Palace," 1902-1904

LOCATION	1902 USE	OWNER	SIZE	COST	1996 USE
SE corner, Linn and College	J. Edwards residence	Koser	150 x 80 feet	$8,500	UI Office of Public Information
SW corner, Linn and Iowa	Calkins Laundry	Lindsey and Foster	160 x 80 feet	$6,500	Three early 20th century homes, now apartments and offices.
SW corner Gilbert and Washington	Griffith residence	Will Musser	150 x 80 feet	$4,500	Chamber of Commerce office, restaurant
NE corner, Linn and Washington	Residence	Bloom family	150 x 80 feet	Not for sale	Senior Center
NE corner, Linn and College	Coldren residence	Solomon Coldren	150 x 80 feet	Not for sale	Meardon, Sueppel, Downer, & Hayes law offices.
SE corner, Johnson and Jefferson	St. John's Church [to be moved]	Iowa City School Board	150 x 160 feet	$5,500	Pediatric Associates.

Sites considered for Carnegie library building, 1902

meeting with a petition asking that the board's site choice be rejected. Their petition, written by Alder, listed several reasons for their objections. The Iowa and Linn corner was not a desirable location for a permanent library building because it was not an attractive or conspicuous spot. It was obscured by university buildings, they said, and was too close and overshadowed by the university hospital directly across the street (now Seashore Hall). Since Linn ended at Iowa and Iowa went only two blocks farther west, they complained that the site was on dark and partly closed streets. Finally, they claimed its surroundings were "encumbered" by the wood and hay market on the north side of Iowa and on both sides of nearby Dubuque Street. It would not look like a city building in this setting, they concluded.

Board President Wade immediately defended the board's site choice against the unexpected attack. He noted the low net price, the size, and the approval of many individuals who had expressed themselves on the subject. The board could not dictate to the council, he said, but in their role as trustees of the library, they deemed this the best place. He asked the council to take immediate action before the option ran out. Owners Lindsey and Foster could easily get more than $6,500 for the site, he explained.

Alder's response was less concrete than the complaints in his petition. He warned that Carnegie might withdraw his gift if he saw the site and suggested that "something about the deal savored of a scandal." He begged the councilors to delay their decision and not select a site that would make the city ashamed afterward.

The council and Alder reviewed the Koser site, which, Alder reported, would cost no more than $5,000 for a piece eighty by eighty feet or $9,000 for the whole eighty by one hundred fifty feet plus the house. Wade questioned Alder's suggestion that the city spend up to $4,000 more of taxpayers' dollars for a smaller site. On motion, the council then voted 4 to 4 to refer the decision to the finance and building committees. Six votes were needed to approve an appropriation, Mayor Stebbins explained, so he voted to refer. The vote, in effect, killed the Calkins site for the option had run out and the owners confirmed they would not extend the offer.

Following this abrupt turndown on the site of its choice, the library board met the next day and prepared a resolution to submit to the council. Because the council had not yet met officially to consider the library board's latest communication and the library would not release the text, *Press* reporter Reizenstein contacted several board members to try to get details. Ball, Hummer, and Wade all gave vague, noncommittal statements—"no bitterness," "we recognized [their] . . . right to endorse or reject . . . but we need a site as soon as possible." One unidentified board member warned that if the council "wrangles long enough and keeps delaying, the board will need a new president." According to the story in the *Press* there was general belief throughout the community that the library board was "very sore over the turn down" and that the resolution message, no matter how carefully crafted sent the message: "You sat on us; now you make your own selection." Enjoying the dispute, Reizenstein offered a paraphrase of Shakespeare to describe the board's feelings. "If t'were done, t'were well t'were done quickly."[24]

Just two days later the headlines in the *Press* read: "Want Koser Corner: Prominent Citizens Will Spend Money to Secure it as Library Site." A group of citizens, spearheaded by John Pickering, local proprietor of a glass and china shop, wanted the library on the corner of Linn and College streets. "Grant us our wish on this matter and we will pay the difference between the net cost of the Calkins site and the Koser site plus pay the City's bill for brick paving College Street in front of the property," the group told the council, according to the newspaper report. (College was already paved but Linn, the front of the eventual library, was not.) They proposed to raise about $1,000—$500 for the difference in cost between the two sites after the house and some of the land are sold and $500 for brick paving. Contributions were already coming in, the group reported. In the war over the library site, all the troops seemed to be fighting against the library board.

The next day the *Iowa State Press* entered the fray editorially by suggesting a third site. Following a recent change in the school board, its members had reversed their decision to build the new high school on the southeast corner of Jefferson and Johnson streets. The school board had purchased this 150-by-160-foot site for $5,500, and the *Press* suggested the board sell it to the city for its purchase price and explained why the paper thought it was a suitable location. The Democratic *Press* seemed to agree reluctantly that the Calkins corner fought for by the Democrats on the council and the library board was not the best place for the library, but no one evidently responded to this alternative suggestion.

The council met on April 28 to discuss the library board's resolution and the request from the group supporting the Koser site. Aldermen Graff and

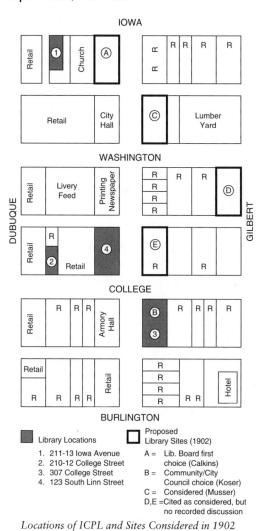

Locations of ICPL and Sites Considered in 1902

Yavorsky argued price and convenience plus some less-than-compelling reasons for reconsidering the Calkins site: It is not in a noisy part of town and it is removed from the stress and turmoil of the business world, they said. Their strongest words, however, were reserved for Koser himself whom they accused of putting an outrageous price on his site. While Koser had already reduced his price from $9,000 to $8,500, the two aldermen reminded the council and the audience that recently when the city tried to raise the assessed valuation of the site from $5,400 to $5,700, the council agreed to cut it back to $5,400 after owner Koser complained about the increase. "Show me how the property adjoining Koser has increased in value to any such extent," Yavorsky asked.

Wade returned to the podium to once again present the library board position in full detail. "Expatiated" was the term used by Reiszenstein in the *Press*. Noting that Carnegie preferred sites large enough for expansion, Wade stressed the need for a lot larger than Koser's if it is cut back to reduce the purchase price. He liked the wide thoroughfare on Iowa. (Improvements to the center boulevard of 120-foot-wide Iowa Avenue were already under consideration in 1902. Linn was only 80 feet wide and unpaved.) He worried that the buildings surrounding the Koser site were neither alluring nor permanent. (The Koser site was surrounded by private homes except for Trinity Episcopal Church on College Street to the north and east, and Armory Hall across Linn Street to the west. The closest retail businesses were on the north side of College Street with Miller Marble Works at 220 East College, near the 1902 public library at 212.) Wade also discussed another possible site on Washington and Gilbert, owned by Will Musser and for sale at $4,500, but alderman Moon countered that Gilbert Street would require $1,500 worth of paving.

At this point alderman Graff moved to buy the Koser site for no more than $8,500 and Moon amended the motion to allow the city to keep the house and rent it or sell that part of it to reduce the cost. Again the council split 5 to 4 and so adjourned without a decision. After the meeting library trustees described the situation to the *Press*. Both the Calkins and Musser sites were large enough and each cost about $5,000. The Koser site, if an adequate size was acquired, would cost the taxpayers $8,500.[25]

The stalemate continued for several weeks, primarily because the council was one member short due to the recent death of F.F. Lee. An election to replace Lee was scheduled for early May and the Democrats hoped to preserve the 5-to-5 Democratic/Republican split on the council by electing Democrat George Sueppel to replace Lee. Sueppel was defeated, however, and Lee's replacement was Republican D.S. Stouffer. The council met in just a few days, ready to let its sixth Republican get them out of the library site crisis. Stouffer, however, said he did not have enough information yet to make a decision and requested that he be excused from casting a ballot. The aldermen who were still maneuvering to get approval for either the Calkins or Musser sites were inclined to grant his request, but the motion to excuse failed, as did motions to buy the Calkins site (5 to 5) and the Musser site (6 to 4). The motion to spend up to $8,000 for the Koser corner then carried 6 to 4. Stouffer had voted "yes" on all three locations. The headline the next day read, "Library Located; Koser Corner Will Be Bought by Council at Price Not to Exceed $8,000." The story said the haunting fear of some of the councilmen had come true. "They were to pay $8,000 for the property that they had assisted in assessing at but $5,400."[26]

Shaken by the failure to get the site they preferred, the trustees felt the need to clarify the relationship between the council and the board concerning the whole process of constructing the new building. At their first meeting after the council's site decision, trustees prepared another letter for council consideration. "The library board desires the city council shall determine whether the new public library building shall be erected by this board or by the city council. . . . [It] ought to be determined as early as possible so that no misunderstanding may arise." They suggested that since it would be a public building the erection should be the duty and responsibility of the city council unless conferred upon the board. They indicated they would like a resolution on the matter and offered to do any part of the process which the council might assign. Once again, they pointed out the need to use the entire Koser corner for a satisfactory building and asked for a prompt response so that construction could still begin in 1902. There is no record of council discussion on these questions, but on May 24 the council unanimously passed a resolution saying the library board was authorized to take complete charge of construction of the library building and to do all that was necessary and proper without further reference to the city council. In June the *Press* reported that the council was not adverse to allowing the whole site to go to the library.

Carnegie Award Is Just Not Enough

With the location and size of the site at last settled, the library board returned to the search for more funds. In a letter to Carnegie dated July 8, 1902, Wade submitted his first request that Carnegie reconsider the $25,000 award. After a short statement about his fear of appearing "presumptuous [or] ungrateful," he reported that the architect believed $25,000 was inadequate for a "suitable building" and noted that "other towns had secured an increase of the original donation upon a proper guarantee of income." He cited Marshalltown and could have mentioned Cedar Rapids whose original 1901 award of $50,000 award was raised to $75,000 one month after the city council promised $7,500 per year support. He attached a supporting note from the mayor and another sworn copy of the council resolution promising at least $3,500 a year in annual support. The Carnegie staff provided a prompt reply dated July 11, just three days later. Unfortunately, it was not from Carnegie or his secretary James Bertram. They were abroad for the summer and the person handling the correspondence in their absence (with the foreboding initials B.A.D) advised them that asking for more money would just delay their project because "Mr. Carnegie bases his allowances for the library buildings on the population" of the community and "the offer made [conforms] to the standard." The cover note attached to the Wade letter and found in the Carnegie Corporation archives summarized the request and added, "Request not sent to Mr. Bertram as the chances are that Mr. Carnegie would not grant the increase. B.A.D., 7/11/02."

Still determined to get the extra $10,000 and with overtures to Carnegie not producing the funds, the board tried another approach to the city council. At a special meeting on July 19 the board adopted a resolution asking the city council to provide an additional $10,000 for the construction of the library. The trustees explained that they had already requested an additional amount from Carnegie and attached a copy of their request, along with B.A.D.'s reply, to this latest council communication. The council asked for a private meeting with the library board to discuss the proposal. From an idea developed by Wade, the trustees suggested that the council give the library the $1,700 from the sale of the house on the site and then issue $8,500 in bonds that the library board would pay off over the next ten years out of its two-mill annual levy. It is the board's opinion, Wade wrote, "that a little less be expended in books and equipment for a few years so that more [can be] put in the building which will serve the needs of the city for the next half century."

Both the *Press* and the *Republican* editorialized against the proposal. The *Press* felt the purpose of the library was to provide books and to shortchange this fund for several years was a mistake. Build what you can with the $25,000, the *Press* said, and use the full two-mill levy to "keep the library abreast of the times."[27] The *Republican* worried about the city's debt and felt the city should not borrow more. If you are already in debt, the paper said, and "a rich uncle gives you a barn large enough to meet all pressing and immediate necessities," would you rush into deeper debt?[28]

The council evidently agreed. At its next regular meeting after the joint board-council discussion, as the final item of business at a session that had lasted past 11:00 p.m., the council produced what the *Press* called "short and sweet" legislation. Graff moved that the library proposal be rejected and the vote was "prompt and unanimous." At the next library board meeting, citing high prices for steel, plumbing, and other components, the trustees agreed to put off the letting of bids for library construction until 1903. It was more than high prices, however, that board members were facing. They had received a quick turndown by Carnegie underlings in July, the city council had said no to their pay-as-you-go proposal, and their leader, Judge Wade, was involved in a political campaign to win election to Congress as Iowa's representative from the Second District.

By December, following his successful first try for national office, Wade was ready to continue the struggle to find $10,000 more to build the size library he and his fellow trustees felt the city needed. Ignoring the response he and the board received in July, Wade wrote another letter to Carnegie on December 17, 1902, requesting the additional funds. This short, rather awkwardly worded letter simply restated the need for more money due to "our inability to construct an appropriate building for the amount donated." He once again apologized if he sounded ungrateful and noted that State Senator Ball and University of Iowa President McLean had gone to New York in August to eexplain the matter to Carnegie but "found you had departed for Europe," a fact they apparently knew from the July 11 reply from B.A.D. If Wade was name-dropping by referring to the visit of Ball and McLean, he overlooked the opportunity to note his own recent election to Congress and signed his name simply as president of the library board.[29]

Just six days later, longtime Carnegie secretary James Bertram sent a terse reply. Recorded in the board minutes of January 23, 1903, and also in the *Press* under the headline, "Carnegie Closes Coin-Holder; Generous Magnate believes Iowa City has had More than her Share Already," Bertram explained in a one-sentence letter that "Inasmuch as the usual sum allowed for library building for a city of the size of yours is about $17,500 and you have been allowed $25,000, Mr. Carnegie does not see his way to give any consideration to the request to increase it." The 1900 U.S. census gave Iowa City 7,887 residents; the 1905 Iowa census recorded 8,497 Iowa Citians. At the standard two dollars per capita, Carnegie could argue that even $17,500 would be a generous award.

At the January meeting where the letter was officially read and acted upon, board members adopted a resolution that "we proceed to build library with funds available." But this was not acceptance of defeat, at least for Wade. Board President Wade was now Congressman-elect Wade after successfully defeating Republican William H. Hoffman for the Second District seat (Wade was only the second Johnson County resident to be elected to Congress and the first Democrat in many years) and he proceeded to use his newly expanded political influence with Iowa's most powerful politician, Senator William Boyd Allison. He sent the senator a three-page letter dated March 11, 1903, explaining the Iowa City predicament vis-a-vis Carnegie, and asked Allison to "personally call Mr. Carnegie's attention to the situation, and see if something could not be done to enable us to construct a building which will meet public needs and which will be worthy the generosity of the giver." Wade, citing his six years as board president as making him "personally familiar with all the details," proceeded to use classic political, demographic, financial, architectural, and statistical arguments for why Iowa City needed and Carnegie, for the sake of his reputation, ought to give $10,000 more for a library building.

Wade's strongest arguments explained how $25,000 would not buy the library as much space as the board currently was renting and that the city was already providing $3,700 a year in support, more than would be required under an increased award. The architects, Wade said, had determined that $25,000 "will not give us a building much larger than 40 to 45 by 80 feet," and yet, he explained, the library was already crowded in larger rented quarters of fifty-five by eighty feet. "Prices are high and if we had ten or twelve thousand more it would enable us to enlarge the building to a very considerable degree."

Strong community support has been shown, Wade argued, by citizens' willingness to tax themselves at the rate of two mills by a vote "carried almost unanimously. . . . The two-mill levy now brings about $3,700 per year and is constantly on the increase." (The fact that the "almost unanimous" vote was for a one-mill levy was ignored by Wade.) He attached a copy of the council's resolution showing that it promised $3,500, not the $2,500 required by Carnegie's $25,000 offer, and added that in addition to the two mills, the taxpayer was bearing the $8,500 for the library site.[30]

On another front, Wade explained, for perhaps the first but certainly not the last time in the library's history, that the presence of the university in Iowa City put special burdens on the local public library. Like the many fund-seekers described by Bertram, Wade objected to the population limit set upon the award by Carnegie and his staff. It is "a gross misrepresentation of our present population," Wade wrote to Allison. "We have over ten thousand within the city limits, and we have a large suburban population . . . who will soon be a part of the city by anexation [sic]. We are . . . a University City and the presence of from fourteen to seventeen hundred students makes a tax upon the public library and especially upon the reading rooms." (Eight years later the 1910 U.S. census gave Iowa City a population of 10,091. University students were not included in the official count until the 1960s.)

Next came the statistical arguments. Wade used the large 1902 circulation, 25 percent higher than just the year before, and the annual number of library visitors to build his case. He gave five years of figures for people entering the library but judiciously skipped over 1900 when the figure dropped by about 8 percent. The size and the recent growth of these indicators made the case for a building larger than the present quarters and larger than $25,000 would buy.[31]

The final point in Wade's case for the additional funds challenged Carnegie's pride in the buildings constructed in his name. Wade noted that "Iowa City is fast becoming a city of fine public buildings." He noted a new university building costing nearly $200,000 (Schaeffer Hall), another $700,000 in university buildings recently approved by the Iowa legislature and a new post office "to be erected under an appropriation already made by Congress . . . [and] . . . just one block from the library site." Wade continued, "in the midst of all these large structures, a $25,000 library will appear very insignificant. It is hardly just to Mr. Carnegie that such a building be constructed, as it will be over shadowed by other building[s] larger in size and of finer types of architecture than we can afford with that much money."

After giving Allison this arsenal of reasons for asking Carnegie to increase his gift, Wade closed with a sentence of acceptance for whatever is given. "Of course if Mr. Carnegie cannot add to his gift, we will do the best we can with the sum already provided, but we feel that if he understands the situation he will see the necessity as we do, and that he may extend his generosity by an additional donation."

Attached to Wade's long narrative was a letter of introduction to Allison from University President George McLean. This was at least the second attempt by McLean to assist the library with its efforts for a larger donation from Carnegie. He confirmed the rate of new buildings scheduled to be built on the University of Iowa campus and closed with, "A building bearing Mr. Carnegie's name, to say nothing of the needs of the community, cannot comport with these buildings of the state unless more than $25,000 is put into it."

It is not known whether Senator Allison ever went through this list of carefully constructed arguments with Carnegie or just drew on his political influence and friendship with Carnegie to urge him to give a little extra money to a deserving community in his home state. Allison, who had been a U.S. senator since 1872, and the soft-spoken but powerful leader of Iowa's Republican Party for as long, had been elected to his sixth term in 1902 and would now welcome Wade, a Democrat, to Iowa's congressional delegation. Senators were still elected by the state legislatures in these years, and Allison's influence at all levels of government was strong. Wade had been an active Democrat all his life and Allison was from Dubuque, one of the other bastions of Democratic strength besides Johnson County in strongly Republican Iowa. According to Wall's history of Iowa, Allison valued the power of his office more than strict conservative principles.[32] Although his roots were in the conservative wing of the Iowa Republican Party, he was known as a compromiser, one who could find a satisfactory middle ground and bring both sides together. Thus good relations with all Iowa politicians would be important to him and doing a favor for the Democrats of Johnson County, particularly Congressman-elect Wade, would be a natural act. It is not known if Allison and Carnegie were close friends. The University of Iowa Library has an 1895 letter from Carnegie to Senator Allison in its manuscript collection. It expresses Carnegie's regrets at being unable to stop and visit Allison while in Iowa as planned.

At a minimum, however, Allison gave Carnegie a copy of Wade's letter. The Carnegie Corporation archives holds a copy of the letter but with this note written across the top: "Increase it to 35 on 3500 from council. A.C" The official 1900 population of Iowa City—7,987—has been noted in the upper right corner.[33]

In just thirty days Wade and the library board received the good news. Writing from Dubuque on April 11, Allison reported that "I saw Mr. Carnegie when in

New York and he spoke encouragingly of your request and . . . if he could have a little time to examine the papers with his sec'y he thought he could come to a favorable conclusion. I have telegraphed him today that I hope he can decide before leaving for Europe. Will send you the response."[34] The telegram, as it turned out, was unnecessary. In a letter dated one day earlier, April 10, 1903, Bertram

The site on Linn Street eventually selected for the new library was surrounded by private homes except for Trinity Episcopal Church on College Street and Smith's Armory west across Linn.

sent another typically terse reply. Bertram wrote: "Mr Carnegie desires me to say that if a pledge is received from Iowa City that Thirty-five Hundred Dollars a year will be appropriated and spent on the Library, he will increase his allowance for building to Thirty-five Thousand Dollars."

Bertram, for seventeen years confidential secretary to Carnegie and secretary of the Carnegie Corporation until 1934, was described by his contemporaries as methodical, systematic, and a stickler for precedent. Brevity was his strong trait; he was inclined to be irritable, but also thrifty, very religious, and a man of irrefutable integrity. His position was difficult, according to Bobinski. "He had to decide on the disposition of a vast sum of money and see that it was properly expended. He judged proposals strictly on their merit. Personal relations or considerations never influenced his judgment. No worthy applicant was to be rejected, and yet, no unworthy one was to be accepted."[35] The phrase "Mr. Carnegie desires me to say" in the March 10, 1903 letter to Wade is not found in other routine notification letters. Bertram, whose life's work had become evaluating and recommending funds for public libraries, was obviously not convinced of the worthiness of Iowa City's appeal but was taking care of a special favor for Carnegie.

At a special board meeting just three days later the board discussed the latest letter from Carnegie via Bertram and adopted two resolutions thanking Allison and Carnegie. Board members also requested that their architect visit Iowa City as soon as possible. The fully funded project was a "go" and they were ready.

Planning the Palace

After the site had been determined in the spring of 1902, board members had turned to the selection of an architect. They asked several architects to submit sketches giving floor space for one- and two-story buildings at a cost not to exceed $35,000. They were still determined to build a larger building than $25,000 would buy. It is not clear how many architectural firms were considered, but at the end of June the board accepted the proposal of Liebbe, Nourse and Rasmussen of Des Moines and authorized the president, Henry Liebbe, to draw up a contract not to exceed $600 for plans for a $35,000 building and for five visits from the architect.

There is no evidence that Liebbe, Nourse and Rasmussen had previously designed a library, but Liebbe, in addition to heading the firm, had been state architect since 1898. The firm was able to cram over sixty listings of current and former design projects on its 1902 letterhead. On the list were many high schools including the one currently under construction in Iowa City, courthouses, banks, churches (including Iowa City's English Lutheran), college buildings, and both Frankels' and Younker Brothers department stores in Des Moines. They named twenty clients for whom the firm had designed homes on Des Moines's Grand Avenue, a prestigious address in 1902, and a few other residences including the home of W.F. Main, prominent Iowa City businessman.[36] The firm had designed Iowa City's "old" high school as well, so there were at least four former and current clients in Iowa City. S.K. Stevenson, as school superintendent, was working with Liebbe, Nourse and Rasmussen on the high school. The architectural firm's lack of apparent experience in planning public libraries did not seem to be an issue with the library board, but there were at least two architectural firms that were designing Carnegie libraries in Iowa during this time period. F.E. Wetherell designed seven Iowa Carnegie buildings between 1902 and 1917, and Patton and Miller of Chicago was the architect for fifteen of the forty-six communities that received Carnegie grants between 1901 and 1904.[37]

The exterior, as designed by Liebbe and company, matched the 90 percent of the buildings Van Slyck describes as having architectural features that Carnegie (in the person of James Bertram) later came to believe were excessive and too costly: domes, temple fronts, triumphant arches, and "pillars and Greek temple features costing much money and giving no effective library accommodation."[38] It had the standard temple front—"a massive portico supported by four heavy columns"—and a lobby ceiling supported by six Corinthian columns and topped by a dome with a stained glass skylight. The 9,000-square-foot building, with its lower level a few feet below grade, featured a grand stairway from the sidewalk to the upper level main entrance.

The interior floor plans were similar to those recommended by the Carnegie staff for awards made after 1908. They did contain a couple of features which Carnegie discouraged and, in later years when plans had to be approved, would reject: radial stacks placed in a semicircular wing instead of bookshelves around the walls of a rectangular building, and fireplaces which Bertram claimed used valuable wall space that could be devoted to storage and display of books. The radial stacks were expensive to build and impossible to expand. (They remain in the building to this day.) Storing the books around the walls of the room saved floor space, opened up the rooms, and were easier to build, expand, and move. Although the building had central heating from the first day, fireplaces were placed in both reading rooms, the offices, and at least one of the seven lower level rooms. They did indeed reduce the wall space available for bookshelves in the reading rooms and, as far as can be ascertained, never were used as fireplaces.

The Liebbe design, however, called for one major feature found in all the plans in Bertram's "Notes on the Erection of Library Buildings": the centrally placed charging desk as the aesthetic and functional focal point of the entire main floor. The small marble-lined vestibule and domed lobby of the Liebbe design led directly to the main desk. There were reading rooms on either side of the lobby with the angled stacks behind the desk. There were two small offices, one for the librarian and the other a staff work-

The Carnegie's centrally placed, octagon-shaped, marble charging desk was the aesthetic and functional focal point of the entire main floor.

room, to the right and left of the stacks. Any staff on duty at the desk (and there would be no other duty posts until the children's room was opened) would be able to oversee all public areas including the radial stacks which fanned out directly behind the desk. Van Slyck notes than when the dome was placed over the desk as it was in Iowa City it offered symbolic opportunities, "literally and figuratively transform[ing] the centrally placed delivery desk into the locus of public enlightenment."[39]

The term "charging desk" was significant. "Delivery desk" was the designation before 1900 when many libraries had closed stacks. The desk served then as a barrier to the carefully guarded collection and as a delivery point for titles requested by library users. After the public was allowed free access to the bookstacks, the process was reversed and the reader presented his choices to the desk for charging out. Today the desk has moved from its central position in most larger libraries and is now called the "check-out desk" or "circulation desk."

Construction: 1903–04

By late spring the architects had finished the plans and prepared the construction bids. The board approved a bid announcement with opening set for June 17, 1903, and received four bids ranging from $37,637 to $30,989. The low bid from Sheets and Freyder was just eleven dollars below the next bid. In addition to Sheets and Freyder as general contractor, the trustees awarded the heating and plumbing bid to C. Hurley. There were no electrical bidders.

Sheets and Freyder's low bid was a fortuitous circumstance for the library. By the luck of the bidding process, the board had acquired the building contractor with the oldest and best reputation in Iowa City. The firm was started about 1855 by three men who learned their trade in Germany: J.M. Sheets and Bernard Gesberg, the original owners, and their talented cabinetmaker, Harry Hazelhorst.

Gesberg arrived in this country first and spent 1854 in Rock Island, Illinois, helping to build the first railroad bridge over the Mississippi. Gesberg and the railroad came to Iowa City in 1855. After thirty years in the construction business as Sheets & Gesberg, Gesberg died in a construction accident in 1885, the same year that Hazelhorst retired. Several Freyders had joined the firm by then and it became known as Sheets and Freyder. After Sheets died in 1906, F.X. Freyder ran the firm under his own name until 1935, eighty years after Gesberg arrived in Iowa City. Freyder lived in Iowa City until he died in 1944—in the house he built at 1010 College Street, torn down to build apartments in 1996.

Photo courtesy of the Freyder family

F.X. Freyder of Sheets and Freyder Construction oversaw the construction of the Carnegie library. The firm built many churches, homes, and other buildings in Iowa City between 1855 and 1940.

According to Weber, the firm built all Iowa City churches constructed before 1908 except the English Lutheran Church designed by Liebbe, Nourse and Rasmussen (now known as Gloria Dei with a new building at the same location). Trinity Episcopal (1871), St. Patrick's (1879), and First Methodist (1907) are still standing. Sheets & Gesberg built the

Opera House on the southeast corner of College and Clinton streets in 1877 and parts of it survive to this day in the Savings and Loan Building on that site. Calvin Hall (1875), the Carson home (1875, now Alpha Phi Sorority), and Close Mansion (1874) are other well-known buildings from this firm which are still standing. Sheets/Gesberg/Freyder were known for their millwork, and until 1983 their own building, which housed a planing mill and a sash and door factory, stood at 320 South Gilbert Street. Weber wrote, "Inside these brick walls the rich heritage of many of Iowa City's finest churches, business buildings, homes and mansions was crafted."[40]

At the same meeting in April of 1903 when the library board celebrated the news that Carnegie would provide the extra $10,000, it received a petition from the local stonecutters' union. Because of strong feelings about how Carnegie mills treated workers, organized labor mounted protests against accepting Carnegie funds to build local libraries in several large cities—Pittsburgh, Detroit, Indianapolis. The award was delayed for over ten years in Detroit. While this opposition was general and consistent in urban areas, the relatively unorganized workers in Iowa left no record of concern about the appropriateness of using Carnegie money. In Iowa City, the issue was one of using local versus out-of-town stonecutters for the work on the library building as the architect evidently had specified. In June after the bids had been opened and the board was ready to write a final contract with Sheets and Freyder, President Wade, who had received the undivided support of Iowa City's labor leaders in the Congressional election the previous fall, proposed that the contractor "be required to cut all stone in Iowa City except the molded stone which may be cut at other places if desired." Representatives of Sheets and Freyder opposed the change and, on motion, the resolution lost and no action was taken. Just four days later, however, at a special meeting to consider contracts with Sheets and Freyder, building committee chairman Coast submitted an amendment to the contract. Sheets and Freyder had agreed to do all stone cutting on the building that could be done without increase in cost to the contractor in Iowa City. The resolution mentioned both the ashlar stone—the blocks used for wall construction—and the ends and fittings for the molded stone—columns and decorative work on the portico. Clearly, the committee had negotiated a compromise between the contractors and the union, for the next document in the minutes is the text of a letter from B. Price, president of the Iowa City Stonecutters' Union. "We, the stonecutters' union of Iowa City, feel that the library board would not be justified in paying six hundred dollars additional for having all stone cut in Iowa City, and that they are doing what they can to have all the stone cut here that is possible."[41]

Construction began in the summer of 1903. The *Press* carried Reizenstein's whimsical report of the July 10 groundbreaking. "Just as St. Mary's clock chimed seven the first man of the gang thrust a spade into the damp earth and the echo had not ceased ere that first spadeful had been tossed aside. The long-awaited step towards a great civic improvement had been taken. . . . As a matter of fact, the surveyors had not finished their work . . . and the groundbreaking was really an error . . . but easily rectified when contractor Freyder arrived on the scene a few minutes later."

The stone, however, not the surveyors, proved to be the greatest barrier to a smooth and timely construction schedule. In January 1904 Coast reported that work was behind schedule due to a delay in getting stone. The pale gray limestone (the 1904 library, the 1907 Methodist Church, and the 1904 post office are the only non-university limestone buildings in Iowa City) came from the large Bedford quarries in Indiana where a two-month strike had just ended about the time the contract was signed. Hundreds of building projects and thousands of workers had been idled by the lack of this popular stone. In Iowa City, that included the new Hall of Natural Science (now Macbride Hall) and other university buildings under construction that summer. While the library's delay was assumed to be caused by the backlog in delivery of uncut stone, there have been

The building's progress was well documented through a series of twenty photographs. Here excavation work is well underway.

Workers placing some of the limestone blocks. Construction had been slowed by a two-month strike at the Bedford stone quarry in Indiana.

unconfirmed stories in Iowa City for many years that the first columns prepared for the new building were too short and had to be redone. If the column story is true, it is an open question whether it was the result of local stonecutters who failed to deliver the skills they petitioned to use, an error on the part of the contractor and the off-site stonecutters, or a rumor started by the locals who still felt cheated out of some work they felt belonged to them.[42]

W.P. Coast, George Hummer, and George Ball were formally appointed to the building committee by President Wade in the summer of 1903 when construction got underway. They actually had been functioning in that capacity since early 1902 when they were the three designated to seek a library site that the city council would approve and buy. As construction got underway and the basic contracts with Sheets and Freyder and with Hurley were confirmed, the responsibilities of the three trustees increased. They coordinated work with the architect who made periodic inspections and with J.J. Hotz, a local contractor they hired to be the board's general superintendent to monitor the quality of the

The front of the new library under construction, facing west on Linn Street

construction work. They approved periodic payments to the architect and contractor after sending confirming documents to Carnegie's staff to get funds released. With no bidders in the first round, they spent a great deal of effort getting firms interested in providing the electrical wiring for the building and had to settle for the only company to bid in the second try, Tri-Electric of Davenport.

As suggestions arose, the committee evaluated proposed changes to the contract and made recommendations to the library board which approved all changes to the original specifications. None of the approved changes entailed dramatic revisions to the original plans, but two provided major savings to the tight budget and released funds for additions identified during the building process. The board saved $3,300, nearly 10 percent of the total project cost, by substituting cork for rubber as the floor material and copper-trimmed tin for copper on the roof.

These major savings, plus the unexpected generosity of the council in giving the project the $1,700 the city received from selling the house that formerly stood on the library site, gave the committee some funds to furnish and equip the building. Otherwise, the basic costs of architect, general contractor, plumbing, heating, and wiring would have taken the entire $35,000 with nothing left to go inside the finished structure.

A rare back view of the original Carnegie building which was enclosed by the addition of 1963

By the spring of 1904 the building committee was getting bids on steel book stacks and lighting fixtures. The search for shelving was assigned to the board's newest trustee, J.W. Rich. With five years of experience as head librarian at the university library, he may have had more familiarity with the specifications for and layout of steel shelving than anyone in the community.

After shelving was underway, the focus of the committee turned to equipping the building for public use. Members reviewed types of light fixtures, ordered sixteen tables—two of lower height for use by children—plus two settees and eight dozen chairs, including a dozen proportioned for children, and selected a charge desk, the most distinctive piece of furniture in the new building. It cost three hundred dollars, was called a "delivery desk" in the minutes, and was ordered from Library Bureau, probably from the 1902 "charging desks" catalog. It was a boom time for equipping libraries and Melvil Dewey's firm was the premier supplier of most kinds of library equipment and supplies. The catalog description noted that "this charging desk is so arranged that the person using it can reach all necessary material with the minimum of effort and without change of position,"[43] a feature that efficiency-driven Dewey would have required. Stressing standardization and library efficiency, Library Bureau catalogs were "teaching tools that spread the lessons of modern library administration far beyond the . . . library school classroom."[44]

According to the post-dedication description written by Reizenstein in the *Press,* the walls were "frescoed, [with] quietly beautiful and harmonious designs and colors [of] red, gray, and green." With board approval the committee dropped the fresco from the general contract and hired its own fresco artist, Charles Morris of Des Moines, for an additional one hundred dollars. They saved one hundred dollars, however, by shortening each row of steel shelving by one section (three feet) to allow easier movement in the aisle on the curved back wall of the stack area. The committee rejected the supplier's recommendation to add a second story of stacks because of lack of funds but this expansion became the board's first priority for post-opening additions when money became available. The board approved bottle-green, color #29 of the Art-Metal Shelving Company, for the shelving and a chocolate color for the cork carpet. Some of the original green stacks remain in the old Carnegie building (leased since 1981 by the University of Iowa for its Office of University Relations). Sodding and grading for eighty-two dollars was one of the final pre-opening expenses.

Who Supervises the Janitor?

At its August 1904 meeting the board heard a first report from Adelaide Lloyd on moving into the new building. This was a repeat performance for her, having directed the library's move from Iowa Avenue to College Street three years earlier. Under her plan no more books would be issued from the old quarters after August 20 and borrowers were asked to return all items currently checked out by August 27. After that the library staff took ten days to inventory the collection, called an "invoice" by librarians of that period. By the second week in September they were moving items to the new building and they vacated the rooms at 214 East College about the middle of September.

While the staff was arranging materials and furniture in the new library, the board held frequent meetings (trustees met twenty-two times in 1904) in the law offices of Baker and Ball, the same place where many of the plans for organizing a public library were launched in the fall of 1896. At one of these meetings the board hired the library's first full-time janitor to start October 1.

The hiring of the janitor gave rise to a pre-dedication crisis similar to the resignation of librarian Howell just before the 1897 library election. Congressman Wade did not resign from the library board until the fall of 1903. The first session of the new Congress did not begin until December 1903, thirteen months after his election to Congress, as was the custom before the Twentieth Amendment to the Constitution. The mayor appointed J.W. Rich to replace Wade and at his first meeting the board also elected him president. Born in 1838 and a Civil War veteran wounded at the Battle of Shiloh, Rich had been a school teacher, editor of the Vinton *Eagle,* and member of the University of Iowa Board of Regents. He had replaced university librarian Ada North in 1892 and had served in that position until 1898. Retired by 1903, Rich was elected to the school board early in 1903 and also served on the board of directors of the Iowa City State Bank.

Rich's transition from university library administrator—with much less oversight than at a public library—to the presidency of a public library board with relatively strong administrative powers, may have confused Rich or caused him, through age and gender differences, to make authoritarian demands on Lloyd and her staff. Whatever the reasons, less than a year after his appointment and election, one week after the hiring of the janitor, and just a few days before the library was due to open, President Rich called a special library board meeting "to settle a misunderstanding between the president and librarian as to the powers and duties of the president." After discussion, the board appointed a committee—Coast, Ball, and Elizabeth Felkner—to draw up rules defining the powers and duties of officers and employees of the board.

In a week the committee was ready, and for the first time that year, all nine board members attended to hear the report. While the minutes do not record the discussion, the response from the committee and from President Rich makes it fairly clear that the appointment of a new janitor brought to a head a conflict about the administrative powers of the librarian. The committee recommended an amendment to the bylaws that would make it clear that "the Librarian shall have direct charge and supervision of the janitor and instruct him as to his work in the library as to heating, cleaning, and doing other work of the library." The report continued, "The President is the executive officer of the Board of Trustees, and as such has general supervision of the Library Building and the employees, subject, however, to the approval and direction of the Board of Trustees. The heating apparatus and the care and management of the same shall be under the control of the janitor, and he shall be held responsible therefor." Trustee Hummer moved adoption of the recommended rules and the motion carried. Immediately President Rich called trustee Ball to the chair and handed in his written resignation as president, asking immediate acceptance. Hummer recommended that Rich's request be deferred until the board's next regular meeting. A week later the board agreed to defer acceptance of the resignation until the December meeting and at the same time by motion they appointed Rich, Ball, and Coast the committee to arrange the program for the formal opening of the library.

Opening and Dedicating the "People's Palace"

On Thursday, October 27, 1904, the new library building opened its doors to the public for the first time. During the first month, while library regulars, after nearly ten weeks of no library service, hungrily checked out books and caught up on their favorite magazines, the dedication committee planned and the board approved the dedicatory exercises. Scheduled for Thursday evening, November 29, there would be speeches and presentations at the Coldren Opera House followed by an open house to let the public inspect Iowa City's newest public building.

The opera house had suffered a serious fire since the 1897 performance of *Honor Before Wealth* which benefited the library in its first year. In March of 1902 most of the upper parts of the house were damaged. Owner John Coldren estimated losses at $20,000. As one of its first major projects the new Commercial Club, started just a year earlier, decided to help raise money for the complete restoration and refurbishing of the 1877 building. Noting that Coldren had donated the use of the house "scores and scores of times to the university, the high school, the academy, commercial colleges, churches, civil, religious, and military organizations, charging no more than his expense of keeping up the institution," club members argued that Iowa City citizens should consider investing in its restoration and remodeling. The club organized a campaign to raise $5,000 through the sale of $5 tickets good for one admission to the revitalized house. The opera house reopened in the fall of 1902 with better seating, a larger stage able to accommodate "the highest scenery . . . used by the biggest traveling companies," and a completely redecorated interior. Reizenstein, the community's biggest theater devotee, described the changes in loving detail several times in the *Press* over the course of the reconstruction.[45] Now able to book larger and more prestigious traveling companies, the new and improved Coldren Opera House also continued to serve the community for the occasions which celebrated Iowa City's progress and growth.

The new Carnegie library at 212 South Linn opened its doors to the public on Thursday, October 27, 1904.

Iowa City Public Library Archives

The dedication of the Carnegie library was one of these historic occasions. The board of trustees issued formal invitations to the event and asked members of the city council to sit with them on the stage. Reporters from the *Press* and the *Republican* attended with notebook and pencil in hand to record the activities. Although his name was not on the program, Congressman Wade was introduced as the evening's master of ceremonies by his library board replacement, J.W. Rich. Wade, Iowa City's most popular citizen, was back from his first session of Congress as well as his unexpected defeat for a second term just three weeks earlier. (Even the *Republican*, fresh from a series of editorials attacking Wade's record in Congress, carefully outlined his long record of service to the library, especially his perseverance in getting a larger Carnegie grant, in its report of the opening ceremonies.)[46]

Dedication ceremonies for the new library were held at the Coldren Opera House. This was also the site of the 1897 benefit performance of Honor Before Wealth.

Photo courtesy State Historical Society of Iowa-Iowa City

Wade's remarks were described as brief, atypical for the congressman. After speaking, he introduced trustee and building committee chairman W.P. Coast who gave a complete report on the money expended in the erection and furnishing of the new structure. Filled with all the details (such as $19.25 income from the sale of dirt from the site), Coast's report listed expenditures of $35,819 from income of $36,719, leaving the board a balance of $900 to fund the variety of incidental expenses expected in the first few weeks. Coast presented the building keys to the next speaker, Mayor Stebbins. Stebbins, after his speech about Iowa

Building the "People's Palace," 1902-1904

City's remarkable progress toward becoming a "metropolitan center," returned the keys in trust to Board President Rich. Rich gave a brief history of the public library movement in Iowa City, a well-researched paper that has been useful since that day for information about nineteenth-century library activities in Iowa City.

After two selections by the grammar school orchestra, the audience was ready to hear the dedicatory address from University President George E. McLean. As a member of the Iowa Library Commission, McLean brought official greetings from that body, but he delivered his principal remarks under the title, "The People's Palace—the Free Public Library—the Sign and Seal of Triumphant Democracy." His theme: The free school, the free press, and the free public library make education universal and with these institutions democracy will triumph. He used the term "triumphant democracy," the same as the title of Carnegie's best-selling book. Through the public library—"the people's palace," McLean said, the great institutions of our society can be coordinated—the school, the church, the press, and the newly developing university extension movement.[47]

The last event on the program that evening was a resolution presented by trustee George W. Ball from the library board, the mayor and city council, and the citizens of Iowa City acknowledging their obligation to Andrew Carnegie "for his noble gift, which has made possible our beautiful and convenient new library." On request for a standing vote, every person in the house "rose at once."

Wade then invited the audience to a reception and "housewarming" and most of those in attendance walked two blocks down College Street and "spent some time going over the structure which kept open . . . until long after its usual closing hour."

Open and properly dedicated, the Carnegie library would stand relatively unchanged for the next sixty years, welcoming generation after generation of Iowa Citians. In the fall of 1904 it joined the growing number of Carnegie buildings throughout the United States that signaled their mission to resident and visitor alike: To serve curious and enterprising minds and to support individuals who seek information, knowledge, and self-improvement. Through the vision and persistence of the library's early trustees, Iowa City's share of Carnegie's legacy was a little larger. They had built the first library building in Iowa City. The university would not follow suit until 1951.

[1] Letter to F.K. Stebbins from James Bertram on Andrew Carnegie letterhead, dated March 14, 1902.

[2] The club was located on the east end of Taft Speedway near the Iowa River. It was destroyed in the

flood of 1918, the first of three golf clubhouses built off of Taft Speedway including the present Elks course.

3 *Press,* Feb. 26, 1902, and May 14, 1902.

4 Vivian Thomas, "The First Carnegie Library," *Wilson Library Bulletin,* June 1995, 53.

5 Wall, *Andrew Carnegie,* 107-08.

6 Wall, *Andrew Carnegie,* 885-940.

7 Andrew Carnegie, *Gospel of Wealth and Other Essays* (N.Y.: Century, 1901. Reprinted by Belknap Press, Cambridge, 1962).

8 Carnegie, 55.

9 From a speech given by Carnegie in Jedland, Scotland, n.d. Quoted by Ditizion, 153.

10 Cited by Bobinski, 109.

11 Carnegie, "How I served My Apprenticeship," *Gospel of Wealth,* 6-7.

12 Wall, *Andrew Carnegie,* 819.

13 Abigail Van Slyck, *Carnegie Libraries and American Culture, 1890-1920* (University of Chicago Press, 1995), 148-51.

14 Other Iowa cities notified on March 14, 1902: Cedar Falls, Dennison, Atlantic, Hampton, Maquoketa, and Oskaloosa. Other lucky communities included Denver, Las Vegas, and San Bernardino, CA. Data from Bobinski.

15 Iowa was fourth in the number of communities receiving Carnegie buildings, surpassed only by Indiana [155], California [121], Illinois [105]. After 1911 the distribution of awards was taken over by the Carnegie Corporation of New York, the major Carnegie philanthropic foundation.

16 Wall, *Andrew Carnegie,* 818.

17 Most of the statistical data and the Carnegie gift requirements are taken from Bobinski.

18 *Cedar Rapids Public Library; The First 100 Years* (Cedar Rapids Public Library, 1996), 18.

19 James Bertram to Melvil Dewey, State Librarian, Feb. 20, 1903, Carnegie Library Correspondence, Reel no. 9. Quoted by Bobinski, 46.

20 *Press,* March 22, 1902. The article contained one of Reizenstein's best alliterative phrases, describing Carnegie as "a multi-millionaire, manufacturing midas and many times maligned money-maker."

21 Letter from Iowa City Library Board and City Council to Andrew Carnegie, July 16, 1901. Carnegie Corporation Archives.

22 *Press,* May 15, 1902.

23 Headline in the *Press,* April 19, 1902.

24 *Press,* April 22, 1902.

25 *Press,* April 28, 1902.

26 *Press,* May 14, 1902.

27 *Press,* July 31, 1902.

28 *Republican,* July 24, 1902.

29 Letter from Wade to Carnegie, December 17, 1902. Carnegie Corporation Archives.

30 The city council resolution to buy said $8,000 but the price cited through history has always been $8,500. Perhaps the offer of some private funds was accepted.

31 The 1901 report of the State Library Commission backs up most of Wade's claims. Of 77 tax-supported public libraries, Iowa City was sixth in total hours open, 8th in annual income, 13th in annual circulation and 23rd in volumes owned.

32 Wall, *Iowa, A Centennial History,* 159-67.

33 The words "from council" are almost unreadable on Carnegie archives microfilm. This is the author's best judgment of what it says.

[34] Letter from Allison to Wade, April 11, 1903. Iowa City Public Library archives.

[35] Bobinski, 26-31.

[36] The home was at the northwest corner of College and Summit streets. The lot extended all the way to Washington and had a three-foot deep swimming pool and an eight-foot iron fence around it. Conversation with Irving Weber, May 28, 1996.

[37] Van Slyck, 60. Kruty, Paul. "Patton and Miller: Designers of Carnegie Libraries." *Palimpsest,* 64, 1983, 122.

[38] James Bertram, letter to Flora Johnson, Feb 13, 1912, Carnegie Corporation Archives. Quoted by Van Slyck, 150.

[39] Van Slyck, 128-29.

[40] Irving Weber, "Sheets and Gesberg were Early Builders," *Press-Citizen,* July 23, 1983, 5B.

[41] Library Board minutes, June 6 and 26, 1903. *Press,* June 26, 1903. The *Press* had noted on Oct. 10, 1902 that all the local labor unions had endorsed Wade: bricklayers, carpenters, stonecutters, teamsters, typographical, and laborers. Other reports indicated that the last two had been organized recently.

[42] Irving Weber heard the story from Will Goodwin, who did architectural work for Sheets and Freyder. Weber never used the story for he could never confirm it. The question always arose, what happened to the discarded columns?

[43] Library Bureau, *Catalog,* 1902. Cited by Van Slyck, 168.

[44] Van Slyck, 48. Dewey had lost control and then sold his stock in Library Bureau by 1902, but his concern for library efficiency was the driving force behind many of the company's products. See Wayne Wiegand, *Irrepressible Reformer, a Biography of Melvil Dewey* (Chicago: American Library Association, 1996), chapter 11.

[45] *Press,* Mar. 19, Mar. 29, May 14, and Sept. 2, 1902.

[46] *Republican,* Nov. 30, 1904. Despite wildly optimistic predictions by his supporters, Wade had a difficult campaign. National Democrats gave him neither the support nor the money they furnished in 1902; Roosevelt's opponent, Judge Parker, got only 40 percent of the national vote; several charges of poor attendance and hypocrisy in regard to Wade's opposition to trusts hurt him in the district. He lost by 186 votes but carried Johnson County by 875, seven times Parker's plurality in the county.

[47] Cooperation between public libraries and university extension activities was a fashionable idea in the 1890s. Melvil Dewey, who was both New York state librarian and secretary to the board of regents at this time, wanted New York to send lecturers and exams to the state's public libraries. He proposed that anyone reading the university-approved books in the library and passing the exams could obtain a university degree without coming to the campus. See Wiegand, chap. 7.

■ 5. Reaching Out: A Public Librarian in the Progressive Era, 1905–1920

Building Iowa City's Carnegie library was the last major initiative of the original trustees. All except Ridgway attended the celebratory dedication ceremonies, but the founding fathers and mothers rapidly dispersed after that November 1904 day. Wade had resigned in 1903 to take up his congressional duties. Ridgway left her university library post, the library board, and the city in the summer of 1903. Ball was elected mayor in 1905, and Coast died in 1906 at the end of his second year as board president. That left five of the originals on the board. Shimek and Mayer attended very few meetings after 1905. Shimek finally resigned in 1911; Mayer was removed in 1914 after attending only ten meetings in eight years. Hummer replaced Coast as president and died in office in 1912. Stevenson and Felkner would continue into the 1920s, serving many more years as secretary and vice president respectively.

The newer members took up a steady but much-diminished level of board initiatives. After J.W. Rich resigned from the presidency in late 1904, he never again held a board office although he remained active in Iowa's professional library organizations and brought suggestions and new ideas to many board meetings, especially in the 1905 to 1912 years. A.E. Swisher, a local attorney who spoke at the 1897 opening day ceremonies, was appointed in 1905 to replace Coast. He offered motion upon motion at his first few meetings, then stopped coming and resigned after less than two years on the board. Four long-term workhorses joined the board during this period: Margaret Switzer, 1904-27, bank clerk; John Springer, 1908-20, longtime editor and colleague of Reizenstein at the *Press;* Willard Welch, 1908-28, popular businessman and owner of the Dresden China Shop; and C.F. Huebner, 1912-57, insurance agent.

Rich-Lloyd Conflict: The Final Round

The conflict between Rich and Lloyd was symptomatic of the gradual lessening of the board's role and the increasing leadership contributed by the librarian. There was some evidence of friction between the two before the janitor issue. After Rich joined the board and assumed the presidency, he requested that the practice of the librarian entering the secretary's minutes into the journal book, including her own monthly and annual reports, be eliminated. This greatly reduced the number of details about library services available from the minutes. In May of 1904, five months before the showdown over the janitor, a committee on rules and regulations consisting of President Rich, Secretary Stevenson, and librarian

J.W. Rich, library trustee, 1903-17

Lloyd was appointed on motion, not on the initiative of the president. Traditionally, board committees had reported within one to two months of appointment but this group lingered until December, after the janitorial conflict had been resolved by others on the board and after Coast had replaced Rich as president. The committee members reported they were unable to agree on a set of rules and they were discharged, the only such instance in the library's recorded history.

Rich's performance on the board was puzzling even after his return to non-officer membership in January 1905. He began introducing a series of harassing motions at each meeting; the library clock, the towel service, the defacing of tables all needed immediate staff attention, he said. He also asked that the librarian not extend her monthly (oral) reports to "any greater extent than now made." The motion on her reports carried. Perhaps Lloyd overdid the details, but Rich's motion appears to have been a public and humiliating way to send the message. And, based on his six long annual reports as university librarian (1893-98), Rich was no stranger to providing detailed reports on library collections and operations. Each of his university library annual narratives had provided an exhaustive review of collection size, collection use, and budget expenditures, and ended, like Lloyd's 1901 ICPL annual report, with recommendations and a work plan for the coming year. He had seemed obsessed with finding out the exact number of books in the university collection, and personally retyped—some say on the university library's first typewriter—the whole shelf list in order to improve the inventory records.[1]

There were a couple of other actions that could possibly be labeled harassing or at least demeaning toward Lloyd. Rich successfully initiated the motion to raise the janitor's salary to forty dollars a month, just ten dollars a month less than Lloyd received as librarian, and when he replaced the recently departed Ridgway as the trustee most able to provide lists of books for consideration by the trustees, he made independent, autonomous decisions while Ridgway had tended to consult with and advise the librarian on this task.

Whatever the amount of tension between Rich and Lloyd and whatever its impact on Lloyd, she left the library in May of 1905 never to return. First she was given a vacation until August 1, then it was extended to September 1, and finally, at the September 20 meeting, Lloyd resigned. There is no record of what happened to Lloyd—physical disease, mental illness, handicapping accident, or ailing parent—but she remained in Iowa City until at least 1918 living with her mother and sisters. While her role during the construction of the Carnegie library was marginal, or at least unrecorded, Lloyd had given the library its first real taste of leadership by the librarian, especially during her first years, 1900-02. Most of all, her nearly five years of service had brought some much needed stability and continuity after a period of rapid staff turnover.

ICPL's First Trained Librarian

If Lloyd left because of her health, it will never be known if it was at least partially intensified by pressure from trustee Rich, but he lost no time in setting in motion his wishes for a different type of librarian. His first motion at the meeting following Lloyd's resignation recommended that "an experienced, trained librarian and one who is a graduate of a library school be engaged as librarian." In addition to the confrontation over supervision of staff, Rich's antipathy toward Lloyd may have been based on her lack of library training, although to employ a librarian with formal college-level library school training for a public library the size of Iowa City's was a rarity in that period. The motion passed and Rich, who had been named along with Hummer and Mayer to a committee to select Lloyd's successor at the previous meeting, immediately suggested "that Lorene N. Webber of Des Moines be invited to visit the library and consult with the board as to the Librarianship." On October 6, just eight days later, the board convened for a special meeting and accepted the committee's recommendation: Elect librarian Webber for one year starting November 1, 1905, at a salary of fifty dollars per month.

Rich undoubtedly knew many librarians throughout the state. Long active in the Iowa Library Association (ILA), he was elected president in 1895 and served several terms on the association's board of directors. He was the ICPL's delegate to the ILA annual conference in the fall of 1905 and convinced the library to host the 1907 ILA district meeting.

Webber's two years at the Iowa City Public Library are recorded sketchily in board minutes but in some detail in her eight-page 1906 narrative annual report. She started an apprentice system enlisting women to give service to the library in return for library training. This system of volunteer or low-pay workers, common in many public libraries of the period, supplemented library staff until about 1940 and channeled many women into permanent full-time library jobs. She changed the charging system, adding a "book card" to each volume. Listing author, title, and classification, the card was removed and filed by due date at check-out. Initially this was a massive clerical project but a better way to keep track of the collection and to record circulation patterns. The system remained essentially unchanged for the next fifty years.

Webber made several changes to basic library service rules in 1905-06. She recommended and the board adopted a policy of letting readers check out more than one book at a time as long as one of them was nonfiction. In 1906 she entered duplicate subscriptions to *Harper's, Century Magazine, Scribner's, Outing,* and *St. Nicholas.* Readers, for a fee of one cent per day, could check issues out of the library, rather than using them only in the reading rooms. The 1907 annual report notes than this service was extremely popular with the public.

In 1906 the library began "summer hours," shortening library hours during the summer months by closing at seven o'clock each evening during July and August. It is unclear whether this was a recommendation of the librarian or was one of the several ideas offered by A.E. Swisher at his first of only five meetings in 1905-06. At a time when the light bill consumed up to 10 percent of the annual budget, the reduction of evening hours saved on electricity. Public usage was lower then anyway, and the reading rooms were "insufferably warm." The time saved allowed assistants to work on library tasks—cataloging, mending, inventory, reference lists—"during the cool hours of the morning," Webber wrote in 1906. Over the years the practice of reduced hours in the summer was gradually expanded from mid-June to mid-September and eventually included closing on Sundays during the summer months. Another basic change introduced by Swisher, with less clear intent unless to reduce staff hours, was to keep the reading rooms open on Sunday but to discontinue book loans. This policy lasted until Sunday service was eliminated all together during the depression years.

Undoubtedly Webber's greatest contribution during her tenure was the development of an independent children's room in the northwest basement room of the new Carnegie building. In 1905, at the request of several local clubs and organizations including the Women's Improvement League, the Natural History

Club, Art Circle, and the three women's club pioneers—Nineteenth Century, N.N., and Raphael—the library board had developed rules of use and designated the northwest basement room as a meeting place for local organizations. When the motion to consider a separate children's room was introduced by Margaret Switzer in February of 1906, the board appointed Third Ward School principal Felkner, school superintendent Stevenson, and ex-librarian Rich to work with Webber on the idea. At the next meeting the committee recommended establishing a separate department using this same room. The board gave the group $150 to set up the new area with the directions that nothing on the main floor could be altered and the "club room" should be moved to the southwest corner.

The children's room opened on May 1, 1906, with Helen McRaith in charge and with 1,846 volumes moved into "spacious and pleasant quarters in the basement. . . . The room is attractive and . . . inviting in appearance with its low tables, small chairs, wall shelving, and fine cabinets," Webber wrote in the 1906 annual report. The committee had spent $157 to outfit it. Webber suggested that a few more pictures and a cork floor would "increase library atmosphere. All the chairs have rubber tips . . . and even when many children assemble for story hour the room has never been in the least disorderly." She gave

The children's room opened in 1905 in the lower level of the 1904 Carnegie library.

Iowa City Public Library Archives

credit for the well-behaved children to "the personality of the person in charge [Helen McRaith]," but added that "she should be aided as far as possible by all the external devices for increasing the general quiet." She thanked several contributors for giving some pictures and sculptures of classic figures: Barye's lion, the *Flying Mercury*, Sir Galahad, and a photograph of Reni's *Aurora*.

Webber credited the popularity of the new room to a much larger book collection by year's end and to the Saturday morning story hours. Children made over 7,000 visits to the new department in 1906 with nearly 2,000 viewing a November "exhibit of Indian relics [and] bead work . . . plus hearing Mrs. Hindman's Indian stories."

Despite being moved from their original meeting quarters, the clubs of Iowa City received a lot of attention from the library staff starting about 1906. The library board had polled them for potential collection ideas in 1897 and 1898. In Webber's 1906 report she said that seven clubs have "their yearbooks on file at the library." The yearbooks that have been preserved from that period—Nineteenth Century and N.N. clubs—probably are typical. In addition to their lists of members and meeting dates, the yearbooks outlined the topics to be addressed at each meeting. "These programs were carefully worked over [by the library staff] during the summer months and reading lists made on each subject represented. . . . This has been very much appreciated by the club women and it is only fair to say that the club work done in Iowa City is of so thorough and thoughtful a kind that it is necessary to make such lists very carefully." Webber told her readers that it has been the policy of the library board to buy liberally "along the lines of club study and [the board book committee] is encouraging the clubs [to submit] their programs early so that book orders may be made with their needs in view." Several clubs, especially Art Circle and Shakespeare Club, contributed to the furnishings of the new meeting room. Although the policy statement used the term "meeting room," it was always referred to as the club room in both the board minutes and in annual reports.

The board was evidently satisfied with Webber's performance. In late 1906 the trustees raised her salary from fifty dollars to sixty dollars a month and she was given a full month of vacation with pay, two weeks longer than previous Iowa City librarians, but a typical benefit for a trained librarian. In these years women were frequently given generous vacations because they were thought to be more fragile than men and to need an extended annual respite.

In November of 1907, just over two years from the date she was hired, Webber told the board she intended to resign because she had a job offer at a library in St. Paul, Minnesota, at a higher salary. Rich immediately moved to raise her salary to seventy dollars a month but the motion failed with everyone in attendance voting nay except Rich. Webber then submitted her written resignation.

There is no record of a search committee to replace Webber, and at its next meeting, following a successful motion to proceed with the "election of a librarian to fill vacancy," the board voted 5 to 2 to elect Helen McRaith at a salary of fifty dollars a month, ten dollars less than outgoing librarian Webber. An unidentified "Miss Shaffer" received the two votes. Bessie Stover, a former apprentice who then went to the University of Illinois Library School according to Webber's 1906 annual report, was elected first assistant to replace McRaith. Was Miss Shaffer a trained librarian from another town recruited by Rich? If so, the board had rejected both his attempt to keep Webber and his recommended replacement. If he felt rebuffed, Rich did not react as strongly as in the case of the janitor and Adelaide Lloyd in 1904. He attended board meetings quite regularly for the next seven years, steadily offering motions and suggestions and making reports. He attended few meetings in his last three years and left the board in 1917 at the age of 79.

The appointment of Webber was an important part of Rich's legacy. She built on the less professional and perhaps more tentative leadership of Adelaide Lloyd and forever changed the dynamics of the board-librarian relationship.

Rich, while probably a demanding, difficult, and petulant personality, continually sought higher and more professional standards for the library and for the staff. As a writer and historian, he is remembered for his book on the Battle of Shiloh, for his article on the unique 1905 engineering feat of moving Science Hall (now Calvin Hall) two hundred feet across Jefferson Street with "nary a beaker of acid upset,"[2] and for his paper on the early libraries in Iowa City given at the 1904 dedication of the Carnegie library. As a librarian he contributed many new initiatives to the university library during his tenure and then turned his attention and enthusiasm to the Iowa City Public Library where he became the first important trustee who was not one of the original ten.

Helen McRaith, Progressive Librarian

If Webber had, in any way, been too much too soon for some trustees, their decision to promote from within rather than seek another trained librarian proved to be a solid move toward an even more active leadership and community role for the librarian. McRaith evidently was a popular choice with the public. Reizenstein, for example, reported that McRaith, "assistant during the past lustrum . . . has been a capable, efficient, and accommodating friend and aid of the public. . . . She merits the promotion and will doubtless give widespread satisfaction."[3]

Unfortunately, we do not know a lot about McRaith's background and education. Born in 1881, she was only twenty-six when the board chose her to be the library's seventh chief librarian. She joined the staff in 1901 at the age of twenty so she may have attended college, but it is doubtful that she earned a degree as did Lloyd and Webber. She got the bulk of her library training after starting work at the Iowa City library. She attended several sessions of the State Library Commission's Summer Library School, two to four weeks of classes held at the University of Iowa each year from 1901 to 1938. Some distinguished library scholars and practitioners served on the faculty and McRaith was active in the annual reunions of librarians who had attended, serving several terms as the chair. After 1907 she was also a member of the Iowa City Library Club, a group of librarians from city, university, law, and state historical libraries which met to discuss topics ranging from esoteric books and bookbindings to famous libraries of the world and practical phases of library work. In 1916 she received six weeks of leave and spent four of them "in practice" at the New York Public Library, evidently some kind of an apprenticeship program. McRaith attended professional library meetings at all levels, including American Library Association conferences when they were in the Midwest. She served as vice president of the Iowa Library Association in 1917 when ICPL hosted its annual meeting.

McRaith's father was born in Massachusetts in 1856 but came to Iowa at least by the time he was a young man. His wife, Mary, and first child, Helen, were both born in Decorah, Iowa. Their son, Joseph, was born in Clinton County in 1882 and youngest child, Abigail, in Scott County in 1884. It appears this Catholic family moved from community to community, perhaps as work was available. They lived in Iowa City when the 1895 census was taken. At that time McRaith worked as a laborer but later city directories list him as a freight clerk at the Iowa City railroad depot. After the elder McRaith died in 1908, the family moved to 519 East Jefferson Street and spent the rest of their Iowa City years there: widow Mary, Helen (often referred to as Nellie), and sister Abigail, longtime algebra teacher at Iowa City High School.[4] Brother Joe spent his life in Cedar Rapids where he owned and operated a chain of ice cream stores.

According to the list of enrollees published by the Iowa Library Commission, this photograph of the 1902 University of Iowa Summer Library School class includes ICPL librarians Adelaide Lloyd and Helen McRaith.

Edna Rummelhart Englert, who spent a lot of time at the library from the age of ten through her teenage years, describes McRaith as tall, not fat, but full-figured with a full face. She was well-dressed, stern, not very outgoing, and "hard to get to know." Quiet rules were always strictly enforced and Englert was a little afraid of McRaith and always fearful of losing her library privileges.[5] We have no other picture of Helen McRaith.

McRaith started her duties as assistant librarian in June of 1901 working under Adelaide Lloyd, her senior by twenty years. She was elected assistant on a 5 to 3 vote from a field of eight candidates and given the same salary as her predecessor, fifteen dollars a month. While there is little specific record of her performance as first assistant, the board raised her salary by five dollars a month each year including an early five dollars in 1905 when she was responsible for all library operations during Lloyd's leave of absence. McRaith's major recorded contribution before her 1907 elevation to librarian was the development of the children's department in the first year of Webber's tenure. Webber, as noted, praised her work in the 1906 annual report and McRaith's interest in service to children and schools was one of the hallmarks of her thirteen years as the head librarian.

During the Progressive Era librarians were optimistic and held high expectations for the vitality and effectiveness of public libraries. They saw the library as one of the institutions for urban reform that might cope with the problems of an industrializing society. Reform initiatives appeared all around them, especially after Theodore Roosevelt became president in 1901. In Iowa, according to Joseph Wall's history, three-term governor Albert Cummins [1902-08] gave the state "the kind of leadership for progressive reform that was surpassed only by La Follette in Wisconsin."[6] Supported by the *Des Moines Register* and a new urban middle class, Cummins pushed through the legislature a remarkable series of regulatory and democratic participatory measures: child labor laws, compulsory education, direct primary elections, food sanitation laws, regulation of railroads, and the insurance industry, and creation of a juvenile court system. In the next decade a constitutional amendment to extend the vote to women in Iowa, proposed in 1916, lost by only 10,000 votes out of 335,000 cast.

Librarians developed their own reform agenda: improving service to children, helping immigrants especially with language and citizenship skills, taking services to neighborhoods and the workplace, and actively and widely promoting the opportunities for continuing adult education that the public library offered.

Except for her lack of a college degree, McRaith was typical of many educated women who were employed outside the home during the first quarter of the twentieth century: unmarried and interested in cultural activities, serving mankind, and initiating reform measures that would help perfect society. The general public considered teaching, nursing, social work, and librarianship the four appropriate professional fields for women, and only nursing had a higher percentage of women. By 1920, 90 percent of librarians were women, with only the top jobs at large public and most academic libraries reserved for men. Educated middle class women flocked to the library field—a cultural career requiring basic knowledge and information but no great physical strength. With emphasis on serving children, creating a welcoming, homelike environment, and nurturing users on a one-to-one basis, the duties were similar to the work of the home and thus, society felt, within woman's appropriate sphere. In addition, the pay was notoriously low, discouraging men, including Howell, Sperry, McElroy, and Switzer in Iowa City. The public wanted the library, funded by tax dollars, to practice thrifty housekeeping and to spend a major portion of the budget on books, not administration.

With limited job opportunities and many women looking for them—by 1900 40 percent of college undergraduates were female—a large number of job seekers picked librarianship and the other feminine professions. By doing so, most of them chose a career over marriage. Fewer than 30 to 35 percent of college-educated women ever married in this period and in 1920 only 7 percent of working women librarians had spouses. The low pay forced spinsters like Lloyd and McRaith to live at home with their parents and unmarried but educated sisters who were also working as teachers, nurses, and social workers.

Having turned their backs on marriage by getting educated and on fortune by choosing a low-pay career, "many spinster librarians," according to library historian Dee Garrison, "felt the need to find high social purpose in their work, partly as a means of defining and justifying their lives as deviant career women. As pioneer professionals, and as a part of the larger professionalism that was transforming many aspects of American society during this period, they believed they were charged with a strong social and moral responsibility to make use of their training."[7]

Melvil Dewey, chief advocate for women in public libraries, felt librarianship offered more opportunity for altruistic women librarians than the ministry or teaching. "Is it not true that the ideal librarian fills a pulpit where there is service every day during all the waking hours, with a large proportion of the community frequently in the congregation? . . . [Is not the library] a school in which classes graduate only at death?" Dewey encouraged women to bypass teaching for a library career; physically less exacting, it avoided the nervous strain and bad air of crowded classrooms. "The genteel nature of library work would compensate," he believed, "for the regrettable fact that women librarians normally received half the pay of male librarians and [often] . . . less than urban teachers."[8]

Through professional organizations and frequent work together in urban areas, librarians and social workers pursued similar goals during the Progressive Era before World War I. As newly energized career women they saw themselves as a "vital force to make society morally pure," as "the inventor of all the peaceable arts of life."[9] If Protestant, they sometimes adhered to the values of the social gospel movement, bringing the kingdom of God here on earth by helping others now instead of waiting for one's reward after death. This kind of social activism infused both professions, but after a few years of work among the underprivileged they frequently found their early ideals overly optimistic. Librarians discovered that the public would not read much of the "higher" literature no matter how cleverly it was presented and social workers found that low wages, unemployment, sickness, and accidents, not moral frailty, caused most poverty. The settlement house movement was underway, library branches became community centers in urban areas, and in the smaller communities the librarians reading the literature and attending the conferences returned home with strong ideas about serving children, immigrants, the workingman, and the poor.

In Iowa after 1900, the enthusiastic and vigorous staff of the State Library Commission led the drive to extend library service to all Iowans by establishing new public libraries and finding ways for rural residents to gain access to established libraries. The biennial reports of this agency display the variety of activities provided by the staff to encourage the spread of public libraries: full reports on each year's Summer Library School; lists of publications developed to help communities get started toward establishing a library and to learn how to provide good service; recommendations for legislative changes or the interpretation of new legislation passed to facilitate library expansion. The lengthy reports, full of photographs of Iowa's libraries, carried the annual count of new libraries established, new buildings opened, and prospective buildings to be constructed, statistics about the number of citizens served, the diminishing number of counties with no public libraries (down to seven by 1915), and all the other descriptive statistics garnered from the reports submitted annually by each library. This enthusiasm was transmitted to every active member of the Iowa Library Association at its district and state meetings and contributed to the passion to serve displayed by McRaith and many of her colleagues throughout the state.

McRaith left a solid record of her years at the helm in Iowa City. She wrote thirteen long annual reports detailing each year's work, and when compared to board minutes it is obvious that she took the initiative away from the trustees— or they handed it to her in recognition of her strong ideas and vigorous and effective implementation. After 1907 the library board settled into a fairly routine pattern: brief meetings, average to poor attendance (nearly 20 percent of the meetings from 1907 through 1920 failed to draw a quorum), no special project committees, few suggestions about titles to add to the collection, and, after a major rules and bylaws revision in 1905, almost no policy statements. The board came to life only to deal with its most basic responsibilities—selecting staff, setting salaries, and dealing with annual budgets and occasional financial crises. The trustees consistently found money to send staff members to training courses and library meetings and formally selected all new staff. The apprentices selected first by Webber and later by McRaith, however, created a pool of candidates for each opening. Until at least 1920, with one exception, no one was hired who hadn't served first as an apprentice.

Serving Children at the Library and in School

McRaith considered services to children and to community schools of paramount importance and she carefully documented each year's accomplishments in these areas in her annual reports. The resulting enormous growth in the use of children's services had a strong impact in two areas—staff and collection. After Stover was promoted to first assistant, McRaith convinced the library board to hire a children's librarian instead of another part-time assistant. Former apprentice Margaret Luse was hired in 1908 and the library has had a designated children's librarian ever since. Many of the children's librarians were recent high school graduates who received their training on-the-job or were graduates of the library's apprentice system. In 1915, however, Gertrude Howell, sister of first librarian A.C. Howell, came directly to the position from teaching at Second Ward Elementary School. In 1920, after five years in charge of the children's department, Howell left to attend library school in California and spent the balance of her career as a branch librarian in that state. As the number of children coming to the library continued to increase, volunteers and apprentices were soon needed to assist the children's librarian.

McRaith enlarged the collection of juvenile books and monitored its steadily increasing use. Circulation of children's materials grew from 12,200 in 1907 to 22,500 in McRaith's last year, representing about one-third of total loans each year, and more than twice the rate of population growth.[10] With such heavy use, books wore out rapidly and McRaith had to struggle to find funds both to enlarge the collection and to replace volumes worn beyond repair. Some years almost half of the book budget was used for juvenile titles. In her 1914 annual report McRaith described her system of selecting books for children: "Juvenile books must be carefully chosen and for that reason very few new titles are ordered." She continued, "There is very little demand from the children for 'new books', and we encourage none, trying to put emphasis on attractive editions of standard and classic books [and] to duplicate these freely. . . . Care is taken to consult the *ALA Booklist*, the bulletins of other libraries and the critical magazines before purchasing."[11]

McRaith praised the picture collection the staff had assembled from purchases and by clipping and mounting photographs from duplicate magazines. These pictures were eventually indexed and relied on by schoolteachers for various exhibits and units of study. The staff used them "to answer many questions not covered in indexes." The picture collection, the library's first "audiovisual" format, consisted of thousands of prints and photographs sorted by subject and serving interests in geography and travel, art, history, holidays, biography, and natural history.

The staff continued to produce children's room exhibits as started under Webber. In McRaith's first annual report, after noting that many books on electricity had been added to the children's collection, she wrote, "In March a small electric dynamo and motor were presented to the children's room by the Iowa City Electric Light Co. It has been found of much interest to boys and during . . . April seventy books on electricity were loaned."

Children's story hours became a Saturday fixture. They were held each week from October through May, but "following the custom of all libraries," none were held in the summer months. Attendance varied from "a few to an overflowing room." In the years after 1911 attendance grew mightily. McRaith reported an average attendance of 30 children in 1913, 86 in 1916, and 150 children in 1917. The staff frequently used themes like Greek or Norse mythology over a period of several weeks, and invited guest storytellers from other cultures. In 1912 using a Victrola, the library's first audiovisual equipment, staff storytellers introduced music during "twilight story hours," a series given daily each year during the week before Christmas.

McRaith and her staff prepared book lists and other forms of reading guidance for parents on a regular basis. By 1912 all titles in the juvenile collection had been "graded" to aid teachers and parents in their selection of appropriate materials. The library's annual list and display of children's books suitable for Christmas giving received widespread recognition from parent-teacher associations and the clergy. The library staff urged parents to build a home library for each child, and they took their lists to local bookstores to guide parents and "in hopes that the local dealer will hereafter use more discretion in his purchase of juvenile literature." They prepared a book list, "The Home and the Child," for distribution at a 1914 child welfare conference held in Iowa City. The State Library Commission provided lists and program ideas for local libraries to use or adapt for their needs. Boys were a popular topic of the period: "Working with boys," "Boys on the street and how to win them," and "Books for boys who like Horatio Alger stories."[12]

McRaith put a lot of effort into getting schoolchildren and teachers to visit the library and in getting library staff into the school and the classroom. In 1906, on the suggestion of trustee and school superintendent Stevenson, the library board had approved purchase of sixteen sets of books that could be loaned to teachers to supplement certain units of study, but McRaith went much further. She established special library cards for teachers, letting them borrow as many books as they needed for as long as four weeks. In the first year thirty-two of the forty-three teachers in the Iowa City school system had cards and had borrowed over eight hundred books and nine hundred pictures. These numbers grew each year. After 1908 McRaith sent letters annually to each teacher and principal in the public and parochial schools outlining the library's services, soliciting their ideas for helpful titles, and inviting teachers to bring their classes to the library for instruction on catalog use and to obtain library cards. In 1909 she sent brochures to each high school student on how to use the library catalog and in just a few years it became the custom for freshmen from Iowa City High School, and later from Iowa City Academy, to visit the public library for serious instruction on methods of research and catalog use as part of their orientation to high school.

In almost every report McRaith expressed a wish that her staff had more time to visit and work with teachers and students in the schools. Worried that children attending North and South elementary schools (in 1911 the two schools were renamed Shimek[13] and Kirkwood) lived too far from the library for regular visits, she established small rotating collections of sixty to seventy-five volumes at each of these two schools. When possible, the children's librarian or one of her assistants spent an afternoon at the school helping teachers and children select materials, telling stories, and urging children to get Iowa City library cards. McRaith was in close contact with English teachers at both the public and parochial schools and purchased duplicates of titles that they required their students to read. The debate team had a special shelf for the materials the library purchased to support its current topics. McRaith cited "disarmament" in her 1913 annual report and "the commission form of city government" the next year as debate materials assembled for the team.

Outreach to Other Groups

In addition to the well-established services to clubs—the library prepared book lists on seventy-five subjects for various clubs in 1907—McRaith reached out to other elements of the community. In a period of intense missionary work in many areas of the world, churches were eager to get the journals and pamphlets that recorded their service into the library. McRaith solicited the appropriate titles from each church and then filled in back issues as needed from various magazine exchange services.

Duplicate copies of indexed magazines and titles that were not indexed were given to local hospitals and to the county jail. Later, discarded books were given to the state sanitorium at Oakdale.[14] The staff prepared booklists for the annual Farmer's Institute and for the Johnson County Fair. In 1915 the library's exhibit at the fair "attracted considerable attention," according to McRaith's annual report. Books were put on display and book lists on farming, gardening, cooking, and children's books were distributed. One of the lists was picked up by the State Library Commission and distributed at the Iowa State Fair and the annual ILA conference.

Early in 1915 McRaith sent letters and application cards to all "foreigners" enrolled in night school. Her report for that year said, "The response was immediate and many of the men and boys have been using the Iowa City Public Library all year long." She also responded to the need for more materials in German and

Bohemian. She commented regularly on the heavy use the foreign language newspapers received at the library and from 1913 on, as Europe heated up, she recorded the demand for more titles and duplicate copies of books in German. In 1914 she cited "the European war and the countries involved" as one of the most popular topics of the year and noted the continued demand for books in German in her 1915 report. "The demands of the German population in Iowa City have been insistent during the year. So many of the older residents can read only books written [in German] and many have read all the German books in the collection. We must buy more to satisfy their requests."

Reading German books, however, and the use of the German language in general became a touchy political issue by 1916. Iowa Governor William Harding decreed that only English could be spoken in both public and private schools and in all conversations on trains, over telephones, and in all public places including church services.[15] Iowa City succumbed to war fever: German language classes were suspended midsemester at the high school[16] and the public library added no new German titles after 1915. Circulation of books in German, which ran as high as two hundred per year before 1916, plunged to zero in 1917 and the category "foreign books" was dropped from the state library's standard circulation record forms.

McRaith asked the clergy for lists of local shut-ins and mailed each person a list of "cheerful books." "There have been many requests for the list," she said, including nurses who wanted it for their hospital patients.

Noticing that parents were using the books at the North School and South School substations, McRaith expressed a wish to have such collections at all schools but realized it was beyond available funds and the ability of the staff to provide. She found a way, however, to serve transients who were ineligible for regular borrower's cards. A book could be checked out with a two-dollar deposit which would be refunded when the book was returned. By 1911 she was also allowing vacation loans. Card holders could borrow five books in the summer and return them by October 1. And by 1917 even Webber's one fiction-one nonfiction rule was dropped in favor of taking "several books on one card." The library had definitely moved away from the strict policy of one book per person for two weeks.

The institutionalized and homebound, those with few skills in English, the farming community, transients, schoolchildren and their parents—McRaith was trying to serve them all. What this required, she discovered, was a planned program of publicity to try to keep everyone informed about the library and what it offered. In her 1916 report she wrote, "Advertising of the library has become as much a part of regular library work as the buying of books. Careful consideration is given to the best way of focussing the attention of the public on the library." She then proceeded to note the month-by-month initiatives of that year alone: She talked at the annual January Farmer's Institute on the advantages of the library; the library sponsored a lecture in February on "how to look at pictures" in association with an exhibit mounted by the Fine Arts Association; March was Baby Week with appropriate library books and pamphlets displayed; in the spring a display in the window of Smith and Cilek featured gardening books from the library along with the store's selection of garden tools; and in the following month the library offered boys and girls a list of references about building birdhouses for a contest sponsored by the Audubon Society. As another regular feature, McRaith's staff posted notices of shows, lectures, and other events recommended by the Drama League and other organizations. They prepared lists of books for the newspaper by and about visiting writers, poets, artists, and others coming to address the public or to perform or exhibit in Iowa City.

Book lists and news stories about the library were appearing weekly in each newspaper, and McRaith, in every annual report, carefully thanked each paper for its generous cooperation. She had posters printed with a picture of the library and its address and hours and distributed them throughout the community. One Christmas season the local department stores—Max Mayer, Yetter's, and Strub's—inserted the fliers in holiday packages.

In addition to the many appearances she made at community events to publicize local library activities and services, McRaith also worked for other community causes and joined community organizations. She served on the city's playground committee and in the Social Service League. She was an officer of the Drama League and served as the 1919-20 president of Art Circle, one of the women's clubs that met regularly in the library club room. On the state level, she joined the Iowa Charities Commission and was elected to the executive board of the Iowa Library Association. In 1917, under her leadership, the library hosted the association's annual conference with meetings held at the library, Commercial Club quarters, and various university halls and meeting rooms.

McRaith was making the library and her role in leading it much more visible in the community. And, as we shall see, she brought even more attention to the library and its relevant community services during the war. Under the presidency of Willard Welch, who joined the board in 1908 and became president on the death of George Hummer in 1912, the library board continued its low-key role throughout McRaith's directorship.

Time for the Basics

In addition to her many community activities, McRaith also carried out her regular bibliographic and reference responsibilities with help from her small staff. The two and one-half regular positions—librarian, first assistant, and the part-time children's librarian—were supplemented by the apprentices who received a small hourly wage after they completed their training. The full-time janitor (now getting only two-thirds the salary of the librarian rather than four-fifths as in the Lloyd-Rich years) took care of cleaning and minor repairs, and the executive committee of the board made recommendations to the full board about coal bids, new equipment, redecorating, and major building repairs.

McRaith reported each year on some of the new reference titles and other important books, especially multivolume sets, that had been added to the collection during the past twelve months. She expressed pride in both the reference collection and the many periodical back files available for school reports, club work, and general information. The periodical back files grew by forty to fifty volumes each year, supplied from more than 135 current library subscriptions, up from about sixty subscriptions at the end of the first five years.

Librarian McRaith frequently attempted to quantify the amount of use made of these materials by the public. Substantive questions were handled by the staff, but no one was ever "on duty" in the reference and periodical room where the materials were housed. As librarians before and after her had done, she reminded her readers that this was an important part of the library's service. In 1909 she wrote, "Following the custom of most libraries of the size of our own, no record has been kept of the number of persons using the reference books nor of inquires coming to this department, yet there is a constant demand for subjects to be looked up."

In 1913 McRaith took up the issue this way: "The use of books supplied by the library is of two kinds. Extensive use is made of the collection within the building, and this use is constantly increasing although not recorded statistically. It includes reference use by the students of the university and the Academy, and by pupils from the public and parochial schools, and . . . by the club women of the city." She then described the second kind of use—circulation of books for home use tallied at 43,803 for the year of the report. She returned to the subject in 1915. After noting the year's recorded circulation, she wrote, "The actual use of the books contained in the library is very inadequately shown by these figures. The so-called "reference use . . . continually increases and no doubt much exceeds the recorded use. No record of the number of volumes consulted or read at the tables has been kept. This should be borne in mind whenever any attempt is made to estimate the efficiency of the library by statistics of circulation."

McRaith summarized in each year's report duties less interesting to her readers but nevertheless necessary—ordering, accessioning, labeling, cataloging, and the binding and rebinding of books and periodicals. Finding a satisfactory bookbinder was an issue she frequently discussed. Like the library's early attempts to place major book orders with local bookstores, McRaith found that the local bindery work, usually done by the newspapers, did not come up to the standards she expected. By late in her tenure books were being sent to Hertzberg's in Chicago, a bindery which is still popular with Iowa libraries. Local vendors for all services were preferred and tried first, but often they could not deliver the specialized needs of the library. Metal shelving, card catalog units, and other library equipment came from library supply houses in Chicago, New York, and other major cities. Various local bookstores, however, were able to handle the annual subscription order for periodicals up until 1920.

After the first five years, almost no board effort went into the selection of specific titles. The majority of books ordered for the library from 1898 through 1922 were supplied by McClurg, a large bookstore in Chicago and a major wholesaler to public libraries. Except for an occasional special title that a board member would bring up during a meeting, the ordering of library books gradually became the responsibility of the librarian during the Webber-McRaith years. The board officially approved a list of books to be ordered at almost every meeting. Sometimes it was printed, but more often read aloud, so there were no surprises about what was going into the collection.

The struggle to find enough money to supply the size and variety of books needed to meet the demands of Iowa City readers continued throughout the 1905-20 period. For the library's first twenty-four years (1897-1920), the amount spent on books each year—excluding binding and periodical subscriptions—ranged from $529 to $1,334. There were more good years than bad after 1916 but the period ended on a low note with only $600 budgeted for books following the city council's refusal to fund the library at the level requested. The record $1,334 spent in 1906 was finally surpassed by $64 in 1921. Postwar inflation, however, meant that $1,400 purchased many fewer books in 1921 (880) than did $1,334 in 1906 (1,300).

Even with less-than-ideal financial support, the public's use of the library, as defined by the number of items checked out, made major gains in the McRaith era. After fairly stable loan levels from 1902 through 1906, despite the opening of a new facility, circulation jumped by nearly 20 percent in 1907 and remained at this new plateau for five years. Between 1912 and 1920 loans increased by 5 to 9 percent a year except for 1918, the year of the flu epidemic. (In 1918 the library, like most of Iowa City—schools, churches, movie theaters—closed down for three to four weeks in October to prevent further spread of the Spanish influenza.)

The leap in 1907 undoubtedly reflected improvements in library operations initiated by Webber, the library's first experienced and professionally trained librarian. But it seems likely that the immense growth after 1912 was generated by other forces. First, it was a period of steady community growth. The population of Iowa City hit 12,000 sometime between 1915 and 1920, more than 40 percent larger than the 8,500 in 1905. Also McRaith's many outreach efforts to both adults and children, along with her careful attention to library operations in general and to the details of collection development in particular, created a more visible library with higher quality services. The annual turnover rate of the book collection remained at a healthy three and one-half to four, a clear sign of a well-used collection.

As suggested earlier, there is little question that fiction was the most popular category at the Iowa City library—and at every other public library in the country. Nearly 80 percent of all check-outs at ICPL were either adult or juvenile fiction. But one of the stories of the library's first one hundred years is the growth in the importance of the general nonfiction collection. In the sixteen years from the opening of the Carnegie to the end of the McRaith tenure, the interest in nonfiction—history, literature, religion, sociology, science—increased by 165 percent, while the check-outs of fiction and children's books went up only 70 percent. As collections improved throughout most of the next eighty years, this trend continued. After the library's doldrums of the 1940s and 1950s, nonfiction became the dominant and most used collection.

Gift books continued to flow into the library and were added to the collection when needed. Less desirable volumes probably were sent on to the hospitals and sanitoriums with the library's discarded titles. In the years 1907-20, gifts accounted for 15 percent of total acquisitions and thus made an essential contribution to the growing collection. The collection doubled in size between 1909 and 1919 to over 19,000 volumes.

The Patterson Memorial Collection

A major gift to the library during these years pumped money into the reference collection and was a primary reason for its growth in both size and quality. In 1905 Mr. and Mrs. Willard Welch gave the library $1,000 in memory of Mrs. Welch's father, Lemuel Bausman Patterson. The following year Mrs. Welch—Lillie Patterson Welch—died after a freak accident while getting off a train. A Christian Scientist, she refused medical attention and died of her injuries. Her will left the library another $1,000. These back-to-back donations became the library's first major gift since the Carnegie award and, in proportion to annual library income, one of the biggest gifts ever received. To make the same impact today, a gift would need to be over $1 million.

Lemuel B. Patterson, Mrs. Welch's father, was born in 1824 and lived all his adult life in Iowa City. As a young man he served two terms as territorial librarian and assisted in writing Iowa's first homestead law in 1849. A lawyer, Patterson and his long-term partner, Levi Robinson, were frequently cited by historians of the period as having the oldest law firm in Iowa. Both Robinson and Patterson had been shareholders in the 1871-74 Iowa City Library Association. Patterson served on the board of directors and oversaw the disposition of the collection and the division of the assets when that library closed down in 1873-74. He was a popular man in Iowa City, known for the number of farmers he assisted in buying land, and, as city attorney, for taking two cases to the U.S. Supreme Court, including one that saved College Hill Park from developers. He built the still standing "Patterson Block," a four-storefront building at 13-19 South Dubuque Street, on the site of his boyhood home. For many years the Dresden China Shop, owned by his son-in-law, Willard Welch, occupied two of the units in the building.[17]

Trustees Shimek and Ball worked with the Welches throughout 1905 to establish guidelines for spending the gift money, and in January 1906, just a few weeks before Mrs. Welch's death, the couple signed an agreement with the board that outlined their plan. When Mrs. Welch died, her bequest was simply added to the total to be spent. The collection, to be called "The L.B. Patterson Memorial Library," would contain books "treating of biography, travel, history, and related subjects" to commemorate the memory of Patterson. The titles, selected under the advice and direction of the board, were to be of such character that they would form a permanent reference library on the

Photo courtesy State Historical Society of Iowa-Iowa City

The Patterson Memorial Collection, started in 1907 with a $2,000 gift from Willard Welch to honor L.B. Patterson and his daughter, Lillie Welch Patterson. This is the only photo showing the interior of one of the Carnegie library's two main-floor reading rooms.

subjects listed. The agreement called for the volumes to remain in the library at all times, housed in bookcases provided by the Welches and subject to library rules governing reference books. The agreement suggested that the Welches would probably contribute more funds in the future, but after Mrs. Welch's bequest following her sudden death, there is no record of further gifts, despite the fact that Willard Welch spent twenty years—the rest of his life—as a library trustee and board president.

The bulk of the collection was purchased in 1906 and 1907 with some volumes added each year through 1910, including two scrapbooks compiled by Welch about the lives of Patterson and his daughter. Webber described the "fine steel wall case with large bronze memorial tablet" bearing Patterson's name. The next year McRaith said the collection was "raising the standard of the entire library as to bindings, editions, etc. . . . It is sufficient to mention as examples the best Frotenac edition of Parkman's works, the Gadshill edition of Dickens, and Brinkley's *Japan and China*." The topics had expanded from history, travel, and biography to include art and literature. In 1915 McRaith noted in her annual report that the collection contained 815 volumes.

The building of the Patterson collection illustrates the great interest in acquiring series and sets of great books that Iowa City and many libraries displayed during this period. McRaith's list of notable additions to the general collection for 1908 demonstrates this predilection: "Shakespeare Variorum edition, 15 vols; Nicolay and Hay, Lincoln, 10 vols; *Historian's History of the World*, 25 vols; Werner's Readings and recitations, 44 vols; *Beacon Lights of History*, 15 vols; Stoddard's Lectures, 13 vols." Multivolume sets, good editions, and fine bindings were coveted in a way that public librarians today would not understand.

McRaith on Public Libraries

In the introductions to her annual narratives of each previous year's library events and accomplishments, McRaith's words reflected her increasing sense of mission and her Progressive Era faith in the power of the public library. In 1909 she offered a rather mild, "Our citizens, realizing the usefulness of this institution, have been our daily borrowers . . . our reading rooms [never] vacant . . . [and] during the fall and winter months . . . crowded to their capacity." By 1912 she notes that "our citizens are recognizing this institution as one of the leading educational centers of the community." The 1914 report opens with McRaith's definition of the task of the modern public library:

> The modern idea of the . . . library is . . . to study the literary needs of its own community and then to endeavor to meet these needs to the fullest extent, even if traditions must be violated in so doing. The old-fashioned library was a cloistral place appealing only to the scholar who moved silently among dust-covered tomes. The modern library possesses a different atmosphere and one more akin to that of a business office; most of the readers have the appearance of seeking information which will be of assistance in their daily problems rather than abstract knowledge. There is a similar change in the appearance and attitude of . . . librarians. Formerly they seemed to look on the library as an end in itself and as a collection of interesting curiosities, they were willing to let it remain a stagnant literary pool. Now they must be alert specialists, keen to keep[ing] a

stream of vital, useful knowledge flowing from the library to all parts of the community.

The very next year, in her strongest statement, she began with a brief mission statement for the library followed by an insightful description of typical library users and her view of the library's unique role in the community.

The great work of our institution—the Public Library—is to build up the mental life of our community, to make people stronger, more efficient, through the infusion of new ideas. The increase of circulation for the year proves that the library is the free and unrestricted possession of all who come to it; the reader in pursuit of information, the leisurely, the student, the scholar, the artizan [sic], and the child are led to feel alike that the library is theirs. The library is the "great school out of school." It is at present practically the only means of education for the people beyond school age. It is next to the public schools the strongest factor in popular education. We are . . . reaching double the number of people and carry on the work long after the school age has passed.

The community probably hadn't heard such library rhetoric since President McLean's "people's palace" speech at the dedication of the Carnegie. This may be the high point in McRaith's articulation of the public library's purpose. By 1917 the library, like the rest of the country, was at war. That year's report was one of her briefest and featured a section called "Library War Work." The first few pages of the 1918 report are missing, but an even longer "War Work" section remains. This second report, probably written by McRaith's first assistant, Ethel Tiffy, ends with the sentence: "On December 20th Miss McRaith left for Camp Dodge, Des Moines, where she will have charge of the base hospital library for three months."

The Library and World War I

In contrast to what would happen during World War II in the 1940s, the Iowa City Public Library was an active participant in the local home front activities during World War I. McRaith wrote in her 1917 report:

Never before has the Public Library meant so much to the community in which it is located as it has this year. People have looked upon libraries as store houses for books, but the war has changed the views of many. This library collected books and magazines for the soldiers at the cantonment during the summer and the response was most generous. Three hundred books—a most interesting collection—were forwarded to Camp Dodge. The library acted as a registration station for the Red Cross . . . many new members were secured. Official directions for all Red Cross knitting have been kept on file and the demand has been great. . . . Food pledge cards were signed by many at the [circulation] desk. Posters calling attention to all government matters are posted in the library."

The following year Tiffy, in the absence of McRaith, wrote, "The war work of the Iowa City Public Library . . . falls into four groups: food conservation, books for soldiers, sale of Thrift Stamps, and general publicity work." She described working with the county's home demonstration agent regarding food conservation. In March the library spearheaded a drive which collected 1,900 books for shipment to camp libraries. With the help of publicity in the local papers the library was able to collect twelve Baedeker travel guides for use by the War Department. The library sponsored competitive games to encourage the sale of Thrift Stamps among children. The staff distributed posters on various government war work campaigns and McRaith and others supplemented this effort by giving speeches to community organizations. The library assisted in various neighborhoods with organizing the Liberty Boys and Girls.

This commitment to helping with the war effort climaxed with the board's approval of a leave of absence so that McRaith could spend three months at Camp Dodge. Women librarians had made one of their first organized protests as women at the American Library Association (ALA) annual conference in the summer of 1918. The special office within ALA to coordinate war activities told women that the War Department would not allow female librarians to serve in camp libraries in the United States or overseas. When one angry librarian wrote directly to Secretary of War Newton Baker about this exclusion, he claimed there was no such directive. At the conference a committee of women challenged the ALA Library War Service committee chairman, Librarian of Congress Herbert Putnam, to produce a copy of the War Department directive. When he could not, the rhetoric heated up: "As chairman, you ruled women out. . . . The fundamental mistake made by you, Dr. Putnam . . . seems to have been the usual one of thinking men are better qualified than women for work in the world."[18] In historian Garrison's report she says the protest brought results. "By the next summer [1919], women headed eight camp libraries," but many months earlier in Iowa City, Helen McRaith was already on her way to Camp Dodge.

McRaith and Technology

There were many technological and recreational developments that some thought threatened the time and resources available for reading and for libraries.

144

Iowa City's first bowling alley rented the second-story quarters at 211 Iowa Avenue after the library moved to College Street. There was hourly interurban service to Cedar Rapids by 1904. Iowa City's first movie theatre, Dreamland, opened in 1906. Automobiles were a common sight on Iowa City streets by 1908. By 1919 radio station WSUI was broadcasting regularly.

Also during this period the term "library economy" emerged to describe the stream of labor-saving gadgets, devices, and methods developed to improve the efficiency of performing basic library tasks—accessioning, cataloging, processing and repair of books, preparation of entries for the card catalog, and procedures for the effective check-out and return of library materials. Pencil sharpeners, fountain pens, dating and numbering machines, embossers, adding machines, typewriters, and card sorters and holders were just a few of the items that filled the catalogs of library suppliers and the advertisements in library journals. Melvil Dewey, one of the original method-and-motion men, loved to find ways to systematize and simplify all kinds of library and general office procedures and his zeal and his ideas influenced library economy for years and years.

Helen McRaith showed little interest in library gadgetry, nor, with the growth in library use she was experiencing, did she worry in print about rival activities. While ICPL prospered under her leadership, not once in thirteen years in over eighty pages of narrative annual reports does she describe the technical end of library operations or the threat of competing media, and she rarely asked for funds for specialized library equipment.

Funding Support, 1905–1920

Limited funds plagued the library throughout McRaith's term as librarian, although a reading of her annual reports, except for her last one in 1920, gave only hints about the static level of funding the library was receiving. Her efforts at improving service to children, schools, and other special groups and her attempts to increase the public's awareness of library resources and services seemed to originate more from a highly motivated and productive staff than from increased dollars to spend.

While many trustees, especially some of the original members, attended board meetings quite irregularly during McRaith's tenure, both old and new trustees worked diligently to increase, and sometimes just to maintain, the library's annual income. They sought contracts with other Johnson County jurisdictions and debated the issue of charging nonresidents for library access. They monitored the return from the city's two-mill levy and after 1915 tried to increase it. They investigated ways to reduce utility costs and used their special fine and building funds to finance building repairs and emergency needs.

During this same period, the board supported its small staff with regular pay increases and expenses for professional activities and continuing education. While overall expenditures increased only 65 percent from 1906 to 1920 ($4,587 to $7,500), salaries went up by 115 percent in the same period ($1,873 to $4,000). Part of the salary increase, and part of the reason McRaith was able to accomplish as much as she did, was the addition of part-time apprentices and assistants working for twenty to twenty-five cents per hour after their apprenticeships were completed. The consistently increasing salary expenditure, plus the regular overhead of utilities, insurance, supplies, and building maintenance, meant that any squeeze in annual income, as it always has for libraries, reduced the amount available for books and periodicals. The library spent $1,562 for books, periodicals, and binding in 1902 yet did not match that amount again until 1913. The amount dipped below the 1902 level in 1918 and did not permanently pass the $2,000 mark until after 1921.

From its earliest days, the library board had an ambivalent attitude about service to nonresidents. The Iowa City taxpayer footed the entire bill, and the income was never enough. Was it fair, therefore, to continue to give free service to those not living in Iowa City? In 1901 the trustees had instructed the librarian not to issue any more cards to people not living in Iowa City but decided not to recall the 108 current cards. No policy statement was adopted. When the board revised the library's bylaws in 1905 its ambivalence was again apparent. The board no longer barred the issuance of cards to Johnson County residents but introduced the privilege with the caution, "as long as the income of the library and the interests of the resident patrons permit it." In 1907 librarian McRaith reported that there were 318 Johnson County card holders and she used Solon high schoolers as an example of the library's service to students. Through 1911 the library listed about three hundred county card holders each year.

Alternating concern about the number of nonresident card holders with the recognition that they were a possible source of additional income, the trustees changed their attitude and their policy on service to nonresidents several times through the years. In the long run, the board had very limited success in creating much income through contracts with other Johnson County officials or by charging fees to nonresidents.

After pressure from libraries and especially from the State Library Commission, whose mission was to spread public library service as broadly as possible, the Iowa legislature granted permission in 1906 for townships adjacent to a city with a public library to contract with the library for free service on the same basis as city residents. Township officers could levy up to one mill on the assessed valuation of property in the township, but each library and township negotiated their own terms. While there was great enthusiasm for this option in the library community, it was many years before there were more than eight or nine such contracts in the state, even after the option was broadened to apply to county boards and communities without libraries.

In 1907 the library board contracted with the trustees of West Lucas Township to provide free library service to Johnson County residents living near Iowa City on the other side of the Iowa River. West Lucas agreed to levy one-half mill, a rate that produced about $175 per year. This agreement lasted until at least 1912. In 1915, after offering two months of free service to encourage townships to vote a library tax under the rural extension library law, the board signed a two-year contract with Penn Township which included a "branch" in North Liberty. While this really was only a revolving collection of fifty to sixty books at the North Liberty School, it took staff time and library resources that offset the agreed-upon three-tenth-mill levy.

In 1911, with only one township under contract despite McRaith's repeated appearances at county fairs, farmers institutes, and farm women's group, the trustees discussed changing their bylaws and charging an annual one-dollar fee for nonresident cards. No formal action was taken, however, until a similar amendment was introduced by trustee Springer in 1914. This time the board voted unanimously for the bylaws changes. The board dropped the phrase about giving Johnson County residents not living in Iowa City library privileges as long as income and interests of Iowa City permitted, and established a one-dollar annual fee, effective April 1, 1914. There was no rush by county residents to pay the fee. Reports for 1914-19 show income of from fifteen to nineteen dollars per year for nonresident cards, representing about 5 percent of those who borrowed when it was free. While the numbers were small, the names are familiar to longtime area residents. Slemmons, Lehman, Brubaker, Meardon, Clausen, Colony, and Moffitt were listed as early fee card purchasers.

Previous to the efforts to secure township levies and the setting of fees for nonresidents, the board had twice sent delegations to the Johnson County Board of Supervisors to ask them to help support the library in return for free access to library services for their constituents. The first time (1905) was at the suggestion of the city council. The city clerk sent a letter advising that the library board ask the supervisors for $1,000 in consideration of the fact that "the people throughout the county have the same privileges as to books as the citizens of Iowa City."[19] Neither the 1905 nor the 1907 visits produced results. At that time, 58 percent of the county residents lived in rural areas.[20] The library would be over seventy years old before the board of supervisors agreed to fund library service for Johnson County residents not living in incorporated cities and towns.

While city council members were the first to suggest that the library board try to get funds from the supervisors, by 1908 the council's financial support for the library was also diminishing. According to a report to the board prepared by trustee Rich, Iowa City property valuations had gone down, thus reducing income from taxes. The 1908 library income was down $350 from 1906 and 1907 levels, a drop of nearly 9 percent, and only thirteen dollars over the $3,500 promised under the agreement with Carnegie. In 1911 the amount dipped below the standard to $3,455. By that point, trustees were advocating a raise in the levy to two and one-half mills. The council granted the change for the 1914 budget and the appropriation for the library went from $4,200 to $5,800, a 35 percent increase. The levy varied from two and one-quarter to two and one-half mills for the balance of the decade. The next crisis came in 1919 during the preparation of the 1920 budget.

Following the Iowa City mix-up in 1897 about the allowable amount of library levy, the Iowa legislature changed the legal limit several times after 1905. By 1913 legislators had increased the limit to five mills. Iowa City followed the two-mill limit until 1913 but in the six years after 1913 and before 1920 with up to five mills allowed, the library levy never rose above two and one-half mills. Despite legislative language that said, "The board of trustees *shall* determine and fix the . . . rate to be levied, collected, and appropriated . . . [and] the city council *shall* levy the tax,"[21] the amount of the Iowa City library levy seemed to be much more of a council decision than during the library's earlier years. The library board had more legal power than it chose to exercise.

The 1919 showdown on the next year's library budget proved to be a breakthrough for library funding but may have also triggered McRaith's decision to leave her position in Iowa City. Shaken by a 1919 shortfall that wiped out the annual $1,000-2,000 carry-over balance the library had enjoyed for over ten years, the trustees were determined to convince the council that they could no longer operate on the two-and-one-quarter to two-and-one-half mill levy that seemed to be reserved for them. Inflation during and after the war plus six straight years of 7 to 9 percent annual increases in library use had stretched both finances and staff. For 1920 trustees asked the council for $7,000, about 25 percent more than the approximately $5,600 they had been receiving since the healthy increase of 1914. This was three hundred dollars less than they had spent in 1919 when they had been forced to use all their carry-over funds. It was even one hundred dollars less than they had originally estimated they would need for 1919. Their 1919 estimate had included language regarding their determination to increase the salaries of the staff by ten to fifteen dollars a month.

The $7,000 request for 1920, which would require a three-mill levy, was prepared for the board by McRaith, but she attached a paragraph explaining why this amount was inadequate. She cited increased utilities cost (coal doubled to $10.20 a ton in 1919-20), a notice of a 10 percent increase for 1920 from their bindery, plus a list of unbudgeted but needed items: another catalog unit for the growing collection, benches for the children's room in order to seat more children, and redecoration of the walls because "the building interior is unsightly." She also noted that raises for staff were not included in the $7,000 budget.

These budget comments came on the heels of her 1919 annual report issued in January 1920. In that document she gave a ten-year overview. She pointed out that while circulation had jumped from 37,000 to 56,000 and the collection had doubled in size, the staff for the same period had stayed the same—three people, one of whom was "little more than half time," a janitor, two paid apprentices, and a page. In one of her shortest reports, with markedly less enthusiastic language than most of her earlier reports, McRaith did not refer to the many new kinds of library services she and her staff were providing and simply said the library needed at least $10,000 in 1920. "The increase in the use of the library justifies a larger appropriation for books, improvements to the building, for the employment of additional help, and increases for salaries." Due to the increased cost of so many items, she wrote, this amount is needed just to operate at the present level.

The board ignored her $10,000 goal and voted to ask for just $7,000. Next they reduced the suggested items in a $7,000 budget by 10 percent to allow a build-up of the carry-over budget needed for emergencies and to help get them through the first quarter of each calendar year before the city's first-quarter taxes were available. McRaith was already unhappy that the $7,000 budget allowed "only $100 a month for purchase of books." The cut to $6,300 reduced that amount by half, less money than the library had expended for books in every prior year except 1903 and 1909. With a 40 percent larger population than in 1905, with annual loans doubled in just ten years, plus the increase in book costs since the war, this was a potentially crippling step.

Was McRaith discouraged by the slow growth in financial support and worn down by her efforts to expand library services in a progressive manner? Did she feel she had made her contribution to the Iowa City library and needed new professional challenges? Was she now able to leave Iowa City due to the death of her elderly mother? Whatever the reasons, McRaith, at age forty-one, submitted her resignation two months after the budget decisions for 1920 and left Iowa City for a position as a branch head at the Portland (Oregon) Public Library. She spent the rest of her life in Portland, seven years as a branch librarian and twenty years as head of the library's order department. She died in Portland in 1959.

A few months after McRaith left, the city council approved a $10,900 library budget for 1921, more than the $10,000 McRaith had advocated for 1920, and more than a 50 percent increase over the $7,000 the board had been forced to settle for earlier. In just two years, 1919-21, after two decades of annual budgets between $3,500 and $5,500, the library had broken through the two-mill limit.

After receiving three mills in 1920, the library captured a full four mills from the city council in 1921.

Compared to other Iowa communities, ICPL was doing well financially. The library's support, at 93 cents per capita, was the third highest among the state's 140 libraries. Only Grinnell at $1.12 and Ames at $1.00 per capita exceeded Iowa City. While the actual millage rate was higher than Iowa City's in many other Iowa communities, a mill returned considerably less in these cities and towns because of their lower total assessed valuations.[22]

Iowa City's financial success recognized both the growth in the size of the community that the library was serving and the new range of library services that McRaith had created. Through the leadership of McRaith, the library had gained a new level of respect and support and would have few financial problems until the painful struggles of the Great Depression in the next decade. Unfortunately, this recognition came after McRaith left Iowa City.

Helen McRaith epitomized the optimism and enthusiasm of the Progressive Era—an optimism that died with the brutalities of World War I. Public libraries and librarians would not return to this level of activism and outreach until the 1960s and 1970s.

[1] The shelf list is a card file consisting of one copy of the main entry card that appears in the public catalog for each title but arranged in the same order as the books are arranged on the shelf. Generally a nonpublic record, the card file details the purchase, price, and withdrawal of each copy of a particular title and provides information about the proximity of each classified title to other titles on related topics. For a layman's view of what is lost when libraries give up their shelf lists, see Nicholson Baker, "Discards," *New Yorker*, April 4, 1994, 64-86.

[2] J.W. Rich, "The Moving of Science Hall," *Iowa Alumnus*, vol. 3, #2 (Nov. 1905), 29-30. Another source that uses Rich is Weber, vol. 3, 19.

[3] *Press*, Nov. 23, 1907.

[4] The first time the author talked to Irving Weber about writing a history of the library in 1994, he said the librarian when he was in high school was Helen McRaith who was a sister to his algebra teacher, Abigail McRaith, and that they lived at 519 East Jefferson.

[5] Interview with author and Suzanne Richerson, May 17, 1995.

[6] Wall, *Iowa, a History*, 171.

[7] Garrison, 176. I have drawn heavily on Garrison's research and ideas for this section on librarians in the Progressive Era.

[8] Dewey as quoted by Garrison, 178. A 1904 study of salaries in small libraries found average salaries for men were $176 a month, for women $115 month. "Small" is not defined but $115 was more than the twice the salary of the librarian at the Iowa City Public Library. Fairchild, "Women in Libraries," *Library Journal*, 29 (1904), 157-62. Cited by Van Slyck.

[9] Anna Edith Updegraff Hilles, "Women in Society Today," *Arena* 16 (July 1896), 163-75, as quoted by Garrison, 197.

[10] Except for the years 1949-73 when records are less reliable, 33 to 38 percent of total library circulation has consisted of check-outs to children or of children's materials. This is a figure found nation-

wide in public libraries. Iowa City population increased by 40 percent (8,500 to 12,000) between 1905 and 1920. Loans of children's materials rose 83 percent.

[11] Iowa City Public Library Annual Report, 1914, 4.

[12] *Iowa Library Quarterly*, vol. 6 (1909-12), 11.

[13] In 1911 Bohumil Shimek became the first living Iowa Citian to have an elementary school named after him. Irving Weber was the second in 1994.

[14] Now the Oakdale Research Campus.

[15] Wall, *Iowa, A History*, 172-173. Wall reports than when five respectable German-American farm wives were arrested for talking German to each other on their rural party line, Iowa and its governor became the laughingstock of the nation despite moderate hysteria on the issue in all parts of the country.

[16] Conversation with Irving Weber, May 16, 1996. Weber's high school German class was stopped in midsemester.

[17] Since 1983 the central portion of the Patterson Block has housed Prairie Lights Bookstore.

[18] Quoted by Garrison who describes this entire incident in *Apostles of Culture*, 221.

[19] Letter to board of trustees from city clerk F.H. Dondore. N.D., ICPL archives. Summary in October 1904 board minutes.

[20] Computed from the 1905 Iowa Census, table 1, 194-95. From 1895 to 1915 the rural share of Johnson County population dropped from 63 percent to 47 percent.

[21] *Code of Iowa*, 1894 through 1921. In 1924 the language is simplified but until 1954 still said "library board shall determine and certify . . . [and] council shall make levies accordingly."

[22] Iowa State Library Commission, *Biennial Report, 1920-1922*.

■ 6.   Reading as Gospel: Jessie Gordon, 1923–1946

One of the casualties of the war in Europe was the optimism displayed by public librarians in the early years of the twentieth century. Before the war the library profession believed wholeheartedly that the powers of creative evolution, with the help of the public library, could carry civilization to higher and higher levels. In their struggle against evil and ignorance librarians asked, "Shall not [the public library] be the most powerful agent for the preservation and perfecting of democratic society that the world knows?"[1] "The library stands for progress . . . [the means] for raising the moral, social, and intellectual standards . . . helping men and women to be more effective in every way."[2] Spurred on by the tremendous innovation and expansion of libraries in the two decades 1890-1910, librarians and others truly believed in the institution's "manifest destiny." They felt, as Helen McRaith explained in her 1917 annual report: "The great work of our institution—the Public Library—is to build up the mental life of our community, to make people stronger, more efficient, through the infusion of new ideas."

One doubting New York trustee, however, asked if librarians were "necessarily the best persons to undertake every job in town." She felt that if libraries were "the highest effort of democracy to crown itself, democracy doesn't know it yet." The men still don't know where the library is and members of the public "still mix [up] the American Library Association with the American Laundry Association."[3]

This New Yorker's skepticism became more widely shared after 1914 but was masked for a few years by the enthusiasm and satisfaction librarians felt about their efforts during the war. The female-dominated profession had been excited by the opportunity to serve large numbers of men in the camps and hospitals of

152

the Allied forces. Based on the thanks and gratitude librarians received from officials and from the servicemen themselves, and based on the popularity and heavy use of camp libraries both in the United States and in Europe, public libraries prepared to open their doors to a rush of new library users as the men returned to civilian life. But these new male patrons did not materialize, and libraries across the country, including the Iowa City Public Library, settled into a pattern of service, stripped of the hope and zeal of both the prewar and war periods. More rigid and conservative than in their formative years, public libraries became a solid source of reading and information for children, students, teachers, editors, ministers, and any person with a love for reading and an inquisitive mind, but libraries made few efforts to reach out to any specific groups except children.

Carolyn Ware, Social Worker Turned Librarian

In late 1920, with Helen McRaith on her way to the Portland Public Library, the Iowa City trustees turned immediately to the job of seeking her successor. Assistant librarian and part-time college student Ethel Tiffy took on the day-to-day responsibilities for the next eight months while the trustees searched for a new head librarian. Tiffy had already served as acting head in 1918 while McRaith spent three months at the Camp Dodge military hospital library in Des Moines.

On March 15, 1921, the board accepted the recommendation of search committee members S.K. Stevenson, S.E. Carrell, and Margaret Switzer to appoint Carolyn Ware of Los Angeles as librarian at one hundred dollars per month effective April 1. With Tiffy working only part time, the library board saved money for the balance of fiscal year 1920, the year of the budget cut which may have sent McRaith looking for greener pastures.

Exactly how Ware found her way to the Iowa City position is a bit of a mystery, but she came with an unusually wide variety of experiences. McRaith and her professional colleagues of the Progressive Era were sympathetic to and influenced by the agenda of social workers; Ware was a social worker who turned, at least temporarily, to the library world. After graduating from the University of Minnesota, she held jobs in Duluth and Chicago: with an Episcopal church, for United Charities of Chicago, and as a probation officer for a Chicago judge. During the war she was a caseworker supervisor for the California Red Cross. This California job was followed by two library posts: librarian for the International Institute in Los Angeles and an assistant librarian at the Los Angeles Public Library.

During her thirty-month tenure at ICPL she left no written records except her annual statistical reports to the Iowa State Library Commission, so the details of her impact on the library are sketchy. While better trained and more experienced than McRaith to work with various nonuser groups, Ware apparently worked mainly on general administrative details, leaving no evidence of giving attention to even the most "sacred" library mission—improving service to children. She convinced the trustees to buy a fireproof safe to protect the shelf list (the official inventory of the library's 22,000 volumes), and she was the first to use a national (and cheaper) vendor to handle the library's 125 newspaper and periodical subscriptions. She fostered the first board-adopted staff vacation policy (four weeks for the librarian, three weeks for assistants, both with full pay), although ICPL librarians had been receiving similar vacation benefits on an annual-approval basis since at least 1905. The library's success in raising the 1921 budget to more than $10,000 was maintained and increased during the three budget cycles of Ware's tenure, and while she must receive some credit, there is nothing to document her role. By the end of 1923 library circulation had increased by one-third over McRaith's last year, probably as much from the increased number of books that larger budgets could provide as from any other direct action of Ware. The money spent for books doubled between 1921 and 1924. The $2,200 book budget for 1923 was more than four times the $503 of spartan 1920.

Ware's work must have impressed and pleased both the library board and the community if the assessment of *Iowa City Press-Citizen* reporter Jacob Reizenstein was shared by others. (The *Iowa State Press* and the *Iowa City Citizen* merged in 1920.) When Ware resigned in October of 1923, Reizenstein, who had been observing and commenting on the public library since its birth in 1896-97, wrote a thirteen-column-inch tribute to the departing librarian. After explaining that she was returning to California to become chief caseworker for the San Francisco YWCA because of better pay and greater proximity to a metropolitan area and her parents, he reported that the library board would have "tendered her alluring inducements gladly, had it been possible to retain her. . . . In Miss Ware's going, the city will suffer a severe loss." Reizenstein continued, "Her gracious personality and exceptional ability in the realm of books have established her firmly in the hearts of Athenians interested in the welfare of the kingdom of . . . octavos and all their kind. . . . Her achievements in Iowa City have been garlanded with success, as the institution has grown magnificently under her guidance. . . . The tremendous increase [in] patronage and usefulness of Carnegie library here during the incumbency of Miss Ware has established a standard that her successor must certainly strive nobly to maintain."[4]

Jessie Gordon Comes to Iowa City

It took eight months to replace McRaith with Ware, but the board moved with amazing speed in the selection of Jessie Gordon. Perhaps Ware had given informal notice earlier, and Reizenstein suggests in the *Press-Citizen* that she recommended Gordon, but Ware did not officially resign until August 21, 1923. At a special Saturday evening meeting just sixteen days later, experienced search committee members Stevenson and Switzer (this was Stevenson's tenth effort to help select a head librarian) recommended the appointment of Mrs. Jessie B. Gordon at a salary of $125 a month, effective October 1, 1923.

In this same sixteen-day period the *Press-Citizen* ran an editorial about a recent report from the Carnegie Corporation on the nation's severe shortage of trained librarians. After a study of the fifteen leading library schools, the corporation found that it was becoming increasingly difficult to find suitable persons for library work. "Librarians are not only called upon for all manner of information but the nature of their work requires familiarizing themselves with the literature, history, arts and sciences of the world. . . . [The work requires] extensive general education and wide reading which take considerable time to acquire." While the report deplores the shortage of librarians, the *Press-Citizen* editors wrote, "It points conclusively to the fact that the American public is coming more and more to use its libraries and [is making] demands upon them." The Carnegie Corporation's recommendation that professional library schools, which at that time were frequently operated by large public libraries, be organized as departments of large universities was already being implemented at several state universities.[5]

Jessie Blackburn Gordon was a 1922 graduate of the St. Louis Library School, run by the St. Louis Public Library from 1918 until forced to close during the depression years. Many of the graduates from public library schools provided trained staff for the sponsoring library, and the schools themselves were outgrowths of apprentice systems similar to the one established by Webber and carried on by McRaith at ICPL. St. Louis may have offered a placement service for its graduates, which might explain ICPL's rapid identification of a suitable candidate for its position despite the shortages outlined in the Carnegie report.

Born in 1892, Gordon came to Iowa City at the age of thirty-one with a background in teaching and library work, a strong interest in the young child, and her certificate in librarianship from the St. Louis school. She was born in Clinton, Iowa, graduated from Wheaton (Illinois) High School, and attended the Chicago Free Kindergarten School. After a couple of years as an assistant children's librarian at the LaCrosse (Wisconsin) Public Library, she spent six years as a kindergarten teacher in LaCrosse. In 1918 she married Albert Gordon in a wedding held in Burlington, Iowa, where her parents resided, but husband Albert had disappeared from her life by the time she reached Iowa City and close associates in Iowa City said she never mentioned him. In her last two jobs before library school in St. Louis, Gordon had been the librarian at high schools in the

Burlington area. The *Press-Citizen*'s announcement of her appointment said she was "at liberty" at the time of her appointment and visiting her parents in Burlington.

The opportunities and outlook of the independent professional woman had been changing rapidly since the war. Less apt to be economically and emotionally tied to family and hometown, women like Gordon and Ware—and even McRaith with her Camp Dodge adventure and eventual move across country to Portland—held diverse jobs in a variety of cities and states. Liberated from long skirts and long hair, having won the right to vote, moving into business and the female professions at even faster rates than at the turn of the century, a growing number of single and divorced women became interested in organizing clubs, organizations, and social groups independent of traditional family and church ties.

When Gordon came to town, Emma Harvat was in her second term as Iowa City mayor, the first woman in the nation to serve as chief executive of a municipality with a population of more than 10,000. Harvat had made her fortune buying and selling bookstores in Iowa City and Missouri, and by 1923 she had just sold a dress shop she owned and operated from 1914 to 1922 with her life-long companion, May Stach. (It was the first Iowa City store devoted exclusively to women's apparel in a period when ready-to-wear clothes for women were the coming thing.) In addition to being mayor, Harvat was one of Iowa City's major business figures and remained so for the rest of her life.[6] May Stach was the same Mary E. Stach who received high praise for her performance in Reizenstein's review of the 1897 library benefit production of *Honor Before Wealth*.

A financially independent businesswoman and successful local official, Harvat (b. 1870) must have been a role model for Gordon. They became friends, according to May Stach's nephew, Carl, and there were interesting parallels in their lives in addition to their connections to Iowa City municipal government. In 1926, just two years after Harvat founded a local organization to promote the welfare of the city's business and professional women—a club that never accomplished many of its stated goals—Gordon became the founder and first president of Altrusa Club in Iowa City. She repeated as president eleven years later. Altrusa claims to be the first national organization for professional women (est. 1917) and to this day the local chapter honors Gordon as the driving force in getting the club organized.

Gordon, like Harvat, was involved in a wide variety of civic projects and remained an active, independent business and professional woman all her life. She joined the League of Women Voters, Child Study Club, and the Iowa City Women's Club. She served as president or as a board member of several local, state, and national organizations including the Red Cross, the Vocational Guidance Council, the Iowa Library Association, and the National Federation of Women's Clubs. In addition to starting Altrusa Club, she was the prime mover behind the formal recreation movement in Iowa City in the early 1930s and one of the original Iowa City playground and recreation commissioners in 1944. Later she helped organize the Iowa City Pan American League. While Harvat owned an electric automobile as early as 1914, Gordon was one of the first local women to learn to fly and served in the Civil Air Patrol during World War II. Harvat started her business career in bookstores; Gordon would spend her later years in the same business.

After arriving in 1923, Gordon lived the rest of her life in Iowa City. She died in 1968 after twenty-two years as businesswoman and community volunteer following her library career. Many Iowa Citians provided firsthand remembrances of Gordon: former library staff members, employees and customers at her bookstore, and friends who shared social gatherings with her and worked with her in Altrusa.

Gordon was about five feet, six inches tall with a slim to moderate frame. She was described as "plain" by several, with conservative, even mannish clothes, flat shoes, and for many years, hair pulled back in the stereotypical librarian's bun. Her eyes were her most remarkable feature—dark and intense. "They sparkled," said one acquaintance, and even when she was playing her most austere librarian's role, "one could see a spirit of fun in her eyes."

There were perhaps two Jessie Gordons. One, Jessie or Jess, was a very social, lively, active professional woman who had friends all over town, was respected for both her accomplishments and ideas, and was sought out as an enjoyable companion. "She was kind of a mentor to me," said one close friend and fellow businesswoman. "Jess had such good sense, and she empathized with people and their problems." "She loved to talk about books and other erudite topics with other educated women," remembers Carl Stach. Many mentioned her sense of humor: "marvelous," said one; "subtle, dropping remarks that went right past many," from another. Soft-spoken—"no matter where she was she talked as if still in the library"—she loved to tell stories about her own worst moments and could hold her audience "even for a repeat telling of a favorite experience." She often entertained and children were always welcome. She was good at matching books and people, according to several old friends, and some remember that she directed them to new paths of reading. Friends with young children were often given advice on reading to their offspring.

The other Gordon was known only as Mrs. Gordon, city librarian for twenty-three years and bookstore owner for almost as long. Both her employees and library patrons remember her as stern and fairly unapproachable, but always as a presence in the library that everyone was aware of. Several people made similar remarks about remembering her sitting, straight, tall, and stone-faced, at her desk near the library's main charge desk. She kept an eye on everything and everyone, employees and library users alike, especially young people. Newspaper pictures of her from the period confirm her serious demeanor.

Those who used the library during her tenure said they were afraid of her, knowing she would reprimand them at the slightest display of excessive talking or failure to follow other library rules. "No one got very close to her at work [the library or the bookstore]; she was very businesslike." On the other hand, Isabel Davis, children's librarian and assistant librarian, 1923-26, remembered her as "fine to work with and a good friend." Gordon had lots of friends and several people who worked for her said they felt they got their jobs because their mother or older sister was one of her good friends.

Thus, Gordon, a humane, fun-loving woman who loved children and parties and storytelling in her private life, when on the job at the library, for reasons we cannot fully understand, became the stereotypical librarian we see in movies, jokes, and advertisements—a lingering image that fuels some people's aversion to libraries to this day.

Except for a short time on Court Street, Gordon lived all her forty-five years in Iowa City on Summit Street, at 112, 305, 428½, and in both sides of the duplex she owned at 410-412. On Summit Street she was a neighbor at various times to A.C. Howell, first ICPL librarian; Judge Wade, first ICPL library board president; Merritt Speidel, president of the library board, 1926-29; and Anita Mercer, who served on the library board in the 1960s. Gordon's renters remember her as a landlord who always paid special attention to their children.

Gordon's First Ten Years

With a budget that had almost doubled between 1920 and 1924—from $6,300 to $12,100—Gordon faced a much different financial environment than the one that frustrated McRaith in her last few years. The years 1921 and 1922 had been a period of great growth in Iowa City. An unofficial census sponsored by the business community revealed a 13 percent population increase between 1920 and 1922 and the growth would continue through the decade, with Iowa City's population a full 36 percent larger by 1930—15,340 residents. In the midst of the booming twenties nationwide, Iowa City and its public library were getting their share of growth.

There were few Gordon initiatives that would receive public notice in the balance of her first decade at the library. The earliest newspaper reports of her tenure were limited to giving highlights of her monthly and annual reports and the routine actions of the library board. Reizenstein either attended board meetings regularly or stopped by afterward for a copy of the minutes and the librarian's report. Whether it was Gordon's or the paper's emphasis, most headlines heralded a new record number of check-outs. Circulation was on an upward spiral all through the 1920s and most every month marked a new high.

In 1925 Gordon announced she would hold a class in library service as part of establishing a newly structured apprentice system. Mention of apprentices disappeared during Caroline Ware's term, so Gordon may have been restarting a broken system. She announced that no apprentices would be taken into library service thereafter unless they had been through the class. The free, six-week, thirty-six hour training was open to anyone who was a senior in high school or older. Two-hour sessions were held three times a week, giving the potential apprentices some of the fundamentals of library operations. By 1926 these classes were scheduled either exclusively or additionally in the summer, with sessions each weekday afternoon. In a 1930 newspaper profile of Gordon, the classes were described as an opportunity for senior high school girls, noting that more than thirty girls had completed the course and that all apprentices currently working at the library were trained under Gordon. One notice for the class cited forty as the upper age limit for enrollees, but other evidence, including Gordon's lifelong interest in fostering reading and library skills in young people and the switch of the classes from fall to summer, points to the probability that young women were the principal participants. Helen Davis Dunlop, children's librarian from 1928 to 1935, says that after completing the apprenticeship class, she spent six months as an apprentice at no pay before becoming the part-time children's librarian while she completed her university degree.[7] The hours, late afternoon and all day Saturday, were ideal for a college student and the position paid her forty dollars a month. Whether apprentices were young or old, Gordon, like Webber and McRaith before her, had created a steady source of trained and experienced library clerks and assistants.

As might be expected from Gordon's teaching and children's librarian background, children's services were always a central focus for her. Descriptions of special library activities for Children's Book Week appeared each November, making it the only library program that got regular newspaper exposure during the twenties. Saturday story hours held during the school year since 1906 must have also continued during this period because "attendance at story hours" occasionally appears in the library's monthly reports.

Use of books in the children's room, open only from 3 to 6 p.m. daily and 9 a.m. to 6 p.m. on Saturdays, increased markedly during the balance of the decade, but the largest growth in the use of children's materials happened elsewhere. Helen McRaith had started small book collections at the old Shimek and Kirkwood schools in 1909 and, when possible, sent staff to the two schools to tell stories and to help children find suitable books to read. These two schools closed about 1918 when Henry Sabin, Horace Mann, and Longfellow schools were built (after a voter-approved $250,000 bond issue). There were never more than sixty to seventy books at each school and McRaith sometimes reported their use—from 250 to 400 check-outs per year—in her long annual reports. In 1924 Gordon immediately established "branches" at Horace Mann and Longfellow, the two schools farthest from the library, and sent staff to set up and check out materials each week the schools were open. The reported circulation, carefully recorded in a journal that detailed activity at the two schools for nearly twenty-five years, reached 10,000 in Gordon's first year and climbed to 21,000 by the end of the decade.

The history of Iowa City's organized recreation program starts with Jessie Gordon.[8] Gordon's concern arose early in her career at the library. In 1934 she told the Kiwanis Club:

> In my work as public librarian, the need of a recreation center where boys and girls of high school age may meet in groups has been evident for many years. . . . Some evenings as many as 100 boys have gathered in the public library because the only place where they can meet in groups is on the streets. The modern home is no longer large enough for groups of eight or ten boys or girls.[9]

While the library's founding fathers and mothers of 1896-97 would have been pleased to hear that young people were gathering in the library, it obviously had become a serious issue for Gordon and her staff. In the late 1920s, she convinced the Iowa City Women's Club, of which she was a member, to study the issue and to produce a plan. Later Gordon organized the Board for Recreation Work and recruited jeweler Harold Hands to lead the drive to find resources for a year-round recreation center and a summer playground program. In a 1967 interview, Hands gave Gordon full credit for the idea of starting a community recreation program. Others said Gordon was very outspoken about keeping all aspects of the program free and fought the idea of charging fees when funds were scarce. The Community Chest, the school board, the University of Iowa Department of Physical Education, and many individual businesses supported the program from 1934 until 1944 when Iowa City voters, in a referendum similar to the 1897 vote to support a public library, approved tax support for the program. Gordon was then appointed to the first recreation commission.

During this period Gordon also plunged into the work of her professional library association. She and ICPL hosted both the Iowa Library Association annual conference in 1926 and the organization's regional meeting the following year. Her local activities, like starting the Iowa City Altrusa Club in 1926 and speaking about the library before many groups, plus her active participation in Iowa professional library organizations, gave her high visibility from the earliest days of her Iowa City career.

While Gordon's more dramatic activities continued to be those outside her daily ICPL responsibilities, the first Gordon decade brought changes to the library as well. At the library she seemed to practice what one critic of libraries called "pure librarianship"—promoting books and reading, whether educational or not, in order to achieve maximum circulation.[10] In these first years, she focused on building larger and better collections with more carefully prepared catalog records, keeping meticulous statistical records, identifying and training young women for future library jobs, and, as noted, giving close attention to the reading and educational needs of children and students. Whether her goal was "maximum circulation" or not, the number of books and magazines checked out from ICPL jumped from 65,000 to 156,500 between 1921 and 1930, an increase of 140 percent. By the last five years of the decade the library was adding an average of 2,650 new books a year, two and one-half times the average for the previous ten years. The budget and the staff continued to expand. After crossing the $10,000-a-year barrier in 1921, library budgets in the twenties peaked at $14,457 in 1928. By 1930 the staff had increased to five full-time positions plus three part-time assistants and apprentices. McRaith had operated with a staff of four, only two of whom were full time. Helped by a booming economy, Gordon had taken the library to a new level of size and operation in her first eight years by concentrating on basics, with children her only special emphasis.

In 1930 Gordon produced a narrative for presentation to the board along with her official statistical annual report for the last year of the decade. The library board minutes for April 1927 through February 1945 are missing, and so, except for newspaper reports, this narrative is the only nonstatistical report about the library available for these eighteen years. The document appears to be notes for an oral report and it is one of the few existing statements of Gordon's philosophy regarding the mission of the Iowa City library. It also confirms what the statistics for the period tend to indicate.

Gordon argued that while it is the librarian's job to seek ways "in which to make the library a more . . . useful part of the community it serves," small libraries like ICPL cannot serve every resident because of limited staff and resources. "I think libraries should concentrate their efforts on the high school boy and girl. Try to keep in close touch with them and their reading," she wrote, in order to "repair the damage that is sometimes done by over zealous English teachers," and to convince them "that we are a friend interested in their reading," for more reasons that just "improving their minds."

Noting that there is always emphasis on circulation because "it is the only tangible measuring stick by which to measure the usefulness of the library in the community," Gordon carefully pointed out some "vital things of special importance to the Librarian beyond the number of books given out over the desk." In addition to her emphasis on high school students, she reported on the ways she had tried to improve the reference department and on her efforts to take information about the library to the community. She told the trustees that she belonged to and attended seven organizations regularly and had made appearances before "almost every club in the city and some more than once." She listed the improvements that had been made to the building and grounds during the past year including "a new hedge, bushes and peonies along the alley, [and a garden to supply] bouquets both upstairs and down."

In her report for 1929 Gordon also pointed with pride to "the harmonious staff . . . each one has tried to do her part and serve the public to the best of her ability . . . and to the cooperation [and] understanding of [the] Board. . . . You have allowed me . . . to experiment even if the results were sometimes doubtful." She ended with this goal: "an outstanding library . . . of service in the community and recogni[zed] in the state."

Other details from the report typify Gordon's style of librarianship. In keeping with her belief in the rewards of reading, she reported that she read "more than one book a day." Her habit of careful records is reflected in the details she gave about the condition of the files for bound magazines and state and national documents. She noted with pride her membership for four years on an Iowa Library Association committee and that she had taken an active part in every ILA district meeting program "even when we were the hostess." Despite her plea to the board to consider more than simply the number of items that passed over the desk, she revealed that the steadily growing circulation had now reached ten per capita, "twice the normal per capita circulation." She warned, however, that "we have surely reached the limit and it is reasonable [now] to expect a loss."

The Depression Years

Gordon and other public librarians had little warning of what would happen to their institutions during the Great Depression. They understood how economic growth and the increasing size of their communities during the twenties had brought them more dollars, bought them more books, and consequently brought them more borrowers and higher use rates. But before October 1929 and the stinging consequences of the economic meltdown, they never would have dreamed that such a large share of the public would turn to libraries as a way to get through the days, weeks, months, and finally years of little money to spend on entertainment and education. Librarians and trustees watched the steady growth of their institutions in the 1920s turn into an almost out-of-control demand for library services, while their budgets just as dramatically dwindled. Residents jammed the reading rooms of their local libraries, placed heavy demands on the staffs, and emptied the bookshelves. Between 1930 and 1935 public libraries throughout the country served record numbers of individuals and checked out books at a rate that would not be matched, at least in Iowa City, until the 1960s.

Historians frequently note the popularity of movies and radio during the Great Depression. The suffering public went to Shirley Temple and Fred Astaire musicals to escape, although even at ten to fifteen cents a ticket, movie attendance dropped 30 percent each year from 1931 to 1933. People listened to the radio because it was free and because some of the best talent of the period appeared weekly. Radio audiences increased by 170 percent in those early depression years. Historians have generally overlooked, however, one "growth industry" of the period—the boom in library use. Book sales, like all retail sales, were cut in half between 1930 and 1933; rental libraries, already popular, expanded for a while, but their traffic, too, fell off after 1933. The free public library became a haven for citizens in every station of life—from those living on reduced incomes and trying to save precious dollars to those who had empty hours to fill in long, jobless, and sometimes homeless days. They came to read magazines, to check newspaper want ads, and to find books that could improve their job skills, increase their knowledge base, give them spiritual support, or let them escape for a while. Sometimes they came to keep warm.

In Iowa City librarian Gordon told the same story when her 1933 annual report was covered by the *Press-Citizen:* "Besides the great demand for books on business, we find that people are also reading to increase their efficiency in their present job or to re-educate themselves for a new one. Books of many kinds which contribute to the maintenance of a spirit of hope and as a substitute for inexpensive recreation are being loaned by the hundreds."

As in most public libraries of the day, ICPL staff members had their hands full. Instead of the downturn that Gordon had predicted in 1930, use of the library continued to climb each year between 1929 and 1933. The 196,000 check-outs in 1933 represented a staggering increase over the 79,000 loans of the year Gordon arrived. After 1920 larger budgets and a larger collection with a greater number of new books each year had fueled growth, but during 1933 the rate of increase took on a whole new dimension. The number of loans per capita increased from the ten which Gordon had labeled "remarkable" in 1930 to nearly thirteen in 1933. By the end of the year the number of card holders had jumped by nearly 2,000 and in 1934 more than 41,000 people used the reading rooms, twice the number recorded in 1930. Library use for 1933 and 1934 was remarkable: Each year the 9,500+ card holders checked out an average of twenty items per person and Iowa City's 15,340 residents made an average of three visits each to use the library's reference and periodical materials. When unemployment eased a bit after 1934[11] library use fell back almost immediately to rates similar to the late 1920s except that Sunday openings had been eliminated. The fifty to one hundred people who had used the library reading rooms each Sunday afternoon had to come another day. The doors remained locked on Sundays for the next thirty-five years, one of the casualties of the Great Depression.

All five Iowa City banks closed between October 1931 and July 1932, but in other ways Iowa City was less severely hit by the depression than the balance of Johnson County, most of Iowa, and the rest of the nation. Iowa City's chief industry was the university, not manufacturing. When factories in many cities shut down, workers were immediately out of jobs; in Iowa City the university continued to operate. Salaries were cut and budgets trimmed. Enrollment decreased and students had much less money in their pockets, but they were still an important factor in keeping Iowa City afloat. As Iowa City historian Irving Weber has written, "Iowa City was something of an oasis in the desert of bad times."[12]

Iowa City income from tax dollars did not take a dramatic drop until fiscal year 1934 (April 1, 1933, through March 31, 1934). When city officials began preparing the budget for that year they realized the size of their problem. The assessed value of local property was diminishing and thus generating less tax revenue. In addition, new construction, the source for expanding the property tax base, had almost come to a standstill. Permits for new houses and businesses had averaged over one hundred per year from 1925 through 1930; only ten permits were issued in 1934. Due to extensive construction activity during the latter half of the preceding decade—many new residents in Manville Heights on the west and the Rundell, Morningside, and Kirkwood additions on the east and south as well as the construction of many commercial buildings—Iowa City officials had become accustomed to generous and regular growth of income from the local property tax base, and over 92 percent of the city's income came from property tax revenues. Another problem of the period: Many homeowners and businesses did not have the funds to pay their taxes. In the worst years, delinquent property taxes were as high as 25 percent in some communities.

The outlook for the fiscal year 1934 Iowa City municipal budget was grim, and the library prepared to take its share of cuts. Loss of Sunday service was minor compared to other cutbacks the library experienced. The budget dropped from $15,400 in 1933 to $11,600 in 1934, nearly a 25 percent cut. To absorb this loss, the library cut its materials budget by 40 percent and prepared to lay off one full-time and all four part-time staff members. In a period of absolute peak use, the staff of nine was down to four and the money to replace and repair the rapidly deteriorating collection due to record levels of use was gone. It took most of the reduced budget to pay library overhead: water, lights, fuel, insurance, and the salaries of the remaining staff.

This was the plight of libraries everywhere. Perhaps no other public institution has ever taken such a double jolt. Already underfunded (and really very good at providing services with the skimpiest of resources), public libraries were being asked to provide nearly twice the service with half the funds. They became one of the essential relief agencies of the period, but unlike other kinds of relief, they received no special funds to provide their enlarged mission and were expected to do it with less money.

The *Press-Citizen* carried an editorial in 1934 supporting the American Library Association's campaign for federal aid to public libraries, noting that "fiscal economies had hit libraries badly . . . just . . . when increased unemployment and [the need to] prepare for different jobs . . . provided an increase of readers with greater demands upon our library facilities."[13]

The titles of articles appearing in library journals in the 1933-35 period describe the grave concern of librarians, trustees, and library scholars: "What the Depression has Done to Public Libraries," "Our Starving Libraries," "Stretching an Abbreviated Library Fund," "Will Libraries Live?" General magazines like *Saturday Review* and *American Mercury*, as well as NBC's *Town Meeting of the Air*, took up the issue, either wringing their hands in despair or offering ideas for solutions.[14] A quote from an Indiana Public Library trustee was typical of the concern of the general citizen or library volunteer. "To cut down on the relatively tiny amounts a community spends on its public library service is to cut down on the intellectual salt which gives savor to most of life."[15]

A 1943 University of Chicago study documented the monumental rates of increased use and loss of funds that afflicted public libraries throughout the country.[16] Using 1930 as the base year (established at 100), the study indexed the growth of circulation and the loss of income for libraries of various sizes in all regions from 1930 to 1935. By 1933, the peak year for most libraries, the average index for circulation reached 127 and the income index fell to 80. In other words, by 1933 libraries, on the average, were doing 27 percent more business with 20 percent smaller budgets. Using a similar method for ICPL demonstrates that both its peak circulation index at 125 and low expenditure rate at 83 were just under the average for the entire United States. The Iowa City figures were less severe, therefore, than the extremes in other kinds of communities. In cities of populations between 50,000 and 100,00, library circulation was up an average 56 percent. In small libraries in the South, income was down an average 69 percent.

To help ICPL operate under reduced hours, with fewer staff and less money, especially for library books, the library prepared some reading suggestions and a few new rules. People were urged to bring their books back on time so others could check them out, to read or reread the classics, to search out older titles that had been missed, and to expect few new ones. Borrowers were limited to four books and four magazines per person. To reduce the cost of mailings and to save staff time, the library eliminated reserves and sent only one overdue notice per book. Fine rates were reduced to one cent per day for those who paid them when overdue books were returned, but remained two cents if the overdue fee had to be posted.

The staff of four responded heroically. They provided library services as best they could, looking for ways to become more efficient and even adding new services where they saw a need. Gordon told the press that her staff had "worked willingly under the added burden caused by a decreased budget and the larger use of the library and they will continue to serve to the best of their ability."

To maximize the number of books available, the library added an outside book return so that books "borrowed in the past" could be brought back without embarrassment, and the staff told homeowners, fraternities, and sororities how to identify library books found after college students or other roomers moved out.

Responding to the reduced amount of money that most households had to spend, the library included a special display of children's books in its annual celebration of Children's Book Week and Gordon assigned a staff person to escort the many new library users through the display in the meeting room and to introduce them to the children's area. In the summer of 1934, the children's room offered its first summer reading program. Children's librarian Helen Davis announced a "new form of hot weather diversion," book clubs for each grade, third through eighth, with some clubs divided into boys and girls groups. In the fall of 1934, during the library's second year of reduced staffing, the library produced a puppet show that attracted over 1,000 children. The staff repeated the performance three times in order to accommodate every child waiting to get in.

In 1935, still under restricted funding, the library mounted a fairly ambitious event for the Carnegie Centennial. Libraries throughout the country marked the one hundredth anniversary of Andrew Carnegie's birth on November 26, 1835. Iowa City had an open house with displays and demonstrations on "how a library works." The city council and other community officials attended and the *Press-Citizen* carried a history of the library and ran a full page of pictures, including one of Gordon sitting at her desk as many in the community remembered her. The paper later described the event: "Ten brilliantly lighted rooms presented a colorful picture to visitors. Bowls of autumn flowers decorated the desks and librarians in various colored smocks displayed the work with which they are daily concerned."

Reading as Gospel, 1923–1946

Iowa City, like communities throughout Iowa and many parts of the nation, had much to celebrate. Local citizens would not have had library facilities without the generosity of Carnegie and various local philanthropists. In 1935 there were 133 public library buildings in Iowa—99 of them built with Carnegie funds and 31 with private gifts. Only Des Moines, Forest City, and Oelwein had spent tax dollars to construct their community libraries.

During the peak use years of the depression era, what kind of books did people actually borrow? Were jobless adults rushing into the library to get materials to improve their work skills and their general knowledge as many, including Gordon, were claiming? This scenario has become the folklore about public libraries during the Great Depression. A comparison of ICPL circulation records for 1929 and 1933 verifies, with some qualifications, the impressions that remain from that period. Fiction still accounted for the majority of loans to adults before and

Photo courtesy Iowa City Press-Citizen

This picture of Jessie Gordon appeared in the Press-Citizen to promote the library's open house honoring the one hundredth anniversary of Andrew Carnegie's birth in 1935.

for a long while after 1933. Fiction made up 81 percent of the library's loans in 1904 and remained at 75 percent in both 1929 and 1933. Thus periodicals and nonfiction check-outs were just one-quarter of all loans to adult card holders. So while the mix of materials, fiction versus nonfiction, remained constant between 1929 and 1933, what changed most dramatically (in addition to the total number of loans) was the ratio of adult loans to children's loans and the type of adult nonfiction materials borrowed. Both adults and children increased their use of the library but adults at twice the rate of children. Between 1929 and 1933 use of adult materials increased by 44 percent, children's materials by only 20 percent. In libraries throughout the country and in Iowa City to this day, the standard juvenile share of total circulation has hovered at about 30 to 35 percent. This standard share of all loans from the library building (that is, not from school deposit collections) had already dropped after 1924 when Gordon started the branches at Mann and Longfellow. In the peak circulation year of 1933 juvenile circulation dropped to an all-time low of 21 percent.

The other major change, and one that continued long after the enormous increases of 1933 and 1934 had subsided, was the type of nonfiction materials borrowed. As noted, use of adult materials increased 44 percent from 1929 to 1933, but loans of certain subjects grew at a much faster rate. Loans of books on the study of English and foreign languages increased 92 percent. Undoubtedly the books loaned were more English than other languages—people learning or teaching English to improve reading and writing skills. Use of books in the sciences increased 64 percent, history and biography, 80 percent. Social sciences, business, and government books went out twice as often in 1933 as in 1929 and there was a 50 percent increase in use of books in the arts and in loans of general magazines and journals. Religion, philosophy, and literature lost share in nonfiction circulation, increasing by 20 percent or less. Practical and pragmatic subjects were more popular than the abstract, and the "loss" in literature probably reflected the relative increased library use by out-of-school adults. Due to school assignments, high school and college students read many more books classified as literature (poetry, drama, essays, speeches, and so on).

Iowa City Public Library Archives

Undated photo of weekly Saturday story hour, probably from the late 1930s or early 1940s.

One more detail supports the finding that practical uses of the nonfiction collection attracted many of those 2,000 new card holders: 36 of the 44 percent increase in use of the nonfiction collection occurred in 1931, two years ahead of the peak in fiction and in total circulation. The level of nonfiction loans remained fairly steady throughout the 1930s at the expense of fiction. There is no way to determine how much of this change was due to new card holders who remained library users and how much to changing reading tastes and publishing patterns. The change was another boost to the century-long trend toward the growing size, popularity, and dominance of the library's nonfiction collection.

There is a final limitation on this attempt to assess the use of the library from loan records. As earlier ICPL librarians have pointed out, we cannot analyze the types of noncirculating reference materials the old and new library patrons crowding the reading rooms were using, how much time they spent there, or precisely what they did. While there are no records of what happened at ICPL, R.L. Duffus wrote a compelling yet charming narrative in 1933 after visiting with staff in ten of the nation's larger public libraries.[17] The most visible change, according to Duffus, was the increase in the number of men.

> Mostly they are strangers to the library, shy on their first visit, not knowing what to expect. Some are here, of course, merely for shelter and a refuge. But by far the largest part are here with a more or less vague intention of turning their time to some good purpose, and look to the librarians for help.

A librarian in Louisville, Kentucky, told Duffus that in the winter of 1932-33, for the first time in the library's history, more men than women came to the reading rooms in the morning. Duffus then goes on to enumerate some of the requests that librarians had received and described to him: a man experimenting at home with a new varnish formula; another trading his city home for a farm and wanting to know about the soil and climate in the new locality; a woman making scarves to sell and looking for attractive designs; a request for the history of famous clowns from a young man who returns to report that he has landed a job as a clown. There were persons wanting to know how to raise bees; how to become bookkeepers, stenographers, cowboys, real estate salesmen, beauty shop owners; how to grow ginseng and other medicinal plants; how to start a candy business at home. Several reported that citizens asked if there was still land in the United States that could be homesteaded and if so, where and what crops could be raised there.

Duffus's reports from other libraries confirm the assessment that new Iowa City borrowers wanted the practical over the abstract. He quotes one librarian, "He [the typical questioner] turns to us for practical help and he wants it in a hurry to solve his personal problems. He cannot afford professional service and brings his legal and medical problems to the library." On the other hand, filling one's hours with inexpensive entertainment also had an impact on reference service. Contests and word games were popular throughout the 1930s; library dictionaries were in tatters and librarians complained about the amount of time required to help people with their contest entries.

Libraries survived the depression but recovery was slow. During the worst years of the depression, the public swarmed into public libraries, borrowing and using everything in sight and leaving the institutions devastated, with worn-out, outdated collections and little money to repair the damage and acquire new materials. Slowly libraries struggled to get funded at levels they had enjoyed before the big cutbacks of the mid-1930s, but in the interim, cities had taken on new responsibilities and lost taxing share to state and federal governments. Burdened with new state and federal taxes, the public became very sensitive to higher tax rates at the local level. Campaigns for homestead exemptions and various kinds of tax rate limitations left cities in several states with levies cut in half and many libraries waited in vain for their funds to be replaced.[18]

In Iowa the twenty-one public libraries in cities of 10,000 or more lost, on average, 20 percent of their income between 1928 and 1934 and were only 2 percent above that level by 1940. Iowa City, down 25 percent, had returned to pre-1934 levels after only three years but remained in the $14,500-16,000 range through 1947, showing less long-term increase than the average for other libraries in its population class.

With money scarce, with book budgets taking the brunt of the cuts, and with collections depleted by the sudden intense use, circulation declined in all libraries, including Iowa City, after the peak years of 1933 and 1934. Iowa City purchased only 1,000 books in 1934 compared to 2,500 or more a year for the previous seven years. After visiting several libraries in similar conditions, Duffus described it well: "A library which does not constantly buy new books is at best a museum and at worst . . . a mausoleum."[19] Circulation totals continued downward nationwide for several years.

Severely injured during the depression, most smaller libraries had neither the will nor the way to investigate technological developments that might make their institutions more efficient or effective. One library writer, while recognizing the limitations facing libraries because of their meager funds, also chastised librarians in public libraries of all sizes for their slowness to change. Compared to modern retail stores, she said, library entrances are obstacles to overcome, not invitations to enter; their record keeping is manual and slow, with a reluctance to use typewriters, automatic numbering machines, mimeographs, card sorters, modern filing equipment, visible indexes, and photostats.

There are only two mentions of mechanization or technology in the less-than-complete minutes of the Gordon administration, but the carefully handwritten daily statistics and the full record of information entered into the accession books during these years do not suggest a search for machine-aided efficiency. In 1930, before major budget cuts, the library acquired a Dickman charging machine and in 1937 offered the public a demonstration of a "reading machine," an early version of a microfilm reader on loan from the Optigraph Company. The *Press-Citizen* report explained that the "film book [had been] squeezed down to microscopic size for storage and transport . . . [and then] the tiny film images are optically returned to normal size or larger by use of a patented reading device."[20] While microfilm was probably the most important technological development for libraries in the 1930s, and while the library offered the demonstration, the article discussed no library applications. Rather the paper suggested lawyers would now be able to take their law library and their reading machine with them wherever they went.

"Books for All Iowa"

One ICPL library service did not change before or after the crisis years. Despite the reduced budget after 1933, library records indicate no reduction in either books or staff time set aside for the two branch collections at Horace Mann and Longfellow schools. Annual circulation from these library outposts, open once a week when school was in session, remained steady at about 25,000 check-outs per year throughout the 1930s.

According to Helen Davis Dunlop, one or two library staff members spent one morning a week at each of the schools. The school janitors helped set up the seven hundred books on tables in the gymnasium from the "trolley" of boxes, then stored them between sessions. (The 1,400 books in the two school branches were about 15 percent of the 10,000-volume juvenile collection at that time.) The collections were chosen and delivered each fall and returned to the library for mending and replacement during the summer. Teachers brought in their classes at an appointed time and children were free to choose two books for a two-week period. The library staff issued a special library card to each child and kept the cards at the school. These cards were in addition to any card the child might have at the main library. All classes came each week, so children could borrow up to two books per week if they wished. Teachers also selected titles from the collection to read aloud to their students, especially those in the primary grades. The books were not intended for curriculum support but rather as a substitute for a trip to the main library. In a newspaper column in 1937 Gordon wrote, "The books we provide are those they can read and enjoy and are not too difficult for their ability."

From Gordon's carefully maintained circulation records we can easily assess what children were reading, or more precisely, borrowing, from the library and the schools. Less than 20 percent of total loans were in a nonfiction category. Fiction was heavily used at the schools, but at a slightly lower rate than at the library. At the school sites, books in the "easy" category were the most popular. These were limited vocabulary readers and picture books aimed at the youngest readers. At Mann and Longfellow, children just learning to read and too young to go to the library without their parents could select books each week that allowed them to read or listen to simple stories, myths, folk tales, fairy stories, and a growing number of general information titles. These books accounted for fewer loans at the library where the average young user was undoubtedly older. One final observation drawn from the carefully formed numerals and the red-inked totals in these old ledger books: Children checked out substantially the same types of materials during the summer months when only the public library was available, as they borrowed during the school year from either the library or the schools.

Service was maintained in these two schools for over twenty years (1924-46) without any funds from the school board and without expansion to Lincoln School (opened 1926) and Roosevelt School (opened 1931). The 1937 *Press-Citizen* column is the only time that Gordon discussed the service in print. She noted the short hours for the children's room during the week—3:00 to 6:00 p.m. daily—and said it was too far (about twelve blocks) from Horace Mann and Longfellow for children to walk to the library after school. Henry Sabin and the two Catholic schools, St Patrick's and St. Mary's, were close to the library (two to five blocks) and children could easily visit on weekdays. There is no record of an attempt to set up branches in Lincoln or Roosevelt when they opened, yet these schools were even farther away, across the river and a walk of at least fifteen to twenty blocks. In her 1937 column, after explaining why Mann and Longfellow were opened, Gordon wrote, "Lincoln and Roosevelt [schools] because of their size are better served with classroom libraries." Did she mean the rooms were physically larger or that there were too many classrooms to serve? Did she feel the parents of the Roosevelt and Lincoln neighborhoods were more apt to make the effort to get their children to the library? Both schools opened in the years when the budget was on the rise, before the depression forced cutbacks.

Its budget now able to support a larger staff and annual purchases of 2,500 or more new books, and with use moderating, the library continued comfortably through the thirties with no major changes to library operations or services. After 1937, Gordon turned her attention to interests broader than the day-to-day operations of the Iowa City library.

Gordon started writing a weekly column for the *Press-Citizen* in 1937 that would be continued by her successors on a more or less regular basis until the early 1970s. Called "Your Library" in the Gordon years, the two-column boxed feature was illustrated with books and carried the byline, "by Mrs. Jessie B. Gordon, librarian." She produced a mix of book reviews, reading suggestions, and general information about the library. Evidently the paper let her be its "reporter" in the early years, for even library news appeared under the "Your Library" heading. Gordon suggested reading paths as varied as Anthony Trollope and Max Brand, gave readers one English professor's choice of the fifty best English and American novels, produced library and budget statistics that pleaded the case for more funds, explained the reserve system and the resources of the reference room, displayed her interest in travel and travel books, and thanked donors for books given to the library. A theme through all her columns was the rewards of reading and the importance of introducing good reading habits to children and young people. There were many columns on juvenile books and activities for children at the library and at the Mann and Longfellow branches. She often had local residents, including children, provide columns on their reading experiences, their views of libraries, or "what I learned at the summer reading club." Gordon's signature sign-off each week was "Know and use your Library."

The columns demonstrated Gordon's wide-ranging interests and further revealed her determination to give people access to books and libraries. Under the banner of expanding library service to those without it, she served several terms as the chairman of the legislative committee for the Iowa Library Association. She traveled widely around Iowa speaking on the issue that Iowa librarians had worked for since the first township law was passed in 1906: providing library service to rural Iowans. By the late thirties the issue had evolved from a failed drive for legislation to permit county libraries to a proposal to establish six state-funded regional branches throughout the state to support and extend library services. "Suitable library facilities should be available to every adult and every child of school age in Iowa" was ILA's goal, and when Gordon was elected president of ILA in 1939, her announced theme for the year was "Books for All Iowa."

She was also busy in Johnson County using her skills and sometimes the library's facilities and resources to provide reading materials to those outside the legal constituency of the Iowa City Public Library. In 1926 the library board approved her "Rural Library Plan" and allowed one hundred dollars for her travel expenses into the county, but the details of this initiative are lost to history. As early as 1928 she had taken small deposit collections to the University of Iowa Children's and Psychiatric hospitals and later to Mercy Hospital. According to Helen Davis Dunlop, Gordon gave cards to teachers from the rural schools whether they lived in Iowa City or not, and let them take twenty or more books when others were limited to three or four titles at a time. In 1939 a "rural library" was set up in the basement of the Carnegie building under a plan to improve service to rural schools. Longtime Johnson County school superintendent Frank Snider announced the plan to the public. Six hundred books purchased by the Johnson County Board of Education would be housed at the public library, "temporarily under the direction of librarian Jessie B. Gordon." Rural schoolteachers came to the library to pick out volumes for their classrooms which in turn would be loaned out to their students. The newspaper report does not mention any agreement with the library, and Gordon's contribution, in addition to offering space and access for the teachers, was undoubtedly to select, order, and prepare the books. The following year she helped Oxford, Iowa, open its new public library by organizing and preparing eight hundred gift books for circulation. With its opening in 1940, the Oxford library became the second public library in the county and the first since ICPL was established in 1897.

Gordon was in the news repeatedly in the late thirties. In addition to her many speaking engagements at other libraries and at ILA meetings, she was "much in demand . . . as an authoritative speaker on books," according to the *Press-Citizen*'s 1939 article on National Book Week. She spoke at several parent-teacher association programs and on one of WSUI's book week interview series, a series she organized for the station. Her message again and again was the need to bring library service to the estimated two out of three "Americans who do not have a good library close at hand. Rural areas and small towns suffer the greatest lack," she said.

When Gordon was elected ILA president in October of 1939 the newspaper and the *Iowa Library Quarterly* noted that the election took place in the same week that Gordon, a student pilot, flew solo. The timing was right. She would join the Civil Air Patrol during World War II and would soon thereafter "fly away" from the world of libraries.

Bookshop I: Competing with the Library?

One item on Gordon's busy agenda did not make the news. In a move that was not revealed publicly until she resigned her librarian's post ten years later, Gordon opened a bookstore, The Bookshop, in 1936 or 1937. Located for three years at 221 East Washington Street, the store moved to 114 East Washington in 1939 after Carrie Wieneke closed The Arcade, a bookstore that had been at that address since 1918.[21]

The store was managed, and possibly jointly owned, by Luella Reckmeyer who was also Gordon's housemate at 428½ South Summit. In February 1934, Luella Reckmeyer had arrived in Iowa City from Iowa Wesleyan College to become the first director of the Iowa City Recreation Center and to work on her master's degree in physical education at the university. She apparently had a very successful first year, with the recreation work an integral part of her degree program. In March of 1935 she resigned from the center to go into business with Gordon and was the visible partner there until she left in 1943 to serve overseas with the Red Cross in World War II.

The Bookshop sold greeting cards, gifts, and party supplies but principally carried books and operated a rental library of popular fiction and bestsellers. Advertisements in city directories of the late 1930s read "THE BOOKSHOP, next to the Englert Theater, RENTAL LIBRARY, Clever Gifts, Party Goods, The Latest Books, Greeting Cards." The first year the phrase "educational toys" was included. "Rental Library" was generally the most prominent phrase after the name of the store.

It is not surprising that Gordon did not reveal her part in the new business venture while still the city librarian. In an era when women were expected to give up their jobs at marriage, the community just might not welcome a female public employee who also owned a business.

There are many reasons why Gordon would start a bookstore. She loved books, and giving people access to them and other reading materials was important to her. For over fifteen years she had purchased most of the library's new acquisitions at local bookstores; she knew the local market and possibly thought her store could compete. Finally, Gordon was an independent woman with no apparent family to care for her in her later years; she would need another source of income after she left the library.

No matter what the reasons, the venture raises some questions, especially the rental library. Rental books were most appealing to persons who were anxious to read new and popular books without a large investment, similar to the audience for popular fiction at the library. If Gordon was fed up with the constant pressure for mysteries and light romances at the library while trying to provide serious books with limited funds, she could have followed the pattern of many other public libraries of that period and started a rental collection at the library. If there were profits to be made from renting books, and managing such an operation took the skills she had developed in her position at ICPL, did she have an obligation to bring those profits to the library?

Most librarians and bookstore owners agree that libraries complement, not compete with retail book suppliers. The library generally has a larger number of titles; the bookstore has fewer titles but stocks multiple copies of the newest books. A rental collection, at the library or at a bookstore, is a disadvantage to the poor but voracious reader only if popular items are available solely by rental or purchase. Others might argue that the type of fiction found in most rental libraries does not merit tax support, or that a library-run rental collection would compete with a legitimate business enterprise.

Whether a rental library operated by Gordon belonged in the library or in her bookstore, whether Gordon's store or her many other projects took her attention away from the library, or whether other unknown community circumstances diminished interest in the library, it is a fact that the library's performance went downhill in Gordon's last years at the library. From 1934 until 1947, the year after she resigned, library circulation steadily dropped. Fiction especially was on a downward spiral, dropping from over 97,000 loans in 1933 to only 38,000 in 1947, lower than Gordon's first full year at the library in 1924. Some of this can be attributed to the general decline of public libraries in this period because of the loss of funds during the worst of the depression years and the failure to recover thereafter. The municipal libraries of all twenty-one Iowa cities with populations of 10,000 or more, like public libraries nationwide, saw enormous gains in circulation from 1929 to 1933 and then watched those high figures melt away as money for books and staff was reduced. By 1947, however, other Iowa libraries on average were only 5 percent below their circulation levels of twenty years before while ICPL was still down over 30 percent.

After the extreme loss of income in 1934, Iowa City, as noted earlier, made a quicker short-term recovery than many of its sister libraries, but by 1946 the average budget of the twenty other libraries was 17 percent ahead of 1928 funding, while ICPL was up only 12 percent. There are too many variables that make a community's use of the library rise or fall—dollars spent on books, astuteness of the staff, growth of the community, changing educational levels, plus the timing and interplay of each variable with the others—to draw many conclusions about Iowa City's poor performance when compared to other Iowa public libraries of comparable size. Few cities in this group, however, showed such a dramatic loss in use or a slower recovery of budget in the post-depression and World War II years.

What happened at ICPL during the last ten years of Gordon's administration besides the possibility that the head librarian was bored by her library responsibilities or absorbed by her new business? The bookstore opened before several of her initiatives of the late 1930s—her assistance to Johnson County rural schools and Oxford and her presidency of ILA after three or four years traveling the state as its legislative chair. We know that Louis Mueller and the Taxpayers Association attempted to keep the lid on library expenditures in 1937. Did this pressure on trustees continue, even if it didn't appear in print? There is no record of library board budget discussions in this period so it is not known if Gordon laid out library needs as clearly as McRaith did for the 1920 budget proposal, or if trustees refused to fight for greater funding. Gordon devoted one newspaper column in 1938 to the static level of the library's budget with clever but bitter references to an "Alice in Wonderland atmosphere" in setting library budgets.

Gordon was running a bookstore, continuing the campaign for a tax-supported community recreation program, and leading the Iowa Library Association. Had she given up on trying to increase the library's share of city resources or did her strong and very broad commitment to increasing the number of people who had access to libraries and books take precedence over daily library service to Iowa Citians? Even service to the schools began to falter in her last years. Annual loans from Mann and Longfellow, which had ranged between 21,000 and 30,000 until 1942, dropped each successive year to a low of 11,500 in 1947.

In Iowa City the downward trend in library use and library support ended in 1948 about the same time that the postwar boom in university education fueled the local economy. It would be the last dip in library use statistics or funding for the balance of the library's first one hundred years.

World War II: The Library as Symbol

When the Low Countries and France were overrun in the spring of 1940, U.S. war preparations accelerated and, in some ways, libraries became a symbol of the conflict. This was a war of ideas, and ideas are a library's major asset. Just a month after Pearl Harbor, President Roosevelt sent a proclamation to the American Library Association: "Libraries are directly and immediately involved in the conflict which divides the world. . . . They are essential [to] a democratic society . . . and libraries are the great symbols of the freedom of the mind."

Unlike World War I when public libraries and librarians performed many useful services to aid the war effort, their participation this time was little more than symbolic. Regular library users were busy with other war-time commitments and there were few library-centered but war-related activities for the staff to coordinate and promote. There were book drives to enrich armed forces libraries and, in Iowa City, a book campaign for Russia chaired by Gordon. In 1942 Gordon announced a war information file had been organized at the library. Trustee William R. Hart was the executive director of Iowa City's civilian defense organization and he and the mayor had designated ICPL the clearinghouse for information about civilian defense, rationing, first aid, victory gardens, and requirements for enlisting in each branch of service. The library also established an honor roll of men in the service and sold books on nutrition to benefit the Red Cross. The war information file was never mentioned again and the library stopped keeping records of reading room traffic after 1938, so there is no way to assess how much the file was used during the war years except for the lower rates of circulation, which usually correlate with less in-library use.

If the war did not specifically engage the library's staff and its dwindling clientele, the library's purchases in the war years certainly reflected the impact the war had on its more active participants. In 1944 alone, when the library purchased just over five hundred nonfiction titles, eighty-nine of them, close to 20 percent, were in some way about the war. Except for Winston Churchill, Ernie Pyle, Eddie Rickenbacker, and Wendell Wilkie, few of the authors are familiar today, but the coverage is global and the emotions universal. Singapore, Tunis, Leningrad, Bataan, Malta, Sevastopol, Wake Island, the Mediterranean, and New Guinea all appear in titles documenting individual battles and campaigns, and in memoirs of war experiences. Titles on determination—*We Cannot Escape Our History, Now Is the Moment, They Shall Not Sleep, We Can Win the War, They Shall Not Have Me*—sat next to books about heroes—*Joe Foss, Flying Machine, Thirty Seconds Over Tokyo*, and *Wingate's Raiders*. Journalists gave us *Here is*

Your War, Pacific is My Beat, and *Pipeline to Battle,* and soldiers described their experiences—*God is my Co-pilot, I Served on Bataan, Letters from New Guinea, Last Man off of Wake Island.* Battles of the war were more than just official engagements between armies and navies. There were descriptions of nations and citizens held hostage and the secret world of the underground: *Singapore Goes Off the Air, The Siege of Leningrad, Lady and the Tigers, What You Should Know about Spies and Saboteurs, The Fighting French, Vichy: Two Years of Deception.* Peace was the goal and it was addressed both realistically and spiritually with *Towards an Abiding Peace, One World, A Preface to Peace,* and *What to Do with Germany.* A brief history of the war could almost be written from the titles alone. Like the civil rights struggle of the 1960s, the birth of the environmental movement in the 1970s, and the long war in Vietnam, the flow of books on a topic at the top of the nation's agenda quickly fills up a once-obscure spot in the Dewey classification system and sends even the smallest of libraries scurrying to find new space in the middle of a once-modest section of the collection.

For a variety of reasons, Iowa Citians were borrowing fewer books in the mid-1940s, but the demand for bestsellers had not waned. Gordon once reported that the library had purchased ten copies of *Gone with the Wind* (published 1936). "Readers wore out seven of them." In 1944 she said the library had thirty-two reserves but only one copy of the current bestseller, *Forever Amber*—certainly not enough copies but proof that Gordon didn't shy away from controversial titles.[22] "The question of banning books has been settled by the policy of assuming that adults have the right to choose what they shall read . . . [and] no official has the right to dictate what people shall read," Gordon told the newspaper.[23] Essential to a democratic society if not the war effort, ICPL appeared ready to defend itself as a "symbol of the freedom of the mind."

Board Leadership, Partisanship, and Membership, 1921–1946

During the 1920s and 1930s the library board continued to take a less active role in the day-to-day operations of the library. It was a trend that started in 1905 after the building of the Carnegie and with the hiring of Lorene Webber, the first professionally trained librarian. Though generally less visible to the public than in the library's earliest days, there were many capable and supportive trustees during the Gordon years. And no cause brought them into the public eye more than a conflict with the city council over the library's budget.

There is no question today that the city council has the final say about how many tax dollars will go into the library's annual budget, but as noted in chapter 5, for most of the library's first fifty years it was not always so clear-cut. As long as state legislation stated library revenues in terms of a maximum mill levy and the library board requested a levy within the limit of the state law, there was always a question of whether the city council could reduce the board's request, although the language of the Iowa Code, which said that trustees *shall* determine the levy amount and the city council *shall* levy the tax, seemed clear. In 1921 and 1923 there were a couple of board-council conflicts on this issue.

The budget process was somewhat convoluted. The library board requested in dollars—$10,000, $11,500—but the council approved the amount for the library and for each major division of city government in terms of mills—three, four, four and one-half. (A mill is one-tenth of a cent so it equals one dollar of property tax for each one hundred dollars assessed valuation.) For instance, the 1921 city budget was reported as totaling sixty-four mills. There was little public discussion of how many dollars that represented, in part because millage represents only an estimate of the actual revenue the levy would produce. Tax collections depended on economic conditions and growth factors, and a high rate of delinquent taxes—failure of property owners to pay taxes due—could reduce the amount collected. For instance, the library might ask for $11,000 and the council might promise two and one-half mills estimated to produce approximately $11,000 for the next year, but the library would get whatever two and one-half mills produced during that tax year, sometimes a little more and sometimes a little less than the $11,000 requested.

While the Iowa Code language seemed clear on who decided what were necessary library expenses, there seemed to be little council respect for the library's power to actually set the mill level within the state's maximum levy. There was no council review of the specifics of the library budget, but since 1918 or so the library board and the council had bickered about what mill level the library should get. The state maximum levy was set at five mills but the library never received more than four.

In 1921 the Iowa City council was under a court order to make "sweeping reductions" on individual assessments to some west side property owners for street paving of a few years earlier. To raise the $12,000 needed, the council cut the fire department and library levies by a half mill each. When the library board informed the council that it could not operate the library under the remaining levy, the half mill was restored. As the *Press-Citizen* explained, "The library board has the right under the law to show its expenses, and the levy necessary to meet that budget. . . . The city council could not do anything else but restore the half mill."[24]

In the fall of 1923 the local newspaper did not cover council proceedings about the next year's budget, but library board minutes suggest that there was another library board-city council disagreement about the amount of the library budget. In July of that year the trustees adopted their annual resolution concerning the amount of funds requested for the coming year. They asked for $11,500, their highest request ever and $1,000 over the previous two years. At a special meeting in early September (the same Saturday evening session when they "elected" Jessie Gordon librarian), the trustees instructed the board president and secretary to confer with the city council to get the proper amount of the fiscal year 1924 budget, $11,500, certified to the county auditor. "If the conference fails," the motion said, the board agreed "that a proper court action be instituted to see that [the] proper amount is levied and certified." The conference was evidently a success. The city clerk and the county auditor agreed that the council needed to change the levy, and the records confirm that the council took the correcting action.

The library trustees themselves could be quite conservative about the appropriate level of funding for the library. Until World War II property taxes remained the major tax for citizens who owned property, often equal to sales and income taxes combined. Trustees and the public were very aware of the level of tax levies. Today, typical library board members serve as advocates for the library, recommending responsible growth and expansion to library operations and letting the city council decide if that request is reasonable in light of other city priorities and doable with city resources. In this earlier period, however, when the trustees still had some power to set the level of library funding, and were not necessarily appointed because of an expressed interest in helping provide better library services, their responsibility to limit the burden on taxpayers was sometimes stronger than their commitment to some vision of a better library.

There were two instances in this twenty-year period when a board member and a former board member opposed the library's budget before the city council. The first is a story difficult to believe in light of the library's history. In 1926, three years before he retired from the library board as the last original member, S.K. Stevenson appeared at a city council budget hearing when library budget chairman William R. Hart was "presenting . . . the needs of the . . . library for the ensuing year," and protested against the library board's request for $13,500. "The council granted the amount requested notwithstanding Mr. Stevenson's objections," Hart reported at the next board meeting. The only other evidence of this internal board dispute is a line in the 1923 minutes that indicates that this was not the first time that Stevenson was displeased with the library's budget request. A Stevenson amendment to reduce the 1924 request from $11,500 to $11,000 failed. Also, Stevenson did not attend the 1926 board meeting when the trustees agreed to ask for $13,500. Thus, Stevenson, the person who convened the original committee to try to establish a public library exactly thirty years earlier, who told the public in 1897 to vote for a one-mill levy to support the library but just two years later, along with the rest of the board, took the full two mill-levy allowed by state law, now publicly opposed his fellow board members in enlarging the library's share of city tax revenues. Was this an act of conscience or an internal board dispute over power and politics? Stevenson, the lawyer who spent ten years of his life as a local school superintendent, resigned from the board in 1929 at the age of sixty-two, just two years before his disbarment for misuse of client funds. His fall from grace may have started with his 1926 attempt to thwart the library's financial condition. When he died in 1938 his obituary mentioned only his early years as school superintendent. His years of volunteer service to the library and his many other contributions to the community had been forgotten.

Louis Mueller was the second trustee to publicly oppose a library budget. Mueller served on the library board from 1927 to 1933, appointed on the death of longtime trustee Margaret Switzer. Born in Iowa City in 1883, Mueller had been a reporter and city editor for the *Republican* but since 1909 he had operated Mueller's, the family shoe store. In the 1930s he was chairman of the Iowa City Taxpayers Association, and in that position was campaigning for a major reduction in the library's 1938-39 budget.

In a long letter written to the Carnegie Corporation in July of 1937, Gordon laid out the problem. "The president of the taxpayer's [group] is maintaining that a library is only a luxury, and support of it should be cut to a minimum . . . [they] are trying to reduce the tax for the library to a few thousand. . . . [The balance] could be raised by charging borrowers for the use of the library."

She explained that while Mueller was a well-educated man, "who at one time was unable to buy books, and used the library considerably. He has either forgotten or chosen to ignore what the library . . . meant to him." She claimed he was formerly on the library board "by a political appointment and when not reappointed, has actively been opposed to its support." Obviously fearful of this threat to library funding—"he is influential with a certain group"—she wrote the Carnegie group at the request of the city council seeking confirmation that (1) the library had to remain free, and (2) the city was committed to maintaining reasonable support, not just paying the minimum $3,500 promised thirty-four years earlier. She asked for a prompt response, in time for an August 9 budget hearing if possible. In a reply worthy of his predecessor, James Bertram, who had left the Carnegie organization just three years earlier, Frederick R. Keppell scribbled a very brief, undated, and barely legible reply on the bottom of Gordon's letter:

In reply to your letter of July 29, 1937, permit me to say that the Carnegie grants for erection of public library buildings were each based on an understanding that the library was to be a free public library, [two unreadable words] supported by the community and free to citizens.

Whether the Carnegie response was received before the budget hearing proved immaterial. The post-hearing *Press-Citizen* headline of August 10 read, "Council Approves Budget; No Protest Made." After Mayor Myron J. Walker asked the audience several times for comments on the budget, he finally directed a question to Mueller: "Does anyone from the Iowa City Taxpayer's Association have anything to say?" Mueller's disgruntled reply: "I think the council should double the budget. . . . Many persons came to me complaining about the budget but they haven't got sand enough to stand up and say anything. I say, double it. It is the only way to wake up the taxpayers!" The council then approved $15,100 for the library, up from $14,000 in the previous year and the same amount Gordon's letter noted was under consideration in the Mueller-library confrontation. Mayor Walker would later leave the library a major bequest. Mueller's next project was to oppose the proposed east side location of the new city high school. His group's attempted legal action to force a more central site could have caused the school board to forfeit its $325,000 Public Works Administration federal grant for nearly half the cost of the new building.

Despite these two minor defections from full library support, the library board was blessed with some capable and loyal trustees during the twenty-three years that Jessie Gordon presided over the daily operations of the library. Willard Welch was near the end of his thirteen-year presidency of the board when Gordon was hired in 1923. Welch had joined the board in 1908, not long after the accidental death of his wife. Together they had given the library its first major gift—the Patterson Memorial Collection—and when the gift became a tribute not only to his father-in-law but also his wife, his tie to the library became stronger. His appointment as trustee seemed a logical step to everyone and he became one of the community-spirited individuals who replaced original library board members in the early years. Welch was a "prominent capitalist and businessman" who served on the boards of several local banks and businesses. He was best known as the proprietor of the Dresden China Shop, located in the Patterson Building on Dubuque Street. In addition to French, German, and English imported china, the store displayed and sold goldfish, some raised by Welch in the goldfish ponds in the backyard of his home at 630 Washington Street. (The garden and pond area was sold in 1950 and is now the site of Agudas Achim Synagogue.) He was an amateur photographer and photos by Welch appear in some pictorial histories of Iowa City. He remained on the board until he died in 1928 and his record of thirteen years as president has never been surpassed. More flamboyant than other old-timers like Stevenson, Felkner, Switzer, and Huebner, Welch was the face and voice of the library board during the 1908-28 period.

Welch was called the "honorary president" in the final three years of his life, but Merritt Speidel, owner and publisher of the *Press-Citizen*, actually held the president's post at that time. Appointed to the library board just one year after he arrived in town following his purchase of the newspaper, Speidel spent four of his six trustee years as president, 1926-29. He was appointed to replace S.E. Carrell who had owned and edited the *Iowa State Press*, one of the newspapers that merged to form the *Press-Citizen*. By the time Speidel left Iowa City in 1939 to extend his growing chain of newspapers as president of his recently organized Speidel Newspapers, he had moved the *Press-Citizen* into a new and architecturally distinguished building at 319 East Washington. His term on the library board was less distinguished, however; he attended fewer than 50 percent of trustee meetings even while president and left no record of outstanding leadership.

Speidel presided over four years of growth and prosperity for the library but his successor, William R. Hart, took the library board through the entire decade of the thirties. He watched the library's popularity with the public and its financial fortunes dramatically rise and fall. Hart was only twenty-four years old when he was appointed to the library board in 1917 to replace J.W. Rich. He was reappointed to four more terms and served through June 1945 for a total of twenty-eight years, a record of service surpassed only by the two long-term board secretaries, S.K. Stevenson (thirty-three years) and C.E. Huebner (forty-five years), plus lawyer F.B. Olsen (thirty-one years). Except for the eighteen months he served in the 305th Tank Corps during 1917 and 1918 (enlisting as a private and leaving as a first lieutenant), Hart attended most of the library board meetings held during his tenure, holding one of the best attendance records of any trustee. He chaired both the budget and building committees during the 1920s, giving almost monthly reports on a wide variety of building improvements or reporting back on a myriad of special assignments. Hart graduated from the University of Iowa Law School and was admitted to the bar in 1914. A lifelong Democrat, he was elected to two terms as city attorney, 1919-21 and 1925-27, both terms while serving as a library trustee. (The fact that Hart was on the library board while serving as the city's solicitor is good evidence of the distance between the library and day-to-day city government at this time.) Evidently an early "organization man," Hart also served as president of the Chamber of Commerce and chaired the Johnson County Democrats while president of the library board. He later served on the Iowa State Central Democratic Committee and received several governor's appointments to boards and special committees. In addition to politics, he was active all his life in veterans organizations, Knights of Columbus, and his local Catholic church.

In the period following the adoption of the woman's suffrage amendment and in a time of growth in opportunities for women generally, it should be no surprise that women increased their representation on the library board. After gaining the right to vote, women had a greater responsibility to participate in public affairs, and the public library was familiar ground for many women. From 1919, following the appointment of Hart, through the end of Jessie Gordon's tenure in 1946, eleven of the twenty appointments to the library board were women. This is the only period in the library's one-hundred-year history when appointments of women outnumbered those of men. From 1921 to 1925, the influence of Emma Harvat, directly responsible for library board appointments during her terms as mayor, was important. With a series of unexpected deaths and resignations, it took until 1930 for four women to serve at the same time, but for six consecutive years women held the majority of board slots. The large number of women, however, probably said more about the soft and feminine image of the library in the community than about political rights for women.

In this period of increased appointment of females, a woman served as library board president for the first time. Ella Van Epps, known then only as Mrs. Clarence Van Epps, joined the board in 1928 and served many years as vice president, the traditional slot for women since the library board first organized in 1896. She was elected president three times—1942, 1943, and 1944.

While many of the women appointed in this era were, like Van Epps, wives of local professional men—professors, judges, attorneys—several independent professional women, women like Jessie Gordon and her circle of friends, also were appointed. Emma Watkins, an Iowa City first grade teacher for thirty-six years and later owner and proprietor of the Copper Kettle Tea Room on Linn Street across from the library, is said to have been the Republican who urged Emma Harvat to run for city council. Watkins served on the board from 1930 until she died in 1939. Public school teacher and elementary school principal Alice R. Davies and genealogist Sarah Paine Hoffman were other unmarried professional women to serve in the 1930s. Despite the fact that single women (about one-quarter of all Iowa City women aged twenty-five or more) have held positions of accomplishment and responsibility, especially in the school system and the university, the appointment of Hoffman in 1938 is the last time an unmarried career woman was appointed to the Iowa City Public Library Board of Trustees.

Bookshop II: Gordon's Last Career

On April 29, 1946, new Board President F.B. Olsen announced that Joyce E. Nienstedt would replace Jessie B. Gordon as librarian of the Iowa City Public Library. This was the first public announcement of Gordon's January 2 resignation—and, as noted before, of her involvement with a local bookstore. The newspaper report explained, "Mrs. Gordon has resigned to become associated actively with the Bookshop, 114 East Washington street, of which she is the owner." If the general public cared then about her dual allegiances, no one today who knew Jessie in the 1930s and 1940s had ever thought seriously about it.

Many did not remember or ever knew she owned the store for more than ten years before she left the library.

The Bookshop is an important part of the bookstore history of Iowa City. The library did some business with most of the general bookstores from its very first days, and Gordon used local bookstores as her principal vendors for the mainstream (trade) titles the library purchased in her tenure at the library. She knew the strengths and weaknesses of them all.

At the time Gordon retired from the library to take over day-to-day operations of The Bookshop there were three other bookstores in Iowa City. The oldest was University Book Store, started in 1899 by Lou Cerny and Eda T. Louis. Cerny had been a member of the cast of *Honor Before Wealth* in 1897. Located in the Dey Building that was built on the corner of Clinton and Washington streets after fire destroyed the St. James Hotel, University Book was probably the first store to specialize in selling to university students.

Lucile Davis (ICPL children's librarian and first assistant, 1923-36) and Jessie Gordon when they received honorary life memberships from the Iowa Library Association in 1965. Davis headed the Clinton Public Library for many years.

Photo courtesy Iowa City Press-Citizen

John T. Ries started Iowa Book Store in 1903, but had been involved in Iowa City bookstores since the 1880s—first the Pioneer Book Store and later Lee and Ries Bookstore, both with members of the pioneer Lee family. ("Wm. Lee Books" opened in 1857.) Son John and Ries's three grandsons ran the store in 1946. Iowa Book Store sold religious materials to the Catholic community, among other specialties.

Iowa Supply Company (not known as Iowa Book and Supply until Ries closed his Iowa Book Store in 1958) was the third store in competition with The Bookshop in 1946. Ownership had just changed from Hugh Williams to experienced college bookstore manager Ray Vanderhoef and his three out-of-town partners. Serving the book and supply needs of university students and faculty has always been their chief focus, and it was their only focus in 1946.

According to Bob Sutherlin,[25] who was hired by Iowa Supply Company in 1949 and spent forty years as its book manager, The Bookshop was the best trade bookstore in town when he came to Iowa City. No other store, including Iowa Supply, could match Gordon's stock of mainstream new and classic, non-academic, non-textbook titles or her strong selection of children's books.

Iowa City became one of best markets for books in the country with per capita sales surpassed only by Princeton, New Jersey, according to Sutherlin. It was not just because Iowa City was a university town with a high percentage of residents who had above average levels of education, he said. There are other communities with these characteristics. Sutherlin feels it is because good books need to be selected, stocked, and displayed well to attract the many potential readers in a college town. A few booksellers in Iowa City were subsequently able to do this, but, in Sutherlin's opinion, it started with Jessie Gordon and The Bookshop.

People who worked at Gordon's store in the 1930s and 1940s agree that The Bookshop was the place to go to find new and interesting titles—to rent or to buy. University faculty members were steady customers, buying for their personal libraries and placing many special orders. After Reckmeyer left in 1943 Gordon shared management and later ownership of the store with Frances McGeoch, widow of psychology professor John McGeoch. (Gordon and McGeoch shared a home on Summit for a few years during World War II and helped Frances's daughter care for her infant son while his father was in the service. Several friends reported this experience to be one of the highlights of Jessie's life.)

In the late 1950s, after both women wintered several years in Florida, McGeoch sold her share of the store and moved permanently to the Sunshine State. Sutherlin feels the bookstore declined in quality in these years. "She spent too much time in Florida," he said. By now Jessie was nearly sixty-five years old. With no partner to help her, Gordon sold the store in 1959 to Joe and Martha Wayner, owners of a jewelry store across the street, but she continued as book department manager. The Wayners combined the two stores at the 114 East Washington location in 1962. Known as Wayner's Gift Shop, the store continued to carry books, especially children's books, until it closed in 1978. The owners always listed their business under both "Wayner's" and "The Bookshop" in the telephone directory and in the yellow pages, and for many years customers referred to the store as The Bookshop.

Gordon left the store in 1965 and started selling real estate for Stella Scott, her only job not associated with children, books, and reading. She spent her last years, however, as the volunteer book department manager at Goodwill Industries, and died in 1968 after a short illness. In 1969 her friends raised funds to establish the Jess Gordon Book Nook at the Goodwill store on East College Street. Her lifelong desire to bring together book and reader was recognized in their tribute.

Jessie Gordon's vision was larger than any single public library. When she recognized a need, she immediately began seeking ways to fill the void: a growing group of business and professional women who wanted a service club; young people who had no place to socialize except in the library; children with no access to books because they were too young, too far, or too rural to get to the library; no local bookstore with a good selection of current and children's books; no state plan or resources for bringing library service to all Iowans. Her goal-driven actions—done quietly but with style—endeared her to those who knew her well but have been generally unrecognized in the records of the library and in the history of the community.

[1] Theresa West Elmdorf from a 1909 issue of *Public Libraries* and quoted by Patrick Williams in *The American Public Library and the Problem of Purpose* (Westport, CT: Greenwood Press, 1989), 32

[2] Gratia Countryman of the Minneapolis Public Library quoted by Williams, 31.

[3] Sarah B. Askew, "Libraries Heresies," *Public Libraries*, 19 (May 1914), 194. Quoted by Williams, 32.

[4] *Press-Citizen,* March 16, 1921.

[5] The University of Illinois, 1893, and the University of Wisconsin, 1902, were two of the first university based library schools. Drexel, Simmons, and Syracuse also started at the turn of the century. Most library schools date from 1930 or later. The University of Iowa's School of Information and Library Science was not founded until 1967.

[6] Anne Beiser Allen, "Her Honor the Mayor: Iowa City's Emma Harvat," *Palimpsest,* summer 1995, 76-96. All the information about Harvat is based on this article.

[7] Telephone conversations with Helen Davis Dunlop, Peoria, IL, January 17, August 1, 1996.

[8] Donald G. Rith, *A History of Organized Public Recreation in Iowa City.* Unpublished master's thesis, University of Iowa, Iowa City, 1967.

[9] Speech to Kiwanis Club quoted in the *Press-Citizen,* Jan. 23, 1934.

[10] Alvin Johnson, *The Public Library—A People's University,* as quoted by Williams, 48.

[11] By 1937 unemployment in Iowa City was only 2.6 percent of the population. No estimate of the size of the work force was given. Another 1.7 percent were unwillingly working only part-time. These figures were lower because 143 people were engaged in WPA, NYA, CCC, and other federal emergency work projects. *Press-Citizen,* January 24, 1938.

[12] Irving Weber, "How's your history IQ?" *Iowa City Press-Citizen,* March 4, 1976.

[13] *Press-Citizen*, September 7, 1934.

[14] J.W. Merrill, "What the depression has done to public libraries," *Public Management,* May 1934, 135-44. R.L. Duffus, *Our Starving Libraries* (Houghton, 1933). "Stretching an Abbreviated Library Fund," *Iowa Library Quarterly*, Jan.-Mar. 1933, 2-3. J.F. Otis, "Will Libraries Live?" *Wilson Library Bulletin*, Sept. 1935, 25-9.

[15] Duffus, 47.

[16] Margaret M. Herdman, "The Public Library in the Depression," *Library Quarterly,* XIII (Oct. 1943), 310-34.

[17] R.L. Duffus, *Our Starving Libraries; Studies in Ten American Communities During the Depression Years* (Houghton, 1933).

[18] Lowell Martin and Arnold Miles, *Public Administration and the Library* (University of Chicago Press, 1941), 142-58.

[19] Duffus, 75.

[20] "Reading Machine is placed on display at Public Library," *Press-Citizen,* March 13, 1937.

[21] Carrie was the daughter of Henry C. Wieneke who ran the short-lived rental library in his grocery store before the Civil War. After managing and then buying Fink's Arcade in the St. James Hotel on the corner where Iowa Book and Supply now does business, he ran a cigar store and let his daughter manage the bookstore next door. When the hotel burned in 1916, Carrie moved her store to 114. East Washington.

[22] Kathleen Windsor's *Forever Amber*, a novel featuring the bawdiness of Restoration England, was the bestselling novel in the U.S. in 1945 and was number four the year it was published, 1944. It is one of the all-time bestsellers with over three million copies sold. Another controversial title, *Strange Fruit*, led the list in 1944 but there is no record of the library owning a copy of it in that period.

[23] *Press-Citizen*, November 30, 1944.

[24] *Press-Citizen*, August 31 and September 1, 1921.

[25] Interview with Bob Sutherlin, August 14, 1996.

■ 7.   Adding On: Joyce Nienstedt, 1946–1963

The formal transition from the Gordon to the Nienstedt administrations took place at the library board meeting of June 4, 1946. Jessie Gordon left the meeting after giving her monthly report and Joyce Nienstedt entered the room and assumed Gordon's place at the table. This back-to-back changing of the guard suggests a seamless changeover from one librarian to the next, but the differences between the two were dramatic.

Gordon had difficulty focusing on the particular needs of the Iowa City Public Library in her passion for bringing readers, especially children, and books together in whatever setting worked, while Nienstedt directed her energies almost exclusively towards improving the resources of ICPL—facilities, staff, funding. Gordon had a wide circle of friends at the library and throughout the community. Nienstedt joined no organizations and her interaction with library users was often limited to enforcing rules and keeping children quiet. Gordon is still a legend among her old friends. Few Iowa Citians today remember much about Nienstedt's eighteen years, speak of her in enthusiastic terms, or even recognize her name.

Nienstedt was not the first choice of the library board. Lucile Davis, an Iowa City native and a first assistant and children's librarian at the library from 1923 to 1936, sent a letter of application just fifteen days after Gordon's resignation was announced. The board offered her the job at two hundred dollars a month with February 15 as the deadline for a reply. This may have been just a gesture of courtesy to a longtime library employee and the daughter of a old Iowa City family. Possibly the trustees thought their modest salary offer would not necessarily convince Davis to leave her position at the Ottawa (Illinois) Public Library.[1] By

189

the meeting on February 19, four days after the Davis deadline and with no record of a response, the board offered a three-year contract at the same salary as

Gordon's to a "Miss Lloyd." Gordon had recommended Lloyd who was from Warren County, Illinois, where Gordon had been a school librarian before she came to Iowa City. The very unusual offer of a multiyear contract at a salary ($225 a month) equal to that of the experienced librarian they were losing indicates the trustees were convinced Lloyd would be a more-than-adequate replacement. In March the search committee members reported that Lloyd had already accepted another position and in April they recommended and the board approved the appointment of Joyce Nienstedt at the $225 salary, but with no long-term contract.

Nienstedt's education and experience surpassed that of any of her predecessors. She earned a bachelor's degree in French from

Joyce Nienstedt in 1946

Lawrence College in Appleton, Wisconsin, and a library degree from the University of Wisconsin. In the six years between the two degrees she taught school in Waukesha, followed by three years as a reporter and feature writer for the Watertown Daily News. After graduate work in literature and "commercial subjects," she was working on a master of arts degree in personnel psychology at the time of her appointment to Iowa City. Nienstedt also had twelve solid years of public library experience before starting her first directorship in Iowa City. She started her professional career as librarian of the joint libraries of Carrolltown and Bowerston, Ohio. After a short stint as a reference librarian at a public library in California, she became a branch librarian, first at Milwaukee and then at Wichita public libraries. Before coming to Iowa City she held positions as head of circulation and personnel officer at Wichita.

All we know about Nienstedt's family background is that she was born in Blackhawk, a small town north of the Wisconsin River in southwest Wisconsin, and that her father was a minister in Jefferson, Wisconsin, at the time she attended Lawrence College. Nienstedt was thirty-five when she arrived in Iowa City.

The First Five Years

Confronted with declining library use, low to moderate financial support, and a physical plant over forty years old, Nienstedt's short-term agenda seemed obvious: Improve services, tighten operations, work for better funding, and initiate a program of repairs and renovations to the Carnegie, its furnishings, and equipment.

Nienstedt, not the library board, seemed to be the source of new direction for the library and the one who took the initiative. Some of the men on the library board were longtime members: lawyer and Board President F.B. Olsen, trustee since 1919; insurance agent and Secretary Fred Huebner, trustee since 1912. Others seldom attended: bookstore owner C.C. Ries, Bremers' manager Julian Brody, and River Products owner James Records. Records died before the end 1947. At the same time, there were four women trustees active in community affairs and probably enthusiastic about Nienstedt's new leadership: Ella Van Epps, a past board president; Marguerite Evans, wife of Judge Harold Evans and a twenty-year veteran of the board by the time she resigned in 1961; Mary G. Martin, spouse of a university biology professor, who would lead the board for three years starting in 1949; and Ruth Beye, another academic spouse. These women took leading roles in the League of Women Voters, the Social Service League, the school board, and many other organizations that put them in touch with the Iowa City community. They had the time to counsel Nienstedt about Iowa City and to be influenced by the new director's ideas for attacking the problems and issues facing the library. In July of 1947 attorney Sam Shulman replaced Van Epps and joined the three women as an active, involved trustee. In these first years the minutes frequently recorded that the librarian had consulted with the mayor or the city engineer on a particular issue; in the past, formal contacts with city officials had been assigned to male board members.

Although little about books or services is recorded in Huebner's minutes (minutes which get briefer and briefer as his thirty-nine years as board secretary stretch on), Nienstedt reported in 1953 that early in her administration she "had offered two alternatives to the library board as [a] means of increasing use of the library." One was to buy many copies of popular fiction, which she warned would "soon be dead wood on the shelves." She called the other a "slower and much more difficult program." She would buy only moderately in fiction and would emphasize books on a "wide variety of subjects of more permanent usefulness to the townspeople." According to Nienstedt, the board chose the latter method.

In her first few months she negotiated a 33 percent discount from Chicago book wholesaler McClurg, dropping the Gordon practice of buying most titles locally, and turned down an offer from Gordon's Bookshop to give the library a 25 percent discount on all trade book purchases.

Nienstedt also received permission from the board early in 1947 to start a rental collection "as a means of providing additional copies of popular books."

This gave library users a source for copies of popular fiction that her collection-building program planned to de-emphasize, and it provided The Bookshop some competition for its much-advertised rental collection. The Bookshop dropped its rental library after 1949 but the library's rental collection continued until the early 1960s. "The majority of public libraries have established rental collections," Nienstedt explained in a long *Press-Citizen* article announcing the new service, "because they feel that tax money should not be spent on . . . 'ephemeral' books—those that people want immediately or not at all." She said it also allowed purchase of more copies of important and popular new titles. "We will continue to buy copies of important new novels for the free collection, and when the rental copies have paid for themselves they will be transferred to the free collection." Nienstedt felt that the rental collection would be welcomed both by those who read bestsellers and those who didn't. "The latter will have the satisfaction of knowing that these books will be paid for by those who want to read them."

No theme is more obvious in the board minutes of Nienstedt's early years than her insistence that the library building and its equipment be upgraded and improved. Almost monthly, she sought approval for some very basic amenities for the public and the staff plus aids for library operations. This interest in facility management became a hallmark of her Iowa City career. In her first three years she received approval for the purchase of a vacuum cleaner and floor waxer, for an adding machine, mimeograph, cash register, and a basic typewriter platen to allow typing of catalog cards. She put venetian blinds in the reading rooms, purchased a water heater and sink so there would be hot water during the warm season when the boiler was off, replaced and moved radiators, resurfaced the floors in all the public areas, added lounge furniture in the reading rooms, and removed the six wooden pillars to increase the space in these rooms. She purchased additional typewriters, a phonograph, fluorescent desk lamps, and some new furniture for the children's room. She gradually added linoleum-topped steel tables and chairs and Sjorstrom blond birch furniture to replace and supplement the forty-year-old dark oak pieces. Bathroom and lighting fixtures were replaced, shelving added, and rooms painted everywhere. She cleaned out a supply room and turned it into a staff lounge and lunchroom. The exterior limestone was cleaned and repointed, loose and missing stone replaced. Windows were caulked and painted and new sills, sashes, and storms installed as required. In 1951 the board approved $3,600 to air-condition the building and add a refrigerated water fountain. The "people's palace" was a much more inviting facility by the end of Nienstedt's first five years.

It is not clear how some of these items were financed in the first couple of years, but by 1949 Nienstedt and the board had convinced the city council that the condition of the library building had reached crisis proportions. For five years starting in 1949, they persuaded the council to levy at least a portion of the three-quarter mill that state law allowed for the maintenance or construction of public library buildings. Over $25,000 was spent on building repair and renovation work from this special levy, thus allowing general building maintenance dollars from the regular budget to be used for some very practical pieces of office, library, and cleaning equipment.

Nienstedt's story of how she parlayed a termite problem into an awareness of library needs and subsequently into a major increase in the library's budget appeared in a 1950 article she wrote for *Library Journal*. It was later reprinted in the *Iowa Library Quarterly*.[2] Termite damage at the library first surfaced in 1943 when a library employee literally fell through the basement floor. The library had to close for seven days while the badly damaged areas of the wood floors were replaced with cement. In 1949 the termites reappeared in another part of the lower level. Nienstedt planned her attack on both the destructive insects and the city's purse very carefully. Her premise in "Even the Termites Helped to Improve this Budget" (Nienstedt offered mimeographed reprints for ten cents each or three for a quarter) was that the discovery of termites in the library proved to be "the well-known blessing in disguise, even though it cost . . . $1,200 to get rid of them." She claimed the library received more than that amount of valuable publicity in letting the community know that the old library building had to be "fixed up . . . that we needed an *emergency* fund [the special levy] as a matter of principle for any building the age of ours."

She goes on to explain in detail how she announced that the discovery of the extensive termite damage would stop all plans for improving the building because the funds were needed to do the extermination work. Nienstedt claimed she had the mayor, finance officer, and city engineer inspect the building and then saw that their comments were quoted in the newspaper story describing the problem. Finally, she investigated all the termite exterminators in the area, compiled the information, and shared it with the city and the general public. The city was facing similar problems in another city building, and the public, made anxious by the library's tale of destructive pests, was told via radio and newspaper that the library's file about termite companies was available to any Iowa Citians interested in having their property inspected for similar infestation. Nienstedt claimed the story brought many people to the building to use the information and consequently to discover the generally poor condition of the library. She wrote that it was her businesslike approach and good news sense that impressed the council.

The *Library Journal* article demonstrated Nienstedt's political skills, her newspaper experience and writing ability, and her practical strategies for convincing the community and the council to spend appreciably more for library service. Nienstedt gave some excellent political and strategic advice that even today would benefit a public library struggling to increase its share of the local tax dollar.

We have no other report on the causes for the library's improved financial condition in this period. We do know the facts: Between 1946 and 1951 the library's income from local taxes increased from $16,500 to $44,380, with the most astonishing increase occurring between 1950 and 1951 when the tax funds appropriated for the library jumped from $22,180 to $44,380. Much of the increase after 1949 was due to the special funds for building improvements, peaking at $12,200 in 1951. The special levy, however, was gone by 1953, and Nienstedt and the library board were able to keep annual appropriations for the library at just under $50,000 for the balance of the 1950s. Nienstedt underplayed the impact of postwar inflation on the rapidly rising budget in her article, but in an early annual report she noted that the same amount of money purchased nearly 20 percent fewer books in 1949 than in 1948. With the building in better physical condition, the funds gradually moved to salary lines and book budgets. With more books and a larger staff, the next building crisis would be one of space.

These same years, 1949-51, were also the last days of Iowa City's one-hundred-year-old mayor-council form of government. In April of 1950 the community voted to adopt the nonpartisan council-manager form of municipal government and by late 1951 the first city manager, Peter Roan, began to install much more sophisticated methods for structuring and analyzing budget requests. Just before this change, the library had engineered a major shift in the city's financial priorities toward library service—a shift even greater than those of 1914 and 1921. For thirty years, since first reaching $10,000 in 1921, library budgets had seesawed between $10,000 and $20,000 per year—higher in the relative prosperity of the 1920s, lower in the depression years—and had improved only marginally in the first years after World War II. After 1950, with some minor setbacks under the increased scrutiny of the city manager, the operating budget remained in the $45,000-55,000 range until the expansion expenses of the 1960s.

As Nienstedt carefully noted in her termite article, to "impress" the city council the library had to do more than show reasons for receiving more tax dollars. She immediately looked for ways to increase income from other sources. The rental collection was not the big moneymaker Nienstedt had predicted, bringing in only about $285 to $400 a year. At two cents a day, it would never make the fiction collection self-supporting as she had hoped. Income from fines increased significantly in these first five years. At about $1,800 per year, fines produced more than twice the income from the same rates as they did in the Gordon years.

Some of her former employees confirm that Nienstedt was obsessive about rules and their enforcement; in contrast, it is hard to imagine Gordon letting her staff turn away anyone, especially a child, because they hadn't paid their library fines.

One of Nienstedt's first moves increased income to the library and improved service to Iowa City schoolchildren. She established library "branches" at all Iowa City elementary schools on the same basis as those that had served Mann and Longfellow since 1923. While expanding the service, she also urged the trustees to seek a contract with the school board to pay for this service. The two boards reached an agreement in just a few months. Undoubtedly it was very helpful that trustee Ruth Beye also served on the school board, and for a few years Beye headed a committee that administered the school-library contract. This contract arrangement lasted for six years, 1948 through 1953, and the fee to the schools increased gradually from $2,100 to $3,200 per year. This amount was said to represent one-half of the cost of serving the schools. It at least paid for the full-time school librarian hired to oversee the service. In 1954, the same year that Mark Twain and Herbert Hoover elementary schools were opened, the school board terminated the contract and told the superintendent to begin planning for elementary school libraries. Thus ended over forty years of Iowa City Public Library book collections in the public schools. They had started with Helen McRaith, flourished under Jessie Gordon, and ended with Joyce Nienstedt insisting on serving all elementary schools and sharing the costs with the school district. It was 1962, however, before the school board approved the funds and the plan. Adding two new school libraries a year, it took the school district five years before each elementary school was equipped and staffed. In the meantime, for the next ten years, children formerly served at the schools swarmed into ICPL.

Nienstedt saw another possible source of library revenue in the massive increase in university students using the library. The campus overflowed with returning veterans, and the number of cards issued to university students doubled in just one year. Ever since 1903, when Judge Wade pleaded Iowa City's case with Carnegie, library officials have recognized the extra load ICPL carries by serving thousands of college students. Like the library's historic ambivalence about serving nonresidents generally, this special subcategory of Iowa City "nonresidents" has caused many to agonize over what is fair to the students who represent the community's principal industry and what is equitable to the local institution supported only by local taxes. Nienstedt didn't agonize for long. The university main library was still on the drawing boards in 1947 and four years away from opening. The enrollment at the university, as veterans returned after the war, shot up from 3,700 in 1945 to over 10,000 in the fall of 1949. It was difficult for many students to find departmental libraries and so they walked east to the Carnegie. The public library's general collection could serve only a fraction of their needs but, as Nienstedt noted, they found the encyclopedias and magazines very useful. In her first year she urged the board to set a fifty-cent per year fee for what she called a "nonresident" university student. By 1949 the board raised the fee to one dollar, two dollars, or three dollars a year depending on the type of service the student chose, three dollars paying for "service on the same basis as other Iowa City residents." By 1952, no doubt based on inquiries from prospective card holders, the board had to define a "nonresident student." The complex and questionable policy statement based residency on age, marital status, and voter registration, and declared all students and faculty living in Finkbine or Stadium Park as residents of Lucas Township, not Iowa City. The new rules and fees did increase the number of nonresident card holders, rising from about fifty per year in the 1930s through 1946 to as high as 934 in 1950, the year after Nienstedt carefully reregistered everyone in order to implement the new policies.

School contracts, rental books, nonresident fees, tighter fine collections—all together they produced about $5,000 a year, but Nienstedt's plan to demonstrate the library's willingness and ability to supplement tax revenues suddenly backfired. During Nienstedt's first few years, indeed, since the day the library opened in 1897, the library board enjoyed full control over expenditure of this miscellaneous income as well as any tax funds that were not spent in the year appropriated. These various fees and fines served as the library's "pin money," giving it funds for miscellaneous and unbudgeted expenses. The power to carry over tax appropriations served as an incentive to spend tax monies carefully so that an emergency fund could be accumulated. This financial arrangement changed dramatically in 1953 and 1954 under a professional city manager administering a new state municipal finance code.

For years, city councils throughout Iowa essentially had ignored state legislative language giving library boards the right to "determine and certify" their level of funding within certain guidelines. In the early 1950s, some of the new state legislation was merely language catching up with political reality. The council-board conflict that developed in determining ICPL's 1954 budget, however, was over control of the library's miscellaneous income and the tax dollars not spent by the end of the budget year. When the library board submitted a request for $48,000 for 1954, the city manager requested information on its estimated other income. With an estimate of $4,000 in hand, the manager recommended that the city appropriate $44,000 in tax dollars and let the library's other income cover the balance. In other words, the manager's action under the new legislation changed the decision that the city council made from, "How many tax dollars do we give the library this year?" to "How much money from all sources do we allow the library to spend?" This change, in effect, reduced the expected appropriation by nearly 10 percent and left the library with no emergency funds to use for unexpected—that is, unbudgeted—expenses.

The library board protested and Nienstedt was directed to write to the State Library Commission. Letters from the state attorney general and from the city manager were noted at the next board meeting. The content of the letters is not recorded, but the library probably received the same answers that public libraries throughout the state were getting. The new state municipal finance code had changed the rules and, except for gifts and bequests, libraries had lost the power to spend any income not first appropriated by the city council. Nienstedt's efforts to enhance tax dollars while impressing the council with the library's ability to generate income were simply bad timing. For a few years library trustees became accustomed to the extra dollars her recommendations had produced, then they learned that suddenly the expenditure of most additional income had to be justified through the budget process just like regular tax appropriations. With no power to accumulate funds, the board was fully at the mercy of the city council for all—not just major—financial decisions. It was from this change that the library board began to realize the necessity of becoming skilled at presenting the library's budget needs to the council and to the community.

The Wullweber Trust and the Van Epps Collection

They may not have realized it at the time, but Nienstedt and the library board would receive more real and unencumbered value from a few major gifts to the library than from raising fines and fees or from renting popular fiction. There were three important gifts during Nienstedt's tenure, two of them in the first five years. In addition, annual income from the Mary Carson Ransom Wullweber trust started appearing some time after 1940.

The Wullweber gift was the first bequest to the library since the Welch-Patterson family had established the Patterson Memorial Library in 1908. Mrs. Wullweber, active in local women's clubs, had been a longtime friend of the library. Helen McRaith had noted her gifts of books in both the 1911 and 1913 annual reports. She gave the library over three hundred volumes of classic fiction and the best in late-nineteenth-century works in travel, history, art, poetry, and oration, including the complete works of Daniel Webster, John Bunyan, Washington Irving, and Lord Byron, the kind of sets that libraries welcomed in earlier times. Income from the Wullweber trust was split each year between the library and Trinity Episcopal Church (where her father and brother had been church officers). For fifty-four years through 1994, when the library's share of the principal was incorporated into the library's general endowment fund, the small but annual check from the trust helped buy books and equipment or funded experimental library services.

In 1947 Clarence and Ella Van Epps gave the library a collection of about 1,000 books—their large personal collection. Ella died just a year later in November 1948. She had spent twenty years on the library board and was the first woman to serve as president. Clarence was on the university medical faculty for over fifty years. In the same year as the gift to the library, the Van Epps, regarded as two of Iowa's foremost art patrons, gave the university their collection of Iowa artists—Lechay, Burford, Lasansky, Stuart Edie, and others. The ICPL book collection included some out-of-print and other valuable editions of well-known titles. This distinguished collection may have been too rich for a public library, which is not the place for valuable copies. With a relatively high loss rate and the promise of heavy use of core titles, the public library needs *any* usable version of a title, not valuable out-of-print or first editions. For the most part, the Van Epps collection was general in scope, with classic and contemporary titles in all disciplines, but the Van Epps had some special interests—Lincoln, Ibsen, Bertrand Russell, Tom Paine, Plato—that went deeper than appropriate for a public library offering a general collection, especially in a community with a large research library. Nevertheless, every title was added; over 950 volumes were entered into the accession books of 1947 and 1948. All books received a special bookplate, went into the general collection, and served Iowa City readers into the late 1970s.

The gradual disappearance of the riches of the Van Epps collection through heavy use, discarding of out-of-fashion titles, and the replacement of classic volumes with newer and easier-to-read paperback editions demonstrates the dynamic character of a typical public library collection. Despite its inevitable destruction in a public library environment, that kind of steady, hands-on use of the collection may be exactly what the Van Epps wanted. In a year when Nienstedt convinced the board to follow her plan for less popular fiction and more titles with long-term value and in a period when she had to spend a great share of the book budget to build juvenile collections to serve more elementary schools, the Van Epps collection complemented Nienstedt's efforts nicely. In fact, her collection development plans may have influenced the Van Epps to make the gift.

The Music Room: A Pioneering Effort

The largest gift of this period funded a whole new service for the library—a music listening room and a large collection of recordings for public loan, the first component of what would become the library's audiovisual collection. The funds came from Jennie Brubaker, a farm woman who was reported never to have used the library. The idea came from Nienstedt who, by the time of the completely unexpected gift, had already convinced the library board that Iowa City should work to establish a record collection similar to those found in 1950 only in the

The Jennie Brubaker Music Room opened in the fall of 1950. Decor was the epitome of 1950s design, with Eames chairs, blonde oak tables, and a full wall mural.

public libraries of larger cities—St. Paul, Denver, Louisville. The trustees, and especially new trustee Sam Shulman, were working enthusiastically to identify funds for the idea. Shulman had systematically contacted local businesses and organizations seeking pledges to support an Iowa City Public Library music room. When the news of the Brubaker bequest arrived, Shulman and Nienstedt urged the board to earmark the entire bequest for the project, and trustee efforts turned from seeking funds to planning the facility. In Nienstedt's own words, from a second 1950 *Library Journal* article,[3] "We had done a lot of pipe dreaming about the kind of music room we wanted," and when the "providential bequest came . . . the reaction of the library trustees could be expressed in just two words: 'Music Room!'"

The board received the $14,000 from the bequest in stages over three years, and the amount was probably larger than the board originally expected. Full settlement was delayed, first over a challenge from Brubaker's caregiver who had been her legal guardian for several years, and then over the discovery of a bequest to Mrs. Brubaker which was not fully settled at the time of her death. The trustees received the final payment, $7,500, after the room had been open for over a year. Although they were free to do anything they wished with the proceeds under the terms of the bequest, board members continued to designate all remaining funds for the purchase of recordings.

The Jennie Brubaker Music Room opened less than a year after the bequest was announced. An eighteen-by-twenty-eight-foot area in the southwest corner of the Carnegie basement had served as a

ICPL was one of the first smaller public libraries to offer a large record collection.

public meeting space since shortly after the building opened in 1904. Generally known as the club room, it had hosted meetings of Art Circle and Shakespeare Club, housed Gordon's displays of children's books during National Book Week, and exhibited the Pelzer Art Library in the mid-1930s. By 1949, according to Nienstedt (with no information about what happened to the room's public meeting function), it was just "a good sized room used by the trustees for board meetings, so immediately we began to visualize what could be done with it."

Local architect and interior designer Henry Fisk was invited to design, furnish, and decorate a room that would "omit nothing which would add to the room's comfort, attractiveness and listening pleasure."[4] The result was a "pièce de résis-tance" of 1950 interior design—a room with good, indirect lighting, a sound-proof ceiling, the building's first carpeting, three Eames chairs (one covered in genuine horsehide), a sofa and upholstered chairs in the popular Danish modern style, unusual oak grille and drapery treatments to block out the mundane views from the sidewalk-level windows, natural oak custom-made cabinetry and desk, plus chartreuse, blue-green, and terra cotta everywhere, colors taken from the wallpaper mural of a rural Iowa scene (to honor the farm background of the donor) which covered the entire east wall. Everything was arranged to focus on the dark mahogany Magnavox Windsor Imperial record player, selected because it provided the period's best fidelity sound for long-playing records.

The decision to buy only 33 1/3 rpm, long-playing records proved right in the long term and was an example of the kind of audiovisual format decisions librar-ies have been making ever since: Where is the market going for this product? Will the consumer purchase appropriate playback equipment? Will this format be easy to loan? Can it be shelved so borrowers can easily find and select their choices? In this case, the LP record remained the principal format for nearly forty years—until superseded by the compact disc in the early 1990s—and the old, heavy, brittle 78 rpm recordings would never have endured repeated library use. A few of the original LP recordings were still in the collection when all LPs were discarded in 1996.

The collection contained about two hundred records when the music room opened for in-library listening in September of 1950. The library held regular concerts each week and, for the first eighteen months, a local radio station broad-cast a library music hour direct from the music room. One of the programs was a memorial concert for Sam Shulman who died suddenly in January 1952, just fifteen months after the opening of the room he had helped to create.

When the room first opened, a visitor would browse through the record jackets and bring a selection to the staff member on duty, who put the recording on the big Windsor Imperial, and everyone in the room heard the selector's choice. There were no individual listening stations or earphones. People came on lunch hours, afternoons, and evenings to listen while studying or reading and, on Saturday afternoons, to hear Metropolitan Opera broadcasts on good equipment without interruptions of children, telephones, or doorbells. The opera lovers could follow along with librettos furnished by the library. On Saturday mornings, story hours moved into the music room from the children's department just across the hall. Music recordings became an integral part of the children's programs, and Nienstedt's idea for a special story hour room for children at ICPL may have started at this time.

Word-of-mouth advertising among music lovers made the music popular. Traffic grew steadily, as did the requests to check out the recordings for home use. Sooner than they had originally planned, therefore, the board drew up rules for loaning records. The rules required a five-dollar deposit to insure the library against damaged records and set fines at five cents per day, but, unlike most record libraries of that time, they made no charge for loans. Borrowers could check out one to three albums for one week.

The collection had grown to over 1,000 albums by 1952 when the library expanded music room services to include the loan of recordings. One-quarter of the recordings were traditional jazz, folk music, children's, and Broadway show albums, the balance a well-chosen selection of all forms of classical and modern serious music. In 1954 an article in *Music Journal* heralded the quality of the Iowa City record collection as well as the surprise of finding such a superior listening room in a small town. "Most small town libraries are going quite a way to have reserved a shelf for records," it said. "More than 400 persons have signed up for free access to the more than 1000 albums in the library files. Whether you want Beethoven's fourteen [*sic*] piano sonatas, the Casals limited editions from Prades . . . an opera by Mozart, Puccini or Verdi (they have them all!) . . . or Louis Armstrong trumpet solos, you'll find them catalogued in [the library's] special music index."[5]

According to the *Music Journal* article, local record stores were not concerned that people could now listen to recordings for no charge; in fact, they found people frequently took library recordings home for appraisal before making a decision to purchase their own copy.[6] Phonograph dealers felt it stimulated the sale of their equipment in the same way that the library's video collection in the early 1980s affected the number of VCRs sold in Iowa City.

The music room continued to be open afternoons and evenings five days a week for most of the 1950s. In 1960, hours were reduced after Nienstedt reported that use was dropping due to an increase in the number of home phonographs and the drop in the price of hi-fi sets and LP phonograph records. Later that year there were "problems with teenagers in the music room," and the library was suffering severe overcrowding in all areas of the building. In 1961 the music room closed and the records were moved upstairs. Later that year Nienstedt moved her office to the music room and freed her small first-floor office for storing and display of library materials.

After the music room closed, Nienstedt ignored the record collection for the rest of her administration. With no documentation in library files, subsequent boards and staff assumed the Brubaker funds had to be used for music-related purposes. The bequest, with no restrictions on its use, had been received during the period when the city had just added a special levy to pay for all the needed library building maintenance and repair. It may have been more politically astute, if not completely honest, to let the public think the Brubaker money was mandated for the music service. Plans to reopen the music room surfaced regularly in the 1960s but never materialized, and Brubaker funds would buy library recordings until 1974.

The Brubaker Music Room was a generous and well-timed gift from a Johnson County farm woman. The bequest had given the library an opportunity to create a unique, tastefully designed, functionally constructed haven for music lovers within the library. The room received national recognition in both library and music journals, and generated visits from many state and local library officials throughout the Midwest. Although the new room spent only a few years in the limelight and although other kinds of library growth and technology developments crowded out its importance, the Brubaker gift established the library's record collection, funded it for over twenty years, and gave the old and never very handsome basement of the Carnegie building a spot of charm and beauty, first for library users and later for staff assigned to spend their working hours in the lower level. The record collection was the first major diversion from an all-print library and it helped set ICPL on a course toward the library's leadership role in integrating audiovisual formats into public library collections in the 1980s and beyond.

The Walker Trust

The third major gift of the Nienstedt years probably seemed modest at the time—the first check was for $94.82—compared to the generous Brubaker bequest, capable of creating a whole new library service. Over time, however, the Walker gift proved to be one of the most rewarding. In the first twenty years the total income, distributed annually, surpassed the $14,000 given by Brubaker and by the end of 1996 the library had received nearly $120,000 with the potential for income in perpetuity.

Myron J. Walker, grandson of two of Johnson County's pioneer settlers, was a local boy who spent much of his life as a naval commander. He served his country in all parts of the world and then came back to his hometown in retirement and served his community. He left Iowa City and the University of Iowa in 1911 to attend the Naval Academy. In his career he commanded gunboats on the Yangtze River, served aboard the first naval vessel to circumnavigate South America after the opening of the Panama Canal, entered naval aviation, piloted some of the early dirigibles, and commanded the first dirigible naval air station at Sunnyville, California.

He retired for the first time in 1936, and by 1937 the citizens of Iowa City had elected him to a two-year term as mayor. It was Mayor Walker who faced former trustee Louis Mueller over issues of proper levels of library funding in 1938. Just as Walker was resettling into life in Iowa City, he was recalled to active service in 1940, retiring a second time in 1945. Active in his church, local lodges, the State Historical Society, and navy societies, he spent the rest of his life managing the real estate holdings he had inherited from his father, Joseph Walker. He died in 1953 and left his property (several farms and apartment houses) in a trust described by one lawyer as a "nearly perfect" perpetual trust. Following the death of each individual beneficiary (several of whom are still living), that person's share reverts to the pool shared by the seven institutional beneficiaries. Eventually the institutions will share in equal parts 95 percent of the entire income from the trust's assets. The remaining 5 percent accumulates as a reserve and may be reinvested to acquire more property or other assets. Two local churches, the University of Iowa School of Religion, Boys Town in Omaha, and the Mary O. Coldren Home share with the library the income designated for institutions.

The Problem of Staffing

When Joyce Nienstedt came to Iowa City from a personnel position at the Wichita Public Library, she had been working on a master's degree in personnel psychology. From that perspective, as a veteran of much larger libraries and with specific personnel experience, she found what must have seemed to her a rather unprofessional operation at ICPL. Not since Carolyn Ware's short administration had attention been given to working conditions and benefits for library employees. Ware, who also had experience in several large organizations including the Los Angeles Public Library, had convinced the 1921 library board to adopt a vacation policy for the librarian and her "first" and "second" assistants. To be fair, the minutes for much of the Gordon years are missing, but Gordon's apprentice training program is the only personnel-related action on the record.

In April 1947, just a year after she arrived in Iowa City, Nienstedt began to bring personnel issues to the board. She first asked for a vacation and sick leave policy. No mention was made of the 1921 vacation leave rules so it is unclear whether this was a revision or the re-adoption of a forgotten policy statement. Primarily, the policy expanded vacation privileges to all full-time staff, a group of six or seven (soon to grow to nine) instead of the two or three staff members of 1921. The new issue was sick leave. The board adopted the vacation policy but deferred the sick leave provisions. Nienstedt brought up sick leave two more times in 1948 and 1949 but never got more of a commitment from the board than a promise to look at the University of Iowa policy. Each time it came up Nienstedt seemed to have a case at hand that illustrated the need for sick leave— a particular employee facing medical problems. Each time the board would make some provision for paid leave for the employee but seemed to want to proceed only case-by-case.

In 1948 Nienstedt asked the board to consider a Christmas bonus for all library employees. A quick opinion from the state auditor found such a gift unlawful, but he counseled that the board could award a cost-of-living pay raise to all staff members. There is no evidence that this was done, but an across-the-board pay raise would be a first step at considering employee salaries in the framework of a library pay plan rather than setting salaries each year on a person-by-person basis.

Nienstedt continued to work on a benefits package for her employees. In 1952 the board gave approval for a funeral leave policy and later a policy granting payment for leave earned but not taken when a person left his or her job at the library. Nienstedt worked to equalize salaries between city staff and library staff, getting 10 percent raises for all employees in 1951. The question of equity with city employees became more difficult after the arrival of the city manager. He argued in at least two budget cycles that the board could find the money in the library budget for salary raises equal to city employees, but refused to recommend a higher salary line to the city council. This forced the library board to choose between money for books and money for library staff.

Nienstedt often brought issues to the board about training and continuing education for staff. She established some formal testing procedures for potential employees in her first year (the apprentice system apparently was discontinued in the late Gordon years) and set standards of education and previous experience for each job. Nienstedt listed "improved salaries and training standards" as one of her major accomplishments in three of her first four reports to the Iowa Library Commission. She regularly sought permission and expenses to send staff members to training sessions and to library association meetings. Also, in addition to regular paid holidays, the board agreed to give employees one paid leave day per year to visit another public library.

Despite improved benefits, recruitment of staff with library experience or training was Nienstedt's most serious and constant personnel issue during her entire eighteen years in Iowa City. In a news article in July of 1946, just weeks after she arrived, Nienstedt announced an entrance examination to be held the next Saturday afternoon to select qualified persons for future library positions. Applicants between the ages of twenty and forty, with two years of college, good hearing and eyesight, and the ability to type, could sign up to take the test. Iowa City was not Milwaukee or Wichita, however, and the call (and perhaps the low salaries) produced few quality applicants. Nienstedt was forced to spend a large share of her time identifying librarians with appropriate library education and replacing and training clerical staff. The larger the size of the staff—nine full-time and four part-time positions by 1952—the more opportunity for turnover. Iowa City's potential work force was primarily women who were "putting hubby through," as one former employee described it, and their commitment to a job was often limited and their tenure short.

Professional positions were the toughest to fill. No university or college in Iowa produced public librarians with professional degrees recognized by the American Library Association until 1968, so Nienstedt was forced to travel to the closest library schools at Madison and Minneapolis to identify and interview prospective staff. Nienstedt received permission and travel expenses to take such trips at least seven times during her Iowa City years. She hired assistant librarians, reference librarians, catalogers, and children's librarians on these trips, but often they seemed to stay only a year or two. She hit pay dirt in 1949 when she recruited fellow Wisconsinite Hazel Westgate to take charge of children's services. Westgate came to Iowa City with her unique vision for serving children, and stayed for nearly forty years, becoming ICPL's best-known staff member. This was Nienstedt's third attempt, however, in just over two years to find a children's librarian who would stay longer than a few months—true of several others she recruited in this period.

There were several possible reasons for the high turnover. Young women fresh from library school would marry and move on, or, like the fast-changing clerical staff, had come to Iowa City because their spouses were attending the university and would leave when husband received his degree. Salaries were still very low in public libraries, lower than teaching and lower even than for librarians in other types of libraries. Nienstedt once said salaries were her prime barrier to effective recruitment, citing differences of between $1,000 and $2,000 per year in the pay rates for local librarians at the public library versus those at the university or the public schools.

The library board always reviewed and approved each new hire and salary change, and so with such heavy turnover, the president appointed the board's first permanent personnel committee to review Nienstedt's appointments and bring recommendations to the board. During the summer months when meetings tended to be less frequent, the board empowered either the committee or Nienstedt herself to fill openings without its official approval. It was the first time any employees, even hourly, part-time shelvers, were hired without board review.

The Essential Nienstedt

Nienstedt's personality also could have contributed to some of the turnover. Although some employees feared her suspicious nature (she used the window in her office to observe operations and would install similar observation posts in both the reception area and director's office of the 1963 expanded library), several persons said it was a good place to work, a relaxed and congenial atmosphere where everyone willingly contributed their share. In addition to her consistent efforts to improve staff salaries and benefits, she was, according to one seven-year employee, "generally fair and never cruel to an employee." Donna Abbott Hogan said she has "warm memories of her years at the library [working with] a close-knit group of mostly women." After Nienstedt created the staff room from an old storage space, the staff members marked birthdays and anniversaries at their midmorning breaks, including an annual holiday brunch for several years. Sometimes Nienstedt, in her traditional smock and with her hair always in braids and pinned back, would join them. "She had a deep hearty laugh when amused," but it was infrequently heard. "If she got to talking, we could end up staying for some time," Hogan remembered. Iowa Citian Don Schallau, who was a page at the library from 1959 to 1962 while a high school student, called her disorganized and inconsistent. He told how Nienstedt first unexpectedly rewarded him with two pay raises for actions he took to keep students orderly and later suddenly fired him for reasons he never fully comprehended. Employees knew that it was important to keep children and students quiet—and out of her way as much as possible. Her impatience with small children was legend.

Employees also described Nienstedt as a loner. She had some strong interests but few friends. After she finished renovating the library building in her first five or six years, she bought a home in Coralville and turned her sometimes ferocious energies toward the house. She traveled a lot, attending professional library meetings at all levels, state, regional, and national. In 1953 the American Library Association appointed her its representative to the US/UNESCO Committee and she attended the Fourth National Conference of the United States Commission for UNESCO.

Several employees and colleagues commented on her pet bird. One said it was a cockatoo, another said parakeet, and a third thought it was a canary, but all agreed that she would sometimes bring it to work where it would sit on her shoulder.[7] When she went across the state to library meetings the bird in its cage went along. Once it flew cageless around the inside of a car that carried six librarians to their destination, and Nienstedt would often be forced to leave meetings early "because of the bird."

Ex-reporter Nienstedt wrote regularly for publication in her first years at the library. She continued the newspaper column that Gordon had written since 1937 with hardly a lapse in the weekly schedule. The content changed, however, from Gordon's wide variety of book, reading, and library topics, to a sometimes deadly recital about new books at the library. Her writing style, like her articles in the *Library Journal,* was lively and probably more interesting when read once a week. She wrote these columns to harmonize with the collection development plan she sold to the board in her first few months at the library. She obviously wanted to demonstrate that the library had more than popular fiction and works of classic literature, history, and ideas. While new serious titles by major writers and thinkers were included in her columns, she looked for the practical and useful in an attempt to attract a broader range of the community into the library. Subjects like child care (a review of Benjamin Spock's *Common Sense Book of Baby and Child Care* appeared in her very first column), gardening, home planning and interior design, cooking, bridge, dog training, bird guides, wedding planning, insurance, and income tax received a lot of attention along with the "bigger" topics like world affairs, atomic energy, and the history of World War II. She frequently urged people to call or come in to reserve books mentioned but also noted that mysteries, Westerns, and "light fiction" were not eligible for the reserve service. A five-column headline over one of her annotated lists in 1950 probably pleased Nienstedt. It illustrated her efforts to attract new, especially male, library users: "Books on Hunting, Movie Equipment, Investments Available at the Library."

The only Nienstedt articles published by national library journals before, during, or after her Iowa City years appeared in 1949 and 1950. In 1949, *Wilson Library Bulletin* published a short Nienstedt article entitled "No Bookworms." As in her later articles, she took the occasion to point with pride to a successful library program, the type of narrative known in the library world as "How I Run My Library Good." In this case she described a children's summer reading program with very worthy objectives: luring reluctant readers into the program and encouraging eager readers to read difficult materials rather than hurrying through books to get awards for the highest numbers.

An article on public libraries written by University of Iowa Library director Ralph Ellsworth that appeared in the December 1949 issue of *Library Journal* may have caused her to write her two 1950 entries, "Termites" and "For Your Listening Comfort." She first wrote a letter in response to the Ellsworth article. It appeared six weeks later and preceded by several months both her commentary on termites and the budget in June 1950 and her description of developing the music room in December of the same year.

Ellsworth, "whose name is synonymous with modern library building planning in the United States," according to the biographical notes published with the article, had been director of university libraries in Iowa City since 1943 and was the principal planner for the university main library then under construction. This article, however, was about public libraries and scolded them for dingy old buildings and old-fashioned collections: "smoldering classics . . . dead novels of yesterday, and its lively but empty stories of today." He believed they were completely unprepared to serve the modern, postwar society of the 1950s, tied to print-only collections, with oppressive librarians demanding quiet and order from their users. The very serious questions to which citizens are seeking answers, he wrote, require serious materials not regularly found in the public libraries of small-town America. The nation needs comprehensive adult education programs and facilities, he said, but the public library "cannot lead because it lacks the manpower, materials, and community prestige." He then postulated a library-community learning center, built near schools and with space for parking and expansion, which would bring together a variety of formats; provide community meeting, group discussion, and individual study rooms; and support facilities for watching film or television and listening to music. In these rooms, he wrote, "Committees could meet and study clubs could plan, refresher courses for doctors and dentists and firemen and lawyers could be held," with the expert on hand or available via television and radio. All persons would use the building, "not just pleasure readers and school children . . . and each reader should have a place where he can work in quiet and comfort." He charged architects to design and communities to build such modern libraries. He warned that utility was in and old-style monumentality was out. Ending with the same phrase as the title of the article, he said the building must be "As Modern in Appearance as the Best Store in Town."[8]

Nienstedt, as the local public librarian in Ellsworth's home community, took many of his complaints personally. "I take violent exception to the article by my neighbor . . . [and] I feel justified in making my reply public, because he might normally be expected to have drawn his observations in part from the nearest public library . . . which I administer."

Contemporaries of Ellsworth and Nienstedt believe it is doubtful that Ellsworth knew much about the current status of facilities and services at ICPL when he gave the talk on which the article was based to the Kansas Library Association. And while the article addressed some of same issues Nienstedt had been struggling with at ICPL, it was obviously meant as a critique of public libraries everywhere.

Nienstedt had already taken some of the steps that Ellsworth recommended. She had made less fiction and more serious collections one of her first priorities; she was, at the very moment the article appeared, planning the music listening room (although she sacrificed a community meeting room—one of Ellsworth's basics—to do so); she had convinced the board and the city to fund major improvements to the building, including the introduction of comfortable lounge furniture, first into the reading rooms and later as an important feature of the music room. The first two paragraphs of the music room story ("For Your Listening Comfort") describe the positive reactions she received from the public for the straight chairs with padded seats and the leather easy chairs she had added to the public reading rooms. "They expressed what we suspected: only avid bookworms and students are willing to endure the conventional wooden chairs for very long."

Complicating her efforts at improving the library and its collection, the university's postwar growth in enrollment had dumped hundreds of students into her reading rooms. The crowding was particularly acute because the university had yet to open its first central library. These conditions made Ellsworth's comment that only in college and university libraries and in the best high schools do you find the "humming vitality" that almost all public libraries lack harder to swallow.

So, feeling in part wrongly accused and in part outraged at the imposition the university's lack of a proper general and undergraduate library placed on her operations, Nienstedt lashed out. She claimed that the impetus for public library development was the same in 1950 as it was seventy-five years ago—"to provide adult education for those the universities have too long ignored: the adults too poor, or even too dumb, to brave the smug intellectual superiority which not infrequently pervades so-called halls of learning!"

Next she took a swipe at the long delay of Iowa and the university in finding funds for a central library. "In my observation, there are two reasons why some universities are now building fine new libraries. They have built all the stadia, classrooms, radio stations and unions they need! What university with a fine new library doesn't also have a big enough field house to build the library inside it?"

She pointed out that "smoldering classics" are asked for by university students because some professors still assign them. She agreed that the "lively but empty stories" are sometimes hard to spend money on, but "one can't start a child eating steak before he develops teeth! The university libraries may blissfully concentrate on buying steak, only when the public libraries afford some pablum for the prospective steak eaters of the future." She said she had seen many who came to get their pablum, "and wouldn't have come if we didn't have any," who have developed "some intellectual teeth, and like a more substantial intellectual diet of the sort Mr. Ellsworth might approve."

Finally, she challenged Ellsworth to "come out of your ivory tower . . . and find out something about the tax situation of the average American town." She explained that public libraries cannot expect to build new buildings "until their towns have adequate police and fire equipment and enough schools. . . . While Mr. Ellsworth is building his fine new library, the city of Iowa City is buying fire trucks and equipment to protect it."

These two Iowa City librarians obviously needed to sit down together and talk, as Nienstedt recognized when she closed with the statement that disunity within the library profession "clearly stems from a lack of information and interest in the problems of each other."[9] It is possible that the two substantial articles that she submitted to *Library Journal* in the next few months were her attempt to demonstrate to her colleagues that in year five of the Atomic Age her library was not one of the hopelessly backward and "dingy old buildings" that Ellsworth, as a library planner, used as a backdrop for his vision of the design of future public libraries.

By any standard, Nienstedt had accomplished a lot in her first five years: a vastly improved financial position, a new direction for the collection, a building renovated and repaired after many years of neglect. She fought for improved benefits, salaries, and training for her enlarged staff, raised educational requirements, and actively recruited trained librarians in a very tough market. She improved library services and operations by establishing collections in all elementary schools, by starting a rental collection of popular fiction, by adding a music room and loaning music recordings, by acquiring projected books (books on film projected onto the ceiling) and projectors to loan to homebound readers. She partially dealt with an almost overwhelming number of university students by getting the board to institute fees for their use of the library. She kept the library visible in the community and throughout the state with her weekly newspaper columns, written regularly through 1952, her articles in both state and national journals, and her participation in professional library groups. She hosted the Iowa Library Association annual conference in 1951 and appeared as a speaker there and at Wisconsin and Kansas library meetings.

She also had some remarkable luck. She succeeded in getting the annual budget raised to a more reasonable level just before the switch in municipal form of government brought in a professional city manager who blocked her access to city elected officials and gave her tighter guidelines for budget preparation and control of nontax funds. Just as she was dreaming about starting a music room, the unexpected Brubaker gift gave her and the board the means to carry it out in a style beyond their greatest dreams.

Adding On, 1946–1963

Looking for a Mission

Something evidently happened in 1952 or 1953 to slow down Nienstedt's rush of activity and accomplishment. For the next several years she literally dropped out of sight. Her newspaper column became infrequent and then stopped altogether. After full and useful reports sent to the Iowa Library Commission through 1953, she failed to even return the forms in 1954, 1955, 1957, 1958, and 1961. Iowa City was the only library in its class (population of 10,000 or more) with no reports at the state library for these years. Her regular news items about ICPL sent to the library commission's quarterly journal ceased with the 1953 issues. She brought fewer projects to the board—mostly personnel appointments, equipment purchases, and building repairs—and the board's regular monthly meetings decreased to only seven or eight a year.

Nienstedt rebuffed an offer by the state librarian in 1956 to have ICPL participate in a library-county extension program even though it would have provided the library with funds from the first federal library legislation, the Library Services Act of 1956. The state librarian made a presentation to the ICPL board, but state officials later confirmed that Nienstedt showed no interest and did not encourage the board to respond. (This federal program later funded the Seven Rivers Library System started in 1964 by Iowa City Public Library director Sallie Helm. See chapter 8.)

Several jurisdictions, organizations, and even a business inquired about contracting with ICPL for services between 1953 and 1958—Coralville schools (they didn't merge with Iowa City schools until 1966), Mercy Hospital, Procter and Gamble, Lone Tree schools, Johnson County schools, and Solon—but there are no records of contracts or agreements. Sometimes the board offered a rate for service (usually equal in millage to what ICPL was currently receiving) but it was generally more than the group wished or could afford to pay. The number of inquiries, if nothing else, was indicative of a strong interest in library service. In contrast to Jessie Gordon, Nienstedt displayed little concern for serving those not in the library's primary service area.

Nienstedt seemed to be in some kind of personal slump, or just overwhelmed by the burgeoning library needs of Iowa City, but it was also not a happy time for public libraries generally. Ellsworth had been biting in his criticism, but not far off the mark about the condition generally of public libraries. The greatest need was for stronger financial support from all levels of government including, in the postwar period, the notion of federal aid to libraries. Benjamin Fine in a *New York Times* editorial in 1953 reviewed the somewhat bleak picture of public libraries in the United States, describing them as in a deplorable condition. Over 24 million people had no access to library service of any kind, with one out of six counties devoid of public libraries. Only three states met the American Library

211

Association minimum standards in terms of money spent for library services. Echoing Ellsworth, Librarian of Congress Luther Evans declared, "Most of our existing libraries are small, substandard institutions, so poor in materials and staff that their potential for community service is largely unrealized." Iowa City was well above these conditions, spending a healthy $1.38 per capita in 1953 when the ALA standard was $1.50 and the national median was about 80 cents, but Nienstedt and the board could identify with the finding that the shortage of trained personnel was one of the major difficulties facing public libraries. Increasing salaries in order to attract better personnel was cited as the most pressing need of public libraries in at least one-quarter of the states.

It seems to have been a classic dilemma. Libraries were bypassed because of their failure to have up-to-date materials and adequate hours of service. Therefore adequate support was withheld. Chronic underfunding kept them from improving their services and modernizing their buildings and collections so the reputation of public libraries sank even lower.

This physical and financial squeeze followed a psychological low point for public libraries following the publication of the Public Library Inquiry in 1949. During the forties the public library community had attempted to plan an expanded role for libraries. The Public Library Inquiry,[10] the most extensive study of public libraries every conducted, was to provide recommendations on how to make libraries more effective educational institutions. The library community felt that citizens needed help dealing with the many taxing problems facing American society since the war—issues related to the United States as a world power, atomic weapons and atomic energy, the menace of communism, industrial relations, and civil rights. A new, more complex world required a new level of intellectual and political sophistication.

Once again, as in the Progressive Era, after World War I, and during the Great Depression, public libraries hoped to become, in addition to an important institution for the student and child, one of the key educational organizations for strengthening the citizens of this democratic society—"to make the public library the instrument of popular education . . . [librarians] devoutly and fervently believed it could be."[11]

As Patrick Williams has written in his long essay on the public library, "The findings and recommendations of the inquiry had a profound and lasting impact on the library community." Librarians were expecting instructions on how to proceed; they received a recommendation that their goals should be abandoned. They were told the public library was not the institution to inform the masses.

Berelson's *The Library's Public*, an extensive 1949 investigation of library users and the use of mass media and one of the essential reports from the Public Library Inquiry, found that libraries attracted the smallest audience of any of the major media. While only 25 to 30 percent of Americans read at least one book a month, half saw a motion picture at least every two weeks and 90 percent read a newspaper and listened to the radio almost daily. Of the books read by American adults, only one-fourth were supplied by libraries.

About 18 percent of adults used their public library once a year, 10 percent once a month. That 10 percent and the 33 percent of children who came that frequently "might be considered the real users of the public library," Berelson reported. Twenty percent of users borrowed 70 percent of the books. Of all books borrowed, half were juvenile, about two-thirds fiction. Nonfiction borrowing and use of reference services was concentrated among a small group of students and well-educated adults.

In findings that have been reaffirmed again and again since the study, the higher the level of education, the more apt a person is to use libraries, women use libraries more than men, middle class more than upper and lower economic classes, young more than older, white more than black. Other findings: New books circulated more than old, few used the catalog or asked a librarian for assistance either for information or for help in selecting books, libraries primarily served opinion and community leaders, most people think libraries are "a fine thing to have" for others to use. Ninety-four percent felt it would make either "a great deal" or "quite a bit" of difference if there was no library in their community, but at the same time 61 percent said it would make "not much" difference to them personally.

The recommendations of the report were simple. Public libraries could not contribute much to the enlightenment of the masses because the majority of the public did not use the library and probably could not be attracted to the library for strictly educational and self-improvement purposes. The library should cease providing light fiction because it serves no acceptable social ends and should concentrate on improving services to those relatively few people who make "serious" use of library materials. Libraries of the future, the report added, will be most affected by changing communication technology and increasing levels of education among their users and potential users. Other than reporting data about library use, the inquiry did not address the impact of public libraries on children.

The Public Library Inquiry was discussed for many years within the library community before it was finally dropped publicly, then set aside and generally forgotten. Every astute public librarian knew you could go too far in reducing the ephemeral on library shelves. Readers of "light fiction and bestsellers" and parents of school-aged children created the public voice that helped get local budgets adopted, and too strong a public vow to be only an educational institution for informal adult education would doom the library to failure. Libraries spent the rest of the 1950s and the early 1960s looking for a new way to articulate their mission. They would finally find it under the rubrics of information services, recreational reading, and the public's right to know.

A follower of professional library literature and active in library organizations at all levels, Nienstedt had to be very aware of the debate over the inquiry's findings and reports. Serving the serious adult user seemed to be the goal of Nienstedt's first efforts at ICPL—light fiction to the rental shelf, purchase and promotion of nonfiction titles to broaden the user groups—but these actions actually came before the publication of the first report in 1949. Her lack of activity in the middle of the decade parallels the rudderless public library community of this period, looking for ways to survive following the tidal wave of the inquiry's recommendations. And there was another tidal wave coming her way—in the form of children and young people.

The Pressure to Expand

Nienstedt tended to translate community demands on the library into facility needs, and the old Carnegie continued to challenge her. The termites returned briefly to the children's department in 1953. The roof needed major repairs in 1954 and 1955. In 1956 she converted the boiler from coal to gas, eliminating the biennial need to clean or paint over the residue left from burning coal. But mostly she bought shelving, tables, and chairs to squeeze into every possible corner, and agonized with the library board over the eroding space for everything.

When Nienstedt had arrived in 1946 the library owned 30,000 books, just 10,000 more than the total in 1920. By 1956, in ten years, the collection reached 59,000, a major increase in terms of space, but still only two books per capita. The population was increasing as fast as Nienstedt could add books.

In 1955, postwar babies began reaching library age daily. First the children's room filled up, and then the demand for materials for that new library category, "young adults," was heard. Every night the reading rooms filled with young people from the junior highs and high schools. The noise and bustle of the younger students discouraged the few remaining university students using the public library. This group, for the most part, had moved to the university main library when it opened in 1951.

Perhaps Nienstedt's mid-decade slump can also be credited to the library's failure to significantly increase anything but use by children, coming in the throng now recognized as the baby boom. The city had made all of the remaining block east along College Street into a parking lot, buying the old Koser homestead next door for $25,000 in 1951 (three times Mr. Koser's price for the library site in 1902). Night and day it was easy to "take the kids to the library." These are the years when Nienstedt frequently failed to file reports, but if her isolated 1956 statistics are accurate, 58 percent of the loans were going to children. Children were not Nienstedt's clients of choice, but they would prove to be her principal argument and her principal reason for advocating the expansion of library facilities.

The pressures on the services and the space of the small 1904 Carnegie library continued to build. When the library opened in 1904, fewer than 8,500 people lived in Iowa City, plus about 1,800 university students. By 1960 university students were included in the count of 33,400 residents in the decennial census, a threefold increase over 1904, but the bulk of the growth occurred after 1940. The library had about 12,000 more Iowa Citians to serve—most of them students of all ages—than when Nienstedt arrived in 1946.

In early 1957, Nienstedt, perhaps for the first time, publicly addressed the need for more space. The *Press-Citizen* coverage of her 1956 annual report included her recommendation to the library board that "attention be given to the need for an addition to the library building." She cited record-breaking circulation of 165,000 in 1956, "all done from the main building" (as opposed to the years before 1954 when loans from school library stations were included in the yearly totals), and reported that the library was issuing new cards at the rate of five hundred every four months.

In this same report Nienstedt also made claims about the increase in adult use of the nonfiction collection, the collection she had been working to improve for ten years. According to the newspaper report, Nienstedt attributed growth in use of the library by adults to her year-by-year improvement of the nonfiction collection. Annual reports that she and Gordon filed with the State Library Commission, however, do not support her assertion. From 1928 through 1946 between 20,000 and 30,000 nonfiction volumes had been loaned to adults, high school and above. (Those below tenth grade or the age of fifteen were not allowed to use the general nonfiction collection until 1962.) After 1946, annual use of the adult nonfiction collection fell below 20,000, as low as 16,000 in 1949, and records show it did not push above 20,000 until 1956. Indeed, all loans to adults dropped during the Nienstedt years and only the enormous growth in student use—first by serving all elementary schools, next by the mounting university enrollment, and then by an exploding school population—kept the library from continuing to fade in popularity since the peak years of the mid-1930s.

No space remained for the books and seating needed to serve the many youngsters crowding into the building. *Press-Citizen* managing editor Edwin Green was a library trustee and gave library needs steady coverage after 1957. Pictures of children stretching to reach books on shelves too high for them, bookcases stuffed to the maximum, and young people sitting two to a seat in the forty-seat reference room appeared in 1958 under headlines such as "City Library Bursting at the Seams," "55-Year Old Building No Longer Adequate," and "Space at Premium in Library Now." Accompanying articles described diminishing services—the summer reading program was discontinued after 1958, the music room was closed, and a policy of limiting the purchase of new children's books only to replace those to be discarded was established.

During this same year the majority of the trustees seemed to accept the idea of expanding the library. At several meetings they discussed financing methods, especially the pay-as-you-go three-quarter-mill levy used by the library in 1949-53 to revitalize the Carnegie building. They also addressed the basic question of whether to add to the Carnegie or to build a completely new facility. Typical Carnegie buildings were notorious for the difficulties encountered in planning additions due to their second-floor entrances, but local real estate authorities told the board that the building would have little resale value. This opinion seemed to convince the trustees to try for an addition. Later they would use the slogan, "We need a new wing," under a drawing of a sad-faced bird with only one wing.

In early 1959 the library board and the city council held their first joint meeting since 1902, when the issue had been how to fund the building if Carnegie did not agree to the extra $10,000. On April 29, 1959, library trustees Marge Rehder, Edwin Green, Bill Jackson, Earl Snyder, and Board President Kenneth MacDonald met with Mayor Philip Morgan and councilors Thelma Lewis, Louis Loria, and Ray Thornberry to discuss the Carnegie's future. Librarian Nienstedt and city manager Peter Roan also attended.

Nienstedt presented a survey of library growth and prospects for future growth with special emphasis on the problems faced "in continuing service in a building . . . built in 1903 for an estimated twenty years of use." The attendees agreed that there was an urgent need "for additional quarters, and that an addition to the building which would double the present size was indicated."

How to finance a library addition, at a cost of perhaps $150,000 to $200,000, turned out to be the main agenda for the group. The mayor suggested that it might be easier to get the money by accumulating funds in the city's regular budget rather than by presenting the community with a bond issue. Other councilors also expressed concern about financing, citing the large and recent school building program which they felt had "left taxpayers highly resistant to bond issues of any kind." (After four highly successful referendums for new and expanded schools between 1949 and 1955, the school board had trouble getting approval for South East Junior High. Three times voters failed to give the proposal the required 60 percent approval. In 1958, just a year before the library-council meeting, a revised proposal received 64 percent approval after advocates went door-to-door to explain the need.) The trustees and councilors also noted that the recreation commission might soon be mounting a campaign for a new building. The community had been without a centralized recreation facility since the old Iowa City Community Building burned in 1952.

By the end of the meeting the council members present had all endorsed the need for a library addition. They were undecided about the best method of financing the addition, but the mayor promised to approve a supplement to the library's 1959 operating budget to provide architectural fees for preliminary plans.

Encouraged by their session with the council, board members, at their very next meeting, approved a 1960 budget request developed by Nienstedt. (There is little evidence of working committees in these years except for the very active personnel committee.) They accepted her proposal to ask for the full amount allowed by the law: three mills for operations and three-quarters of a mill for the building levy, with the suggestion than any money left from the operations fund be added to the building fund. Sparked by city manager Roan's information that the recently abandoned fire station on Gilbert Street was available, Nienstedt also proposed that the children's room be moved to that site until new space was available. Board members disagreed, saying that the move and the separate operation would use money better saved for the building fund. The council notified the board in September that the city would begin to levy the three-quarter mill in 1960 for a library building fund, but the library received only a nominal increase in operating funds, not the more than 30 percent increase that the full three mills would have provided.

The council also refused to make the requested exception of allowing Dr. Kenneth MacDonald to remain a trustee after his move to a new home outside the city limits. MacDonald, the only member of the university medical faculty ever to give extended service on the library board, left his six-year post as president on July 1. Marge Rehder, the spouse of a university administrator and already a seven-year veteran on the board, took on the presidency for the next two years.

Despite the loss of MacDonald, the momentum for the building addition was already underway. With the funds to select and engage an architect in hand, the group wasted no time in getting started. In the next few months members interviewed three firms: Henry Fisk of Iowa City who had designed the music room for the library in 1950, Savage and Ver Ploeg of Des Moines, and a third firm identified only as Architects Associated. The trustees made their final decision in February of 1960. Some trustees cast votes for each firm, but after several ballots they settled on Savage and Ver Ploeg. Started in 1953, Savage and Ver Ploeg was a relatively young firm and this project would be its first library and first work in eastern Iowa.[12]

The trustees recognized Nienstedt's role in developing ideas for the new addition when they gave her expenses and permission to travel to nearby libraries for building ideas. Several communities in Iowa had already enlarged their original Carnegie buildings by 1960. Ames had added space in 1937 and more recently Dubuque, Newton, Cedar Rapids, Council Bluffs, Burlington, and Davenport had expanded. Ottumwa had renovated and built a branch; Keokuk was building a new library.

Planning the Addition

The closest thing to a statement of building needs came from Nienstedt and paralleled her comments of earlier years. In a 1960 *Press-Citizen*, after reciting once again the stories of overflowing shelves, young adult collections squeezed into a former office, and students sitting two to a chair, the paper quoted Nienstedt directly:

> It would seem to me that a new wing, approximately the same size as the present building, which would contain a children's room and a young adult's room on the main floor and a large room for public meeting on the ground floor plus additional stack space for books and with the library entrance inside the building instead of outside as at present, would take care of Iowa City's present library needs and provide for necessary expansion for some 30 years to come.

Earlier she had argued that the original Carnegie was meant to last only twenty years, thus falling into the pattern of many who campaign for new facilities: Underestimate the planned useful life of the previous building and overestimate the probable useful life of the proposed one. Taxpayers resisting a new expenditure take an opposite tack. They always claim they were promised that the current facility would last through five generations, but do not want to pay for more than enough space in the proposed one to take it through the next ten or fifteen years.

With a city parking lot starting just a few feet east of the back wall of the library, one of the first tasks of the library board was to negotiate with the city about space for the proposed addition. In the summer of 1961 trustee and insurance agent Dale Welt met with city manager Roan to discuss the approximately fifty feet the preliminary plans indicated the library would need. He reported back that this fifty-foot strip (reduced later to forty-six feet) would cost the library $30,000. City officials figured the cost to remove twenty-four parking meters at $1,250 each. The space needed by the library was part of the $25,000 Koser property the city acquired in 1951, and the income from the parking meters was paying for the land and improvements. State law required that the parking fund be reimbursed.

According to the architect's preliminary plans, the extra 46 feet would be used to build a wraparound wing approximately 64 feet by 128 feet, extending from College Street on the south to the alley connecting Linn and Gilbert streets on the north. This two-level rectangle would incorporate the complete curved stack area within its dimensions, thus extending only forty feet beyond the Carnegie on the east. After subtracting the square footage of the half-circle stack area from each level, the addition would produce about 14,000 square feet of new space for a total completed building of over 22,000 square feet. The preliminary plans also called for, in effect, turning the building around. The old entrance on Linn would be closed, the steps removed, and the old foyer turned into a new stack area between the two reading rooms. The main entrance would be on College with a gentle ramp leading up to a recessed front entrance. This entrance reversal is rare among Carnegie additions, and, according to architect Ver Ploeg, created the multilevel problems at the main door and beyond.[13]

The trustees had their first major review of the plans in the fall of 1961, now more than two years since the 1959 meeting with the city council. The membership of both groups had changed. July 1961 marked a major turnover of library trustees: Five board positions changed hands, causing some loss in continuity for the building program, but adding several energetic individuals ready to take on the responsibility of completing the project. New members Myrtle Aydelotte, Karl Kammermeyer, Anita Mercer, Ardith Melloh, and William Tucker joined 1959 appointees B.W. "Bud" Sheridan and Dale Welt plus ten-year veteran Edwin Green. These eight trustees would be the major players in the campaign for and the construction of the 1962-63 library addition. Sheridan took on the presidency for the next two years, a job that included an endless stream of decisions and paperwork related to the construction project. For example, it was his task to invest the building funds that were accruing to the library at the rate of $22,000 a year.

The October 1961 review of the plans with the architect introduced the new trustees to the project. Additional reviews were held in January and February of 1962, after which the plans were accepted and revealed to the public in a newspaper story on February 28, 1962. The building's main features were much as Nienstedt had described them in 1960. The children's room, at over 2,800 square feet, accounted for nearly one-fourth of the new area. One of the two old reading rooms was turned into a young adult department which would house the growing young adult collection and provide reading and study space for junior high and high school students. The other became the adult reading room with lounge furniture, current issues of periodicals and newspapers, and some display space. The semicircle stack area was labeled "browsing" and became a balcony overlooking the new main floor. Beneath the children's room was a thirty-five-by-fifty-foot public meeting room and below the new main floor was a large periodical storage room and an almost-as-large children's story hour room, said to be the first such room in the state. All in all, the only nod to adult needs was an exclusive reading room, access to a larger reference room (an area that would be dominated by high school and university students through the 1960s), and provision for larger collections. Both the old and the new stacks would now be two stories high, creating a low-ceilinged, windowless attic that allowed quiet browsing in the adult nonfiction collection and, for two or three readers, lounge chairs secluded from the rest of library traffic.

Total square footage was not given but the announcement said the overall building size, "including both the old structure and the addition, has been planned to afford 150 percent more space." Adding 14,000 square feet to an 8,000-square-foot building was more than a 150 percent increase, but this phrase would be repeated again and again. Another but less obvious inaccuracy was the description of the new entrance.

> . . . in an attempt to give improved service to people of advancing years and enable them to enter the library without climbing steps . . . the library entrance has been planned with a ramp to provide easy access to the main service area where most patrons will be. [They can be] served in the main area for all essential services without the need to climb to the upper levels.[14]

The plans published with this February 1962 story clearly show that the visitor entering the ten-by-twelve-foot foyer inside the entrance doors at the end of the long outside ramp would find eight steps. The visitor had to climb these eight steps to get to the "main service area," the card catalog, and the materials in the reference collection and then climb eight to twenty-eight more steps to reach the adult, children's, and young adult collections. Also, from both the ramped main entrance or the ground-level secondary entrance on Linn Street, visitors had to take several steps down in order to attend events in the meeting room or the story hour room. An architectural study of the completed building made in 1978 revealed that the structure had a gross building area of over 25,000 square feet, but so much space was used for stairs and other building circulation that the "net usable functional area" was only 14,000 square feet.[15] The seven levels of the proposed building did not appear to be a concern to either the planners or the voters, but they would bedevil both staff and library users for the next twenty years.

The construction cost of the 14,000-square-foot addition plus some renovation of the old building was now estimated at $235,000. This included a new boiler and a twenty-ton air conditioner for the new section. The architect estimated that constructing the addition in phases would add at least 5 percent to the cost and that general costs would increase from 2 to 3 percent for each year of delay.

At this juncture, with the costs and future costs laid out before them, trustee Tucker worked to dissuade the board from waiting to begin construction until the funds had been accumulated. He argued that with rapidly rising construction costs, it could take ten to twelve years to stockpile enough funds to pay for the type of building they currently had on the drawing board. The three-quarter mill levy, he said, could be used to pay off the bonds purchased following a successful referendum. The community would have the building ten years sooner, the cost of interest on the bonds would be known and fixed, and taxpayers would pay no more for the library addition than they were already paying with the annual building fund levy. Tucker claimed the arguments favored building the addition now, and a bond issue that did not raise taxes should pass easily despite the 60 percent voter approval required.

The board was persuaded by Tucker's analysis and decided it was time to meet again with the city council. In preparation for a joint meeting the board compiled a list of building addition costs. With furnishings, equipment, land, and architects' fees added to construction costs, the project totaled $332,000, almost $300,000 more than was spent fifty-nine years earlier for the original building. Subtracting the $67,000 that had accrued from three years of collecting the building levy, the board agreed to ask the council to support a bond issue of $265,000.

Trustees discussed two other issues which had concerned them at a special meeting in preparation for their discussion with the city council. Tucker had attended a meeting of the Parks and Recreation Commission to explore the commission's plans for a bond issue for a new building. While worried that they might be seen as competing projects, Tucker counseled that both buildings were needed and each should proceed at its own pace. On the second issue, Tucker warned the board that city council members might require that a public hearing be held on a bond issue before they would approve submitting the question to the voters, or that they may ask for a petition. A petition would require signatures from 25 percent of the voters at the last election, and would take time and volunteers.

Thelma Lewis was the only person remaining from the council who met with the library board in 1959. Civil engineer Dorr Hudson and university personnel director Fred Doderer, both candidates approved by the Council-Manager Association (CMA), had won seats on the council in 1959. In a close race with a record voter turnout in November of 1961, real estate broker William Maas and house mover Max Yocum were elected as independent candidates, and CMA founder and former Mayor Lewis was reelected. Maas and Yocum were the first councilors not endorsed by the CMA to be elected since the adoption of council-manager government in 1950.[16] Lewis, Doderer, and Hudson maintained a CMA majority, but there had been many 3-2 votes since Maas and Yocum took office in January, and their position on a library addition was unknown.

On March 23, 1962, William Maas and Max Yocum toured the library in preparation for a joint library board-city council meeting to follow. Exactly what happened at this meeting was never recorded. Just four days later Mayor Hudson died of a massive brain hemorrhage, and on April 3, city manager Peter Roan resigned. For a time, city government was in turmoil and the minutes for the council-library meeting were evidently forgotten. The four remaining councilors had to elect a replacement for Hudson and start the search for a new city manager. Worried about a 2-2 vote, the library board was advised that the council resolution to put the library issue on the June 4 primary election ballot should be postponed until the new council member was appointed. Similar to the situation that delayed the city council's decision over the library site in 1902 while a replacement for a deceased alderman was elected, the library board's request was put on hold.

During this delay, trustee Tucker prepared a long memo requested by the late mayor which outlined the arguments for a bond issue versus waiting for the building fund to accrue. It detailed the estimated increases to library operating costs. Through narrative and charts, Tucker outlined the advantages of bonding the debt and building the library addition promptly. According to his figures, even with increased operating costs—estimated at $9,500 per year—it was cheaper over twenty years to build and pay back at 3 percent than to wait and be at the mercy of inflationary construction costs.

In April the council voted unanimously to appoint ex-mayor Leroy Mercer as Hudson's replacement. On May 8, after a one-week delay to investigate a minor legal aspect of the bond issue proposal and forgoing the possible public hearing and petition drive, the reconstituted council voted unanimously for the resolution approving the referendum vote. Its action on that day just met the deadline for getting the proposal on the June 4 primary election ballot.

The Campaign

The time available for a campaign had been shortened by the delay, but an optimistic library board planned and prepared the essential campaign activities. The board had agreed in Tucker's letter to the council to absorb all costs of the campaign and to take the responsibility for informing the electorate about the issues.

The trustees had been planning a Friends of the Library organization since the fall of 1961, and after some delay in finding an organizing chairman, former board president William R. Hart agreed to serve. In late May, I was one of many general library users and Iowa City parents who attended the only meeting of this group in the children's section of the old Carnegie basement. We were briefed on all aspects of the campaign including the costs and details of the proposed addition. With a late start, a relatively easy case to sell to the public, and a seventy-year-old retired trustee returned to serve the library one more time, neither a mandate nor a mission for the organization was outlined beyond the election. After June 4, the 1963 Friends never assembled again. Hart, former city attorney and longtime Democratic party chair, as well as a ten-year library board president, was very good at making politically sound and quotable statements, and the Friends of the Library title gave his remarks added force. In response to the pay-as-you-go plan which would continue if the bond issue failed, Hart said,

> If we fail to vote for this bond issue and wait until 1975 to build we shall be denying adequate library facilities to a whole generation of school children. In the thirteen or so years it would take to lay aside enough money for the addition, children who will be in kindergarten this year will be graduating from high school before the addition is built.

Once again, despite a continuing belief by librarians and core library supporters in the importance of the public library for the out-of-school adult and for the health and well-being of a democratic society, campaign rhetoric defaulted to the needs of children. In 1962 the library was still an institution for schoolchildren, students, and a minority of compulsive adult readers.

Trustee Myrtle Aydelotte headed the publicity committee for the campaign. As dean of the University of Iowa School of Nursing, Aydelotte was a skilled organizer and quickly appointed community women to take the message to Iowa City groups and organizations. Jessie Gordon, still active in Altrusa, agreed to work with women's service clubs. Jean Lloyd-Jones, soon to become a library trustee, wrote fact sheets and composed letters for parents, teachers, and business and professional people. The school board allowed letters to parents to be sent home in the hands of schoolchildren. Artist Ellie Simmons created the one-winged bird which symbolized the need for an addition to the library on campaign bookmarks and brochures.

The board and volunteer campaigners used one interesting fact to highlight the cost of public library service in Iowa City. First the fact sheets and newspaper articles noted that for the last sixty years, the only capital expense for taxpayers was the $8,500 for the site. Then they claimed that the total tax bill for fifty-six years of library service to a person paying taxes on an average home in Iowa City from 1904 through 1960 was about fifty dollars, or eighty-eight cents a year. They never mentioned, however, how much the twenty-three-year levy would cost the average taxpayer, and since the levy had already been in place for three years, it seems no one asked.

Few issues arose in the campaign and there was no organized opposition. The library claimed that the efficient design of the new plan would allow the current staff to operate the much enlarged facility, although its list of increased operating costs given to the city council projected a modest increase in staff. Expanded services were promised. The music room, closed and used as Nienstedt's office since before 1960, would be reopened, campaign spokesmen said, even though this would make it the only public service in the lower levels except for events in the meeting or story hour rooms. The drive-up window, designed to allow both the return and pick-up of materials, was touted as a unique feature, but there was no plan on how to staff the pick-up service nor was the service ever offered.

Campaign literature pointed out that parents and teachers would be able to select and check out materials from the children's department anytime, even though on weekdays no staff would be on duty in the room except from 3 to 6 p.m. Nienstedt hoped that children unaccompanied by parents would enter the library from the secondary entrance on Linn Street, climb the full flight of stairs that led directly to the children's room, and leave by the same route. Based on my personal observation at the time, Nienstedt designed the glass-paneled doors on the west wall of the children's room which led to the rest of the library to keep children out of adult areas as much as to provide a convenience for parents and teachers during daytime hours.

All the arguments for voting yes were summed up in one of the campaign slogans: "We need the library addition and we need it now. We're paying for it now. Let's build it now." And that was what the electorate thought, too. On June 4, 1962, over 80 percent of 3,661 voters pulled the "yes" lever, giving the issue one of the highest approval rates of any bond issue to date.[17] Only one precinct, Mann School, gave the issue less than the required 60 percent. Voters on the west side of town, voting at Lincoln School and the UI art building, favored the proposition by over 90 percent.

In a long editorial praising the wise vote of the Iowa City electorate, the *Press-Citizen* used Jacob Reizenstein's comment in the *Iowa City Republican* following the 1897 election to establish the library:

> The library tax was overwhelmingly carried. There was absolutely no politics whatever in the matter and the lovers of good citizenship and happy homes voted unanimously for it. Only a few mistaken voters opposed them.

Reizenstein died in 1961 at the age of ninety-three, but nobody would have cheered louder or longer about the prospects for a new era at the Iowa City Public Library.

Construction, Dedication, and Resignation

Things moved quickly after the successful vote. President Sheridan's term as trustee ended just twenty-six days later and the board elected Bill Tucker to the presidency. Tucker, a lawyer fresh from several years in the county attorney's office, including two years as the elected county attorney, exhibited leadership and contributed many ideas during the referendum campaign. He was a natural choice for the board.

Librarian Joyce Nienstedt watches as work begins on the library addition in the fall of 1962.

With a group of active bidders, the bonds sold readily. At 3.128 percent for twenty years, the interest would cost taxpayers $90,000 by the time the bonds matured in 1981. Few changes were made to the preliminary plans and the architects had the bid documents ready just eight weeks after the election. Five of the six bidders for the construction contract were Iowa City firms, with Frantz Construction Company submitting the lowest bid. When the winning construction, electrical, mechanical, and book stack contracts were added together, the total bid, at $203,574, was 13 percent or $31,400 below the estimate.

Thus there was a generous level of funds available and the library board could afford to make a few adjustments to the building program. From the board's decisions it is evident that the original budget had allowed very little to renovate the existing building, and that the plans for some of the new areas were bare bones. Also there is no evidence that the $53,000 budgeted for furniture and equipment was much more than a rough estimate, to be spent until it was gone. Meeting about every two weeks and working as a committee-of-the-whole rather than through committee assignments, the trustees gradually sifted through the many options and decided how to spend about $85,000—the $53,000 furniture and equipment budget plus the nearly $32,000 gained from the low bids. It was a process of investigating costs and alternatives for various options and then, as a group, coming to a decision.

The trustees spent a large share of their extra funds on the story hour room.

225

A Century of Stories

The add-ons were fairly basic: a west wall to enclose the room, acoustical ceiling tile and light fixtures, carpet, coatracks, and special wall paint to cover the raw

The new addition, seen here under construction, completely enclosed the east side of the original Carnegie building.

cement block. Another area that received major attention was the main floor of the existing building, especially the reading rooms and the area in between. The trustees approved vinyl floor coverings, acoustical ceiling tile, and new light fixtures, as well as renovation of the exterior parts of each room's fireplace. The women on the board took the initiative to furnish the staff room, first choosing a

stove and refrigerator, and later adding a sink unit with a disposal, lockers, and new lounge furniture. Plaster and floors were repaired in the old children's room, soon to become the library's major workroom. In addition to the story hour room, the carpet bid also included the librarian's office and boardroom. They upgraded the fixtures in the restroom of this office from white to aqua to match

the color scheme chosen for the drapes, carpet, and furniture fabric. The room was furnished with a couch and walnut desk, conference table, coffee tables, and built-in cabinets. After sixty years of librarians working from a very public ten-by-eight-foot cubicle—the architects turned the former librarian's office into a stairwell to the new second-level stacks—future librarians would find this four-hundred-square-foot office an oasis of comfort and privacy.

The original east wall of the Carnegie can be seen behind the check-out desk. The dumbwaiter to the left was used to send materials downstairs for sorting where another dumbwaiter carried books to the upper levels for reshelving.

The restrooms here and in the staff room were tiled and luxurious compared to the barely refurbished public restrooms left in a rather remote area of the basement of the existing building. Public restrooms were not yet a basic library service.

For the auditorium the board selected 120 handsome, comfortable, and sturdy folding chairs. Seemingly built to last forever, many are still in service in various city government departments. One change order to the construction contract added a concrete platform to the meeting room and upgraded the quality of the floor covering. Finally, the board ordered soffits in many parts of the lower levels to cover heating and water pipes along walkways and in restrooms.

Nienstedt was fairly invisible during the construction period, but obviously she was very busy scouting out information for the board on all these options, presenting price and other details for the trustees to chose from, and then following up on their decisions. While the minutes describe in some detail the many choices the board was making, both architect Ver Ploeg and trustee Rosalie Braverman believe that Nienstedt was the powerhouse behind the entire project. Few board members would contradict her or override her recommendations, according to Braverman.

The paperwork generated by the administration of several contracts and the purchase of mounds of equipment and furniture was a full-time job. At one point the board authorized Nienstedt to hire some hourly employees to help relieve the workload brought on by the construction activities, but the bulk of the work fell to the librarian and the board president. No employee was assigned to clerical and accounting duties until after Nienstedt's administration. She reviewed the invoices, prepared the checks for the board president's signature, and kept the ledgers on all the building funds. Also, the library board was responsible for handling the more than $300,000 that had to be put into short- and long-term investments and paced so that cash was available when payments to contractors were due. Most of the trustees had the pleasure of shopping and spending and choosing, but Nienstedt and presidents Sheridan and Tucker had to establish procedures and records to ensure secure and intelligent handling of funds. Perhaps because of the heavy clerical work involved (and the city did not have a separate finance department until 1970), this was one financial project the city was content to let the library handle on its own.

Several times in 1963 the board took time out from its many decisions about library furnishings, finishes, and equipment to address some policy issues related to services and facilities to be offered in the expanded building. The trustees planned to establish a charge for the use of the meeting room to cover janitorial and maintenance costs, and although this was discussed several times, no fee schedule was adopted through 1963. They established a separate library card for young people of junior high age. It was an "identification card" to use the adult nonfiction collection and the new young adult room where a much-enlarged

227

young adult fiction collection would be housed. While this collection included "many adult department titles," the announcement about the new card made it clear that there was no change in the policy that borrowers must be in ninth grade or fifteen years of age before using the adult fiction collection directly. Finally, as they watched the dollars poured into the construction and furnishing of the library mount, they raised the nonresident fee for the fifth time since Nienstedt had first suggested that it should apply to university students as well as county dwellers and residents of neighboring communities. When the new library opened, they agreed to charge all individual nonresidents seven dollars a year for an ICPL library card. About the same time, they again offered to give library service to any Johnson County jurisdiction for a levy of two mills on the community's assessed valuation, but, despite frequent inquiries, once more there were no cities or towns interested in paying the full cost of library service.

By late spring of 1963 the library needed to close down operations so that workmen could make major changes in the existing building. The library staff encouraged all card holders to check out materials for five to six weeks in order to reduce the number of books that had to be moved to their new locations. The newspaper ran pictures of empty shelves and reported that all circulation records were shattered. Both the *Press-Citizen* and the *Des Moines Register* quoted Nienstedt, "It's much easier to move a slip of paper telling where a book is than to move the book itself." The library closed on Memorial Day and hoped to reopen after July 4. Work took more than three months, however, and the library didn't reopen until September.

On November 10, 1963, on a Sunday afternoon during National Book Week, the library board held simple dedication ceremonies. Before a crowd of about three hundred, President Tucker presented the keys of the building "to recently retired Board President Bernard W. Sheridan under whose leadership the successful bond issue campaign and building erection took place." Tucker's large role was gracefully understated in the press release announcing the event, but the release noted that the building was "the largest public library edifice to have been constructed in Iowa since World War II."

Among the features of the new building that the press release writer (former newspaperwoman Nienstedt?) chose to highlight: a "browsing balcony," the greatly expanded children's room, an auditorium seating 120 people, a drive-up book return window, and enough additional shelving to hold a book collection of up to 150,000 volumes. "The charcoal brick and Indiana limestone building . . . is reached by a main entrance featuring a ramp rather than stairs," the release explained. The interior layout is credited to librarian Joyce Nienstedt who also designed the "unique" story hour room. "The tiers of carpeted steps, arranged in a quarter circle around the storyteller [with] special lighting focused on the storyteller somewhat in the fashion of a small theater . . . It is believed that the design is unique in present library buildings," the press release concludes.

One month later, in a letter to President Tucker on December 5, 1963, with copies to all board members, Nienstedt resigned her position effective the middle of January, 1964. She said that

The addition was dedicated on Sunday, November 10, 1963. The library's press release for the event said it was "the largest public library edifice to have been constructed in Iowa since World War II."

with the completion of the building program, the last in the goals "I had set up when I came here has been achieved, and I now feel that I can fairly consider my own future first, with no feeling of leaving things uncompleted." She had accepted a position as director of the public library in Tempe, Arizona. Some staff members believed she was asked to leave; others remember that she was very bitter just before she left, but no board member would say more than the library "needed new blood and they were happy to see her leave."

Hired to become Tempe's first "graduate librarian . . . to guide the [library's] expansion program," according to that library's January 1964 minutes, Nienstedt resigned after only three years at Tempe. Current library officials there could not provide much information about Nienstedt's years in Tempe, but one document shows that the library was still in "temporary quarters" in 1971.[18]

Nienstedt returned to her Coralville home in the fall of 1967, and although the Iowa City library board issued her a lifetime library card, to my knowledge she visited the library only once, sometime in the middle to late 1970s. She came, she told Hazel Westgate, on the request of a former ICPL employee who was visiting her. I was sitting at her beautiful walnut desk, and would have liked to have told her how much I enjoyed the office she had designed and furnished. She looked in my office door very briefly, taking no notice of me, and remarked to her friend that we still had the lovely drapes that she had selected.

Nienstedt was fifty-seven when she returned to Iowa City and perhaps sixty-five when she made her one visit to the library. To the best of my knowledge, she never worked again. She entered a nursing home in Cedar Rapids just a few years later. She died there in the early 1980s. Her eighteen years at ICPL was the primary library position of her career and the addition to the Carnegie her principal legacy. Her contributions to the library were major but mixed. Today she is re-membered more for the parakeet on her shoulder or the unsatisfactory Carnegie addition than for the many accomplishments of her early years.

[1] Lucile Davis spent three years as children's librarian and ten years as first assistant (1923-36). She was head librarian at Spencer, IA, Owatonna, MN, and Ottawa, IL, before spending fifteen years (1949-64) as director of the Clinton Public Library.

[2] Joyce Nienstedt, "Even the Termites Helped Improve the Budget," *Library Journal*, June 15, 1950, 1007-11. *Iowa Library Quarterly*, vol. 16, fall 1950.

[3] Joyce Nienstedt, "For Your Listening Comfort," *Library Journal*, December 15, 1950, 2113.

[4] Ibid., 2114.

[5] Marvin Weisbord, "A Public Library Discovers Music," *Music Journal*, July 1954, 6.

[6] Ibid., 8.

[7] An undated *Press-Citizen* clipping says it was a parakeet named Jackie and cites several phrases in the bird's vocabulary: "Let's read a book," "Hi, Sweetie," and "Parakeets can talk!" The cleverly written article appears to be a Nienstedt-authored press release.

[8] Ralph Ellsworth, "Appearance as Modern as the Best Store in Town," *Library Journal*, December 15, 1949, 1851-53.

[9] Joyce Nienstedt, "Public library buildings," in the letter column, "They Say," *Library Journal*, February 1, 1950, 130.

[10] The Public Library Inquiry was a $200,000 study financed by the Carnegie Corporation and conducted by the Social Science Research Council. Researchers were political scientists and University of Chicago Library School faculty. From the seven books and five reports published as parts of the final report, two were the most important: Bernard Berelson, *The Library's Public* (1949) and Robert D. Leigh, *The Public Library in the United States* (1950), both published by Columbia University Press.

[11] Williams, 66. I am indebted to Williams for his general discussion of the Public Library Inquiry.

[12] Interview with Stanley Ver Ploeg, October 15, 1996. Ver Ploeg was the project architect for the addition. He doesn't remember who, but assumes someone asked the firm to apply since this is one of the few jobs the firm has had outside of central Iowa.

[13] Interview with Ver Ploeg.

[14] *Press-Citizen*, February 28, 1962.

[15] Hansen Lind Meyer, P.C., *An Architectural and Engineering Study of the Existing Library Facility, Iowa City, Iowa.* Iowa City, 1978.

[16] The Council-Manager Association was formed in the late 1940s to lead the campaign to change the form of municipal government from mayor-council to council-manager. The new form was nonpartisan and after its approval, the association took on the job of identifying and backing candidates, a task formerly handled by the local political parties. The association faded and finally disbanded after the 1961 election and after the community's commitment to council-manager government seemed secure.

[17] In December 1962 the Recreation Commission took its building needs to the voters and received 88 percent approval for a $650,000 community recreation center. The building was built on the same site as the first such facility which was destroyed by fire in 1952. This vote may still hold the all-time approval rating for an Iowa City bond issue referendum.

[18] Correspondence with Donald Koozer, Tempe Public Library, August 25, 1995.

■ 8. Planting the Seeds: The Birth of a Modern Public Library, 1964–1969

There were many difference between the styles of Jessie Gordon and Joyce Nienstedt, but the library itself did not change dramatically over the forty-one years of their leadership. It remained a typical Midwestern small-town public library with somewhat better-than-average tax support and per capita use. Directors Sallie Helm (1964-68) and Mary Croteau (1968-70) would change all that. These two experienced and astute librarians showed the library board, the staff, and the community how to shape a first-class library capable of giving a full range of library services while cooperating with other libraries, agencies, and organizations to broaden the library's reach and effectiveness. Helm and Croteau set in motion a number of initiatives that would fundamentally change the library, and they influenced staff members and library trustees that served with them and after them.

Sallie Helm Moves Five Blocks East

Joyce Nienstedt's successor was already in Iowa City and facing the need to find another position when Nienstedt resigned. Helm had been on the staff of the University of Iowa Libraries since 1960. Although she had been promoted to the head of her department just a year after she arrived, she would soon be terminated because her husband, on the university music faculty, was about to receive tenure. Unrelated as these two events may seem, at that time it was the university librarian's unwritten policy to refuse employment to a librarian (usually a woman) whose spouse was a tenured faculty member. The librarian felt women in such positions might unduly influence the library's holdings in their spouses' fields and would join them for long vacations, professional meetings, and other academic opportunities to travel.

Helm had already spent three years as a member of the professional staff of the Dallas Public Library (1955-57) where she became head of a branch, then personnel director and head of reference services in a very short time. One university library staff member believes Helm would have applied for the ICPL position without the pressure from losing her university job. "Her abilities far exceeded the responsibilities of her position [at the university library]." Helm herself said she was considering attending law school, but "the directorship at ICPL sounded like too much fun to pass up."[1] She had been happy

Sallie Helm in 1964

working in a public library, she said, and was committed to the mission of the public library in American society. There were seven other applicants, but it didn't take the library board long to realize the talent that was available "just down the street."[2]

Born in Louisiana in 1931, Helm grew up in Crowville, and by 1955 had both a bachelor of arts and a master of library science degree from schools in that state plus four years experience as a teacher-librarian. She spent three years in Dallas while her husband earned an advanced degree, then one year at Wayne State College in Nebraska, and one year in Europe before coming to Iowa City in 1960.

Helm combined the strong interest in literature, art, music, and things cultural of the traditional librarian, with political savvy and aggressive and original ideas for change and improvement, all somewhat masked by her appearance: a very attractive, middle class, young matron. Full of endless exuberance and optimism, she could charm, use feminine wiles, or be tough and firm—whatever the occasion called for.

The thirty-three-year-old librarian reported to work on March 1, 1964, and, according to those who worked for her, immediately changed the environment of the library for the staff and the public. Dayle Hughes Tucker, whom Helm promptly promoted from the children's room to the position of office secretary, said, "It was a breath of fresh air when Sallie arrived. Her energy and enthusiasm inspired everyone—staff and library board. She asked what we thought about library operations, and she began holding staff meetings for the first time."[3]

At Helm's first board meeting she convinced the trustees to consider plans that would soon be formally proposed by the state library to provide, with the aid of federal funds, library service outside the city limits on a contractual and cooperative basis. After she planted the seed for the Seven Rivers Library System to follow, her list of eight immediate needs for daily library operations impressed the board, and they assigned her the task of assessing the financial status of the recent building project and producing a priority list of ways to use the unencumbered funds.

Finishing the Library Addition

One month later the trustees received a five-page report summarizing all receipts, bond purchases and sales, transactions with each contractor, a list of encumbered funds, and a demonstrated unencumbered balance of $17,269. First, the bids for the building addition had come in 13 percent under the estimate. Now those responsible for closing out the project were given funds equal to a healthy 5 percent of the total project cost. This enabled the board to flesh out rooms and furnishings and to address various details which could not be planned for or sometimes even predicted beforehand. While the layout of the enlarged building would receive criticism almost from the first day, the balance in the building fund allowed library officials to add equipment and amenities gradually, on a priority basis.

After failing to convene a quorum in May, the trustees reviewed Helm's recommended list of uses for the $17,000 at her third board meeting in June. Her top two categories, using about one-half of the funds, entailed basic work to the basement rooms of the old library—now work areas for the staff—and installing public restrooms on the first floor so that library visitors would not have to depend on the sixty-year-old restrooms in that same basement area. The basement needed new locks, panic bars, and alarms to make the area both safe and secure, and the rooms required new plaster, new flooring, painting, and major electrical work.

The library board approved most of these recommendations in June and July, and by then Helm had estimates and details for spending most of the rest of the money.

The most interesting expenditure was another $1,000 for the story hour room—interesting because it included the honorarium given to local artist Ellie Simmons for the mural she painted on the walls of the room. The mural was completed in 1965 and was featured in color on the cover of the *Des Moines Sunday Register* "Picture" section in September of that year. Working with children's librarian Hazel Westgate, Helm first recruited Simmons, author of two wordless picture books and illustrator of several others, and then solicited original works from twenty-eight other well-known illustrators of children's books while Simmons completed her mural. These framed originals decorated one wall of the story hour room while the Simmons mural covered the other three. The library board hosted a reception to dedicate the mural and honor the artist in late 1965 and Simmons produced a charming narrative aimed at children about creating the mural.[4] ICPL's unique story hour room was only a partially completed bare room in the original plans. Through financial good luck, the commitment to a concept by Nienstedt, and to artistic excellence by Helm, it developed into a visual wonderland for children and a spot of beauty and delight for all in an otherwise prosaic and unimaginative library addition.

Helm continued her efforts to brighten up both the public and staff areas of the expanded library. She used the balance of the funds not only for minor library equipment and additional shelving, but also to furnish and refurbish both public reading rooms and the music room (which at this point Helm and the trustees hoped to reopen). She was particularly proud of the young adult room. She replaced the battleship gray steel tables and chairs with fruitwood finished wooden ones and added brightly colored drapes, an area rug, and reupholstered easy chairs. Helm, in one of her regular newspaper columns about the library, said she wanted to replace the sterile, institutional atmosphere with a friendly, homelike one—here and in all areas of the library.

Helm's 1996 comment about the library addition was: "Nienstedt had devised a clever addition to the old Carnegie, built and furnished a luxurious office suite for herself, but seemed more interested in [building] the facilities . . . than in taking services to the public."[5]

Seven Rivers Library System

Staff members working at the library today occasionally come across a reference to the Seven Rivers Library System and wonder about its connection with the Iowa City Public Library. Few know its history or understand its influence on the long-term development of the library.

Seven Rivers Library System logo (1965)

Under the leadership of Sallie Helm and working with the same state library officials that had approached Joyce Nienstedt almost ten years earlier, ICPL signed an agreement with the Iowa State Library in 1965 to head a fourteen-county cooperative public library system in eastern Iowa. They named it the Seven Rivers Library System.[6]

The Iowa systems were funded primarily by federal dollars matching state and local appropriations for library service. The federal program had started under President Eisenhower in 1956, was renewed in 1960, and was expanded in scope and in funding by Presidents Kennedy and Johnson. Early in his administration, President Johnson signed the Library Services and Construction Act, known thereafter as LSCA in the library community. By 1964, the same year that Helm took over the directorship at ICPL, LSCA was offering nearly $55 million a year for distribution to state libraries that met federal guidelines. All states received some funds; those states that appropriated matching dollars for their state libraries above a certain level could increase the number of dollars coming into their state libraries by as much as two-thirds. Iowa never received its full share because year after year the Iowa legislature failed to give the state library a budget large enough to qualify it for maximum federal funding.

In her first year Sallie Helm convinced the library board and the city administration that directing one of the state library's planned regional cooperative library systems was an important opportunity for Iowa City and the surrounding areas. By that date the three libraries that had signed on in the 1955-58 years when Nienstedt had shown no interest had each brought over a half million dollars of federal funds into their multicounty areas. In less than ten years, through the stimulation of federal aid, the local budgets of libraries in those cooperative systems had increased an average of over 200 percent.

For the first time since the beginning of the public library movement in the nineteenth century, and especially during the 1960s when money flowed generously from Washington for many educational and cultural purposes, LSCA and its predecessors provided federal aid for the development of the nation's public libraries. The funds were intended to improve established public libraries and provide library service to those currently without it by encouraging cooperation between libraries, stimulating increased state and local funding for public libraries, enlarging the pool of library materials within the state, and improving the ability of each state library to advise and support public library activity in its state.

The federal administrators of LSCA required a carefully developed state plan to be approved before any funds were released. Any plan for public library development in Iowa had to face up to certain facts: When the program began in 1956, there were already some 430 municipal public libraries, yet over a million and a quarter Iowans (nearly 45 percent) did not have legal access to a public library. Only six counties in Iowa provided library service to rural residents, either through a county library or by contracting with the libraries in their county for service to rural residents. And, as Frederick Wezeman, the founding director of the University of Iowa School of Library Science, had pointed out at a state library meeting in 1956, despite years of professional meetings and exchange of ideas, there were almost no programs of cooperation between Iowa public libraries.

> The most conspicuous thing about librarians working together is that they don't. Public libraries are virtually next door to each other and they have no contact, bibliographic, or even social. Public libraries and school libraries in the same community have no contact—no area of cooperation. There is no cooperation between academic . . . and public libraries, even in the same community.[7]

Iowa's plan was based on strengthening the materials and staff available at the state library, providing financial assistance to smaller public libraries (those in communities under 10,000), and organizing public library systems—groups of public libraries of all sizes working together to improve library service to the citizens of Iowa. Financial assistance to libraries Iowa City's size came by their taking a leadership role in the operation of one of the regional systems. Many in the library community of the 1950s and 1960s (indeed it was one of the recommendations of the 1949 Public Library Inquiry) believed that the nation's thousands of small, independent municipal public libraries could flourish only if they joined forces and worked together in systems. Wezeman's 1956 vision called for "a network . . . lines drawn from one institution to the other . . . instead of dots representing little isolated bibliographic centers untouched by each other."

Iowa's cooperative library systems required no changes in the governmental status of existing libraries. Each local library board retained its identity and control over its affairs but agreed to enter into contracts with a central library to work to improve library services to the residents of its community and to those in nearby areas. The library that agreed to serve as the administrative center of the region, in turn, contracted with the Iowa State Library to perform the supervision required by the state agency and the federal guidelines.

The central library received LSCA funds to oversee the recruitment of libraries into the system and to hire staff to provide a variety of services: centralized ordering and cataloging of each library's books; in-service training on reference service, book selection, and children's literature; and professional advice to library boards and librarians on all phases of good library service.

Each contracting library, in addition to meeting certain minimum standards for collections, hours, and staffing, agreed to spend at least 15 percent of its total budget (and no less than two hundred dollars) through the central library and to work with other libraries in the system to develop cooperative service programs. In addition to buying and sharing the books purchased (at much larger discounts) through the administrative library's centralized service, the members also developed policies for reciprocal borrowing between libraries, uniform lending rules, and loan of materials to other libraries. By linking each of the state's administrative headquarters libraries through joint meetings, uniform policies on interlibrary loans, and later by a teletype network for identification and exchange of materials, the state, for the first time, formed a network of public libraries that were sharing information about their collections and services, exchanging materials, and working for common goals.

This was the system in process of development when ICPL became the headquarters library of the Seven Rivers Library System. In 1965 the library received $15,000 to administer the system and signed up its first member, the Blairstown Public Library. The Grinnell, Brooklyn, and Victor public libraries also signed contracts in 1965. By 1966 Seven Rivers received $100,000—$28,000 for administrative salaries and expenses and $72,000 to purchase books. ICPL's simple workroom suddenly expanded into a full-fledged "technical services" department, ordering, cataloging, processing, and rotating thousands of books to member libraries.

The Iowa plan to increase the books available to card holders in small public libraries was a clever one. Each library selected books to be ordered and processed at ICPL from the funds it had promised to spend through the system. After three months on the "new books" shelf at the home library, the books joined the system's rotating collection for one year before being returned to the owning library. All purchases by member libraries were matched dollar-for-dollar by federal funds, and with this money the ICPL-Seven Rivers staff selected additional books permanently assigned to the rotating collection. Every three months each cooperating library exchanged its current allotment from the rotating collection for a fresh one. Each year, therefore, the number of titles available to readers at their local libraries was increased as much as ten times over the number purchased from each library's local funds.

The next development for Seven Rivers was a pilot program for enhancing reference service to its member libraries. Few small libraries had the resources to field any but the simplest reference questions. A survey by Wezeman revealed that 33 percent of Iowa public libraries did not have telephones and less than 60 percent answered reference questions by phone. Federal funds distributed by the state library had given nearly $104,000 in $200-500 reference grants to over three hundred libraries between 1958 and 1966. For all but the largest libraries, however, this purchased only the basic reference titles. Helm and state library officials tried another method. They selected four other major libraries in the region—Cedar Rapids, Marshalltown, Clinton, and Davenport—and each, including Iowa City, identified a subject specialty. Iowa City selected literature and art; others were business and economics, science and technology, history and the social sciences, and language and psychology. The program depended on the state library for its holdings in history and public administration. Each of the five public libraries received $12,500 in federal dollars over a four-year period to buy materials in depth in its specialty. At the same time, each member library was given a telephone credit card and additional training in negotiating reference questions. Staff members were encouraged to call the reference center at Iowa City. Answers to their questions were sought, or materials on specific subjects were identified at Iowa City or at one of the satellite reference libraries, and mailed to the inquiring library as soon possible.

By 1967 the Seven Rivers rotating collection had grown to over 20,000 volumes, large enough to supply nearly six hundred volumes per quarter to each of the thirty-four members. Therefore, one-fourth of the matching federal funds earmarked for purchasing books was used to buy titles for the Iowa City permanent collection to build strength in areas of heaviest reference and interlibrary loan requests. Between the two programs, thousands of dollars were pumped into ICPL's book collection.

As the administrative headquarters of the Seven Rivers Library System, Iowa City staff gained experience in many areas and the library itself benefited. Ordering and processing books for over thirty libraries required quick mastering of methods and techniques used in larger libraries as well as learning management, supervision, and personnel skills formerly needed only by the library director. The professional staff was enlarged with the help of federal funds, and all librarians learned to build larger and deeper collections, especially in art and literature. Also, in these years before local library users provided a steady stream of questions, information requests from member libraries throughout the fourteen-county area allowed librarians to practice their research skills on a wide range of topics and levels of difficulty.

In addition to richer, larger book collections and valuable bibliographic and reference challenges, the library staff acquired expertise in preparing publications, book lists, and training materials. Federal monies helped purchase shelving and card catalog units, a small press and related printing equipment, the library's first of many photocopiers, and a postage meter used at the library until 1995. All in all, these standard library experiences and the basic library equipment were nothing revolutionary, but after living under the inch-by-inch, dollar-by-dollar incremental increases awarded by municipal governments, they proved to be giant steps toward an increasingly sophisticated level of staffing, book stock, and accoutrements for the Iowa City Public Library.

"A Cheerful, Inviting Place to Be"

The Seven Rivers Library System remained financially healthy and growing during the Helm years. Once she had gotten it staffed and running, and after using the balance of the construction funds to complete and furnish the new building spaces, Helm turned her energies toward improving library services and increasing the library's visibility in the community.

Helm's vision of a public library was broader than that of a reading and study agency. She saw it as one of the cultural centers of the community, and she joined those who believed that, in a university town, the cultural interests of the average resident were frequently slighted. While the university offered quality programs of music, art, drama, lecture, and study, these programs did not necessarily trickle down to children, young people, or the average working family. In 1965 there were few non-university cultural institutions other than the public library. Helm used her university connections to tap the talent of the faculty and staff for library programs and she encouraged other creative people in Iowa City to come forward.

During her second year on the job and for the balance of her short time at the library, Helm lined up a striking array of programs and exhibits. She used the new auditorium, story hour room, and display cases for lectures, book signings, panel discussions, art exhibits, concerts, puppet shows, poetry readings, film showings, and literary forums. Musicians, writers, and poets from the university community, many of whom had never before stepped off the campus for public appearances, agreed to participate in library-sponsored programs. Poets Donald Justice, Marvin Bell, George Starbuck, and Frederic Will gave readings; novelists Vance Bourjaily and William Cotter Murray joined the library's Literary Forum series; the Iowa String Quartet gave a concert for children; classics scholar Peter Arnott presented adult puppet plays of Greek and medieval drama.

Local talent was showcased, too. Elementary, junior high, and high school students mounted their best artwork annually. Garden expert and author Gretchen Harshbarger gave a lecture series. Local children's authors Ellie Simmons and Lois Muehl participated in the Literary Forum programs. Members of local study clubs presented a panel on "Books and Civil Liberties." From a collection of 8mm films purchased with Seven Rivers funds, the library sponsored heavily attended film showings of silent comedies and classic silent films like *Intolerance* and *The Hunchback of Notre Dame*. Sometimes the programs had to be repeated when the free showings in the 150-seat auditorium were filled.

Community and public affairs were not ignored. The library obtained copies of an early urban renewal proposal and advertised its availability for check-out. In March 1967, area state legislators Robert J. Burns, Minnette Doderer, and Earl Yoder participated in the first of a now thirty-year library tradition of presenting reports and question-and-answer sessions by Johnson County's state legislative representatives. ·

A Century of Stories

The twice-weekly story hours and the summer reading program remained the principal events for children throughout the Helm years. In addition, Helm worked with the public schools to organize a Junior Great Books discussion program. In 1965 I was one of twenty women who completed an eight-week training program sponsored by the Great Books Foundation of Chicago. Following the training Suzanne Richerson, future library trustee, and I jointly led one of the eight groups of fifth and sixth graders that met every two weeks at the library or at one of the elementary schools. The program expected young readers to form and express their opinions about works by core writers like Stevenson, Kipling, and Dickens. It enrolled over 150 children for two consecutive school years.

In addition to the 8mm films which were available for loan to all Seven Rivers member libraries, two other nonbook formats took center stage under Helm's direction. First, she revived the recordings collection which had been more or less ignored by Nienstedt after the music room closed in 1960. Plans to reopen the basement music room never seemed to materialize. The space adjoining and perhaps the room itself was needed to house the growing regional processing center. The recordings were moved to a more prominent spot on the main level. Staff members selected new copies or fresh versions of major classical titles using Brubaker funds and published lists of the new recordings to reenlist former borrowers.

Sallie Helm with Library Board President William Tucker (1964-67)

In mid-1965 Helm introduced the library's new circulating art collection to the public—framed reproductions of famous paintings and prints. Only ten pictures could be purchased during the first year, but the library staff repeatedly emphasized its goal: quality reproductions of important examples of all styles and periods of art in sturdy, suitable frames. Long-range plans called for some original works and many more reproductions. According to the library brochure about the new format, "The art collection is part of the public library's effort to contribute to the cultural growth of the Iowa City community."

A year later, Helm called the art loan program an unqualified success. With a collection of thirty-five reproductions of oils, watercolors, drawings, tempera on wood, and gouache paintings, and with hopes of buying fifteen to twenty prints a year, Helm said the sixty-day loans were "encouraging the appreciation of art" to those lucky enough to get a turn to check one out. "Often families like a picture so much that they want it in their home permanently. This is the reason we started the collection," Helm told the *Press-Citizen* in 1966.

New formats did not push book reading to a secondary position. The book collection was growing rapidly thanks to larger city budgets and Seven Rivers funds. With improved in-house printing capabilities the library staff began offering readers a weekly list of new acquisitions. Nonfiction titles received top billing, many times accompanied by short annotations. This weekly list survived many years, with and without annotations, and finally was dropped when changes to other parts of the cataloging process made its production more complex and too costly. It was always popular with regular library users who continue to ask for a similar report to this day.

From the library's earliest years, gift books have enriched its collection, but Helm was the first to publicly solicit money for books. Under her direction the library staff issued a

First brochure published by the library to describe its services (1967)

brochure explaining the importance of gifts to the library and created appropriate gift bookplates and forms to use for memorials and other types of gifts. With the machinery in place, the public began to designate the library for small contributions given in memory or in honor of particular persons, and money started to flow into the library's gift and bequest fund.

The weekly new books list and the memorial gift materials were just two of the many kinds of publications the library began to produce in the Helm years. In 1965 Helm and her staff created the first all-purpose brochure that introduced library users to general library services, materials, and rules. This first "intro"— obviously involving the work of a graphic designer—included a floor plan, a must for users of the confusing, multileveled, enlarged Carnegie.

Aside from the 1902 book catalog, and one or two printed booklets of library bylaws and rules, the Helm publications were the first of hundreds and hundreds of fliers, brochures, signs, book lists, bookmarks, calendars, and announcements that the library would issue in the remaining years of its first century. The scrapbooks kept by the library from 1923 through 1970 dramatically reflect the change that took place after 1964. Garnering the funds, equipment, and creative staff to produce the giveaway materials needed to explain and promote library programs and services was an important step toward becoming a mature public library.

Helm squeezed more noncontroversial newspaper coverage out of the local paper than any library director of the one-hundred-year period. In addition to long columns written by staff librarians and submitted every other week, there were pictures and reports on most library programs, feature articles about "what librarians read," long summaries of the past year's accomplishments, feature stories on each new collection or service, pictures and bios of every new library board trustee, and stories about donors to library collections and gift accounts. When Helm announced her resignation in 1968, the *Press-Citizen* editorialized about the high standard of performance any successor would have to match, and the writer successfully captured the spirit of the Helm library.

[After just 4½ years] the Public Library now is a lively, busy center of activity, about as far removed from the musty, gray image libraries often had as is possible. Not only has the collection of books been improved, but the library has offered programs by local authors, it's made available some movies of a bygone day; it's had dramatic presentations, and there's art and music for loan to patrons.

Inside the cheerful open, even noisy, building are cheerful people, whether employees or readers. The library is an inviting place to be and to go.[8]

The Power Struggle Continues

The newspaper is also the best remaining record of some turbulent times during Helm's reign. The library board's long-festering question of how best to serve nonresidents met head-on with the city's ongoing desire for closer control of library operations and a new city council attempt to negotiate contracts for any city services delivered to residents of other Johnson County jurisdictions. Provisions in the Seven Rivers contracts about reciprocal borrowing and the liberating effect of federal funds on ICPL activities added spice to the developing stew.

Principal players in the two years of on-again, off-again conflict included able and articulate Board President William Tucker, library director Sallie Helm,[9] city manager Carsten Leikvold and his replacement, Frank Smiley, in early 1967, Mayor William Hubbard and city council members James Nesmith, Robert Lind, Richard Burger, and Loren Hickerson, plus, at various times, the Johnson County Board of Supervisors, the Iowa City Community School District Board, the University Heights City Council, and citizens of all the affected areas who wrote letters to the newspaper or appeared before their respective governing boards.

Tucker, president and chief spokesperson for the library board since the construction of the library addition in 1963, continued to appear regularly before the council on behalf of the library. His presentations during this period often caught the ear of reporters and he was frequently quoted in newspaper reports.

The library had done fairly well in negotiating budgets with the city council for the first two budget cycles after Helm took over. The 1966 budget, at $124,000, was double the 1963 budget of $62,000 . . . and the council was beginning to notice the size of the change. The *Press-Citizen* reported in the summer of 1965 that, in developing the 1966 city budget, "the most closely examined part . . . was the expenditures planned for the public library." Councilman Jim Nesmith asked Tucker and Helm the reasons for such an increase. Tucker took the opportunity to bring the council up-to-date on several matters. A larger staff, now with nineteen employees, was required to handle the growth in the public's use of a larger facility, although staff members had received no raises since 1962 and salaries were not yet equal to those of other city employees. The larger operation and general demand, he said, called for a larger book budget: $25,000 instead of only the $4,000 of "several years ago." ("Several years" was actually eighteen; 1948 was the last year the library had only $4,000 to spend for books.) Even with the larger budget, the library had only 63,000 volumes instead of the 100,000 "a city of this size should have," Tucker told the councilors. Nesmith questioned the addition of 1,500 record albums now available for loan and noted that "this thing keeps growing by leaps and bounds." (His questioning the record collection was the first in what became a regular custom over the next twenty-five years of councilors wondering aloud at budget hearings about the wisdom of buying nonbook materials.) The council cut a modest $3,000 from the 1966 proposal.

By the spring of 1966, the city had mounted a three-pronged attack on library independence. First it asked the board to cease issuing nonresident cards under a new council policy of only extending services to nonresidents by way of a contract with the receiving jurisdiction. (In September of 1965 the city had lost in a referendum on merging Iowa City and University Heights, a small town of 1,000 completely within the city limits of Iowa City, and the city was looking at new ways to squeeze University Heights into submission.) The library board agreed in January of 1966 to a nine-month moratorium on issuing fee cards. This allowed the city time to negotiate a contract with University Heights for fire and police protection, garbage, airport, cemetery, recreation, and library services as one package rather than letting the town choose to buy some services and letting others, like library service, be picked up by individuals who were willing to pay for them.

A few months after agreeing to the moratorium on the sale of nonresident cards, the second blow to library autonomy was the news that the city intended

A Century of Stories

to cut $10,000 from the library's 1967 budget request, a larger reduction than in any previous budget cycle. The city claimed that the proposed amount exceeded the three-mill limit on library expenditures. Helm told the library board that the lower amount was less than the minimum she needed to continue operations at the present level. The council denied a request to replace $3,000 of the cut.

Salaries remained an issue. Four librarians were leaving for higher-paying positions, and Helm worried about how she would replace them. (University salaries for librarians ranged from $1,000 to $1,5000 a year higher.) The city was planning another round of salary increases which again would exclude library employees. The squeeze play was in place.

Perhaps offering a method for restoring the lost funds, the city manager issued the third challenge. "Library Urged to Join the Family," was the front-page headline describing Leikvold's visit to the library board meeting of June 1966. Describing the library as the city's only "autonomous" agency, Leikvold told the trustees that the library could be brought under the city's central administration. He posed four areas where the library could benefit from the city's "greater efficiency": accounting, personnel, purchasing, and planning. Board members asked many questions and Helm spoke against the change. The trustees agreed to consider it, but after a special meeting on the topic, they voted unanimously at their next regular meeting to reject the invitation to "become closer allied" with the city. As they had done ever since the first city manager, Peter Roan, began making similar but much less public appeals in 1953, the trustees accepted accounting and clerical help where feasible, but rejected any move that they thought diminished library board autonomy.

At the August 1966 budget hearing Tucker made headlines by offering some surplus equipment to the city to sell—a one-wheeled grocery cart, a two-burner hot plate, a small steel cabinet, two folding kiddie gates, one electric clock, and three fans. Tucker told the council, "We discussed the sale of such property to supplement our recent budget reduction but felt that in view of the fact that such items were originally purchased through tax funds and the city obviously has need for any monies available, that such items should be returned to the city for their benefit." The paper noted that the council recently trimmed $10,000 from the library budget to help finance a new traffic program. Tucker's final jibe: "The fans should be of particular value during these heated times."[10]

By fall the city had successfully negotiated a contract with University Heights for 1967. Still $10,000 short for budget year 1967, the library asked the council for the $4,000 the city would receive as part of that new contract, but the council refused. Residents from University Heights were given immediate access to all library services after the contract was signed, but regular library users from other parts of the county were still shut out.

244

The city next turned its attention to getting a similar contract with the county board of supervisors at least for library and recreation services. The supervisors were unwilling to make a commitment and with some reason. The Farm Bureau was against tax money being spent for library service and many of the letters in the newspaper and many of the farmers in the area were arguing against the new tax. One farmer bragged that he "hadn't been in the city library for fifty years and that most farmers can buy the books they want for less than the tax."

The *Press-Citizen* supported a county library tax editorially, and Tucker wrote a long letter to the editor outlining why it was unfair to force rural individuals and families to pay fees if they wanted library service. Both gave the standard reasons about funding library service: the need of all citizens to have access to a library, the indirect value to the community even for those who do not use a library, and the fact that taxpayers do not have the right not to pay for other governmental services they may never use such as public schools and fire protection. Both Tucker and the newspaper acknowledged that the nonresident fee of seven dollars per year was about half what Iowa Citians were paying and if left on a fee basis, the amount would need to be doubled or tripled. The *Press-Citizen* claimed that no matter what the cost to the county, if it was based on a fair share of the library's operating cost, county residents would be getting a bargain for they had not helped to pay for any of the seventy years of development costs: the library building and its recent addition, an extensive collection, and a program and staff already in place.

In the hope that the board of supervisors might change their minds when they were preparing their next annual budget in spring 1967, the library board voted in late 1966 to reject current city policy and to resume the selling of nonresident cards for the next six months, December 1, 1966, through May 31, 1967, at nine dollars per card.

All spring the debate continued, and the closer it got to the May 31 deadline, the more intense the discussions became. The library board held an open house and encouraged rural residents to visit the library to see what was available. The city council remained adamant about getting a contract but the supervisors still resisted, saying there was not enough demand for it. In May council members softened their language if not their stance. Mayor William Hubbard said, "I appreciate the problem the board of supervisors has in financing." And he said he could see why they "have difficulty justifying the expense because of the failure of people who wish the service to express their opinion." Nevertheless, the council said nonresident service would end May 31.

In an attempt to placate some petitioners who seemed to blame the city more than the county for the failure to agree, the council asked City Attorney Jay Honohan to contact school authorities and try to work out an agreement with

A Century of Stories

the Iowa City school board to permit nonresident schoolchildren to use the library. That plan was promptly overruled by the school board. Members were not interested in a contract with the city, nor did they think it possible to let only nonresident children use school libraries in the summer. Dr. Michael Bonfiglio, school board president, declared, "The problem should be taken up with the county board of supervisors."

In late May on the same day that the council voted 3-2 to deny use of the Iowa City Public Library to nonresidents, the *Press-Citizen* recapped the eighteen-month struggle over library use and profiled two county women who had been working for the past three months to change the minds of either the city council or the board of supervisors. "We do not want to stir up turmoil, we just want and need to use the library," Mrs. Harvey Henry and Mrs. Harold Mulford told the newspaper. While willing to pay a "reasonable" fee, they felt a library contract of $25,000 was too much to expect the county to pay. The fee may not adequately cover costs, the women said, "but it could be a way of extending a welcome. . . . While the kids are in the library, the parents are in the store buying."

Just a few days later, the library board ignored the council vote directing the library to terminate the practice of allowing nonresidents to purchase library cards as of May 31. The trustees voted unanimously to extended the fee card option three more months until September 1, 1967. In a statement issued by the library board, President Tucker said the board agreed with the council that non-residents should be allowed to use the library only through contracts with their governing body; however, he continued, "The board does not feel that strict application of the policy at this time is in the best interest of . . . the community." Noting that the majority of rural residents do not want to pay for library service, Tucker argued that it was not fear of the tax dollar, "but failure . . . to make these people aware of our splendid library facility and the worthwhile service which . . . can be available to them."

Following the issuance of the board's statement, Mayor Hubbard said he had no comment. He noted, however, that "the matter undoubtedly will come up at our budget hearings in July." He was right. The council cut $25,000 from the proposed 1968 library budget and set off a controversy that received statewide attention.

Cutting the budget was really the only tool the council had to "discipline" the library board. Unlike the recreation department, which cut off service to nonresidents under the council's first directive in early 1966, the library board had the power to decide who could use the library and clung to that right throughout this period.

With director Helm on a six-month leave through August 1967 (in Europe with her academic husband, just like the university librarian had predicted),

246

Tucker, more than ever, spoke for the library. He served as chief spokesperson during the nonresident fee card squabble with the council and the subsequent budget cut. The library board held formal meetings only every other month during Helm's absence and if there were special strategy meetings they were not recorded.

The cut came late in the budget preparation cycle. Normally, the library got feedback in May or June about the council's preliminary decisions, time to prepare a response. With Helm in Europe and no notice about the proposed cut from the council until July 3, Tucker had few options. He appeared before the council on July 7 and warned that the $25,000 decrease, leaving a total budget for 1968 somewhat lower that the current one, would result in decreased library service. He compared the cut with closing down a swimming pool after it had been built, not really a valid comparison unless the library faced a major reduction in hours. No details of consequences were given except that the cut could affect the required match to federal funds coming into Seven Rivers by as much as $14,000.

The five councilmen directed their new city manager, Frank Smiley, to meet with Tucker—but not until July 19, four days after the deadline for publication of the proposed budget hearing set for July 24. This action meant there was little possibility of a change in the council's decision about the library for, under state law, a city budget can be lowered but not raised after the public hearing.

At the regularly scheduled library board meeting of July 20, Tucker reported on his sessions with the council and the city manager. At an informal budget session with the council "when the budget was filed" (sometime before May 18 and before the board's vote on continuing nonresident fee cards), Tucker reported that the only question he and acting director Marilyn Greve were asked concerned an unusually large salary jump for two employees. "There was not any informal discussion of the budget, as had been the practice in the past." At the July 19 meeting, Tucker told the board, city manager Smiley "intimated council displeasure at the library practice of transferring unused funds from salary to books. They want a more exact estimate and close following of the budget."

The board discussed three options: Ask council to amend the budget and schedule a second hearing; meet informally with the council and ask if it will give some of the liquor fund or salary adjustment fund to the library; or ask for an attorney general's opinion on the legality of council's action. The board decided on the latter and also to ask for restoration of library funds at the July 25 budget hearing, more for publicity than results. There evidently would not have been enough councilors in town during August to hold a second hearing anyway before the county auditor's deadline for receiving certified budgets.

At the July 25 budget hearing the only comments came from library supporters. At the opening of the meeting, Tucker, who always tried to make his points without creating long-term animosities, presented a single long-stemmed rose to the council as a "peace token" from the library board. Tucker said he offered the rose because "some feel there is a feud between the board and the council." He wanted to show, he said, that it is "simply a disagreement on policy matters."

He then proceeded in strong and vigorous language to explain how the $25,000 reduction would affect library operations. "Something is wrong with someone's figures," Tucker said. "We have 15,000 registered borrowers and circulate 250,000 books a year. Ours is a substantial service and should not be curtailed by this drastic budget cut." Admitting that the library budget had been increased by 225 percent since 1963, Tucker noted that nine different departments of the city had received increases of 350 percent in the same period.

Next Tucker emphasized that the cuts put the library in "substantial jeopardy" in regard to federal library funds. He explained that to retain eligibility for the funds, the library must have 15 percent of its budget allocated for purchasing library materials.

Fellow trustee Jean Lloyd-Jones was less forgiving. She said the cut must have had some connection with a council directive to halt service to nonresidents. "I believe very firmly [in your goal] of extending services to rural residents only through governmental units. I question the means by which we are trying to achieve it." Also, noting that the main purpose of the federally financed library services act was to extend services to people in rural areas, Lloyd-Jones said she felt the library had a real moral obligation if not a legal one to serve these people if possible. "I don't believe we have really attempted to reach a reasonable compromise with the rural residents on the library." In the mid-1960s relatively powerless women were more able to speak the truth of a political situation than the businessmen and lawyers who had to do daily business with each other.

Councilor Richard Burger, serving that night as mayor pro tem, denied the connection and said the cut was a result of council efforts "to keep a rising tax burden within tolerable levels." He responded to the objections raised, however, by setting a special meeting between the council and the library for the following Thursday "to work out budget difficulties."

The results of the special meeting seem to indicate that the councilors were most moved by the possible loss of federal funds. They asked the library to prepare three budgets: details of the original budget, one showing the effects of the $25,000 cut, and a compromise budget restoring about $7,200 which Burger indicated the council could probably grant to settle the disagreement. He asked that all three budgets show in detail all items affected by federal money.

On August 29, 1967, with all councilors back from vacation and Helm back from Europe, the two groups met once again. After Helm made an informal presentation of the three requested budgets, the council agreed to restore $7,200 to the library's 1968 budget. This decision put the budget at just $3,900 above the 1967 level, what the library board called a "minimum level" without losing federal support. Councilman Nesmith noted that he didn't "see why there has been a reluctance to show these things in the past." "Don't say reluctance," Tucker replied with a smile, according to the newspaper report. "That's a mild choice of words," Nesmith retorted. "To my knowledge we've never been asked for information that we haven't provided," was Tucker's last comment. City councilman Loren Hickerson observed that the city-library relationship "is awfully important" and he hoped future councils would have "the benefit of a close relationship." The council had flexed its muscles and library independence took another blow, but on principles of library operations and serving the public, the board had come out unbruised.

Reports of the budget hearing appeared in several regional newspapers and the *Des Moines Register*. How library boards fare in the battle for funds always seems to be considered news. There is no record of how the attorney general responded, but the power struggle between library boards and city councils over the council's degree of oversight continues to rise and fall with the skill and philosophy of participants in every budget cycle. Sallie Helm's comment that she would "go home and cry" when asked by the mayor what she would do if the library had to accept the full $25,000 cut would have been understood by library boards and library directors throughout the state.

Following their marginal recovery from the 1968 budget cut, library board members continued their policy of being "reasonable" until they could convince the county of the merits of a contract for library service. They voted in September to "reinstate" their nonresident fee at eighteen dollars per year and continue to negotiate. Perhaps pleased with the library board's understanding about the issue, as opposed to the council's take-it-or-leave-it stand, the board of supervisors agreed tentatively in the fall of 1967 to put $5,000 in its 1969 budget for library service. At an informal meeting with Tucker, Lloyd-Jones, and Helm, the supervisors were given assurances that as soon as the budget was adopted in the summer of 1968 county residents could begin using the library and continue through the balance of 1969, "in order that we may determine how many people would use the library under those circumstances." At last, ongoing free public library service for county residents was a strong possibility, and for many years thereafter the library board, not the city council, controlled library service contracts with other jurisdictions.

From Helm to Croteau

With an attitude of "I was just getting started here," Helm left somewhat reluctantly in 1968 when her husband received an attractive academic opportunity at the University of Maryland. In addition to the congratulatory editorial quoted earlier, Helm received a Community Service Award from the Iowa City Optimists Club in recognition of her work at the library.

After leaving Iowa City, Helm spent a few years working for the Fairfax (Virginia) Library System, entered Georgetown University Law School, and graduated in 1974. She spent four years as an assistant district attorney for the District of Columbia and, in 1978, joined a large Washington law firm, where to this day she "litigates anything in the civil rights area."

Photo courtesy Iowa City Press-Citizen

Mary Croteau in 1969

Helm submitted her resignation in April to be effective September 1. Her hand is evident in the employment ad that appeared in the May 1968 *Library Journal.* "Ours is a stimulating, university-centered community of 41,000. Our vigorous public library is a center for a 14-county co-operative system. The director we seek will also be the administrator for the Seven Rivers Library System."

The board interviewed two applicants. In June when Betty Kohler, Helm's assistant in 1965-66, refused to make a commitment until July, the trustees next called Mary Croteau in Lansing, Michigan, who accepted their offer. In July they made the appointment official, setting Croteau's salary at $13,500. Of this, $1,200 would be paid by the Seven Rivers Library System.

Croteau was a Michigan girl—born and educated in the state, with all her library positions there. After receiving her library degree from the University of Michigan in 1960, she became director of the Escanaba Public Library for three years. In 1963 she became a consultant for the Michigan State Library, first as a field representative in the Upper Peninsula and later in Lansing, responsible for the state library's book collection, the development of public library collections, and an adult literacy project.

Dayle Hughes Tucker, who served as secretary to both Helm and Croteau, has pointed out the differences between the two women. While Helm was upbeat, joyful, energetic, and *always* optimistic, Croteau was low-key and laid-back. Less interested in her appearance and less social, she was a hardworking, quality librarian, Tucker thought, and just as earnest as Helm about doing the best for ICPL. "As employees we knew little about her interests and personal life. She preferred to talk about items related to the library."

Carol Spaziani, who started work at the library on the same day as Croteau, described her as "informal." She was less attached than Helm to doing things according to traditional library methods if she could find a better or cheaper way, or perhaps easier for the public. Spaziani found her fair, open, never power-hungry or unwilling to share ideas and results with fellow librarians.

I found her politically aware, a "politico" who loved to talk libraries and politics in small social settings. A good storyteller, she seemed to attract similar kinds of talkers, librarians, and armchair politicians who enjoyed exchanging ideas and stories with her one-on-one. She was fun to be with.

Croteau was fairly astute at quickly developing or assessing proposals and ideas—ideas scratched out on yellow legal pads and explained informally. She issued few formal communications. Her casual way of making assignments gave you wide berth to succeed—or to fail—on your own merits. There were no formal evaluations; she either assumed, or unobtrusively observed, that you finished the assigned project. Her assumptions about your abilities were empowering; she gave staff members many opportunities.

Croteau's list of library "firsts" was a substantial one—paperbacks, a copier for public use, Sunday hours, the art and music room, popular music recordings, special services to the business and handicapped communities—and, for the most part, her accomplishments were logical extensions of initiatives started in the Helm administration. Her experience at the Michigan State Library, a bigger organization in a much more populous state, gave her a level of sophistication about library practices beyond the experience of the balance of the staff.

The Complexities of Serving More Than Iowa Citians

At the top of the agenda when Croteau arrived at the library was the contract for library service to Johnson County rural residents that Helm and the library board, as well as many librarians and trustees before them, had fought for. The board of supervisors followed up on its promise of the previous fall to give county library service a try. The supervisors put the $5,000 in their 1969 budget, and as soon as the budget was approved, at a meeting attended by both Helm and Croteau on Helm's last day, the library board opened its doors to rural residents.

It fell to Croteau to make the experiment work. She had to mount a campaign to inform rural residents about library services, monitor their use of the library, and make regular reports to both boards. At the October 1968 board meeting Croteau reported that her staff had already issued 171 library cards to people living in rural Johnson County, more than four times the number who had fee cards before the contract went into effect. Six months later, in March 1969, the number had risen to 460, and rural card holders were checking out about 1,300 items per month.

251

In January the library mailed a brochure to all rural households. Besides describing current library services, it promised to mail library books to any county resident requesting them, but without lists and catalogs from which to select, few chose to use that option. In retrospect, information about library hours would probably have been more useful in a publication written to attract new library card holders.

Croteau surveyed other area public libraries—Cedar Rapids, Coralville which opened in 1965, and Solon, started in 1966—for the number of rural residents holding cards. In the spring she analyzed the location of the new rural card holders at ICPL. The two studies proved what librarians already knew—when there is a choice, most people go to the nearest or most convenient library. In that period neither Coralville nor Solon charged rural residents for cards.

In the spring of 1969 the library board began negotiations with the county on the 1970 contract. No records survive to tell us the number of county card holders or the total use they made of the library during the trial period, but the supervisors must have felt satisfied. The library board asked for $12,000 but agreed to $10,382 or seventy-five cents per capita. This amount qualified ICPL to get an extra $5,000 book grant from federal funds distributed by the state library.

The signing of the 1970 contract ought to have been a moment of closure for the library board, which since 1905, had tried various ways to responsibly bring library service to area residents not living within the city limits. But the tangle of boundaries, contracts, fees, and reciprocal borrowing agreements would continue. Lone Tree contracted the next year at the county price of seventy-five cents per resident. University students charged discrimination in the library's rules defining which university students were eligible for free cards. After considerable publicity and much board discussion, the definition of an Iowa City resident eligible for regular service was broaden to include all but single students living in university dormitories. The question, "Who can use the library?" would go on, and on, and on.

Seven Rivers: A Short but Rewarding Adventure

One requirement of Seven Rivers membership added another variation to the "Who can use the library?" question. All libraries agreed to reciprocal borrowing privileges between members. After sixty-five years of being the only public library in the county, ICPL saw Coralville and Solon establish public libraries shortly after the beginning of Seven Rivers.[11] Before long they asked to join Seven Rivers, which meant that not only their card holders but also county residents with cards from either of the libraries could have free access to ICPL. Bringing libraries into cooperative agreements, with ICPL leading the way, suddenly changed from an idealistic quest to a problematic issue when other public libraries, especially small and relatively underfunded ones, appeared on ICPL's doorstep. They could undermine the long-sought county contract by offering free service to county residents, and they could put pressure on ICPL resources if their residents used the Iowa City library in any great number.

Sallie Helm had brought the Coralville application to the board's attention just a few months before she left and before the trustees would be asked to approve the contract. Usually the board approved the Seven Rivers membership contracts without question if they carried the director's recommendation, but Helm had realized that this was not routine.

At ICPL some felt it had been a mistake for Coralville to establish a library. They saw the area as natural expansion territory for ICPL and Helm believed strongly that one library system with branches in outlying areas would provide the best, most economical service for the larger community. Iowa City and Coralville had recently gone through a bitter battle, however, before merging the Iowa City and Coralville schools. It was not a good time to discuss merging other institutions.

But that is exactly what they did. At a joint meeting of the Iowa City and Coralville library boards, Iowa City offered an Iowa City-Coralville merger in five years as one option, but insisted most strongly that to join Seven Rivers, Coralville would have to raise its nonresident fee to match Iowa City's and levy the same millage rate as Iowa City for its annual operations. One month later the Coralville board said it could not comply with Iowa City's stipulations. The Coralville library never joined Seven Rivers.

Solon was smaller and farther away, and with Croteau's recommendation, the library board approved its Seven Rivers application in the fall of 1968. This approval came after the trustees had signed their first county contract so they may have felt less threatened. The Iowa City board held a preapproval meeting with the Solon board but there are no minutes of the meeting.

During Croteau's two years at the library Seven Rivers continued to add members. There were thirty-four in 1970, her last year. As the system grew the funds increased, the processing center and other services were busier, and the staff was enlarged. Neither the federal funds nor the county contract monies were subject to line-by-line budgeting so the library added staff and purchased equipment as needed. Both Carol Spaziani and I, new library staff members in 1968 and 1969 who would stay with the library into the 1990s, spent our first year on the Seven Rivers payroll. We moved freely between work for Seven Rivers and ICPL. There were really no sharp distinctions.

The intrasystem reference and interlibrary loan services expanded, and in October 1969 the state library established a teletype exchange, linking all ten cooperative systems in an interlibrary loan network. Every day specific title requests and difficult reference questions were routed around the network to all major Iowa public libraries. Libraries that had not joined any system were literally "out of the loop." The technology would change and the participants would increase, but this early I-LITE system was the start of Iowa library networking.

Federal funding had been threatened but not cut in 1968. There were some reductions in 1969 and new regulations required a higher rate of matching funds from members. In January of 1970 President Nixon vetoed the Department of Health, Education and Welfare's budget and Iowa's LSCA funding was cut by $285,000. The state library reorganized the ten cooperatives into seven and laid off forty-five staff, including seven in Seven Rivers. The processing center at Iowa City was shut down and the state library established a statewide processing service, first in Des Moines and later at the site of one of the oldest cooperatives, North Iowa Library Extension (NILE) at Mason City. Iowa City used the services of NILE into 1975.

The final days of the Seven Rivers system and the other Iowa cooperatives, and their replacement by a state-financed regional library system is a story of the 1970s, but the system was at peak performance in the middle to late sixties under Helm and Croteau. It was a short, intense period which changed the course and broadened the vision of the Iowa City Public Library.

The Doors Reopen on Sundays

In 1968 trustee Kent Braverman asked why the library wasn't open on Sundays. Considering the condition of library archives and the short tenure of ICPL librarians and trustees in 1968,[12] it is doubtful anyone could have answered that question from a historical perspective. Very few public libraries offered Sunday service at that time.

Both the number of hours a week and the number of days per year that ICPL was open had gradually diminished since the library's opening day. The first trustees set the hours from 8:00 a.m. to 10 p.m. six days a week plus four hours on Sunday afternoon, every day of the year. Librarian Howell probably left because of the impossible schedule, and successors Sperry and McElroy convinced the board to eliminate 8:00 to 9:00 a.m. and 9:00 to 10:00 p.m. in 1898. Adelaide Lloyd used attendance data to successfully petition the board to close on the major holidays, Christmas, New Year's, Thanksgiving, and the Fourth of July, starting in 1901. Memorial Day and Presidents' Day were added soon after. About 1906 the library first reduced hours during the summer, eliminating Sundays and evenings during June, July, and August. The 25 percent, depression-driven budget cut in fiscal year 1934 closed the library on Sundays all year long, dropping total weekly hours from seventy-six to seventy-two. Nienstedt gradually eliminated the custom of reducing hours in the summer during her tenure, but was forced to drop the 9:00 to 10:00 a.m.hour after a budget squeeze in the early 1950s. The library eliminated Saturday night openings soon after when stores changed from Saturday to Monday nights as the one evening they were open for business. These changes dropped the total to sixty-four hours per week, where it remained until 1969 when trustee Braverman asked his question.

The board requested funds for Sunday openings in its 1970 budget proposal and followed this request by offering trial service in the fall of 1969. In just a few months loans per hour were higher on Sunday than on any other day of the week. Sunday afternoons became a favorite time for family visits, programs, and other special events. In the 1970s and 1980s the library board would learn that there were political consequences to cutting this highly valued community asset.

Serving Special Constituencies

With the 1960s emphasis on warring on poverty and protecting the civil rights of minorities, the idea of services designed for those with special physical needs— simply called "the handicapped" in those days—was strongly advocated by many in the library community. Public libraries were tax-supported institutions and all citizens deserved library services they could use. The visually handicapped received the first wave of support because libraries were primarily about reading, but those who were physically unable to come into the library to select reading materials also received high priority.

The library's first special materials, "projected books," had been a gift from the Lions Club in 1950. These books on microfilm could be projected onto the ceiling one page at a time to serve persons flat on their backs or unable to hold a book. This service received repeated promotion over the years but was seldom used.

Seven Rivers provided the seed money for large-type books, probably the most popular and certainly the largest collection in most libraries for use by those with some visual limitations. The early titles were simply enlargements of already published books, and the oversized volumes that resulted proved difficult for many to handle. As soon as the technology allowed for smaller, lighter-weight editions, popularity soared.

Under Sallie Helm's direction, the local Optimists Club began the library's first "shut-in service" in January of 1967. Card holders called the library to request specific books or certain types of materials. Optimist volunteers picked up the items and delivered them to the home of the caller. As the service grew, the post office took over the delivery of materials, and the library started keeping records on what regular callers had already read. The service was used by those temporarily confined to their home or to a hospital bed, but the most consistent customers were people permanently disabled. With the many levels and steps in the building, few of them could make it into the library.

In 1969 Mary Croteau convinced the Iowa Library for the Blind, which claimed at the time to be the largest library of its kind in the world, to break with tradition and place some "talking books" and "talking book machines" on deposit at ICPL. This allowed the library staff to demonstrate the service to new or potential users, although regular loans to persons who qualified for services were mailed directly from Des Moines to the borrower's home. Any person "who could not use conventional library materials," both the legally blind and the physically handicapped, had free access to the recorded books and the machines to play them on. The library for the blind also had books in braille for those who had the special skills to use this method, but it was the convenience and ease of the "talking books" and their migration to cassette tape format that led eventually to a widening audience. Persons with tired eyes, busy hands, poor reading skills, or long hours in cars became fans of recorded books and became the users of the books on tape collections of today's libraries.

One of my first assignments as a reference and adult services librarian in 1969 was to create a publication about the library's services for the "handicapped and homebound" and to promote their use through special events and talks to service clubs. On the first afternoon of the new Sunday schedule, which happened to coincide with National Employ the Handicapped Week, we invited the public to visit a display of all the special library materials and equipment the library could provide. The *Press-Citizen* ran a comprehensive article, including pictures, about the event and the services. That particular effort made a fairly small splash. Its importance was that it signaled the growing staff awareness that library users had a wide range of abilities and needs that required constant and consistent monitoring.

Croteau next targeted the business community for special attention. A large and politically powerful group, many did not think of the library as their first source of information but merely as a safe and rewarding institution for their spouses and children. Croteau told the press in announcing the plans, "We believe that the library, as a tax-supported institution, has a responsibility to serve the information needs of the Iowa City business community as well as the educational and recreational needs of individuals."

Croteau felt that beefing up the library's resources in areas of business, economics, and government information was a first step in legitimizing the library in the eyes of the nonacademic sector of the business community. It would also build an information base on which a stronger general reference service could be offered. "The library staff [wants to provide] vital information quickly and efficiently for the busy executive or secretary . . . aid the independent salesman or investor analyze his markets—in effect, act as a research department for firms and business people of the Iowa City area," Croteau explained in her original announcement.

Using mostly gift monies for start-up costs, the library began to select a wide range of business and government materials. Some items were so basic that today it would be difficult to operate without them: income tax forms and publications, codes and administrative regulations, business and marketing directories. Others proved to be too specialized or expensive for the use they received.

Photo courtesy Iowa City Press-Citizen

Librarian Carol Spaziani introduces the new Business Services Center to the public in 1970.

The business service was just getting under way during Croteau's tenure, but she identified the money, assigned the staff, and gave shape to its basic goals and direction. For the next twenty years, under the direction of Carol Spaziani, business services and resources were fine-tuned to match the needs of and actual use by Iowa City's business and commercial sector, and were eventually merged into the powerful information services of the 1980s and beyond.

The oldest of the library's young card holders had received special attention at the library ever since Nienstedt started the young adult book collection in the mid-1950s. She had designed a special room for them in the new addition and Helm followed up by furnishing the room to suit its potential audience and by hiring the library's first young adult (YA) librarian. The room offered a collection of books considered interesting and suitable to people of junior and especially senior high age.

Croteau felt it took more than books to retain high schoolers as regular library users, and noting that there was only light traffic into this comfortable reading area, she made major changes in the assigned uses of the building. She moved the young adult collection to the balcony area and turned its former reading room into the music and arts room. When an opening allowed her to hire a new young adult librarian, she picked a young woman ready to provide programming rather than a reading room for this age group. Under Lori Parker, the YA room became the young adult department, more of a service than a place or a collection. Working with a council of teenagers from the high schools, she planned programs of folk singers, student-produced films, and poetry readings of student works.

A Century of Stories

Parker strengthened the YA fiction collection by removing titles like *Sue Barton, Nurse* and adding more classic titles of interest to young people such as *Catcher in the Rye* and *The Hobbitt*. She added posters to the art print collection that would appeal to a younger audience: pop art, "black light and psychedelic" work, and some with "comments on contemporary life." The YA fiction collection continues to this day and is the one exception to the philosophy that the library must have specific titles, formats, and programs of interest to young people throughout the library rather than just in segregated areas and collections.

Croteau started two of the library's more consistently popular collections in her two years at the library: uncatalogued paperbacks displayed on browser racks and popular music recordings. These collections changed the tone and atmosphere of daily life at the library. They were less formally arranged collections and both signaled "popular culture" to library visitors.

Paperback readers would bring grocery sacks to carry home piles of the small and light volumes, arranged in those days absolutely randomly on the spinner racks. No need to search the catalog first, no reason to know the author or even the title of your favorite type of novel, mystery, or adventure. The covers gave many clues to those readers too impatient or unschooled to search systematically for what they wanted. Sometimes the reader would get fooled—a dense Faulkner novel with a cover featuring a voluptuous blonde in a low-cut blouse, for example. Sometimes this mixed message introduced the reader to a higher quality of fiction—the traditional goal of library founders and librarians, sometimes it merely warned readers to look deeper than the cover to get the type of stories they wanted.

Purchasing the books for the racks could also be a pleasure. Traditional library vendors all required lists or order slips giving full title, author, and publisher information—and a delay of several weeks between order and delivery. To buy new paperbacks we drove to a Cedar Rapids paperback and magazine distributor, took a grocery cart, and walked up and down the aisles selecting from the many bins of popular fiction and nonfiction titles. Back at the library, as soon as the books received a pocket and a spine label they were ready to add to or replace the torn and well-used volumes on the racks. Quick, easy, cheap, and popular, the adult circulation rate, flat for the previous four years, jumped 25 percent in 1969, the year of the paperback.

The revision of the former young adult room into an arts and music room included a major refurbishing of the LP recordings. They were removed from the drab leather albums of the music room days, reunited with their original jackets, and inserted into plastic covers. Croteau purchased waist-high units with bins, record store style, and suddenly borrowers could browse through the collection, reading program notes and making their selections almost as easily as twirling the paperback racks.

Adding current popular music and moving the recordings collection to the arts and music reading room (along with the large collection of art books purchased with LSCA funds as the subject specialty of ICPL), probably attracted as many teenagers into the room as did the former arrangement. Their own paperback browser rack near the formal YA collection also encouraged more young readers to feel at home in the library.

The Helm-Croteau Legacy

In this period before long-range planning and goal-setting, in a small library like Iowa City where most staff had little experience outside their current jobs, both staff and board members depended on the experience and vision of the director to chart a future and to suggest initiatives for improving and enlarging library services.

Croteau and Helm, different in work styles, personalities, and backgrounds, shared a similar library philosophy. Croteau's accomplishments, for the most part, built on Helm's initiatives and formed a continuing stream of ideas and projects rooted in the Helm years.

Croteau, street-smart, with no ties to an academic community, was probably more comfortable with the popular arts and the mainstream library user than her predecessor. Helm wanted her art collection to "contribute to the cultural growth of the community," and she expected the user to master her perfectly assembled card catalog. Croteau understood the need for easier methods to locate popular materials for some of the public and gave them paperback racks and recordings in browser bins full of bestsellers and current pop artists. Both had a strong belief in the articulated mission of public library; Croteau was simply closer to what might bring the average man, woman, or kid-on-the-street into the library. Helm might have been content running a quality library for those opinion makers that the Public Library Inquiry concluded were the core users of public libraries. More politically astute, Croteau observed and courted the opinion leaders while still striving to find ways to serve everyone. Helm taught us how to operate a more sophisticated, professional public library; Croteau gave us the vision to bring these services to everyone—and some political insights on how to do it.

---

[1] Interview with Sallie Helm, July 18, 1996.

[2] Interview with William Tucker, library board president (1963-67), August 1996.

[3] Interview with Dayle Hughes Tucker, October 12, 1996. Tucker is one of the few remaining persons whose tenure bridged the administrations of Nienstedt, Helm, and Croteau, 1961-69.

A Century of Stories

[4] Simmon's narrative is in ICPL's archives. The mural itself is gone. When the new building was constructed several methods of transferring the mural from the cement block walls were investigated but none proved feasible. The university, which rents the old library, used the room for news events and photography and painted the walls a uniform color in 1982. A video of the mural with Hazel Westgate narrating is in the library's collection.

[5] Helm interview.

[6] The name describes the seven rivers in the fourteen-county area: Iowa, Cedar, Wapsipinicon, English, North Fork Maquoketa, South Fork Maquoketa, and Mississippi.

[7] Quoted by William M. Cochran in *A Century of Iowa Libraries in Association; a History of the Iowa Library Association, 1890-1990* (Des Moines: Iowa Library Association, 1990), 27-28.

[8] *Press-Citizen*, July 31, 1968.

[9] In August of 1966 Helm asked the board to change her title to Director. "Referring to her as Librarian seems to deny that title to other professional librarians on the staff," the minutes recorded.

[10] *Press-Citizen*, August 4, 1966.

[11] The Oxford Public Library opened in 1940, but with its short hours, voluntary staff, and distance from Iowa City, it did not have an impact on the Iowa City area.

[12] Edwin Green, trustee 1951-63, is the last board member to serve two full terms.

260

■ 9. Growing Pains: The Search for New Patterns of Service, 1970–1979

After the assassinations, moon walks, and Woodstocks of the 1960s, Iowa City (like the rest of the country) was changing rapidly in 1970. The number of university students had doubled since 1960, and both the university and the community had built extensively and with haste to educate and house the hordes of postwar babies who were now college age.

Following several years of legal action and political bickering over urban renewal, 1970 saw the beginning of the destruction of much of downtown Iowa City in order to renew and rebuild a thirteen-block area. Many plans, proposals, and recommendations had been considered and rejected; more lawsuits, litigation, demolition, delay, and debate lay ahead.

For almost a decade many Iowa Citians had been giving serious attention to the conditions and rights of local minorities as well as lending strong support to the national civil rights movement, learning phrases like "black power," "gay pride," "Gray Panthers," "Wounded Knee," and "boycott grapes!" In 1963 Iowa City had become the first city in the Midwest to pass a fair housing ordinance. By 1969 attention was turning to an emphasis on women's rights. There were many more women than blacks and other minority groups in 95 percent Caucasian Iowa City, and women were organizing and starting to flex their muscles.

Since 1965 teach-ins and local protests against the Vietnam War were common, with serious incidents in 1967, 1968, and 1969. The Citizens Committee Against the War in Vietnam and RESIST represented the left and the far left of local protestors. Action peaked in May 1970, forcing university officials to allow students the option of leaving campus two weeks early, dropping final examinations and commencement ceremonies. In just two days, 11,800 of 17,500 students had elected to go home. A broad-based peace movement mounted demonstrations against Dow Chemical, armed services recruiters, and the Iowa City Post Office as the local headquarters of the federal draft throughout this period.

In early 1970, shortly after the deaths at Kent State, director Croteau had forbidden library employees to wear armbands and other antiwar symbols while on the job in order to protect the library as a source of reliable information on all viewpoints. Staff members had participated in various protests and for seven years often joined Fred Wezeman, director of the University of Iowa School of Library Science, each Friday noon in a silent antiwar vigil at the corner of Washington and Clinton streets.

The first Earth Day, April 22, 1970, launched the environmental movement. The library participated in this much-publicized event. The staff purchased fifty copies of a handbook for novice environmentalists and spotlighted the trash that was fouling our community by inviting the public to collect discarded pop and beer cans to add to a growing pile on the library's soon-to-be-carpeted first floor.

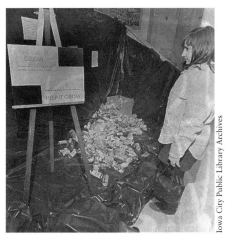

These various political and intellectual movements were challenging the established social and culture traditions of every part of society. At the library people were asking for books and information on a wide range of new topics: drugs and the drug culture, natural foods, changing sexual mores, running and fitness routines, cooperatives and communes, solar energy, nuclear

The library participated in the first Earth Day, April 22, 1970. Here Mary Seelman (Mascher) views pop and beer cans deposited at the library for recycling. Eventually more than 10,000 cans were collected.

power, global clean-up, astrology, acupuncture, transcendental meditation, Scientology, the human potential movement, Jung, Hesse, Casteneda, macramé, bead and leather crafts, organic cosmetics, waterbeds, earth shoes, leisure suits, and hot pants. The surge of new interests, ideas, writers, and fads represented by these examples kept the library staff actively engaged in identifying and acquiring materials.

In July 1970 Croteau joined the then-popular back-to-nature movement and resigned effective August 30. She had taken a job heading a library system in the northern woods of Minnesota in order "to seek the simpler life," she said.[1] She recommended to the board that I be made acting director. The board moved quickly to fill the vacancy and by November 2, 1970, new library director Jack Hurkett was on the job.

Jack Hurkett, 1970–1974

In some ways, the administration of Jack Hurkett may have been doomed before it started. He was the second choice of the board, appointed to save $1,000 in salary over that demanded by the board's top candidate. Hurkett came from a library system in upper New York state that, while somewhat larger than Iowa City and Seven Rivers, did not yet face many of the elements of the social revolution already playing themselves out in university communities like Berkeley, Madison, and Iowa City. Hurkett said in an interview four months after taking his first job in the Midwest that he found Iowa City "far less provincial and far more sophisticated that he'd expected." He brought his 1950s and 1960s library experience directing small public libraries in Clinton, Connecticut, and Westerly, Rhode Island, to a public library staffed with politically sophisticated women wanting to make the library an institution relevant to a community awash in change and upheaval.

We were married women in our thirties and forties who had returned to graduate school in the 1960s for a professional library degree and were steeped in the philosophy of progressive librarianship of the period. In some ways as hopeful and naive as many of the public library's early advocates about the power of the library to change lives, we were intent on designing services appropriate to all age groups, ability levels, and socioeconomic classes. Experienced parents, knowledgeable community volunteers, and enthusiastic neophyte librarians, we held strong opinions about the library and many of the revolutionary social and political movements that had been gaining momentum in Iowa City since the early 1960s. We were seldom reluctant to speak or act on their behalf.

Hurkett inherited a number of situations that would have challenged the most talented manager, and conditions in Iowa City did not ease up after he arrived. The oil crisis forced new energy management requirements on city buildings. Federally imposed wage controls made salary computations complex and controversial. Congress reduced funding for the Library Services and Construction Act (LSCA), threatening the generous funding that the Seven Rivers system had been receiving since 1965. The Occupational Safety and Health Administration (OSHA) had inspected the library and ruled that both the auditorium and the third floor needed a second exit. The roofs over both the old Carnegie and the new addition were leaking, the air conditioners were failing, and the city was changing access to the library front door by remodeling the parking lot adjacent to the library.

At city hall, some bright young men ran the new departments of personnel and finance. Eager to impress the city manager, they worked with gusto on the city's goal of bringing the library into closer step with city operations. Not long after Hurkett arrived they began pressing for changes in financial and personnel procedures that the city had long wished to impose on the library. Their approach was less straightforward, however, than city manager Carsten Leikvold's appeal to Board President Tucker and library director Helm in 1967 described earlier. Incremental requests for policy and procedural changes and financial information kept Hurkett on the defensive. The library board held many special meetings and responded to the director's requests for committee reports and investigations to help him address both general problems and city-imposed challenges. Relations between Hurkett and his colleagues deteriorated during 1972 and 1973 as city staff, library staff, and trustees became increasingly aware of his limited ability as a manager. When Ray Wells became city manager in 1973, Hurkett became one of his favorite whipping boys.

When the city council made a major cut to the library's proposed 1974 budget in the summer of 1973—partially, we suspected, because of the director's poor performance in handling financial matters and in preparing the newly required "program" budget—the impact on the library board was profound.[2] With little assistance from their director, the trustees were forced to reduce library hours (Sundays plus Thursday evenings) and eliminate planned raises and expanded health benefits for their employees. The demise of Seven Rivers at the end of 1973 required additional employees to perform some basic library tasks which had been done by system employees for the last eight years. The only bright spot was the council's approval of federal revenue sharing funds to take care of some of the building's physical problems.

Problems continued to multiply during the balance of 1973. The library staff was petitioning the board for the same salaries and health benefits as those given other city employees. By the end of the year library employees had joined with other city employees to form a municipal union and, with permission from sympathetic Mayor Edgar Czarnecki, were engaged in bargaining by early 1974, one year before the Iowa legislature passed the public employees collective bargaining law.

The county board of supervisors was as unhappy with the library as the public over the reduced hours. The supervisors felt they would not get the full value of their contract (now costing the county $13,200 per year) if the library was open fewer hours than promised. The library staff filed a grievance with the library board regarding Hurkett's failure to follow the recently adopted personnel policy about posting job openings. As part of its response to the grievance, the board told Hurkett to stop having the city personnel director screen applicants for library jobs.

Hurkett faced a threatening city staff, a hostile library staff, and an increasingly dissatisfied library board. Trying desperately to please them all, he satisfied no one. In January, the library board asked Hurkett to resign.

The Search for a New Director

When Jack Hurkett announced his resignation on January 31, 1974, the board of trustees not only felt great relief but also some optimism about getting a new library director who could provide the leadership needed to operate in a rapidly changing financial, legal, and social environment, leadership that had been sorely lacking in the past three years. Instead, by July the trustees were embroiled in a bitter and very public dispute with the library staff over their choice to replace Hurkett, a dispute that turned the spotlight on library officials and staff instead of library services for several months of 1974.

Recruitment and hiring practices were changing rapidly in the late 1960s and early 1970s and, at least in the public sector, the traditional "old boys" network was disappearing. Since 1972 municipalities had been covered under the 1964 Civil Rights Act and were obligated to take affirmative action to actively seek minority and female applicants. Selecting a new employee had become a complicated task involving carefully worded ads, widely distributed job postings, and precise documentation of the process of selection from multiple applications, as well as rigid guidelines on acceptable and unacceptable questions to ask in the job interview. Library board members received notice in several forms about these changes but did not seem to understand the potential seriousness of failing to follow them carefully.

Iowa City had a very active women's movement by 1974, with many women keenly aware of and informed about the new law. Several library staff members were deeply involved with these issues. Many helped establish the Iowa chapter of the Women's Political Caucus and organize the Johnson County Commission on the Status of Women in 1973. Some library staff members were working to obtain equity in programming for girls' athletics in the Iowa City Community School District.

By February 1974 the City of Iowa City was under an Equal Employment Opportunity Commission (EEOC) conciliation agreement based on a charge of serious discrimination against women in rates of pay and job opportunities. Staff librarian Carol Spaziani and I, along with Iowa City residents Clara Oleson and Elizabeth Diecke, had filed the complaint against the city in the spring of 1973. The action was taken on behalf of all women employed by the city, not just library staff. In fact, six of the seven highest paid women employed by the city were library staff members. We also became concerned for librarians, however, when the new 1973 classification plan placed librarians two steps below male-dominated professional categories such as engineers and planners.

The local Commission on the Status of Women analyzed both the city's old pay plan and a new pay plan that started on January 1, 1973, and found that 50 percent of the city's female employees, including cashiers, secretaries, account clerks, and parking meter readers, were paid less than males doing unskilled labor. Job classifications dominated by women and requiring a high school degree, some college, and up to three years of specialized experience were ranked lower than male-dominated classes requiring an eighth grade education and no experience. In addition, it was found that under the old plan 20 percent of the men were being paid at salaries that were up to three steps higher than the officially adopted plan, making the gulf between male and female salaries even wider. Except at the library, there were no women at the management level.[3]

The negotiated EEOC agreement, signed by city officials on February 26, 1974, not only committed the city to all the standard provisions of the 1964 act but to specific requirements for affirmative action advertising, recruitment, hiring, reporting, classification, and dissemination of policy. In return for not having to admit to any violation of Title VII of the act (called a predetermination agreement), the city additionally agreed to build a work force of 33 percent women within two years and to fill the next three top-level city jobs with qualified women. It was assumed by some that the EEOC agreement applied to library jobs, but this was never confirmed by the EEOC and no one had discussed it with the library board, although board members had received copies of the agreement in May.[4]

In addition to new affirmative action requirements and the presence of an active women's rights movement in the community and on the library staff, there had been at least two other changes in the employment environment since the last time the library board had selected a director. With the trend toward more openness in hiring, professional-level employees, especially in government and academic areas, expected to help with the selection of their colleagues and supervisors. And with stricter requirements to ensure open and fair employment practices, there was a renewed awareness of and attention to Iowa's open meetings laws. These laws were greatly strengthened in 1971 with strong penalties for failure to conform. In 1973 the League of Women Voters had cautioned the library board about the need to follow the precise procedures required by Iowa law when holding executive sessions, but library board bylaws in 1974 still contained language about reasons for executive sessions that were not in harmony with the Iowa Code.

At the same January meeting called to accept Hurkett's resignation, Board President Robert Downer appointed a three-member search committee: University of Iowa psychology professor Arthur Canter, a past board president and member of the search committee that hired Jack Hurkett; retired professor of library science Louane (Jerry) Newsome; and high school media specialist David Kirkman. Newsome and Kirkman were both librarians and new trustees. The council had appointed them six months earlier. Canter, a trustee since 1969, was keenly aware of the problems the board had faced over the last four years. The committee immediately set up traditional search procedures with a target date of June 27 for naming a new director.

Having sampled the job as acting director between the administrations of Croteau and Hurkett and having spent the Hurkett years managing the cataloging and technical services department, I decided to seek the position and was one of the first to apply. On May 22, when the committee gave the board a list of the forty-five applicants I was rather surprised to be included as one of the five finalists. Subsequently two of the five dropped out, and when the board made no move to enlarge the finalist pool, I hoped it meant that mine was more than a courtesy interview for the in-house candidate.[5]

Board members were on their own during the final phases of the selection process with no one to assist or advise them. Hurkett left at the end of May and the board appointed me to be the acting director, but since I was one of the candidates for the permanent position, naturally I was not given access to the applicants' files or search committee plans. For the fifth time since Hurkett had arrived in 1970, the office secretary had resigned. The latest one was gone by June 1. The search committee made no effort to include library staff, especially librarians, in the process of evaluating or even meeting the candidates. The committee told the staff that there was no legal way to include them, but offered to accept and consider ideas for interview questions if staff members wished to submit some.

Throughout the process, the committee displayed no recognition of how much the environment for selecting and hiring employees had changed during the four years since Canter had helped select Hurkett. Nor did they seem aware that local citizens were watching the library board and other officials and agencies to see that hiring and job promotion were done in a manner that provided equal opportunity for women and minorities and that they were done with open and legal procedures.

The Firestorm

The library board's decision on July 2 to select Charles Kauderer as the next director of the Iowa City Public Library was like setting a match to a carefully laid fire. It produced a conflagration that quickly consumed the board's hopes for a quick and smooth transition to stronger leadership from a new director and for some relief from the financial and personnel crises of the past few years. It sparked a controversy that burned out quickly but not until its flames touched all involved.

The issues emerged as the board's choice became public and the process used became known. Kauderer did not meet two of the board's published job requirements: a master's degree in library science from an accredited library school and public library experience at the administrative level. In explaining their choice the trustees ignored their published requirements and cited Kauderer's business experience as a deciding factor although only public library experience was required. In addition, they explained the reasons for their choice to staff members only after the decision had been made, and evidently without checking to see if their candidate had actually done the things he claimed on his application and in his interview. They used a secret ballot in a closed session without documenting the vote or recording the discussion. Finally, a majority evidently expressed a gender preference. In 1995, Canter told me that many on the board at the time preferred a male to control the "clique of radical women librarians" and because they felt a man would be better able to deal with the city staff and city council. Some trustees, Canter said, were interested in an outsider as a way to moderate what they saw as a troublesome group on the staff but, after the turmoil erupted, were told by Mayor Ed Czarnecki that being an outsider was not a "bona fide employment qualification."[6]

On July 3, following the official action of the evening before, newly installed Board President Vivian Buchan assembled the library staff in the director's office to tell us of the board's decision and to describe the experience and credentials of the new director.[7] When we heard that Charles Kauderer had a 1965 library degree from the University of Iowa and that he was a community college library director who administered an Illinois public library system, we immediately started asking questions.

We knew, for instance, that you couldn't get the required master's of library science degree from Iowa in 1965. The University of Iowa School of Library Science[8] did not open until the fall of 1967. In addition, the Illinois public library systems were highly visible, much-admired entities in public library circles in the 1970s, and it was common knowledge among public librarians that the systems were not administered by community college librarians. Unlike Seven Rivers and the other cooperative systems in Iowa that were dissolving at that very moment, the Illinois systems had solid state financial support as well as LSCA funds.

Kauderer's M.A. degree in education was not equivalent to the degree specified in the ads and in the job description. Moreover, an accredited M.L.S. was a requirement found in the job descriptions for all librarians at ICPL. In fact, search committee member Canter, as board president in 1972, had written to the city manager to support this requirement when the city was revising its pay and classification plan.[9] Kauderer's M.A. in education with emphasis in library science had been designed to prepare school librarians before the university library school was established. Search committee member Newsome had headed this former program before the new UI library school opened.

Fueling staff shock about the prospective director's degree was the knowledge that ICPL librarian Joan Tucker and I had delayed getting our library degrees in Iowa City until the library school opened, Carol Spaziani had left town for one year to seek the accredited M.L.S. degree from another institution, and Maureen Moses had been denied a professional position at ICPL despite public library experience and a *bachelor's* degree in library science until she completed her M.L.S. degree.

Staff research revealed nothing about a system of public libraries that the director-elect administered or any evidence that he had any kind of public library experience. It simply raised more questions about the veracity of his credentials. Kauderer directed the library of the Lake Land Community College in Mattoon, Illinois. The city of Mattoon and Cole County were served by the Lincoln Trails Library System headquartered in Champaign. Lincoln Trails was one of eighteen state-funded library systems in Illinois at that time which provided back-up services to public libraries. Illinois law required that administrators of these systems hold an M.L.S. degree from an accredited library school.

Despite Kauderer's claim, via Buchan's report, that Lake Land served as the public library for Mattoon, the Mattoon Public Library was a viable institution open sixty-three hours a week, loaning its 37,000 volumes about 165,000 times a year.[10] This was six times the number of annual check-outs made by the Lake Land library to both students and nonstudents. Lake Land Community College was nearly four miles from downtown Mattoon and, when asked, local people at the library and at bookstores seemed to know little about the college or its library.

After struggling for nearly four years with financial and other operating problems created by its last director and now facing union negotiation for the first time, the library board was very impressed with Kauderer's claim that he had spent two years managing his father's extensive business enterprises in New York state, including dealing successfully with a union. According to employment records at both Lake Land Community College and Kauderer's former post, the similarly named Lakeland College in Wisconsin, however, there was just about one year between his jobs at the two schools. The records showed he had left Lakeland College in Wisconsin to run a single dairy store owned by his father.

The possibility of constructing a new library building in Iowa City was on the agenda of most of the board members, so they were also impressed with Kauderer's claim that he had experience planning and constructing a library.

One library board member told me at the time that this was one of his reasons for selecting Kauderer, and Board President Buchan told the press that the construction of a new library while Kauderer was director "played an important part in his selection."[11] The Lake Land library was in a multi-use building that was under construction but nearing completion when Kauderer arrived there. According to the Lake Land business office, Kauderer's only contribution was to eliminate a couple of exits from the library.[12]

Through research, telephone calls, and a visit to Mattoon and Lake Land by librarian Jeanette Carter and me on July 12, we identified several areas of possible falsification of Kauderer's credentials. In addition, his degree was a source of concern to several recently credentialed staff librarians. The impact of his not having the required degree, we felt, not only would tarnish the reputation of the library but could threaten the library's eligibility for federal and state funds according to the 1974-75 state-federal plan for Iowa libraries.

Many staff members felt that the library board should be made aware of these discrepancies, so on July 12 seven of the eight staff librarians, myself included, signed a letter to the board requesting a hearing to go over these findings with members of the board. The one-page request briefly outlined our concerns regarding Kauderer's degree and his lack of public library experience. "Until July 3," we said, "we had . . . assumed that the person finally selected would be the best qualified candidate. We now have reason to doubt that this is true and therefore request an immediate hearing." We never received a formal reply to our request but President Buchan called on July 24 to say we should attend the regular July board meeting scheduled for the next day.

Realizing that by challenging the board's decision we had crossed over some kind of invisible line, we hired a lawyer to advise us and to represent staff concerns at the July 25 board meeting. Before that day our lawyer, Pat Kamath, shared some of our findings informally with fellow lawyer and library trustee Bob Downer. Kamath reported that the board was angry. Our trip to Mattoon and Lake Land had shocked and outraged even my supporters on the board. They interpreted the complaints of the staff as a challenge to their authority and as a determined effort to make me director, not as a plea for truth-finding, professionalism, and concern about what would best serve the long-term needs of the library.

Like the library board, the staff had been very frustrated during the directorship of Hurkett. Most of us had laughed now and then at his vagueness on library issues, his frequent off-mission concerns with administrative trivia, and his general good-hearted and well-meaning incompetency, but his lack of ability to direct the staff or advise the board was more serious. We were enthusiastic and energetic librarians, full of ideas on how to improve library service in Iowa City and, like the library board, we needed a leader.

According to a 1974 staff report there was considerable discussion among library employees about their wish to be involved in the director selection process, "somewhat the same way that academic faculty in a university department might express their opinions to those in charge of making the final appointment."[13] They had decided, however, that since a current staff member was among the applicants the initiative would have to come from the board. "Such a move on the part of the staff might be interpreted as an attempt to promote her candidacy."

While I would have been a satisfactory choice for many of the staff, they felt they had been careful to remain neutral and to be open to other outcomes. They felt that a highly qualified librarian, one with more experience than I had at that time, could be an even more satisfying choice. Several staff members had worked under or observed the work of two experienced and creative ICPL directors, Sallie Helm and Mary Croteau, and were eager to continue the growth and progress made in those years (1964-70) as well as to build on the staff initiatives of the 1970-74 period.

Based on President Buchan's invitation to attend, we thought that the staff's concerns about Kauderer's qualifications were scheduled for discussion at the July 25 board meeting. As noted in our request for a hearing, the staff had widened the circle of concerned librarians to include faculty from the university library school, a few staff from the university libraries, some Iowa public library directors, and the executive board of the Iowa Library Association. We had prepared a fully documented statement that we felt explained our concerns about the director-elect.[14]

To accommodate the many persons who wanted to attend, the site of the July 25 board meeting had been moved from the director's office to the library's auditorium. The morning edition of the *Daily Iowan* reported that "lawyer Pat Kamath, representing some staff members, and Frederick Wezeman, Director of University of Iowa School of Library Science, were planning on making statements." Wezeman, the story said, would try to clarify the difference between the department of education degree received by Kauderer in 1965 and the traditional master's in library science degree offered by the university library school since 1967-68.

These statements were never heard. Board member Arthur Canter opened the meeting by reading an eleven-page statement vigorously denouncing the protesting staff members, describing the board's rationale for selecting Kauderer and declaring that they would not even consider changing their decision on the appointment of Kauderer as director. Calling us the Iowa City "plumbers," a timely reference to the scandals caused by the Watergate "plumbers" and to our trip to the Mattoon Public Library and the Lake Land campus, Canter said, "The dissenters can cool it and join forces with the new director . . . or they may resign. . . . If the dissenters choose to remain but hinder or obstruct the work of the new director, they will be asked to resign. . . ."

The board unanimously adopted the statement without discussion and abruptly adjourned. They allowed no formal statements, questions, or comments from the roomful of citizens and library users.[15] But in the face of an uproar from the audience, board members stayed an additional two hours to listen informally to complaints about their actions. Individual board members accepted copies of the twenty-five-page, staff-prepared statement but no minutes were taken and no record was kept of these informal proceedings.

Lawyer Kamath charged that the board statement "was not an answer a responsible agency gives to the public." It is never rude, she said, "to go to a board and ask for information." Kamath also charged, on a subject she would later discuss in detail with the city council, that the trustees had not conformed to Iowa's public meetings law. The board had held a meeting earlier in the week without public notice, and, on Canter's admission, voted in secret on the director decision on July 2. Canter said they voted in secret to "reduce friction among board members." It was a split vote, he said, but no one knew for sure how everyone voted.[16]

Sometime during that same week Charles Kauderer was in Iowa City, perhaps to meet with the board, perhaps to look for housing, perhaps to look over his opposition at the library. I cannot remember if it was before or after the tumultuous July 25 board meeting. At a meeting he requested with staff librarians (which no one but me now seems to remember) we sat in the librarians' offices in the former Brubaker music room and discussed, as I recall, rather innocuous items about the library and its operations. He made no accusations and discussed nothing pertaining to his directorship slated to start in just a few days.

On July 30, a few days after he met with staff librarians and just two days before August 1, the day he was scheduled to take over as ICPL director, Kauderer submitted his resignation to the library board, citing criticism of him and his professional background. He refused to talk directly to the media, but his resignation statement put the library dispute back on the front page of the *Press-Citizen*. The statement was addressed to "the Iowa City Library Board and the People of Iowa City," and in it he was critical of "certain individuals in Iowa City . . . attempting to subvert the resources of the public library to serve their personal goals of self-aggrandizement and empire building." He repeated the library board's charge that the professional staff would accept no one but me as director.

"The situation in Iowa City today, as I see it," Kauderer wrote, "is the reluctance of certain individuals to give up their private dreams of power over a public facility."[17]

On hearing the news from a reporter that Kauderer had resigned, I acknowledged that I was "pleased to hear of the resignation of Charles Kauderer as director of the Iowa City Public Library," and said, "I will not seek nor do I want the directorship. . . . The library board is now in a position to resume their search for a director. I am confident that they will select a person who meets the basic qualifications for the job and that they can find a public librarian who will have the full support of the staff."[18]

Cleaning Up after the Storm

Ever since the abrupt ending of the meeting on July 25 the library board had been under pressure to make amends to its public by holding a special meeting to officially hear comments and complaints. The events had made headline news in the area papers so the number of interested residents had increased. Many letters to the editor supporting both sides of the dispute were appearing in the *Press-Citizen*. "It is time [to] pay more attention to human values than . . . to the alphabet of education following one's name," said one writer. On the other side of the question, another wrote, "The library staff and the citizenry are entitled to a full explanation of the appointment of a candidate with apparently inferior qualifications."

The special meeting was already scheduled for July 30, in the evening of the day Kauderer's resignation statement appeared in the *Press-Citizen*. To a crowd of over fifty people gathered in the social hall of the Iowa City Recreation Building, President Buchan announced that an open discussion period would follow the business meeting. The board officially accepted Kauderer's letter of resignation and Newsome, Canter, and Kirkman were directed to renew their search for a library director.

While the majority of the audience was evidently soothed by the news of the resignation, they still addressed the board for nearly two hours. Several individuals stressed the need for staff input into the selection process and expressed dismay about the way the public and the staff were treated at the July 25 meeting. The trustees took no action, however, on repeated requests for reconciliation with the staff or a reconsideration of their approval of the board statement about the library staff. "I'm afraid I'll go down in history as an ogre," Canter told the audience.[19]

The dispute received wide newspaper coverage: the *Cedar Rapids Gazette*, the *Des Moines Register*, and the *Davenport Times-Democrat* in addition to the two local papers. Details were carried in state and national library journals throughout the fall. *Press-Citizen* columnist Andrea Herman tried to place the dispute in the context of "the times." In this new era "of minority advocates, human relationists, legal counsel and affirmative actionists," she said, "serving on a search committee is the hardest job."[20] On August 6 the *Press-Citizen* carried an editorial reminding the library board that no matter the rightness or wrongness of the controversy, the board must comply with Iowa's open meetings law. It reviewed the missteps the board had taken and charged that it had been careless in notification of meetings, in reasons given for executive sessions, and in procedures used to reach decisions. "At least part of the fiasco which ensued may have stemmed from that failure," the editorial concluded.

The board was publicly castigated about its actions—at a city council meeting, by people attending library board meetings, and through letters to the editor and editorial comment—but what about the staff? Should we have attempted to confirm or deny the director-elect's credentials and to seek to share this information with the board? Was it bad judgment to travel to Mattoon, Illinois, and visit Lake Land College? As the acting director, was it my job to carry out board decisions without question? Was there a method we could have used that would have avoided the very public confrontation? What are staff members to do when they have direct evidence that a job applicant has apparently falsified his credentials?

I believe our research on Kauderer, which must be seen as the principal reason for his resignation (some trustees say he was advised to resign), saved the library from an unproductive and possibly destructive few years. Today, I believe our biggest mistake was not trying harder to find a less public and confrontational method.[21] Probably the same could be said for the library board. After the battle we all better understood the powers and responsibilities of the library board, yet we staff members also felt proud about our stand for integrity and truthfulness.

As mature women in our first professional positions, used to making our own decisions, infused with the idealism of our new professionalism, and empowered by the gender liberation ideas of the period, we were ready to act upon those ideals and to live by the new values. In our inexperience, we stumbled ahead righteously and were undoubtedly naive about the lasting effect of the old ways, of the traditional, casual, informal methods of making decisions and of the shock that challenging authority would be.

The most serious mistakes were obviously Kauderer's falsifying or misrepresenting the facts about his library and other experience, the board's failure to understand the distinction between a degree for a teacher-school librarian and the standard M.L.S. degree and to stick to its advertised criteria. All three members of the search committee through their academic or library connections should have been sensitive to these distinctions. Perhaps they were overruled by the balance of the board. Another problem was the failure of the board to independently check references for its top candidate or to share the applications and resumes with a representative of the professional staff or a public librarian from another institution.

The amazing end to this story is how quickly both the board and the staff were able to recover from this emotional confrontation. The July 30 public meeting was the board's first step in trying to smooth relations with its public. And just seven days later the reappointed search committee held a meeting with representatives from all five library departments seeking ideas for the second search and for improved staff-board relations. The board appointed two staff members to help the search committee develop criteria and screen applicants. The board showed a new respect for the professionalism of the staff which has continued to the present day.

I continued as acting director for the next seven months, solving some of the problems facing the library and giving the board advice on how to proceed with others. I gave them what they wanted most: some relief from the day-to-day operating decisions that Hurkett had forced upon them. Things went so well that after six months, on January 28, I reapplied for the directorship and two days after my second-round interview, on March 13, 1975, I became the fourteenth director of the Iowa City Public Library.

From my perspective, at least, the next twenty years brought a period of most cordial, professional, and effective board-director relations. We had all learned from the terrible days in the summer of 1974. Both sides forgave and moved on. We forged an alliance, became a team where each member knew his or her role, and together we built the foundation for the library's great accomplishments of the 1980s and 1990s.

Library Service in the 1970s

While the most public story of this period was the long dispute over the directorship, there were many changes and developments during this decade in the diversity and quality of services offered and in the public's perception of what constituted public library service. Working from the seeds sown by Helm and Croteau in the last half of the sixties, the staff developed new methods for building library collections that matched the interests and needs of the Iowa City community and did the spadework for an information service which would become one of the major strengths of the library. Efforts were made to reach people not currently using the library via outreach services to the institutionalized and homebound and a greatly stepped-up publications and public information program.

Despite his weak leadership and management skills, Hurkett had worked tirelessly for the library and made several contributions to the well-being and services of the library during his three-plus years at ICPL. Like Joyce Nienstedt, Jack Hurkett had an affinity for the physical and maintenance needs of the building. He fought roof leaks, as had many before him, but now the roof included the flat and far-from-seamless covering of the 1963 addition. He repaired and landscaped the long-neglected west face of the Carnegie, and he built a glass-enclosed vestibule—dubbed Hurkett's Hall by staff—to reduce energy loss during periods of extreme temperatures. He exhibited serious concern about the inability of the handicapped to use the multilevel building. While his proposal to install an elevator got nowhere,[22] he fully understood the inadequacies of the seventy-year-old Carnegie and its ten-year-old addition and laid some of the groundwork for planning a new facility.

Undoubtedly Hurkett's greatest contribution was the "permission" he gave children's librarian Hazel Westgate to unleash her creative imagination and transform children's programming. He both allowed her and inspired her to increase the level of programs: more story hours, children's film showings, and summer activities expanded beyond reading incentive programs. He championed the addition of a 16mm film service to the library's growing roster of audiovisual materials, partially at least to provide the children's librarian a source for her film programs.

By the time I became acting director in June of 1974, the activist staff had undertaken most of the initiatives that would shape library services for the rest of the decade and into the 1980s. In retrospect, it seems questionable whether under a more watchful director we could have proceeded as broadly and as rapidly. With no leadership from the top and with the library board distracted and occupied with Hurkett's managerial blunders, our team of librarians designed and created services that we felt a contemporary library should provide to the community. With recent degrees from graduate library schools but little hands-on public library experience, we knew from our textbooks and our observations the model of service advocated by leading public librarians of the 1960s and 1970s and, somewhat naively but boldly, did what we thought was "right." Most of the changes and improvements we made were not cost-intensive at the onset, we were relatively inexperienced in relating service objectives to dollars and resources, and the librarians and the rest of the staff were inspired by the challenges of the times. We started with a fairly simple agenda, an agenda that would be found—enhanced and refined—in every set of goals and objectives developed in the next twenty years:

- Provide an information service capable of handling all kinds of inquiries from all types of library users.

- Improve the collection in scope, size, and format and take measures to make most-wanted materials more available.
- Keep the broadest possible number of community residents informed about library services and resources.
- Provide service to those who cannot come to the library.

We worked to provide a reliable information service, an increasingly rich and varied collection, a high-profile public information program, imaginative children's programming, and services in forms acceptable and attractive to all members of the Iowa City community.

In other words, we tried to establish the public library as a key Iowa City cultural institution, a respected information delivery system working with and serving individuals, businesses, organizations, local government, and social service agencies. We defined "information" broadly to include all the data and ideas of humankind's creative endeavors and we saw ourselves as reliable agents who would channel people to the sources that met their needs—at the library or through the library to whatever agency or place that could provide them. Our timing was right. The response of the information-and education-hungry public to these efforts sent all library service indicators skyward and we spent the rest of the 1970s and beyond seeking funding, staffing, and other resources to adjust to the new level of library use that our initiatives generated. By the end of the decade, overwhelmed by growth and seeking to house new library technologies, library board and staff were focused on building a new facility.

Information Services: A Major Advance

Requests from individuals for library staff to provide information and answer specific questions are almost as old as public libraries themselves. As soon as librarians moved past the barrier of thinking of themselves as merely custodians of books, they began to develop ways to serve the varied needs of their readers. Inexperienced library users, especially, have always needed help using the card catalog, finding appropriate materials on particular subjects, and looking for "good books" that satisfy their reading preferences.

It may have been in the depression years of the 1930s that the questions asked of public librarians first veered very far from the educational, cultural, and scholarly, at least at libraries outside large metropolitan areas. McRaith's efforts (1907-20) in Iowa City to reach out to immigrants, transients, the homebound and hospitalized were premised on giving them access to reading materials, not answers to their questions about learning the language, finding a home, or understanding a medical treatment. In the library she prided herself on helping students and teachers and providing resources for the women's study clubs. The questions that Duffus had found "new" library visitors asking during the depression—questions about finding jobs and supporting other income-producing ventures—probably foreshadowed the direction of information services for public libraries in the 1960s and beyond.

Until at least the 1960s, in small public libraries like ICPL, librarians were kept busy helping high school students, club women, and the occasional individual who needed specific information. While doing their best to help students with their assignments, they were careful to not "spoonfeed" them. One library historian wrote, "They would show them where to look for an answer but would no more hand them a fact than they would the key to the vault."[23] With adults librarians were more likely to search out the answer, but only if it was narrowly factual enough to find in a standard reference book—encyclopedia, directory, yearbook, almanac, dictionary, handbook, or atlas. Few people really thought of asking the library for specific information, anyway, and librarians treated requests informally and never thought about counting questions or setting guidelines or procedures.

As everyday life increased in complexity, individuals needed competent and trustworthy sources of information. Technological and scientific advances, government programs and regulations, the proliferation of consumer products and of advertising designed more to persuade than inform, plus postwar patterns of increased mobility in seeking educational degrees and jobs all complicated the life of the average citizen. Although individuals tend to query the most convenient person or institution that happens to cross their path, libraries began to see themselves as the institutions that could supply information to guide the public through the maze of government and private agencies spawned by a complex society, as a first-stop center for all information needs. At ICPL the professional staff bought into this concept. Inspired by the first steps taken by Croteau in 1969 and 1970, and relatively unhindered by director Hurkett during his three and a half years, Iowa City's reference and information staff was handling nearly 25,000 information requests a year by 1975.

Not until Croteau requested special funds in 1969 to begin information services for the business community did the library make any effort to advertise its ability to field questions and inquiries, nor was it previously prepared to answer those not of the standard literature, history, and help-with-your-book-report variety. A 1970 brochure directed at the business community declared, "Make our Business Center your Research Department." Through the brochure and a business newsletter sent monthly to over four hundred business and professional people, the library promoted its enlarged resources related to business, marketing, investments, and government regulations as well as the staff's ability to field related questions. Sample inquires in the brochure included "What is the outlook for the mobile home industry in the coming year?" and "How do the hourly wages I pay compare to the national average in my field?"

To take the message about our information services beyond the traditional student and female user, Mary Croteau in 1970 started me on a speaking tour of local service clubs—Kiwanis, Rotary, Lions, Altrusa—and I spoke to many groups during the Hurkett years. I would outline the number of occasions in one's business, school, or personal life that required information for intelligent decision making, explain the special efforts and files the library made to acquire and organize this information, and close with a representative list of questions that had been handled recently by our reference librarians. The list of actual questions proved to be the most effective part of the presentation, drawing both chuckles and gasps from the audience. Telephone calls always increased after these appearances, and information questions answered by phone increased from a trickle in 1969 to a flood of over 12,500 in 1975.

To improve the visibility of information and reference services in the building, we rearranged the main floor of the library, placing a designated reference desk in a prominent position with a sign overhead, "Information." More of a counter than a single desk, it and the qualified librarian on duty faced the public and invited questions by their very appearance. It was apparent that this was the place to ask questions, and library users caught on quickly. In-library inquiries handled at the information desk, never even tracked before 1969, topped 11,000 in 1975.

Offering assistance to those who came to the library because they knew it to be the repository for standard humanities, science, and social science materials was quite different from promising to be a research department for a business or office and fielding requests for specific pieces of information, whether by phone or in person. First, the librarian had to be prepared to answer the inquiry, not just point to the encyclopedias or find a useful subject heading in the catalog. Second, she had to be prepared to answer questions that could not be found in standard reference books. Whom did the governor appoint to the Supreme Court three weeks ago? What local agency inspects restaurants? Who is the local representative for World Book Encyclopedia? How can I reach members of local Kiwanis clubs?

In a rather short time, ICPL reference librarians developed a data base of local information based on an analysis of the questions received, the subjects and areas of interest to library patrons obvious from circulation patterns, close reading and clipping of local publications, and monitoring the actions of many local governmental and agency meetings. As word of the service spread, questions became more specific and more locally focused. This whole endeavor required a larger staff to handle questions whenever the library was open and to collect and organize the local, state, and regional information needed.

A Century of Stories

Between 1969 and 1974 the library staff, primarily through the work of Carol Spaziani and Jeanette Carter, started many of the basic components of today's information services. In addition to undertaking the service-to-business initiatives, they established the local documents collection (minutes, reports, budgets, and other publications of official bodies in Johnson County and Iowa state government); created the organization file (the contact person, purpose, and services of five hundred local organizations); set up an events notebook (information about local and area concerts, theater, lectures, conferences, and so on); organized a business and consumer table (business directories, investment guides, and consumer product information); instituted methods to track appointments of city, county, and state officials; and published the first edition of the library's now twenty-five-year-old publication, "How to Contact Your Local Officials." The tax center including tax forms first appeared in 1971, followed later by a permanent display of information on local job opportunities, career education, and publications of the Small Business Administration. The pamphlet file grew from four to sixteen file cabinets with newspaper clippings added and the number of government publications and other pamphlet materials greatly expanded. We added microfilm back files of the *Press-Citizen* and its predecessors, the *Des Moines Register,* and the *New York Times.* To collect miscellaneous bits of difficult-to-find-information, the staff started a rotating file of two-by-four-inch cards full of local trivia (highest point in Iowa City), elusive information (incidence in 1,000 words of each letter in the alphabet), important statistics and telephone numbers (the monthly consumer price index, number for personal credit ratings), and answers to hundreds of other frequently asked questions.

To expand the definition and the utility of the reference collection, the staff added telephone books for all of Iowa and hundreds of U.S. locations, Iowa and nationwide college catalogs, all kinds of college directories, many federal publications and, with larger budgets, purchased newly published reference sources and new editions of standard reference tools more frequently. All staff members were on the prowl wherever they went to find any kind of printed matter that could increase the library's effectiveness in handling information requests, especially about local affairs.

Improvements didn't stop after 1975, but they certainly slowed down. The major components of a collection able to answer almost any kind of local inquiry were in place. Now it was a matter of fine-tuning, updating, and learning to manage the overwhelming response. The telephone became one of the principal resources of the department. It became common to call local, state, or federal agencies to find an answer or to get help on where to find more information. Staff visits to local agencies and special libraries helped librarians become acquainted with colleagues in other locations and with the services or resources they provided. Clients of our service soon learned that staff members would go to great lengths to find answers to their queries, and they regularly expressed gratitude and appreciation for the promptness and quality of the information received. It was obvious by mid-decade that we had made a good beginning on assembling the resources needed to deliver accurate and complete information on demand as well as a service ethic for doing so.

By decade's end the library staff's reputation for quality information service had spread to a large group of regular users. Many writers, researchers, office workers, students, homebound persons, and the frequently curious were exchanging stories about the amazing ability of the staff to find an answer. Stories appeared in the local media about unusual or humorous questions.

Managing the Collection

Except perhaps for the heavy emphasis on collecting and dispensing local information, putting together a highly respected information service was not unique. Most large public libraries had been providing similar services for many years. We broke new ground, however, with our efforts to develop and manage the library's general collections.[24]

In early 1971 Hurkett asked me to head the technical services department which was responsible for ordering, processing, cataloging, repairing, and eventually discarding all library materials. From this vantage point I found the whole process of buying and circulating books relatively random and unexamined. When we had money we purchased books; when we had time we looked at old books to see if they should be discarded. No one seemed to worry much about whether the books we selected were used, and certainly no one took the time to discover if the books described in the card catalog were still in the collection.

The check-out system we had used since the Helm years was certainly not user-friendly. It produced a sequentially numbered due date slip for each loan and microfilmed the borrower's card and the bibliographic information on the book pocket. We then checked the microfilm record and prepared overdue notices for those transactions for which the numbered slip had not been returned by the due date. There was only one possible response we could make to a question about the location of a specific title: "If a book is not on the shelf, then it must be checked out." It took a trip to the basement to consult the shelf list to determine if the library even owned more than one copy of a particular title. If a reader placed a reserve for a title, we would hunt for it every time a batch of books was sorted and reshelved. Many were missed and others were never found. In the short term, we forced people to rely on the titles that happened to be on the shelf on the day of their visit. Older circulation control systems gave better information about the status of books checked out than ICPL's Regiscope microfilmer, but were slower at point of check-out and required hours of filing and retrieving the "book card" each time a volume was loaned and returned. In those days before computers, most high-traffic libraries had to resort to the faster and cheaper microfilming systems—faster and cheaper for the library, perhaps, but a disaster in terms of customer service and responding to the needs of library users. A store where your favorite product is out of stock can be frustrating. When that "store" is the public library, you have no alternative place to "shop."

While this unfriendly check-out system was all we had until the library entered the computer age in 1979, we looked for ways to counterbalance its disadvantages. We decided to try to build a more responsive collection with its associated services and, through trial and error, learned to manage the whole system more effectively.[25]

The first task was to describe the size and scope of the problems. Although librarians have always been accused of too much counting, we really counted only the easy and the obvious—the number of books owned and checked out and the number of card holders. Certainly, we didn't know much about the shape, age, or content of the ICPL collection. It had been at least twenty years since anyone had taken an inventory, and therefore missing volumes remained in the card catalog long after they were lost. Except for reserve lists, we had no hard data about which books or which subjects were in demand, and except for evidence from its physical condition, we had no idea how many times a book had been checked out, or how long it may have been sitting on the shelf unused. We seldom purchased more than one copy of a title except for bestsellers with long waiting lists. We had no knowledge about how long it took a returned book to get reshelved and we seldom checked the shelves to see if books were in proper order. Although our part-time shelvers were assigned the task of "shelf reading" when all other duties were completed, it was definitely a low priority. We had no objective data about our users except the number who held adult or children's cards. We knew nothing about the age, gender, or frequency of visits of library borrowers, or what type of items they checked out.

So we spent the first half of the decade developing methods and procedures to find out what was in the collection and how it was used and then finding some rational way to decide what we should buy and what we should get rid of. We surveyed library users, gathering demographic and reading preference data as well as their opinions about library collections. One of our first and most important decisions was to date stamp each returned book before it was reshelved. By the end of the first year, we could identify every book that had not been checked out in that time as well as the titles and subjects of those that had gone out frequently.

We analyzed each year's purchases by category and compared the results to each year's circulation in those same categories by sampling data from the microfilmed circulation records. From the data compiled from circulation records and from the feedback we received from questions and inquiries at the reference desk, we identified topics on which people were unable to find material despite ample listings in the catalog and then conducted inventories. For subjects which did not appear even in the catalog we identified suitable titles and purchased them. The results of these mini-inventories were so shocking (20 to 35 percent of popular topics like gardening, auto repair, amateur radio, medicine, and health were missing) that we constructed a random sample of the entire adult collection from the card catalog, searched for the books on the shelves, and allowing time for those checked out to be returned, we concluded that about 9 percent of the entire collection was missing.

The number of missing volumes and the number of subjects without adequate materials indicated that we needed each librarian to become a subject specialist— to select new materials, monitor use, and discard dated and unused volumes in her assigned areas. Formerly, selection had been a group activity. This old method focused our attention on new titles recently published and reviewed and gave no one the responsibility to attend to the growth and development of particular subjects, finding titles to fill out holes, identifying particularly popular titles or subjects for duplication, or replacing worn, outdated, or lost materials. As subject specialists, we had to see that missing titles were replaced or else removed from the catalog, and, especially as we moved through the 1970s and space for books became tighter and tighter, we had to get rid of unused titles. Several years of date stamping each time a book was checked out was a tremendously valuable supplement to a librarian's other knowledge about user interests and her growing familiarity with her collection's growth and development.

All our numbers and analysis began to paint a picture of a collection and thus a library that was not performing very well. When we found in 1973 than there was only a 58 percent chance of finding on the shelf a book randomly selected from the card catalog, when a reader-placed reserve took an average of four weeks to locate, when we found books that had lingered in the reshelving area for over seven days, when we discovered that 60 percent of the auto repair books, 75 percent of the science fiction collection, or 95 percent of the newest fiction was checked out, or that all the books on planning a wedding, witchcraft, or fixing a 1970 Volkswagen seemed to be missing, we put a name to the problem and called it "availability." Our task was to improve the chances of readers finding what they came for. If the most-wanted materials were rarely available, the borrower was not satisfied and the library was not fulfilling its mission.

Our list of options and possible fixes was long, and it got longer as we learned more about the movement of books in and out of and around the library. Lost and stolen books, unused books, unshelved books, overdue books, reserve books, highly popular books, new books published and not yet ordered, books on order and not yet received, and new books not yet listed in the card catalog—each category had procedures to allow the information or the books themselves to move through the system. We analyzed them all and found ways to speed them up, reduce errors, eliminate duplicate effort, identify problems, and satisfy requests.

In addition to inventories, strict discard guidelines, date stamping, subject specialists, analysis of circulation and acquisition records, we also set standards for reshelving, sought reader ideas for purchases, bought more copies of books on popular topics, leased extra copies of bestsellers, and after 1975 added electronic theft detection equipment, raised fines, changed loan periods, and refined our statistical reporting system to collect and record all aspects of library service beyond the simple counting of the number of books checked out.

Also in 1975 we established a system of "core" titles—seven to eight hundred basic fiction and nonfiction titles beyond the current bestsellers, titles that readers came for again and again. These titles were checked regularly to see if a copy was on the shelf, and if not, a new copy was purchased until the title was almost always available. By the end of the decade we had raised the average availability of the whole adult collection from 58 percent to nearly 75 percent. For those core titles, checked out more frequently than any others but monitored and duplicated more regularly, we found that copies of as many as 82 percent of them were on the shelf on any particular day.

Comparative studies of other public libraries indicated that ICPL's high circulation from a relatively small collection was based, at least partially, on the careful selection and discarding of titles. Iowa City, in 1978, had the seventh largest public library collection in Iowa, but was third in the number of unique titles (titles found only at ICPL among Iowa's largest public libraries) and first in circulation per capita and in circulation per volume owned.

By 1979, with the prospect of a computer-assisted check-out and catalog system on the way, we were eager to turn over some of the routine chores of keeping the collection up to date and available to this new miracle machine. Our system of managing the collection was indeed working, but it badly needed electronic assistance. We had learned that library demand is truly elastic in the economic sense; the more materials are made available and easy to obtain, the more they are requested. Good service creates a demand for more service.

Serving Everyone

There were two parts to the goal of serving "everyone": first, making sure everyone in the community knew the full range of services so they could decide which were useful to them, and second, taking library materials and services to those unable to come to the library. The library staff worked on both during the 1970-74 period and continued to refine them throughout the decade.

The more general goal of publicizing library services succeeded more from diligence and consistent efforts than from original ideas. We created newsletters, wrote press releases, and compiled mailing lists of targeted groups—elected officials, school librarians, newsletter editors, social service agencies, and so on. We published a list of weekly events and sent it to all media (reprinted every week by the *Press-Citizen* for over ten years), spoke about library services to local service clubs, held special events to attract a wide range of audiences, and met with representatives of local organizations and agencies to explain services or offer library assistance. We prepared essays about new books and used them as newspaper columns and, for a while, as KRNA radio shows. (The newspaper column carried on the tradition started by Gordon in 1937, continued for a while by Nienstedt, revived by Helm, and then published regularly through June of 1980.) For three years (1972-74) we turned the public's appetite for lists of new acquisitions into a newsletter called *NEW at the Iowa City Public Library*. It combined new titles with articles about library services and general comments about the library's mission. One popular feature was a column called "You Asked Us Last Month" which featured interesting questions the library had answered. One article, "An Overview of Overdues," reminding people that returning materials on time was one of the basic premises of a free public library—sharing costs for a large collection which we also share by taking turns—was reprinted as an editorial by the *Press-Citizen*.

We also publicized our services through library staff who were active in the community. With librarians selecting materials in various assigned areas, working at the information desk, and attending meetings of groups and agencies related to their specialties, we had a network of staff increasingly alert to the interests and needs of various constituencies of the library. Aware of their collections and of the special resources of the information department, individual staff members offered help and information to various groups and in return picked up more clues about what the library needed to acquire and to do in order to better serve the organizations, businesses, and individuals of Iowa City.

We believed that special events at the library must have their own intrinsic value, but they also served to publicize the library both to those who attended and to those who only read the notices in the media. In the early 1970s, programs were a mix of the Sallie Helm type—art, literature, film, and music programs— and those of Mary Croteau—business, tax, consumer topics, and public affairs. Poetry, film showings, and photo exhibits were mixed with programs on insurance, money management, investments, and consumer topics. Hundreds attended Sunday afternoon concerts, an antique identification fair, the annual model railroad show, and films and panels about new educational methods and sex stereotyping in children's books. A "creative reading group" read and published its short works via a library-sponsored series. The 16mm film collection added a new dimension to the film programs, with more documentaries and newer productions added to the comedies and classics on 8mm film. The film showings drew audiences of 50 to 150 per program throughout the 1970s. As the years went on and the staff became busier with the steady increase in library use, there were fewer programs and more often they were done because a program or other event was the best way to address a particular topic and because no other organization seemed to be filling the need. A parliamentary procedure workshop and free tax assistance for elderly and low-income people were two examples. Frequent interaction with a wide variety of community organizations and social agencies led to the custom of cosponsored programs. The library provided the facility, the publicity, and sometimes a resource list on the topics covered, and the cosponsor recruited speakers and planned the event.

Because a parallel series of year-round programs in the children's department (drawing an audience in 1976 of over 25,000) sometimes conflicted or competed with those planned for adults, the library established a programming committee about 1976 to coordinate children's, young adult, and adult programming plans. Both departments did some joint programming with the city recreation department.

Under Judy Kelley, young adult programming changed from the folk singing and poetry readings of the 1960s to a concentration on more practical issues: drug-related problems, baby-sitting clinics, tips about getting summer jobs. The young adult librarian was in contact with the schools and with other youth-serving agencies to identify interests and ideas for the collection and for program or book list ideas. Kelley started annual tours for all sixth graders in 1975 with emphasis not only on using the library for school assignments, but on how the library can be a lifelong resource for reading, information, and leisure time activities.

The other side of trying to serve the whole community was getting services and materials to community residents who could not come to the library. Since Sallie Helm started the service in 1965, homebound people had been receiving library materials—first delivered by the Optimists Club and later mailed. The number of registered readers had grown to over 220 by 1975 and ranged between 150 and 225 for the rest of the decade.

In 1974 the library started weekly service to the county jail using volunteers and funds from an anonymous gift.[26] The service soon became institutionalized, the library contributing staff and the county paying for library materials.

Whether volunteer or staff, the person assigned the responsibility of visiting the jail each week and taking orders for specific books always developed a strong commitment to the value and importance of weekly visits. Carol Spaziani, the chief designer of this service and the person who struggled with jail officials for several years to get reasonable jail procedures established, always reminded the staff and the public that most of the individuals in the county jail were local residents and thus easily fell within our goal of serving everybody. Spaziani's knowledge of jail service was used by public libraries throughout the state.

A third component of outreach service developed into a long and always changing list of local institutions that either accepted paperback collections for their clients (usually residents) or a "deposit" collection of books checked out to the agency and exchanged for a different selection every two to three months. Either type of collection required regular monitoring to keep the books fresh and useful. Only gift money was used in the 1970s to buy materials not available from the general collection or from the many gift paperbacks (see below), but literally thousands of volumes were either loaned or given to institutions and agencies like Oaknoll, Beverly Manor, Mark IV library and social center (now called Pheasant Ridge Apartments), United Action for Youth, boys and girls group homes, Youth Emergency Center, Women's Resource and Action Center, and Johnson County Health Care Facility. Others were added to the list throughout the 1980s and 1990s.

Also in this decade, we worked on "serving everybody" by adding nonprint formats as well as new categories of books to broaden the library's base of users. Recorded books, books for adult literacy training, books for learning English as a second language, and books in other languages provided reading and book-related materials for adults not generally considered mainstream library users. Tours for new adult readers and for special education youth featured information about music recordings, magazines, and other illustrated materials that could be of interest to those with limited reading or English skills. We taught all categories of users with special needs to call the library when they needed specific information or had questions. Providing information by telephone soon became a prime outreach service.

Mainstreaming Audiovisual Services

Joyce Nienstedt and Helen McRaith share honors as the library's first "audiovisual" librarians. McRaith was especially proud of the picture file of photographs and illustrations that she developed in the 1910-20 period, and Nienstedt, of course, started the music collection on long-playing records in 1950. Sallie Helm added art prints and 8mm films about 1965, and Hurkett was a prime mover behind our first venture into 16mm films in 1971. During the seventies, the LP collection—moved, refurbished, and enlarged several times since its inception—was the most popular in terms of loans, but in this time before video, 8mm and 16mm films were popular both for check-out and for library film showings.

We realized by this period that audiovisual services was a much larger issue than providing alternative formats "to people with special needs." To maintain and broaden the base of its users, the public library had to lose its reputation for being a print-only institution. The number of nonprint formats continued to multipy, and their use in public schools, community colleges, and business and industry intensified. Children in school (both through classroom instruction and in their learning resource centers) and adults in many kinds of post-high school training and jobs expected to find a variety of print and nonprint resources at the public library. A new generation of taxpayers, constituents, and policy makers, accustomed to listening and watching as well as reading, wanted a diversity of formats at the public library or would find them from other sources.

While books and magazines required little more than good light and a dependable, orderly system of access, most of the new formats could not be used—or even browsed—without their corresponding hardware. Films and early varieties of videotapes were expensive, the appropriate playback equipment even more costly and frequently difficult to use. Both the software and the hardware required regular inspection and maintenance. Most formats didn't fit on standard library shelving. The budget implications alone were enough to discourage most public libraries, institutions that had been much less favored with increased funding than public schools and colleges during the postwar education boom.

At ICPL the library board's first policy statement on audiovisual services (and the first official use of the term "audiovisual") appeared as a 1975 goal in its 1974 annual report. In this report the new objective was to "establish a modest audiovisual department under the direction of a trained technician who will supervise the purchase, distribution, and maintenance of nonprint materials and hardware." It noted that "the preservation of the human record in nonprint form is a vital necessity." "Preserving" was probably the wrong word. ICPL, a small public library, was not aiming at major preservation projects but wanted to give its users full access to all forms of the human record. Some learned more easily through oral or visual presentations. Everyone could use the alternative formats to fully understand and appreciate a musical performance, a painting, a scientific concept, a historical event, or the power of the spoken word in poetry, theater, or public speaking.

The growth of audiovisual services in public libraries has been gradual and often has had to confront strong resistance from the reading public. As in most communities, Iowa City book lovers and heavy readers traditionally supported the public library either as regular library users themselves, as trustees, or by lending political support when needed. There is both a generation and a format gap between many traditional print-oriented readers and younger individuals raised on a multiplicity of sound and visual sources. The traditionalist dislikes seeing funds buy tapes and films when books must be passed over. McRaith's pictures were free or of minor cost; gift money purchased recordings for twenty years, started the art collection, and funded 16mm films and equipment. Seven Rivers federal funds paid for the first collection of 8mm films. With no local tax dollars involved, many policy makers saw these collections as attractive frills capable perhaps of luring people into the library to find the real meat—books and journals. The debate heated up as soon as staff suggested that a larger portion of the library's budget be earmarked for AV materials, equipment, and staff. Trustees Kirkman and Newsome, a school media specialist and a retired library school professor, helped build board support.

By August of 1976 the library had hired an experienced audiovisual librarian. Connie Tiffany came to the library from a college library in Wisconsin with a reputation for leadership in the growing discipline of audiovisual materials, equipment, and presentations. Her impact on the library's budding media services was immediate and lasting. She could clearly articulate the purpose and scope of audiovisual services. She taught us how to make these services user-oriented and integrated into the fabric of the library rather than segregated into an isolated audiovisual department.

In her first year Tiffany analyzed all library systems—collection development, shelving, cataloging, processing, and circulation—and recommended revisions to meet audiovisual requirements. She converted a small storage room near the south reading room (the remaining part of the old librarian's office left after the 1963 remodeling, with the boarded-up fireplace still visible), into an AV preview facility allowing in-library, self-service viewing and listening. My annual report for fiscal year 1977 reported the spot was chosen for "its public location and the fact that it contained the library's only unused electrical outlets." Turntables and headsets were put in the art and music reading room and the children's department. The playback equipment required to allow in-library use of all AV materials put us in a technical mode that would give us a step up toward the video and computer revolutions that would soon engulf us.

In the annual report that year Tiffany noted that the library was expanding the AV collection to included spoken-word audio cassettes, slide sets, slide-tape programs, super 8mm sound films and filmstrips. Many new terms and concepts entered our vocabulary: "booking forms," "preview sessions," "equipment security devices," and "intershelving." By March of 1977 all audiovisual materials except LP recordings and 16mm films had been intershelved with books. Staff learned to operate and maintain various kinds of audiovisual equipment, and plans to train card holders to use AV equipment were underway. We developed many rules, policies, and instructions to deal with all this nonbook material. Libraries had been designed to collect, store, and circulate books, and now that we were increasing the type and number of other formats and were trying to treat them as equals to printed materials, many adaptations had to be devised to make the facility work for these new-

In 1977 a supply closet (on left) was remodeled to make the library's first audiovisual area shown on right.

est modes of information delivery.

In 1978 the library purchased its first half-inch videotapes, a relatively new format which looked like it might be of some value for public libraries and home use. Tiffany also helped the staff and library board understand the library's options in relation to the proposed local cable television system and she was a critical participant in the city's decisions related to implementing practical and legal oversight for the company the voters chose to receive the franchise.

Used Books Prove Their Value

Many people in communities all over the country try to give their old books to libraries. It seems to be part of the same impulse that started public libraries in the first place—a reverence for the printed word and books in particular. People dislike having to discard books as just another form of trash; they would rather find them a new home. As a consequence, unless a library puts a large warning sign at the entrance, "your old books are not welcomed here," it receives boxes and boxes of dusty, moldy, smelly books with yellowed, brittle pages and faded, broken covers. Some donors, finding publication dates before 1900, are sure they are offering valuable first editions.

Over time however, as people moved more and had more disposable income, and as books themselves became relatively cheaper, the chances increased of finding some very attractive, even valuable volumes in the boxes upon boxes people brought in. From this change, and from each library's need to dispose of discards, library book sales were born.

The full story of ICPL's successful experience with used book sales belongs to the history of the Friends of the Iowa City Public Library, but it was the staff in the mid-1970s that first decided to hold a sale. A new city attorney in 1974 freed the library from the former attorney's opinion that the only way the library could lawfully dispose of books purchased with tax dollars was to quietly send them to the dump. Selling them at a public sale was a much more enlightened, profitable, and satisfying method. The staff organized book sales in 1974 and 1975 using as stock the combination of discarded library books and the used books that came in regularly from the public. It was another way to bring attention to the library and the sales also raised funds. The 1974 sale was the first ICPL fund-raising event since the benefit theater performance and lecture series in 1897 and 1898.

We did not realize at first that Iowa City was such fertile ground for used book sales, full of book buyers and collectors who would welcome the opportunity to give their surplus volumes to the library for use in the collection or for sale to benefit the library, plus collectors, dealers, and voracious readers who would buy and buy when offered good books at a low cost. We quickly learned that, instead of refusing old books or reluctantly accepting boxfuls of primarily worthless volumes, we should invite people to give us their unwanted books. We found practical treasures for the library's collection and gave the Friends thousands of items for their book sales. By the end of the decade the Friends sales were earning $5,000 a year, much of which was returned to the library in the form of gifts designated for library materials and equipment. Those items siphoned off for library use stocked most of our outreach paperback collections and many of our in-library paperback racks and accounted for over 20 percent of the books and recordings added to the library's regular adult and children's collections, often about 2,000 volumes a year. It had become an operation valued at over $20,000 (1979 dollars) annually.

Painting a Statistical Portrait

One of our greatest strengths by the end of the decade was knowing a lot about the library and how it functioned. In 1974 we had issued *Users and Uses of the Iowa City Public Library*, a forty-page report based on the registration forms of 15,000 card holders (called "borrowers" in the report) and questionnaires completed by 4,700 building visitors on six different days in January and September of 1973 (called "users" in the report). On survey days we monitored the use of equipment and information services in the building, found out how long people stayed, and analyzed materials checked out. The report also included 1973 studies on title availability (sampling from card catalog to shelf), two years of periodical use studies, and an analysis of 1972 and 1973 acquisitions by classification number and unit cost. We had demographic information—age, gender, occupation, and education level—of both our "borrowers" and "users" to compare and contrast. Finally, we summarized the content of over 3,000 open-ended and volunteered comments made by those filling out the questionnaires. In our studies we found, for example, that 60 percent of visitors stayed thirty minutes or less, only 42 percent checked out materials, and 23 percent of all visitors read at least one magazine or newspaper. Only 10 percent asked for help. These and other results gave us many new insights into library operations, and while some were gross measures, they helped us plan the library's future.

By the end of 1979 we had five years of data about every service and collection we offered. Whether it was planning for a new facility, preparing to automate the check-out and catalog functions, designing a new phase or feature of a current service or collection, or just solving an operational problem, we knew enough about our users, services, and collections to make informed decisions and projections.

Closer analysis of all aspects of library operations helped us understand what happened to library business in the years since the addition to the Carnegie. The fresh face that Helm and Croteau put on the library in the 1960s plus the growth in the size and variety of materials and services afforded with eight years of help from the federally funded Seven Rivers Library System created one of the library's greatest growth spurts. In the ten years between 1963 and 1973 Iowa Citians more than doubled their annual borrowing rate (203,800 to 454,225).

During the next eight years total circulation leveled off and even fell a bit, but there were major changes in the types of materials circulated and in the user base of the library. The children that descended on Nienstedt's staff in the 1950s and regularly marched through the enlarged children's room of the new addition were accounting for 50 to 60 percent of all library loans between 1950 and 1971. The number of children in the community decreased rapidly after that and by the mid-1970s loans of children's materials dropped back to the historic pattern of about one-third of the library's annual business (where it has remained to this day).

In a period of little change in total circulation, the reduction in children's loans concealed the great 1970s spurt in service to adult users. Adults (some of them, of course, were the heavy juvenile users of the 1950s era) increased their use by 75 percent. The growth of information services and programs brought more people into the library (nearly 300,000 a year as counted by the electronic theft detection gate installed in 1975). A larger share of audiovisual loans plus service to homebound borrowers and jail residents increased the complexities and time required to check out, retrieve, and reshelve materials. The general improvement in the availability of the adult collection and its stronger coverage of subjects identified as of interest to a wide variety of adults created many new regular users. Finally, new contracts and reciprocal agreements increased the number of people eligible to use the library.

County-wide Service . . . Briefly

The decade of the 1970s turned out to be the golden age of ICPL serving county residents. After seventy-five years of seeking contracts and setting non-resident fees which would equitably reimburse the library for service to those not paying Iowa City property taxes, and after an equally long period when nonresidents wanted library service but not enough to pay anywhere near its actual cost, several disparate circumstances suddenly made county-wide service a real possibility. For three years, from 1974 through 1976, everyone in Johnson County, both rural and town residents, could borrow materials from the Iowa City Public Library. Through a combination of court rulings, contracts, short-term state funding, and reciprocal agreements, residents of University Heights, Lone Tree, North Liberty, Hills, Tiffin, Swisher, Shueyville, Coralville, Solon, and Oxford and all university students were eligible. Between 1967 and 1976 the population served by ICPL jumped from 22,000 to 67,000, plus another 7,650 if those communities with public libraries served through reciprocal agreements were included.

The details make a complex story, with jurisdictions dropping in and out for reasons not always controlled by the ICPL board. In the same year as the first contract with the Johnson County Board of Supervisors for rural residents (1968), a court ruling regarding university students ended the board's many efforts to define which of those students were eligible users. University enrollees were counted as Iowa City residents in the 1960 federal census if they spent the majority of their time in Iowa City—which most students did—and thus could not be denied local services. UI students and rural residents added about 20,000 eligible users. University Heights was contracting directly with the city for all services from 1966 to 1978, and the library board signed service contracts with Lone Tree in 1971 and North Liberty in 1972.

The establishment of the new state-financed regional library system in 1974 (Seven Rivers officially ended December 31, 1973) was the final step in making service in Johnson County universal, at least for a few years. To encourage communities without public libraries to contract with a local library, as North Liberty and Lone Tree had recently done, the new Iowa legislation authorized funds for a four-year demonstration program. Residents of all towns without libraries could get service at an area library, and the serving library would receive twenty-five cents for each loan. For the next four years residents of Hills, Tiffin, Swisher, and Shueyville gained free use of the library and ICPL earned a few hundred dollars from the state. A statewide reciprocal borrowing agreement was another requirement of the new regional system if institutions wanted to receive other services. This opened ICPL's doors to area residents living in Coralville, Solon, and Oxford, although Solon and Iowa City had exchanged services since Solon joined Seven Rivers in 1968. Card holders from public libraries in neighboring counties—West Branch, West Liberty, Kalona, Wellman—also started using the library under this agreement. At the same time many Iowa Citians living on the west side started using the Coralville library.

Universal coverage was short lived. Lone Tree dropped its contract in 1977. University Heights ended its contract with Iowa City in 1978, the same year that the state-funded demonstration project closed. None of the four Johnson County towns chose to continue library service by using local funds. North Liberty's last contract was in 1981. This brought ICPL back to serving only rural residents by contract and continuing reciprocal agreements with the other libraries in the county, a situation that would hold through the end of the library's first century.

The library board continued to increase the contract price for library service throughout the 1970s. It first went to two and then three dollars per capita, and in 1977, after experimenting with contracts based on share of total circulation for a few years, the trustees settled on a formula that for the first time added a 15 percent surcharge to the per capita share to cover part of the library's long-term capital costs which were not reflected in its annual operating budget. This brought the county's annual fee to nearly $45,000 for fiscal year 1979, a long way from the original $5,000, and nearly 10 percent of the library's 1979 budget. The county would continue to account for about 10 percent of total library loans and pay 10 percent of annual operating expenses until a new library-county formula and competition from a new statewide reciprocal borrowing program in the late 1980s would change all the rules.

The county's increased share of library operating costs was rewarded by representation on the library board under the home rule legislation of 1975. The new legislation required all municipalities operating public libraries to adopt an ordinance setting out the powers and responsibilities of the local library board. It contained language similar to the just-deleted state legislation. Because home rule was designed to give local jurisdictions more control over their own affairs, and fearing the abolition of library boards, trustees throughout the state fought for inclusion of a clause in the model ordinance that required a referendum by the citizens of the municipality before city councils could alter or eliminate powers held by library boards. Iowa City adopted the model ordinance in June of 1975, exercising the one option the new legislation allowed: appointment of a county resident to serve on the library board if the county has a contract with the library. For reasons not recorded nor now remembered, the city did not exercise this new option until 1981 when stockbroker Herbert Lyman became the first county representative.

Budget Battles of the 1970s

Although library boards of Iowa won the 1975 battle to preserve their powers under home rule, the Iowa City struggle between council and board was far from over and the skirmishes continued, although generally in a less public manner than under the unsympathetic and confrontational tactics of city manager Ray Wells.[27] It was less public because the referendum protected the library board from frontal attack by the council, and because the appointment of Neal Berlin (1975-85) to replace Wells gave the library not only an avid and regular library user but also brought ten years of his support for library needs. That changed the balance of power. All of us, trustees and staff, benefited regularly from his advice. In the middle to late 1970s the library had yet to demonstrate its strong public support through success at the polls, but without a city manager to urge council members on, the council's conflicts with the library board were a little less one-sided.

Year after year, the library's chief need and the library board's principal request was for increased staff. The steady growth in library use—information, special services, public information, long-term planning, as well as the core library tasks of collection development, purchase, processing, and circulation of library materials—required more and more people. We were reaping the overwhelming "rewards" of the wider scope of services initiated by our eager, competent, but inexperienced professional staff during the Hurkett years.

Although I believe it happened on my watch, it is unclear just when the council decisions about additional staff changed from granting a salary budget to approving each additional staff position. As salaries and benefits increased and union contracts and federal law narrowed the council's flexibility, the council became reluctant to add permanent positions which, in times of cutbacks or layoffs, required complex procedures to ensure fairness and respect for seniority. Since the late 1960s the library had used every work/study, CETA (Comprehensive Employment and Training Act), Mayor's Youth, and vocational rehabilitation employee that federal and state funds would supply. The number of "temporary" employees also had increased. But these young people could only supplement and assist the regular, committed, long-term permanent employee, and council approval for such positions was becoming harder and harder to obtain.

There were two concepts that the council and library board frequently squabbled over. Both would continue to be contentious issues throughout the 1980s and '90s. The first was a disagreement over the term "level of service." When council members decreed that there would be no increase in the level of service for the coming budget year, they believed that any increase in resources given the library (or other city department) increased the level of service. The library board claimed, on the other hand, that the library offered a limited set of services and if it required more staff to deliver those services because more members of the public were using them, this was not an increase in the level of service but simply an increase to the resources to continue the current program. Like inflationary increases, it required more money to do the same thing.

While "level of service" may have been a somewhat arcane or semantic argument, the other disagreement could have a more dramatic impact. In years of most serious need, if the council did not approve at least some of the staff requested, the library board would vote to reduce library hours rather than reduce services. After cutting service on Sundays and Thursday evenings in 1974, the board threatened to do the same following a major reduction in its proposed fiscal year 1978 budget. That year the council and the board reached a settlement but in the process the board adopted a policy statement concerning its position:

> The public's benefit from library services is affected more by the variety and quality of services provided than by the length of time they are available. Therefore, offering the fullest service possible while open must take priority over longer hours at lower levels of service.[28]

In support of this position, the board argued that a library has certain standards for quality library service. If there is less quality with longer hours the public just assumes it is a poor library. Also, cutbacks of staff and materials, if and when they are restored, are generally viewed as additions to the "level of service" by future councils and not as replacements for past cuts. Whatever services are cut in a situation where hours are maintained, those services can then be judged by others as extra, not priority, and thus candidates for future reductions. If some services are reduced part of the time (no information service on Sundays, for example) then the library visitor is confused about when services are available or goes away unaware that his request would have been handled on another day.

In January 1978 there was a classic budget battle on these issues. After a review of the proposed city budget, Library Board President David Kirkman announced, "We will have to close on Sundays and Thursday evenings. We won't be able to provide the same levels of materials that we have had, and we'll have to shorten the hours we are open for business." The *Press-Citizen* quoted me as telling the council that Sunday was the most costly day to operate. "It is a time when the library is heavily used, but it stretches our resources in every department to have to add six hours on Sunday. . . . We are producing about as much as we can produce with the current staff."[29]

Three days later the council voted to add $30,000 to the library's fiscal year 1979 budget. My quoted comment: "We think the $30,000 will enable us to beef up our staff enough to stay open on Sundays and Thursdays and continue approximately the same level of library services that we have now. We will have to . . . stretch a little, but we can do it." The story goes on to describe the two part-time clerks and part-time librarian we planned to hire.[30]

In a few days Mayor Robert Vevera and councilwoman Mary Neuhauser said they were surprised to learn of planned additions to the staff for the next fiscal year, "after settling last week on a library budget that was supposed to maintain services at their current level." According to the newspaper I told the council I thought they understood that more staff would be needed to maintain current services in the face of greater use. In a formal memo to the council justifying its plans for $30,000, the library board said it had only two options without the added funds: "Maintain the same quality of service whenever the library is open and reduce the number of hours [or] maintain the number of hours the library is open, but reduce the quality of service offered. . . . In either case, the level of service is reduced." The council voted 4 to 3 to reverse its decision on the additional $30,000, and the library board closed the library on Sundays and Thursday evenings starting July 1, 1978.[31]

Preliminaries to a New Building

All the trustees responsible for the 1963 addition to the Carnegie were gone by 1969. Despite overlapping terms, the modern custom of only one six-year appointment for library trustees gave less continuity to library operations than in the days of members spending ten, twenty, even thirty years on the board.[32] The nineteen trustees who served between 1969 and 1981 generally viewed the library building, both old and new parts, with equal disdain. While the original Carnegie was honored for its historic value, the addition was considered poorly planned and of little merit.

Comments about the building from the public in the 1973 user study were equally damning. The needs for handicapped accessibility, warm and ventilated restrooms, and quiet places to study were most frequently mentioned. "My [handicapped] daughter has never been able to use this library." "I'd like a quiet and large enough spot to research a term paper and not have to carry home all the needed materials." "Expand! You need more room here." "I freeze my b— in the rest rooms!" (When Helm converted two closets to public restrooms from what was the former front entrance, no heating or insulation was added.) Seating had already been reduced to ninety places, with additional shelving scheduled to take out more tables and chairs in 1974.

The building itself seemed determined to prove its own unworthiness. Fire, roof leaks, and equipment failure caused several emergency closings during 1974 and 1975. A fire set in the library's book return on December 2, 1974, resulted in major damage to that room and extensive smoke damage to the rest of the build-

ing. We had to clean, paint, or replace fixtures, drapes, walls, carpets, books, and shelves throughout the building. The continuing problem of minor roof leaks escalated into a major one in 1974. The Linn Street entrance was closed for four days because of the volume of water coming down the back stairwell. The problem spread to other parts of the building the next summer when three major leaks oc-

Conditions were chaotic in the sorting area where all materials had to be transported by two small dumbwaiters.

curred during torrential rains while the roof was being replaced. Contents of one supply closet were destroyed, including, we believe, official library board minutes for 1927-45. A boiler breakdown also closed the library for one day in 1974.

By early 1974, the city council, library board, staff, and many regular library users agreed that a completely new facility was the only answer to a modern public library program. University library school director Fred Wezeman also met with the trustees and encouraged them to seek a new facility. Even if failing mechanical systems could be corrected, the building's plan and structure was an insurmountable barrier to universal accessibility and efficient operations. That summer the entry in the city's Capital Improvement Program (CIP) changed from "a new or an addition to library" to "study, design, construct a new building" with a cost estimate of $3 million for fiscal year 1979 or 1980.

After a visit to Iowa City in April 1974, building consultant Robert H. Rohlf was asked to submit a proposal for assisting in planning a new building. Rohlf, director of the Hennepin County (Minnesota) Public Library, was recommended by Wezeman and had a nationwide reputation for his work in planning public libraries, including the many architecturally interesting branches of the Hennepin system. In his proposal letter a few months later, Rohlf made it very clear how he felt. "It would be economically unfeasible, if not irresponsible," he wrote, "to attempt another addition to your present building . . . my proposal is . . . only for a new project [and if this is in conflict with board wishes] I withdraw the proposal."

Rohlf's initial task was to develop a written building program and recommend a site. To better understand the library's program and the board's intentions, he asked the board and staff to produce some long-range goals. This request gave staff members the opening they had wanted—to discuss the library's developing values in more depth with members of the library board. After the conflict of the summer of 1974, this task, which took several months, gave both groups a valuable agenda for dialogue, and the set of goals produced reflected much of what the staff had been working for during the previous five years. The goal statement became the first official document to formally express these ideas, and the goals would guide the design of the building from the very first day of planning.

The three-page document listed twenty-four goals under eight headings. Some goals were restatements or enhancements of the simple agenda noted earlier that staff librarians had been pursuing since about 1969. Other goals were additions, recognizing activities already underway or developed through discussion. Several statements concerned ambitious political and interjurisdictional ideas about a county library and written service agreements with the university, Kirkwood Community College, and the school system and were never seriously pursued. Most, however, would be recognizable to anyone familiar with the library's history since 1975. They spoke to the value of planning, measurement, and evaluation and to the central role of competent, fair-minded, service-oriented staff. The goal concerning the library's environment was transferred to one of the early pages of the final draft of the written building program. It described an informal public "living room" where people borrow materials, seek and are given information and referrals, attend community events and library programs, and spend leisure time in an atmosphere where suggestions and contributions are welcomed, individuality and privacy honored.

Other goal statements still of interest twenty years later include the concept that persons unaffiliated with educational institutions—from preschoolers to adults out of school—would receive the library's primary support, while the task of assisting public school curriculum would be secondary. Programs for school-age students would emphasize their nonstudent roles with only backup services for their school-related needs. Collections, "in whatever medium is most acceptable to the user," should be more than educational and practical. They should serve an individual's "self-realization, self-expression and mental recreation" needs and recognize the "many levels and varieties of cultural taste and appreciation."

The information service was described as the "first place to call for general information and as the switching point (referral center) for more specialized information sources." If not provided elsewhere, the library should provide "in-depth" information "essential to living and functioning in the community." The public catalog, all library resources, and the building itself should be organized so they are "understandable to those with limited skills and/or library experience," with guides or other suitable materials produced to "promote, describe and interpret the library's collections and services."

There was a long list of groups and organizations to be served at the library or through outreach: "the geographically remote; the handicapped and/or homebound; the institutionalized; community organizations and government agencies with special needs and interests; and those groups who seldom use traditional library services: farming, labor, and business personnel, elderly, low-income groups and those with limited reading skills."

Finally, the goals included a determination to "make full use of video and cable TV as it develops" and to "provide public access to audiovisual production and playback facilities." In retrospect, these goal statements provide a fairly accurate picture of the library as planned and eventually built. Only automation, central to library operations by 1979, is missing from this 1975 document.

From the day I became the permanent library director in March of 1975 until the new facility opened on June 15, 1981, at least 50 percent of the time and attention of senior staff and board members focused on the building project. None of us had any hands-on experience with planning and constructing a library—or any other kind of public building. We knew we had a lot to learn. We attended workshops, visited other public libraries, and interviewed people who had built libraries, including those who had been ICPL trustees in the time of the Carnegie addition. We were guided by our consultant and by trustee David Kirkman who had written about the planning process for designing school libraries as his master's thesis and who had some practical experience as an electrical contractor.

Our understanding of the components of the task, the steps in the process, deepened, and before long we all could have recited the litany: set goals, write a program, select a site, hire an architect, develop preliminary plans, estimate costs and adjust plans, determine the dollar amount of bonds required, set date for election, mount an informational campaign, get voters to the polls, analyze the victory or defeat, and plan the next steps. We saw lots of hard work and planning ahead, but nevertheless it seemed a straightforward, relatively rational process. We were given the standard advice for such an undertaking, "Think big because it will be compromise, compromise all the way." We expected to make concessions, adjust differences, strike bargains; we were not prepared for the many alternative agendas that arose to threaten or delay our major objective—to build a library capable of delivering library services in the variety of ways our goals described.

Steps to Seeking Voter Approval

In June 1976 the board approved the *Recommended Building Program, Iowa City Public Library*.[33] The first version was received in January of that year and the staff and board immediately formed task forces to develop ideas to answer issues raised by Rohlf's draft. This was another opportunity for staff and board members to work together, and six months later when approval was given to the program we all helped develop, there was fairly unified opinion among board and staff about what the library should be. The written program outlined in words the size and kind of physical spaces required to fulfill library goals. It would be given to the architect to guide his design ideas.

Site selection . . . site fight. With the written program approved and the optimum square footage determined, Rohlf's next assignment was to help the city select an appropriate site. In the summer of 1976 there were still several empty and unsold urban renewal parcels left in downtown Iowa City. Court action had stayed progress on the city's Urban Renewal Project R-14 and Rohlf was counseled by city officials to "investigate the possibility of a new library location within the central business district development area."[34] Rohlf was looking for a location large enough to accommodate a minimum first floor of 36,000 square feet. In addition it had to meet the generally accepted criteria for public library siting: a location central to all segments of the community on a primary street, preferably at an intersection, with dense pedestrian traffic and close to public transportation and parking. He looked at all the possible sites in the thirteen-block redevelopment area and for various reasons eliminated them all except block 64 and block 65. Using a point system to rate various factors, he described and ranked six sites, four in and two outside the urban renewal area [see diagram]. His first, second, and fourth choices were 45,000-square-foot sites on the southwest, northeast, and southeast corners of block 64. His third choice was the southwest corner of block 65. The biggest drawback of this site was its small size. It was only 27,450 square feet and the study noted it required vacating all of College Street south of the site to reach the desired 45,000. Rohlf's final recommendation was that the city give the library 45,000 square feet somewhere on block 64. The library board sent this recommendation along with a copy of the site study and the building program to the city council on July 14, 1976.

After clarifying with the council that this was a request, not a demand, the council's initial rhetoric cooled and members spent several weeks discussing the site recommendation. Mayor Neuhauser said she realized the consultant looked for the best possible site in library terms, but believed a majority of the council considered "block 64 too valuable as commercial land to be used for a library." Hoping for a hotel and parking ramp on block 64, the city and business community wanted to market it as a unit. David Perret and other council members expressed interest in locating the library in a "multi-purpose building—perhaps including shops, offices, apartments or parking—in the renewal area."[35] Finally, the council turned to its urban redevelopment consultant, Donald R. Zuchelli, for a recommendation. In February 1977 councilors and, somewhat reluctantly, library trustees accepted his choice of block 65 on the northwest corner of Linn and College streets. By giving the board permission to use up to forty feet of the College Street right-of-way, the smallish site was stretched to 34,000 square feet. This was the first major compromise. The site was smaller than the desired footprint for the first floor and allowed for no on-site parking.

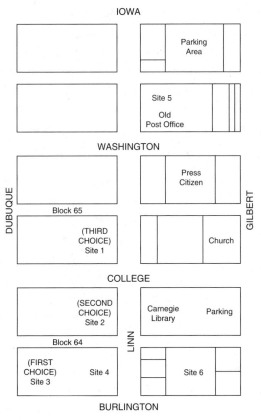

Library Sites Recommended by Consultant Robert Rohlf, 1976

Board and staff members thought that when the council gave official approval to block 65 in July of 1977, step two in our pursuit of a new library, "select a site," was over. The location for the new library, however, would prove to be even more of a contentious issue than the struggle in 1902 when the site for the Carnegie was chosen. After the brief wrangle with the council over block 64, it soon became apparent to the library board that the business community and many others did not like block 65 any better than the library's original request. They did not want the library on *any* urban renewal land. Consultants Rohlf and Zuchelli both argued the case for the library as an attraction to bring people downtown. Zuchelli said the library would "anchor" the east end of the pedestrian mall and, like the shopping mall on the west, would draw people to the shops and businesses in between. Many site opponents looked at the consultants as the hired guns of the city and the library board and did not trust their opinions.

From the day it was announced and throughout the next eighteen months, the site became the major issue. In the fall of 1977 former trustee and downtown merchant Tom Summy asked the board to "rethink" the site; trustee and downtown merchant Roz Moore reported, "Downtowners are unhappy!" In the spring of 1978 when board members appeared before the Chamber of Commerce Board to inform them about the specifics of the library plans, I noted in my building project journal, "They were only interested in talking about the site. They dislike the site overwhelmingly." The pressure forced the library board, at some expense for a professional evaluation, to explain why an addition or a complete new building could not be built on the parking lot next to the current library. Finally, convinced it could not persuade the library board or the city council to change their minds, the Chamber voted to oppose the referendum. The *Press-Citizen* joined the Chamber editorially. This opposition became the engine that drove the whole campaign and probably decided the outcome of the election.

Before the library ever selected its architect, or developed a preliminary design, or set an election date, many Iowa Citians were voicing their dissatisfaction with the site. The campaign debate was supposedly still four "steps" ahead in the process, but we began to discover it was not all as rationally ordered as we had hoped.

"Select an architect" . . . **but do it twice.** The first round of steps to select an architectural firm was textbook perfect: proposals, interviews, visits with former clients, decision. The board voted 7-2 to hire Hansen Lind Myer (HLM) in June of 1977. Three months of negotiating a contract and initial design work ended suddenly in October when HLM's assigned design architect, Douglas Barker, left the firm. Upset at losing the person who had most influenced their choice, board members voted to cancel the contract and re-interview the final four firms. Somewhat to their public chagrin, the trustees again selected HLM when the firm offered an even more engaging and articulate design architect, Charles Engberg. Engberg turned out to be a solid choice and Barker's departure a fortuitous development. No compromise here; the board held fast and got much in return.

I was extremely pleased with the change to Engberg. I had already noted in my building project journal that I kept during much of the preliminary design and referendum campaign period (1977-79) that I had reservations about Barker's willingness to listen to staff ideas. An August entry read, "Although he espouses the view that staff input is important . . . I can see that he is not always listening . . . seems anxious to write his own program . . . he needs a lot of education about how a library operates." In October of 1977 when we began working with Engberg, I noted after his first session with the staff, "Engberg . . . sounds good. I think we can work well together. Staff responds to him. He seems to *want* our information." I don't think our opinion on Engberg ever wavered after that. After warnings from many librarians about architects who want to build monuments instead of functional libraries, we were extremely pleased with the relationship that developed between Engberg and those of us trying to work out operational details. We were hoping for a successful and rewarding architect-librarian team and Engberg proved to be the perfect partner. Working on his first library, he was open to our ideas but firm about who should make the architectural decisions. "Describe the problem," he would say, "and let me find the architectural solution." He was flexible, quick to grasp the issue we were addressing, and produced a stream of possibilities, especially at the early stages of concept design.[36]

"Develop preliminary plans." The staff and board went into the preliminary design phase well-equipped to judge options offered by the architect. In addition to their joint development of the long-term goals and many aspects of the written program, the board had held four public hearings in September of 1977 requesting ideas and comments for features and facilities of a new library. On the weekend before the first hearing, board members had handed out fliers about the hearings at four shopping areas and talked with many citizens. Every community organization received a letter inviting it to send a representative. Over one hundred people attended the four meetings held in the library auditorium and a few groups sent letters. Amidst mostly positive suggestions and information-seeking questions, there were a few angry comments about the site and some skepticism about the trustees' ability to plan a facility that would be better than the Carnegie addition. Since late 1976 library visitors had filled three notebooks with their suggestions and comments about the building, the collection, and services. The 1973 user study had produced over 1,000 unsolicited comments about the library. Filtering all these ideas through the technical and professional skills of the staff and the financial and political views of the board, our vision of how the library should function was fairly firm.

Working out a site plan and distributing functions between two floors and a basement was more difficult with the smaller site. We even considered an option or two that allowed for some parking on the site, but they were quickly discarded to protect the valuable first-floor space. Using the basement for more than storage, mechanical equipment, and future expansion was looked at and also dropped. In a series of meetings in January and February of 1978 a plan very similar to the final building layout received approval from the staff, the building committee (myself, staff representative Susan McGuire, city manager Neal Berlin, and trustees Bezanson and Kirkman), and finally, from the entire board. We had rejected library consultant Robert Rohlf's recommendation to put children's services, the meeting rooms, and media production on the second floor. Our ideal had been to have all public services on the first floor, and in this configuration we put them all there except the adult nonfiction collection and some seating and study areas. Engberg had taken us through about ten different schemes, had worked out details on those we thought plausible, and had brought us to a relatively easy agreement on "Concept H-1."

"Estimate costs and adjust plans." We had reached accord on what seemed the best possible preliminary plan for a library to be built on a busy corner in the "new" downtown Iowa City along the pedestrian plaza. Consequently, it was hard to swallow the news that we couldn't afford it. HLM cost estimates placed a $5 million price tag on the design. We were told that $3.5 million was all the city could afford and the maximum that the public would approve. With that warning, the cuts were quick and sharp. Eliminate the basement. Reduce the total space by 5,000 square feet. Cut out one elevator, combine stairways into a central staircase, and omit the two-story spaces above several first-floor areas. The saved space reduced the gross to net space ratio, that is, made more efficient use of the total space. First-floor spaces remained essentially the same with each area slightly smaller, but the second floor was made compact and L-shaped. Shelving and seating space accounted for about half of the reductions "because they would be the easiest to build when expanding." The northwest corner was eliminated completely, reserving about 9,200 square feet for future expansion. Mechanical units were moved to the roof; the boiler, mechanical controls, and storage were located on the second floor.

As Engberg and HLM staff worked on these proposed changes, the board and staff debated how best to proceed. Some board members felt that furnishings, AV, and computer systems should be reduced to save space and architectural features; staff and other trustees argued for slight cutbacks in all areas rather than eliminating whole functions. In the final project budget, furniture and equipment costs were reduced by $250,000 under a strategy of using interest from the bond money to flesh out those categories later. (Interest rates were very high in 1979-81, peaking in 1981 at 13 percent.) The changes were less radical than we first imagined and the best of the first-floor ideas were preserved. Expansion to the basement had never been very attractive and the original second story was fairly chopped up with the architect's two-story open spaces. We compromised, but on aesthetics more than function.

"Decide the dollar amount and set an election date." By the time everyone agreed on the changes for a smaller, less costly library, it was May 1, 1978, and the board was hoping for a fall referendum. There was no wiggle room on the $3.5 million after the city finance director promised to say publicly, if asked, that it was all the city could afford. Setting an election date took a little longer. Trustees had studied the results of other library bond issue elections and decided they wanted the issue on the ballot alone. The recently elected auditor and commissioner of elections, Tom Slockett, was preparing for his first general election in November and said "no" to an October date. He determined for us that it would be legal to have the issue on the school board election of September 12, but a meeting with the school board revealed its lawyer not only interpreted the Iowa Code differently, but also school board members didn't want to tempt fate by bringing out "new voters" to their election. Only one possible time was left; put it on the ballot in the general election of November 7, 1978.

"Organize a campaign to inform the public." During these years, as was true during 1902-04 and 1961-63, board members gave an inordinate amount of time and thought to library matters. In 1977 and 1978, for example, the board held nearly thirty meetings each year and average member attendance surpassed 85 percent. Board Presidents Ron Farber (1976-77), David Kirkman (1978), and Randall Bezanson (1979-80) made many public appearances and public statements. Other trustees worked behind the scenes developing plans, recruiting volunteers, talking to influential community members, writing campaign materials, and speaking to groups.

As soon as the library board saw a possible new facility in Iowa City's future, members started making plans to establish a Friends of the Library organization. Beginning in 1974 trustees Jerry Newsome and Ron Farber reported regularly to the board on progress towards this goal. Newsome especially, a former public librarian in Petaluma, California, and a navy librarian during World War II, recognized the value of such a support group for helping with a referendum campaign. By early 1975 the committee of two had prepared a list of five goals under the rubric, "Why organize a Friends of the Library?" Goal four said Friends can help "build public support for expansion of the library's physical facilities." A year later Newsome reported that an organizing steering committee under the chairmanship of Ann Bagford had been organized, and in the fall of 1976 bylaws and articles of incorporation were completed and the first membership meeting was held. By the end of the fiscal year, June 1977, Bagford had completed the first Friends year with over three hundred members, a treasury of $3,000, and newly elected co-presidents Dottie Ray and Ann Feddersen ready to take over. The library's 1977 annual report listed the new organization as one of the year's major accomplishments. Friends had taken over the annual book sale from the staff and were planning a long list of other activities.

In the fall of 1977 the Friends board heard ICPL Board President Kirkman review the status of the building plans and in response the Friends officers promised to take the question of bond issue support to the membership at their annual meeting in April of 1978. The promised discussion, however, was never taken to the membership and the Friends board agonized over the organization's proper role for several months. By the time Board President Randall Bezanson met with the Friends board a year later, the Friends had agreed to host a public meeting on the issue in September before the vote and conduct tours of the old building.

They had given the "New Library For Everyone" committee access to the Friends membership list, and individual members were giving financial support and serving as volunteers in several capacities. Bezanson told them that the "library board was concerned that the Friends had not come out publicly in favor of the bond issue."[37] The Friends board of directors, however, decided that the best route for the Friends was to remain officially neutral on the bond referendum.

The directors explained that the Friends intended to continue to support the library whether the bond issue was approved or not, and, in the words of one director, it "definitely should not be a one-issue organization."[38] If the library board thought they were forming a group whose first task would be to support a new library, the resulting organization did not agree. The Friends continued to expand its membership, take on other kinds of library promotion and advocacy activities, and provide major financial support. It became a powerful support group for the library but always remained in the background when the library was in the political arena.

ICPL board and staff felt that one of the first steps in a successful campaign was to prepare information about the need for more space and the major inadequacies of the present building. After nearly seventy-five years on the corner of Linn and College, the library was a fixture of Iowa City to many who never entered its doors. We needed succinct and dramatic data about needs and conditions. While I worked on a series of background papers that could be given to library trustees and staff, city council and staff, and other supportive individuals, part-time employee Susan Craig used the data to create a slide-tape show for use with groups. Entitled *Growing Pains* and originally done as work towards Craig's M.L.S degree, the slide show became the campaign's major visual presentation about the inadequacies of the existing library. It featured a series of dramatic pictures showing the many levels, the crowded shelves and reading rooms, inefficient operations, and below-code physical conditions. It was updated a couple of times as the campaign proceeded and the photographs used in the production were later featured in displays at the library, at the Sycamore Mall, and in windows of downtown businesses.

The library board's public information committee, Lynda Ostedgaard and Suzanne Richerson, started meeting with me weekly in early 1977 to begin to plan a referendum campaign, to create and distribute information about the need for a new library, to select someone to direct the final phase of the campaign, and to hold my hand whenever events heated up or new strategies were called for. They had read about other campaigns, digested the staff-produced data, prepared "frequently asked questions" to distribute to anyone interested in the details of the library project, lined up speaking engagements, wrote press releases,

In the late 1970s crowded conditions became a major problem as illustrated here in the children's room.

and planned the September 1977 hearings held to gather input from the general public.

By late 1977 the three of us were meeting with councilwoman Carol deProsse. She was first elected to the council in the fall of 1973 and from her first day in office had been a strong supporter of the library and the building project. She, councilwoman Mary Neuhauser, and city manager Neal Berlin were generous in their help and support for a new library, but when the trustees could not find someone to head the election campaign, when the idea of a paid campaign coordinator was dropped for lack of funds, deProsse volunteered to take the job. First we searched for someone to cochair with her—several past trustees and community leaders were approached—but when this too failed, deProsse offered to take on the job alone, if the board would give her a fairly free hand. It took board members a while to accept her challenge, to evaluate the effect of her name alone at the top of the campaign organization. A local elected official heading a citizens committee advocating the expenditure of local funds was fairly unusual, but deProsse was never a typical councilor and had always been open about where she stood and what she stood for. It worked.

The city attorney had ruled that the city's campaign election laws would apply to the referendum campaign: No one could contribute more than fifty dollars, the names of all who gave at least ten dollars had to be recorded, and a committee officer had to officially register the committee and record and report all income and expenditures. While trustee Dick Hyman served as the treasurer of the committee, deProsse set the strategy, recruited volunteers, reported regularly to the library board, and used trustees as key players in her plan.

By the summer of 1978, with a preliminary building plan scaled back to meet the city-imposed budget, an adequate but controversial site, and a skilled and tough-minded campaign chair, the staff and trustees were eager for the last round in a process that had started more than three years earlier. The summer months were filled with discussion about how to frame the issues, what to put in the campaign brochures, and how to respond to the Chamber of Commerce's insistence that the best plan for the public library was to add on or build anew on the present library site and parking lot. The library board commissioned HLM to do an evaluation of the Carnegie library and present the options and rough costs of a new building or an addition to the present library on the Carnegie site.

On September 11, 1978, deProsse held a news conference in front of the information desk at the library to kick off the campaign. She said the overall theme, "A New Library For Everyone," was chosen "because the goal of the Library Board and the City Council is to be able to provide an adequate and accessible library that will allow everyone, including the young, the handicapped, and the elderly, to use the library with ease and convenience—something that is not possible in the present building."

deProsse outlined in some detail the various opportunities for citizens to inform themselves about the issues: brochures distributed house-to-house, library tours, newspaper and radio advertising, leaflets to parents of schoolchildren, displays at several locations, radio interviews with library trustees, presentations to both the public and Catholic school boards. She explained that the brochure had been designed to "forthrightly explain the need [and] answer the most commonly asked questions." A random sampling of people who receive the brochure would be called, deProsse said, to determine their attitudes toward the library project. She emphasized the willingness of the referendum committee to provide any additional information that the voting public might need to help them make their decision. Finally, she stressed that this was a huge volunteer effort—"I believe it will be one of the most extensive volunteer efforts Iowa City has ever seen for a local issue"—and assured the public that "absolutely no expenditures of public funds will be involved in the effort to pass the referendum."[39]

City councilwoman Carol deProsse, seen here (standing) in the library's 1978 University of Iowa homecoming parade entry. DeProsse coordinated the referendum campaign for the library.

There were not many surprises during the final nine weeks. In late September HLM presented its *Architectural and Engineering Study of the Existing Library Facility, Iowa City, Iowa* to the library board. Renovation and an addition was estimated to cost about $400,000 more than the

The "New Library For Everyone" campaign was kicked off September 11, 1978. This display was in the library.

current proposal. Even the proposed building built on the old library lot would cost more because of demolition and relocation costs. The report gives the best-ever description of the Carnegie addition's multilevel conundrum and the near-architectural impossibility of using the space efficiently.

The Iowa City Education Association, the city employees' labor union, and the editorial staffs of both high school newspapers endorsed the referendum, and support letters began appearing regularly in the *Press-Citizen*. On October 19, just three weeks before the vote, the Chamber of Commerce announced that it "cannot support" the proposed bond issue for a new public library on "prime retail space." Instead, it said, the Chamber stood ready to give full support to a new plan and new bond issue to build on the "half block which includes the present site."

The responses from Library Board President Randall Bezanson and from referendum coordinator deProsse were immediate and strong. "The Chamber's suggestion will involve considerable added costs to the taxpayer," Bezanson noted, because "of demolition and temporary library location. . . . The proposed site [on City Plaza] will be good for downtown development now and in the future." Councilwoman and campaign coordinator deProsse noted that the city's original urban renewal plans had a parking ramp on the proposed library site. Questioning the Chamber's sincerity about the commercial value of the proposed site, she said, "If the city wanted to put another public facility, a parking ramp, there today the Chamber would be 100 percent for it."[40] The sale of the old library would balance the loss of tax revenue from commercial use of block 65, deProsse and Bezanson argued. A debate between deProsse and former mayor and councilor C.L. (Tim) Brandt at a community forum sponsored by the First Christian Church on the next day covered much of the same ground but also received detailed newspaper coverage.

Four days after the *Daily Iowan* wrote a strong "anti-establishment" endorsement for the library issue, the *Press-Citizen* followed up its May 1978 editorial questions about the site with a strongly worded, long editorial advising a "no" vote on November 7. In retrospect, I think the *Press-Citizen* probably gave the best-reasoned arguments and scenario for building on the old library site, but by then the paper was seen only as a mouthpiece for the Chamber.

After the official Chamber declaration, interest in the bond issue campaign broadened. More letters of support appeared (seventeen of eighteen letters on the issue published in the last ten days urged a "yes" vote), the telephone survey promised by deProsse showed strong support, and on November 3, the usually neutral city manager released copies of a letter to Iowa City Chamber of Commerce President Donald Hebert. It was front-page news in the *Press-Citizen* of that day. In his letter Berlin said that the Chamber's proposal to sell the planned library site for commercial use could "injure" urban renewal development. He noted that the city, "under a carefully tailored program to prevent creating a new blighted area due to over building new retail space" will be placing about "240,000 square feet of new leasable space" on the market "within a year or two." He charged that the Chamber "provided no factual information to support its premise that this site can be integrated into the retail market without seriously injuring the redevelopment project."

The same day, the newspaper devoted two full pages to a review of all sides of the controversy and outlined all the planning steps that had taken the community to this point. Charges from letter writers that *Press-Citizen* publisher J.C. Hickman, as a member of the Chamber board of directors, was using both positions to oppose the library were successfully explained by the paper, but the rumor did not help the Chamber-*Press-Citizen* image in the short term.

"Get voters to the polls." No standard "get out the vote" techniques were used, but radio and newspaper ads were prominent during the last few days. The ads were simple and frequently humorous—historical figures mouthing library-related puns to urge a yes vote ("The need is well defined," Noah Webster) and a typical endorsement ad whose long list of supporters all turn out to be literary characters. The one exception to this light approach was a half-page, text-heavy ad describing in detail one more time why it would be more costly and less satisfactory to build the library on the site of the existing library and parking lot.

Staff and trustee confidence in the outcome was shaken a little during the very public debate of the closing days even though the phone polls sounded positive. On my way to vote early on November 7, I saw an enormous "vote no" sign two blocks from Helen Lemme School. Visions of losing and having to repeat the last few years and months all over again left me panicky and distressed for the rest of the day.

There were many still-familiar Iowa and Iowa City names on the ballot that day—Robert Ray, Terry Branstadt, Jim Leach, Richard Myers, Jean Lloyd-Jones, Minnette Doderer—but most of us deeply involved in the campaign saw only the tiny box in the upper right hand corner squeezed between a constitutional amendment about home rule for counties and a referendum on a local hotel-motel tax. To help others find that box, volunteers in high-support precincts had distributed highlighted sample ballots door-to-door the day before.

"Analyze your victory (or defeat)." We heard the news at an hour somewhat later than with today's computer-produced election results. Board President Bezanson took the call just after he announced, "No more campaigns for me. The tensions are too great." The issue had passed by a margin of 2 percent, just 244 votes. Almost 90 percent of those who voted that day found the library issue on the ballot, and 7,427 of these 12,371 voters approved the resolution permitting the sale of bonds for construction of an new library. Only two precincts failed to produce the required 60 percent approval. Less than 50 percent of the voters at Herbert Hoover and Helen Lemme schools said "yes" to the library. Board, staff, and campaign volunteers enjoyed an evening of celebration and rejoicing at a house smack in the middle of the Hoover-Lemme neighborhood.

Iowa City legend holds that the Chamber of Commerce and *Press-Citizen* opposition to the library bond issue is what put the vote over the top—by a narrower margin than those who just focused on the 62 percent approval rate realized. Who were the extra 244 voters who made the difference? Veterans from the urban renewal wars? University students and some of the faculty who generally ignore community issues? Anyone in this highly educated, academic community who interpreted a vote against a public library as a vote for the forces of evil and ignorance? We have never gathered hard data on just who voted, but the legend remains.

1979—A Year of Getting Ready

Celebration soon turned into hard work and tedious detail. There were several weeks of negotiations with HLM over particulars of the contract, a lengthy debate over using a fast-track construction management technique that was ultimately ruled illegal by the city attorney for a publicly bid project, protracted discussion with the city engineers about who would "run the show" during the construction period and with the city attorney about who "owned" the building and who should sign certain documents.

More exciting was the development of the plan, fleshing out the details and finding and solving the problems and issues never plumbed in the prereferendum phase. We wrestled with terms, techniques, and regulations unfamiliar to most of the building committee: party walls, fast-track construction, soil borings, slippage lanes, foot candles, hardware schedules, building codes, maximum occupancy rates, alternates to base bid, transformers, diffusers, projection ratios, and on and on and on. It was sometimes like two foreign delegations searching for a common language. To us "circulation" meant checking out books; to the building trades it was air velocity rates of the heating, ventilating, and air conditioning systems; to the architect, how people moved around in the building. Just as we mastered some of the terms of one specialty, we would move to another building system and another jargon-speaking expert.

After hours and days of meetings, three volumes of memos and minutes, nine months of arranging schedules for the out-of-time experts, many—and generally optimistic—cost estimate updates, and a plethora of short-term crises and compromises too complex and too painful to relate, HLM produced and the board approved the final bid documents, including a long list of alternates to protect us from an unexpectedly high bid. The library building would have been less attractive and less functional if high bids had forced us to drop these optional features: skylights, automatic entry doors, Linn Street entry canopy, the stained glass skylight moved from the old building, brick planters on the east front of building, brick pavers in the lobby, a stairway from the children's room to the second floor, movable partitions in meeting rooms, and wall coverings of cloth and vinyl.

Our work was done and our architect had neither over-designed nor underestimated. We received solid bids from six contractors, all below the HLM estimate—the top dollar we could spend and still have adequate funds for fees, equipment, and furnishings. Vawter and Walter of West Des Moines was the low bidder. At $2,664,300, its bid with all twelve alternatives included, was $74,000 under our estimate. This provided a comfortable cushion that would allow for minor changes and additions throughout the construction period.

Electronic readiness. Automating the library's circulation and bibliographic records was one of the "other costs" planned for the balance of the $3.5 million approved by the voters. The library board, especially trustee Randall Bezanson, had been adamant that these costs be included in the total new library package presented to the voters, and it turned out to be one of the wisest decisions of the campaign. In planning the project we always considered the estimated $300,000 cost for automation as one of the components of the $3.5 million price tag, but other issues crowded out public discussion of the proposal. Today I can find only three references to the automation plans—only one about its cost—in all the newspaper clippings, brochures, and scrapbooks that documented the campaign. No one was trying to hide the expense but the dramatic shortcomings of the old library and the raging controversy over the site tended to block out discussion of many of the proposed specifics of the new facility. Trustees and staff members had talked about automation so thoroughly that I am sure they would all be surprised today at how infrequently automation surfaced during the campaign.

Nevertheless, as soon as the election was certified we were on the phone talking to vendors about systems, bid procedures, and time frames for getting started. Both the staff and board had attended demonstrations and read materials about circulation control systems. We had done a massive in-house study on the cost and functional benefits of converting our bibliographic and card holder records to machine-readable form and then using this data base plus appropriate software for both the public catalog and for circulating library materials.

Not many companies in 1979 were marketing turnkey computer systems suitable for public libraries. Only one had been in business for as long as five years, had several libraries with functioning circulation control systems, and was planning to introduce an on-line computer catalog. Therefore, the decision was fairly easy. By January 1979 we had signed a contract with CL Systems (CLSI) of Newtonville, Massachusetts, for the circulation component plus an option to purchase software and equipment for an on-line catalog in the next fiscal year.

In February, the auditorium was closed and turned into a computer room holding our first minicomputer and several keyboard terminals. By June 30, the equivalent of twenty full-time employees were in the middle of a six-month project of keying 125,000 bibliographic records into the computer. They worked in two shifts matching edited shelf list cards with the books they represented, entering bibliographic data into the computer, proofing the results, and attaching matching bar codes to books and other library materials. We staff librarians with cataloging experience carried bundles of shelf list cards with us everywhere, editing the cards to eliminate unneeded information and coding for proper entry into the correct field of the record. In between regular duties (like planning a new library) we worked at home, on road trips, in meetings, and just about anywhere in order to keep ahead of the data entry operators. This conversion project cost several thousand dollars extra for books which had to be rebound before they were worthy of the cost of conversion and a bar code, and for lost or missing books needing immediate replacement.

By midsummer we added the re-registration of all card holders to the project. Volunteers, working at a table in the small vestibule below the famous eight steps to the main level of Joyce Nienstedt's "accessible" library, helped borrowers to fill out a form to be used for computer entry, issued new yellow plastic library cards with their assigned bar code attached, and asked each card holder to continue to use the old library card until the new system began operating. Staff members all wore yellow buttons and distributed yellow bookmarks urging people to get their new cards. The *Press-Citizen* aided this process by printing a picture of the new card in color on the front page followed by weekly reminders about applying for a card throughout the summer and fall.

The new building plans captured the public's interest throughout 1979, but the library staff felt that the installation of the computer-assisted circulation control system was the prime accomplishment of that or any year of the library's history.

Since their beginning, libraries had operated under rather rigid procedures for ordering, organizing, accessing, and circulating their collections. Filing rules, cataloging conventions, and circulation methods were based on years and years of local and profession-wide practice, precedent, and policy. In just a few months we had changed most of our basic files and procedures, discarded the eighty-year-old shelf list, entered 90 percent of the collection and 10,000 patrons into the computer, wired the building, installed the equipment, trained the staff, and had started up the circulation control component on the exact day targeted nine months earlier, October 1, 1979. We finished the conversion process with new confidence that we could take on any project and survive. In about one year we would take a more revolutionary step: Close the card catalog and introduce the public to a user-operated electronic catalog which would integrate bibliographic records and circulation transactions for complete public access to the holdings and status of all cataloged materials.

Ready to use volunteers. The volunteers who helped the library re-register 10,000 card holders in the summer and fall of 1979 were part of the first major project demonstrating how a planned and structured volunteer program was benefiting the library. The library's earliest volunteers may have been the apprentices recruited by librarian Webber in 1905, although some of those women were working to prepare for regular employment at the library. There were a few volunteers in the 1960s, including Hulette Belle who volunteered for many years after resigning from a regular library position that began in 1948. Mary Unrath was another former employee who gave many hours of work as a volunteer in the 1970s. Former Seven Rivers administrator Nelle Neafie worked on several volunteer projects before her sudden death in 1980. Isabel Turner started doing a variety of tasks around the library under Sallie Helm and remained until she became active in the Johnson County Planning and Iowa City Human Relations commissions. Probably the longest serving volunteer is Mig Judiesch who was first given volunteer work by Jack Hurkett in 1971 and was on the active roster until the early 1990s.

During 1979 Carol Spaziani added Volunteer Coordinator to her list of titles and, working with Friends member Linda Goeldner, developed a plan for volunteers for the library that was subsequently adopted as a policy statement of the library board after extensive review by ICPL department managers and the Friends board. This policy defined the purpose, guidelines, basic requirements, recruiting, recognition activities, responsibilities, and rewards of being an ICPL volunteer. The policy has been amended several times over the years as circumstances have changed and experience has indicated, but it is still basically the same plan and has been used as a model by libraries throughout the United States.

A Century of Stories

Regular and short-term volunteer jobs requiring one or two persons have been less dramatic and less visible, but they have provided many valuable services that have enhanced and enriched the library. Organizing the volunteer program so that massive numbers could be recruited when required seemed like good insurance for the library when the policy was developed in 1979. In the next decade it would turn out to be one of the lifesaving resources the library staff would use to survive, especially in the high-growth, static staffing years before 1987. The crew that signed up card holders for their new cards was just the first example.

Breaking new ground. At the close of the decade the library's annual statistical report reflected the changing patterns of library service. In the minds of the public, the library was now much more than a place to get favorite reading materials. There was more use by adults (65 percent of loans and 77 percent of card holders). There were more requests for information (a 300 percent increase since 1969) and for nonprint formats (13 percent of all loans). There were requests for special kinds of spaces: for tutoring, for small group meetings, for video viewing and editing, for quiet study and reading areas. It was satisfying to know that responses to these requests were reflected in the plans for the new library.

On October 11, 1979, just ten days after launching a new computer-assisted circulating system and just ten years after the initiatives of Helm and Croteau were taking root in a new generation of librarians, we held groundbreaking ceremonies for the new building. We hoped this traditional ceremony symbolized the library's future. We hoped to continue to break new ground throughout the 1980s.

---

[1] In an interview in September 1996, Croteau said it was the humidity that drove her away.

[2] When the city found an $88,500 error in its proposed budget, the manager recommended they make up the entire shortfall by dropping the city's annual contribution to the county health department ($45,000) and by cutting $36,000 from the library's budget. Wells cited the library policy of allowing thirty-day vacations for "all employees" as one he was "not in agreement with." The library said loss of Seven Rivers and work/study federal funds already had the library in financial difficulties. *Press-Citizen*, Sept. 9, 1973.

[3] "The Status of Women Employed by the City of Iowa City," unpublished study in the archives of the Johnson County Commission on the Status of Women held by the author, 1973.

[4] In September 1974, after correspondence between City Attorney John Hayek and officials at EEOC, Hayek recommended that the library board ratify the EEOC agreement with the exception of Article II about hiring goals. It was unanimously agreed to at the Sept. 19, 1974 meeting.

[5] The list of forty-five included several librarians who have subsequently taken major jobs in public libraries. Dan Bradbury is currently director of the Kansas City [Mo] Public Library and was named Librarian of the Year by *Library Journal* in 1991.

[6] Interview with Arthur Canter, June 21, 1995. Interview with Robert Downer, July 17, 1995. UI Professor Edgar Czarnecki was mayor 1974-75 during his 1971-75 term on the city council.

[7] Based on notes taken by Carol Spaziani at the meeting in the personal files of the author.

8 Since 1983 called the University of Iowa School of Information and Library Science.

9 Letter from Arthur Canter to city manager Ray Wells, September 23, 1972. Appendix item 7 in staff-prepared packet for July 25, 1974. In library board minutes for that date.

10 *American Library Directory; a classified list of libraries and statistical data,* (R.R. Bowker, 1974).

11 *Press-Citizen,* July 3, 1996.

12 Interview with Lake Land administrative staff, July 12, 1974.

13 Attachment 1 to the July 25 statement of staff to the board of trustees. Written by Carol Spaziani, et al.

14 Memo to the Iowa City Public Library Board of Trustees. July 25, 1974. Six-page memo with seventeen attachments. In library board minutes for that date.

15 Downer believes the plan to adjourn without discussion had been agreed to beforehand. Interview, July 17, 1995.

16 Canter interview, June 25, 1995.

17 *Press-Citizen,* July 30, 1974.

18 Ibid.

19 *Press-Citizen,* July 31, 1974.

20 *Press-Citizen,* August 1, 1974.

21 Both Downer and Canter today believe the staff should have approached individual board members privately and attempted to convince them about the seriousness of their findings. Downer and Canter interviews, 1995.

22 Hurkett identified a source of matching funds if the city would authorized $23,000. In 1972 the board sent the request to the council and got a quick and heartless reply to find $23,000 in its own operating budget—about 10 percent of its 1972 appropriation.

23 Samuel Rothstein, "Reference Service: the New Dimension in Librarianship," *Reference Librarian,* Number 25/26, 1989.

24 There was professional research and literature about theories and techniques of collection development and management, but very few public libraries were using them. A simple article I wrote in 1976 was reprinted in several library journals, indicating perhaps lack of information about practical applications. "More Effective Management of the Public Library's Book Collection," *Aardvark,* July 1976, and reprinted in Phyllis Van Orden, *Background Readings in Building Library Collections,* 2nd ed., Scarecrow Press, 1979. p129-36.

25 The basics are in the article cited above.

26 Fred Wezeman, former public librarian and director of the UI School of Library Science from 1967 to 1980, gave the anonymous gift of several hundred dollars in 1974.

27 City manager Ray Wells and others were irritated by the fact that librarians with M.L.S. degrees received twenty-two days of vacation after their first year. He often mistakenly said that all library employees received the same vacation. Adelaide Lloyd, 1900-05, was the first ICPL librarian to receive the traditional librarian's four-week vacation, given by most libraries throughout the country.

28 Library board minutes, January 27, 1977.

29 *Press-Citizen,* January 24, 1978. Since the return of Sunday service in 1969 the library has given employees six hours comp time for each four hours worked on Sundays.

30 *Press-Citizen,* January 27, 1978.

31 *Press-Citizen,* February 22 and 24, 1978. The library returned to regular hours on Jan. 1, 1980, based on staff hours saved from putting the circulation system on line on Oct. 1, 1979. In the next (FY1980) budget cycle the council approved two and one-half library positions.

32 After the adoption of council-manager government in 1951, only two persons have been appointed to a second six-year term after serving six years: Kenneth MacDonald in 1953 and Suzanne Richerson in 1977. Richerson resigned in 1981 after ten years.

[33] This version was dated June 1976. It was later revised to include more specifics regarding audiovisual facilities and is known as *Revised Recommended Building Program, Iowa City Public Library*, October, 1977.

[34] Robert H. Rohlf and David R. Smith. *Iowa City Public Library Site Study*, July 1976, 2.

[35] *Press-Citizen*, October 12, 1976.

[36] After the Iowa City assignment, Engberg left HLM to start his own firm in Milwaukee, WI. His credits now include many public libraries in Iowa, Wisconsin, and Minnesota, including the Ames and Sioux City public libraries.

[37] Friends of the Iowa City Public Library Board of Directors, minutes, Sept. 20, 1978.

[38] Background paper by Friends board member Steve Hedden attached to the August 1978 Friends board minutes.

[39] Press release, New Library For Everyone Committee, Sept. 11, 1978.

[40] *Press-Citizen*, Nov. 19, 1978.

■ 10. Building a Library and a National Reputation, 1980–1991

The 1980s was a tumultuous decade of strong library board leadership, astute adjustments to controversy and change, and unsurpassed community support.

The public had shown its satisfaction with and support for the library in its solid approval for a new library building. The library staff had become a spirited team of professionals eager to see their visions of library service played out in a building designed to deliver them. The library board supported the ideas and values the building plan represented and incorporated them into a set of operating principles for the library's first long-range plan. By the end of the 1980s the library would be known nationally for its innovative audiovisual services, active cable television channel, first-in-the-nation on-line public library catalog, original methods for developing a collection valuable to the widest range of library users, fund-raising capabilities, successful volunteer program, quality long-range plans, and roster of creative librarians. At the same time, this new mix of innovative and quality services produced such a surge of library use that library officials would spend the decade working to find enough resources to keep the library afloat at the level the public rapidly came to expect. The library board used every possible type of public and private support: grants, gifts, endowment, volunteers, political persuasion, donated books, and finally, a special tax levy. The honors and awards and accolades vied with the crowds, the computer failures, and the service reductions for the attention of staff and board.

The Construction Period

Relatively few problems surfaced during the construction of the library building from October 1979 through February 1981, the date the library officially

319

took possession of the building. There were only a few minor change orders—about $45,000, about 1.6 percent of the construction budget. Vawter and Walter, the general contractor, proved to be a steady, conscientious firm and, with oversight from HLM, managed all aspects of the project. The firm finished its work just a few weeks later than originally planned. There were no hostile relationships

Construction of the new library, October 1979 through February 1981, was directed by general contractor Vawter and Walter with oversight by architects at Hansen Lind Myer (HLM).

and few bungled details and we ended the project as trusted associates and cohorts. The chief carpenter for the building, Kevin Watt, became a firm friend of the library and built equipment and repaired or remodeled building features throughout the decade and beyond.

While the building was taking shape across College Street, the board and staff worked on many building-related components that needed development and decision before we could move into our new dream house and, as we believed at that time, live happily ever after. Furnishing and equipping the library was a high priority and through good luck and the library's first attempt at fund-raising, we accumulated a comfortable budget. The $3.5 million in library bonds, sold in April 1979 at a rate of 5.32 percent for thirteen years, earned the project $390,000 in short-term interest during the peak interest rate years of 1979-81. This paid for the initial computer system and left the balance of the approved $3.5 million, after construction and fees, for carpet, shelving, furniture, and equipment.

Because I was too inexperienced to know better, I took on the general coordination of the project—with a lot of help and support from staff members and the board building committee: Ed Zastrow, Randy Bezanson, and Lynda Ostedgaard. The general contractor watched over the subcontractors, the architect watched over the general, and I watched over, evaluated, and tried to assist them all. A lot of equipment and several systems were installed after we took official possession of the building—carpet, shelving, audiovisual, telephone, furniture, signage, security, computer, cable television. These required my supervision or that of a specialist on the staff. Already understaffed and on reduced public service hours following a city budget crisis in 1980-81, we somehow squeezed in enough time to "work both sides of the street" through long hours and seven-day weeks.

Our consultant, Robert Rohlf, convinced the library board to let him contract for the interiors, to the disappointment of design architect Charles Engberg who took great interest in this aspect of all his building designs. Engberg wanted HLM's interior design department to select the furnishings and colors. Rohlf worked with DVR&W, Inc., a design firm in his community of Minneapolis.

Paula Vesley, the "V" of DVR&W, headed the project and her ideas were sometimes controversial. At one point, the head of HLM's interior design department offered a long critique of the interior design package offered by consultant Vesley. The HLM representative felt the gray was too cool a color, noted that deep wine "connotes sophistication," and said that research on human response to color indicated it was the least likely to be selected by individuals choosing from a full spectrum of colors. He recommended minimizing both the gray and wine and introducing warmer hues to the color palette. He also objected to the two-person seating units for the lounge areas. Vesley argued at a board meeting a few weeks later that the gray was a background color and that the palette was not just wine, but wine, rust, and gold, with bright reds and blues for the children's room. She had reduced the number of two-seaters and added a few pull-up chairs with arms. I argued for items and colors easy to maintain and suggested that we probably couldn't pick colors by committee. The board approved Vesley's package pretty much as presented. The building's color scheme was never considered one of its strong points and I doubt if there has ever been a single staff member who would champion it.

As any new homeowner knows, unplanned but necessary items can quickly eat a furnishings budget. In our case, book trucks (never before needed or practical in the old seven-level building), a space heater, a mail cart, a handrail for the east-side entry, hanging devices for four hundred framed art prints, door closers, fire extinguishers, coat racks, building plaques, and initial supplies for many new pieces of equipment were just a few examples of the hundred or more unplanned items suddenly needing purchase from our general equipment budget.

Therefore, the board decided to try some private fund-raising to enhance the equipment and furnishings budget even beyond the rich windfall of interest income. The majority of steps taken for the new building project were carefully planned months before the action; the decision to solicit money from individuals and organizations in the community developed late and slowly, partially stimulated by the generosity of local residents—the 350 who gave money to the referendum campaign and the more than two hundred that worked on the library campaign. It was a small effort, but the first since the citizens of 1896 and 1897 had contributed to the fund to start the library.

A Century of Stories

By the time the building opened, board members had raised $50,000, including three major gifts. The Sunrise Optimists gave $5,000 to build the large display case in the children's room and to help start the Child and Family Resource Center that was established in the new library. When the gift was received in the spring of 1980 the Optimists vowed to support the library annually, which they have done, giving the library $1,000 a year through 1996. At about the same time, the *Press-Citizen* gave the library $5,200, via its parent company's Gannett Foundation, for the purchase of both microfilm and microfiche reader-printers. The third large pre-opening gift was from the Friends of the Iowa City Public Library. At their May 1980 annual meeting, the members approved $10,000 to buy the signage system for the library. Designed by HLM's environmental graphics director, Mitchell Neymeyer, the plan provided over 350 stack, directional, room, and departmental identification signs.

Making the building "legible" through good signs was one of my personal goals for the new facility. I had standardized the signs in the Carnegie building in 1974 and had gotten immersed in the ideas of wayfaring—the manner in which people orient themselves and find their way in complex environments. I believe that a library is a complex institution, with all its materials, from fiction bestsellers to items in a pamphlet file folder, arranged in a variety of systems—complicated systems if you do not understand the "codes." Making the building legible meant helping people find their way and locate what they needed without having to ask too many questions. It was a long-standing rule in the old library and later in the new building that signs had to meet certain basic standards of color, size, and design and that no new sign could be posted without my approval. Every manager has a few idiosyncracies and this was one of mine. The system in the new library was never perfect or complete and I fiddled with it as long as I was director.

We dealt successfully with the general contractor, the architect's staff, all the construction subcontractors, and the interior designers. We juggled times and dates to please the installers of carpet, telephones, the computer, cable television, security systems, shelving, and furniture—and kept the project on schedule throughout. Then as we were coming down the homestretch we ran into a major obstacle. In May, after the dedication and opening day events had all been planned and announced, the city's building inspector denied our certificate of occupancy. He claimed, after making no comment in several earlier inspections, that the back stairway was four inches too narrow. These stairs would be used almost exclusively by the staff but also served as an emergency exit, so they had to meet building and fire code requirements. The inspector's finding depended on how some terms in the building code were defined and interpreted. On May 28, seventeen days before the scheduled opening, we challenged his interpretation of the term "stairway" before the city's board of appeals and received an exception to his ruling.

Stretching the Staff

Finding enough staff to operate the new enlarged facility had been a major concern of the library board and administration ever since the referendum was approved in November of 1978. Despite the battle with the city council over the 1978-79 budget just nine months before the election and the subsequent reduction of library hours in July of 1978 (described in chapter 9), there was surprisingly little discussion during the campaign about staffing the new building. The response to the few questions asked by the public—they were generally prefaced by referring to the library's recent difficulties in getting additional staff—was to point out that the increased efficiency of the new building plus the automation of several procedures would make each employee more productive. "The need for additional staff beyond this will depend on the level of services provided and the size in the increase in library use generated by the new building."[1]

Prompted, perhaps, by the strong referendum vote, the city council gave the library two and one-half full-time positions in the 1979-80 budget approved just weeks after the election. On the first day of the new fiscal year, July 1, 1979, the library reopened on Thursday evenings and the board promised to look at Sunday openings after October 1979 when the first phase of the computer system would be up and running. In December the library announced it would reopen on Sundays starting January 1, 1980, because staff previously committed to typing overdue notices and sorting transaction slips could now be reassigned for public service duties.

Sunday hours were short-lived, however, for during the next round of budget negotiations underway during the same month that Sunday service resumed, the city, faced with a financial crisis, reduced the number of employees throughout the city. To preserve our hard-won permanent positions, but following the city's directive to lay off the least senior employees, we chose to reduce our hourly-pay staff, termed "temporary" in city and union contract terminology. The cut, totaling $34,000, meant four fewer full-time equivalent people in 1980-81 than the year before. Sunday service was again dropped.

In January 1981, during the last budget go-around before the new library was scheduled to open, we convinced the council to allow Carol Spaziani to increase from one-half to three-quarters time in recognition of her increased duties coordinating volunteers. Additionally, we were given back some of the funds for temporary employees lost the year before. A sharp reduction in the number of federally funded employees during this period, however, meant that we would enter the new building with fewer staff members than we had five years earlier in a smaller building.[2]

Even if no increased use occurred, the new building required us to staff at least three additional public points: the audiovisual desk, the switchboard (formerly handled by circulation staff), and an additional check-out point at the circulation desk as 35 percent of the library's annual loans moved from the children's department to the new centralized department. Additionally, beginning in late 1979 when the computer circulation system went into operation, someone was always on duty to monitor the computer.

The larger building also would require more hours of cleaning and maintenance. We knew by this point that the employee hours saved by automating circulation and the catalog could be stretched to cover the new positions required at the audiovisual desk, the switchboard, and the circulation desk, at least for the sixty-one hours a week of service budgeted for 1981-82. We had decided during that budget cycle that instead of using our limited ability to get council approval for new maintenance staff, we would contract with a local cleaning firm for the hard-core cleaning work and upgrade our one maintenance staff member to a building and equipment manager.

The building manager's job was just one of the many ideas produced by a staff task force drawn from all ranks and departments that worked throughout 1980-81 to decide how to staff the new building effectively and equitably. A massive "job sharing" program was designed, with implementation to start the day the old library closed. Departments were reorganized, combining some (children's and young adult into youth services) and establishing others (audiovisual and community services), and audiovisual librarian Connie Tiffany was designated assistant director. Forty distinct positions were identified and the library's twenty-eight permanent employees had the opportunity to apply for those jobs within their skill and qualification ranges. The result: Twenty-eight persons took on the forty jobs, with only five staff members assigned to spend all their time in one department. At ICPL job sharing meant one person having two jobs in two departments with two supervisors, not two persons sharing one job as found in many other organizations. The equivalent of five and one-half full-time positions was reallocated to direct public service desks. Almost everyone spent time at a service desk, including some evenings and some weekends. This staff-generated solution placed persons on duty at all service points in the new building, yet gave individuals important behind-the-scenes duties to perform when shifts changed or during periods when traffic was less heavy. We reaped the benefits of interdepartmental understanding and commitment to the library as a whole. The flexibility proved to be an advantage in developing versatile staff able to move from department to department and to take on new or expanded positions, but it would always be a scheduler's nightmare. The task force proved to be an effective method for making group decisions about the library, and it became one of the problem-solving methods that would get us through the surge of library use that lay ahead.

On-line and On the Air

Two other important developments reached the operational stage during the last few months before we moved to the new library. Both were ground-breaking accomplishments that would help shape the library's distinguished service record of the 1980s. On October 1, 1980, just twelve months after we switched to the computer-assisted circulation system, technical services department staff installed two "touch" terminals near the card catalog and invited library visitors to try out the nation's first public library on-line catalog capable of retrieving ICPL catalog information by author, title, or subject. From that day forward we ceased updating the card catalog and planned to leave it behind when we moved across the street in June of 1981. The touch system allowed the public access to the catalog without having to use a keyboard, but required a somewhat laborious search through progressively finer alphabetical headings to reach the desired entry. The traditional card catalog demanded familiarity with alphabetical order, but this computer display requiring the same skill seemed to discourage some users. The bulk of those who first tried out the new system were inquisitive, technical types, eager to test their abilities. Those not yet open to computer technology generally ignored the new system and continued to consult the card catalog. It would be a few more months before we would hear the howls from this latter group. From almost the first day of making the on-line catalog available, "Eggers's first law of library catalogs" became evident: People blame their own inadequacies for any failure to find what they want in a traditional card catalog; when the same information is transferred to a computer, they blame the computer system.

The benefits of the new catalog for both the public and the library rapidly became apparent to the staff and most library users. In tandem, the catalog and the circulation systems increased the number of hours of staff time already being saved since the introduction of the circulation component one year earlier. In addition to the elimination of traditional clerical duties in the circulation department, the on-line catalog relieved technical services staff from the typing and filing, revising and refiling of catalog cards and allowed them to enter a bibliographic record only once and then update it or remove it easily. The public got a more accurate catalog, knew if the desired item was checked out and when it was due, and received faster service when a reserve was placed.

The library staff, if not the borrower, was pleased with the simple and quick access to information about fines and lost materials. In just one year fine income tripled, helping to pay some of the costs of the new systems, and the library had a data base it could depend on for accurate information plus regular statistical reports about library users and what they were borrowing. As long as the system was working, user and staff benefited. In a very short time, we all become very aware of the need for steady and reliable performance by our minicomputer.

After the move and after the card catalog had been dismantled, we conducted surveys on the use of the new on-line system. Similar to surveys of card catalog users we had done prior to automation, the studies found that nearly three times as many people were using the on-line catalog as used the old card catalog based on a ratio of catalog uses to items checked out during the survey periods. Despite the pleas from a small minority to "bring back the card catalog" (one complainant offered to help retype the cards), it was obvious that the system was being consulted by a much larger proportion of library users.

The second system launched in this period was the library's new cable television channel. About the same time as the on-line catalog was installed, our small cable operation in the basement of the old library began cablecasting. Ever since cable television companies petitioned Iowa City for a franchise (the franchise election was held just a few days before the library referendum in 1978) audiovisual librarian Tiffany had headed the task force appointed to write the cable television ordinance and assist in the development of cable television in Iowa City. In the election campaign, eventual winner Hawkeye Cablevision had promised a channel for the library as well as four other public channels. Tiffany also chaired the committee that selected the broadband telecommunication specialist (BTS), the person hired by the city to oversee the specifics of local cable operations to ensure that the company fulfilled the requirements of its franchise agreement. The cable studio, control room, and reception area in the new building were being constructed under Tiffany's supervision, and the BTS and the Hawkeye employees assigned to operate the public access functions would be housed in the new library.

By the end of 1980, channel 20 (later channel 10) had produced thirty-five hours of programming and the library's computer-driven "character generator" was displaying messages about library hours, programs, and services. A $37,000 grant from the National Telecommunication Information Agency (an agency of the Department of Commerce) purchased production equipment earmarked for use by the public channels. It would be housed in the audiovisual lab of the new building. Intense staff training and the use of volunteers and interns kept the shoestring operation going during the first few months. Among other things, the new video equipment was being used to document the construction of the library. As one of a very few libraries in the United States with a dedicated cable channel, calls and visitors interested in what we were doing began to flow in.

Where Do Old Carnegie Buildings Go to Die?

The old Carnegie library served the public for the last time on Wednesday, May 27, 1981. After closing at nine o'clock that evening, staff and board members as well as some other old friends of the library gathered to tell stories and to honor the many years of library service the building had contributed to the community. For the length of the short ceremony, at least, there were some warm memories and honest regret to see the structure end its days as Iowa City's first library building. The knowledge that the building would be preserved and restored via sale and private redevelopment soothed our limited guilt about leaving.

The city had already taken steps to market the Carnegie. At the time of the library referendum the city council had promised to put the building into private hands to offset taxes lost because of the use of part of block 65 for the new library. The old building was estimated to be worth $200,000 and council members were determined to sell it for at least $155,000 in order to replace the money they

One of the last persons to be served at the old library, May 27, 1981

had been required to transfer into the urban renewal fund in payment for the library site. In 1980 the council had commissioned Zuchelli, Hunter, and Associates, the same firm that recommended block 65 for the library, to evaluate the old building's redevelopment potential.

Just about the time the new library opened, the Johnson County/Iowa City Arts Council asked the city council to convert the Carnegie building into a community cultural center. The council rejected the idea and, in a letter sent by city manager Neal Berlin, the council reminded the arts group of its promise to Iowa City taxpayers to sell the building for private redevelopment.

In Zuchelli's $12,500 study, received just a few weeks later, the consultant told the council that the old library could "most advantageously" be redeveloped for a restaurant and specialty shops, although offices, private club, dinner theater, and restaurant-tavern-exclusive lodging were also suggested. Invitations to bid went out in the spring of 1982. The minimum price for the building was set at $155,000, and for the adjoining parking lot $205,000. Any purchaser would have to agree to reinvest a minimum of 300 percent of the building's bid price in "hard construction costs for renovation." Purchasers wanting both sites would be preferred, according to press reports of the time, although separate bids were permitted.

Just before the bids were due, the Johnson County Board of Supervisors asked the city council if the county could buy the old library. The county badly needed office space at the time and the supervisors felt the council would work with them on the idea. "The people of Iowa City are also people of Johnson County, and I think they could help us out. It certainly wouldn't hurt to put our foot in the door," supervisor Don Sehr explained. The 23,000 square feet at the library "could solve our space needs forever," Board Chairman Dennis Langenberg said. Mayor Mary Neuhauser said it was unlikely the council would renege on its promise to the taxpayers.[3]

The council received only two bids for the property. One was so flawed it was eventually discarded. The only valid bid was from GWG Investments who offered $165,000 with an option to buy the seventy-seven-space parking lot for $205,000. GWG said it planned to renovate the library for leased office space with some space reserved for retail shops or a bar and restaurant. GWG bought the building in January 1983 and six months later signed a three-year lease with the University of Iowa for the entire building. The university rented the space for about $1.75 per square foot and agreed to do its own necessary renovations. The city council grumbled a little, but said GWG could do the promised $495,000 in renovations after the lease was up.

In 1996, fifteen years later, the University of Iowa still occupies the building, with renovation limited to adequate heat, air conditioning, a repaired roof, carpeting, and a paint job at the university's expense. The university now pays $60,000 a year ($2.40 per square foot) in rent and still maintains the building. GWG retained its option on the parking lot and in 1994 the firm finally purchased it at the 1983 price. In 1996 the site was sold for high-rise housing not considered feasible or suitable in 1982. As the *Press-Citizen* editorialized back in 1982, "The old library deserves better."

Moving In

One of the major contributions that community members made to the new library was their help in moving books and other library materials across Linn and College streets from the old to the new building. After finding out it could cost up to $40,000 to employ a professional moving company to do the job, and with the buildings less than two hundred feet apart, we decided it would be an ideal undertaking for Friends and volunteers.

Moving a library collection is physically taxing and potentially disastrous if the order of materials is disturbed. Once the shelves are filled it would be a tedious job to shift thousands of volumes should the books get out of order. We read about lots of successful moves but one bad one stuck in our minds. A move to a new public library in a Wisconsin community was poorly planned and executed. Half the nonfiction collection was incorrectly shelved and in the heat of

Hundreds of volunteers, including Mayor John Balmer, helped move the books across Linn Street on June 7, 1981

operating a new facility, no one could correct it for six months. The wooden moving boxes were too heavy, too few, and dispensed splinters. The conveyor belt from the second floor was too steep and many boxes fell off. Several very young and some elderly volunteers were hurt trying to carry heavy loads. Many volunteers quit in midmove because of the poor organization. We took heed and planned carefully.

Reference librarian Susan Craig was the strategist. She designed the method and wrote the precise procedures. Retired University of Iowa College of Education dean Howard Jones and his longtime administrative assistant Mildred Wilslef served as cochairs for recruiting and assembling the six hundred volunteers required to fill the three shifts of eleven teams each for Craig's plan. Carol Spaziani developed the recruitment forms, the publicity, and all the rules of the day. She prepared a sample box weighing twenty-five pounds for applicants to test-lift before signing up. They were told they would work for four hours with one rest period. Those unable to lift and carry could staff registration desks, refreshment stands, or first aid stations. Others, working in the basement of the old Carnegie on the days of the move, addressed thank you cards and invitations to the pre-opening party to all the people who participated. Two-wheel handcarts were borrowed from downtown merchants. Grocer and former trustee Ron Farber delivered eight hundred beer cartons from Graf's Beverage Company, the type used to transport bottled beer, with folding lids and cutouts for handles—standard, stackable, and waterproof.

Volunteers could sign up at the library, at local churches and schools, and at the UI library. And they did. One-half of the goal of six hundred had signed up by May 1, just three weeks after the first announcement. Former trustee Jerry Newsome received forty-five responses the first day that she recruited librarians at the UI library, and she had seventy-five names by the end of the first week. According to Spaziani, 105 librarians from a dozen area towns participated. Many organizations signed on as teams of twenty—churches, clubs, businesses, scout troops. Mayor John Balmer and State Representative Jean Lloyd-Jones

Move strategist Susan Craig (on landing) checks on progress.

were just two of the familiar faces in the throng of participants. On the weekend before the major move, one hundred volunteers from the Iowa Homebuilders Association and its auxiliary moved bound periodicals, recordings, tables, and other miscellaneous furniture.

On June 7, enthusiasm was high, the weather hot (90 degrees by 9 a.m.), and turnout was near 100 percent. The task was to move about 120,000 books without mixing up their alphabetical or classified/numerical order. Each team had an assigned section to move and a designated route to follow. Team members removed books from the shelves and packed them into the beer cartons. Others on the team carried the filled boxes out of the building, placed them on the handcarts, and wheeled them across the street. Team members waiting at the door toted the boxes to the appropriate spot in the new building where the team volunteers with library experience pulled the books from the cartons and shelved them in the correct order. Empty boxes and handcarts were returned to the old building and the cycle was repeated until the assigned section was finished—about 3,000 trips for each four-hour shift.

Success depended on Craig's careful planning, her measuring of the collections and the spaces each required, and on volunteers who followed her instructions to a T. And they evidently did. All three shifts finished at least an hour early. Ray Muston, university associate dean for academic affairs who served at the command post on Saturday, told the press, "You want to see the height of planning? This is a most carefully organized operation. I organized field marches in the army and I know the army could learn something from this." The teams competed informally with each other, calling out the number of boxes they had loaded. With so much enthusiastic effort, "The whole move could have been completed on Saturday," said Craig, but knowing that 240 people were signed up for Sunday, she sent the Saturday teams home early and left the final 20,000 books for the Sunday shift.

The project seemed to intrigue the press, which gave the move extensive coverage before and after the event. Pictures of volunteers wheeling boxes across the Linn and College intersection appeared everywhere. The *Des Moines Sunday Register* noted the smiles on all the workers' faces and marveled at the precise planning. Calling it a "monumental achievement," the *Press-Citizen* reporters caught the weekend's spirit in their follow-up story: "Names, jokes, and jests were traded in a project that may have created some lasting friendships and helped lay the foundation for community involvement in the new facility."

During breaks volunteers explored all parts of the building. Many who were not regular library users seemed eager to visit the library again, and many old-timers were ready to sign up as volunteers or to join the Friends. The event bonded many people with the library and the relationship lasted all through the decade. In addition, the great community turnout dramatized the library's new volunteer program, and from that point on volunteers became a major component of library operations.

All those who participated in the June 7-8 weekend move were special guests at "a gala preopening celebration" held Saturday evening, June 13. In addition, construction crews, trustees, Friends, referendum workers and donors, local officials, and all staff, former staff, and volunteers were invited. Live music in two locations, hourly tours, refreshments, special displays, slide and video shows, plus a chance to try out the many new machines and computer terminals and to poke around informally in the new facilities kept hundreds of guests, many wearing their "I Moved the Library" badges, busy for several hours. The idea of celebrating with champagne was squashed by the city attorney. His requested opinion reminded us that the consumption of alcoholic beverages is prohibited in any public place not covered by a liquor control license. There were rumors of champagne celebrations in the staff room, but I never investigated. The intense activity of the past three years may have driven some to drink, but fortunately they could not see into the future or their partying may have been even greater.

The next day, starting with a ribbon-cutting ceremony, the general public was invited to attend the formal dedication ceremonies. Most of the activities of the night before were available and the speeches of the dedication ceremonies were carried throughout the crowded building on closed-circuit television. After remarks and "thank you's" from Mayor John Balmer, Board President Lynda Ostedgaard, Friends President Jo Catalano, and me, first District Congressman Jim Leach made the dedicatory address. Dramatic rhetoric had gone out of style since the bold speech that UI President McLean made at the dedication of the Carnegie library in 1904, but Leach also delivered a strong message. The freedom of ideas represented by our country's public libraries make our embassy libraries the most-attacked institution in many foreign countries, Leach said. Use your library not just for fun and adventure, but for the "maturing of the intellect through reading. Our libraries give all of us the means to take responsibility for our own lives, and we owe this to ourselves and to our society if our way of life is to survive."

First District Congressman Jim Leach was one of the speakers at the dedication ceremonies, June 14, 1981.

The First Year in the New Library

I will never forget opening day. We were scheduled to open at 1:00 p.m. Here is my account of the day, written five years later:

> About 10:00 a.m. the heavens let loose with a rain storm which was as heavy as any I can remember. The [south side] windows on the first and second floor were leaking everywhere. We spent hours (or so it seemed) mopping up. I was thinking that our beautiful new library was going to be marred and stained before the public ever got to use it. I don't know what we had planned to spend those morning hours doing, but we did open at 1:00 p.m., and when the doors were opened the crowds rushed in—and they have been rushing in ever since. More than two and a half million visitors [eight million by 1996] have gone through the lobby gates, and any marring or staining that is around now is simply the inevitable marks of enthusiastic use.

George Orwell's *Animal Farm* was the first book checked out of the new library. When this shabby paperback was later retrieved from the shelf to put into the library's archives, an unbelievable coincidence was discovered. We had also saved the first book entered into the computer and bar coded in 1979—another copy of *Animal Farm*.

We were delivering a full range of library services from the day we opened, but all I can remember of the first two weeks is the blur of books coming in and going

Iowa City Public Library Archives

The Iowa City Public Library at 123 South Linn Street

The children's room in 1981. Paddington Bear makes a rare visit inside the children's area from his regular post at the room's entrance.

The circulation desk as it appeared in 1981. It was later remodeled to accommodate the frequent long lines of library users waiting to check out materials.

out. We had been closed for eighteen days. A lot of pent-up library demand had accumulated, as well as a very large pile of books read and returned for reshelving. We were checking out about 240 books an hour in June, almost twice the rate of the previous year, and throughout the first two weeks the backlog of unshelved books never dipped much below 9,000. Staff was reassigned, extra help was hired, and volunteers moved into the check-in area—a spot they occupy to this day. On two Sundays in June and July we recruited thirty local librarians to come in and help us shelve, and one or two volunteers were soon on duty at all hours the library was open. I told a reporter in August that "a more efficient sys-

333

tem to handle returns is the long-range solution, but we need to get to ground zero first."

Crowds waiting to use the catalog terminals and the in-library VCRs and lines of people waiting to get library cards and to get help at the information desk also created problems, but the overwhelming obstacle of being unable to get the books back on the shelves was our primary concern for several weeks. We were pleased with the public's response, but we were not keeping up with it. At one point, I suggested that only "brownies and elves coming in at night to reshelve" could rescue us.

The flow of books in and out of the library leveled off somewhat in July—only two hundred items checked out each hour and an average backlog of only 4,000 books—but because the prospect of getting more staff was dim and because we had two fewer people than we thought we would when the building opened, I knew we were in trouble. Quality would diminish rapidly if we didn't find time for administrative and other essential behind-the-scenes work.

While many functions and formats have changed since 1981, the audiovisual desk today looks very similar to this opening day photo.

Iowa City Public Library Archives

Library traffic, already higher than any library in the state while still in the crowded and inefficient Carnegie building, started its astronomical upward climb. By the end of the summer the patterns were clear: 50 percent more people entered the building every day, library card applications doubled and then tripled the old rate, and questions at the information desk increased from 2,200 to 4,400 per month. By comparison, the 15 to 20 percent increase in loans seemed modest even though those 8,000 additional check-outs and check-ins each month were bankrupting our staffing budget and reducing our ability to get other work done.

Visitors to the new library seemed dazzled by what they found. There were services and facilities many had never seen before, services and features found in few libraries anywhere at that time. It was a mind-expanding experience for many—regular and infrequent users alike.

The building's interior was simple and understated, informal and unpretentious, designed to be more inviting than most public institutions. In the oak and carpeted setting, the library's many technical features stood out: the terminals of the on-line catalog, the remote listening stations, the user-operated audiovisual equipment, the study room and special gear for wheelchair users and the visually and hearing impaired. With the audiovisual playback equipment distributed throughout the building instead of concentrated behind the doors of an audiovisual department, everyone was instantly aware of its importance to the library's operations. The public access cable television studio and the audiovisual production lab added to the impression that this was the library of the future—"a futuristic dream" the *Press-Citizen* called it in a special section honoring the library's opening.

Others commented on the library's many amenities: automatic doors; comfortable reading areas near windows and skylights; a six-foot Paddington Bear greeting children at the entrance to the children's department plus a child-sized toilet in the restroom; a small but cozy story hour pit in the farthest corner of the children's area and that department's own stairway to the second floor; lobby pavers that matched the brick of the pedestrian mall just outside; and the 1904 stained glass window from the dome of the old Carnegie restored, framed in oak, and vertically displayed between the entry and exit gates in the lobby.

The lobby itself, furnished with racks and bulletin boards bearing all types of local information and a rear projection screen for displaying visual materials, led into a multimedia meeting room complex planned to shelter and assist every kind of library program or community meeting and designed to be used before and after regular library hours.

A legacy from the original Carnegie library, this stained glass window by an unknown artisan graces the entrance to the 1981 building.

A small collection of permanent artwork by local artists Mauricio and William Lasansky, James Lechay, Byron Burford, Howard McKenzie, Jim Ochs, Keith Achepohl, Stan Haring, Mildred Pelzer Lynch, and Norval Tucker was scattered throughout the building, with the art-to-go collection displayed on other walls and ready for check-out.

A public lounge with vending machines, tables, and chairs for eating, drinking, and reading, and soundproof study rooms, wired for audio and video signals, immediately became popular destinations. Tall, round display units stood throughout the building ready to present library information and exhibit community projects.

One critic reviewing the building said the library passed one test for the value of any structure or institution: "Whether or not you would stay there willingly if you didn't have to." He said it was "a community displaying its best intentions." He welcomed the opportunity to "know the building as a friend."[4]

The new library rapidly became a popular place to visit for Iowa Citians, area residents, and their out-of-town guests. Children brought their parents, who brought friends, who brought relatives. Grandparents and other guests were urged to meet Paddington Bear and try out the on-line catalog. The audiovisual desk was probably the prime internal destination point, booking videos and films, all kinds of audiovisual equipment, and the three meeting rooms. During the summer of 1981, before videocassette players became commonplace in many homes, young people lined up in the lobby each morning and when the grille was raised at 10:00 a.m., they would race to the audiovisual desk to be the first to request earphones for one of the four videocassette player stations. Adults lined up on the first of each month to book the video player, the video camera, and other equipment available for overnight check-out. The meeting rooms were used eight hundred times in the first year by a wide variety of Iowa City groups which represented the rich organization life of the community. (This early rate of heavy use has continued to the present day.) The audiovisual staff handled over 10,000 bookings in the first twelve months and tallied another 7,770 requests for films, equipment, and rooms already in use.

In just a few months it was clear than our intent "to make the library a community resource center that used automation, telecommunications, and audiovisual services to provide modern information services in a friendly, easy-to-use, and informal setting"[5] was succeeding beyond our greatest expectations. The new glamorous audiovisual and computer services received the most acclaim, but the overload at the information desk and the steadily increasing use of print materials were still causing the biggest bottleneck.

The Sunday Hours Crusade. It didn't take us a full year to realize the size of the monster we had created and that something had to be done to keep the whole system operating. In October, eight months before relief was possible in the form of additional staff for the next fiscal year and several months before the council would even consider the issue of staffing, the board began to discuss some service cutbacks designed to ease the burden that daily growth was placing on the library. Because they had no funds in the 1982-83 budget for more staff, the trustees announced several changes aimed at reducing the number of check-outs. The library would close Thursday mornings, card holders would be limited to ten items per check-out, reciprocal agreements with all area libraries except Coralville would be canceled, and children's weekly story hours and film showings (which produced long lines to check out after each event) would be reduced from ten to six. "One of the most time consuming and costly things we do is to put a book back on the shelf," I told the newspapers. "It takes us four or five times as long to put it back as it does to check it out. We are hoping people will be a little more selective for a while and not scoop up more books than they can read."

The changes had little effect. We learned that if you place a limit on the number of books, many who formerly took only three or four books now felt compelled to take "their share" and would check out ten. Circulation from Solon, Oxford, West Liberty, and West Branch dropped off, but many residents from these towns purchased nonresident fee cards so they could continue to borrow. Shorter hours and fewer children's programs spread check-outs more evenly into the remaining times open and provided the overwhelmed staff a few more uninterrupted hours to sort and reshelve library materials.

These hours and service reductions on December 1, 1981, followed the library's formal budget request for the next fiscal year and set off a concern about getting the library open again on Sunday that involved the Chamber of Commerce, the city council, and the board of supervisors, and held the attention of the community throughout the winter of 1982.

The library board asked for funds to revive Sunday service but not unless the council first approved funding for two additional positions to handle current rates of use and to restore the December 1 service cuts. "The Sunday hours are our second priority," Board President Ed Zastrow told the council. "We are already unable with the present staff to meet the recent 50 percent increase in use of library services."

The old debate about reducing hours versus reducing other services was regenerated. Eager to use their new library as much as possible, many persons in the community gave Sunday hours a higher priority than some library services. The problem was that no one could agree which services to cut—some wanted to cut hours other than Sunday, some wanted to continue to limit children's programming in exchange for Sundays, and others wanted to close whole departments such as information or audiovisual to get the doors open on Sunday. The variety of their demands supported the library's long-standing position that when the library was open, all services would be provided. Any other arrangement, the board reiterated, would be both confusing and unfair to library users.

In addition to several letters to the editor and a *Press-Citizen* editorial on the subject, John Hughes, president of the Chamber of Commerce, appeared before the library board to ask for Sunday hours. The business community felt Sunday library service would help increase traffic at the Old Capitol Mall on Sundays. By the end of January, impressed with the number of residents and out-of-towners visiting the new library, the Chamber ignored its 1978 opposition to the library's location and gave ICPL its 1981 Economic Development Award.

As the council debated the 1982-83 budget, the Johnson County Board of Supervisors added to the library's concerns about adequate funding. The supervisors had fought a major increase to their library contract a year earlier. The county's share of library operations had increased 50 percent over a two-year period due to the library's increasing budgets, increased use by county residents, and a surcharge to help cover new building costs. The surcharge especially rankled the supervisors. They felt it was unfair because the county did not own the library. In 1981-82 they had bargained their $82,600 share down to $69,500 by threatening to cancel their contract. Now they joined the Sunday hours debate and told the library board that without Sunday service they would not contract.

The library trustees had vowed they would not open the library on Sundays until after they got the money they needed to run the library without Sunday service, but if the county's $80,000 contract was canceled, there would be an even larger hole in the library's budget. At the same time, both the supervisors and the city councilors were under great pressure from their respective publics to provide the requested funds. Finally, in late rounds of budget discussions, the council identified some undesignated funds and approved both levels of library funding: $24,000 for a one-quarter-time permanent position and one hundred hours of shelvers, and $19,500 for Sunday openings October through May. The funds were accompanied by several scoldings from city councilors about limits on funding for the library in the future. They felt the council was being bludgeoned by the library board on the issue of Sunday hours. "The library sort of uses this as a club against us," Mayor Neuhauser said, "and I think people are getting very annoyed." Councilman Larry Lynch said he wanted the increase to be the last for a while. "We know the library is swamped . . . but there has to be a limit to it." He said he didn't want to see the library come looking for more staff additions the next year.[6]

Editorials in the *Press-Citizen* and the *Daily Iowan* praised the council for its decision. "Applause for restoring Sunday library hours," headlined the *Press,* noting that the library's budget, called "too much" by the council, was "still a modest 8 percent of the general fund budget." The council decision came just two days after the paper had published a survey form asking people their opinions on the issue. Only eight of the thirty-eight who responded to the brief survey said they could "live without Sunday hours," the paper reported.[7] The *Daily Iowan* seemed more aware of the political forces at work. "The squabble between the city council and the library board . . . is only the latest of feuds between the two groups that predates the construction of the new building. . . . The compromise over Sunday library service represents, at best, an uncertain standoff in this ongoing conflict, and it does not address the basic issue: the library board still wants additional funding, which the council is reluctant to provide."[8]

In April, after the budgets had been approved and money for Sunday hours was assured, *Cedar Rapids Gazette* columnist Tom Walsh interviewed Mayor Neuhauser, asking, "Will Sunday library hours survive?"[9] She said she felt the library board understood how the council felt about the issue. "They can't just keep raising [the issue] year after year as a means of winning council approval of [library] annual budget requests." She claimed some people were so distressed by the cutoff of Sunday service that they had suggested the Iowa legislature "rescind the current political protection provided library boards." Neuhauser felt it was important the library adapt its hours to the changing habits of Iowa Citians, including those who shopped in downtown Iowa City on Sunday afternoons.

The *Gazette* column also included excerpts from a letter Board President Zastrow had sent Mayor Neuhauser in response to her insistence that the library never again eliminate Sunday hours. "The Library Board is very interested in providing Sunday service to this community. . . . I can't, however, permanently commit future library boards to this service any more than you can permanently commit future councils to a particular level of funding. The board, like the council, carefully endeavors to allocate available resources to the maximum benefit of our constituencies."

For the fourth time since service on Sunday was revived in 1969, the library reopened on Sundays following a battle with the council over funding. Sunday service started again in the fall of 1982 and except for summers ICPL has never again closed on that popular day.[10] We had learned Sundays were sacred to both library users and community officials. In budget battles near the end of the decade, the board would stick to its policy of reducing hours rather than specific services when faced with funding shortfalls, but when closings were necessary, they would be shifted to other days of the week.

After Sunday hours were funded for 1982-83 and their principal objection was gone, the county supervisors quietly agreed to the $80,000 contract. It took only twelve months, however, for them once again to object to the cost of the library contract. For the third straight year the supervisors threatened to cancel their contract, and perhaps with some reason if viewed from their perspective. Under our then-current formula, the library asked the county for $107,000 for 1983-84. The supervisors said they would not pay a 34 percent increase and offered 10 percent or $88,000. The growing library budget and a larger share of total use by county residents were driving the increases to the county. Not only did the library's budget increase 20 percent between fiscal years 1982-83 and 1983-84, but loans to county residents increased 25 percent and accounted for over 12 percent of all check-outs from the library.

After negotiating for several months, including one period when both sides doubted if an agreement could be reached, there were two major breakthroughs. Fearing public pressure if library funding faltered and realizing the large shortfall in the library's budget if the county failed to contract, the city council decided and the library board agreed that the council, not the library board, would negotiate and execute the contract with the county. The councilors, especially Mayor

Neuhauser, felt they had more negotiating power with the county than did the library board because of such city-county joint ventures as the Senior Center and SEATS. Both the city and the library board were eager to end this annual stalemate over the county contract. Most important, the library and the city produced a revised, open-ended agreement, with the help of County Attorney Patrick White, that simplified the process and eliminated the necessity of annual negotiations unless the city or the county wanted to change the terms of the agreement. All references to library capital costs and city administrative costs were eliminated; the county would pay a simple 10 percent of the library's net operating budget (excluding grant, gift, state, or federal monies).[11] This formula would keep both sides content for nearly ten years.

Computer Calamity. The last major crisis of the first year in the new building was a series of computer breakdowns that lasted for much of April, May, and June. Like television sets in the early 1950s, computer systems in this period were "at the shop" with a frequency that would be considered absolutely unacceptable in the 1990s. These were the days before backup systems and affordable built-in redundancy.

After a few short breakdowns in August of 1981 due to an inadequately air-conditioned computer room, performance had been quite remarkable. In the spring of 1982 when our computer trials began, the system had been operating more or less reliably since it was purchased and turned on in March 1979. After more than three years, therefore, we were upgrading both hardware and software for some much-needed power, space, and functionality. At the same time that the city was putting utility wires underground and paving the alley north of the building, right below the computer room, our computer gurus were installing the new equipment. Day after day, with occasional hours of relief, the system refused to operate. "The first library in the U.S. with an on-line catalog" was down and apparently out for unknown reasons. (ICPL was one of the showplaces for the company's turnkey system and news of our problems spread like wildfire throughout its customer base.) Was the electrical supply compromised? Was the room still overheating? Was the problem caused by undetected bugs in the new software? Could all four replacements for the "#3 circuit board" be defective? While computer experts from Boston debated these questions, the staff alternately waited and watched, then worked like crazy to check in, check out, consult the catalog, and add a few new materials whenever the computer was up for a few hours.

The public quickly learned just how much library operations depended on the computer. Every day that the computer was not functioning (nearly one-half of April, one-fourth of May, and one-third of June), we all bore the burden of facing the public once again saying, "We still don't know why." It didn't enhance the reputation of the computer, the computer company, or those of us who had purchased it. After the turmoil of the first few weeks in the new library the previous summer, staff members felt they could handle anything, but they were suddenly back in a familiar predicament—thousands of unshelved books—but this time they faced somewhat angry crowds instead of delighted new customers.

After seventeen consecutive days of a dead system in late April and early May, the public began to soften and to feel sorry for us. We were *all* at the mercy of the machine. Every one of the two hundred transactions per hour that took place when the computer was inoperative had to be recorded by hand. That at least was a partial substitute for the regular check-out system. The loss of access to the catalog was more crippling. It was impossible to determine if the library owned a particular title, books by a particular author, or material on a particular subject, although those library users who had rarely asked questions before were sometimes impressed with the amount of help our information librarians could supply.

By mid-June, we began to accept that our long computer ordeal had been due to four defective circuit boards in a row, as improbable as that may seem. The in-house hero was systems coordinator and technical services manager Diane Ingersoll who gave us straight answers and ignored our desperate pleas for more optimistic progress reports. The experience became one of the building's first legends. Those who had worked through it loved to share the awful details whenever a minor system problem upset a newer employee.

The first year was much more than crowds and lines, unshelved books, budget and contract battles, and computer catastrophes, however. In the first year's annual report, I issued a report card on the new building, giving it mostly "A's":

> The building works. Most people are able to find the new services (and discover the old ones), locate major collections, favorite reading spots . . . with relatively little help. While much less hidden than in the old building, the trail to the second floor nonfiction collection is probably the least obvious. . . . All corners of the library are . . . used for reading. Supervision of the 2nd floor is awkward but problems have not been serious.
>
> Though well planned . . . audiovisual services are probably the most crowded. Spaces should have been larger. . . . Storage space is limited . . . will force us to save only what is necessary. Sound absorption is excellent . . . normal conversation and this library's tradition of an informal social atmosphere continues without . . . disturbing others. The meeting room complex and the cable television wing are able to provide their different kind of activities without interrupting mainstream services. . . .
>
> The cost for utilities has been less than predicted. Careful lighting poli-

cies and conservative temperature settings helped the building to perform well in this area. . . . There have been a few acts of vandalism but generally the public respects and enjoys the new building.

The public lounge—a rare feature in an American public library but common in England and Europe—seems to have satisfied the public's need to eat and drink while reading and studying. . . . Public is spending about $1,000 a month at the vending machines.[12]

Visitors came from all over the nation and several foreign countries for tours of the new facilities and to observe the new on-line catalog. Delegations from other public libraries were drawn by feature articles about the building in several national library and cable television publications. The formal visits were just a small part of the guest traffic. After many weekends, I would find notes from old friends or complete strangers giving rave reviews of what they had seen.

After a couple of years, as local residents became accustomed to the popular features of the new building, the informal visits from out-of-towners became less visible. The formal visits, however, from libraries and from various foreign delegations (Netherlands, Australia, Japan, China, Canada) continued throughout the decade. Most departments, especially audiovisual, information, technical services, and community services, received a continuing stream of requests by mail and by phone for advice and for copies of various library brochures and policies. Staff members were invited to speak at many state, regional, and national library meetings.[13]

Near the end of the building's first year, both staff and board realized they needed to take action on several fronts if they were going to keep the library operating at the levels of quality and direction they had in mind when the building was designed. They turned to long-range planning; they decided to seriously seek other forms of support; they needed to make great efforts to protect and enlarge library collections in order to serve the needs of an ever-growing reading and viewing user base; they had to find ways to help the information department continue to offer quality information services under the burden of so many new users.

By the spring of 1982 the board had a fifteen-member committee working on a long-range plan. The board had also taken the first steps to establish the Iowa City Public Library Foundation, an independent, nonprofit corporation, to raise funds for larger material budgets. They had strengthened the volunteer program by squeezing ten hours of additional professional time for volunteer recruitment and coordination from the council's austere 1982-83 budget. They knew this was just the beginning.

Learning to Plan

Neither board nor staff members brought planning experience to the process, the project took twice as long as originally planned, and we probably collected too much data and took too many surveys, but we established a baseline of information about the library and had a wonderful time discussing new ideas about library services. Once again, the 1975 agenda was advanced and, most important, some simple priorities were established.

After preparing comprehensive community and library profiles and conducting five community opinion and library use surveys, the original group (four trustees, four staff members, and seven community volunteers) struggled to make sense of all the data and opinion. By the time they reached their original nine-month deadline, they had produced only a "preliminary report." A restructured and smaller committee took another nine months and the help of six staff-trustee-volunteer committees to produce a brief five-year plan. The plan, *Library Priorities for the '80s*, adopted by the library board in July of 1983, and its revised version five years later, set library service priorities for the next ten years, 1984 through 1993.

There were several firsts in the 1983 plan: a mission statement, operating principles, library roles defined and placed in priority order, plus brief goals and objectives for the 1984-89 period. The goals and objectives were crude and simple, obviously the work of people new to the task of long-range planning. More original for the time were the operating principles and the roles. The principles incorporated many of the values the library was already trying to adhere to in giving library service to Iowa City; the roles became a shorthand method of describing to the public and ourselves the multiple functions public libraries traditionally provide and of explaining the priority, effort, and resources these functions would receive in the next five years.

The operating principles addressed issues of intellectual freedom and the importance of keeping library services free. They acknowledged the library's commitment to collections in all formats, arranged and labeled to allow independent use. One statement promised that all users' interests, levels of intellectual achievement, and physical abilities are of equal weight and everyone's opinions and suggestions must be sought in designing services. The principles incorporated the long-held board position that whenever the library was open, all services offered would be available. They described the skills and values sought when selecting and developing library staff. Finally, one principle characterized the informal, friendly, and productive library environment the board and staff hoped to achieve by following these standards and beliefs.

These principles, although never distributed except as part of the five-year plan, guided board and staff decisions throughout the decade. It was useful and effective to be able to cite official board operating principles when explaining to the public or local officials why the library did not charge for services; why the library board chose to reduce hours rather than cut back services; why calls to increase resources through special fees were inappropriate; why time was spent surveying library customers, collecting data on how they used the library, and seeking their suggestions for improvement. It became our "constitution" and complemented the American Library Association's Library Bill of Rights, another policy statement adopted by the trustees.

The six roles defined in the 1983 plan were based on ideas in a January 1983 article by distinguished librarian and scholar Lowell Martin[14] and were later adopted nationally by the Public Library Association for the second edition of its planning manual for public libraries.[15] Martin's ideas were an important breakthrough for the planning team. The six terms, succinctly defining and describing obvious public library functions, allowed members of the planning committee to communicate with each other, the rest of the board, staff, and eventually the general public about the scope of library services and the plan's recommendations for setting priorities. The planning committee, the full library board, and all staff members ranked the six roles to determine their priority for the next five years. There was a clear consensus among all groups on the rankings. The roles and their definitions listed in rank order were:

Information Agency—Collects and dispenses information essential for daily living.

People's University—Materials for self-education and personal enrichment.

Children's Door to Learning—Programs and services for youngsters entering the world of reading and learning.

Popular Book Store—The free source for recreational reading, listening, and viewing.

Student's Auxiliary—Supplementary resources for elementary and secondary students.

Community Center—Multi-use facilities and resources for group interaction and community participation.

The four goals of the new plan addressed general administrative or library-wide issues. They were stated in somewhat simplistic or vague terms, but they staked out four areas for action: improve services and resources for individuals and groups with special needs; "increase public awareness and understanding of specific services, collections, and facilities"; "educate the public about the distinct purposes of the public library" (referring to a plan to try to reduce curriculum-related use of the library by university faculty and students); and help the public understand how the new information technologies will change but enhance the library.

Each of the six planning subcommittees adopted objectives and strategies for its assigned role and wrote position statements that tied its role to the operating principles and the four general goals. These fifty pages are a textbook of dreams and possibilities for library service in a fully funded environment. They display the originality and idealism of library trustees and staff as they set out to deliver the library services that local residents, through the 1982 surveys, helped them envision. The many objectives developed by the subcommittees were also ranked to get a list of the twenty-two top objectives that would constitute the basic five-year work plan.

A sampling of some of the more jargon-free objectives includes items, large and small, typical of our attempts to fine-tune library operations in the 1980s: get staff for the audiovisual lab, adopt an unattended child policy; target one special needs group each year for review of related library services; institute an all-purpose user suggestion procedure; set a three-hour standard for reshelving high-demand materials and a two-day standard for all other items; increase the numbers of story hours and other children's programs on cable channel 20; teach children and adults on-line catalog searching techniques; provide public access to microcomputers and microcomputer software. All were eventually accomplished although the one most heatedly debated, microcomputers and microcomputer software for the public, was short-lived and finally declared undoable without using an unacceptable level of staff time and staff training.

The plan document, although awkward to use and graphically uninteresting, was consulted frequently throughout the period. It lacked any procedure for evaluation, but we checked off items, circled accomplishments in red, and revised objectives each year as circumstances changed.

Information Agency: The Priority Role

As the top library priority for the next five years, the information department received a lot of attention. The surveys conducted in the summer of 1982 gave information services high ratings on every scale. Two-thirds of those surveyed had received help from department librarians to locate materials or find answers to questions; nearly 40 percent had telephoned the library for such service. The committee assigned to this role quoted the comments of the public in its report: "Information services should be the highest priority" and "Basic information resources should have the highest priority for funding." Serving all segments of the community, the report explained, "children, students, adults—information is the easiest kind of library service to obtain, since it is available by telephone . . .

a service which can specifically aid the elderly and disabled," groups targeted by the library plan. "There are alternative resources for most of the other roles which the library serves, [but] there appears to be no other agency in town which can assume the functions of the Information Agency as provided by the Iowa City Public Library."[16]

The information subcommittee developed many objectives and strategies for maintaining and improving information services, but they all required staff time, a precious commodity made more scarce by the overwhelming increases in the number of questions handled since the opening of the new building. (Information transactions jumped from 32,000 during the last year in the Carnegie to 44,000 in 1981-82. By 1984-85 they reached nearly 54,000.) There were no strategies in the committee report on how to find staff time to accomplish any of the plan's objectives, let alone handle the new level of business. Ideas developed within the department, however, and some general restructuring during the next few years helped give the librarians some relief.

The department needed two librarians on duty at the desk whenever the library was open, but it would take nearly two more years to reach that goal. To begin to provide this level of staffing, all librarians on staff served some time at the information desk, including taking turns for evenings and weekends—a much more intense version of the staffing pattern used in the old Carnegie. Volunteers took over some routine clerical tasks and shelvers were reassigned from the central pool in order to have one person—known as the information page—on duty at all times to put away materials, care for the copiers and microfilm equipment, and retrieve items from storage. By 1985 we were able to add more hourly-pay or permanent library assistants qualified to assist librarians at the information desk. One librarian and one library assistant became the minimum staffing standard, and this further stretched our small pool of librarians.

The information department had grown from one librarian on duty most of the time in the early 1970s to a large crew with varying levels of skill and expertise. It was the blast of business from the new facility that forced us to staff the department, and the desk itself, more efficiently with no loss in the quality of the service provided. Technology also pushed the process. The information pages proved invaluable. Today they command their own service point in the back of the information area, oversee use of study rooms, and have become well-trained if unfortunately low-paid techies who, with supervision from regular technical staff, can deal with CD-ROM networks, the Internet, and the World Wide Web, as well as the many print and storage files of the department.

Strengthening the Collection

All librarians worked on a public service desk somewhere—information, audiovisual, children's—and we all shared responsibility for the collection. The same pattern had been followed, more or less, since the subject specialist system was adopted in the mid-1970s. We each had responsibility for a part of the collection based on subject, intended audience, and/or format. The new organizational chart produced during the 1981 staff restructuring showed all selectors reporting to the director for that aspect of their job. This simply formalized what had been in place for several years. Ever since 1970 when Jack Hurkett assigned me to head the technical services department, my strongest professional interest had been managing all aspects of the collection including developing the materials budget and dividing it equitably between the many selectors.

Our particular collection assignments changed from time to time as people left, or as librarians were added and the whole task could be divided into smaller parts. Librarians became specialists in business or fiction or history or cookbooks or science or medicine, and then sometimes, they gave up a subject for a new topic or two. Others held on to favorite subjects for years and years and became experts on the bibliography of their assigned areas. When Mary Croteau left the library in 1970, I handed myself the record collection and spent more than twenty years developing first the LP and later the compact disc collection.

As the collection manager, however, I had to face larger issues than the almost hobby-like pleasure of building a comprehensive collection of music recordings. Almost all the roles identified in the 1983 five-year plan were based on the premise of a larger and richer collection, but developing that collection had become much more difficult than we had ever envisioned.

The 1981 building provided the space, the special facilities, and the equipment to support the size and variety of collections the community required. Each year since the doors had opened, however, with higher-than-expected increases in the use of all library services, it took all increases in funding to rebind and replace rapidly deteriorating basic collection items and to hire additional staff for public desks and for reshelving materials.

Inflation had badly damaged our purchasing power. Rapidly increasing costs for salaries and other expenses had squeezed the most flexible part of any library's budget—the book and materials fund. During the early 1970s, the library purchased approximately 11,000 new volumes a year. In that period, with a smaller user base and lower book prices, we regularly strengthened the range and depth of the collection. Hit by the heavy inflation of 1978-81, annual acquisitions dropped to a low of 8,800 volumes in 1981, just as we opened the new building. By 1982 the average cost of a hardcover book hit $25.50 compared to $9.50 just ten years earlier. Both the periodical and hardcover book price indexes rose more rapidly than the general consumer price index.

To compound the problem, from 1981 to 1985 card holders had nearly doubled and circulation had risen by 50 percent. This reduced the total items available for loan from five per card holder to three per card holder in just four years. The additional borrowers increased the share of the total collection checked out at any one time from 18 percent in the first year of the computer to nearly 23 percent in the mid-1980s.

In a period of rapidly rising circulation the library must buy more and more volumes each year just to stay even. Between 1981 and 1984, with the help of gifts plus some generous increases in tax dollars, the library had increased its expenditures for library materials by more than $50,000 a year, reaching $135,000 in 1983-84. However, 11,000 items purchased in 1970 represented one new volume for every two library users and for every twenty-five items circulated. By 1984-85, 13,300 purchased items represented one new item for every four library users and for every thirty-five items circulated.

In the face of continuing large increases in the use of the collection, the additional effort had allowed the library merely to maintain the collection and prevent its deterioration. It had not enabled real growth. At the rate of use in the middle of the decade, the library needed to add at least 17,000 volumes per year in order to substantially enlarge and broaden the collection. This rate of acquisition would not be reached until 1991. Until at least 1986, a large share of the book funds had to be spent to replace lost, worn, and out-of-date materials.

This combination then of reduced purchasing power and increased maintenance costs caused by more borrowers checking out a larger proportion of the collection thwarted the long-term goal of enlarged and expanded collections in many subject areas. We also needed to purchase all kinds of nonprint materials— video, 16mm films, slides, audiotape, and disc recordings—to fulfill one of the library's newly adopted but long-striven-for operating principles: "Information . . . will be supplied in whatever medium best serves the needs of users." Although the library had been lucky in securing a $31,000 grant for developing the audio-visual collection in 1980 and 1981, the proliferation of nonprint formats and the library's decision to provide them in quantity further diminished resources available for print.

Additionally, the 1981 building was planned with no knowledge of the approaching popularity of the videocassette player and the accompanying explosion of movies and other forms of drama, information, and art on half-inch video. In the late 1970s and early 1980s we were buying a small number of videotapes because they were cheaper and easier to use than 16mm film but still too expensive for most individuals.

When the VCR revolution hit the consumer market, our movies on video circulation went "off the charts." In 1981-82 the library loaned 3,285 videos under an overnight booking system. In 1984-85, with the loan period changed to two days, 20,392 videos were checked out. By 1988-89, the loan period had been extended to seven days and loans totaled 67,700. As the library approached its centennial, this format, which we were barely aware of fifteen years earlier, accounted for 22 percent of all adult loans—135,000 movies and 41,000 nonfiction video titles. In 1996, the library's 10,600 videos of all types—movies, nonfiction, and children's—were loaned 220,000 times. Long-range planning helped us take a clearer look at where we thought the library should go but it could not predict the future.

Looking for the Voluntary Dollar.

That first-ever plan did not anticipate the continued high level of growth in the use of the new library. We assumed that increases would level off after the first few months, or at least the first two years. Nor did we foresee the rapidity with which the financial outlook for the library would change. There was nothing in the plan about seeking additional sources of support.

Per capita support for ICPL appeared healthy when compared to other communities. Iowa City's twenty-two dollars per capita support in 1984 was 35 percent higher than the average for Iowa libraries and the highest of any city in Iowa with a population over 10,000. Also, Iowa City was receiving nearly 10 percent of the local municipal tax levy in the mid-1980s, compared to less than 4 percent for most Iowa public libraries in communities of similar size. The problem, however, was that Iowa City had the same number of card holders and annual loans as many cities three and four times its size. For instance, when annual budget was divided by total card holders rather than by total population, Des Moines (population 193,000) was spending sixty dollars per card holder versus twenty-four dollars at ICPL.

With these kinds of comparative "riches," the library's financial predicament was difficult to explain to city officials and to the public. The library had received budget increases of 7 to 20 percent every year from 1980 to 1984. Faced with ongoing staff and collection shortages, the library board began to realize that the library's 10 percent share of the city budget was most likely an unsurmountable barrier. In addition, there was a strong possibility it could become 10 percent or less of a smaller pie. Federal assistance had been cut drastically and growth in the local tax base had leveled off. The state of Iowa, hit by the farm debt crisis, was also reducing the size and scope of its services, including municipal assistance. To top off the suddenly gloomy picture for the city, university enrollment peaked in 1984 and was predicted to decline over the next few years.

Thus, while the library was supported at a rate unmatched by any other Iowa public libraries and by few nationwide, Iowa City's public funds seemed inadequate. Under then-current trends, and based on statements of some city councilors, the library did not expect to obtain a larger share of the local tax dollar.

The board, determined to expand nontax resources to enhance services and to increase the materials budget, took its most public step when the trustees established the Iowa City Public Library Foundation in June of 1982. The trustees' efforts in this direction had been underway for several years, before their most recent concerns about municipal support. The lack of attention to this topic in *Library Priorities for the '80s*, adopted one year later, was probably attributable to our urgent need to create some priorities for library services. At that time we saw service plans and the resources to support them as two separate tracks.

The board had taken several steps as early as 1975 to increase library-generated revenues. The climate, if not the policies, for urging contributions, gifts-in-kind, and voluntary assistance was reflected in the goals written to start the building planning process (chapter 9). These efforts had begun to pay off. Between 1980 and 1985 the library increased from 7 to 15 percent the share of its operating budget which came from income other than the local property tax.

The library found a variety of ways to increase its nontax income. The contract with the county, while it sometimes took hours of negotiation and painful confrontations with county officials, was the largest county contract in Iowa at the time. (The contract fee came from rural tax dollars, not from Iowa City's local tax base.) Also, the library board continued to set the rate for nonresident fee cards equal to the cost per household for Iowa Citians and marketed the card to residents of neighboring jurisdictions that wanted access to Iowa City's wide range of services. The fee was also the highest in Iowa at the time and produced annual income of about $8,000. Miscellaneous income came from the sale of vended snacks and drinks, photocopies, discarded library materials, book bags, public telephones, and copies of the library-produced newspaper index and the information department's association file.

Since computer-controlled circulation was inaugurated in 1979, fines for overdue library materials had increased from $15,000 to more than $60,000 a year. (A policy of stiff fines was part of the library's operating principle regarding keeping services free. "All services should be free . . . but limits, fines, and penalties will be designed to promote fair and equal access to limited resources.")

In addition, other activities—contributions, gifts-in-kind, Friends, and volunteers—produced support valued at close to $75,000 a year by the mid-1980s.

Friends and Volunteers

Since the Friends took over the book sales shortly after they were organized in 1976, used books and records had accounted for 15 to 20 percent of all acquisitions. These gifts-in-kind included additional copies of heavily used titles as well as valuable titles which the library had been unable to purchase. The Friends' eight-year program to encourage people to contribute books and records to the library had added 15,000 hardbound volumes and recordings to the collection, saved thousand of dollars on the purchase of paperbacks for browsing racks and for jail and nursing home collections, and by 1985 produced about $10,000 a year on the sale of books not needed by the library.

This joint Friends-library activity became a highly developed production line of librarians first searching incoming boxes for possible candidates for the collection and then turning over all remaining items to the Friends for sorting and sale. By 1985 the Friends had to hire a part-time book sorter. Anything less than a weekly sort produced gridlock in the library's mail room and garage. Book sales were increased to four or more a year. At each Saturday sale, held in the library's garage, the pre-opening lineup often stretched for a half a block.

Income from these sales was the main source of funds for the Friends annual gift to the library. Between the annual gift and the value of the used books added to the library's collections or to various outreach collections, the annual benefit to the library, estimated at $20,000 in 1979 (see chapter 9), had increased to at least $35,000 to $40,000 a year by the mid-1980s.

The Friends of the Iowa City Public Library had been the first formal link between the community and the library in the library's search for additional support. Besides their book sales, the Friends also lent early support to the volunteer program. In addition to assisting Carol Spaziani develop the volunteer policy in 1979, members took library volunteer positions (in addition to their volunteer work for Friends events and projects), and starting in 1982 they hosted the annual volunteer recognition event.

The library had used a large crew of volunteers to issue library cards for the new computer-assisted circulation system in 1979, but it was the seven hundred volunteers moving the library in 1981 that was the breakthrough event for publicizing volunteer opportunities at the library. Then, in the summer of 1981 during the crisis of returned books logjammed in the back rooms of the library, the volunteers again came to the library's rescue. Volunteer coordinator Spaziani recruited and trained a pool of forty volunteers to work two to four hours a week checking in materials and rough-sorting books in the circulation department. This major volunteer responsibility continues and has accounted for about half the hours contributed to the library ever since that first year. Volunteers who work in every other library department, doing a wide variety of regular and special project tasks, make up the other half of the annual 6,000 hours. Equal to almost three full-time employees, even at minimum wage, volunteers contribute at least $25,000 worth of work to the library each year.

A Century of Stories

The Iowa City Public Library Foundation

There had been a long record of gifts throughout the library's history: Welch/ Patterson (1907), Wulwebber (1946), Brubaker (1949), Walker (1955), and the estate of Jacob Reizenstein (1961) all provided gifts, bequests, or trusts to benefit the library. These gifts suggested that the library was capable of attracting others. More recently, the $50,000 raised by the library board during the construction of the 1981 building demonstrated there was a willingness to contribute despite the library's major support from local taxes.

After the building opened in 1981, volunteer applications rose dramatically, community organizations offered money for special projects, and contributors donated larger and larger numbers of used books and records. The library had created several avenues for voluntary support and the public had responded. Consequently, the library board, primarily at the urging of Board President Lynda Ostedgaard, decided to establish the Iowa City Public Library Foundation. Ostedgaard felt that a well-managed, reliable, nonprofit organization ready to accept gifts and bequests plus an experienced fund-raiser helped by a motivated board could mount an annual fund drive and eventually build an endowment for the library.

The board set three short-term goals: (1) start an annual fund drive which would build a base of regular donors, (2) dramatize the library's need for additional collection and program support, and (3) stockpile enough money to fund a major capital drive.

Trustee and lawyer Jean Bartley developed the bylaws, drew up the articles of incorporation, and helped the new organization get its tax-exempt status. The ten-member foundation board of directors included four library trustees and six other directors representing various segments of the Iowa City community. Ostedgaard was the first president.

With $7,000 of seed money from the library's gift fund, the nonprofit corporation established an office in the library and hired Pat Forsythe as its part-time executive director and fund-raiser. Forsythe had a library science degree and three years of experience fund-raising for the California Institute of Technology.

In its first three years, through June of 1985, the foundation established a donor base of 850 people and raised $85,000. The foundation funds and accounting were handled by the city finance department with funds going into the city's pooled investments. The foundation decided it would invest its money independently and under its own guidelines when the fund reached $250,000.

Three successful annual fund drives confirmed that many community members would support the library with regular financial contributions. Consequently the foundation directors and the library trustees began planning a major capital drive, setting a goal of a $1 million Centennial Endowment Fund to be in place by the time the library completed one hundred years in 1996.

In some ways the case statement developed for the Centennial Endowment Fund became an update to the 1985-89 long-range plan. The statement identified four areas of concern. The principal need, the statement said, was to create a $500,000 Fund for the Humanities. Reflecting the interest rates of the early 1980s, the foundation hoped to raise $50,000 a year from this first fund to provide the 4,000-5,000 additional volumes needed to get the library above its current inadequate level of purchasing and to overcome its inability to enlarge and enrich library holdings.

Three other funds were named and defined. The Newsome-Westgate Fund for the Preschool Child recognized the importance of the preschool years in the development of the young child and the importance of the library in serving the preschool child. The fund was named for children's librarian Hazel Westgate and former trustee and professor emeritus of children's literature Jerry Newsome. The Fund for the Year 2000 was dedicated to keeping the library in the forefront of information technologies. The Fund for a Free Public Library earmarked money for the identification and development of additional funding sources.

NEH Challenge Grant: Endowment and Acclaim

The Fund for the Humanities represented a serious need for the library but the emphasis on the humanities was a somewhat calculated move to improve the library's chances for getting a National Endowment for the Humanities (NEH) Challenge Grant. We defined the humanities as broadly as possible to include any book or other format that presented ideas as well as information. We could use other parts of the materials budget for science and for the very practical and the very popular.

A challenge grant required the local institution to raise three dollars for each dollar of the grant, and to do so within a five-year period. The foundation decided to ask NEH for $125,000. The library would then need to raise $375,000 between 1985 and 1990, but would finish the period with $500,000, one-half of the Centennial Endowment Fund goal. There were some restrictions on the gifts eligible for the match, based on rules designed to build a larger donor base and involve more people. One wealthy patron could not simply give the required $375,000, and in fact, only the increased portion of gifts from donors who had contributed in the twelve months before the offical NEH fund drive began could be counted as local matching funds.

To qualify for a grant, a library, college, university, museum or other humanities institution competed with other applicants for the limited pool of funds available for each year's award cycle. Each institution had to demonstrate to the satisfaction of the NEH review board that it was an institution with significant humanities activities, that it had a plan and the ability to raise the matching funds, and that it would use the funds in an effective and significant manner. NEH looked favorably at endowment building for institutions that met its criteria.

I worked closely on the library's proposal with foundation director Forsythe and former trustee Suzanne Richerson. I built the arguments, but Richerson edited and edited and edited until my words were cogent, concise, to the point, and within the forty-page limit. With over 8,000 public libraries in the United States, our job was to convince NEH that a public library in a small to medium-sized community could have a role in the promotion or development of the humanities important enough to qualify for a grant, and that the work was ongoing and worth helping build the library's endowment fund. Few public libraries had been awarded NEH Challenge Grants (only about two a year for the past several years) and those which had written successful proposals were generally much larger or were asking for funds to restore a historical building.

We started by pointing out the importance to the humanities of public libraries in small cities and towns all over the country, suggesting that in many such communities the public library is "the only humanities institution, serving the newspaper editor, the school teacher, the minister and other generalists, building political and fiscal support for the humanities generally, and, especially through service to children, fostering the development of future humanities scholars."[17]

In thirty-four pages we argued that since public libraries are an essential link in the strengthening and support of the humanities in the United States, Iowa City's public library, already known nationally for its innovative services, was serving as a model for other small and medium-sized libraries across the country. Through the presence of the University of Iowa, the library had a rich source of humanities scholars and resources as well as a large audience for serious humanities-related programs and services. The university also brought students, including library science students, and young faculty and professional staff to Iowa City. These individuals and their families took an active part in library activities while they were part of the community. When they moved to other locations throughout the United States, as future librarians, potential library board members, or other library activists, they took with them the experience of good library service.

By documenting our large user base; giving details about the current strengths of our collections, programs, displays, publications, cable channel, and support for community organizations; and outlining the fiscal problems faced due to dramatic increases in use, the squeeze of inflation, and limited local tax resources; we made the case for NEH helping us build an endowment so we could continue to serve the humanities by serving as a model public library.

While the grant application was not due until April 1986, under the terms of the Challenge Grant program, any money raised after December 1, 1985, was applicable to the match. The foundation started its Centennial Endowment campaign in December, distributing a handsome brochure written and produced by trustee and foundation board member Charles Drum. From the start, the campaign made it clear that the grant had not yet been awarded but, since the library was going ahead with the campaign whether it received the NEH grant or not, pledges and contributions were being taken in a manner that made them all eligible for the Challenge Grant match—just in case.

On December 10, 1986, we received a call from NEH headquarters informing us that ICPL was one of forty-one institutions in twenty-two states that received grants in the 1986 cycle. There was only one other public library on the award list. Providence, Rhode Island, received an award for renovation of its historic library building. We were also told it was exceptional when an institution was awarded a grant the first time it applied. By that date the library foundation had already raised $200,000 of the required $375,000 and we had four years, until December 1990, to raise the remaining $175,000. The NEH Challenge award was a great honor for the library and one of the high points in my library career.

The "Cadillac" Gets Some New Drivers

Even as the library received congratulations for the NEH award, the library board was in the middle of its most serious effort to date to increase local tax support for the staff required to provide the new levels of service attained since the opening of the new building. The trustees were trying to provide a reasoned, low-key response to library difficulties, but, like Sunday hours in 1982, their efforts would become politicized before the issues were resolved.

Early in 1986 the city council had turned down the library's request for additional staff for the fifth consecutive year. The board had asked for four positions essential to maintain quality library services. In five years of increasing library use, visitors were up 85 percent, card holders 96 percent, materials used in the building and checked out each 60 percent, and information requests 78 percent.

After that fifth turndown, the library board spent the next five months reviewing library operations and debating financial alternatives. Board members analyzed long lists of staff ideas for reducing workload. They reviewed their five-year plan. They looked at library hours and work schedules. They found the staff was already squeezing maximum service out of its current resources. The new library was built to provide a larger collection and modern library services and neither could adequately be done under current staffing.

Until the city could provide additional tax support, the board faced the same old dilemma: Eliminate some services or reduce hours. Reducing services important to some constituencies betrayed the board's charge to "serve everyone with equal vigor" as Judge Wade had phrased it in 1897. Reducing expenditures for an already small collection would require heavy costs later to bring it back to standards. Reducing the total hours of access to the library for everyone and using the saved staff time to keep collections growing and services in shape was the most equitable and least costly option. Furthermore, when the requested positions were provided, the library could quickly reopen to a full schedule.

Following this in-depth, detailed look at library services and after long discussions of the options, the trustees developed a plan and announced it to the public in late August. "Due to inadequate funds to increase staff in proportion to increases in library usage," their formal announcement said, "certain services . . . will be curtailed beginning September 1." They added that "beginning March 1, 1987, and continuing for an indefinite period, the library will be closed Thursday evening and all day Friday."[18]

"Library faces its popularity," the *Press-Citizen* wrote in its editorial following the announcement. "Iowa City loves its public library too much—too much for its current staff to keep up both quality and quantity service under its budget. The board of trustees decided something had to give. They picked quantity."

The September 1 changes announced by the board would not have a dramatic effect on the user, but the board felt that the cutbacks would allow the library to reduce next year's staffing request from four to two and one-half positions. The trustees postponed some of their five-year plan objectives such as improving services to the elderly and adults learning to read, eliminated telephone requests for various audiovisual and meeting room bookings, reduced the number of displays, programs and publications, and closed the library on three minor holidays—Veterans Day, Presidents' Day, and the day following Thanksgiving.

Because the major change—reducing library hours by eleven hours per week—was not scheduled to begin until after the next budget deliberations, the decision sounded to some observers like more of the blackmail the board had been accused of in the Sunday hours debate of 1982. "This is not the first time the library board has threatened drastic changes to pressure the city council to give them more money," one editorial remarked.

Aware of this potential charge, the trustees noted in their public statement that they were well aware of the city's financial problems and that they realized that the library already received a larger-than-average share of the city budget. Trustees met individually with council members and gave them materials that explained their plan in detail. The trustees hoped this early announcement would minimize controversy and help build a cooperative plan with the council to find a reasonable solution to the library's desperate need for staff.

Appearing before the city council a few days later to answer questions about the board's decision, Board President Riley Grimes received some kudos for the way the board was dealing with its problems, but also several sharp rebukes from individual councilors. "It's an embarrassment for Iowa City to have to close it," council member Kate Dickson complained. In a heated and lengthy exchange with Grimes, Ernie Zuber said the library should cut back on some of its services. "To me," he said, "a free library is books, periodicals, and reading maps."

The idea of finding the needed funds by reducing or charging fees for audiovisual services, especially movies on video, was a popular suggestion. In addition to some city councilors, both the *Press-Citizen* and the *Cedar Rapids Gazette* ran editorials recommending fees for loaning videos. There were similar remarks from a few library users who attended a library board-sponsored public hearing on the proposed changes. The idea that library videos competed with local video rental stores was discussed widely in this period and public libraries were on the defensive nationwide.

Board members were determined to keep the public informed about the reasons for their actions. The library had strong support from the many volunteers, Friends, foundation contributors, and core library users, but without adequate staff, which only regular tax revenues could finance, the library would gradually lose the quality of services that motivated this overwhelming level of support. "These painful steps were not taken easily," the board explained in its announcement. "The library is a popular and extremely successful service, but it is success and popularity, coupled with the city's fiscal restraints, that makes these steps necessary. . . . The library is a service institution, [and without adequate staff] it would be no more than a warehouse of unsorted, rapidly obsolescent materials unaccessible to the public." Some steps must be taken, the board said. "Good organization and management can no longer compensate for the work hours necessary to perform essential tasks."

The board and foundation were also in the middle of a major fund-raising campaign for the Centennial Endowment Fund. The decisions behind the August announcement had been balanced against the momentum of the CEF drive. It was difficult to tell a donor who had just made a multiyear pledge that the library would have reduced hours for an indefinite period. In some ways, the NEH Challenge Grant made the ongoing public information about the library's serious staffing needs even more difficult. When the NEH award announcement was made in December the board cautioned that "the money cannot be used to hire staff, so it will not solve the library's current budget problem that is forcing it to close Thursday evenings and all day Friday beginning in March."[19]

While the trustees took care to keep the public informed about the library's predicament, they also spent the fall looking into alternative sources of funding for the city and for the library. They studied an analysis of Iowa property tax rates prepared by the University of Iowa Institute of Public Affairs, they gathered information about the local sales tax option, and they heard representatives from Cedar Rapids Public Library explain their city's successful vote for a special library levy allowed by the Iowa Code. The trustees knew that until the city's financial situation improved, until the council was willing to increase the property tax levy, or until the city or the library had new sources of tax revenue, the prospects for adequate library staffing were dim.

The budget sessions in the winter of 1987 went much as predicted. There was no money for more library staff and new Board President Charles Drum—Riley Grimes had left town in early January to head the staff of newly elected Congressman Dave Nagle—made a conciliatory and supportive statement to the council during the library's budget hearing. He reviewed the library board's decisions and why they had to be made, but suggested that letting city services deteriorate (the transit system was also facing a financial crisis) was not healthy in the long term for the community. Drum asked that the council heed the new city manager's call for boards, commissions, and citizens to work with the council in seeking a solution. "Everything we hear from library supporters leads us to conclude that Iowa Citians are willing to pay taxes to keep their excellent services," he said.

The city council was looking for ways to increase city revenues without councilors taking the heat for raising property taxes. Shortly after city manager Steve Atkins (Atkins replaced Neal Berlin in July 1986) had finished his first Iowa City budget cycle (1987-88), he appointed and coordinated, with the blessing of the city council, a task force called the Citizens Committee on City Revenues. The council had asked for background information on the local sales tax option in the budget cycle before Atkins arrived. Working with this directive, Atkins had assembled a group of city employees to gather information from sales tax campaigns in other Iowa cities during the previous fall and the sales tax option became one of the major items on the agenda of the citizens committee.

While the citizens group debated the pros and cons of property tax and local option taxes, the library board and staff prepared the public for the new schedule of hours to begin March 5, 1987. They sent out a new round of press releases, changed the hours on all general library publications, and issued a bookmark distributed to each person checking out materials that not only listed the new hours but also included the statement, "This schedule will remain in effect until there are sufficient city funds to allow for additional staff positions at the library." The board told the public that the weekly eleven-hour reduction would

358

give the library about one hundred hours (equal to the requested two and one-half positions) to take care of the less visible but essential tasks of library operations.

News stories and library statements tried to make it clear that, while closed to the public on Fridays, the staff would be either in the building working or taking a day off for scheduled weekend work. The staff had recommended the Thursday evening and Friday closings based on five years of traffic counts which showed these to be the periods of lowest use. The board readily agreed, hoping to avoid past criticism for closing the library on Sundays, the library's busiest day. Sunday closings had merely reduced overtime pay and the amount of scheduled time off during the week. Fridays provided nine full hours for uninterrupted attention to major projects.

It was very weird to be in the building with people pounding on the door, peering in the windows, and ringing the phones incessantly. The library staff was accustomed to working for and around the public most of the time, but the productiveness of the nine-hour days was sometimes astonishing. We tried not to get used to it. After the first month I told the newspaper, "It's a bit easier to get caught up on reshelving, cataloging [and other routine operations] when you can do it without being interrupted. But the staff and I miss those interruptions." No matter how many ways we tried to remind people that the library was not open on Fridays, people forgot and came to the door anyway—including Board President Charlie Drum whose University Relations office was just across the street in the old Carnegie.

After March, the total number of people coming into the building went down, but everything else continued to rise. The check-outs per hour rose precipitously and Mondays became nightmares of lines and phone calls and elbow-to-elbow people. In March the library checked out 3 percent more items in 13 percent fewer hours than the previous March. The library was 20 percent busier when open to the public, but the library staff was keeping abreast of essential tasks, and completing long-term projects in record time. The city manager commented that the library had saved money and the staff was able to cope with the normal duties of daily traffic, but "it means the library is more efficient and less effective." As I said in the annual report, it was ironic that in the same year the library received national recognition for excellence in library services, the board was forced to reduce services and hours to maintain that excellence.

The final recommendations of the Citizens Committee on City Revenues, published in late May, were overwhelmingly in favor of maintaining all city services, but by a 2-to-1 ratio the group preferred a property tax increase to the local sales tax. Despite the committee's position and after some heated debate, in June the city council agreed to put the sales tax option on the ballot for an October 6 vote.

359

At this June session, President Drum asked the council if money from the proposed tax could go toward reopening the library on Thursday evenings and Fridays. Councilors Darrell Courtney, Kate Dickson, and George Strait said they would favor increased funding for the library; councilors William Ambrisco, John McDonald, and Larry Baker were more cautious. Ambrisco declined to state his position. "I'm not going to be painted into a corner by you or anyone else tonight," he told Drum. Zuber, whose term ended before the next budget preparation, said he believed the library could operate more efficiently. In explaining the city's financial situation to an individual who objected to the sales tax, Courtney first blamed Washington, D.C. for taking money away from cities, but also said that Iowa Citians "could quit voting for Cadillacs"—citing the library and the new Mercer Park indoor swimming pool as examples—that put the city in debt and cost a lot to operate.[20] The term "Cadillac" became a popular figure of speech used to describe the library by those least interested in seeing library funding increased. The way it was frequently quoted to me was: "Yes, a good library is important, but do we need a Cadillac?"

Although the board received less than full support from the council for funding additional library staff if the proposed sales tax was approved, board members nevertheless felt they had no other option that summer and fall than to endorse the sales tax campaign. They voted 8 to 1 to issue a public statement urging a "yes" vote on October 6 and mail it to Friends and foundation contributors. Trustee Nancy Willis and husband Craig (who had chaired the Citizens Committee on City Revenues) became the chief spokespersons for the campaign. Both were long-time supporters of the city's recreation and library services. Although Iowa City initiated the referendum, the Iowa Code required elections be held in all Johnson County cities and towns. There was almost no support for the idea outside of Iowa City. Citizens Against Unnecessary New Taxes (COUNT) campaigned against the tax.

While the question lost by only fifteen votes in Iowa City, it was overwhelmingly rejected everywhere else. "County zaps sales tax," headlined the *Press-Citizen*. In fact, it carried in only eight of the fifty-two county precincts, all eight "in upper-income neighborhoods," according to one local analyst. Voters in Manville Heights gave the issue a 78 percent approval while "no" votes in some county towns were as high as 94 percent. Some campaign statements and most post-election analysis stated that the "no" vote did not represent opposition to the possible uses of the new funds—library staff, human services, property tax relief—but opposition to the tax itself as regressive and unfair to those with lower incomes.[21]

By October, after the failed attempt for a local sales tax, board members were back to preparing another budget proposal—their seventh since first striving to get additional staff—as well as hoping the November city election campaign would clarify who supported library funding. Two new councilors, Susan Horowitz and Randy Larson, appeared to be strong library supporters, but would there be additional money for the council to spend? The city was not at the general levy limit but, hurting after the loss of federal funds for transit and other programs and boxed in by its own policy of several years to limit budget increases to 6 percent, it was uncertain what the city council might do.

City manager Steve Atkins did not recommend more staff for the library for the 1988-89 budget; under his guidelines, departments could not even submit requests for additional staff. In fact, his three-year budget plan, based on holding staffing and services at then-current levels, meant that the library could be on its reduced schedule for three more years. President Drum was inspired by this revelation to write a guest opinion for the *Press-Citizen* noting that at the end of the three years the new library would be ten years old, the same age as the library board's annual request for additional permanent staff. Drum's column went on to review all the reasons for needing more staff including the fact that use of the library continued to increase. "Just this month we experienced the two busiest weekends in our history—checking out an average of seven items every minute the library was open." As in his previous year's budget message, Drum again said he felt many local residents were ready to pay more taxes to preserve city services.[22]

In his remarks to the council at the January 25, 1988 budget hearing, Drum covered much of the same ground, reminding the council that the number of permanent staff had remained virtually the same since the day the library opened and before the astronomical increases in use. The library was increasingly dependent on temporary, hourly-pay staff. He described how the library had used automation of library procedures and established a volunteer corps and a fund-raising arm to try to adapt to the pressures of growth. "Support activities, however, can never make up for core staff," Drum explained as he described the many tasks and decisions that can only be made by professional and trained permanent staff. Although, he continued, "nearly a year later . . . the library is still closed Thursday nights and Fridays . . . we remain optimistic that funds will be found to reopen and we are dedicated to working with the council toward that goal."

The day after the hearing the library received a request from the council for information on the costs of the two and one-half positions the library board had requested in previous years. Just a few days later, there was a surprising turnaround at the council table. Overruling the manager's recommendation, the council voted unanimously to give the library an additional $64,000 for the oft-requested two and one-half positions. Searching the entire budget carefully, the councilors agreed to eliminate from the proposed budget items valued at

$140,000. They cut $12,000 for police accreditation, reduced equipment replacement funds for fire and transit, and postponed the payback of money borrowed from the recreation facilities fund. After giving $64,000 to the library, the changes reduced the total budget by $76,000 and lowered the property tax increase by a small amount. Whether this was wise budgeting or not, it was a smart political move by the council. It eliminated the pressure on the council to fund the library and reduced the proposed budget while staying below the self-imposed 6 percent limit. It was an unexpected victory for the library.

As a thank you to the taxpayers of the community and to those who had been inconvenienced for fifteen months by the shortened library schedule, the library reopened on Friday, June 2, 1988, one month before the library could even hire its new staff. We hung a banner, "Open Again Thursday Evenings and Fridays," on the front of the building. The two and one-half positions would fill several of the holes which were plugged by staff borrowed from public service desks during the fifteen months. In my annual report I noted that the "sixty-four Friday closings were used to great advantage. No one wants to repeat the experience but in many ways the library is now in better shape because of it." That year's report is full of references to what was accomplished.

The library trustees were the heroes of this long fight to preserve the quality of library services. An unusually determined and talented group, they stood their ground for nearly two years, from early 1986 until the budget victory of February 1988. They articulated library needs, protected the staff from acute overextension, and defended the library's operating principles at a time when many said just charge fees or cutback services and get the library open. In his last statement on the long affair, Drum said simply, "The staff could no longer run a library sixty-four hours a week and provide the quality service the board was committed to and the community expected."

Annual loans totaled 487,000 in 1982 when the board first asked for additional staff. By the time the library returned to full schedule after a six-year wait (including two years under reduced circumstances), loans totaled 654,000, a 35 percent increase. With a return to sixty-four hours per week in 1988-89, circulation increased another 11 percent. To the general public we needed to show our gratitude for the additional resources; privately we knew we were already in a hole and unless service indicators suddenly leveled off we would be facing the same shortfall of bodies and minds that had plagued us since the doors of the new library opened in 1981.

On Track for the '90s

By the time the new staff members were on board in the summer of 1988, we were heading toward the 1990s. Our first five-year plan would end in just twelve months. To prepare for writing a new plan, a small group of staff and trustees began meeting as a "planning to plan" committee in the fall of 1986 just after the library made the first public announcement about the service cutbacks and hours reduction. Our task was to decide what needed to be addressed in the next planning cycle and how it should be done. We had learned a little about planning in the first five years and hoped to produce an improved document the second time around.

By spring of 1987, the board received the committee's recommendations for a planning group of ten to eleven people including representatives from the board, staff, Friends, foundation, and the general public. They would be chosen and oriented during the summer of 1987, start work in September, and provide a report by July 1, 1988. Over twenty people applied to be community representatives and seven people were chosen, including director of the university school of library science Carl Orgren, future trustee Kathy Moyers, former trustee Suzanne Richerson, long-time volunteer and Friends member Mary Parden, and future foundation directors Dave Johansen and Rebecca Reiter. Meeting about twice a month for ten months, the group met its deadline and presented its plan to the board for approval. *On Track for the '90s,* a long-range plan for 1990-94, was adopted in July 1988.

The most obvious change in the new plan was its readability and logical sequence. It contained a useful executive summary and a procedure for evaluation and revision. While the plan contained goals and priorities for five years, only two years of objectives were developed, with updates planned for the last three. The ten operating principles became twelve, with one divided into two and a new one added: "The library protects the confidentiality of library users."

In a move that proved of little help because of unexpected changes, the committee developed a list of assumptions about the economic, financial, and demographic characteristics of Iowa City and local government during the next five years and their possible impact on the library. Library roles were put in priority order again. The community members, the board, and the staff ranked each role and agreed easily on the priorities for the next five years. Library services to children and improved information services emerged as the areas for prime attention for 1990-94.

After five years of emphasis in the previous plan, information was still struggling to reduce the wait for services at the information desk. As an alternative to waiting, the department would try strategies to help some clients find information independently or through library-prepared lists and research guides. More systematic collection of local history and efforts to coordinate the collection and dissemination of local community information with other local service agencies were also on the agenda.

The library had long given the library needs of the young child special emphasis but this was the first time this age group would receive extra resources and attention and have a written plan to guide service development. The department would attempt to reach a larger share of the community's young children, taking some library activities for children out into the community. Plans for building larger collections of children's materials and for urging parents and other adults to read aloud to young children and to bring them regularly to the library were also included.

There was great irony and sadness in this decision, for just six weeks before the board adopted the *On Track* plan, and thirteen months before she would complete her fortieth year at the library, Hazel Westgate, children's librarian since July 1949, died suddenly. (Her story and the story of children's services at the library are told in the next chapter.)

Although lower in the priorities, the "popular bookstore" and "people's university" roles gave us a single task: making the general collections as responsive as possible to the needs of library users, a directive welcomed by most librarians who generally love their collection development responsibilities. Collection quality was an important goal, but we also wanted to buy more copies of popular titles, shorten some loan periods, and improve methods of displaying and shelving materials. The nonfiction collection, especially the humanities, would be enlarged, with some plan objectives designed to aid children ages nine to fifteen to find suitable materials in their nonstudent lives—independent learning, hobbies, sports, and other avocations.

Despite generally large but diverse constituencies, the "community center" and "student's auxiliary" roles again were ranked the lowest. The definition for the latter was carefully worded. "The library assists elementary and secondary school students and adults in non-university continuing education programs to meet the educational objectives of their formal courses of study." We carefully excluded university students in their classroom mode from the definition, after making some progress in the previous five years toward educating university faculty, administration, library staff, and the students themselves that, except for local history materials, ICPL was *not* the first place to go for class-related assignments.

The activities represented by the concept of the library as a community center have been extremely important to the library and the community. From the day it opened, the new ICPL had extraordinary facilities for making the library an important community activities center—well-equipped meeting rooms, varied display facilities, giveaway racks, audiovisual lab, and the ability to cablecast from several locations in the building. The nearly 1,000 meetings a year held by over 250 different sponsoring organizations made the library ipso facto a community center whether this role was ranked high or low by library planners. Indeed, it was the many services that these various facilities provided to a wide range of organizations that built much of the support for the library throughout the community. People active in organizations are apt to be the most politically active and issue-oriented individuals in the community. Many library board members never seemed to understood this connection, while library staff, especially in audiovisual and community services, stretched themselves to the limit to help the many community groups and organizations asking for services. There was never enough staff to train individuals to use the meeting room projection booth, to properly produce programs for the cable channel, or to have the audiovisual lab open sixty-four hours a week. These facilities were all victims of unexpected levels of interest in their use plus chronic understaffing. The priorities we set were not wrong, just sad in the face of such possibilities.

Unlike our first plan, *On Track for the '90s* also addressed administrative goals including fund-raising, a newly organized development office, a computer replacement fund, monitoring information technology developments for library applications, long-term financial planning, and a committee to prepare a long-term facilities plan. In this planning cycle, we realized that services, resources, and financial needs of the library belonged in one coherent plan.

This second plan proved to be much more practical, useful, and usable than its predecessor, but as always, "our eyes were bigger than our stomachs." There were many more ideas than time or resources would ever allow us to pursue. Planning had become central to our operations, however, and if too many options were recorded, a lot of others got discussed and discarded. We had a fairly reliable road map, useful for guiding us through the expected, somewhat helpful for evaluating unexpected events and opportunities, and completely off-base about growth which we said would plateau. As the pace of change continued to increase along with the rates of library use, our long-term planning efforts at least helped keep chaos at arm's length.

Controlling Chaos

We claimed to be "on track for the '90s," but derailment always seemed a possibility. No area seemed more out of control in these years than keeping abreast of technological changes—and finding ways to pay for the required updates to library computer equipment. Our quiet smugness about incorporating the cost of our first computer system into the referendum package for the new building rapidly changed to obvious naïveté about automation and technology. We had planned on maintenance costs to keep the system operating and we had expected to add a few terminals and printers as we were able, but we certainly did not understand in 1980 that replacing computer systems every three to five years was the industry standard. It took us several years to figure out how to pay for these major equipment "upgrades," a politically acceptable way to describe the gradual but complete replacement of one system for another. The library was ahead of most city departments in installing a major computer system so the city was not prepared for our large budget requests. We were very dependent on our vendor to guide and advise us. Without the vendor's daily technical support to keep our systems operating we would be back to the computer chaos of 1982. We tried lease-purchase plans, we borrowed from the endowment fund, and we used every combination of year-end surplus and capital equipment dollars we could find. Susan Craig, who spent four years as technical services department manager and then continued her oversight of computer needs when she became assistant director in 1986, lobbied for a computer replacement fund. This simple solution, planned in 1989 and first funded in 1991, marked the long-overdue official recognition that computers, like police cars and firetrucks, were essential and their replacement had to be planned. Learning to finance and buy computers, like learning to undertake long-range planning, was nothing unique to ICPL. It had become a rite of passage for any manager in the 1980s.

Part of the urgency of funding computer upgrades was our desire to offer the public a second-generation catalog. One of the costs of being the first public library in the on-line catalog business was our purchase of a system more primitive than those that would follow later. After a few years it became clear that if we wanted a catalog with the capabilities becoming standard in the most sophisticated versions of the day, our vendor had to move from its unique "short record" to the bibliographic record standard in the library computer world—MARC (machine readable cataloging). MARC was capable of holding much more information about each title. In other words, much of the 30,000 hours spent entering our collection into the computer during 1979 had to be redone using the new, expanded MARC record, only this time we had to conduct our "retro-conversion" while keeping the old system operating.

We estimated the project would take seven years. A $25,000 grant from the state library helped us get started. When the grant was not renewed with 130,000 records left to convert, the technical services team, under Hal Penick, used volunteers and snatches of regular staff time to chip away at the momentous task. Through intelligent strategies, some extra staff time during Friday closings in 1987-88, and sheer perseverance, Penick and company completed the task in six rather than seven years.

The payoff of all this work was COMPASS. It replaced the more primitive catalog and its often awkward and hard-to-use touch terminals. The new system had a keyboard, on-screen instructions, and more powerful searching abilities. During most of 1990 staff committees worked to configure the catalog to provide the best possible access to the library's collections. COMPASS was named by long-time staff member Kathy Henderson to connote the new catalog's ability to guide users into the world of ICPL collections and eventually to those of other libraries. COMPASS was introduced to the public in January of 1990. Just eighteen months later, its direction-finding abilities were enhanced when a little more software and equipment gave library users phone access to COMPASS from their home or office computers.

To be fair to library history and to those who worked so hard to make this part happen, another chapter on microcomputers and their care and feeding during the 1980s should be included here, but is almost beyond my ability to describe. The 1981 building was planned and constructed without a notion of the role microcomputers would play in all aspects of the life of the library during the 1980s and 1990s. From messages on our cable channel, to a backup system when the main system was down, to access to hundreds of data bases, to my own private fetish for recording and comparing every kind of library statistic to the month, year, and decade before, these machines changed everything. Sitting first here and there on discarded furniture in awkward little corners of the building, and later, linked to one another in networks and resting grandly on newly designed ergonomic furniture, we wrestled with microcomputers most of the decade.

Many of *On Track for the '90s* goals and objectives about improving and enlarging the collection derived from the public's demand for every variety of library subject and format. The number of items purchased grew from 13,000 in 1985 to 19,000 in 1990. Bestsellers, picture books, videos, compact discs, magazines, books on tape, and the regular parade of practical, political, and philosophical nonfiction were returned to the library every hour of the day, yet the resorting area was no larger than it was in 1981 when opening day logjams of returning books almost shut the library down. Now, with twice the traffic and at least as much more know-how, the library staff and the many loyal volunteers struggled daily to keep ahead of the mounds of materials that accumulated when the department was temporarily short-staffed. On summer Sundays when the library was closed, or on two-day holiday weekends, library staff came in to empty the book drop so that materials could keep sliding down the chutes all weekend long.

There were more new items indeed, but also the variety within certain types of formats was increasing. The astounding popularity of movies on video was described earlier, but other types of video also earned a spot on the library's most-popular list. In 1988 the John D. and Catherine T. MacArthur Foundation gave money to libraries to purchase some of the classic programs and series produced for PBS—*The Story of English, Civilization, Ascent of Man, The American Short*

Story, and several others—at less than half the then-current price charged by distributors. The heavy response from public libraries demonstrated there was a market for these materials and the unit price dropped almost immediately. Subsequently the price of all such videos—documentaries, music, drama, how-to, every category except commercially distributed motion pictures—dropped dramatically. ICPL had been building a strong collection of what we called nonfiction video since about 1979, but the new pricing stretched budgets and allowed faster growth. Annual loans reached 30,000 in 1991, the same year movies on video approached the 90,000 mark.

Compact discs and recorded books also saw spectacular growth in this period. After their introduction in the fall of 1986, CDs bounded ahead of the LP collection in just two years. Each compact disc was checked out an average twenty-eight times versus four times for the LPs that year. As the keeper and molder of both collections, it was exciting for me to build the new one but a little sad to see the LPs fall into disuse. I could never bring myself to dump the LP collection, but it was done promptly soon after I retired.

Books on tape—full-length books, mostly fiction, popular history, and biography read by professional readers and actors—have always been one of the most popular and one of the most expensive formats in the library. Offered by the library since the early 1970s, use of these recorded books boomed in the late 1970s and 1980s as people spent more time in their cars commuting to work or traveling, and as they learned they could listen to great literature while they washed the dishes, built cabinets, exercised, and pursued other routine activities. ICPL consistently resisted buying recordings of condensed versions of books, and so the unit price of $50-100 for eight or more cassette tapes per title always limited the number the library could buy. In 1988 Bill and Eleanor Hageboeck gave a large gift to purchase books on tape, and since 1988 the James L. Shive Memorial Fund has been dedicated to this purpose. Throughout the 1980s we had regular requests for additional books on tape to "read."

And old-fashioned book reading did not diminish in the face of all these alternative formats. In 1988 we started Fiction Express, leasing copies of the current bestsellers to supplement the library's copies which were often tied up filling reserves for several months after publication. Hills Bank and Trust Company started its annual fall Reading Month in 1988 which put great emphasis on the value of reading and was popular enough to become an annual event.

The importance of reading was being promoted everywhere and perhaps we were seeing the results. In calendar year 1990, almost from the first day of the year, record hikes in circulation occurred every month for six consecutive months. Loans increased by 33 percent in March over the previous March and, for the six-month period, increases averaged 22 percent. In my annual report for that year I noted that "large increases in the use of children's books, paperbacks, and general nonfiction indicate that a lot more reading is going on." Percentage growth in these large collections surpassed that of the small audiovisual collections "for the first time in years and years."

One lucky defense against this sudden spurt of loan activity in the winter of 1990 was a reorganized shelving system. "The circulation staff developed improved reshelving procedures in the late fall, so despite the increased circulation, many books were getting back on the shelves faster than before," my report continued. This change also fueled the increase, however, because books in the back room don't get checked out; books out on the shelves do.

Nothing feeds library circulation like new materials and popular formats—unless it is more users. ICPL participated in a pilot program of statewide reciprocal borrowing called "Open Access" starting January 1989. A year later this program was expanded to all Iowa libraries that wished to participate. State funds paid fifty cents for each item a library loaned to card holders of other participating libraries. This was considered a form of state aid to public libraries (a first for Iowa except for federal Library Services and Construction Act money funneled through the state library) and was popular with legislators as well as Iowa library users. ICPL was soon earning $40,000 or more from this program—funds that by state law could not be used to reduce local tax effort. Along with gift funds, this new money gave the library some flexibility in funding special projects, but it also brought hordes of new card holders to the library who carried away armfuls of books, videos, and compact discs. There were 1,500 to 2,000 new Open Access card holders in the first three years and they borrowed 35,000 items, excluding loans to Coralville. Another plus of the state program was that both Coralville Public Library (CPL) and ICPL were getting reimbursed for the loans made to each other's card holders. This CPL-ICPL reciprocal agreement was important to both libraries. After ten years and 222,000 loans between them, CPL had loaned just 256 more items to ICPL card holders than ICPL had loaned to Coralville residents.[23]

Developing clear, board-adopted policy statements and then distributing them widely in a variety of formats was an important method of keeping chaotic growth and change under some semblance of control during the first ten years in the new library. Carol Spaziani was our in-house "policy wonk." Her insistence on "getting it in writing" and then distributing the resulting policy to those most affected helped us to serve more people with less staff intervention and to limit most complaints and objections to those with honest disagreements with library regulations.

By 1986 board members were reviewing twenty major policy statements on a regular three-year cycle, or more frequently if conditions changed or a complaint revealed a hole or discrepancy in a policy's language. This process kept the board closer to day-to-day aspects of library operations but still focused on one of its principal responsibilities—setting policy to guide library development.

In 1987 a new financial policy revamped the process for developing the library's annual budget. It gave both board members and staff managers greater involvement and more specific input into budget decisions. As the budget grew—in my administration from $350,000 in 1975-76 to $1.5 million by the end of the 1980s—and as the sources of revenue multiplied, I discovered I could no longer be the only budget officer. I needed more guidance from the board and more ideas and preliminary budget work from my colleagues. In 1975 we had a small gift and bequest fund and 98 percent of all monies came from the annual city operating budget. By 1990 there were ten funds in addition to the city operating budget and together these ten funds accounted for 25 percent of total revenue. This was the financial component of the increasing complexity of library operations in the 1980s—grants, contracts, trust funds, replacement funds, and the foundation, an independent nonprofit corporation.

Many library policies were translated into attractive and cogent publications that informed the public about library services and the policies and procedures governing their use. Thousands of copies were mailed or distributed in the lobby information racks and at appropriate agencies throughout the community. Through *The Window*, the monthly library newsletter established in 1987, as well as calendars and press releases, we kept the public informed about special events and new services or provided other information we thought would enhance an individual's use of the library. We had a highly structured and up-to-date mailing list that allowed us to target specific audiences.

Some of our policy statements and publications had their short moments of fame. Our first-of-its-kind unattended child policy (adopted in the height of the child-snatching scares of 1983 and after a library board member found a three-year-old who had wandered out of the library to the pedestrian mall beyond) was the subject of a lengthy article in *Library Journal* in 1987, but the term "unwanted" was accidentally substituted for "unattended" and the library received some "unwanted" and unjustified complaints from children's librarians across the country. A brochure aimed at university students and explaining the difference between the purpose, facilities, resources, and hours of the university library and the public libraries of Iowa City and Coralville was featured on the cover of another library journal followed by hundreds of requests for copies. Our jail, meeting room, and volunteer policies plus anything we would supply about the foundation received the most out-of-town requests. The first appearance of the unattended child policy in a 1983 library periodical produced over one hundred requests for copies in just a few weeks. At the library, the policies on meeting rooms, displays, bulletin boards, and giveaways were the most frequently consulted and also the most frequently challenged by library users.

We also depended heavily on our suggestion forms to gather opinions from library users on our policies and services. We received about two hundred written suggestions or complaints a year. Many individuals who would not confront staff with complaints or suggestions would write down their concerns. If a name and address were included, each one received a written reply from the appropriate staff member within seven days and then both question and answer were filed by broad topic so we could review and look for trends at the end of the year. For a few years I summarized these communications in the library's annual report, calling the section, "Library Users Annual Report." The simple and not uncommon process seemed to please the suggestion makers—glad that their concerns had been listened to—and it gave us practical suggestions and good insight on how the library was perceived by our various publics.

Summing Up the Decade

At the opening of the decade we had built a state-of-the-art library. Our unique facilities and applications of technology plus innovative services brought recognition throughout the national public library community. The public's response to our menu of services and facilities had been so overwhelming that by the third month after opening the doors, cutbacks were required to keep library operations afloat.

The city council approved additional staff for the library only once during the building's first ten years, so there was chronic understaffing the entire decade. By July 1988, when staff was added, the continuing increases in library use and other changes during the intervening years made the additional positions too late and too little to improve the library's position significantly. Reduced hours were in effect for more than three of the ten years.

Strong board leadership, regular long-range planning, organizational restructuring, careful policy development and review that reflected library values, healthy support from volunteers and financial contributors, a robust and persistent public information program, and a loyal and creative staff that prevailed through every emergency and crisis kept the library operating during an increasingly chaotic period. Information technology developments, new and very popular audiovisual formats, disagreements with city council and county government about fair and adequate funding and appropriate services and hours, plus a major population increase that no one predicted or prepared for, presented problems never dreamed of when the building was planned and constructed.

In June of 1991 we celebrated ten years of service from our no-longer-new library. We reenacted the June 15, 1981 ribbon-cutting ceremony and rededicated ourselves to excellence in library services for Iowa Citians. The increases in use during the ten years had been greater than any reasonable projection; funding sources, except for staffing, had expanded more than we ever imagined possible. When compared to the annual Index of American Public Libraries[24] between 1980 and 1990, ICPL's circulation had increased 58 percent more than the average for the national sample while expenditures were 15 percent above the average ten-year increase.

Five million people had entered the building and some major refurbishing was needed, but the question of whether or when to expand was unanswered. The unexpected 17 percent growth in population from 1980 to 1990 demolished some of our formulas regarding future space needs and overwhelmed our carefully developed five-year plan for 1990-94.

By the time of the ten-year celebration in June 1991, a referendum on whether to permanently increase the local levy for the library was already scheduled for November. Dramatic technological advances were changing the way information was organized, formatted, and delivered. Space was dwindling and more space would be needed to house new forms of computerized equipment. We needed key staff members to lead us into this new environment, and the rest of us would have to be trained and retrained if we were to enter the 1990s able to continue to assist library users find the information they needed and to keep the public library the place where everyone continues to have free access to information in all its many forms. The last five years of the library's first century would be a very important period.

---

[1] *Frequently Asked Questions about Library Building Program.* Typed fact sheet. Iowa City Public Library, May 1978.

[2] Between 1977 and 1981, CETA, Mayor's Youth, and work/study programs dropped from five to fewer than one full-time equivalent position.

[3] *Press-Citizen,* May 13, 1982.

[4] David Groff, "Learning to appreciate new Iowa City Public Library," *weekly news*, Feb. 11, 1982.

[5] Connie Tiffany, "An Electronic Public Library for Iowa City," *Library Journal*, Oct. 1, 1982, 1816.

[6] "City revives Sunday library service," *Press-Citizen*, Feb. 4, 1982.

[7] "Applause for restoring Sunday library hours," *Press-Citizen*, Feb. 9, 1982.

[8] "Open on Sunday," editorial, *Daily Iowan*, Feb. 17, 1982.

[9] *Cedar Rapids Gazette*, April 23, 1982

[10] Sundays were extended to September in 1992 and were slated to be funded year-round starting in the library's 101st year, July 1, 1997.

[11] The contract actually said, "10 percent of the net budget for operating costs of the public library, or 85 percent of the maximum allowable levy for county library contracts (27¢ per $1,000 assessed valuation of unincorporated areas, Chapter 331.421, Section 10, ACTS 1981, 69 G.A.) whichever

shall be the lesser amount." This would become a controversial point in the 1992 argument over the library-county contract.

[12] 1982 Annual Report, 6-7.

[13] The department reports in the library's annual reports for these years frequently list all the libraries, communities, or other institutions that requested information or asked for specific help.

[14] Lowell Martin, "The Public Library: Middle-Age Crisis or Old Age?" *Library Journal*, Jan. 1, 1983, 17-22.

[15] Charles R. McClure, *Planning and Role Setting for Public Libraries* (American Library Association, 1987).

[16] *Library Priorities for the '80s*, D1.

[17] *Iowa City Public Library Challenge Grant Application*, April 29, 1986, 1.

[18] Library press release, Aug. 21, 1986.

[19] Library press release, Dec. 9, 1986.

[20] "Sales tax discussion heats up city hall," *Press-Citizen*, July 14, 1987.

[21] Tom Slockett, "Unfair tax rightly voted down," *Daily Iowan*, Oct. 26, 1987. This is the most complete recorded analysis of the campaign and the October 6 election results.

[22] Charles Drum, "More staff for the library," *Press-Citizen*, Jan. 30, 1988.

[23] In 1995-96 ICPL loaned 125,000 items to reciprocal borrowers (including CPL) and earned $60,000. This amounted to 11.5 percent of all loans for the fiscal year.

[24] An annual sample of fifty public libraries serving communities of 25,000 or more gathered and reported each year by the Library Research Center at the University of Illinois.

■ 11.   Serving Children, 1897–1997; Hazel Westgate, 1949–1988

The public library began as an institution for adults. Children were tolerated if they were quiet, did not linger too long, and knew how to care for books. The typical child user before the turn of the century was at least ten years old and could come to the library without parental supervision. Children were not encouraged to browse. A rule at the Cleveland Public Library in the 1880s: "Select the book, draw it, and depart."[1]

By the end of the century, as Progressive Era ideas about the needs of children developed, public libraries also began changing their rules, their collections, their attitudes, and finally their facilities to accommodate and even cater to children. The history of the rules governing the Detroit Public Library, founded in 1865, illustrate this evolution. Between 1865 and 1903 the minimum age for children allowed to borrow books dropped from "over eighteen" to seven years, with stops along the way at "high school students" (1868), fourteen years (1881), and twelve years (1894). During this period, loans to children at Detroit, and at most every other U.S. public library, grew from a few percentage points to nearly 25 percent.[2]

As the number and variety of books published for young people increased and the debate over the morality of reading fiction and dime novels heated up, so did the desire to control what children were reading. With free public schools increasing the general levels of education, publishing of children's books exploded. Some children, long before the distractions of radio, movies, television, or computer games, became caught up in reading the cheap literature of the day. Teachers and librarians began to feel they should direct the reading of young people into "proper channels." By 1897 the statement of Detroit public librarian Henry

M. Utley was fairly typical. "It is coming to be felt in all wide-awake [libraries] that special efforts should be made to interest young people and to direct their reading."[3]

By 1896 larger public libraries were creating the first children's reading rooms. Boston, Denver, Minneapolis, and Cleveland all opened children's departments in this period, and many others had set aside alcoves, dedicated tables, and hallways for the exclusive use of children as early as 1885. In 1900 children's librarians founded their own section in the American Library Association. Service to children was becoming a major force in the American public library movement.

ICPL Established to Serve Children

In 1896, the children of Iowa City had no need to worry about their place in the proposed new public library. It was founded, as we have seen, to serve children first. The motivating incident, the rhetoric of the campaign, and the language of early documents—the minutes and constitution of the Iowa City Public Library Association—made it clear that children, at least older children, were a priority. Access to a wider variety of books, newspapers, and magazines may have been an attraction for many of the adults leading the campaign, but the reasons articulated at public meetings and at the library's dedication all stressed the commitment to young readers. S.K. Stevenson, for example, told the audience that the library would "destroy the habit of reading vicious, yellow backed literature that is ruining so many young lives."[4]

From the day ICPL opened its doors, children rushed in. The first rules required a child to be ten years old (and there seems to be no record of when this changed). Children could choose from 359 volumes in January 1897, and the collection had grown to only 862 five years later. With juvenile annual circulation rates at 8,500-11,000 in these first five years, the competition for favorite books must have been fierce. Each volume was being used an average of thirteen times a year.

A few statistics on the numbers of loans plus the titles of all the juvenile books purchased are about all we know about children's use of the library in the first five to eight years. Trustees, occupied first with getting the library operating and then planning and building the Carnegie library, seemed to pay little attention to the specific needs of children despite their campaign promises.

In 1906 the board started action toward establishing an independent children's room in the basement of the new library. Helen McRaith, while still first assistant to librarian Webber, was given $150 to set up the new area and the room opened in May of 1906. McRaith's long annual reports after she became librarian in 1907 document these first years (covered in chapter 5). The first designated children's librarian, story hours, displays, picture files, book lists, class visits, and a variety of services to schoolteachers were all part of the McRaith legacy.

Worried that children at the north and south edges of town could not get to the library regularly, in 1910 McRaith established small rotating collections at the two elementary schools farthest from the library. This began a major service to the public schools that would continue until 1955.

There was nothing revolutionary, however, about McRaith's decision to put public library books at the schools. Since the 1870s, despite their early reluctance to shape services for children in their own institutions, public librarians throughout the United States had been the principal advocates of getting a greater variety of reading materials into the public schools. For many years and in many places, teachers resisted. Garrison's 1979 study of public librarians between 1876 and 1920 quotes one 1880 Boston teacher, R.C. Metcalf, who resisted and then was converted.

> . . . for a long time the public library has been looked upon by teachers as an enemy of the public schools. We fought against the introduction of light literature within the sacred walls of the schoolroom. . . . We have coaxed, we have scolded . . . yet the library . . . beat us every time.

After finally bringing in some library books and assigning daily supplementary readings, Metcalf was impressed with the student interest the program excited. This stimulation of student interest by supplementary reading was a revelation common to all early descriptions of school-library cooperation, Garrison noted. Teacher Metcalf advised that teachers unwilling to take on this "extra load" of supplementary reading should know that it is "rather a help to bear what is now imposed."[5]

By 1892, William Brett of the Cleveland Public Library could report that there was hardly a city library in the country that was not making a special effort to introduce books into the schools.[6] Librarians and other educational reformers were helping to change the public schools from the rigid discipline, curriculum, and recitation routines found in classrooms since the Civil War. They wanted to introduce the notion that reading for pleasure—especially if channeled into good literature by librarians and others—could motivate learning and improve reading skills. "Proper food for the intellect and soul" was the frequently used metaphor, and in this case young readers need only avoid the "overseasoned" variety.

The children's department in the basement of the Iowa City Carnegie, decorated and furnished especially for children with art reproductions, displays, and books to intrigue and motivate reading provided a common library experience for Iowa City children for nearly sixty years. Carnegie philanthropy coincided with the rise of the children's room so the Carnegie library became the first library experience for thousands of young readers nationwide. According to Van Slyck, who has tried to analyze this experience and found it universal but fairly undocumented, "to the extent that Carnegie libraries established a model of library design prevalent until the post-World War II era, they provided similar library encounters for children in hundreds of American communities for at least half a century."[7] Van Slyck believes that no matter what their class or cultural background, the generations of children using Carnegie libraries learned well the complex meaning of the simple phrase "free to all." For children of the working class families that could ill afford the cost of an annual subscription fee, a library that lent books free of charge was "a clear and undeniable boon." The library upheld the best hopes of Judge Wade and the other founders of ICPL. The price paid by children of all backgrounds was one of demeanor. With some feelings of fear and wonder at all the "idiosyncratic and sometimes inscrutable rules of behavior," and at the librarian in charge whose persona often made the task of visiting even more fearsome, most children conformed in order to be allowed to stay and to check out books. "The classical portals that graced many Carnegie libraries were not simply symbols of public welcome," Van Slyck concludes, "they also marked, it was hoped, a gateway to a common American culture grounded on self-improvement, individual achievement, and the principles of Protestant liberalism."[8]

Jessie Gordon followed McRaith by a few years and was at least as zealous in her concern for serving children as her very successful predecessor. The schools McRaith had served with small collections were closed in 1918 and Gordon immediately established "branches" at Longfellow and Mann schools as a stopgap service for children who lived too far to walk downtown after school. Gordon provided larger collections and sent library staff to the school sites once a week to help children choose books.

Gordon continued the practice of hiring and training high school or college-trained young women to serve as the children's "librarian," but retained for herself the responsibility of selecting materials. The children's librarian visited schools, helped children select books, conducted story hours, mounted displays, and maintained discipline and control in the children's department. After McRaith hired Margaret Luse, Ada Sample, Lois Sample, and Gertrude Howell, Gordon followed in her twenty-three years with seven more children's librarians including the three Davis sisters (Isabel, Lucile, and Helen), Louise Slemmons (Cox), Mary Louise Schulze (Cone), Dorothy Reha, and Betty Utterback (Chudacek).

The newspapers for the Gordon years frequently ran articles about the special children's activities offered by the children's department. National Book Week was always a period of high activity, Saturday afternoon story hours continued, and, as described earlier, summer reading programs and puppet shows began in the depression era as a way to provide additional activities for children. After Gordon started her weekly newspaper in the late thirties, her commitment to children and reading became even more abundantly clear.

Hazel Westgate Joins the Staff

Joyce Nienstedt made three major contributions to children's services in her eighteen years. She expanded library service to all elementary schools, oversaw the construction of a large children's department and a unique story hour room, and hired Hazel Westgate, the library's first professionally trained children's librarian.

Nienstedt found Westgate on one of her frequent trips north to recruit librarians. Hazel had just graduated from the University of Wisconsin in the spring of 1949 and Iowa City was her first library job. Her degree in library science from Wisconsin followed by two years her graduation cum laude from Northland College in Ashland, Wisconsin, where she majored in English and biology.

Hazel was born in Ashland in 1925. One of Wisconsin's major ports, Ashland sits at the south tip of Chequamegon Bay on Lake Superior with only the peninsula leading to the nearby Apostle Islands and a few Wisconsin cities—Superior, Bayfield, and some small towns—farther north. It had a population of about 12,000 before World War II and in this post-mining and lumbering period, many people, including Hazel's father, worked for the Chicago Northwestern Railroad. Hazel's parents—quiet, conservative, and starting parenthood later than most—were unprepared, perhaps, for the interests and pursuits of their precocious but plain elder daughter. Hazel's one sister was five years younger. Hazel was the valedictorian of her high school class, played the French horn, drew cartoons for the school paper, and, according to a classmate, wore her hair in braids, even through her first years in college. With her parents' conservative lifestyle and her strong academic record, she may have received a scholarship to allow her to attend Northland, a four-year liberal arts college.[9]

While Ashland had a public library, it was not the inspiration for Hazel's career. She once described the librarian as a "shushy lady who collected dolls. She would follow me around and tell me what I should read. And of course I didn't. That's why I never discovered *Winnie the Pooh* until high school."[10]

From high school on Hazel became absorbed in the world of children's stories—Pooh and Babar and Paddington—and never stopped wanting to share with children the fantasy and imaginative adventures she evidently missed as a young child. With unsurpassed knowledge about children's literature—and many other topics—Hazel took great pride in her expertise, but in many ways remained a child like those she spent her life serving. The public library, especially the children's room, was a refuge from "real life" for her, but as a result, two generations of Iowa City children benefited from her gentle, yet commanding presence at the library and from her steady prodding to explore the books and stories that excited their imaginations and satisfied their curiosity about the world.

For the nearly forty years she served Iowa City children, and continuing in many ways to this day, Hazel's philosophy that children should be treated like real people—people who will learn faster and more willingly in an informal, comfortable, welcoming place—has been the modus operandi in the library children's room. In a 1977 interview with Mary Jane Odell on Iowa Public Television, Hazel said, "[children] are awfully nice little people and they are nice to know. Treat them straightforward." When asked to define a library, she responded:

A library is a special place to be. Everybody has special interests . . . of wanting to learn about the things they like, about the things they want to do and be, about things that are fun, about the things that teachers tell them they should know. It is a place to be welcomed and to belong—and to know that you can come to it always for whatever you want.

This was a typical Hazel statement, spoken in a very soft voice—a device to keep children quiet and under control some of her fans believe—and using simple, one-syllable words. Her philosophy about children's behavior was also fairly simple. "I don't expect them to sit around like cabbages," she once said. "If they get terribly loud, we ask them to knock it down a couple of decibels. If they get too rowdy, we recommend the rec center." Another time she told a mother whose son's behavior had been almost unacceptable at a story hour, "He needs to go home and `practice' before he comes back."

There are many stories about her custom of dealing with the child, not the parent, whenever possible. When a mother requested a first-time library card for her four-year-old, Hazel looked past her, saying, "I think the young man can speak for himself." And turning to the boy she said, "Now, sir, may I have your name?" To a child who was running in the children's room while his mother did nothing, Hazel said, "I think you forgot to walk."

Hazel often worked ten- to twelve-hour days and rarely took vacations or sick leave. On Wednesdays, her traditional midweek day off, she could be observed, especially in her healthiest years, walking all over town—buying groceries, getting food for the birds and cats at home (and the fish, snakes, gerbils, and hamsters that sometimes lived at the library), or carrying one of her cats to the vet.

Hazel had many hobbies that filled the few hours she spent away from the library. She generally rose at four o'clock in the morning in order to work on one of her original-design knotted rugs for a couple of hours before she left for the library. (Her rugs can be found hanging in several small public libraries and in homes of friends, and one entitled *Not All Dragons are Alike* is one of the original art pieces displayed at ICPL.) An ardent collector, Hazel loved arrowheads, paperweights, stereoptican slides, music boxes, and most of all, bookmarks. She wrote to many libraries and printers asking for samples, and while she never traveled much, cosmopolitan Iowa City friends brought her bookmarks from all over the world. Completely uninterested in housekeeping chores and cleaning routines, her house (as well as every desk or storage cupboard ever assigned to her at the library) was filled with the trappings and remains of her many interests and avocations. Some of her closest associates were employees at all the companies where she ordered yarn, books, bird feeders, bookmarks, and other paraphernalia. She had a particular person at each vendor—her "mail order" friends—with whom she could carry on business and a friendly exchange of letters with no fear of unwanted intimacy. Through the years she had many cats—Maine coots were a favorite—and they were her daily companions at home, her second-floor apartment at 1019 East Washington.

She loved to work jigsaw puzzles. Former children's room assistant Mary Seelman Mascher remembers that she would assemble them from the back side, claiming that the manufacturers used only six or seven cutting patterns. Once you learned the patterns you could finish the puzzles much more quickly if not distracted by all the designs and colors.

Hazel's creative talents and her humor were apparent throughout her life. She loved to draw and had a wry and very quick sense of humor. These traits obviously surfaced early. Her high school yearbook predicted that in twenty years she would be drawing cartoons for syndication. At the library she wrote stories, designed simple crafts, collected originals from well-known children's book illustrators, and decorated children's room publications with animals and fanciful figures. A small mouse drawn on a document was almost like her signature. She never used a typewriter and her "hand" was recognizable by all who received her letters or brief memos or saw her library annual reports. She told Odell that her favorite writers were people who play with words, naming without hesitation James Thurber, Leo Rosten, Joseph Wood Krutch, Robert Benchley, and E.B. White.

Hazel the Librarian

There is universal agreement among all who knew her about Hazel's greatest strength as a librarian: her knowledge of the collection and her ability to use that knowledge to match reader and book and to find information about a very specific fact or topic. She had the ability to build a great collection and to know it intimately. She had an encyclopedic memory about children's books and could identify a particular book using the smallest clue or fragment of memory—a character's name, the briefest plot, sometimes even the color of the binding.

Someone called her a "walking card catalog" and others noted that until the late 1970s, she not only had selected every book in the collection, but also had ordered, cataloged, processed, read, checked out, and sometimes reshelved every book, and along the way she somehow seemed to commit the contents of each one to memory. She took great pride in her almost-total recall; give her a clue and she would perform. It was more than a trick, however. She made invaluable suggestions about books to read and subjects to pursue. She loved creating the collection and valued any compliments about it she received.

Debate among her fans and colleagues swirls around whether her ability to approach children in a straightforward manner was insightful or a just a matter of dealing with her "peers." Almost everyone describes Hazel as childlike. At the minimum, this brilliant woman (who received academic honors at high school and college) remembered how she wanted to be treated as a youngster and she was determined to pass it on to those she served. The soft voice sometimes served as an instrument of control. When it didn't, she tended to ignore the problem. She was absolutely non-confrontational with other adults, but used passive resistance to fend off interference in her domain.

Hazel had complete autonomy over children's services for at least twenty-five years. For the first twenty, under Nienstedt, Helm, and Croteau, her options were limited by a restricted budget and by benign neglect from the director. Nienstedt, who preferred not to be confronted with children at any time, gave Hazel a completely free hand in selecting juvenile materials and in services to children and to the public schools. Hazel complained later about the rigidity of Nienstedt's rules, which gave Hazel no choice about days off or vacation (which Hazel apparently took now and then in her early years).

For fifteen of the Nienstedt years, Hazel operated out of the same children's room that opened in the basement of the Carnegie in 1906. Children in the 1950s, including Mascher and my three sons, loved to enter the library through the iron gates and darkened archways of the lower doors beneath the steps to the main entrance. "It was like entering a mystical other world," Mascher remembers. "The darkness and the archways at the entrance, and all the nooks and crannies of the library basement added to the mystery." She remembers being at first a little afraid of Hazel, who had a witchlike appearance that fit with Mascher's impression of the mysterious place. As soon as she heard Hazel's soft voice, however, she felt safe and secure. Mascher was one of the many children and former employees who kept in regular contact with Hazel. Hazel advised her when she was studying to become a teacher and invited her to be a guest story-teller many times. Mascher became part of Hazel's large network of children, former children, parents, student teachers, teachers, librarians, and anyone else Hazel found interesting enough to keep in touch with.

Nienstedt was responsible for getting Hazel out of the basement and moving children's services to a large new room in the 1963 addition. As described in chapter 7, Nienstedt may not have enjoyed the company of children, but in those years the young ones were the library's principal clients and she had to accommo-date their needs. By including the story hour room in the addition, she gave Hazel a new theater in which to perform. After Sallie Helm worked with Hazel and Ellie Simmons to create the wonderful story room mural, Hazel had a theater of some renown. The 1965 color photograph of Westgate that appeared on the cover of the *Des Moines Sunday Register's* famous "Picture" section added to her growing reputation around the state. The picture now hangs in the Hazel Westgate Story Hour Room at the library.

Photo by David Penney. Copyright 1965 The Des Moines Register and Tribune Company. Reprinted with permission.

Helm remembers Hazel as "one of the most unusual persons I ever knew. You took her as she was or not at all. She had strange dress and living habits, yet I valued her work

Hazel Westgate and the story hour room mural painted by Iowa City artist Ellie Simmons were featured on the cover of the Des Moines Sunday Register's Picture Magazine in 1965.

and thought she was great with children."[11] Hazel went on being Hazel and was working on her second generation of young readers, while Helm, in her project-laden four years, developed many new services and collections that had little to do with children.

Few individuals ever stepped inside Hazel's door, but director Mary Croteau was once invited to the apartment for dinner. Croteau loved "kiddie lit" and enjoyed following up on Hazel's reading recommendations. During her two years at ICPL, Croteau fielded complaints from Hazel's sometimes-frustrated staff. She issued one directive that upset Hazel but delighted the children's room employees who had to reshelve the rapidly increasing numbers of picture books: All picture books were to be arranged in order by author. Hazel—and probably her prereading clients—preferred to group the books into subject categories.

Books about cars and trucks, books about dinosaurs, alphabet books, animal books, and so on were shelved or piled together. A young one who was wild about trucks, like a couple of my boys, knew just where to go to find more of his favorite topic. But it was very difficult for the staff to sort the returning books into these rather loose categories and it was impossible to find a specific book. With some soft-voice grumbling, Hazel made the change, and probably none too soon. Today, there are over 21,000 picture books with ten or more different people regularly sorting and shelving them.

Hazel and Jack Hurkett

In 1970, at age forty-five and probably at the peak of her abilities and energy, Hazel was fortunate to have a library director for four years who clearly recognized her creative abilities and who was willing to give her a free hand to try out new ideas.

Hazel added twice-weekly film showings using the library's new 16mm film service. She also added more story hours for preschoolers on weekdays so that soon after Hurkett arrived the total number of year-round weekly events for children rose to six. Guest storytellers were added, including representatives from a variety of foreign cultures.

The summer of 1972 was typical of the summer programming during this period. In addition to the regular story hours and film showings, children's room staff read and told stories weekly at three of the city's organized playgrounds and at some community daycare centers. Once a week, a series called "Music Matters" featured a variety of musical activities and concerts designed for schoolchildren. There were also special sessions on bicycle repair, stamp collecting, archeology, magic, and words and their meaning, and a session by local children's author Lois Muehl. There were two children's film festivals featuring award-winning children's films and a series of performances at the library and at community playgrounds by the Popo Puppeteers, a library-sponsored puppet group.

During the Hurkett years Hazel began her story writing, bookmark, and drawing contests. To stimulate the writing of imaginative stories by young authors, Hazel would compose several "story starters"—or in some cases, "story enders"—which were distributed throughout the city's elementary classrooms along with the rules for writing and submitting stories. These sentences demonstrated Hazel's whimsical bent and her love of fantasy and just sheer nonsense. In the 1976 Odell television interview, she gave examples of three of her favorite starters. "It was most embarrassing and too late to return to the North Pole, but Santa had grabbed his bag of dirty laundry instead of the bag of toys." "It was the best pumpkin pie she had ever eaten, but it seemed to be making her feet grow." "People in the valley were worried. The giant in the mountain had swallowed the weather and he had the hiccups."

Through the years these writing competitions grew in participation and in production. After the teachers had sorted out the best to submit to the library, a team of judges read those chosen and granted awards to one story at each grade level. Copies were made for distribution to the public. Prizes varied from year to year, but what the young authors liked best was autographing copies of their stories at the children's room annual awards party.

Hazel always placed emphasis on creative activities. Those who didn't write could draw. The best drawings were printed on bookmarks and distributed at the library. Another contest involved drawing cats to mark the annual appearance of Jerry Newsome telling her favorite story, *Millions of Cats,* by Wanda Gag. The mostly junior high-aged Popo Puppeteers made puppets and wrote scripts and music for their performances. Several talented women, including puppet master Monica Leo and future children's room assistant Deanne Wortman, volunteered through the years to supervise the puppet troupe.

During the fall of 1972, parallel to the presidential campaign, the children's room conducted an election in which children voted for their favorite literary characters for president and vice president. Snoopy, one of Hazel's all-time favorites, got the nod for vice president, and Jo March of *Little Women* fame was elected president. Like the summer programs that featured bicycle repair, magic, and story writing, Hazel liked to translate the real world into the child's world of fantasy and make-believe, or at least the basic child topics of toys and pets and hobbies. Not wrong, not right—just Hazel.

Hazel never liked the traditional summer reading program held at ICPL before her days and by most public libraries throughout the country. "Summer reading programs are dog and pony shows," she once said. She did not want children racing through a great number of books in order to win an award for having read the most or the required number of books. Thus her emphasis was on creative activities or informational programs geared to the school-age child. She told a reporter in 1973 that children's programs were planned to provide "as much participation as we possibly can, even in the story hour." One program that summer was called "make-a-story" hour during which the children manufactured the story themselves. One such effort was pinned to the wall of the children's room. It was a five-foot mural with captions underneath telling the story. Hazel commented that having children create stories or design bookmarks "makes the library far more their [place] than it would be otherwise."[12]

Throughout the Hurkett years Hazel produced annual reports that showed off her writing skills and her sense of humor. The reports were fifteen to twenty pages long, with a Snoopy or a Pooh or a Cat in the Hat theme, and were filled with bits of poetry and nonsense lines to surround the required statistics. A graph could be a giraffe's neck, or a graceful flower stem, or stars on the horizon watched by Pooh and Tigger.

Her monthly and annual statistics were sometimes as fanciful and creative as her other endeavors. She would automatically renew all loans to contract areas—Johnson County, Lone Tree, North Liberty—assuming that since members of these communities lived farther away they would probably need the books longer. This practice also doubled the number of loans to those areas. She would add on extra loans for collections made to teachers on the theory that the teacher would loan them to

Jack Hurkett (library director, 1970-74) and Hazel Westgate with Iowa state librarian Barry Porter (on right) in 1975

children four or five times before the books were returned to the library. In 1974, Hazel's extra tallies for school loans amounted to nearly 42,000, a 20 percent bump to total children's circulation.

The stretching of her statistics may have been part of her eagerness to show her gratitude to Hurkett. These numbers meant little to her personally, but high ones would indicate that all the freedom he had given her to take children's services in new directions was paying off. Their relationship was important to Hazel. Hurkett enjoyed her wit and wordplay and gave her some of the adult attention she craved. He was her fairy godfather, Prince Charming, or as she would ever after refer to him, "My Dragon."

Hurkett Leaves, Disappointment Follows

When Hurkett left and the controversy over the next director erupted, Hazel was the one librarian on the staff who did not join our concern over the proposed successor. From her perspective, she did not see the failures of Hurkett's administration and she blamed the rest of us for making life difficult for him. Her first read on Kauderer was that he might be an adequate substitute.

I am sure she was disappointed when I was named permanent director. One of my goals was to convince the community that ICPL was more than a children's library and in the process I know I gave less attention and probably less priority to children's department needs. Also, we were very different in our approaches to library matters. No one ever thought of me as whimsical, or clever, or witty. I wanted support services centralized; Hazel was still receiving and processing new children's materials in the children's department. I wanted long-range plans, budget needs, and statistical data from the staff, items that would always be of little interest to Hazel. I wanted to articulate the goals and values of the library so that we were all pointed in the same direction; Hazel knew exactly what she wanted for children's services but wouldn't commit it to writing—it might change after her next creative notion. Her principles regarding children were firm and of great value, her ideas were original and popular, but the specifics could shift and fluctuate. She had never been asked to provide budgets or plans; she preferred to take what was given her and turn it into her kind of something special.

For several years we made do with each other's peculiarities and moved ahead. "No room is an island" started Hazel's 1980 annual report, as she recognized some of the profound changes the organization and the children's department were making. And as library collections, budget, and staff grew larger, and the complexity and size of library operations increased, I saw a need for change.

The building was planned with little input from Hazel except for a strong insistence on a story hour pit in the children's area. There were hard feelings over the decision to intershelve the children's upper elementary nonfiction collection with the adult collection on the second floor, and a feeling of loss about combining all check-outs at one main circulation desk. Children's staff felt they would lose their regular contact with children when staff members didn't chat with children as they checked out their books. The compromise was to retain registration for library cards in the children's room so that staff members could introduce the services and resources of the department to newly enrolled children. It was hard for the staff to envision that they would actually have more time to interact with kids when they were no longer strapped to circulation routines and records. The introduction of "Mr. Machine," Hazel's term for the computer system, two years earlier, however, had already relieved the staff of many of the more onerous parts of the old circulation system and thus made it even harder to adjust to losing a check-out point in the children's area.

In many ways, the children's room was leaderless, or at least voiceless, when representing children's needs to the rest of the library staff. Always full of ideas about what materials to buy and how to make children enthusiastic about learning and reading, Hazel's inability (or unwillingness) to plan, or at least to organize and articulate her ideas, became clearer during the building planning process. In addition, the style most of us used to solve problems and evolve workable ideas could be very threatening to a person who disliked, indeed always avoided, confrontation. We were often loud and wordy and sometimes sharp in our comments, but when we left the meeting we would immediately forget any friction fired by the discussion. Hazel, along with others before and after, did not operate well in this environment. During the building planning period, we would hear rumors that certain proposals were unpopular but we seldom received concrete responses. In looking back, I wonder why I didn't sit down with Hazel and discuss the controversial ideas with her.

As part of our restructuring in the spring of 1981 we completely reorganized the departments and the management lines of the library. One major change was to create a youth services division and to make Judy Kelley, young adult services and reference librarian since 1972, the coordinator. All children's staff, including Hazel, would report to her and she would be responsible for all management-level decisions. Hazel was made senior librarian for children's services. I thought this was a good solution to our leadership problems in the children's area. Hazel could do full-time what she did best: select materials, plan children's programs, and help individuals find the information and books they needed in the children's room.

I don't believe, however, that she ever fully adjusted to losing the autonomy she had enjoyed for thirty years. Earlier directors respected her work and found it easiest to give her full rein within the bounds of money and staff available to her. But later she may have felt betrayed in several ways. She felt a clique of feminists had schemed to get rid of Hurkett, the best director for whom she had ever worked. Then they took away her independence when the new building opened by combining young adult and children's services under the management of Judy Kelley and removing the check-out desk and half of the juvenile nonfiction collection. She was no longer the queen of ICPL children's services. She must have felt demoted and dethroned.

In the meantime, from the day Hurkett left to the day Hazel died, she continued to provide new program ideas, to select the best in children's books, to conduct story hours in her familiar style, and, when directed to begin some kind of summer reading event, to come up with a unique twist on a summer reading program—Hear Me Read. She continued to astound people with her ability to find the hidden treasures of the collection and to inspire many children and adults to explore the world of children's literature.

Hazel introduced several new formats to the children's collections—toys, games, book-cassettes, and tiny Ladybird books imported from England. She selected frequently used, classic children's 16mm films for the library's growing collection. Films continued to play a large role in children's programming and her goal in this period was to have at least one story hour, film showing, or "special" every day except Wednesday, her day off.

From 1974 to 1980 the number of children in Iowa City declined sharply.

This, plus loan-period changes and our refusal to let Hazel make automatic renewals, caused her annual statistics to drop, a situation that bothered her despite her public disdain for such numbers. Between 1972 and 1980 the number of card holders in the children's room dropped from 6,200 to 2,700 as fewer and fewer children followed the huge earlier generation. She noted, however, that more and more toddlers were brought to story hours by their parents—baby boom parents eager to introduce their children to the library as soon as possible. Service to and materials appropriate for the really young child started in these years.

One of her creative touches in the new building was a six-foot Paddington Bear, a personal gift to the library from Hazel. She took great joy in telling the story of Paddington's arrival as a passenger in the front seat of Mr. Anderson's car. (Anderson, according to Hazel, was a "salesman Santa with six bulgy bags of puppets and puzzles." He once sold Hazel a pair of spider puppets that she used as mittens.) Paddington became a symbol of the new library and received so much attention from the throngs of young children that he had to be replaced regularly. Paddington V was purchased in 1990.

In her 1980-81 annual report, her last before she handed that managerial task over to Judy Kelley, Hazel noted "a great change of everything-that-was," but added:

> None of this [the contents of her report] would be important if there weren't the children to work with and for. They find themselves welcome, and encouraged to participate in what we do. They draw bookmarks, they write, they sing and join in the programs. They read, they read what pictures tell them, they find out how to take care of their tarantulas and toads and puppies. They "forget" their jackets and mittens and saxophones. They want to make chemical volcanoes that erupt. They want to know why trees get bald in the winter. They are why.

Hazel never forgot Jack Hurkett. Every new employee heard about the days of her "dragon." For several years he was in Des Moines as assistant director of the Iowa State Library and Hazel often directed her attention in that direction, attending state meetings on children's issues, creating the annual prize drawing for one of her rugs conducted by the state library, and, in 1977, establishing at the state library the Hazel Westgate Endowment for Small Public Libraries. As she did with many of her distant friends, she sent Hurkett gifts and stories and clippings on topics they had shared and laughed about together.

While Hazel continued as a one-of-a-kind children's librarian, Judy Kelley mapped out a slightly broader road for children's services. She worked quietly, less in the limelight than her famous children's librarian. Kelley gave new organization and direction to the style of children's librarianship that Hazel had long advocated and delivered. She began using the skills of other children's staff members and shifting to them some of the children's room responsibilities. For example, Wortman produced outstanding displays for the large display case and became a popular storyteller, channel 20 interviewer, and voice for Popo. She used her artistic skills for library publications and, like the other departmental clerks and library assistants, took her turn helping at the children's information desk. Staff were sent to continuing education events to sharpen their library skills.

In addition to greater use of staff members' talents, Kelley initiated closer cooperation and communication with the schools, child care and parent organizations, the recreation center and other city departments, and many university and community cultural groups. Using gift funds, she developed within the children's room the Child and Family Resource Center, generally called the parent center, and for five years coordinated programs for parents produced jointly by the library and Coordinated Community Child Care (4Cs). These well-attended programs were also cablecast live on channel 20 and the taped version added to the library's video collection. Story hours, live and taped, appeared on channel 20 almost daily and featured staff and guests as storytellers.

Children's Day during Artsfest, the new puppet show featuring Popo and Don (Benda), and an all-day puppet festival were some of the regular and annual events added to Hazel's traditional writing and drawing contests, piñata parties, and the "no-ring circus." Ideas were generated by all staff through regular meetings.

Iowa City Public Library Archives

"Popo and Don," with library staff member Deanne Wortman and volunteer Don Benda, was one of the all-time favorite program series in the children's room from 1981 until Don's untimely death in 1993.

Coordination with other agencies and organizations required planning, delegation, cooperation, and follow-up. Kelley handled these tasks smoothly and with skill, managing to use Hazel's outstanding skills and the under-utilized skills of other staff members, and along the way developed a corps of adult and junior volunteers to help with the many tasks required to carry out an enlarged and more complex program. Because of the smaller population of children in the first part of the 1980s the children's room experienced less growth after the opening of the new building—

about 25 percent—and growth leveled off a little sooner than in other parts of the library. This gave the children's room a little breathing space to adjust to the new facilities and to develop programs for the increasing number of very young children and their very concerned parents. When Kelley left at the end of 1988, she had helped lead the library planning staff to making children's services the top priority for the new five-year plan.

Not Quite Forty Years

To the best of our knowledge, Hazel never saw a doctor during her years in Iowa City. A friend of hers once told me that she, the friend, had tried unsuccessfully to convince Hazel to see a doctor about a badly infected thumb. Other more serious ailments began to surface. Hazel became tired and breathless after walking or climbing stairs and was always ready to sit down. There were some signs of untreated diabetes. When she had not appeared at work by ten o'clock one morning, Susan Craig and another staff person went to her apartment. They found her unconscious on her couch, with the book *Listen to Your Body* next to her. She never regained consciousness and died the next day, May 17, 1988.

Iowa City today is full of Hazel's kids—young and middle-aged adults who have spent their entire lives in Iowa City. They grew up going to Hazel's library and many still feel a strong attachment to the library because of this relationship. Before Hazel's sudden death, the library was already making plans to celebrate her fortieth year at the library in 1989. Her "kids," library staff, and trustees all felt robbed of the opportunity to formally express their gratitude for her life at the library. And we knew that whatever form the celebration might have taken, Hazel would have enjoyed receiving best wishes and congratulations from her many friends and admirers in Iowa City and around the country.

Instead of a celebration, however, we had a funeral and a memorial service. The local papers published extended stories of her life and wrote editorials praising her contribution to the community. Larry Lynch, local lawyer and former part-time library employee, remembered the day in 1952 when he got his first library card. "Hazel had a rule," he said. "When you could write your name, you could get a card." Lynch had already taken his four children to get their library cards from her.

The city declared June 19, 1988, the day of the memorial service at the library, Hazel Westgate Day. "The world of delight whose door Hazel could open with the simple phrase, 'Once upon a time,' is one we all seek to share," Mayor John McDonald's proclamation affirmed. "The community in which Hazel chose to live and work is forever enriched because of her stay here. . . ."

Meeting room A was full the afternoon of June 19. Friends and coworkers told Hazel stories. We enjoyed some of her past appearances gleaned from the library's video archives. Jerry Newsome repeated her telling of *Millions of Cats*, and then story book treats were served in the children's room—Captain Hook poison cake, Winnie-the-Pooh coconut honey cookies, and Queen of Hearts strawberry tarts.

About a year later there was another ceremony when the story hour room was named in Hazel's honor and a plaque and picture of Hazel were unveiled. Again, old friends and children's room em-
ployees shared their remembrances. Jody O'Mara, children's room associate for many years, in explaining why naming the story hour room for Hazel was a good choice, reminded the audience that Hazel was an expert on stories. She read them, she judged them, and she wrote them. Hazel always said a good story has a beginning, a middle, and an end, recalled O'Mara. "For Hazel's life and career which were one and the same, the ending is the hardest part. . . . Her story needs to be rounded off," O'Mara said. "It

Hazel Westgate with Jerry Newsome (library trustee, 1973-79) in 1985

Photo courtesy Drake Hokanson

needs a punctuation mark. Today, perhaps we can supply an exclamation point."

By the end of the year, library staffer Greg Kovaciny had gathered together over one hundred of Hazel's stories and printed them in a book, *The Stories and Tales of Hazel May Westgate*. All the short, one- and two-page stories, and a few poems, are in Hazel's handwriting, carefully printed on plain paper, or in her script on sheets from a lined tablet. Copies of this book are in the library's collection and they offer a direct route to the fantasy and make-believe world of Hazel Westgate.

After Hazel

By the time of the story hour room dedication in the spring of 1989, Debb Green, the new coordinator of youth services, had been on the job for over six months. Judy Kelley's plans to resign were underway before Hazel died. She left in July of 1988 to become head of children's services for the Newport Beach Public Library in California.

We hired two part-time children's librarians plus Green as the new coordinator. The department badly needed more librarians to give assistance at the children's desk and to share responsibilities for selecting the rapidly expanding children's collection. Green, former head of children's services at Tampa, Florida, gave up a "bigger" job to return to the Midwest and a library where there would be more front-line work with children than was possible as a full-time manager in Tampa's multibranch system. And, as it turned out, not just any smaller library would have satisfied Green. In the early 1980s she had stopped in Iowa City to see the new library and met and visited with Hazel. "She graciously gave me a tour of the children's room, and shared some of her ideas with me. I discovered that she and I agreed on what a children's library should be—informal, user-friendly, full of popular materials, non-quiet, and active." Hazel told Green that she wanted the room to be "a comfortable place to crawl around in." "I remember thinking at the time that maybe someday I'd get to work somewhere as wonderful as the Iowa City library," said Green.

Green turned out to be a very appropriate choice. The public, especially, had to adjust to seeing a new face as ICPL children's librarian, and Green soon proved that she harbored the same visions for children that library users had found in Hazel. While she said she sometimes feels she was "meant" to follow Hazel, she doesn't mean that she slavishly followed what Hazel did. Green notes, "There is a good healthy respect, but I used what worked and discarded what didn't."

Green greatly expanded the summer reading program, offering lots of choices and a variety of incentives to ensure that it was more than just a numbers game. While she agreed that Hazel's collection was a major strength of the program, it was also one of its weaknesses. There were not enough copies of standard titles, too many shabby and worn volumes and out-of-date nonfiction (depression era kids have trouble throwing things away), and too many titles in fiction that may have had historical value but no longer interested contemporary readers. The collection, Green thought, had simply become too large with too many subcollections for one person to manage. With three or more librarians working together, subject and format assignments could be made and long-term decisions could be planned together as adult collection librarians had been doing for over ten years.

Green never met Kelley, but she inherited the best from both Westgate and Kelley—a basic philosophy of service that had guided the library for nearly forty years, spruced-up departmental operations that used the skills of all employees, and closer ties with other groups and agencies that work with the young child.

In the last eight years of the library's first century, Green has led an increasingly varied and expanded staff—talented, committed, eager to serve children and to serve them well. "Expanded" because Green convinced the board and management team about the drastic need to enlarge the staff assigned to her department, pointing out the very few hours in a week available for management and background tasks.

Serving Children, 1897–1997

One of the least visible but most important transformations was the improvement in service offered from the children's desk. It is a sea change from the days in the old library when "the desk" was primarily concerned with checking out materials and getting them returned and reshelved. Questions were welcome, of course, but it was a secondary function when the room was busy. Now, the desk is always staffed with one, sometimes two persons well-trained to take on any type of inquiry. Keeping track of what is asked helps the staff improve the collection and their own ability to provide the kind of information frequently needed.

The goals of the 1990-94 long -range plan were honored and outreach efforts rose to all-time highs. Interpreted broadly, reaching out meant every kind of effort to let children and their parents know about library services and resources. Cable programs, Dial-A-Story, publications and calendars mailed to agencies dealing with children, booths at the fair or at a shopping mall promotion, work with neighborhood centers, story time kits, visits to kindergartens to sign up young new card holders, and regular press releases helped tell the ICPL children's services story. In addition, staff members were available for appearances at preschools and daycare centers on request.

In addition to the major overhaul of the collection started almost the first day Green arrived, the department continued to add and delete formats as circumstances and technology changed. Compact discs, books on tape, and many more videos were added. The Peanuts collection was retired, while a homework center for elementary school students and board books for the youngest page-turners were added. The parent center became the parent-teacher collection and changed its focus from child development issues to resources for those who work and live with children—storytelling, preschool programming, home schooling activities, and recommended children's literature.

For the first time, parents were surveyed about programming for children at the library and adjustments were made in the types of programs and the times they were offered. The survey was repeated at least two more times in order to confirm or update the original findings. Many of Hazel's favorite programs were replaced with those that appealed to the child of the nineties. For example, the audience for the very popular film showings of the 1970s gradually fell away as videos of many of the same stories—and many more—could be checked out and viewed at home. Viewed from the perspective of 1996, the 530 children's programs and the 26,000 people that attended them in 1975 can now be seen for the major accomplishment it was—although Hazel's creative numbers must also be a consideration. In 1996 the children's department offered 280 programs to an audience of just over 19,000. The children's room has kept Hazel's tradition of providing programs and stories for children fifty-two weeks a year, no preregistration required—a tradition that distinguishes ICPL from many other libraries.

A Century of Stories

The typical child coming to story hours and programs today is two to four years old. The trend toward serving younger and younger library users, first noticed by Hazel in her 1979 annual report, reached its limit in 1991 when the library and Hills Bank started presenting new mothers with "Begin with Books" packets while they were still in the hospital. The packets contain a book for baby plus information to encourage the new parents to read to their children and take them to the library.

Perhaps Hazel would view the current summer reading programs as just a "dog and pony" show, but in the fifteen years since the first Hear Me Read in 1981, to the several divisions and activity options of today, participation has increased from 80 to 2,000. There are more elaborate trappings and awards due to the support of local businesses and service clubs.

Hills Bank, with its Begin with Books project and fall reading month, is one of the best examples of the new cooperation ("partnership" is the in-vogue term) between the library and community businesses. In the 1980s businesses gave major gifts to the library's endowment fund, but it has become more satisfying for many to link their name with a specific library program or event in return for their financial support. Anything to do with children is one of the easiest to "sell," and the foundation and Green have done a good job of matching program and business.

So we have come full circle. The library started one hundred years ago because of broad community support—26 of those first 150 pledges to the 1897 library fund were from local businesses—and after many years of depending almost entirely on local taxes, we again have businesses reaching out to assist with the work of the library.

And for the sake of the children we have had Helen McRaith, Jessie Gordon, the Davis sisters, Hazel Westgate, Judy Kelley, and Debb Green along with over one hundred trustees and many ought-to-be-named volunteers and employees who have worked to keep the promise of Judge Wade:

> Parents may feel that their children in coming here for books whether they
> be rich or poor, are placing themselves under obligation to no one. . . . to
> promote this spirit . . . it was made absolutely free to everyone.

The children of this community have been the prime targets of library efforts since that first day one hundred years ago.

[1] Clarence H. Cramer, *Open Shelves, Open Minds* (Cleveland: Case Western Reserve Press, 1972), 64.

[2] Frank B. Woodford, *Parnassus on Main Street; A History of the Detroit Public Library* (Detroit: Wayne State University Press, 1965), 229, 233.

[3] Ibid., 228.

[4] The full quote is in chapter 1.

[5] Garrison, 54-60. This section covers much about public librarians and the public schools at the turn of the century.

[6] Cramer, 65.

[7] Van Slyck, 201-02. Van Slyck reviews the descriptions of three writers who have written about their childhood public library experiences (Eudora Welty, Jackson, MS; Helen Santmyer, Xenia, OH; and Susan Toth, Ames, IA), but wonders if writers can represent the "average" child library user.

[8] Ibid., 216.

[9] Interview with Betty Marx, Feb. 2, 1997. Marx grew up in Ashland and graduated from high school with Hazel in 1943.

[10] "A World for Children," *Iowa City Press-Citizen* editorial, May 20, 1988.

[11] Helm, telephone interview, July 17, 1996.

[12] *Daily Iowan*, July 6, 1973.

■ 12. Voting "Yes": The Library Levy and Other End-of-the-Century Stories, 1991–1997

It was "déjà vu all over again" for the library in the winter of 1991. Facing another year of severe staff shortages, the library board decided to seek a referendum on a special library levy.

The road to this destination had been long and winding. The trip started the day the new library opened its doors, with the only relief stops along the way the successful 1988 bid for two and one-half staff positions following fifteen months of reduced hours, and the 1990 "compromise" that gave the library two of the four positions requested. "The new positions slipped in and disappeared like ice on a hot day," I wrote in the 1989 annual report, but the comment could just as well have been made in 1991.

Each time we added staff we knew we had gained little ground—two or two and one-half positions instead of the four or five we had honestly needed. And "honest" was a key term. In all the budget battles with the city council over staffing, going back to the mid-1970s, the library board had presented honest needs or had whittled them back voluntarily, feeling that accurate estimates of staff needs were too much to ask for. Inevitably, the council refused the requests or offered compromises. By the time budget negotiations were over, the library was still in the hole. It was just a little deeper in some years than others.

By 1991, on a daily service level, the library needed a third person to handle phone questions at the information desk and two people at the children's desk at busiest times. The circulation and audiovisual departments required ten people on duty on weekends to keep lines reasonable and to keep the more than four hundred books and audiovisual items returned each hour flowing through the system. Every hour the library was open, over one hundred current magazines had to be reshelved or people could not find the issues they needed. There was a similar problem in the nonfiction stacks. Ignore shelving and straightening for a few hours and materials were in unacceptable order for either browsing or finding books systematically. In 1991 the seven managers worked a total of fifty hours a week on public service desks, including scheduled evenings and weekends. At least one additional librarian would be required to let these department coordinators reduce their hours directly serving the public in order to have time for administrative or collection development work. The coordinators and six other librarians had almost no clerical support to assist them in the routines required to select the thousands of new and replacement items added each year. By 1991, with increased money to spend, both the selectors and the technical services crew had to complete work on seventy-five to one hundred items a day just to keep ahead of the flow—a rate 25 percent higher than just two or three years earlier.

The staffing shortages, however, went much deeper than what was represented by simple increases to the number of items loaned, reference questions answered, and materials processed. Tasks and the skills required to accomplish them were increasingly technical and specialized. Fund-raising ($1.6 million since 1982); seeking business and organizational partners for special events and new services (ten partnerships in calendar year 1990 alone); providing public access to reference tools on CD-ROM through linked microcomputers; planning for dial-up access to COMPASS, the new version of the on-line catalog; keeping abreast of the ever-changing formats and playback equipment of modern library collections; programming and operating a cable television channel—these all required in-house skills and facilities not fully understood when the library building was planned in 1977-79.

We seemed to be spinning our wheels. We were stuck in a cycle of growth which continued to increase faster than resources, with a staff attempting to maintain quality services in the face of ever-increasing demand. Up-to-date, quality library services generated such a response in the community that the more we offered, the more out of balance library resources versus library service levels seemed to become. The economic theory that demand can be continuously elastic just kept snapping us where it hurt.

A couple of developments in the 1989-91 period helped board members deepen their understanding of the library's ongoing financial squeeze. In 1989, as described in chapter 10, the trustees revised and lengthened their budget preparation process. Spending at least twice the time as in previous years, the board heard from departmental managers giving chapter and verse details about day-to-day operations and current problems, as well as compelling descriptions of each department's requirements. These presentations were much more specific and informative than when I alone had briefed the board on the whole array of library needs and activities.

In order to describe ICPL's circumstances more clearly, the staff developed comparisons between Iowa City and libraries in larger cities. Identifying cities with libraries equal in use to Iowa City, we demonstrated that these were communities with populations two to three times larger. The libraries of these cities, on average, however, had more than twice the resources of ICPL (staff, collection, annual budget). We also compared ICPL use statistics to libraries in other college communities of similar size to show that even in cities with comparable demographics, ICPL's often smaller staff, smaller collections, and smaller budget were producing library service at equal or higher rates.

While it didn't solve the library's problems, these comparisons plus better budget information strengthened the board members' resolve and their ability to articulate the issues.

Looking at the Levy

In the negotiations for the 1991-92 budget in the winter of 1991, the library board, reeling from the impact of a two-year, 25 percent increase in use and armed with more specific details about library requirements, told the council that the library needed five, not two, additional positions. The city council not only failed to provide the two slots it had half-heartedly promised a year earlier, but the city manager warned that the city had reached the maximum general levy allowed by state law ($8.10 per $1,000 assessed valuation), and recommended that no more staff be added in any city department unless money to cover the salaries was identified.

Thus the library board faced a serious dilemma. The library was at least five positions short of what it needed. Only five new positions had been received in the last twelve years, and now the council said the city could not afford to add employees to the city budget unless a new source of funding could be determined. The prospects looked dim for relieving library difficulties via the traditional city tax route. As detailed earlier, the library had been receiving about 9 to 10 percent of the city's property tax dollars since the mid-1980s, a generous share compared to most communities. Also, some city councilors had already vowed that funding for the "Cadillac" would not surpass 10 percent.

Although the library board believed that core library staff should be paid from tax dollars, the trustees had supported all staff efforts to enhance the library work force. In addition to adding the equivalent of three staff members through the contribution of volunteer hours each year, the library had squeezed a second half-time position from city cable franchise fees in 1992 to partially reimburse the library for time spent operating its cable channel. (Cable fees were funding at least three people working on the city's channel.) Also, the development office, organized in 1989, now had two full-time employees, both paid primarily from foundation dollars and both contributing to library operations in areas beyond the scope of Friends and foundation activities. We used every kind of special work program to supplement the hourly-paid crew: work/study, Mayor's Youth summer programs, vocational rehabilitation placements, and library school interns.

After the disappointing budget decisions for 1991-92 were completed, the trustees realized they needed both a long-term and a short-term strategy. They had to face the approaching budget year with no new staff, and they had to decide whether potential service cuts made in order to get through the coming budget year should be permanent. Was it time to permanently cut back on the services provided? While the library had received kudos from local, state, and national bodies for its outstanding array of services, quality collections, and innovative ideas, the pressure put on ICPL from the ever-increasing number of users without comparable increases in staff would, in the long run, destroy the quality of services and collections and deplete the energy of the small staff to keep all the wheels spinning.

Before they made any decisions about services, the trustees took a long-term look at alternative ways to support the library. They had worked for the council's unsuccessful local option sales tax referendum in 1987. They had been raising private funds since 1982, but they did not think fund-raising could be expanded enough to support rather than enhance library operations. The city could renew its efforts for a local sales tax or an increased hotel-motel tax (also defeated in 1987), but there was no guarantee that any of it would be earmarked for the library.

Board members had looked at the special library levy in 1987 and had talked about it periodically ever since. In 1991 the levy suddenly took on added appeal. By March the trustees' strategy was pretty well formed, but they waited until April, following a special meeting with the city council, to take formal action. They would put the levy on the ballot in November. In the meantime they would design a combination of temporary service cuts and hours reduction to get the library and its staff through 1991-92. If the levy failed, the board would look at permanent cuts to library services. "We'll let the people decide," Board President Ellen Buchanan said.

Lowdown on the Levy

The levy is authorized in the Iowa Code as an additional tax that cities may levy under certain circumstances—for cultural facilities, transit systems, bridges, airports, and so on. If not done on the motion of the council, the levy requires a petition signed by qualified electors (eligible to vote but not necessarily registered) equal to 10 percent of the voters in the previous city election. After the required number of petition signatures has been submitted, the question goes on the ballot of the next city election (odd-numbered years) and requires a majority vote to approve. The maximum levy varies from purpose to purpose but the one associated with cultural institutions had always been twenty-seven cents per $1,000 of assessed valuation. The question on the petition and the ballot must cite the amount of the requested levy and the length of time, if limited, the levy will be in effect.

A special levy to support public libraries was the newest addition to the twenty levies allowed by this section of the code. It was still only proposed legislation when the library board briefly considered a levy vote in 1986. At that time a library was eligible under an older, more general levy to benefit cultural and scientific facilities. In 1987, after lobbying by the Iowa Library Association, the legislature added the special section for public libraries. It carried a clause that made it different from all other special levies. The code section for a library levy stipulated that if approved, the levy shall be imposed. Under the other levies the city council retained an option not to use the levy, even after voter approval. "Shall" versus "may" was a big difference.

The library board decided to go for the maximum levy—twenty-seven cents— and for an open-ended time period. This would generate an estimated $330,000 a year, about a 20 percent hike to the annual budget. Board members argued that the Iowa Code provided this opportunity for libraries when city government is unable to provide additional funding, and that if an open-ended levy is approved, it would be a clear message from the community about its willingness to pay for the wide range of services the library currently was providing. It would enable the library to plan for the long term.

Several political problems confronted the board as soon as the decision was made. First, the trustees had to get an informal agreement from the city council that if the levy was approved, the council would not cut back on the library's current share of the general fund and thus negate the effect of the additional money from the levy. Such agreement could only be informal and would have to be renewed with each new council and councilor. These issues were discussed with city council members in April prior to the board's formal action. Several councilors said successful passage would be a clear message from the voters about their wishes concerning the library and they would honor it. Later, I told the board that, as one concrete way to monitor the level of council support, it would be easy to continue to compute each year's share of property tax and/or total general fund monies (excluding library levy income) that was allocated to the library.

Also there was a problem about the date of the levy election. Iowa Citians would go to the polls at least two times before November 5, the next city election. The Iowa City Parks and Recreation Commission had scheduled a June 25 vote on a $4.6 million bond issue for a softball and soccer field complex and a redesign of Napoleon Park. The school board was already planning an October vote for $11.1 million to build a new elementary school plus additions and remodeling at the two high schools and a junior high. Board members realized the danger of following two other ballot issues that could raise local taxes, but since the library levy question could only be on the ballot of a city council election, it meant a two-year wait if not done in the fall of 1991.

A *Press-Citizen* editorial asked, "Why so many special elections?" and took all three governing bodies to task for wasting money and the voters' time. While the editorial didn't bother to explain the Iowa Code requirements for various kinds of elections, the newspaper did add up the tab. It told readers that the three votes could cost the owner of an average $75,000 Iowa City home about $83 a year in additional taxes.[1] The library levy, at $16.20, would be about 20 percent of that total.

The third political problem the library faced was that before the levy campaign could get organized and gather momentum, the trustees had to decide on the scope of the service cuts they would make for the coming budget year, 1991-92. The changes would take effect July 1, 1991. On the one hand, reduced service levels would dramatize library needs, but it also could antagonize some voters, who might feel that once again the library board was holding the library hostage to get the resources they felt they needed.

The library board started looking at possible service reductions almost as soon as the budget decisions for the coming year were completed and printed. The staff had been preparing lists of service reduction ideas, each suggestion accompanied by the estimated hours per week it would save. The goal, similar to the process used in 1987, was to assemble a combination of temporary service cuts and hours reductions that equaled the 115 productive hours per week that the three and one-half positions from tax monies would have provided if the council had approved them for the 1991-92 budget.

All the old arguments for and against reducing hours versus eliminating services surfaced. "When you cut hours, you cut everyone equally," assistant director Susan Craig told the board in March. "But [you] have done that in the past and been accused of playing political games." All-day closings, dropping reserves, closing the meeting rooms, discontinuing tax forms, and eliminating special children's programs were some of the ideas examined.

Following discussions on March 7 and March 28, with a March 8 news story in the *Press-Citizen* inviting public comments,[2] board members made their decision about service cuts in late April immediately following their eight to one vote on pursuing the levy. Avoiding the more productive but also more controversial all-day Friday closings of 1987-88, the board agreed to closing the library on Wednesday and Friday mornings, Thursday evenings, and on four minor holidays. These closings averaged about eight fewer hours a week for public service and eighty hours a week of staff time transferable to other tasks. Combined with a few permanent and temporary service changes worth about thirty hours per week of staff time, the total savings approached the board's 115-hour per week goal. Children's film showings were permanently discontinued based on low attendance and changing technology. The loan period for compact discs was permanently changed from seven to twenty-one days. This five-year-old collection had grown to 3,000 discs, and the change would reduce the number of loans and thus staff time spent sorting and reshelving. Adult programs and displays repeated their 1987 temporary disappearing act, and telephone reference service on Sunday was temporarily discontinued. In an attempt to reduce circulation growth, some money for popular materials would be funneled temporarily into reference materials. Children's and information services, the top priorities of the long-range plan, were protected at the expense of other library efforts.

The Levy Campaign

The first task before mounting the public campaign was to get the full story ready to pass on to the campaign committee. As the board had requested in similar efforts, we prepared a question-and-answer sheet and updated it whenever new information or unexpected questions surfaced. These campaign materials capsulized the issue: There has been an explosion in the use of the library, and the board and staff are unable to keep up with the demands the community is making on the library. Unable to get enough staff through the budget process for the library's current program, the library board needs some indication from the community about what levels of service it is willing to support. "The levy is needed to maintain services, not expand them," Ellen Buchanan explained in the press release announcing the board's decision. "It will be used to hire staff [50 percent], improve the collection [25 percent], and to begin to refurbish the 10-year-old building [25 percent]. The public faces reduced service hours, deteriorating collections, and a narrower array of library services and programs unless the library is supported at a higher level of funding," Buchanan said. Lawyer Tom Gelman, a former board president, noted that, "The Iowa Code offers this option [the levy] for public libraries in communities that cannot provide sufficient funding from the general property tax or for libraries with extraordinary needs."

It was relatively easy to find volunteers to serve on the campaign committee. Bob Burns, former county supervisor and state senator, joined Suzanne Richerson, ten-year veteran as library board trustee, to lead The Committee for the Library Levy. Board members, former board members, and former Friends board presidents comprised the fourteen-member leadership group. Gelman and trustee Kathy Moyers served as co-treasurers.

Just one mailing to Friends, volunteers, and foundation contributors produced a bevy of enthusiastic supporters. They sent money (232 contributed a total of over $6,000), signed up to seek petition signatures (considered a positive first step to introducing the issue), agreed to yard signs (over fifty households), autho-

VOTE YES
TUESDAY, NOV. 5
FOR THE
LIBRARY

Iowa City Public Library Archives

rized the use of their name in ads of support (250), or agreed to send letters of support to the newspaper (at least twenty were printed with only two opposing).

Good graphics and concise slogans—"Make your vote one for the books" and "Iowa Citians love their library to pieces"—filled campaign brochures that also gave full information and explicit graphs about the library's dilemma. The last section of the brochure asked and answered the question, "What if the levy does not pass? Library services will be permanently scaled back."

The referendum for a special library levy received approval by 68 percent of the voters in the fall of 1991.

The staff prepared background papers for speakers to use before groups. These documents detailed and personalized the many library jobs required to run a modern public library and tried to dispel commonly held misconceptions about the library: "Ten Reasons Library Service is Essential to a Community," "Who Uses the Library besides School Kids and Bestseller Readers?" and "What Does a Library Staff Do besides Check-out and Reshelve Books?"

One of the most fortuitous developments of the campaign was the discovery that the thirteenth and final bond payment for the construction of the library would be made in 1991-92, the year before the new levy would start. In addition, the annual payment for these bonds had averaged about $335,000, almost the exact amount the levy was estimated to produce in the first year. Consequently, the campaign committee could honestly say that the levy would not increase taxes that currently supported the library. No one realized this when the decision to seek the levy was made. I will never forget the day at my desk, when, rifling through the city budget, I eyed the debt service payments for the library bonds and realized this happy coincidence. Fortunately, we made the discovery in time to include it in campaign materials. (A similar situation was described in chapter 7.

Trustees in 1962 asked voters to approve a building levy which already had been on the tax books for the previous three years in its pay-as-you go form.)

The campaign went fairly smoothly, but there were some dark moments. Two of them were on the days when the results of the other referendum issues became known. On June 25 only 17 percent of those voting said "yes" to building the proposed recreation facilities, and on October 15 the $11.1 million school board proposal also went down to defeat, 8 percent short of the 60 percent approval needed. Many were predicting that Iowa Citians were not going to vote to raise their taxes and would be saying "no" to all proposals that year. Pessimists did not give the library proposal a chance. The argument that the levy would not raise taxes because of the end of the library construction bond payments now seemed more important than ever.

With the library vote in the offing, the library was news and the local papers gave good coverage of library activities. Details of our annual report (always full of the remarkable increases in service), a profile of our information services, and an article about changing information technologies and the library's efforts to keep abreast of them all made the front pages of the *Press-Citizen* between late August and November 5. The paper also printed graphs and a detailed story about the comparison between ICPL and eight similar public libraries, derived from material we had prepared for the campaign. It dramatically illustrated the library's high use versus its small staff, collection, and budget. In May, a *Press-Citizen* editorial had said the city could not afford the proposals then before the electorate. By November, with two proposals defeated, the paper supported the library levy. "Keep library standards high," it editorialized. "Vote yes for the levy."

Except for a couple of letters in the newspaper, there was no public opposition to the levy. Our nemesis in the last campaign, the Chamber of Commerce, twice printed details about library needs and levy plans in its newsletter. One of the letters to the *Press-Citizen*, complaining about UI student domination of the library, gave the new library board president, Kent Swaim, the opportunity to respond with a guest column that detailed the actual facts about UI student use at ICPL. He noted that while students were quite visible—they often filled the library's study tables, especially during the day—their use really was an insignificant part of total library business. For example, Swaim explained, even if every person in the city between the ages of 18 and 21 (22 percent of the Iowa City population) was assumed to be a university student, this group accounted for only 8 percent of library card holders and 4 percent of library loans.

The newspaper ads and other campaign materials emphasized how little the $16.20 average per year tax bill was when compared to other costs. "Less than the price of one hardcover book" and "4 cents a day or $1.35 a month," the ads pointed out. "What can you buy in Iowa City for $1.35? One well-used paperback, or one well-used library. Have we got a deal for you," said another.

There was no last-minute crisis, no marches for or against the library issue. People quietly went to their precinct voting sites and 68 percent of them voted "yes"—a 5 percent higher approval rate than 1978 voters gave for building the library, and 18 percent higher than was needed to secure the levy. Four councilors were reelected in fairly easy races, yet the vote was 10 percent higher than the previous city election and 40 percent higher than 1987 and 1985. The 9,637 votes set a new record. The levy carried in every precinct, with the percentage approval rate ranging from 54 to 95 percent. My own precinct, which had deserted the library on the bond referendum in 1978, had voted 455 to 299, a 60 percent margin.

Cedar Rapids Gazette columnist Tom Anglin, commenting on both the library and the two earlier referendum losses, said, "Well, you can't lose them all! . . . Iowa City voters finally said yes to something . . . the levy passed with 68 percent of the vote. That's a rather extraordinary level of support for a public spending proposal . . . in the midst of a pesky recession. . . . Give Iowa Citians a spending choice on something we use all the time and feel great pride in—the library certainly is that—and we will come to our senses."[3]

In the thirteen years since the 1978 election, the affection and respect for the library had grown substantially, and trustees, staff, and volunteers were buoyed by this show of approval. The board had asked for an opinion on the future of the library and the resounding response seemed to be, "We like what you're doing. Keep it up." One voter, quoted after the results were in, said that the large vote for the levy did not surprise him. "This library . . . has a very broad base of support."[4]

The levy vote was a crucial moment in the contemporary history of the library. Without additional funds and the firm community support those funds represented, the last few of the first one hundred years would have been another story.

The Last County Battle

The levy vote came in the middle of the budget preparation period and we hustled to get our expanded budget plans into shape and on the required forms. One of the routine budget tasks was to send the county a copy of the library's proposed budget by January 1 so that thirty days later, the supervisors could return a "resolution of commitment" to fund 10 percent of the library's operating costs as required by the 1983 contract. That contract had been signed after three years of disagreement about the county's equitable share of library funding that several times threatened to end free service to rural residents.

This time, however, the budget procedure was not routine. Due to the new levy, the county's share, like the library's budget, would increase 24 percent (from $182,600 to $225,900) and the supervisors were not happy. Shortly before the February 1 deadline—which had rarely before been adhered to—the county board held a special meeting to set the county share for 1992-93 at $166,150, almost $60,000 less than the city and the library were planning on.

The February 1 news article announcing the supervisors' decision began, "Johnson County and the city of Iowa City are having another difference of opinion." This turned out to be more than a slight understatement. Before it was all over, barbs would be hurled in both directions, the county and city attorneys would provide starkly different interpretations of the library contract, the library board would be accused of mismanagement and of misinforming county residents, and the county of trying to renege on a contract and of crying wolf about its lack of funds. The library board would ask the city to consider court action, and the county would complain that it suffered from taxation without representation.

The story made headline news more than twenty-five times between February 1 and late April 1992 with a rich variety of verbs used to describe some of the heated meetings—squabble, spar, dispute, "sparks fly," "tempers flare," and "city blasts county," to name a few. By the time the terms softened to "both sides agree to negotiate," "compromise sought," and "deal would split the difference," an agreement had been struck and both sides were on their way to fashioning another contract and formula for funding library services to rural residents. After the fiery debates over nonresident cards versus a contract for service which preceded the first and very tentative library-county contract in 1968, each decade had its contract controversy. In 1974 it was the failure to stay open on Sundays, next the 1982-84 extended conflict, and now the 1990s round was about to begin.

It was a somewhat complicated dispute. Upset by the large increase to their annual bill for library service, the supervisors had the county attorney's office search the contract to see if there was a loophole—and they thought they found one. In the contract language, the promise to pay 10 percent of the library's budget was coupled with an alternative: 10 percent or 85 percent of the maximum allowable levy for county library contracts, "whichever shall be the lesser amount." Although the 1984 state legislature had eliminated the maximum levy cited in the 1983 city-county library contract, and although the county had been paying the library a full 10 percent share even though the amount had been more than the now-repealed limit for several years, the supervisors quickly computed the amount due under the 85 percent rule—$166,150—and sent a letter declaring this was all they would pay in budget year 1992-93. They took the position that this was a legal option in the contract that they simply had not chosen to exercise before.

Stung by the possibility that the county might put a $60,000 hole in its newly expanded, hard-fought 1992-93 budget, the library board immediately asked for a legal opinion. I gathered together all my charts, memos, and contract drafts from past county negotiations and the city manager asked City Attorney Linda Gentry (Woito) to prepare an opinion. Two days later Gentry responded: The county's position was untenable. It not only relied on repealed code language, but by paying 10 percent a year for nearly ten years, a "pattern and practice" had been established. She said the contract was in full force until it was renegotiated or one of the parties gave notice of termination.

County Attorney White's response was not unexpected. He had written the contract in 1983 and had pointed out the loophole to the supervisors. His argument was simple. A contract is a contract and the language rules unless a change is mutually agreed upon. He recommended that both sides work to make revisions.

Both the city and county attorneys felt very strongly about their positions. The supervisors felt they were at the mercy of an Iowa City decision on which county residents were not allowed to vote. The library board argued that for the past nine years county residents had accounted for over 11 percent of library circulation and that paying only 10 percent of the cost was more than fair. Also, the board felt strongly that Iowa Citians should not subsidize the cost of library service for nonresidents.

Board members Gelman and Swaim tried to craft a compromise that would phase in 10 percent of the new levy portion of the library's budget over a period of five years, and the library board offered to accept $208,000 for the first year. Only two supervisors were interested in that amount, but after a few more hot sessions, three of the supervisors agreed on $192,000 (a 5 percent increase) as a counter-offer.

The trustees rejected the offer, saying $192,000 was a number without basis, and then outraged the supervisors by posting signs in the library warning rural card holders that their library service was threatened and suggesting they contact county supervisors and ask them to continue to pay their 10 percent share. The supervisors were inundated with letters. With tempers high, one supervisor criticized the library of poor management, spending too much money on videos and artworks, and reducing hours instead of reducing services. Library board members accused the supervisors of covering up the amount of county funds available, although it was true that county expenses for libraries had expanded considerably in the past ten years as the other four public libraries in the county (Coralville, North Liberty, Solon, and Oxford) asked for their share of supplementary funding from the county. None had a contract with the county but they were awarded amounts ranging from $2,500 to $19,500 for 1992-93.

Tempers flared a final time at the annual joint meeting between the supervisors and the city councilors. The library board had asked the city council to discuss the contract standoff with the supervisors at the meeting and to consider court action if nothing was resolved. After a fairly heated exchange, the two bodies emerged with an agreement to appoint a joint committee to negotiate a settlement. Two supervisors and two councilors joined three board members, including the county's representative on the library board, Anne Spencer. In two weeks the group came to a preliminary agreement: The county would pay $208,000 for the coming year, and by August 1 the committee would negotiate a new contract.

The meetings to find common ground for a contract took place during May and June in the supervisors chambers at the county administrative building. In preparation for the first meeting, I put together a thick package of history and charts about county contracts; library ordinances, policies, and budgets; contract comparisons with other Iowa counties; and surveys on use of the library by county residents—undoubtedly more than anyone, especially the county representatives, wanted to know about the topic. The information showed, among other facts, that there were nineteen Iowa counties spending more per capita for library service than Johnson County, and that in the last ten years both the number of county card holders and loans to county card holders had increased at almost twice the rate as that of Iowa City residents.

Most of the arguments of the previous three months were rehashed and negotiations were pretty much at a standstill until County Attorney White presented some ideas in late June that got the trustees, supervisors, and councilors off dead center and on their way to an agreement. Working from the 1983 contract, White suggested that after the city determined the amount of property taxes necessary for library operations each year, the county would pay a share of that amount based on the average three-year circulation to rural residents. In 1983 the formula for computing the county's share had been revised to eliminate a surcharge for the city's overhead costs in serving the library not reflected in the library budget and for debt service costs on library construction bonds. This time, all miscellaneous library income to the general fund—fines, fees (including cable TV fees), and sales—was excluded on the grounds that rural card holders contributed their share to this type of library income.

Despite some unresolved issues on both sides, the group reached agreement fairly quickly after White's suggestions, and all bodies—board of supervisors, city council, and library board—had officially adopted the new agreement before the August 1 deadline. The library board, in fact, was not an official party to the contract; the policy of 1983 was continued, letting the city council contract with the supervisors. The trustees had been promised, however, that they had to agree to the terms before the council would sign.

The use of the three-year average circulation to rural residents as the multiplier instead of the flat 10 percent has saved money for the county, and I feel I should have spotted the developing trend and pointed out the probable effect. The rapid rise in the number of loans to card holders from other communities through the state reciprocal program, Open Access, has dramatically changed the ratio of loans to Iowa Citians versus rural residents. Although circulation to the county has risen about 6 percent since 1992, its share of total circulation has dropped from over 10 percent to 8.6 percent—not much of a change, but enough to save the county about $30,000 a year over what the county would pay if the former 10 percent a year formula had been retained.

The idea of serving rural residents and the desire to charge equitably for that service have been tackled by almost every library board throughout the last one hundred years. With the advent of a contract with the supervisors in 1968 the wrangling continued and at times became quite bitter. As when a kaleidoscope is passed from person to person, each viewer sees a slightly different version of the county-library relationship. There are issues of equity and equal access and fair representation that can never be completely settled in a contract environment.

Cooperation between the public libraries of Johnson County has been strengthened in recent years, and this growing collaboration could form the basis of something completely different for county service in the future. In the meantime, thousands of rural residents have had free access to all the libraries in the county and have borrowed over two million items since 1968.

Library Housekeeping

There are several essential tasks that keep the library wheels spinning but do not produce the interesting stories that readers—and editors—prefer. They are important to the history of this library, however, and can be skipped by those readers not interested in the last few years of ICPL planning, fund-raising, and collection development. Coverage will be brief.

A New Strategic Plan. By 1993 it was time to prepare a new long-range plan. *On Track for the 90s* had been extended to a sixth year, through June 1995, because of the attention given to passing the levy, the required follow-ups, and the county contract dispute. There were enough unfinished goals and objectives in the plan to keep us busy until the end of the century, but the plan's faulty assumptions—no population growth and a leveling off of library use—plus the impact of that unplanned growth, the new levy funds, and rapidly developing information technologies made the 1988 plan wildly out of touch with our real library world.

The time needed to create and adopt a plan ready to be used for preparing a budget for the first year of the new planning cycle always led to a confusion of dates and fiscal years. We needed a new plan in place by July 1994 (also my retirement date) as the basis for preparing the 1995-96 budget, which meant work had to begin in 1993. This long lead time was a handicap to developing a plan that reflected current conditions—as the 1990-94 plan developed in 1988 so vividly demonstrated—and we were determined to condense and simplify the process.

Note the word "strategic." Our planning skills (and general planning jargon) had advanced by the year 1993 to the point where we could use the term "strategic planning" and sound like we knew exactly what we were doing. Theoretically, strategic planning is not as time-specific as long-range planning and is more dynamic, able to be changed from one year to the next as priorities shift or circumstances change. This sounded very attractive after the failed assumptions of the last plan. Most of all, however, we were very serious about improving, simplifying, and shortening the process, and producing a plan that people could easily and quickly read and understand.

To help us direct our planning efforts toward these goals, we hired Roger Boldt, a frequent ICPL user. Boldt was an experienced planner with a library degree and a strong commitment to public libraries. He helped us design our planning process and served as the facilitator for a two-day planning retreat and several of the follow-up sessions, the basic framework for developing this cycle's plan.

To provide background for the retreat participants, we prepared materials in two areas. I assembled appropriate data about the library's financial condition, collection, and circulation patterns, and, as in the levy campaign, made comparisons of ICPL to other libraries in formats that highlighted ICPL's strengths and weaknesses. The second component prepared for the planning team summarized information gathered from library users, community officials and leaders, the staff, and the general public about the strengths and weaknesses of the library and the critical issues the library faced in the years ahead. The results of these phone interviews, mail surveys, and discussion sessions were compared, where possible, to the results of the massive user studies done in 1982.

As seems inevitable in formal planning efforts, the process took longer and was more complex than we envisioned. Our impressive team of twenty-one volunteer planners had promised us two full days in January 1994 plus three short follow-up sessions before and after we reviewed their preliminary plan with the library board, staff, and the general public. A few extra meetings and several written reviews of plan drafts by the participants extended their work into April. Staff committees worked throughout the spring to develop appropriate tasks to implement the new goals and objectives.

The process produced a viable plan in much less time than the eighteen and nine months of the 1982 and 1987 planning teams, but proved again that planning was hard work, sometimes difficult to translate for those not directly involved, but worth the effort even when specifics in the final written plan proved undoable or just plain wrong.

The new plan, *Building on a Century of Service*, has strong roots in the 1975 goals and the operating principles of both long-range plans written in the 1980s. We had been the first public library to use stated roles as a communication and priority-setting device, but this time, just as many in the public library community were beginning to choose their roles, we deliberately eliminated them for a more comprehensive mix of services, finances, facilities, staff, technologies, and community participation. The topics were so intertwined and basic to continued library health that we could no longer ignore the nonservice aspects as we did in the plan of 1982, or label them "administrative goals" as we did in 1988 and then struggle with them alone. Events leading up to the levy vote had taught us that.

The core elements of the plan, subtitled "Iowa City Public Library Strategic Plan for Centennial Year 1996 and Beyond," are available in an attractive six-page flier distinctly different from the forty-to-eighty-page stapled or spiral-bound monsters of the past. The larger and more diverse community component of the planning team enriched the content of the final plan and added the zest and enthusiasm of serious library users. The intense sessions let these lay people dig into the details of funding, planning, and delivering library services for longer and thus more productive periods than the two-hour, biweekly meetings of the previous planning efforts.

Since this would not be my plan to administer, I served as an aide to our facilitator and as a resource person, though I am sure I wasn't as quiet as I intended to be. Working on this plan for the last six months of my directorship allowed me to look forward instead of back and to assist in sending the library into its second century. The library board officially adopted the plan in June 1994 at my final board meeting as library director.

The last task of the two-day planning retreat in January had been the writing of a library mission statement that reflected the values and ideas that the planning team had developed through their decisions about specific goals and objectives. Members fought over the meaning and nuance of every word. I hear language in this statement that satisfies my library soul. It speaks to every issue we had striven for since I started my career at the library in 1969—and to the values the library has proclaimed since its founding in 1897:

The Iowa City Public Library is an innovative, dynamic resource central to a literate and informed citizenry. The library reflects and responds to the community and is committed to

- intellectual freedom
- equal accessibility for a diverse population
- lifelong learning beginning with the young child
- enhancement of cultural and leisure activities.[5]

Fund-raising in the '90s (and before). By 1991 the Friends were celebrating their fifteenth year and the foundation was one year short of its tenth birthday. The reorganized development office, as a department of the library rather than an office for the foundation's executive secretary, had been in place for nearly two years.

Pat Forsythe had done the hard work of getting the foundation started. She developed the prospect files, educated the staff about the ways and ethics of fund-raising (the giving records of contributors are as confidential as the circulation records of library users), wrote the first funding appeals, designed publications, and planned events (including two unforgettable dinner parties) to make the community aware of the existence and plans of the new organization. Forsythe launched the Centennial Endowment Fund (CEF), helped recruit valuable people for the board, installed the Giving Tree for donor recognition in the library's lobby, and patiently and helpfully answered all the requests for information that poured in from other public libraries seeking to duplicate the success of the ICPL Foundation. She left with the new quarters for the development office about to open, her small office overflowing with files, a part-time assistant, and a crew of regular volunteers. In her last year, the endowment fund was approaching $700,000 and the annual fund raised $40,000, both from a base of over 1,000 regular contributors.

In 1989 Deborah Sales succeeded Pat Forsythe and became the library's second development officer. Sales came to the library from the Iowa City Community School District Foundation with broad experience as a community volunteer and a wide acquaintance among Iowa City business people and individuals active in local organizations. She was the master of the $10,000 gift. She rapidly filled in the "boulders" beneath the Giving Tree with the names of businesses and organizations giving $10,000 or more to the library. She gathered each donor group together, snapped their picture, and sent it to the *Press-Citizen's* weekly "Community Album" page of organizational events, accomplishments, and awards. Almost every week one or two donors to the foundation were featured. Sales didn't neglect the smaller gift. She returned many of the city's service clubs to the rolls of library contributors. Probably overlooked in the early years of the foundation when the emphasis was almost entirely on unrestricted gifts, these local organizations preferred to give money for equipment, materials, and programs that complemented the purpose and goals of their clubs. Sales worked with many of the service clubs to find suitable gift opportunities and in 1991 alone she arranged seven successful partnerships with service organizations. The NEH Challenge Grant plaque was installed that same year, featuring large donors and listing all CEF donors. When the library had a chance to buy a valuable Tadashi grand piano at a bargain price, she quickly took up the cause and "sold" individual keys to contributors whose names appear on the unusual piano-shaped plaque near the piano in meeting room A.

The Friends flourished under Sales. She helped them celebrate their fifteenth year with a $15,000 gift, their largest annual gift to that date. As the Friends and the foundation grew and each expanded its activities, the confusion that had existed from the foundation's first day became more intense. Large contributors to the foundation, for example, did not understand why their gifts did not qualify them for free admittance to the Friends "membership hour" at the beginning of each book sale. Friends sometimes felt their less glamorous activities were undervalued in comparison to the gifts of the foundation's major donors. Tension between the groups increased and Sales felt the duplication of organizations wasted development office time as well as damaged the library's image. She got the two groups to form an exploratory committee to consider a merger. By the fall of 1992 each group had approved the substance of the plan and former trustee Tom Gelman had contributed the legal expertise to guide them through the maze of rescinded, revised, and reenacted articles of incorporation and IRS tax-exempt authorizations needed to make the new Iowa City Public Library Friends Foundation a legal entity. Sales helped them become a unified organization with a newly structured board of directors and a continuation of most Friends activities now coordinated by a new Friends committee. Unfortunately, a fund-raising consultant who helped us focus on the possibilities of merging also focused on our development director. They married and Sales moved to Minneapolis in the spring of 1993.

One major Friends Foundation fund drive overlapped the administrations of Sales and the next development coordinator, Larry Eckholt. Early in 1993, John and Ellen Buchanan promised the library a $525,000 deferred gift with the stipulation that the foundation match their pledge on a 3-to-1 basis with other deferred gifts. Consequently, the foundation board approved a $2.1 million "Funding the Future" deferred giving campaign. Sales returned a few times to oversee aspects of the campaign started before she left, but soon new director Eckholt was fully in charge. Eckholt, a former reporter for the *Des Moines Register* and former fund-raiser for the University of Iowa Foundation, had returned to Iowa City after a four-year absence to take the library post.

The Funding the Future campaign raised $2.2 million in deferred gifts and $100,000 in cash in just nine months. Eckholt followed up on this new emphasis on deferred giving with a Cumulative Giving Wall to recognize past and future gifts, and a regular deferred giving newsletter that reminded current contributors about the many methods of making a bequest or other deferred gift to the library. The new plaque featured an engraving of the Buchanans.

Eckholt increased the number of business partnerships, a trend started under Sales. Children's Day during the June arts festival, the annual Popo Puppet Festival, Begin with Books, and the Books for Giving and Liking (now Book Gala) all benefited from business sponsorship. Early on Eckholt showed his flair for managing events, and in the last four years of the library's century, he coordinated many major and minor social functions and special occasions: the day in 1993 when the library made its first millionth loan for the year, the launching of Duncan the Meter Reader, the annual contributors' fall reception, the amazing and gratifying events planned for my retirement (Lolly Finale), and probably his finest event to date, the library's one hundredth birthday celebration. His journalism experience made it natural to shift editorial responsibility for *The Window* to Eckholt in 1996. All these events and skills exhibited how much more than a fund-raiser we get when the library has an office designed not only to gather gifts but also to present its best face to the public.

The Centennial Endowment Fund reached $1 million in 1995, one year ahead of its goal and two years ahead of the library's actual centennial year. At the end of 1996 the endowment fund was valued at $1.1 million and income from the fund was approaching $350,000 for the first nine years. Since the Friends organization was founded in 1976 they have contributed $265,000 to the library. During the last twenty years, since attracting private gifts became a goal and not just an accident, the library has received $1.4 million from all sources of private giving.

Reliable tax support is necessary and vital to the library, but an institution cannot make many grand leaps forward with the incremental increases gained through the annual budget process. Alternative sources of funds—private gifts, grants, state aid, or a voter-approved levy increase—have given the library the flexibility, the independence, the courage, and the means to step into its future by experimenting with new services and new technologies. In addition, the library now has hundreds of "stockholders" (stakeholders in current planning jargon; volunteers is the old-fashioned term) who have invested time and money in the library and want it to remain viable.

Collections are still number one. The 1994 planning team voted by a wide margin to make the goal concerning library collections the number one priority. In their statement about that goal, team members wrote, "The most important responsibility of the library is to develop, maintain, and offer to the public collections of books and other materials. It is critical that the staff anticipate the community's needs and, when it doesn't, that methods exist for gathering input from the community."[6] This was not a revolutionary idea; it reflected what we had been trying to do for many years, but this planning team, dominated by community representatives, provided strong library user support for our professional beliefs.

The resources needed to provide the range and quality of library materials that the strategic plan requires have been gradually accumulating, especially since the levy was passed. The annual materials budget, first enriched by gift books, contributions, and endowment income in the mid-1980s, has increased by one-third since the levy began to supplement the budget in 1992-93. (The $373,000 spent for library materials in 1996 is more than the entire library budget in 1975, the first budget I prepared.) And of course, more money translates into more items purchased. The library now adds annually twice the number of new items it could afford in 1986 and one-quarter more than before the levy—nearly 25,000 items in 1996, 21,000 of them books.

The library has continued to keep the management of its many collections distributed among all the staff librarians (fifteen in 1996), but is currently writing a collection development plan that will help to keep these subject and format specialists moving in the same direction and pursuing goals that match those of the strategic plan. I feel strongly that the wisdom and experience of fifteen minds produce collections superior to those developed in a more centralized mode. Many larger libraries delegate this responsibility to only two or three individuals who devote full time to deciding what materials the library requires. At first glance, multiple selectors may seem to be an inefficient method because of the many procedures and policies necessary to accomplish the task—budget allocations, ordering procedures, reports, and other communications—but every type of evidence from statistical to anecdotal confirms the ongoing quality of this library's collections. Fifteen individuals from different backgrounds and experiences who are involved in a variety of other library and community responsibilities give the library's relatively small collections a richness, scope, and quality found in few other community libraries. These hard-working and experienced librarians keep the collections lean but nourishing, and the constant positive feedback from the public about the collection is confirmed by a very respectable turnover rate. On average, each item in the collection was used nearly six times in 1995-96—a rate that has slowly increased from less than four in the early 1980s.

A library the size of ICPL does not archive any materials except local history. All other items in the collection must pass the use test.

The collection development plan that is in the works will provide the public, for the first time, comprehensive narratives about each of the twenty major collection components, with information about the scope and character of each. Each narrative will describe the intended purpose and audience, the planned size and rate of duplication, the special subtopics included, special maintenance requirements, selection criteria, and the particular aids (review journals, local experts, popularity lists, and so on) used to assist purchase and withdrawal decisions for that part of the collection.

As we discovered in the 1970s when we first inventoried the collection and found high rates of missing volumes and low rates of duplicates of popular titles, availability is a continual challenge in a public library. Although each reserve represents a failure of a borrower to find what he or she came for, the ability to promptly fill and deliver these requested items is extremely important.

Two major improvements to the reserve system in the fall of 1995 gave library users a much-desired boost toward getting materials more promptly. For the first time since 1977, the library removed the fee for placing a reserve. The fee had been installed after a strong message from city hall that the library should make at least a token effort to raise fees or it would receive a budget reduction. (The fee never raised more than $2,000 a year.) Ever since that time, a strong desire to remove the fee was balanced by fear of the number of reserves the public would place when there was no charge. Chronically understaffed and with reserves a personnel-intensive process, we rationalized the fee for these reasons despite an operating principle that said "services of [the library] are available free to all people of the community."

The second improvement to reserves in 1995, however, made the first possible. COMPASS, the library catalog system, could now allow card holders, using their bar code number and a password, to place their own reserves directly into the system. The results were as expected. The number of reserves tripled, from 7,000 to 21,000. The task of capturing this increased number of items at point of check-in required more staff effort, but much of it was offset by the time gained at all public desks from no longer assisting borrowers to fill out reserve cards.

After seven months under the free, place-your-own reserve system, an analysis of all items reserved revealed that the new and much busier system did not tie up large parts of the collection. Only 4 percent of all library titles received reserves, and of those titles, 86 percent had only one or two requests. Traditional reading favorites—fiction, mysteries, and science fiction, plus two hot topics—computer books and multimedia (interactive CD-ROM), a new and still small collection, accounted for most of the titles with multiple reserves. Several very popular categories—compact discs, movies on video, and books on tape—surprisingly recorded fewer reserves than the average for the entire collection. The report demonstrated the quality and range of the library's collections and the wide variety of interests represented by the library's card holders.

The new multimedia collection is symbolic of the changing nature of library collections. Since the doors opened in 1897 with just six print collections (adult fiction and nonfiction, juvenile fiction and nonfiction, reference books, and periodicals), the library has added seventeen more print collections (genre fiction, young adult fiction, large print books, foreign language fiction, picture books, uncataloged paperbacks, books for adults learning to read, and story time kits, among others). In addition, since 1950, the library has started twenty-two audiovisual or nonprint collections in a variety of formats, age levels, and content groupings. Ten of these twenty-two, including LPs, 8mm and 16mm films, software on floppy disc, and filmstrips, have subsequently been discontinued. Some librarians are making the case that World Wide Web sites appropriate to library users are another "collection" the library must monitor as it already does the CD-ROM data bases on Refnet, the library's local area network. (For a history of all ICPL collections, see appendix F.)

A New Director

Compared to twenty years earlier, the transition to a new director on July 1, 1994, was almost seamless. I moved out and Susan Craig moved in from her office just next door. I turned the reins over to a woman with whom I had worked for almost twenty years and who had been my closest associate since 1986. Craig has been one of the major players in the present administration, a person whose ideas and service helped build the library's reputation for excellence.

The board, however, did not just hand her the job. She earned it by surviving the competition of numerous applicants and three other finalists. Search committee members had the advantage of a retirement announced early enough to enable them to take as long as they needed to complete the process and make their decision. A resignation or the sudden death of a director can force a much faster track. The long time frame allowed the committee to gather a lot of information from the applicants, request written answers to questions about basic library issues, talk to references and associates of the candidates, and hear reactions and recommendations from the staff.

One interesting step in the final round of selecting the new director was a series of public forums held to introduce the four finalists to the community. At each forum one of the candidates made a brief statement about his or her library experience, concerns, and philosophy regarding public libraries. A question-and-answer period and a social hour followed. The large number of people who attended these forums testified to the community's interest in who would be the next library director.

Craig grew up in Waterloo using the public library as a child and working there in her high school years. She came to Iowa City in 1970 and started at ICPL in 1975 as a work/study employee doing filing and general clerical tasks in the same month that she began work on her graduate library degree. Following the birth of her first son later that same year, she continued work on her M.L.S. part time. As soon as she completed her degree, she became a substitute librarian in the information department, followed by an appointment to a permanent librarian's position in 1977 and promotion to manager of the technical services department in 1982. She replaced Connie Tiffany as assistant director in 1986 when Tiffany left to head the Glendora (California) Public Library. In 1990-91 Craig was a member of the inaugural class of the Iowa City Chamber of Commerce Community Leadership Program and served as chair of the committee that directs that annual program in 1993-94.

Craig has continued to play a leadership role in state and local library activities, serving on several state library committees and as founding chair of the Johnson County Community Network. JCCN is a new nonprofit organization committed to building an electronic network of local information.

"Tell Me Your Story"

I have told the stories of many of the earlier trustees and library directors who have written important chapters in the library's story—the budget battles, the struggles with the county officials over service to rural residents, the approval, planning, and construction of two library buildings, the attempts to serve schoolchildren before the days of school libraries, the changing relationship between the library board and the librarian as she became more professional and the board more advisory. This history has also traced the development of the library's collections, documenting the changing formats, noting the gradual growth of adult nonfiction as the dominant collection component, describing the development of information, audiovisual, and children's services, and relating the growth of support groups that give time and money to enhance library activities.

In telling these stories of conflict and development and change, the essential part played by individual library staff members is inevitably under recorded. Today the library director is the vital link between the trustees and the staff and volunteers who carry out the day-to-day operations of the library and deliver services to the community. No longer the chief cook and bottle washer—secretary to the board, purchaser and processor of new books, library hostess at the charge desk, reference librarian, library advocate with the public schools, and

418

sometimes, building custodian (with or without dusting)—the contemporary director leads an ever-growing team of managers, librarians, technical and subject specialists, clerks, shelvers, and volunteers.

Since the mid-1920s but especially during the last quarter century, the library's story is only partially told through the trustees and directors alone. Helen McRaith's staff of two and one-half is now 95 full- and part-time employees and 120 regular volunteers. In addition, there are countless donors, businesses, organizations, and Friends that contribute to the daily life of the library. The staff includes artists, publicists, fund-raisers, catalogers, building and departmental managers, computer and audiovisual experts, storytellers and puppeteers, subject and personnel specialists, and the wizards of information retrieval and handsomely processed library materials. They represent the bevy of skills required to operate a contemporary public library.

Iowa City Public Library Archives

The library staff continues to be involved in community events. Pictured here is the 1996 Hospice Road Races team—including friends and family—decked out in party gear celebrating the library's approaching centennial.

Public libraries generally and ICPL in particular attract talented people with wide-ranging interests and an urge to share them with fellow employees and the public. Typical library employees enjoy serving people of all shapes, colors, ages, levels of knowledge, and abilities. The only prerequisite is an inquiring mind. To a committed library staffer, all new programs or procedures are tested by the question, "How will this change affect the service the library gives?" This urge to serve is at the root of all successful library workers, and the question becomes an analytical tool for library effectiveness.[7]

To the degree I remembered to pose this question at all levels of the library organization, we were able to develop services that pleased and satisfied library users. Staff members from all departments and throughout all my years made the defining contributions that earned ICPL its reputation for quality and service. It is impossible to adequately portray their skill, dedication, and ingenuity.

The ICPL staff revealed their typical generous spirit, originality, and good humor through the three-day "Lolly Finale" of July 1-3, 1994, planned to celebrate my retirement. This weekend of staff gatherings, banquets, open houses, speeches, gifts, video tributes, banners, flowers, jazz concerts, and other surprises showered on me will always be one of my favorite library stories. The events themselves and the many tributes I received, however, were merely another reflection of the many outstanding individuals that contributed the ideas and performed the services that brought fame to the library. Too often I received the credit for what they did.

I cannot begin to tell all the stories that would document the contributions that the library's rich mix of employees and volunteers has produced, so I have chosen two persons who represent this myriad of staff and volunteer talent. Along with a variety of other services to the library, each has pursued a topic basic to one of the values or goals of the public library.

Carol Spaziani and Intellectual Freedom. Carol Spaziani retired in 1995 after completing twenty-six years as a library employee. She had been full-time and part-time; a regular and a Seven Rivers employee; a manager and a librarian; an information specialist; and the volunteer, community services, and audiovisual coordinator. Her key roles in the development of information and business services, the volunteer program, book sales, jail service and other outreach services,

Photo courtesy Iowa City Press-Citizen

Carol Spaziani retired in 1995 after twenty-five years of service.

library publications, public information, and library policies have been noted throughout the latter half of this history.

On her retirement, however, the library chose to honor her for her work for intellectual freedom by establishing an annual series of events to be held each fall in conjunction with Banned Books Week—the Carol Spaziani Intellectual Freedom Festival. Spaziani had always been an articulate spokesperson for First Amendment rights, and during her tenure had served as the library's watchdog, trying to ensure that library policies and practices were inclusive, not exclusive. She mounted the library's Banned Books Week display for many years. The displays proved to be one of the library's best advertisements for intellectual freedom issues, generating broad newspaper and television coverage and exclamations of surprise from display visitors about the range of titles that someone, somewhere, had tried to remove from the shelves of school and public libraries.

This book has probably slighted issues of intellectual freedom, not because they are unimportant, but because Iowa City is a community relatively free of serious complaints and full of people who take academic freedom and civil liberties very seriously. It was always comforting to know that potential support was "out there"; librarians in other communities have sometimes paid a high price for taking a courageous stand against censorship.

Despite an enlightened community, Spaziani never allowed the staff or the board to get too comfortable. In the early 1970s, at Spaziani's urging, the board broadened the meeting room policies to make them more inclusive, and in the 1980s she developed policies to ensure equal access to other library facilities such as display equipment and bulletin boards. She kept us all informed about new interpretations of the Library Bill of Rights, an American Library Association document that most libraries adopt and try to follow.

There are almost no references to censorship complaints in the library's official minutes during its first eighty years. This indicates, and newspaper records tend to confirm, that there were no public controversies about the library owning specific titles. We know that children under fifteen were not allowed to use adult materials until Sallie Helm took over the directorship on 1964. The children's room kept sex education books on a special shelf as long as Hazel Westgate had complete control.

During my tenure between 1975 and 1994, most complaints were about giving children access to adult materials, but we were usually successful in convincing parents that it was their responsibility, not the library's, to monitor what their children checked out. We also received several complaints regarding displays on topics distasteful or objectionable to the viewer and requests to restrict access to R-rated movies. In 1990-91 there was a long conflict about giveaways and posters provided by groups on opposing sides of the abortion issue. Before any such complaint went to the board (and few did), the objector was in my office demanding changes in library policies. Spaziani was always supportive, helping to interpret the existing policy and to develop a strategy which allowed us to stand firm on our principles while letting the complainants have their say.

The 1996 Spaziani festival included four days of events: a talk about the former Des Moines library director who wrote the original Library Bill of Rights; a showing of the film *Fahrenheit 451*; an exhaustive look at children's books that censors have tried to remove from libraries by children's librarian Debb Green; and a talk by the director of the ALA Office of Intellectual Freedom. The festival will be an annual reminder to the library staff that active advocacy of intellectual freedom is a responsibility of all libraries, and for the community, a celebration of the fact that libraries will continue to be open to all—except the censor.

Ellen Buchanan and Local History. Trustee, library board president, volunteer storyteller, foundation board member, major donor—Ellen Buchanan has held almost every kind of library position except that of an employee. In 1989 she began a local history project that has produced one of the library's most valuable resources. Her seventy-five interviews with some of Iowa City's most interesting and influential citizens were recorded on videotape and added to the library's local history collection. They are cablecast frequently on the library's cable channel and copies are available for check-out.

Ellen Buchanan has produced seventy-five video interviews with well-known Iowa Citians as well as serving as library board president, foundation director, and volunteer storyteller. She and her husband, John, are major library benefactors.

Buchanan says, "Everyone has a story to tell; stories can entertain, inform, enlighten, and teach," and quotes Robert Coles and William Carlos Williams on the power and influence of personal stories. The forty interviews in the first series, *Tell Me Your Story*, were taped between 1989 and 1992 and concentrated on older people who Buchanan felt had made an impact on the community. The fact that more than a quarter of these individuals have since died testifies to the urgency of recording this kind of oral history. In her second series, *One of a Kind*, she had interviewed thirty-five Iowa Citians by the end of 1996—choosing people who have interesting, distinctive stories to tell. For most of this latter series, Suzanne Richerson served as Buchanan's research assistant. Richerson was another library volunteer whose name appears in ICPL history as frequently as Buchanan. Her *One of a Kind* story, however, had to be related by friends after she died in the spring of 1996.

Buchanan's two series have won awards and a lot of attention from viewers. In 1992 *Midwest Living* magazine gave *Tell Me Your Story* one of its historic preservation awards, and in 1995 the Johnson County Historical Society named Buchanan the winner of the 1995 Irving Weber Award for distinguished contributions to the research, writing, interpretation, or preservation of Johnson County history. One commentator wrote, "With infinite grace, charm and professionalism, she [Buchanan] elicits fascinating stories of lives well-lived, the adversities, the triumphs, and joys."[8] The "polished, engaging thirty minute interviews" were all taped in the PATV cable studio at the library, with editing and the addition of photographs done by members of the library's audiovisual staff. In the first newspaper report about her series in 1989, Buchanan said, "I might be doing these for a couple of years."

Local history has always been a special responsibility of public libraries. Some libraries work alone if there are no local history organizations; many house the local historical society and its archives. In Iowa City the library cooperates with all local history institutions and organizations, archiving and indexing local newspapers, preserving basic local reference books like telephone and city directories, and providing a collection of minutes and other documents produced by

Johnson County governmental units. Since 1980, the library's cable television and video facilities have allowed ICPL to concentrate on collecting and sometimes producing local visual history. Buchanan's interviews are outstanding examples of this capability.

Unfinished Stories

Technology and the Public Library. As the format changes described earlier illustrate, the library has survived and flourished through decades of technological change. Electric lights were available from ICPL's first days, but it was just a few years earlier that libraries lacked artificial light and were open only in the daytime when few working men and women could visit. ICPL added typewriters and telephones in its first five years. The typewriter made a card catalog easier to compile and improved its readability. The telephone was the library's first technical link to other sources of information and a necessary predecessor to the electronic networks that libraries depend on today.

When advances in photographic processes produced microfilm in the 1930s there was a lot of talk about converting the world's books and other printed information into this new format so readers could have these materials at their fingertips—similar to today's dreams about digitizing all print resources.

The excitement over the capability of making copies is hard to appreciate today. In the past scholars hired copyists to provide handwritten copies of rare works and more recently students spent long hours writing down information from periodicals and other reference materials. ICPL got its first copier in 1966 and the public now makes over 200,000 copies a year from library resources. The more recent development of computer printers that can make attractive copies easily and quickly and the availability of printouts from searchable, on-line or CD-ROM data bases offer other easy substitutes for the laborious work of note taking.

The invention of the phonograph, moving pictures, radio, and television produced new kinds of creative efforts that a library could not ignore, and since 1950 ICPL has added and discarded formats as technology and the market have ordained. Now the computer has linked audio, visual, and the "printed" word, and the library must expand and refine its resources in order to continue to be the free and neutral location for access to all forms of the human record.

Futurists have predicted the end of reading, the book, and the library several times in the last one hundred years. Movies, radio, microfilm, television, computers, and now the Internet all have been cited as causing the end of reading, the death of print, and the demise of the library. Movies, radio, and television were seen as a replacement for reading. Edison predicted movies would eliminate textbooks. Microfilm and computers threatened to replace books and now Internet devotees argue that libraries will soon be obsolete.

As long as libraries are supported at a level that enables them to extend their information resources to all media, and as long as they have leadership that understands that these changes are just the next steps in the evolution of libraries, they will remain central institutions in the educational and cultural life of our society, and public libraries will have an essential role.

I have tried to trace the impact of technology on ICPL throughout its history. During the last quarter century as a director with limited technical skills, I surrounded myself with competent and trustworthy staff members and was guided by their recommendations. Craig, first as technical services manager and then as assistant director, provided the vision and enough technical know-how to see that we went in the right direction with very few missteps. Her selection as library director, following eight years as the library's chief planner for technical developments, gives the library a leader not only schooled in basic public library values, but also with the experience required for directing a public library headed for the electronic unknowns of the twenty-first century.

During the last two decades ICPL moved ahead technically at a fairly steady rate, sometimes leading, sometimes behind in the various streams of technical change necessary to provide the best resources and services for our public. The last five years have produced especially dramatic and far-reaching changes. Craig put a computer on my desk in late 1992 and forced me to move beyond the charts and graphs of my spreadsheet mentality. E-mail and local area networks entered our administrative lives, and at the same time public users and reference librarians learned to use Refnet, the library's network of CD-ROM data bases. We were still putting quotation marks around the term "internet" that year. By 1994 these two networks were linked and, following profound changes to our main catalog/circulation computer system, a staff member could access all our internal systems as well as much of the Internet world from one workstation. In 1995 and 1996 the public gained free library access to the Internet and the World Wide Web. Five staff members now make up the core "systems group" at the library, planning upgrades, staff training, and future electronic adventures. The library is a founding member of JCCN, the consortium of local educational and government agencies organizing local information resources into an on-line network. JCCN is the electronic version of a twenty-year library goal to cooperate with community agencies to improve the availability of local information.

Alongside this thick and complex web of arcane terms and intricate connections, reading is not a lost art. "Reading was the first virtual reality," proclaimed a 1993 article in *American Libraries*.[9] Libraries have provided data organized into information ready to provide enlightenment for many years—some of it identical to the information "discovered" on the Internet by inexperienced library users. While there is no question that computers are the most efficient medium for storing, searching, retrieving, and reordering data, facts, and information of all kinds, libraries and society in general will continue to treasure books—"print on paper"—for sustained reading, for assembling knowledge, and for acquiring understanding. One of the most efficient devices every invented, the book provides compact, portable, eye-saving, and in many forms (such as paperbacks) the cheapest access to the world's accumulated knowledge as well as recreational escape, life experiences, and practical advice and information on thousands of topics. In a 1995 short but powerful book, *Future Libraries: Dreams, Madness & Reality,*[10] librarians and library automation experts Walt Crawford and Michael Gorman give philosophical, physiological, technical, and economic reasons why society will not abandon books and libraries nor attempt to digitize all print resources to become a paperless world. Last year, for instance, ICPL card holders checked out more than 130,000 children's picture books. This collection and many others will be supplemented by, rather than replaced by, electronic formats.

The virtual library will not replace books, physical libraries, and library staff. Libraries are about respecting *all* forms of knowledge, using technology intelligently to aid the effort of providing free access to knowledge in *all* its forms, and giving instruction and assistance in the use of *all* collections to people at *all* levels of ability and experience. That job will continue, indeed will become more important, as the electronic revolution changes the mix and increases the complexity of our choices.

Only a fool would predict where technology will take us, but I will put my money on a long life for the public library.

Expanding the Library. The expansion or replacement of the present library building is the second story that remains unfinished at the end of the library's first century. While the final chapters will be written in 1997 and beyond, it seems important to report the story up to the end of 1996.

Nearly ten years ago when we were developing our second long-range plan, we included an objective to "have a long-term facilities plan ready for board approval by June 30, 1991." With no extreme sense of urgency—perhaps even a little pride that we were looking that far ahead—we took more than two years after the adoption of *On Track for the '90s* in the summer of 1988 to get a committee appointed and a committee charge written.

The committee held its first meeting in November 1990. The board and staff members adopted an ambitious schedule of staff reports, surveys, guest speakers, and focus groups to help them determine the answers to the board's major request: "If the building is not considered adequate for ten more years, review options of remodeling, expansion, and providing additional outlets." The committee decided to work under four assumptions: the present building could be enlarged but not abandoned; parking will continue to be limited, possibly more so if the old library parking lot and the block south of the library are sold for private uses; increased cooperation with the Coralville and North Liberty libraries should be considered in any branch recommendations; and use of the library will continue to increase at a faster rate than was assumed when the plan directing the formation of this committee was adopted.

The committee held five meetings and had moved through only a small part of its agenda before all work stopped in April 1991 to turn full attention to the levy campaign. The most useful product of these meetings was a survey of building visitors in January and February of 1991. Of the 645 visitors interviewed, 47 percent had driven to get to the library, and there were significant differences between drivers and those who walked, biked, were dropped off from a car, or took the bus. While over 75 percent of the drivers found parking within two blocks of the library, twice as many drivers as those who came by other means said they came downtown specifically to visit the library, said parking was a factor in the frequency of their library visits, and showed interest in the idea of another library outlet where parking was easier. About one-fourth of those interested in another location qualified their answer to include "only if it had the same resources."

When the committee was reactivated eighteen months later, the changed circumstances following the levy vote and nearly two more years of space-eating growth in staff, collections, and daily use quickly convinced the group that they needed professional help with the decisions about future facilities for the library. David Smith, a well-respected library consultant from Minneapolis, was hired to do a space needs study. Smith had been familiar with ICPL since his days of assisting our 1976 building consultant, Robert Rohlf.

Smith issued his report to the board in July of 1993.[11] The library, he said, was already serving a population 10 percent larger than the "design" population of the 1978 building plan projected for 1995. Noting the huge population increase in the 1980s and the smaller but additional increases projected for the next two decades, Smith recommended an increase of at least 28,000 square feet to serve the library until 2010. Smith told the board that the lack of general space and the congestion in the building were the major physical limitations. Inadequate storage space and the lack of work space for staff were serious deficiencies, he said, and the children's room and the circulation area were two of the most critical areas.

Smith's comments on branches were short and succinct. Until the using population exceeds 100,000 (sometime after 2010 according to 1993 population projections) and has dispersed substantially beyond a two-mile radius of the library, he said, the community should not consider opening branch libraries. Concentrating the library's resources in one building in Iowa City's commercial and service center will result in their best and most efficient use. In another part of the report Smith noted that, "The location of branch libraries in other high traffic areas of the community would not remedy the space problems of the Iowa City Public Library. However, it would dilute the concentration of resources and possibly the quality of library service."[12]

In July 1993, the library board hired Smith to help the staff prepare a written building program for remodeling the current facility and adding 30,000 square feet. Because of the complexity of the project and on Smith's recommendation, we also selected an architect at this early stage. A year later, by my retirement in June, we had a board-approved building program and an architect. By the end of the summer the city council approved $50,000 for preliminary design work.

After Minneapolis architect Jeff Scherer of Meyer, Scherer, and Rockcastle had developed a fairly detailed plan for a full third floor addition which called for moving virtually all nonpublic space to this new level, the engineering and cost estimate reports were discouraging. Originally considered feasible, it was decided that the cost and inconvenience of adding footings to a building never designed to carry a third floor were prohibitive. The cost estimate was $11.5 million, much of it for the additional structural costs. Either relocating the library temporarily or constructing around an operating library would add to the cost.

In January 1995, with one option eliminated, the board decided to look west and consider a plan that would include the purchase and replacement of the Lenoch & Cilek building. This, in effect, brought the proposed third floor functions to a much-enlarged second floor while the first and basement levels of the new structure could be sold or leased to private concerns. In a meeting with the library board in May of 1995, the city council encouraged the board to provide commercial space as outlined.

By April 1996, with an offer to purchase property contingent on successful passage of a referendum, the west expansion option had been investigated, designed, and prepared for presentation to the city council. The floor plans and elevations were accompanied by cost estimates and an architect's rendering of one possible exterior design for the block-long building.

The response to the proposal was dramatic. Reaction to the rendering seemed to split the public right down the middle. Many found it an exciting attempt to link the old and new buildings and thought the tower on the southwest corner would provide a distinctive architectural landmark in downtown Iowa City. Others found it too distinctive, too "gothic," or just plain ugly. The council's concerns were less architectural. They didn't like the price tag: $12.1 million for

427

This proposed library expansion to the west of the present library was rejected by the city council in 1996. The design, by architects Meyer, Scherer, and Rockcastle, proved to be highly controversial.

the library, $2.1 million for the portions to be leased, plus the cost of purchasing the building and outstanding leases, an estimated $1.6-1.8 million. Council members were also worried about the political price of moving businesses out of their current locations for up to two years while the building was constructed, and the economic cost of failing to lease all the space once it was constructed.

In July 1996 councilors expressed their dissatisfaction with the library proposal and refused to place the issue on a referendum ballot. After delays in discussing what they wanted to do, the council agreed in December to look at ideas and costs for a multi-use facility on block 64 across the street from the library. They authorized the city manager to engage an architect to develop some concepts that would include an 80,000-square-foot library, a 30,000-square-foot conference center, room for cultural activities and a 500-seat auditorium, parking, and the possibility to add on some commercial space. The architect could use the current library space as part of the project if it incorporated an appropriate link to the principal site. Preliminary concepts from the architects were reviewed in February, the conference space was eliminated, and in mid-March of 1997 the council informally agreed on a $20 million proposal that would need voter approval.

While this is indeed a story in process, there are a couple of interesting links to the library's past. Block 64 was the first choice in the 1976 site study prepared for the library board by consultants Rohlf and Smith. One of the architectural firms chosen to prepare the conceptual drawings for the multi-use facility is headed by Charles Engberg. Engberg, now an experienced builder of public libraries, was described in chapter 9 for his work as the HLM design architect for the 1981 building, his first public library. Finally, if a new library is built across the street, making it the third public library in less than one hundred years constructed at the intersection of College and Linn streets, this university community can claim this convergence—probably unique in the world—as another symbol of Iowa

City's commitment to learning, intellectual endeavor, and the arts. It certainly reflect's the city's ongoing love affair with its public library.

A One Hundredth Birthday Celebration

On Sunday, January 19, 1997, the library held a grand birthday party, celebrating one hundred years of service to the Iowa City community. The entire day was perfect. The January weather cooperated—the flags mounted on the roof for the occasion floated in a gentle breeze rather than the thirty-mile-an-hour gale of just forty-eight hours earlier. Huge arches of brightly colored balloons framed entrances and areas set up for the day's special activities. A special history room displayed information, photographs, and artifacts from the past one hundred years, and people leafed through the 1897-1901 registration book looking for relatives and other familiar names.

A special display of library memorablia was popular.

Tables loaded with birthday cakes were scattered around the building, and children loved eating cake "right in the library!" In the children's room kids made libraries of their own from graham crackers and frosting (five gallons used) and watched as Greg Black, UI Memorial Union food director, created a "real" gingerbread library styled after the 1904 Carnegie building across the street.

The library building displayed its amazing acoustics when three groups, Maramel String Quartet, Sweet Adelines vocal quartet, and Acoustic Mayhem, performed comfortably for the assembled audiences in front of the fiction stacks but could not be heard just one hundred feet away. In the meeting room young and old lined up to participate in a series of "book walks," modeled after a traditional cake walk but with books as prizes for standing on the winning number when the music stopped.

Children built libraries of their own.

The library was open for regular service that day and those who just happened to wander in to check out a book or ask a question often joined the more delib-

A Century of Stories

Over 3,000 people attended the celebration on January 19, 1997.

The Honorable Dick Myers, State Representative delivered the opening day speech from January 20, 1897.

erate revelers for cake, party favors, and a chance to win one of the many door prizes. Many visitors inspected the wares at the official "Centennial Headquarters" in the lobby in front of the stained glass window. Bookmarks, t-shirts, book bags (all carrying the special centennial logo), and note cards with color photographs of internal library scenes sold briskly.

In the middle of the six-hour party—the library was open from noon to six that day—three to four hundred spectators squeezed into the meeting room complex. In front of a spectacular rainbow of balloons, Mayor Naomi Novick read a proclamation, Library Board Vice-President Jesse Singerman made a statement, and library director Susan Craig read letters of congratulation from President Bill Clinton, Vice President Al Gore, Senators Tom Harkin and Charles Grassley,

Library director Susan Craig welcomes the first card holder of the library's second century, three-day-old Mark Christopher Coretsopoulos, shown with his parents.

and Congressman Jim Leach, the featured speaker at the dedication of the 1981 building. After I read a few short excerpts from the early chapters of this book to set the scene, State Senator Dick Myers read Judge Wade's now-famous speech from the 1897 dedication ceremonies. The afternoon ended with a sing-along of 1890s songs led by the Voices of Experience, a choral group from the Senior Center.

One paper in 1897 had called the dedication ceremonies "a love feast." One hundred years later the Iowa City Public Library had more than 3,000 people attend a remembrance of that event. They feasted on cake, good music, and family fun and, indeed, showed their love for the library.

A few minutes after opening that day, a library staff member issued the first card of the library's second century to three-day-old Mark Christopher Coretsopolous, one of the more likely of the day's guests to be able to attend the next such party in January 2097.[13]

[1] *Press-Citizen,* May 2, 1991.

[2] "Library weighs service cuts," *Press-Citizen*, March 8, 1991.

[3] *Cedar Rapids Gazette,* Nov. 11, 1991.

[4] "City shows strong support for the library," *Press-Citizen*, Nov. 6, 1991.

[5] *Building on a Century of Service; Iowa City Strategic Plan for Centennial Year 1996 and Beyond* (Iowa City Public Library, 1994), cover.

[6] Ibid.

[7] Walt Crawford and Michael Gorman, *Future Libraries: Dreams, Madness, & Reality* (American Library Association, 1995), 8. I am indebted to Crawford and Gorman for some of the best ideas about the motivation of library workers that I have ever read.

[8] Eleanor Chappell, "Two locally produced series turn television into art," *Press-Citizen*, Jan. 1, 1994.

[9] Kathleen de la Pena McCook, "The first virtual reality," *American Libraries*, July/Aug 1993: 626-628.

[10] Crawford and Gorman.

[11] David Smith, *Iowa City Public Library; Library Space Needs and Alternatives*, July, 1993.

[12] Ibid., section 1: 2; section 4: 6.

[13] Thanks to Susan Craig and Larry Eckholt for ideas and whole sentences borrowed from *The Window* for February 1997.

■ Appendix A

Library Board Trustees
Iowa City Public Library, 1896–1997

Alice Luscombe	1896–1898	Emma Watkins	1930–1939d
Bertha Ridgway	1896–1904	Harry Shulman	1930–1942
Martin J. Wade	1896–1903	Maude Hands	1932–1938d
George W. Ball	1896–1905	Anna Bittner	1934–1943
W.P. Coast	1896–1907	Sarah Paine Hoffman	1938–1943
Bohumil Shimek	1896–1910	C.C. Ries	1939–1959
George Hummer	1896–1912d	Marguerite Evans	1941–1961
Max Mayer	1896–1914	Joseph Braverman	1943–1944d
S.K. Stevenson	1896–1929	Mary G. Martin	1943–1952
Elizabeth Felkner	1898–1920	James L. Records	1943–1947d
Joseph W. Rich	1903–1917	Ruth K. Beye	1943–1952d
Margaret Switzer	1904–1927	Julian Brody	1943–1945
A.E. Swisher	1905–1908	Rueben Flocks	1947
John Springer	1908–1918	Kenneth MacDonald	1947–1959
Willard J. Welch	1908–1928d	Sam Shulman	1947–1952d
Frank Horak	1911–1917	James Parden	1947–1953
C.F. (Fred) Huebner	1912–1957	Edwin B. Green	1951–1963
S.E. Carrell	1915–1922	Charlotte Shulman	1952–1954
Paul A. Korab	1917–1929	Marge Rehder	1953–1961
W.R. Hart	1917–1945	William Jackson	1953–1961
Laura Rockwood	1919–1921	Clark Houghton	1953–1955
F.B. Olsen	1919–1950	Earl Snyder	1955–1961
Alice R. Davies	1922–1928	Rosalie Braverman	1955–1961
Merritt C. Speidel	1922–1929	B.W. (Bud) Sheridan	1957–1963
Louis F. Mueller	1927–1933	Dale Welt	1959–1965
Glenn A. Kenderdine	1928–1937	William Tucker	1961–1969
Ella Van Epps	1928–1947	Ardith Melloh	1961–1965
Elsie C. Davis	1930–1935	Karl Kammermeyer	1961–1967

■ Appendix B

Presidents
Iowa City Public Library Board of Trustees, 1896–1997

Martin J. Wade	1896–1903	Tom Summy	1970
J.W. Rich	1904	Clayton Ringgenberg	1971
H.P. Coast	1905–1906	Arthur Canter	1972
George Hummer	1907–1911	Robert Downer	1973–1974*
Willard Welch	1912–1925	Vivian Buchan	1975
Merritt C. Speidel	1926–1929	Ronald Farber	1976–1977
W.R. Hart	1930–1939	David Kirkman	1978
Harry Shulman	1940–1941	Randall Bezanson	1979–1980
Ella Van Epps	1942–1944	Lynda Ostedgaard	1981
F.B. Olsen	1945–1948	Ed Zastrow	1982–1983
Mary G. Martin	1949–1952	Carolyn Cavitt	1984–1985
Kenneth MacDonald	1953–1959	Riley Grimes	1986
William Jackson	1959 [6 mos]	Charles Drum	1987–1988
Marge Rehder	1960–1961	Tom Gelman	1989–1990
B.W. [Bud] Sheridan	1962–1963	Ellen Buchanan	1991
William Tucker	1964–1967	Kent Swaim	1992–1993
Louis Loria	1968	Stephen Greenleaf	1994–1995
Kent Braverman	1969	Charles Traw	1996–1997

*18-month term. Since 1975 president takes office July 1 to match fiscal year.

■ Appendix C

Dec. 1896–Mar. 1897	Andrew C. Howell
Apr. 1897–Oct. 1898	Samuel H. (Harry) Sperry
Oct. 1898–Aug. 1899	Gilbert A. McElroy
Aug. 1899–Feb. 1900	Leslie Switzer
Feb. 1900–Oct. 1905	Adelaide C. Lloyd
Nov. 1905–Oct. 1907	Lorene N. Webber
Nov. 1907–Sept. 1920	Helen McRaith
Oct. 1920–Apr. 1921	Ethel Tiffy (acting)
Apr. 1921–Aug. 1923	Carolyn E. Ware
Oct. 1923–May 1946	Jessie B. Gordon
June 1946–Feb. 1964	Joyce Nienstedt
Mar. 1964–Aug. 1968	Sallie Helm
Aug. 1968–Aug. 1970	Mary Croteau
Aug. 1970–Nov. 1970	Lolly Eggers (acting)
Nov. 1970–June 1974	Jack Hurkett
June 1974–Mar. 1975	Lolly Eggers (acting)
Mar. 1975–June 1994	Lolly Eggers
July 1994–present	Susan Craig

*Title was Librarian until 1964

■ Appendix D

Presidents
Friends of the Iowa City Public
Library*, 1976–1997

Ann Bagford	1976
Dottie Ray & Ann Feddersen	1977
Carolyn & Michael Cavitt	1978
Sandra Keller	1979
Dallas Hogan	1980
Jo Catalano	1981
Mary Jo Langhorne	1982
Leslie Menniger	1983
Tom Gelman	1984
Della McGrath	1985
Steve Gerard	1986
Ellie Densen	1987
Linda Crim	1988
Maggie Hogan	1989
Vera Dordick	1990–91
Anne Spencer	1992
Mary Lea Kruse	1993
Kay Loeffelholz	1994
Tom Hulme	1995–96
Linda Dellsperger	1997

Presidents
Iowa City Public Library Foundation,
1983–1992
Iowa City Public Library Friends
Foundation, 1993–1997*

Lynda Ostedgaard	1983
John Koza	1984–85
Carolyn Cavitt	1986
Nancy Willis	1987
Randy Bezanson	1988
Russ Schmeiser	1989–90
Kathy Moyers	1991–92
Marvin Hartwig	1993–94
William Burger	1995–96
Brad Langguth	1997

* The two organizations merged into the Iowa City Public Library Friends Foundation in 1993. Friends is now a committee of the Friends Foundation and Friends presidents are called "chairs."

437

■ Appendix E

Chronology
Iowa City Public Library, 1896-1997

1896	Aug. 28	First organizational meeting at the First Christian Church.
	Sep. 21	Mass meeting about establishing a library held at Smith's Armory.
	Oct.	Iowa City Public Library Association formed and board of directors appointed.
1897	Jan. 20	Pre-opening dedication ceremonies held at library, 211 Iowa Avenue.
	Jan. 21	Opening day of library under the aegis of the library association.
	Mar. 1	Election to make the library supported by tax dollars. Approved 1,283 to 299.
	Mar. 15	First Iowa City Public Library Board of Trustees appointed. Same nine as on the association board.
	Nov. 26	*Honor Before Wealth* performance to benefit the library by St. Mary's Lyceum (Drama) Company.
1901	June 20	Library moves to 214 East College, second floor of Cannon & Pratt Building.
1902		Library book catalog published.
	Mar. 14	Carnegie awards Iowa City $25,000 for library building.
1903	Apr.	Carnegie agrees to add $10,000 after intervention of Senator William Boyd Allison.
1904	Oct. 27	Carnegie library opens to the public.
	Nov. 29	Carnegie library dedication held at Coldren's Opera House.
1906		Welch-Patterson Memorial Collection established.
	May	Children's room opened in basement of Carnegie library.
1911		Library service to schools begins.
1933		Library closes on Sunday due to depression era budget cuts.
1935		Library open house to celebrate centennial of Carnegie's birth.
1937		Jessie Gordon begins weekly newspaper column that continues until 1980.
1942		Trustee Ella Van Epps becomes first woman library board president.

Chronology

1946		School board begins to share the cost of library service to all elementary schools.
1947		Clarence and Ella Van Epps give the library their personal library of over 1,000 volumes.
1949	July	Hazel Westgate hired as children's librarian.
1950		Music room opens and recordings collection started from bequest of Jennie Brubaker.
1955		Library service to public schools ends.
		Myron J. Walker Trust begins annual income to library.
1962	June 4	Referendum on building addition to Carnegie library is approved by 83 percent of voters (2,929 to 742).
1963	Nov. 10	Dedication cermonies for new building addition.
1965		Library becomes headquarters for the Seven Rivers Library System.
1967		Service to shut-ins begins.
1968	Aug.	First contract with Johnson County Board of Supervisors for library service to rural residents.
1969		Services to business begins.
		Library reopens on Sundays for first time since 1933.
1974		Seven Rivers system ends and state-funded East Central system headquarters opens in Cedar Rapids.
		Library holds first used books sale.
		Reciprocal borrowing with area public libraries including Coralville and Cedar Rapids begins.
		Library service to county jail started.
1975		Planning for new library begins; building consultant hired.
1976		Friends of Iowa City Public Library founded.
		First audiovisual librarian hired.
1978	Nov. 7	Referendum on bonds for a new library carried by 62 percent of voters (7,427 to 4,944).
1979		$31,000 grant helps build audiovisual collections.
		First volunteer policy adopted.
	Oct. 1	Computer-assisted circulation system goes on-line.
1980	Oct. 1	Library's on-line public catalog is first in a U.S. public library.
	Oct. 11	Groundbreaking for new library.
	Nov.	Library cable channel begins.
1981	May 27	Carnegie library closed after seventy-seven years.
	June 14	Dedication ceremonies for new library.
	June 15	Library opens to public.
1982		Audiovisual lab opens.
		Iowa City Public Library Foundation established.
1983		*Library Priorities for the '80s*, first long-range plan, approved.
1985		Centennial Endowment Fund established by foundation.
		Library awarded a $125,000 National Endowment for the Humanities Challenge Grant.
1986		$125,000 bequest from Edwin Green received.
1988		*On Track for the '90s*, second long-range plan, approved.
1989		Open Access, statewide reciprocal borrowing program, begins.
1990		Public Libraries of Johnson County Association formed.

Chronology

1991	Nov. 7	Referendum on a permanent special levy for library approved by 68 percent of voters (6,426 to 3,041).
1992		Refnet, CD-ROM reference network, installed.
		Children's outreach plan adopted.
1993		First year of 1 million loans, 100,000 reference questions, and 20,000 new items added to collection.
		Ellen and John Buchanan challenge bequest of $525,000 raises $1.5 million in deferred gifts for library foundation.
		Friends of the Library and library foundation merge.
		Space needs study for library expansion begins.
1994		*Building on a Century of Service*, the third long-range plan, approved.
1995		Audiovisual lab closed.
		Public access to the Internet.
		First Carol Spaziani Intellectual Freedom Festival.
1996		Celebration of library's centennial begins.
		Public access to World Wide Web.
		City council denies board-recommended building expansion, wants library in multi-use facility.
1997	Jan. 19	Library's one hundredth birthday party.

■ Appendix F

History of Collections
Iowa City Public Library

Adult Collections

1897	Fiction
	Non-Fiction
	Reference
	Periodicals
1920s	Mystery Fiction
	Western Fiction
1950s	Science Fiction
1950–96	*LP Recordings
1950	Young Adult Fiction
1950–69	**Young Adult Non-Fiction
1965–84	*8mm Films
1965	Art Reproductions
1966	Large Print Books
1969	Paperbacks (Browsing racks)
1970s	Recorded Books
1972–75	*Cassette tapes (music)
1972–86	*16mm Films
1977	Comic Books
1978–81	*Sculpture Reproductions
1978	Movies on Video
1978	Non-Fiction Video
1978	Slides and *Filmstrips
1982–95	*Games
1985	Foreign Language Fiction
1985	Easy Reading (Adult New Literates)
1987	Compact Discs

1987–90	*Software on Floppy discs
1995	Multimedia

Children's Collections

1897	Fiction
	Non-Fiction
1905	Periodicals
	Reference
1905–30s	*Picture File: prints and photos
1920s	Easy Readers/Picture Books
1950–94	*LP Recordings
1960s	Holiday Books
1970s	Paperbacks
1970s–81	*Book/LP
1972–81	Framed Art Reproduction Minatures
1979	Book/Cassette
1981	Toys and Games
1981–85	*Filmstrips
1985	Video
1990	Compact Discs
1991	Board Books
1993	Recorded Books
1994	Music on Cassette

* Discontinued collections. Children's LPs in with general collection until 1981.
** Young Adult non-fiction combined with general non-fiction. Upper elementary non-fiction moved from children's to adult in 1981.

■ Sources

Iowa City Public Library Archives
Accession books, 1897–1958
Annual reports
       Narrative—1900–1920, 1971–1996
       Statistical only—1897–1899, 1921–1953
Architectural records—1904, 1963, 1981
Circulation records—1897–1901, 1923–1947
Grant proposals
Minutes Board of Trustees—1896–1927, 1945–1996
       Friends of Iowa City Public Library—1976–1992
       Iowa City Public Library Foundation—1983–1992
       Iowa City Public Library Friends Foundation—1992–1996
Newsletters
       Business Newsletter—1970–1973
       NEW at ICPL—1972–1974
       The Window—1987–1996
Newspaper clippings—1970–1996
Planning documents: plans, surveys, studies—1982, 1988, 1994
Publications—1965–1996
Scrapbooks: 12 covering various periods—1897–1991
Video and pictorial archives

Newspapers
Iowa Citizen, 1896–1920
Iowa City Republican, 1896–1920
Iowa State Press, 1896–1920
Iowa City Press-Citizen, 1920–1996

Sources

Personal, Corporate, and Club Papers

Carnegie Corporation Archives, Rare Book and Manuscript Library, Butler Library, Columbia University, New York, N.Y.

Citizens' Library Association (Iowa City), State Historical Society, Iowa City.

Iowa City Book Club, State Historical Society, Iowa City.

Iowa City Library Association, State Historical Society, Iowa City.

Nineteenth Century Club, State Historical Society, Iowa City.

N.N. Club, State Historical Society, Iowa City.

Joseph W. Rich papers, State Historical Society, Iowa City.

Willard Welch notebooks on Lemuel Bausman Patterson and Lillie Patterson Welch, State Historical Society, Iowa City.

Books and Articles

Acton, Richard Lord, and Patricia Narsif Acton. *To Go Free; A Treasury of Iowa's Legal Heritage.* Ames: Iowa State University Press, 1995.

Allen, Anne Beiser. "Her Honor the Mayor, Iowa City's Emma Harvat," *Palimpsest,* Summer 1995: 76–96.

Aurner, Charles Ray. *Leading Events in Johnson County, Iowa, History.* 2 vols. Cedar Rapids: Western Historical Press, 1912–13.

Baker, Nicholson. "Discards," *New Yorker,* April 4, 1994: 64–86.

Bell, Michael J. "The Jews of Iowa, 1840–1990," *Annals of Iowa,* 53(1994): 85–95.

Berelson, Bernard. *The Library's Public.* New York: Columbia University Press, 1949.

Bial, Raymond. *The Carnegie Libraries of Illinois.* Champaign: University of Illinois Press, 1991.

Bobinski, George S. *Carnegie Libraries; Their History and Impact on American Public Library Development.* Chicago: American Library Association, 1969.

Brass, Linda J. *Eighty Years of Service; A History of the Children's Department, Seattle Public Library.* Seattle Public Library, 1971.

Carnegie, Andrew. *Gospel of Wealth and Other Essays.* New York: Century, 1901. Reprinted by Cambridge: Belknap Press, 1962.

Carrier, Esther Jane. *Fiction in Public Libraries, 1876–1900.* New York: Scarecrow Press, 1965.

———. *Fiction in Public Libraries, 1900–1950.* Littleton, CO: Libraries Unlimited, 1985.

Cedar Rapids Public Library; The First 100 Years. Cedar Rapids Public Library, 1996.

Cochran, William M. *A Century of Iowa Libraries in Association; A History of the Iowa Library Association, 1890–1990.* Des Moines: Iowa Library Association, 1990.

Cramer, C.H. *Open Shelves and Open Minds; A History of the Cleveland Public Library.* Cleveland: Case Western Reserve University, 1972.

Crawford, Walt, and Michael Gorman. *Future Libraries: Dreams, Madness and Reality.* Chicago: American Library Association, 1995.

Croly, Mrs. J.C. *History of the Women's Movement in America.* New York: Henry Allen, 1898.

Dickson, Paul. *The Library in America; A Celebration in Words and Pictures.* New York: Facts on File Publications, 1986.

Ditzion, Sidney H. *Arsenals of a Democratic Culture.* Chicago: American Library Association, 1947.

Duffus, R.L. *Our Starving Libraries; Studies in Ten American Communities during the Depression Years.* New York: Houghton, 1932.

Eggers, Lolly. "More Effective Management of the Public Library's Book Collection," in

Sources

Phyllis Van Orden. *Background Readings in Building Library Collections.* 2nd ed. New York: Scarecrow Press, 1979: 129–136.

———. "The Public Library in the Political Process." Unpublished paper, 1969.

Ellsworth, Ralph. "Appearance as Modern as the Best Store in Town," *Library Journal,* December 15, 1949: 1851–1853.

Garceau, Oliver. *The Public Library in the Political Process.* New York: Columbia University Press, 1949.

Garrison, Dee. *Apostles of Culture; The Public Librarian and American Society, 1876–1920.* New York: Free Press, 1979.

Gerber, John G. A Pictorial History of the University of Iowa. Iowa City: University of Iowa Press, 1988.

Glenn, George D. *Opera Houses of Iowa.* Ames: Iowa State University Press, 1993.

Hackett, Alice Payne. *80 Years of Best Sellers, 1895–1975.* New York: Bowker, 1977.

Harris, Michael H. "The Purpose of the American Public Library; A Revisionist Interpretation of History," *Library Journal,* September 15, 1973: 2509–2014.

———. *A Reader in American Library History.* Washington: Microcard Editions, 1971.

Hoeltje, H.H. "Notes on the History of Lecturing in Iowa, 1855–1885." *Iowa Journal of History and Politics,* 25 (January 1927): 62–128.

Koester, Eleanor. *Public Library Movement in Iowa, 1930–1957.* Unpublished master's thesis, Case Western Reserve University, 1958.

Kruty, Paul. "Patton and Miller; Designers of Carnegie Libraries," *Palimpsest,* 64 (1983): 110–122.

Mansheim, Gerald. *Iowa City; An Illustrated History.* Norfolk, VA: Donning Company, 1989.

Martin, Lowell. *Public Administration and the Library.* University of Chicago Press, 1941.

———. "The Public Library: Middle-Age Crisis or Old Age?" *Library Journal,* January 1, 1983: 17–22.

McCook, Kathleen de la Pena. "The First Virtual Reality," *American Libraries,* July/Aug. 1993: 626–628.

McGuire, Letha Pearl. "Public Library Movement in Iowa," *Iowa Journal of History and Politics,* 35 (1937): 22–72.

Monson, Mary. "Library Fire of 1897," *Palimpsest,* 61 (July/Aug. 1980): 118–123.

Musmann, Klaus. *Technological Innovations in Libraries, 1860–1960; An Anecdotal History.* Westport, CT: Greenwood Press, 1993.

Nienstedt, Joyce. "Even the Termites Helped Improve the Budget," *Library Journal,* June 15, 1950: 1007–1011.

———. "For Your Listening Comfort," *Library Journal,* December 15, 1950: 2113–2115.

Noun, Louise. *Strong-Minded Women; Emergence of the Woman-Suffrage Movement in Iowa.* Ames: Iowa State University Press, 1969.

Ohmann, Richard. *Selling Culture: Magazines, Markets and Class at the Turn of the Century.* London: Verso, 1996.

Old Settlers' Association Yearbooks, 1866–1925. Reproduced by the Johnson County Historical Society, 1978.

Our Live Ones: Iowa City (Caricatures of Iowa Citians in about 1907). Publisher and date unknown.

Portrait and Biographical Record of Johnson, Poweshiek, and Iowa Counties. Chapman Brothers, 1893.

Sources

Rith, Donald E. *A History of Organized Public Recreation in Iowa City.* Unpublished master's thesis, University of Iowa, Iowa City, 1967.

Sears, Roebuck and Company. *1897 Sears Roebuck Catalog.* Broomall, PA: Chelsea House, 1968.

Shambaugh, Benjamin F. *Iowa City: A Contribution to the Early History of Iowa.* Iowa City: State Historical Society, 1893.

Shera, Jesse. *Foundations of the Public Library; The Origins of the Public Library Movement in New England, 1629–1855.* University of Chicago, 1949.

Throne, Mildred. *History of the State University of Iowa Libraries.* Unpublished master's thesis, University of Iowa, Iowa City, 1943.

Thomas, Vivian. "The First Carnegie Library," *Wilson Library Bulletin,* June 1995: 52–53.

Tiffany, Connie. "Iowa City Library's new building helps make it a 'Library for Everyone,'" *Community Televsion Review,* October, 1981: 50–51.

———. "An Electronic Public Library for Iowa City," *Library Journal,* October 1, 1982: 1816–20.

Tuchman, Barbara. *Practicing History.* New York: Knopf, 1981.

———. *The Proud Tower: A Portrait of the World before War, 1890–1914.* New York: Macmillan, 1966.

Van Slyck, Abigail A. *Free to All; Carnegie Libraries and American Culture, 1890–1920.* University of Chicago Press, 1995.

Wall, Joseph Frazier. *Andrew Carnegie.* New York: Oxford Press, 1970.

———. *Iowa; A Bicentennial History.* New York: Norton, 1978.

Watts, Blanche. *Iowa Summer Library School.* Unpublished paper, University of Iowa Library School, 1970.

Weber, Irving. *Historical Stories about Iowa City.* 8 vols. Iowa City Host Noon Lions Club, 1976–1994.

Wiegand, Wayne A. *Irrepressible Reformer; A Biography of Melvil Dewey.* Chicago: American Library Association, 1996.

Weisbord, Marvin. "A Public Library Discovers Music," *Music Journal,* July 1954: 6–8.

Williams, Patrick. *American Public Library and the Problem of Purpose.* Westport, CT: Greenwood Press, 1988.

Woodford, Frank B. *Parnassus on Main Street; A History of the Detroit Public Library.* Detroit: Wayne State University Press, 1965.

■ Index of Proper Names

Index of Proper Names

Index of Proper Names

Index of Proper Names

Index of Proper Names

Index of Proper Names

Index of Proper Names

LOLLY PARKER EGGERS grew up in Des Moines, Iowa and graduated from Grinnell College in 1951. She moved to Iowa City that same year when she married fellow Grinnellian, Del Eggers. In June 1969, with a new library science degree from the University of Iowa, she joined the staff of the Iowa City Public Library. Eggers served as director from 1974 to 1994. She and her husband have three sons and five grandchildren.

Photo courtesy Sue Young